Praise for

THE PRICE OF SILENCE

"Meticulous . . . evenhanded . . . Mr. Cohan captures brilliantly the theater of the absurd that is played out on campuses every year over one controversy or another. . . . Our tour guide in this chamber of horrors, Mr. Cohan, is remarkably dispassionate as he sets forth the fallout from the initial charges: the lacrosse season canceled, three of the team's players indicted, a community in upheaval as a bitter debate over race, sex, and class raged, fueled by (often intemperate) media attention."

—*The Wall Street Journal*

"At once a masterwork of reporting and a devastating critique of a university that has lost its way . . . What Cohan has done, to superb effect, is to bring a forensic level of reporting to the event, so that we are forced to throw out its long-accepted narrative and look at it with new eyes. . . . Every parent planning to send a child to an 'elite' college dominated by an overly powerful athletic program should buy this book. For those with children thinking of Duke, it is required reading."

—*The New York Times Book Review*

"Exhaustive, surprisingly gripping . . . *The Price of Silence* proves its worthiness. . . . When the story broke, it had plenty of salacious aspects . . . but the story turned out to be far more complex, a drama made rich by the characters' apparent refusal to play their assigned roles. . . . Remarkable . . . Cohan has added a lot of new details to the narrative . . . extremely impressive . . . Ultimately, Mr. Cohan's account is valuable for what the case says about wealth and our legal system."

—*The New York Times*

"Fascinating . . . What Cohan's extraordinary six-hundred-page tome shows is that there is a yawning gap between the lofty rhetoric and grubby reality of American elite universities. . . . It is around the issue of sports that the tangled questions of power, money, racism, and culture crystallize particularly clearly . . . As anthropologists know, every society has power networks and rituals that enable groups to coalesce. But another truism of anthropology is that rituals are most effective in upholding power structures—however distasteful—when nobody talks about them at all, be that on Wall Street or university campuses. In that sense, then, the good news about the 2006 scandal was that it spurred debate about standards."

—*Financial Times*

"*The Price of Silence* is the definitive account of what happened up to and after Crystal Gail Mangum made her accusation. Its six-hundred-page length might at first seem more appropriate to a presidential biography or a history of one of the world wars, but *The Price of Silence* earns its heft, and unlike most biographies and histories, it rarely loosens its grip on its reader's attention."

—*Salon*

"In his new book *The Price of Silence*, William D. Cohan presents the first authoritative account of what happened on the evening of March 13, 2006, and the chaos that followed. Cohan's clear-eyed reporting tracks how administrators, lawyers, police, media personalities, Mangum, and the exonerated players reacted to the spotlight and the shadows it cast. In the book, Cohan speaks with a number of important figures who had never before spoken publicly about the scandal, including both Mike Nifong and former Duke University Board of Trustees chairman Robert Steel."

—*Men's Journal*

"Unsavory as the facts are, *The Price of Silence* reminds us that the relationship between the university and athletics goes beyond big television contracts, payment of players, and academic standards. It questions how, and if, the two can properly coexist."

—*Sports Illustrated*

"Cohan's book is as exhaustively researched as it is fair and objective. The level of detail and the rare interviews he scored with disbarred prosecutor Mike Nifong and the accuser, Crystal Mangum, are accomplishments but not the endgame. What makes this book a worthy read is the perspective. Mr. Cohan convincingly places the Duke lacrosse scandal within the context of America's most prestigious universities' too-often unchecked ambitions."

—*Pittsburgh Post-Gazette*

"Top-notch investigative journalism defines this examination of 'one of the most improbable legal sagas in American history' . . . meticulous . . . not just an edge-of-your-seat courtroom drama and a cautionary tale but also an illuminating fable about the power of status, talent, authority, and belief. Throughout, Cohan's spare prose and objective tone cast his subjects in a humane light, even when their behavior is stunning . . . the definitive account of the case."

—*Publishers Weekly* (starred review)

"Lessons emerge . . . Cohan notes the ceaseless challenges Duke and many other universities face in limiting the influence of alcohol . . . The book also cautions against the power of athletics."

—*The Washington Post*

"Cohan seemingly leaves no stone unturned in covering all aspects of the case . . . undeniably gripping drama . . . A comprehensive, illuminating, and highly readable study of a notorious episode in the annals of the American justice system."

—*Kirkus Reviews* (starred review)

"[Cohan] is sharp about following the money . . . [he] receives extra points for fairness."

—Karen Long, *Newsday*

"The relationship between sports and the academic side of college life has long been troubled . . . Cohan explores the social dynamics that clouded every aspect of the case . . . [He examines] the usual disconnects that occur in high-profile crime cases between what is reported in the press, chronicled in official records, and perceived as public opinion and what really happened. A gripping account of a sensational case."

—*Booklist* (starred review)

"Acclaimed investigative journalist Cohan turns from his previous focus on Wall Street to the 2006 Duke lacrosse scandal . . . Cohan tells the complex story, drawing on public records and interviews to portray the sports players and the three indicted students, the police investigators, the expert defense team, the academic leadership, and the district attorney who generated a media storm over the case until it was dismissed and he was disbarred. With both detail and clarity, the author engages the reader in the paradox of the emergence of Duke as a nationally ranked university where scholastic excellence vied against a 'party hard' social scene. . . . This excellent presentation of media-generated hysteria over a criminal investigation offers insights into police work, prosecutorial excess, and an extensive and expensive legal defense, set in a North Carolina city where the wealthy university was neighbor to an economically stressed black community and seemed to echo national tensions."

—*Library Journal* (starred review)

"William Cohan's fascinating *The Price of Silence* shows that the Duke lacrosse case was not just a controversial legal investigation that became a heated media circus but also a conflict that illuminated the fierce pressures on America's elite universities as they battle for power and prestige and money. Cohan's deep character study of the principal figures involved also reveals the case as a crucible of fate that created distinct winners and losers."

—Bryan Burrough, *Vanity Fair* contributing editor and author of *Public Enemies* and *The Big Rich*, and coauthor of *Barbarians at the Gate*

"William Cohan's scrupulously reported and grippingly written account of this elite campus horror story makes clear that if you thought you knew what happened at Duke, as I did, there is much more to learn. This is a story that ought to disturb anyone who cares about contemporary college life. For the first time, Cohan gets many of the central characters to speak—and what they have to say is eye-opening."

—Jane Mayer, longtime staff writer at *The New Yorker* and author of *The Dark Side*, and coauthor of *Strange Justice* and *Landslide*

Also by William D. Cohan

Money and Power:
How Goldman Sachs Came to Rule the World

House of Cards:
A Tale of Hubris and Wretched Excess on Wall Street

The Last Tycoons:
The Secret History of Lazard Frères & Co.

THE PRICE OF SILENCE

The Duke Lacrosse Scandal, the Power of the Elite,
and the Corruption of Our Great Universities

WILLIAM D. COHAN

SCRIBNER

New York   London   Toronto   Sydney   New Delhi

SCRIBNER
An Imprint of Simon & Schuster, Inc.
1230 Avenue of the Americas
New York, NY 10020

First Scribner paperback edition April 2015

SCRIBNER and design are registered trademarks of The Gale Group, Inc.,
used under license by Simon & Schuster, Inc., the publisher of this work.

For information about special discounts for bulk purchases,
please contact Simon & Schuster Special Sales at 1-866-506-1949
or business@simonandschuster.com.

The Simon & Schuster Speakers Bureau can bring authors to your live event.
For more information or to book an event, contact the Simon & Schuster Speakers Bureau
at 1-866-248-3049 or visit our website at www.simonspeakers.com.

Manufactured in the United States of America

1   3   5   7   9   10   8   6   4   2

Library of Congress Control Number: 2013043923

ISBN 978-1-4516-8179-6
ISBN 978-1-4516-8180-2 (pbk)
ISBN 978-1-4516-8181-9 (ebook)

The author gratefully acknowledges Houston Baker for his generosity in granting permission
to reprint his letter, and the News & Observer Publishing Company for its permission
to reprint Barry Saunders's "ditty" from his column as it appears herein.

For Deb, Teddy, and Quentin
and for my wonderful parents, Suzanne and Paul

We may never be able to uncover the truth. But we have to try. The truth is out there, and we, in principle, can find it.

—ERROL MORRIS

CONTENTS

CAST OF CHARACTERS

Selected Members of the Duke Lacrosse Team Present at 610 North Buchanan Boulevard on the Night of March 13, 2006

Kevin Coleman
David Evans, a resident of the house, later indicted
Collin Finnerty, later indicted
Dan Flannery, a resident of the house
Kevin Mayer
Ryan McFadyen
Peter Lamade
Reade Seligmann, later indicted
Matt Zash, a resident of the house

Strippers

Crystal Gail Mangum
Kim Roberts

Selected Durham, North Carolina, Police Officers

William Barfield
Mark Gottlieb
Benjamin Himan
John Shelton

Duke University Hospital Personnel

Tara Levicy, sexual assault nurse
Dr. Julie Manly, fourth-year resident

Selected Duke University Administrators and Officials

Richard Brodhead, president
Robert Steel, chairman of the Board of Trustees
Mike Krzyzewski, men's basketball coach
Peter Lange, provost
Tallman Trask, executive vice president
John Burness, senior vice president for public affairs
    and government relations
Larry Moneta, vice president of student affairs
Sue Wasiolek, assistant vice president for student affairs
    and dean of students
Joe Alleva, athletic director
Chris Kennedy, senior associate athletic director
Mike Pressler, men's lacrosse coach
John Danowski, new men's lacrosse coach

Selected Duke University Professors

Peter Wood, professor of history
William Chafe, professor of history
Wahneema Lubiano, associate professor of African
    and African-American studies
Houston Baker, professor of African-American literature
Orin Starn, professor of cultural anthropology and history

Durham District Attorney's Office

Mike Nifong, District Attorney
Linwood Wilson, investigator

Selected Defense Attorneys

Joe Cheshire
Bradley Bannon
Kirk Osborn
Bob Ekstrand
Bill Thomas
Bill Cotter
Wade Smith
Jim Cooney

North Carolina Bar Association

    Lane Williamson
    Katherine Jean

North Carolina Attorney General's Office

    Roy Cooper, attorney general
    Jim Coman, investigator
    Mary Winstead, investigator

THE PRICE OF SILENCE

Exactly Who Is In Charge at Duke

On June 28, 2004, three days before the start of his tenure as the ninth president of Duke University, Richard H. Brodhead was mentally unpacking his bags in his office in Allen Building, on the main quad of Duke's stately West Campus, when Joe Alleva, the university's athletic director, burst in on him with some momentous news: The men's legendary basketball coach Mike Krzyzewski, known to all as Coach K and the one force at Duke seemingly as immutable as the school's soaring Gothic cathedral just outside Brodhead's new office, was thinking about leaving to coach the Los Angeles Lakers.

It turned out that a few days earlier Krzyzewski had been at Madison Square Garden in New York City for the 2004 NBA draft and had watched, disheartened, as the team's future seemed to go up in smoke. Coach K's first loss to the NBA that evening was Shaun Livingston, a high school senior from Peoria, Illinois, who had committed previously to Duke as the team's point guard. But he decided to skip college and turn pro. The Los Angeles Clippers made Livingston the fourth overall pick. Three picks later, the Phoenix Suns drafted, and then traded to the Chicago Bulls, the prodigiously talented freshman Luol Deng, who had just completed his first year as Duke's small forward, averaging 15 points per game.

The outcome of the draft had put Krzyzewski in a foul mood, and again lamenting the state of college basketball, where the lure of big money in the pros had repeatedly proved too tempting to young players unable to fully appreciate the long-term benefit of a college degree, at least when compared to an immediate cash infusion of millions of dollars. Krzyzewski favored a minimum age requirement to play in the NBA. But Krzyzewski knew, too, that this change was not going to happen on his say-so, even though he had reached exalted status not only at Duke but also nationally and internationally. At fifty-seven, Krzyzewski had compiled a 621–181 record at Duke, a winning percentage of 77 percent, leading the team to national championships in 1991, 1992, and 2001. By 2004, under Coach K, the Duke basketball team had secured ten Final Four appearances, eight Atlantic Coast Conference tournament championships and ten conference regular-season titles. His Duke teams had been ranked number 1 in twelve different seasons, including each of the last seven. With his team's success on and off the court, Krzyzewski—like John Wooden at UCLA and Dean Smith at North Carolina—had become the personification of Duke basketball and one of the more powerful members of the Duke community.

In December 2004, the basketball court in Cameron Indoor Stadium was named Coach K Court in his honor and the patch of bluegrass outside Cameron—known as Krzyzewskiville—is where the faithful camp out, often weeks in advance, in order to watch a live game. In October 2005, he was named the coach of the U.S. national team that would compete (and win a gold medal) at the 2008 Summer Olympics. In 2010, Duke won its fourth NCAA basketball title under Krzyzewski, and then, early in the 2011–12 season— his thirty-second year at Duke—Krzyzewski became the all-time winningest coach in Division I men's college basketball. In 2012, he again coached the Olympic basketball team to a gold medal. "Sports has often been likened to the front porch of a university," observed sportswriter Liz Clarke in the *Washington Post*. "Hardly the most significant part of the structure, but the part that nonetheless forms the first impression. For the past three decades, Duke has basked in the splendor of a front porch embodied by the Duke Blue Devils basketball team and Coach Mike Krzyzewski, who, when not leading the team to national championships, can be found extolling the virtues of character and leadership in national TV commercials and in books."

Coach K had a "lifetime" contract at the university, which was then paying him around $2 million annually, more than double Brodhead's approximately $800,000. He also earned millions more in endorsements and from his various media enterprises, including book writing and hosting his own radio and television shows. He was also a professor at the Duke business school and a "special assistant" to the president of the university. To put it mildly, at Duke, Krzyzewski was at the center of his own solar system. "It is clear that his is the national face of Duke University," Keith Brodie, a former Duke president, explained following the news of the Lakers' offer. "No one can get in the *New York Times* like he can. He has become a symbol for us and for all of college athletics."

As Krzyzewski watched Livingston and Deng slip into the ranks of professional athletes at Madison Square Garden, Mitch Kupchak, the Lakers' general manager and a former forward at Duke's archrival, the North Carolina Tar Heels, sidled over to him and asked if Coach K would be interested in doing the same thing. In the wake of Coach Phil Jackson's recent announcement that he was going to leave the Lakers, Kupchak was in the market for a new man. Did Krzyzewski want the job? Coach K was not only one of the best college basketball coaches of all time but was also the preferred choice of Kobe Bryant, the Lakers' prima donna, who had specifically recommended Coach K to Lakers owner Jerry Buss. Like Livingston, Bryant, too, had jumped from high school directly to the NBA. Had he decided to go to college, he would have played for Krzyzewski at Duke. Adding to the intrigue of Kupchak's question was the fact that Krzyzewski had considered coaching in the NBA twice before: once in 1990 for the Boston Celtics, and then again in 1994 for the Portland Trailblazers. Both times, he decided to stay at Duke, despite a personal appeal from the Celtics' legendary leader Red Auerbach and the unlimited checkbook of Paul Allen, the Trailblazers' owner and Microsoft cofounder.

This time, Joe Alleva, Duke's athletic director, was sufficiently concerned that Krzyzewski might make the jump that he rushed into Allen Building to see Brodhead, who had been the longtime undergraduate dean at Yale University and was a scholar of nineteenth-century American literature. "The first day he was in his office, I had to go in there and tell him that Coach K was talking to the Lakers," Alleva recalled. "His first day on the job." Brodhead remembered the moment as being somewhat "hilarious" because he had been in his office all of one hour that morning, passing the time "very pleasurably," when Alleva demanded to see him. "Well, maybe he just wanted to say hello," Brodhead recalled, "but he gave me my first news about the Lakers. I had been president of Duke for about five hours when all of a sudden this crossed my bow."

In the days that followed, there was the usual wooing, with Kupchak coming to Durham, North Carolina, where Duke is located, to meet with Krzyzewski and his wife and closest adviser, Mickie, and to take them to dinner and talk about the idea. Then there was the money. The Lakers had offered Coach K a five-year, $40 million contract, or $8 million a year—seriously big money, and multiples of what Duke was paying him at the time (and a third more than the Lakers had been paying Jackson). "It was intense," Brodhead said later. "It wasn't the week I'd been expecting. And yet, I have had university administrative jobs for years, and the main thing you know about them is that you never can know on any given day what's going to happen."

Inevitably, news this hot leaked out. After keeping the conversations quiet for nearly three days, on the afternoon of June 30, the Duke student newspaper, the *Chronicle*, broke the story. When asked by Michael Mueller, a *Chronicle* reporter, about the rumors swirling around campus, Alleva confirmed that the Lakers had contacted Coach K, and the team and the coach were in "serious discussions." The *Los Angeles Times* further confirmed that Kupchak had flown to North Carolina and offered Coach K the job that day. "It's his for the taking, his job to lose," a Lakers source told the paper.

Alleva then released a statement, evidence of his growing concern that Krzyzewski might actually leave. "We have long believed that Mike is the best coach in the country," he wrote. "The Lakers' interest in him merely confirms what we have known. We hope that Mike will decide to stay in college coaching at Duke, a place that has been so special to him throughout his outstanding career. Mike has been an incredible asset to our institution, and on a much larger scale, to the sport of college basketball." He noted that he and Brodhead had met for dinner with Krzyzewski "to express at the highest level our desire for him to finish his coaching career at Duke."

Later that afternoon, Alleva also held a press conference at Cameron Indoor Stadium, one of the nation's meccas of college basketball. Seth Davis, a 1992 Duke graduate and a writer at *Sports Illustrated* (and the son of Lanny Davis, a former legal counsel to President Bill Clinton), would later refer to Alleva's press conference as a "farce" because the press release about the "serious discussions" under way had already conveyed all that was going on. "It may have been a gesture, on Alleva's part, to demonstrate to Coach K how much they want him to stay, but I think it was unnecessary," he said. "It's hard to tell what Duke was thinking."

One thing that was clearly on Alleva's mind that afternoon was getting Krzyzewski to stay. "Obviously, when you have the best coach in the country, it's not unusual when one of the best franchises in the country comes after him," he said. "He has meant so much to Duke basketball, and so much to college basketball, that obviously we're going to do everything we can to keep him in college basketball."

Later that Thursday night, one hundred summer-session students—as well as Brodhead—attended a candlelight vigil and rally at Krzyzewskiville that had been organized using social media. For ninety minutes, the students cheered for Coach K, in absentia, and urged him to stay. At one point, Brodhead picked up a bullhorn to lead a discussion with the students about the crisis and then joined with them, sitting on the grass strewn with beer cans, to form a giant *K* by linking arms. For his part, Krzyzewski and his family were sequestered at their house in Durham, trying to decide what he should do.

The third time seemed like it was going to be the charm for Krzyzewski and professional basketball. He had become good friends with Kupchak. He greatly admired the skills of Kobe Bryant. He respected the family and team values espoused by Lakers owner Jerry Buss. The money was of course seductive, even though he had often spoken about how little money mattered to him. Once again, though, he had to think about whether his true calling was as a professional basketball coach or as the world's best college coach. Word was that Coach K would take the weekend to decide what he wanted to do. "He's going to have to measure what the opportunities are in front of him in L.A. against what a quarter of a century has provided him here," Tom Butters, the former Duke athletic director who had hired Krzyzewski from Army in 1980, told the *Chronicle*. "If he were to leave and go to the Lakers and win twenty championships, he will always be associated with Duke basketball."

Over the weekend, Coach K's nerve-racking decision was the top news story in the country. ESPN couldn't get enough of it. The media speculated that his growing frustration with the ease with which the pros picked off his best players would lead him to make the move to the NBA. (Of course, there was no mention of the irony that now he was potentially in the process of being picked off by the pros, too.) Prior to the 1998–99 season, no nonsenior Duke player had ever gone pro; since then, eight had done so, with Livingston becoming a professional without ever having set foot on Coach K Court. "What he loves the most—it's not beating people—it's taking an eighteen-year-old kid and producing a twenty-two-year-old man," Chris Kennedy, Duke's senior associate athletic director, explained that weekend. "To have these polished, accomplished, admirable individuals come out of our program—that's what he's seen as his central mission. Now it's sort of leaking away. . . . What bothers him more than anything else is the way things have gotten so out of kilter."

He got plenty of unsolicited advice. Pat Forde, a columnist at the *Louisville Courier-Journal*, urged him to reject the offer. He wondered if Coach K had "LOST YOUR FLIPPIN' MIND?" and then observed: "Mike, you love all that rah-rah stuff—the stuff that makes Duke everything that the NBA isn't. You built Duke's corny camaraderie—the coaches love the players, who love the students, who worship you like some kind of ancient god. It's basketball set to the *Barney* theme song: I love you, you love me . . . Annoying, but apt. The cloying word that envelopes your program is 'special.' And it's true. Duke is smug, Duke is sanctimonious . . . but Duke is special."

He also received an e-mail from Duke undergrad Andrew Humphries, from Waynesboro, Virginia, that supposedly influenced his decision. "Duke basketball is the reason I came to this university, plain and simple," Humphries wrote Coach K over the weekend. "One of my essays was about [1990s team member] Bobby Hurley's assist record and watching [Hurley's teammate] Thomas Hill cry his eyes out. Without knowing it, or perhaps fully knowing it, you have been an integral part of the lives of hundreds of thousands of people who you've never actually met. We watch you coach, we come to Cameron and hear you speak . . . and most of all, we admire you. We admire you because you take kids from all over the country and you make them into a family that seems second only to your actual family in your life. We admire you because you taught us that five people together is a fist, while one person is just a finger. We admire you because you are just an old Polish guy in the dark, looking for some heart. And you always find it."

Humphries wrote that while he had dreamed of playing for Krzyzewski when he was a kid growing up, he knew that he didn't have a prayer. "And then I got to Duke," he continued, "and discovered that, yes, I am going to play for Coach K. I am going to be his sixth man. We hear about it on TV, how the Crazies are like a team member, and we think: Sure. We're a team member as soon as we [make] a jumper. But then we get to Duke, and we watch players from all over the country stare wide-eyed at us as their jumpers start to clang off the back iron. We get to Duke and we hear you speaking, imploring us to be louder, try harder, to give 100 percent. We get to Duke and we realize you are our coach. Not just the coach of our team, but you are also our coach, because you believe that we give you something no one else can and we know that you give us something that no one ever could. Please still be my coach. I know that we can find more heart to offer an old Polish guy in the dark next year." Soon enough, Humphries had his fifteen minutes of fame.

The consensus seemed to be—not surprisingly—that there would be no way for Duke to compete with the Lakers financially for Krzyzewski's services but that on the margin the school could improve life for him—for instance, by building a new practice facility for the team that Krzyzewski had long coveted and continuing his various ancillary roles around the campus. "My heart tells me that he'll stay, but evaluating everything that's been going on, and everything the Lakers can offer him, and his own kind of thirst—he's a very, very competitive guy," Chris Kennedy continued. "And I think that maybe in the back of his mind for a long time he's thought, 'I could compete with Phil Jackson or Red Auerbach or whoever you think of as a great NBA coach.' . . . But from time to time, he's had to have wondered how he would do on that stage." In the end, it seemed it would come down to his wife Mickie's counsel. "Mike places a lot of stock, and rightly so, on what Mickie thinks," Kennedy said. "If Mike comes to her and says, 'We have a great life here and a great home and people love us and we're secure, but this is something we have to do,' then Mickie's going to say, 'Follow me, I'm going to lead us out there.'"

Late Sunday night, Krzyzewski and his family made the decision to stay at Duke. He called Kupchak first. "I figured the person that I was not going with needed to be told first," he said. Then he called Brodhead and told him of the decision. Then Krzyzewski told his players.

On Monday morning, word began to leak out that Krzyzewski would stay at Duke. That afternoon, Mickie Krzyzewski left a message on Andrew Humphries's phone. "You don't know me, we've never met, but my name is Mickie Krzyzewski. I'm Coach K's wife," she said. "I read your e-mail to him, and he read it too, and I wanted to let you know on his behalf that he is still your coach and we are staying here at Duke. There's going to be a press conference over at Cameron at 5 [p.m.] in the media room, and if you're available at five, I would love to say something to you. I don't want you to go out of your way to do that, but I wanted to let you know, and I'd love to say hello to you. Thank you for your e-mail, it meant a lot—and he's your coach." Needless to say, "when Mrs. Krzyzewski called," Humphries recalled, "I got goose bumps. I was tearing up a bit. It was unbelievable."

At the five o'clock press conference on July 5, both Brodhead and Alleva flanked Krzyzewski. Clearly relieved—but in a rare public display of inarticulateness (it was his first moment on the national stage since coming to Duke)—

Brodhead heaped praise upon the coach. "So early in my appointment do I have the happy task of confirming the news that Mike Krzyzewski, the famous Coach K, will be staying on at Duke and hopefully finishing his career here," Brodhead announced at the start of the news conference. "When I say that this is a great pleasure, you will note why: it partly has to do with this man's records and achievements as a coach—all those games won, all those great seasons; but I must say that in . . . my own personal sense, that this is a man whose success as a coach has to do with far more than the strings of victories he's compiled." He noted Krzyzewski's excellence as a teacher who espoused the importance of character, teamwork and integrity. "I've been here a great deal in the last six months, and I must say that I have learned even more, and every visit here I see that you embody so many of the kinds of values that this school prides itself on," he continued. "You are a person that has competed at the highest level year after year [and] that level of competition has always been associated with maintaining the highest level of integrity, dignity, and many other virtues." He announced that Krzyzewski would remain an assistant to him, and that "I'll be relying on you in lots of ways."

Brodhead's relief was palpable. "It's not surprising that a person on this level would be gone after by a range of people, most recently by the L.A. Lakers, and I'm sure I don't even know a half or a tenth of what the last week has been like for you," he said. "At the end of the day, you have to decide what choice is best for you. You have one life to live and where is it going to be best lived and where are you going to give what's best in you to give. I had to face the fact that I might arrive here just in time for you to leave. If that's the choice that you decided you needed to make at this time, I would have had to respect that and urge this community to thank you for your good work here and pre-pare themselves for the post–Coach K years. I must say that I am enormously excited that, at the end of the day, you decide[d] that your place was in college basketball."

Alleva, too, was nearly giddy with the news, as he had been since he first heard it. "Thank you all for being here today because this is a happy day," he said. "It's a happy day for Coach K and his family and it's a great day for Duke University and college basketball." He praised the Krzyzewskis for "the way they have handled this situation," especially since "it's human nature in this world, when they had an opportunity of the magnitude that they had, for things to go through their mind" like taking the money and moving on to the NBA. Instead, they decided to stay, in Durham. "It's a real tribute to Mike as a man and to Mickie as his spouse the way that they handled this situation," he said. He then praised his new boss. After recounting how he had had to dis-turb Brodhead on his first day, he said, "He handled this situation with great leadership and great vision. Let me assure you that, in the Duke world, this university is in as good hands as our basketball program is."

When Alleva turned the stage over to Coach K, he was his usual gracious, public self. He thanked the Lakers for the opportunity and Duke for letting him explore it thoroughly, which he took as a sign of institutional strength. He said he took the opportunity seriously because, at fifty-seven years of age, the time had come to reflect upon where he had been and what the future likely held for him. In the end, though, he said the decision was easier for him than he'd thought it might be. "You have to follow your heart and lead with it"—a reference to the title of his first bestselling book, *Leading with the Heart,* published in 2000—"and Duke has always taken up my whole heart," he said. "I've been very fortunate in my adult life to be part of something bigger than me. Obviously I've been that with my family and my faith, but I've always had that with being a part of the United States Military Academy, with Duke and with college basketball. Those three entities are bigger than any individual, or any group of individuals."

He also mentioned Humphries's e-mail and how it reinforced the idea of the bond between the team, the coach, and the fans—and moved him to tears. "That's the type of relationship that has made this place just different, where it's not just been our team," he continued. "It's been OUR team, with everybody involved. And hopefully we can keep that going."

By all accounts, Brodhead had passed his first major test at Duke. And he seemed to know that he had dodged a bullet, one that came out of nowhere. "Yale has wonderful athletics, and I was a devotee of them and I was a very good friend of the athletic director there," Brodhead recalled of this experience. "But, of course, nothing prepared me for competition at the level that would soon be my daily life. Let's just say the L.A. Lakers weren't trying to recruit anyone from Yale." Asked a few years later if anything he had experienced at Yale had prepared him for the firehose that he was drinking from after Alleva barged into his office, Brodhead conceded that when it came to a sports-related crisis, the answer was no. "I admired the level at which sports are played down here," he said, referring to when he was at Yale and thinking about Duke. "It's not just basketball—that's our most famous—but Duke had soccer teams, lacrosse teams, cross-country teams, golf teams in the national championships last year, and it's all part of this sort of culture of excellence, of people trying to do things at a very, very high level. And, of course, when you get into that level, then all of a sudden there are new kinds of pressure, but there weren't when you play in a less competitive league. What did I have for preparation? All I'm going to tell you is, if anybody wants preparation for the job of a university president, you have to be prepared for the unprepared to come up every five minutes or so."

But it didn't take long for the cynics to point out the irony of the situation: to wit, that in his first week as the university's president, Brodhead, who had been selected in part because of his world-class intellect and impeccable academic credentials—with the expectation they would rub off on Duke and help the school continue its long march into the very top tier of the world's elite universities—had been confronted with the potential loss of the school's most high-profile and important icon: its basketball coach. And Brodhead had not even been Krzyzewski's first call after he had made the decision.

Many sportswriters believed that the coach had played the university and its new president like a Stradivarius. Krzyzewski "could have listened to the Lakers' offer, then quietly and politely declined the same day," observed Phil Taylor in *Sports Illustrated*. "But then he wouldn't have been in the headlines for the entire weekend, with each speculative story raising his profile even more, not to mention his public speaking fees and his endorsement possibilities. It wouldn't be surprising if he parlayed the Lakers' interest into a few more perks from the Duke administration. Stretching things out was a great career move. All in all, Coach K played this situation out as masterfully as any game he's ever coached." Added *Kansas City Star* columnist Jason Whitlock, "It was a great score. It was old-school. Coach K never raised his voice or his hand, but he let his new president know exactly who runs things on Tobacco Road"—the way locals refer to the area around Duke and Durham. "He also sent a similar message to basketball recruits across the land: Coach K is the unquestioned king of amateur hoops. Check *SportsCenter* and *USA Today* if you doubt it.... Coach K, without uttering a word or meeting face-to-face with owner Jerry Buss, had us all believing he might uproot his family and move to the West Coast for the privilege of coaching a young man"—a reference to Kobe Bryant—"who is scheduled to stand trial for rape this year. I feel stupid for falling for it. Brodhead shouldn't. He had no other choice."

Whitlock expanded this observation a few days later, after Kupchak had leaked the news that Roy Williams, the new coach at Kupchak's alma mater, had quietly turned down the Lakers job, too. "When you've just lost your two best teenage players, this sort of free publicity can be very beneficial on the recruiting trail," he wrote. "And when your number one rival (UNC) has recently backed up a Brinks truck to land the coach of its dreams, a little public flirting with the Lakers is the easiest way to modify your 'lifetime' contract, the one Krzyzewski signed in 2001. 'We were able to do a few things for Mike in his contract,' Alleva sheepishly acknowledged on Monday. And Krzyzewski was able to let his new school president, Brodhead, know exactly who is in charge at Duke."

But it wasn't only outside observers who got the message about the starring role athletics played in the Duke firmament. The symbolism of the pas de deux between Krzyzewski and the Lakers, and the humbling part Brodhead was expected—indeed, forced—to play in it, resonated powerfully inside the Ivory Tower, too. "What you saw there was the lay of the land," explained Orin Starn, a Duke professor who specializes in the anthropology of sports. "The fact is that it's the basketball coach, Coach K, who's the most powerful person at Duke, and in Durham, and maybe in North Carolina—much more powerful than the college president himself. So Brodhead—I mean, there was almost this kind of ritual humiliation, this ritual obeisance, or fealty, that was required of him."

Krzyzewski clearly got what was going on—"I am Duke every second of my life," he has said about the essential role he plays at the university, even as he feigns modesty. "Duke basketball is not the most important thing here," he explained to *Duke* magazine in 2012. "I know that. I work for Dick Brodhead and [new athletics director] Kevin White. But Duke basketball is the biggest marketing arm of the university." He then likened the basketball program at Duke to a street-level, Christmastime window display at Saks Fifth Avenue in New York. "You look at them and say, 'Wow!'" he continued. "'How did they do that?' So you walk in the store and you go to the first floor, the sixth floor, the seventh floor. Well, we're the window of our university. We bring a lot of people in, and then they find out what's happening in medicine, law, business, history, English. As long as we understand that, and use it, it's nothing but good. I've understood that from the get-go. Getting the right people to come in the door opens up development, research, enrollment—it opens up everything. We know we're part of that team."

But the good news about Coach K masked deeper institutional problems at Duke about the often uneasy relationship between academics and athletics. Three days before Alleva burst into Brodhead's office in Allen Building with the news that Krzyzewski might actually be leaving Duke for the Lakers, another Duke administrator and professor of medical psychology, Robert Thompson—then in his fifth year as the dean of Duke's undergraduate program—received a two-page, single-spaced, letter from Peter Wood, a longtime Duke history professor and former Rhodes scholar. Wood, then sixty years old, had been teaching history at Duke for nearly thirty years and briefly coached the women's lacrosse team when it was a club sport. In his letter to Thompson, Wood worried that during the previous decade "mission creep" had occurred "regarding the time demands of student athletes." He noticed that "slowly" and "sport by sport and year by year" it had become "more acceptable and common for players to miss classes and spend inordinate time on the road." Why, Wood wondered, were injured athletes required to travel with their teams? Why were nonconference, midseason games scheduled in western time zones? And why were varsity coaches allowed to call a "required" practice during "morning class time in the last week" of the semester? "I was shocked to lose at least a dozen students for this reason this spring," he wrote Thompson, "during the important last week of class. They had no option. Needless to say, even when such drills are billed as voluntary, students on athletic scholarships feel that they must give their first allegiance to coaches, not to professors."

Wood wrote that he found "even more troubling" the second trend involving the "attitudes of some varsity athletes toward their professors and their schoolwork generally," who are "part of a larger minority of disaffected, uninterested, and openly hostile students." He made clear this wasn't just a conclusion he had reached based on his own personal experience—although he had been confronted with the attitude in his own classes—but had heard the same from other professors and teaching assistants, too. "Unfortunately, this trend may well dovetail with the increasing centrality of sport for some at Duke," he concluded. He mentioned that at an alumni reunion event in 2003, he was "surprised" to hear a varsity coach "downplay the importance of course work and academic majors." He professed his hope that with "adequate leadership from all of us," he could see "no reason why this troubling antiacademic attitude cannot be addressed and repaired." Still, he ended his letter on an ominous note: "In my experience, we have gone beyond the 'few bad apples' stage."

Wood had been prompted to write the letter to Dean Thompson after the end of the spring semester in 2004, during which he taught a class in Native American history. There were sixty-five students in the class, ten of whom were varsity lacrosse players. He was reviewing his teacher evaluations and read the following comment from one of the students: "I wish all of the Indians had died; then we wouldn't have had to study them." Wood suspected that the author of this comment was a lacrosse player. He had become increasingly convinced that "the play-hard cohort was poisoning the campus culture" at Duke, "and that lacrosse players were at the heart of the problem."

Wood never heard back from Thompson. But it was not hard to see why Thompson did not respond. And why Brodhead, in his first week as university president, had no choice but to indulge Krzyzeswki in his very public flirtation with the Lakers. Duke had seemingly become the embodiment of a still-credible aspect of the American Dream: the ability to have it all in just four quick years. There was the first-rate education; the top-notch Division I athletics; the seemingly infinite job prospects upon graduation, especially on Wall Street; the gorgeous campus; the handsome student body; and the temperate climate. Who could ask for anything more? "Duke's rapid rise to prominence over the past several decades was perhaps without precedent in academia," observed Buzz Bissinger in *Vanity Fair*.

But Wood's warning about the shifting priorities of student-athletes at Duke would be driven home—for good—less than two years later, when Duke confronted its worst crisis in a history that traces back 175 years.

CHAPTER ONE

"We've Got Dancers Coming"

Although no one knew it yet, Duke's perception of itself, as well as how the university was perceived by the rest of the world, began to change sometime around midnight on Monday, March 14, 2006, after a night of shenanigans and heavy drinking by forty-one of the forty-seven members of the tight-knit varsity lacrosse team—all but one of whom were white. The party took place at a nondescript rental house at 610 North Buchanan Boulevard, off Duke's East Campus, where three of the lacrosse players lived. It was spring break, and the rest of the Duke campus was quiet. Two days before, the Duke lacrosse team, then ranked third in the country, had defeated twentieth-ranked Loyola 9–7 in San Diego, improving its record to 5–1. After the Loyola win, coach Mike Pressler said, "Now we look ahead to one of the most difficult weeks in Duke lacrosse history," a reference to the team's upcoming March 18 match against rival University of North Carolina, followed by games against Cornell and Georgetown in quick succession. Little did Pressler know that for whatever reason—boredom, feeling sorry for themselves for having to be in town when everyone else was on spring break, or simply because they could—most of the guys on his lacrosse team would decide to have their own version of *Girls Gone Wild* on North Buchanan Boulevard in Durham, North Carolina.

After lacrosse practice on March 13, at around 3 p.m., Dan Flannery, a twenty-one-year-old senior cocaptain from Garden City, New York, ran a few errands and then went home to 610 North Buchanan. He found a number of his teammates already there. According to Jason Bissey, who lived next door, he and his roommate, Derek Anderson, remembered that the drinking began an hour before Flannery returned home. A group of guys were playing "washers," whereby a player tries to toss metal washers into a cup from a defined distance. "I remember in particular one young man wearing a sort of suspenders-like harness that would hold two cans or bottles of beer," Bissey said. Anderson remembered that as the day turned into night at 610 North Buchanan, more and more people showed up at the party. He remembered seeing as many as thirty people in the backyard, playing washers. "They were pretty loud that night," he later told police. "They had been playing washers for about seven hours."

Flannery confirmed that the drinking began early that day. "We decided

13

to start drinking [because] we were on spring break," he explained. At least once a week, the team usually went together to Teasers Men's Club on Ramseur Street in Durham, a topless bar—it boasted of being the "area's finest"— where to be admitted one had to be at least twenty-one years old. Since some of the players at the house were not twenty-one or had lost their fake IDs, they decided to see if they could hire two strippers to come by at 11 p.m. that night to dance during the party for a couple of hours. This was, apparently, a spring break tradition for the Duke lacrosse team. Recalled Ryan McFadyen, a six-foot-five defenseman from Mendham, New Jersey, "The tradition is: 'Hey, it's spring break. We're the only guys on campus.'" McFadyen remembered March 13 was a gorgeous day. At the practice that morning, they did a running workout with the speed coach. He also remembered that Coach Pressler came to the practice with something like $10,000 in cash that he handed out to the players for "meal money" for the eight days of spring break. "Coach Pressler handed out meal money for the week to every guy on the team that Monday," McFadyen said. It was like, 'Yeah, here's five hundred bucks. Here's five hundred bucks. Here's five hundred bucks.'" Afterward, he got a message on his cell phone from David Evans, Flannery's housemate and another cocaptain of the lacrosse team. "I remember the message he left," McFadyen recalled. "He said, 'Hey, we're having a barbecue over at 610. Get yourself and the sophomore guys over here. I need a six-foot-five-inch hunk of meat in my backyard right now. Get over here.' So people were making their way over. Some guys were there early. Some guys were there at two or three."

The idea was just to have some fun while the rest of the students were away. McFadyen got to the party around two o'clock. "Guys were drinking," he said. "We were hanging out. I don't think I had any beers yet, 'cause I know I went back to eat and went to the gym, worked out again." When he was at the party the first time, he noticed some of the guys were betting some of their meal money on games of beer pong. "Who wants to play?" he recalled people saying. "Who wants to play?" He then went to work out and got a ride back to the party. "We were there all day, grilling, having beers, playing washers, beer pong, just having a good time, playing some music. . . . Everyone was drinking, and someone said, 'Oh, let's go to the strip club.' Someone's idea was like, 'Let's just have dancers come to the house as opposed to risking people going out and getting in trouble. We'll just order dancers to come here,' a very common occurrence on campus. I know Duke tried to issue some sort of moratorium, make a rule against it after the fact, but between keeping the frats on campus, sororities doing it during their rush week and people doing it during random events, it happens all the time, so it's common for sure. For us, it was just 'We'll just do it here. It'll be very casual.' It'll be the smarter choice, because there won't be anyone outside the team to screw anything up or get into trouble or risk anything."

After searching Google for the phone number of the Allure Agency, Dan Flannery called and spoke with the woman who answered. They discussed the rate for each stripper—$400, half of which the dancers could keep—whether certain ethnicities of strippers could be selected and if there was a maximum stripper-to-partier ratio. He gave the woman a fake name—Daniel Flanigan—but his real cell phone number. "She called me back twenty to twenty-five minutes later telling me that she had two girls," Flannery recalled in a subsequent written statement. "The first had brown hair with light brown highlights, measurements 35-25-35 (vaguely) and a 36C chest. The second girl was [H]ispanic with roughly the same measurements. The lady on the phone told me the girls were in their mid- to late twenties and had worked together before."

Flannery shared this information with his buddies, and they decided that hiring the two strippers was a good plan. Flannery then called his other teammates, not already there, and invited them over for the party, which was going to be a night of drinking, watching TV, and playing "Beirut," another name for the drinking game beer pong, where cups partially filled with beer are arranged in a pyramid shape on a table and each team takes turns trying to bounce a Ping-Pong ball into the cups. If the ball goes in, a member of the opposing team has to drink the beer. The skill required to get the Ping-Pong ball into the cups is pretty low, so the consumption of beer is pretty high—which is the point, after all. Another housemate, David Evans, also then twenty-two and the cocaptain of the lacrosse team along with Flannery, collected $25 from each lacrosse player at the house to pay the $800 cost of the two strippers.

McFadyen remembered when he got back to the party for the second time, "People were collecting money, like, 'Hey, we've got dancers coming. Instead of going to Teasers, they're coming here.' All right. The whole team's here. I'll hang out."

Around 6:10 p.m. that night, "Melissa" from the Allure Agency called Kim Roberts, also known as Kim Pittman, a thirty-one-year-old half-black, half-Korean woman who had been working at the agency for about six months. She lived at 1602 Albany Street in Durham, had a young daughter and was in some trouble with the law. She had been convicted of embezzling from a previous employer in Durham County and had then run off to California, in violation of her parole. She returned to Durham, even though there was an outstanding warrant for her arrest for missing a meeting with her parole officer. Her job prospects were pretty dim. Dancing as a stripper was a way to get some steady work and pay her bills. Allure told her to show up at 11 p.m. at the house on North Buchanan for a bachelor party of about fifteen guys. "I went to Priscilla's to purchase an outfit for the evening and proceded [sic] to get ready for the night," she wrote in a statement given to the Durham police about a week later. She believed the party would be relatively small and tame because she assumed the guys would be older—the friends of a guy getting married—and that she would be dancing with another, more experienced woman in case things got out of control.

When Roberts arrived at 610 North Buchanan around eleven o'clock, she decided not to stop at the house. She had quickly realized that this was not likely to be a bachelor party but rather a Duke student party at what looked like some off-campus house. She was right. "At first I didn't want to stay, because I saw all these young guys," she said. She drove around the block and then pulled up to the house.

Flannery—known to her as "Dan F."—met her when she got out of the car. She still didn't like the setting but Flannery got her to relax, although her anxieties were not much allayed when she saw player after player coming out onto the front lawn of the house to take a piss. Flannery told her that actually the party was a gathering of friends, not a bachelor party after all, and that they were all graduate students on sports teams at Duke. Flannery described Roberts as the "Hispanic" stripper—even though she was not—and "very friendly and outgoing." He said she told him she had graduated from the University of North Carolina at Chapel Hill—even though she had not—and that the other stripper, described as a black girl, would be arriving shortly. "She drove her own vehicle, seemed very concsious [sic], sober and eager to start the party," Flannery explained in his written statement. She waited another thirty minutes or so for the other dancer, Crystal Gail Mangum, to arrive at the house. While Roberts was waiting, she saw a Durham police car drive by the house a few times. This made her nervous—there was the outstanding warrant for her arrest, after all—so she moved to the back of the house. Evans made Roberts a drink—Diet Pepsi and whiskey—and she and Flannery hung out in Evans's room for a while, waiting for Mangum to arrive. She went outside at one point to smoke a cigarette and Flannery accompanied her. She also collected her $400.

She had been told that members of the Duke baseball and track teams were at the party, but then learned that the party comprised Duke lacrosse players. One player told her the guys were expecting one of the strippers to be white and the other to be Hispanic. Even though Roberts was not Hispanic, she looked like she would fit the bill, so the general expectation was that the other stripper would be white. "As we waited, I met a few of the fellas in the house," Roberts said, "and chitchatted for several minutes. The guys were anxious and asked me to call Melissa and check on the second girl. We were told that she was on her way."

When Mangum, who is black, finally arrived, there was some initial concern about whether the dancing should proceed, given the boys' preference for white dancers. Like Roberts, Mangum was a single mother—of two children—and a student at the predominantly black North Carolina Central University in

Durham. She also seemed unsteady on her feet. "When the black girl arrived," Flannery explained, "she was dropped off by a male and was suspected to be high and drunk. She could hardly speak and her words were slurred and at times incomprehensible. . . . Guys on the team were commenting on how messed-up/high the black stripper was." Added Evans, "She was obviously on some kind of drug from the start, the black stripper. She couldn't walk or talk clearly."

But Flannery and his buddies decided to move ahead with the evening entertainment as planned. "People are kind of shoveling up money," McFadyen recalled. "I heard Dan saying, 'These girls are coming. Let's go. Everyone get around.' And I'm in the back playing washers with Kevin Mayer and having a couple beers. But nothing was out of the ordinary. Every party there is somebody who is the DD"—designated driver—"and someone who's drunk, and every level in between. And guys were just having a good time. I remember Dan telling people, 'Hey, the girls are coming. Let's get inside.' So we file in. The main living room is packed. I hopped into someone's bedroom. Eddie Douglas was in there. We sat down. We were watching baseball on TV." McFadyen also remembered what Flannery said about the two dancers. "He was like, 'Oh, we have two girls, both blondes, in their late twenties, 36-24- . . .' He gave some measurement. All right, great." But then, after the players had assembled and the dancing was about to begin, McFadyen remembered that Flannery had told everyone: "'Hey, both girls are here, and they're chocolate.' I was like, 'Whatever.' D. Wood"—Devon Sherwood, the only black player on the team— "gets up and goes, 'Hell yeah, bring them in.' I said, 'I don't care if they're black, white, whatever. They're just here to dance, show some skin and that's it.'" (In an interview, Sherwood denied making this comment to McFadyen.)

Mangum—whom Roberts referred to as "Precious," while she referred to Roberts as "Nikki"—went to the back of the house, met Roberts "for the first time" and then went inside to get her $400 payment, which she then showed to Roberts. Flannery and Evans then spoke to the women about "the routine and the logistics of their dance." They also spoke about the need to be "respectful" during the performance. "Okay, you guys seem very respectful," Roberts recalled telling the guys. "If everybody acts as you are acting, I'm sure we'll have a fun time. I'm sure we'll have a good time." Roberts said, "They completely assured me that everybody in there were good guys—'Everybody in there is respectful, and you will be fine and safe.' [I was] completely assured of that."

With the decision made to proceed, Roberts told Flannery to go back inside the house so she could speak with Mangum alone and "get to know her" before the dancing began. "We talked," Roberts explained later. "We joked a little bit. I told her I was new to this and didn't really know what I was doing. [She] told me that she danced at a club and was a little more experienced. She told me about her kids. . . . It was a regular, normal conversation, nothing that set off any alarm bells in my head." Roberts disputed the notion that Mangum was incoherent when she arrived, even though later the statement that Mangum was "loopy" would be attributed to her.

They headed into the house, into Evans's bathroom, to get changed and prepared, even though Mangum was already in costume. (She also showed up at the house with cuts on her knee and foot, according to pictures of the event.) "We conversed about our plan for the dance," Roberts explained. While the two women were in the green-tile bathroom, "there was a knock on the door," Roberts continued, "and we were handed two drinks of equal amounts." They sipped the drinks but soon "Precious's cup fell into the sink," Roberts said. They finished getting dressed, and then Flannery led the women out of the bathroom to the living room "to do our show," Roberts continued.

At that time, most of the students were in the front room of the house, drinking, watching TV, listening to music, and waiting for the dancing to begin. "There were about twenty to twenty-five young guys there who were all sitting down," Roberts recalled. "Precious and I began our show, which, in my opinion, seemed to be going well." Observed Flannery, "Guys were cheering and yelling." Roberts noticed that the guys had been drinking more than just beer—she saw a large bottle of Jack Daniel's going around—and remarked at how young many of them seemed. "The girls entered the room, began to dance and make out with each other," Flannery continued. "The black girl fell to the ground and the [H]ispanic girl sat on her face, engaging in or mimicking oral sex." Recalled McFadyen, "So they come in. I remember hearing when they come in and start dancing . . . I remember when I first saw [Mangum], you could just tell. Her movements were wishy-washy. She was really fucked-up on something."

Evans noted that Mangum "couldn't talk or stand up straight, she was so high," and that Roberts "took of[f] her bra" but "never her underwear." Mangum, he said, "only pulled her top down halfway" and "never took off her underwear," either. "The girls were sloppily dancing due to the black stripper's state of mind and began to kiss," he observed. Still, there seemed to be the expectation among the team members, Roberts later thought on reflection, that the dancers "would fully degrade each other during the course of the performance." Evans reported that that was, in fact, what happened next. He said Mangum "went down" on Roberts. Neither Roberts nor Mangum recalled having oral sex.

At the time, Roberts said she was increasingly nervous for their safety. "As soon as we showed ourselves in our costumes, it was on," she said. "They were ready to see whatever they were going to see, and so it got loud from there and there was no time. There was no time. There was no wait. It was just a go from there. . . . You have to think of two little girls among how many big boys? That in and of itself is intimidating if they are not being respectful of my feelings, my space. . . . How is someone supposed to perform a show if they're wondering, 'Okay, what's this guy talking about over here? Am I going to have to worry about my safety?' Things were said that made me concerned for my safety."

After the women got up off the floor, according to Flannery, Roberts asked the guys, "Who was going to step up and take their pants off[?] No one would." Peter Lamade, then twenty-one, from Chevy Chase, Maryland, and a graduate of the Landon School—a feeder school for Duke athletes—asked Roberts "if she put objects up her vagina." Her response, according to Flannery, was "something along the lines of 'I would put your dick in me but you're not big enough.'" Then Lamade grabbed a broomstick, showed it to Roberts and said, "Would this do?" (Another version of this incident, according to Matt Zash, had Lamade wondering if the dancers had brought with them any "sex toys," to which Roberts supposedly responded, "What's wrong, white boy, is your dick too small?" To which Lamade responded by grabbing the broomstick and telling Roberts, "Here, you can use this" and "I'm gonna shove this up you.")

With events having taken a seemingly nasty turn, Roberts decided to stop the show. "That statement made me uncomfortable, and I felt like I wanted to leave," Roberts explained. "I raised my voice to the boys and said the show was over. The commotion riled Precious up and caused her to get irate." Roberts was "half-naked" at that point, according to Flannery, and Mangum was wearing a "glittery-type dress or getup." He said Mangum had not taken off her clothes. Roberts was very upset at this point. She was "yelling and screaming about how we had disrespected them," Flannery recalled. Roberts then grabbed Mangum and both women headed into David Evans's room. "So, three minutes later, all of a sudden I look up and I see the one girl stepping over the couch and getting out of the room," McFadyen remembered. "The guys were saying shit to each other."

Flannery and Evans, as well as players Kyle Dowd and Tony McDevitt, followed the women into Evans's room. "We tried to apologize and reason with the [H]ispanic stripper," Flannery recalled. "The black stripper was mumbling and stumbling. I was apologizing to the [H]ispanic stripper and she offered to give me a private dance that I refused." Roberts and Mangum then went into the bathroom and closed the door. "I told her I wanted to leave," Roberts recalled. "Precious felt we could get more money and that we shouldn't leave yet. She was uncontrollable at this point and was yelling at the boys, who were knocking at the door, to leave us alone."

With the show over, a number of the lacrosse players were angry, as if they had paid $800 for next to nothing. "Guys on the team were upset and wanted their money back," Flannery said. "Some guys wanted to call the police." He tried to convince the women to continue the show, but that did not happen.

"At that point I was demanding our money back, because it appeared they were hustling us," Evans recalled. Said McFadyen, "I remember the two girls were in the bathrooom. They had locked themselves in. I guess they had already pooled all the money together and paid them up front for, like, two hours; it was $400 an hour for two, 'Here's $800,' and it had been, like, ten minutes. So then it was 'Hey, listen. We understand your friend is really fucked-up. She's not fit to dance. She needs to be taken somewhere, or you need to take care of her. But we paid you for two hours. Can we get some of the money back?' I remember walking by and seeing Dan and Evans were having this conversation."

According to Evans, it took another $100—that Flannery paid—to get the two women out of the bathroom and to leave the house. Jason Bissey, the next-door neighbor, heard the commotion brewing outside about the feeling of being cheated by the dancers.

Meanwhile, Roberts changed her clothes in the car and just wanted to drive away but didn't want to leave "Precious" by herself in the house. She said the guys came to her car window and asked her to help get Mangum, who had passed out on the back porch of the house. "By this point, it seemed that the fellas may have been ready for the evening to be over," Roberts said. "I told them that if they could get her to my car, I would get her out of their hair."

That is what happened. "The [H]ispanic stripper stomped out the back door with the black stripper in the midst of changing back into her clothes," Flannery remembered. "I was talking to the [H]ispanic the entire time she was walking to her car, apologizing. . . . The [H]ispanic girl entered her vehicle and was very angry. I tried to calm her down. [S]he wouldn't leave without the black stripper. We both thought the black girl was still in the bathroom. However, she was passed out on the back stoop of the house, half-naked. At this time I went to the back of the house w[ith] Kevin Coleman"—another teammate—"who photographed her passed out there and picked her up. I put her arms around my shoulder and walked her to the other girl's car."

When Mangum got into Roberts's car, Roberts noticed that she did not have her bag. Roberts asked her if she "had the most important thing, her money." Mangum told Roberts she did have the money. "But she did not seem coherent," Roberts recalled. "She then told me that we should go back to the house because there was more money to be made there." Roberts asked Mangum again if she had her "things" and Mangum said yes, she did, but Roberts didn't see them. "So in my opinion, she was talking crazy," Roberts recalled. She locked Mangum in her car and went back into the house to try to find Mangum's bag. She and Flannery looked around for Mangum's bag but couldn't find it. "I said, 'I've done all I can,' and went back to my car," she said.

Evans was growing concerned that the Durham police might come by, what with all the yelling and screaming and the fact that Mangum was stumbling around barefoot and, apparently, without her top on. "The [H]ispanic girl was in her driver's-side seat, while the black girl was circling the car, yelling," Evans remembered. "Her boobs were exposed and I thought that we were going to get a noise violation and that she was going to get a public nudity charge." Evans tried to convince her to go back inside and get her purse and shoes. But she wasn't going back inside.

Frustrated by the scene outside, Evans said he went back into the house and told everyone to leave because of the commotion outside. "Everyone was like, 'Everyone's got to go. Let's go to Charlie's. Let's go to a bar. Everyone make your way out,'" McFadyen said. "Guys were all over the house, walking out the front door, walking out the back. I think we were out of beer at that point. People just kind of dispersed." Evans said his teammates were still miffed. "They kept [asking me,] 'Did we get the money back, because we got hustled'; they had only stripped for maybe five minutes," Evans recalled. "I said, 'No, and I would gladly pay to have them leave.' This would be bad publicity for our team; otherwise I would have called the police then. Ryan McFadyen said that he wanted to take the money from the black girl's purse. I told him he was stupid 'cuz the girl had a driver who prob[ably] had a gun and would kill us." McFadyen had stayed behind briefly to use the bathroom. "Most guys are exiting to the backyard," he said. "Some guys are leaving. Some guys are walking down to the one bar. Some are walking to the other. Most of the guys are walking this way, toward East Campus so they can go to Charlie's. I was taking a pee. I remember seeing the one girl"—meaning Roberts—"walk out. I don't know. I guess everything is settled. I'm walking out and Dan Loftus was there. Dan said something . . . Dan opens the door and says, 'Oh, you're welcome,' and she's like, 'Fuck you.' Dan looks at me. Dan does a really funny face. His face was like, 'Oh, she's a little testy, huh?'"

As the women were getting ready to leave in Roberts's blue Honda, and then again as they were driving off, racial epithets started flying. Jason Bissey, who was already concerned about all the noise and the partying, said he heard one of the players yell, "Hey, bitch, thank your grandpa for your nice cotton shirt!" Roberts said the verbal assaults were even more offensive than Bissey recalled. "They just hollered it out, 'nigger,' 'nigger,' 'nigger,'" said Roberts. "They were hollering it for all to hear. They didn't care who heard it." Flannery remembered that some of his teammates were on top of the stone wall that surrounds Duke's East Campus and were yelling at the Honda as it pulled away. He saw that Roberts had stopped the car, gotten out, and yelled something back. Roberts later conceded she may have provoked a response by yelling "You limp-dick white boys, you're not real men. You had to pay for us" at them. At that point, Flannery said, the guys on the wall screamed, "Go home and feed your kids." Roberts replied, "Fuck Duke, I'm calling the cops. That's a hate crime." For his part, Matt Zash remembered overhearing one of his teammates say,

"Well, we asked for whites, not niggers," whereupon he heard Roberts say, "That's a hate crime, I'm calling the police." As she drove away, Roberts said, she kept thinking to herself, "It was almost unbelievable. All I kept going back to was, 'I can't believe these are Duke students.'" Recalled McFadyen, "We're sitting on the East Campus wall. Five minutes later, the girl comes out, gets in her car, pulls her car around. Dan Flannery walks out with the other girl, who is passed out in his arms. . . . He's carrying her out, puts her in the car. There was an exchange of words between some of the guys sitting farther down from me on the fence with Kim Roberts, whatever her name was, and she drives off."

Since he didn't have his fake ID with him, McFadyen and some of his younger teammates went back to their dormitory room at Edens Quad, on Duke's West Campus. "That was probably around midnight at that point," he said. "Hung out for a bit. I wrote my e-mail. I go to sleep." The e-mail he wrote, although in exceedingly poor taste, was supposedly a riff on the Brett Easton Ellis novel *American Psycho*, which many Duke students were required to read. The book and the movie based on it were favorites of McFadyen's. "To whom it may concern," McFadyen wrote, "Tommorow [*sic*] night, after tonights show, ive decided to have some strippers over to edens 2c. all are welcome. however there will be no nudity. I plan on killing the bitches as soon as the[y] walk in and proceding to cut their skin off while cumming in my duke issue spandex . . . all in besides arch and tack[.] please respond[.]"

In any event, it was bedtime after a long day and night. The Duke lacrosse team had a practice the next day at 11 a.m.

Meanwhile, Roberts said, she called the police on her cell phone and relayed the incident to them, as she had promised she would, but she did not give the police her real name—remembering the outstanding arrest warrant—plus she did not want it to be known that she was a stripper who had just come from a job. She also did not know what to do with Mangum, whose real name she did not know. Nor did she know where Mangum lived. She could not ask Mangum, either, since by this time the other woman had completely passed out.

According to a transcript of Roberts's 911 call, she spoke with the dispatcher at 12:53 a.m. from her cell phone. "Hi, I don't know if this is an emergency or not, necessarily," Roberts said, "but I'm in Durham, and I was driving down near Duke's campus, and it's me and my black girlfriend, and the guy—there's, like, a white guy by the Duke wall—and he just hollered out 'nigger' to me. And I'm just so angry I didn't know who to call." She noted that she had just come from 610 North Buchanan Boulevard—a "frat house," she said—and that although she had not been harmed and was not going to press charges against the guys, she did want to report to the police how offended she was by their use of a racial slur. "So I don't know what's gonna happen—I can't—I'm not gonna press the issue, I guess," Roberts continued. "But I live in a neighborhood where they wrote *KKK* on the side of a white station wagon, and that's near right where I'm at, you know what I mean. And they didn't harm me in any way, but I just feel so completely offended, I can't even believe it. I thought, you know, saying, times have changed, and I don't even know what the hell is going on. . . . So, I'm not going to press the issue, but, whatever, however Durham city feels about racial slurs and stuff, however you guys want to handle it, you can handle it however you do. I'm not hurt in any way, okay."

After making the call, Roberts again asked Mangum where she lived so that she could drive her home, but Mangum still did not respond. Roberts then called Melissa at the Allure agency to try to contact the driver who had dropped Mangum at 610 North Buchanan a few hours before. But Melissa was of no help, either. Roberts decided to drive to the Kroger supermarket, on Hillsborough Street in Durham, which was relatively nearby and which she knew was open twenty-four hours a day. She drove into the parking lot, found a security guard, and asked her to call the police. At 1:22 a.m., the security guard, Angel Altmon, called 911. About Mangum, Altmon said, "Um, the problem is . . . it's a lady in somebody else's car, and she will not get out of the car. She's, like, she's like intoxicated, drunk or something. She's, I mean, she won't get out of the car, period." After Altmon explained to the dispatcher the make and color of Roberts's car and the fact that Mangum was unarmed, not dangerous, and barely talking, Roberts added, "And she's fairly drunk. She has no weapons, not dangerous or anything." Shortly thereafter, the dispatcher said she would send a police cruiser to the Kroger parking lot to investigate and to be helpful if he could.

By this time, things had quieted down considerably at 610 North Buchanan. Neighbor Jason Bissey recalled that "within five minutes" of the women leaving, the noise at the house had ended. "It was total silence," he said. Zash, the third housemate, told everyone to go home, and that was when a number of the players started walking toward the East Campus wall. After everyone had left the house, Flannery and Zash moved their cars around the corner to 1105 Urban Street, where a group of their lacrosse teammates lived. "We were afraid the[y] might come back and damage our cars," Flannery said of the two dancers. Flannery and Zash then went inside 1105 Urban Street and one of their teammates told them the police had stopped by 610 North Buchanan. Flannery stepped outside the Urban Street house and could see that a police officer was outside, inspecting his house. He and Zash waited there, watching TV, until the officer left before returning home. It was around 1:30 a.m. "We then went back to the house and went to bed," he said. "The next morning, Matt found the black stripper's purse outside our house." At around 3 a.m., Zash heard a police radio outside the house. He woke up and saw an officer looking inside a car window with a flashlight, but the officer did not come to the door of the house.

David Evans also went to his teammates' house on Urban Street after the party broke up at North Buchanan. He was thinking the "cops might come because of the 'racial slur'" remark, although he said he did not know exactly what was said by his teammates to the women as they drove away. He remembered, too, that Flannery had given him $260 left over from what people had paid the dancers. He then gave Flannery back a $100 bill "because he had paid extra," and he noted that Flannery had also won $100 playing beer pong. He put the remaining $160 on his desk.

After Roberts's 911 call, Durham police sergeant John Shelton was dispatched to 610 North Buchanan Street to check out the alleged disturbance. "The narrative of the call stated that several males [were] yelling racial slurs at passersby," Shelton later recalled. When he arrived at the house, no one was outside or could be seen leaving the house. After some other officers arrived, Shelton knocked on the door of the house, but there was no answer. When he looked inside the house—from a window—he could not see anyone, either. "There were beer cans and bottles, a beer keg, and several empty plastic cups strewn about, leading me to believe that there had been a party," Shelton continued. "There were also two or three full trash bags on the front porch." Shelton saw Jason Bissey on the porch of his house and spoke with him. Bissey told him the "party had just broken up and that it was rowdy, causing him to contemplate calling 911." Shelton left 610 North Buchanan after he concluded the party was over and no one was at home.

A few minutes later, Shelton was dispatched to the Kroger because of a "woman refusing to get out of the complainant's car." Shelton arrived at the Kroger around 1:51 a.m. He was the first police officer on the scene. Roberts walked over to his car and explained that she had called 911 earlier about the "racial slurs" being spewed by the Duke students and that—lying here—she had seen Mangum walking along the wall of East Campus near 610 North Buchanan and had stopped and picked her up. Roberts told Shelton, who noted it in his report, that she "did not know if the female was drunk or high but that in any case she did not appear that she could take care of herself, and she was afraid of what the white men might do to the woman." Roberts told Shelton she had offered "the woman" a ride home, and now Mangum would not get out of her car. She also said she did not know the woman. "I cautioned her about picking up strangers," Shelton said. (Some forty-eight minutes later, several other Durham police officers concluded that Roberts had lied to them and that the two women had met earlier in the evening at 610 North Buchanan.)

Shelton then saw Mangum slumped down in the passenger-side seat of Roberts's car. He reported to the dispatcher that she was "breathing" and "appears to be fine. She's not in distress. She's just passed out, drunk." He said she was wearing a "see-through red garment," no underwear, and "one white high-heel shoe." He "grabbed her lightly," "jostled her," and spoke to her "loudly" in an effort to rouse Mangum from her stupor and get her out of the car. As she remained unresponsive, Shelton opened an ammonia capsule and put it under Mangum's nose, which revived her instantly. Mangum "began mouth-breathing, which is a sign that she was not really unconscious," Shelton observed. He was concerned that she might "wake up quickly" after smelling the ammonia capsule, and so he "grabbed" Mangum and "attempted to pull her from the vehicle."

But Mangum did not want to cooperate with Shelton. She grabbed hold of the Honda's emergency brake as Shelton tried to pull her from the car. She lost her grip on it, though, after Shelton applied pressure to her right hand and arm. "At this point, I applied a bent-wrist come-along [maneuver] to her right hand and arm," Shelton said. Once she was out of the car, Shelton released the pressure. "She collapsed to the ground," Shelton observed.

By this time, another officer, Willie Barfield, had arrived at the Kroger. He and Shelton conferred about what to do. Roberts said she did not want Mangum to get into trouble. At first, Shelton and Barfield decided that Mangum's "bizarre behavior" was the result of either drugs or alcohol and determined she be taken to the Durham County Jail and placed on "twenty-four-hour lockup status." Echoing Shelton's observations about Mangum, Barfield communicated to the Durham Community Communications Center, or DCCC, "She's breathing, appears to be fine. She's not in distress. She's just passed out drunk."

Without any identification—her pocketbook was still at 610 North Buchanan—and since Mangum would not talk to the officers and Roberts did not know her name or where she lived, the officers revised their thinking and decided instead that Mangum was "too intoxicated" to be brought to jail overnight and decided to take her to Durham Center Access, a halfway house and emergency room that helped indigents through substance-abuse and psychological crises. Shelton determined Mangum "met the criteria for involuntary commitment," since she had no identification, wasn't speaking and seemed unable to walk voluntarily. "Based on his experience, both on patrol and in his training of officers on the methods of making such distinctions, Sergeant Shelton identified signs and symptoms of a severe mental illness," according to court documents. "Sergeant Shelton further concluded that Mangum was imminently dangerous to herself or others, and that she was in need of immediate psychiatric care. Shelton withdrew his twenty-four-hour-hold order and directed the officers to initiate emergency involuntary commitment proceedings." Shelton then "withdrew from the call." (The DCCC recordings relating to Shelton's change of heart have been destroyed.)

To some participants in the unfolding drama, this was considered a crucial moment. If Mangum had been brought to the Durham County Jail, as originally planned, she would have been held for twenty-four hours and likely slept off her drug or alcohol frenzy. Instead, by bringing her to Durham Access, a series of steps was initiated that could have resulted in Mangum's two young children—at that moment alone at her home, asleep—being taken away from her.

Mariecia Smith, a supervisor at Durham Access, met Mangum first in the parking lot of the center. It was around 2 a.m., Smith later told Durham police, that Officer Barfield did not know Mangum's name because she was "nonresponsive." Smith introduced herself to Mangum and asked her to get out of the police car. Smith told the police that Mangum "appeared nervous and was shaking." Mangum told Smith her name was "Honey" and that she did not want to go to jail. Smith told Mangum she was at Durham Access, not jail. Mangum "grabbed her and started crying," Smith explained. Smith noted that she smelled alcohol on Mangum's breath. Barfield and another officer stood by while a staff nurse, Alycia Wright, asked a reviving Mangum the usual list of questions about risk of suicide, substance abuse, danger to others and victimization. These questions were part of the normal process by which someone would be admitted to the center. Mangum refused to answer Wright's questions. Instead, Mangum wrote the names of her children on a piece of paper. Wright and Smith ascertained that Mangum's children were five and six years old and were home alone. Smith said she then asked Officer Barfield to check on the children, and he made a number of calls on his police radio to do that.

"Did something happen to your children?" Wright asked.

"No," Mangum replied.

"Did something happen to you?" Wright wondered.

"Yes," Mangum answered.

"Were you raped?" Wright asked.

Mangum nodded yes.

At that instant, in the eyes of the Durham police department—per police protocol—the incident went from being one involving a noncommunicative, drunk stripper to one involving a possible rape victim, a serious criminal charge. The involuntary commitment procedures at Durham Access were immediately stopped—ending, at that moment, anyway, the possibility that Mangum's children would be taken away from her—in order to administer a so-called Sexual Assault Examination. At first, Smith told police that Mangum did not want to go to the Duke Hospital—"No, no, no," Mangum reportedly said—and that Mangum "was talking about her children and that was a big concern of her[s]." But, in the end, Mangum agreed to go. Smith "escorted" Mangum back to Barfield's police car and put her in the backseat. From previous run-ins with the police, the athletes' attorneys later argued, Mangum would have known that the involvement of the Department of Social Services could very well lead to her children being taken away from her—an outcome no mother, no matter what her mental or economic condition, would permit without a fight. Barfield reported Mangum's rape allegation to Shelton, who told Barfield to take Mangum to Duke Hospital. He would meet them there. Mangum mentioned nothing about the rape on the ride to Duke Hospital, but insisted that Roberts had stolen her $2,000, her ID, her cell phone, and her bag.

Mangum was checked in at 2:45 a.m. to the Duke University Medical Center. Five minutes later, the written police report on Mangum was "changed from passed out drunk to alleged rape." Then she was taken to the hospital's emergency room, where a university policewoman, trying to reassure her, reportedly saw her "crying uncontrollably and visibly shaken." By this time, Mangum was now willing to talk with Shelton. She told him that she was a stripper and had been hired by Angels Escort Service to dance at 610 North Buchanan along with Nikki, as she called Roberts. They put on a show for the men and then went outside and got in Nikki's car. She said "someone from the party" wanted them to come back into the house—and presumably continue dancing—but that the two dancers disagreed about the wisdom of going back in. She said she did not want to go back, but Nikki did. According to Shelton, "She said that she and 'Nikki' got into an argument about going back inside. She said at that point some of the guys from the party pulled her from the vehicle and groped her. She told me that no one forced her to have sex. She then mentioned that someone had taken her money." Shelton went outside, called his "watch commander" and told him that Mangum had "recanted her rape allegation." Moments later, Shelton heard that Mangum had changed her mind again and was now insisting she had been raped. Shelton called back the watch commander and told him that "she had changed her story back to being raped." He then went back to Mangum's room and asked her whether she had or had not been raped. "She told me she did not want to talk to me anymore and then started crying and saying something about them dragging her into the bathroom," he explained. He soon thereafter left the hospital after calling back to police headquarters in order to suggest that officers be dispatched to 610 North Buchanan to see if in fact it was a Duke student house. "I think she is lying," Shelton proclaimed after speaking with Mangum at the Duke emergency room.

Durham police officer Gwen Sutton then interviewed Mangum at the Duke Hospital. She knew from Shelton that the last known place Mangum had been was 610 North Buchanan. Mangum told Sutton she had been there to dance at a "bachelor party" where "twenty men were present." She told Sutton that "five men raped her in the bathroom at the bachelor party." She said that one of her five attackers—"Brett"—had "penetrated her vagina with his hands and penis" and that she was "bleeding vaginally." She also slightly revised her story that Roberts had stolen her money. She told Sutton that she may actually have deposited the money into the ATM account of her escort agency. She also told Sutton that she had danced at 610 North Buchanan with three other women dancers, "Nikki," "Angel" and "Tammy," which defense attorneys later speculated referred to Roberts; Angel Altmon, the Kroger security guard; and Tammy Rose, her contact at the escort agency.

At 2:53 a.m., Jeni Hauver, a registered nurse at the Duke Hospital, examined Mangum. She told Hauver she had been "sexually assaulted." Hauver noted that she seemed "anxious." The nurse asked her to rate her pain on a scale of one to ten, with ten being "worst ever." Mangum said her pain was "a perfect ten" or the "worst ever." Hauver then conducted a series of tests to determine whether Mangum was indeed experiencing such intense pain. The tests concluded that she was not. "Nurse Hauver tested Mangum for symptoms associated with pain and found none," according to court documents. "In Mangum's chart, Nurse Hauver noted that Mangum appeared to her to be 'in no acute distress, no obvious discomfort.'"

At 3:14 a.m., Dr. Jaime Snarski examined Mangum, the first doctor to do so. She told the doctor she was "stripping at a bachelor party" and "the bachelor [and] the other guys . . . put their fingers and penises" in her "vagina against her will." She also complained of "extreme pain" but denied to Snarski "being hit." She said the pain was "only in her vagina," but Snarski found no evidence of pain in her vagina.

At 3:28 a.m., another nurse, Carole Schumoski, examined Mangum. Schumoski asked Mangum to score her pain, and Mangum again reported the pain as a ten "down there." The nurse examined Mangum for symptoms of extreme pain but, like Dr. Snarski, found none. "Shortly thereafter, Nurse Schumoski found Mangum alone, resting quietly in no apparent distress," according to court documents. Dr. Joshua S. Broder, the attending physician and Snarski's boss, also examined Mangum. He found that she had no pain in her abdomen and that she was "well nourished, visibly upset, crying, alert, cooperative, no acute distress." After these early morning exams, Mangum was wheeled out of the examining room and allowed, at last, to try to get some sleep.

In the midst of the various medical examinations of Mangum in the wee hours of March 14, another seemingly momentous decision occurred. After determining that the alleged rape had happened at 610 North Buchanan Boulevard, a home owned by Duke University and rented to three Duke students, Sergeant Shelton and his supervisors concluded that the matter fell under the jurisdiction of the Duke University police department and should be turned over to the Duke police for further investigation.

At 3:08 a.m., Duke police lieutenant Jeffrey O. Best headed to the Duke Hospital to begin Duke's investigation into the alleged crime. When he got there, he found that Duke police officer William Mazurek had arrived first and discovered that the Duke Hospital medical staff had been examining Mangum. Mazurek later reported that what Mangum was saying seemed "almost not real" and she seemed to be "possibly faking," although he "was not sure," since he had "never seen a rape victim before." Furthermore, he said, "at no point did he smell any alcohol on her," although "she seemed like she was in a daze." He noticed her clothes were ripped and two laces on her shoes were broken. He never asked Mangum any questions. He informed Best that Mangum had claimed she had been sexually assaulted at a "frat party"—not a "bachelor party"—at 610 North Buchanan.

Per protocol, Duke police officer Sara Beth Falcon, the only woman on the Duke police force, was then asked to assist Mangum. Falcon noted that her supervisors had gone out to the loading dock of the hospital to confer with Durham police officers. They shared what they had discovered to that point and officially handed off the case to the Duke police officers, who dispersed shortly thereafter. Best then dispatched three Duke officers to 610 North Buchanan to see if they could find any residents awake, which they could not, since it was now after 3 a.m.

Later that day, one of the three Duke officers, Christopher Day, filed the first operations report about what had been learned. Day wrote that Mangum "was claiming the she was raped by approximately twenty white males at 610 N. Buchanan Street." Day concluded his brief, three-paragraph report with the observation that Mangum had "changed her story several times" and "eventually Durham Police stated that charges would not exceed misdemeanor simple assault against the occupants of 610 N. Buchanan. There were no charges filed by Duke Police Officers. No suspects have been identified at this time."

From this moment on, there would be confusion—some of it said to be deliberate—about the roles that the Duke police and Durham police played in investigating what occurred. Despite the order that transferred responsibility for the ongoing investigation to the Duke police, the Durham police continued to make inquiries. At 3:47 a.m., Sergeant Lori Fansler "paged out" Durham police investigator Buffy Jones, who was on call that night, and dispatched her to Duke Hospital. At around 4 a.m., Jones interviewed Mangum. She noticed immediately "a strong smell of alcohol" coming from Mangum. Asked if her name was "Crystal," Mangum said her name was "Precious." She also first said she lived in Durham and then changed her story and explained, untruthfully, that she lived in Raleigh. She did not claim to have been attacked or raped, and mentioned the name of one person—"Brett"—but not in the context of any attack, as she had told Officer Sutton about an hour earlier. To Jones, Mangum said Brett "knew the deal" and "the guys weren't with it." She also told Jones that Kim Roberts, her fellow dancer, had stolen her purse and phone. She would not answer Jones's questions about the rape allegation. "All I want to do is go home," Mangum told Jones, before falling back asleep on the gurney. At 4:44 a.m., Jones spoke with Fansler about the "incident" and the "victim's condition."

At around 7 a.m., Mangum was awakened by Tara Levicy, an in-training sexual assault nurse examiner, or SANE. Per Duke Hospital policy, anyone claiming to have been raped had to be examined by a trained and certified sexual assault nurse. At that time, the hospital employed fourteen, "enough so there is at least one on-site during all shifts," although it was not clear why one of them had not already examined Mangum during the nearly four hours she had been at the Duke Hospital.

Levicy arrived at the hospital at 6:45 a.m. and the head nurse asked her to perform the rape exam on Mangum. Although still technically in training— she would get her certification in the mail when she got home that night, and it was effective as of March 2—Levicy went looking for Mangum. When Levicy first found Mangum, she did not notice any smell of alcohol, nor did Mangum appear to her to be impaired or "intoxicated" in any way.

They were together for the next six or seven hours, until Mangum was discharged from the hospital in the early afternoon of March 14. Levicy explained that the examination would take "hours to do" and was "very personal." Levicy reported that Mangum said she was "able to do that." When Levicy first started her examination of Mangum, she noted that Mangum "spoke clearly," was "very articulating in her words" and was "complaining of pain to her lower areas." At one point, Levicy left the examination room to get a wheelchair down the hall, leaving Mangum alone with a white male "Rape Crisis" worker. Mangum "started screaming" hysterically and Levicy had to run back down to the room to reassure Mangum she was not going to be hurt. The man left the room, and another woman, Amy Wilkinson, was brought in to assist Levicy.

Mangum had quite a story to tell Levicy. According to the sexual assault exam report, Mangum said that she and Roberts were dancing for the lacrosse players at the party. "They were getting excited and they wanted more," she explained. "They kept saying 'more, more, more,' and that's when . . . Brett asked Nikki [Roberts] for a threesome with me." Roberts then asked her, "Girl, are you down?" Mangum did not want to participate. She said she wanted to "go home and see her kids," but Roberts told Mangum she wanted to "stay and make some money." Mangum wanted to leave. "Something did not feel right," she told Levicy. Mangum said she then "stormed out of the house." She and Roberts got into Roberts's car and started "fighting." Roberts said to her, "Girl, I swear, if you don't act like you have some sense, I will leave you right here." Roberts then told "Brett" to get Mangum out of her car, and Brett and Roberts walked alongside Mangum as they all went back into the house. Mangum said she protested again, but Roberts said to her, "Girl, you want some more to drink, we got to make some money. . . . Girl, we got to put on a show." Mangum said she heard Brett reiterate his desire for a threesome. But "what really scared me" was when "Adam" closed the door and said to Mangum "You can't leave," and she could "not see [Roberts] anymore."

After the door to the bathroom closed, Mangum told Levicy that "Adam, Brett, and Matt" asked her to take off her clothes. They were together in the bathroom off the master bedroom, and Mangum said she heard voices of other men in the bedroom. She said "Dan Flanagan"—Dan Flannery—was the "fake name" he gave the agency, and his real name was "Matt." She said that Matt said he was "getting married tomorrow" and couldn't "do this"—the original ruse was that Mangum and Roberts were to perform at a bachelor party—but "Adam" said "Yes, you can." That was when Matt put "his private part in me and did not use a condom, and he said, 'Oh yeah, I love black pussy.'" Adam then asked Matt if he was "enjoying it," and he said "Oh yes, I am enjoying it." Mangum then said Matt "wanted to try something different," and that was when "Adam came around back and put his private part in my butt and it was hurting and stinging, and I kept saying, 'Stop. Please stop.'" But the door was locked, Mangum told Levicy, and "they said I could not leave."

Mangum said she again asked Adam to stop because she was in a lot of pain. He did not stop. "They kept calling me 'Nigger bitch' [and] kept grabbing me and [saying] 'I swear, I'll kill you if you don't go through with this.'" Mangum said that after this comment the scene "escalated"—the boys kept "using racial slurs and . . . getting excited." Mangum told Levicy that they said, "Yeah, we fucked a nigger bitch and we fucked her good." That was when someone started knocking on the bathroom door to let them know "it was time to go." Mangum said she started to cry. She said Roberts was on the other side of the door, and the two women started arguing again. She said the men put her clothes back on her and took her to Roberts's car. Levicy asked if the players "assaulted her orally," and Mangum said, "Yes, Matt put it in my mouth, [and] that's why my breath smells so bad."

Mangum told Levicy that she and Roberts drove off, and eventually Roberts "pushed me out of the car" before the police came. Mangum said Roberts "took my stuff" and then told her to "get back in the car" and that she would find someone else to drive Mangum home. "The next thing I knew, the police arrived," Mangum told Levicy. She told the police that she lived in Durham and her name was Crystal. Of Roberts, Mangum said "she took all my money and everything."

Levicy asked Mangum again if the attackers had used condoms and she said no, but Levicy also later conceded Mangum wasn't sure. "Victims can never be sure if condoms are used, because if they can't see them, how would they know for sure?" Levicy said in a statement. "You can't feel them, so you have to realize that there is always a possibility that a condom could have been used." Mangum told Levicy that she was "unsure" if the boys ejaculated in her anus or in her vagina but knew that one of them had ejaculated in her mouth and that "they wiped her with a rag in the bathroom."

Since Levicy had not then received her SANE certification, she was not authorized to do the pelvic exam of Mangum. That task fell to Dr. Julie Manly, a fourth-year resident at the hospital. At around 9 a.m., while Levicy took notes, Manly performed the pelvic exam of Mangum and then also took oral, rectal, and vaginal swabs and collected hair, blood, and skin samples. These samples became part of the kit that is required in any rape investigation, and would prove to be essential pieces of evidence in the weeks that followed. Levicy noted that Manly had done the examination correctly. The only physical trauma on Mangum's body were three small scratches on her lower leg, which she had had before she started dancing the previous evening, according to photographs of Mangum taken by one of the lacrosse players at the party. In her notes, under a section titled "Brief Account of the Assault," Levicy wrote, "Patient sexually assaulted by three men at party. Persons unknown. Vaginally, rectally, and orally assaulted. No condoms used." Levicy also checked that Mangum told her there were "verbal threats" used and that there was "actual" penetration of her vagina, anus, and mouth, and that she was sure that one of the men had ejaculated in her mouth. She also said she had had intercourse "one week ago" before the assault, and without a condom.

The pelvic exam was complicated by the fact that when Manly inserted the speculum into Mangum's vagina, Mangum writhed in pain. "Ms. Mangum was gripping the table and showing pain," Levicy observed. According to Manly, however, though Mangum's screaming was intense, there were no other recorded signs of her severe pain, "such as sweating, facial distress, changes in her vital signs such as heart rate, or changes in her body position." After Mangum calmed down sufficiently to be examined—which took an hour because of the disruptions—Manly's only observation was "diffuse edema of the vaginal walls," or generalized swelling. Because of the pain—Levicy noted that Mangum had "extreme tenderness" and "vocalized extreme pain upon insertion of speculum"—Mangum insisted that the examination be stopped. "Clinical decision by Dr. Manly not to do colposcope exam because of patient's pain," Levicy noted, and added that the "objective standards of pain" were the facts that her "muscles [were] tight" and she was "gripping [the] bed." Levicy continued, "Crystal had no idea that these people were at a lacrosse party—every person she spoke to documented that she believed she was at a bachelor party."

Instead of trying to figure out the source of the pain, treating it, and allowing the examination to continue, Manly stopped. No thorough pelvic or rectal examination ever occurred. No forensic toxicology reports or blood tests were taken. The sexual assault exam was never completed.

There was one other finding that Manly made in her incomplete pelvic examination—a "whitish vaginal discharge"—that for some reason was not mentioned by either Manly or by Levicy on the sexual assault examination report, which Levicy signed as the examiner even though she did not do the examination. At the time, Manly assumed the white discharge was semen, although she did not test the fluid. Later, she would concede that it could have been from a yeast or other vaginal infection.

As for the vaginal swelling, it was the only finding from the examination that Manly thought could have been evidence of the veracity of Mangum's claim that she had been raped. Still, there were other possible explanations for the swelling, as attorneys for the athletes were only too happy to point out later. Swelling is a symptom, not an injury. Edema "can be caused by smoking, sex within twenty-four hours of the vaginal exam, frequent sex, antidepressants, or taking Flexeril [a muscle relaxant]," according to their filings. "It is known that Mangum used a vibrator, had sex with her driver, and may have had a yeast infection just prior to March 14, all of which could have contributed to the vaginal swelling."

Despite the lack of compelling physical evidence, Levicy was convinced that Mangum had been raped. "Based on what she reported to me and the physical findings of tenderness, there was a congruence between her report and the findings," she later testified. On this point, Levicy's critics are legion. They complain she was not qualified to make a judgment because she was not then fully certified as a SANE nurse and that she had not been properly trained as one. They point out that she had graduated from the University of Maine with a degree in women's studies and a minor in outdoor studies. They note she did not study nursing as an undergraduate. While at the University of Maine, she produced and directed a version of Eve Ensler's *The Vagina Monologues*, an "event she recalled with fondness." After graduation, she worked as a whitewater rafting guide and became certified as an emergency medical technician. She also volunteered at Planned Parenthood.

She has been labeled a feminist, apparently making her predisposed to conclude that another woman had been raped despite the lack of physical evidence. This assumption is based on her time with Planned Parenthood and an article she wrote in 2003 about medical problems women experience in the wilderness. "A few years ago I produced and directed Eve Ensler's *The Vagina Monologues*, a whole night dedicated to hearing women's stories about their vaginas," she wrote. "I can clearly remember people's startled response to the word 'vagina' when I was promoting the play. . . . If saying the word 'vagina' feels foreign, then I recommend looking into a mirror and saying, 'Vagina . . . vagina . . . vagina.'" In late 2003, Levicy returned to school at the University of Southern Maine for a fifteen-month "fast-track" program that allows liberal arts majors to obtain a nursing degree, to help rectify the shortage of nurses. On February 8, 2005, she received her nursing license. Her first job was at the Duke University Hospital Emergency Department. In August 2005, after working for five months as a nurse, she started working on her SANE certification—even though the International Association of Forensic Nurses requires at least three years of nursing practice before a SANE certification program can be started.

Levicy's critics singled her out for blame. According to a court document filed by attorneys for the athletes, all the doctors and other nurses who examined Mangum on the morning of March 14, 2006, "concluded, upon examination, that Mangum's head, back, neck, chest, breast, nose, throat, mouth, abdomen, and upper and lower extremities were all 'normal,' and Mangum was consistently noted to be in 'no obvious discomfort,' even when she was scoring her pain as a '10 out of 10.' With the exception of Levicy, every provider who examined Mangum for symptoms to corroborate Mangum's pain scores found none." At the conclusion of the examination by Levicy and Manly, the rape kit and other evidence was collected and given to Duke police officer Joyce Sale. Nevertheless, Levicy wrote in her notes that accompanied Manly's examination that Mangum's condition was "consistent w[ith] sexual assault emotionally and physically" and that she had "signs of Rape Trauma Syndrome," evidenced by the "first sign," when she started "screaming at [a] male" nurse in her room. Levicy noted that Mangum had "no signs of intoxication" and had "consistent responses," including "periods of crying" and "deep sadness." Levicy also quoted Mangum telling her: "I am so embarrassed to say what they said to me."

At around 1 p.m. that day, Mangum was released from Duke Hospital but told to set up a subsequent doctor's appointment to check for bacteria in her throat, anus, vagina, and cervix. At around 2 p.m., Mangum called Durham police investigator Buffy Jones and left her a voice mail message seeking the return of her "stolen property," which she still believed Roberts had taken from her. She made no mention to Jones of being raped the night before. Jones agreed to meet with Mangum at 7 p.m. at Durham police headquarters. But Mangum did not show up for the appointment. Later that night, at 10:30, Mangum's "boyfriend" called Jones to explain that Mangum had missed the appointment because she had "gone back to be seen by a doctor again due to medical problems." Jones set up a new appointment with Mangum for the next day, March 15, at 7 p.m.

At 7:30 on the morning of March 14, while Mangum was being examined at Duke Hospital, Robert Dean, the director and chief of the Duke Police Department, arrived at his office and read Officer Day's report that Mangum had claimed that "twenty white males" had raped her at 610 North Buchanan and that had she had changed her story several times about the details of the incident. He then called Sue Wasiolek, the assistant dean of students, and informed her of Mangum's allegations. This was the first time the Duke administration had been informed of what may have occurred at 610 North Buchanan. Dean told Wasiolek that "the accuser was not credible," that her story had changed repeatedly—including that between three and twenty men had raped her—and that "this would go away." He also said that neither the Duke nor Durham police officers familiar with the case believed what Mangum had told them.

"I've relied on what they have told me more times than I can count," Wasiolek said later. "Their judgment has always proven to be something I could depend on. . . . [I]t did not appear that this case was really going to go very far, because there were some real inconsistencies in some of the information that the alleged victim was providing."

That afternoon, Wasiolek called Mike Pressler, the Duke lacrosse coach, on his cell phone. Pressler was at a bowling alley in Durham, a few hours after the end of lacrosse practice for that day. The occasion was the team's annual bowling tournament. Wasiolek told Pressler about the party, the dancers, and the rape allegations. Pressler then confronted the four cocaptains: Flannery, Evans, Zash (who lived together at 610 North Buchanan), and Brett Thompson. "I told them they were being charged with rape," he recalled in an interview with *Men's Health* magazine. "And, look, I was livid that they had the party. Livid. But when I told them they were being accused of rape, the look of absolute astonishment in their eyes told me that they were innocent." He said he knew instantly that they did not do what they were accused of doing. "I spent every day with those boys," he said. "I know their parents, their brothers and sisters. I sat in their living rooms, recruiting them, and they spent time in my house with my family." Ryan McFadyen remembered seeing Pressler and the cocaptains having a "very serious" discussion in the corner of the bowling alley. "We're all like, 'What the hell is going on?'" he said. "We have no idea. . . . It kind of sparks some interest between us, but nobody knows what's going on. The captains haven't told anybody. Coach P hasn't told anybody."

The cocaptains called Wasiolek back using Pressler's cell phone. Wasiolek said Flannery told her that "it was a bad scene" with "two strippers" and "thirty people were there," "all of them . . . on the lacrosse team." Flannery told Wasiolek that "they [had] paid the women and then they paid them more to leave," and that one of the women—Mangum—"was passed out on the porch, patio, deck and had to be carried out to the car to leave." He further said that "at one point he was going to call the police" but decided not to because "there was never a reason as to why he would call the police." While the lacrosse captains conceded to Wasiolek that "two exotic dancers" had been hired for the party the night before, they "emphatically and unequivocally denied Mangum's rape allegations and assured Dean Wasiolek that nothing of the kind had occurred at the party." Wasiolek then told the players she believed them and that the police had assured her that Mangum's story was "inconsistent and not credible."

Wasiolek, a former attorney who had worked at a law firm in Durham for nine months in 1994, then told the cocaptains that they did not need an attorney and that they should keep the rape allegations to themselves and not even tell their parents. This was another fateful decision. "Right now, you don't need an attorney," Flannery recalled Wasiolek telling him. "Just don't tell anyone, including your teammates and parents, and cooperate with police if they contact you." Flannery later elaborated, "We believed, albeit falsely, that these people would look after our best interests." Pressler passed Wasiolek's advice about keeping quiet about the incident on to the rest of the lacrosse team. For the next several days, in accordance with Wasiolek's advice—which would later be alleged to have violated Rule 4.3 of the North Carolina Rules of Professional Conduct—the team did not talk about the incident to their parents. No one on the team hired an attorney, despite the allegation of criminal behavior. "I was told to keep it quiet," Pressler explained. "Everybody . . . thought it was going to go away. There was no reason to bring more attention to it. So I interpreted that as being, 'Hey, guys, it's going to go away, let's keep it in-house here. Don't tell your parents yet; don't tell your girlfriends. Keep it in-house.'"

After receiving the report, Dean Wasiolek also contacted Joe Alleva, Pressler's boss and the athletic director, and Chris Kennedy, the associate athletics director. She also called her boss, Larry Moneta, the dean of student affairs, and Tallman Trask, the university's executive vice president. Consistent with Day's report, Wasiolek's message to these administrators was essentially that Mangum's accusations were not credible and would not be proceeding much further. Kennedy recalled that Wasiolek said "there had been a party hosted by the lacrosse captains, that a woman had alleged that she was raped and the allegations were not credible, and the police thought they were going to go away."

Matt Zash arrived back at 610 North Buchanan around 3:30 that afternoon after the bowling tournament. The lacrosse team's freshman players came to the house to help Zash clean up from the party. They picked up the trash and vacuumed the living room while Zash mopped the floors and cleaned up the bathrooms. In the "green-tiled" bathroom, he found "three or four red plastic nails"—which Mangum had lost there the night before—and threw them in the garbage can in the bathroom. Zash then went outside "to straighten up" and found his housemate Dave Evans's Dopp kit, including a Fusion razor, some shaving cream, and a toothbrush. Zash also found, on the ground outside the bathroom window, Mangum's makeup, cell phone, ID, and a "purse-like bag." He brought all the detritus into the house, placed Mangum's bag and its contents on top of the mini-fridge and noted Mangum's contact information "just in case we found anything stolen."

That night, McFadyen and a few other lacrosse players went over to teammate KJ Sauer's house, around the corner from 610 North Buchanan. They still had not heard about Mangum's accusations. The only reaction McFadyen had received from his late-night e-mail was from his teammate Erik Henkelman. "I distinctly remember Erik Henkelman getting my joke," McFadyen recalled. "I walked in and he was like, 'Dude, that e-mail was so funny.'" After practice, a group of the lacrosse players decided to investigate whether there was any truth to the long-standing Duke rumor about there being tunnels under East Campus, including a mile-long tunnel that connects East Campus with West Campus. "We had made a pact that night, 'Let's go find these tun-nels,'" McFadyen recalled. Afterward, they ordered some food. "We're walking toward East Campus, and there's a cop car parked in front of 610," McFadyen said. "We're like, 'What the hell is that?' Sauer goes, he's like, 'Dude, I'm not a captain. I'm not really involved. Apparently that stripper called the cops or something.' He's like, 'The cops are saying it's bullshit.' They're just giving them, you know, statements or something. He says it very casually, and we go about our day and that's it. Two days later, or maybe it was the next day, Coach P finally breaks the news that someone is claiming they were sexually assaulted at this thing. Then that's when everything just kind of becomes a mess."

The next day, Zash sent an e-mail to a group of his friends describing what had happened on the evening of March 13. According to Benjamin Himan, a Durham police officer who investigated the alleged crime, Zash's e-mail said "something to the effect that 'he doesn't split dark wood.'" Zash quickly real-ized that the e-mail he sent was not in the best of taste. "I am embarassed [sic] and ashamed of the incensitive [sic] language I used," Zash explained a few days later in a statement he gave to the police. "At the time I thought I was just telling an interesting story. Prior to the police search of my house, I wrote a follow-up e-mail to them describing how things escalated and [that] we got in trouble with our coach and administration for having strippers over. I also made them aware that a false report was filed against us alleging that there was a 'gang rape.'"

About the time Zash sent his rogue e-mail, Sergeant Mark D. Gottlieb, of the Durham Police Department, was working off-duty at Durham City Hall when he got a call from Buffy Jones. According to notes Gottlieb wrote some five months later (but which were dated as if they were contemporaneous), he said Jones told him she was "handling" a new case in which "there was a rape reported at 610 North Buchanan" in Durham's police District 2, which had been Gottlieb's territory. Gottlieb's notes make no mention of Jones's skep-ticism about Mangum's allegations, saying only that Jones "had very little information on the case" because of the "victim's condition" while she was at the Duke Hospital emergency room. (Other accounts of the conversation claim that Gottlieb found out about the alleged incident and called Jones, who told him that Mangum's claims were "false" and she was about to rule them "unsubstantiated." Gottlieb, Jones's superior, told her not to close the case, not to make any ruling, and to turn it over to him.)

According to Gottlieb's notes, though, Jones told him that Mangum had left her a message on her answering machine on March 14 around 2 p.m. and that the two of them had been due to meet at seven that night. She explained that when Mangum didn't show, Jones had heard from her boyfriend that Mangum was "being seen" by a doctor and that was why she had missed the appoint-ment. Jones told Gottlieb, according to his notes, that she had set up a new appointment with Mangum for March 15 at 7 p.m. According to Gottlieb, Jones "wanted to know if District 2 Investigations wanted the case, since she had not had a true interview with the victim to this point." Gottlieb asked Jones if a canvass had been done or a search warrant issued to examine the crime scene, or if "identification of any potential suspects" had occurred, and told Jones that he and his team "could take over the case" if Jones "needed our assistance." He said it would be best for Mangum "to limit the number of inter-views of the traumatic event."

Gottlieb suggested that they "consult" with their superiors about whether it made sense for his team to take over the investigation. If Gottlieb were to take over the case, the appointment with Mangum—then scheduled for a few hours later—would need to be rescheduled so that the new investigator, to be assigned the next morning, could make arrangements to meet with Mangum. Although Jones said she would check with Fensler to get the sign-off for the transfer of the case, it was a pretty much a done deal at that point—marking yet another important turning point in the saga.

Nine minutes after finishing his conversation with Jones, Gottlieb says he sent out a "basic e-mail" to the District 2 community Partners Against Crime listserv—a digital bulletin board on Yahoo! for Durham residents interested in information about local crime—asking for information on the event from the community, although that e-mail is now gone. The only available e-mail Gottlieb sent to the District 2 Partners Against Crime went out at 4:49 p.m. on March 15, explaining that his investigators had worked another "17+ hour day in less than a week" and had arrested a man for a series of small robber-ies in the neighborhood. There was no mention of an incident at 610 North Buchanan or request for information about an alleged rape.

At 5:20, Gottlieb spoke with his boss. "She advised me she thought it would be a good idea if District 2 was able to continue with the case," he wrote. "I agreed to adopt it, and told her to have Inv. Jones cancel the interview as we discussed earlier, and to have the victim contact me in the morning." Five min-utes later, Gottlieb spoke with Jones and informed her that the case had been reassigned to himself and Division 2.

Meanwhile, earlier that day, Mangum had been experiencing what she called "neck pain" and had gone to get treatment at North Carolina Memorial Hospital in Chapel Hill, where she had been treated for her various ailments in the past. At UNC, she met with Dr. Yvonne E. Lai. Mangum told Dr. Lai she had been hired to dance at a bachelor party and wanted to leave but was pushed into a bathroom, where three men raped her. "She was knocked to the floor multiple times and hit her head on the sink during one of these episodes," Dr. Lai wrote in her notes. "She states she was drunk and had a lot of alcohol that night. She denied any pain in the emergency room because she was 'drunk and did not feel pain.'" According to Dr. Lai's report, Mangum had "a rape kit done" at Duke Hospital the day before, had been given "the morning-after pill" as well as medications for sexually transmitted diseases, and was "set up for rape counseling and sent home." She had returned to the UNC Hospital because, "after sobering," her "neck was very painful" and she was "unable to move her head." Dr. Lai also noted that Mangum had "bilateral knee pain and right ankle pain," as well as "a headache and facial pain." Mangum told the UNC doctor that after being discharged from Duke Hospital she fell because her legs were "wobbly," and she still felt "wobbly on her legs." The doctor noted that Mangum had suffered an "assault last night" and had "new neck pain after the . . . trauma." She sent Mangum up to the emergency room for X-rays, and prescribed Flexeril and told Mangum to keep taking ibuprofen for the pain.

As for the alleged rape, Dr. Lai wrote that Mangum had "contacted the police" and was "plugged in to a rape support group." She noted that Mangum's boyfriend was "very upset with her currently because of this rape" and that Mangum felt "responsible partially for drinking and going to this party" and that she was "unable to trust any men anymore, since in the past she has had a similar situation with African-American males, and this party was white males." Dr. Lai noted that Mangum had no loss of bowel or bladder function, but had a "past medical history of bipolar disorder and multiple somatic complaints." She concluded with the notation that, because of Mangum's "long psychological history, she is at very high risk of narcotic abuse," and that the clinic should not prescribe her any narcotics.

Despite the swirl of events and the various conflicting stories about what had happened in the bathroom at 610 North Buchanan, it certainly seemed that *something* untoward had happened to Crystal Mangum in the early morning hours of March 14 at the hands of a bunch of white Duke lacrosse players. What *precisely* had happened and who did what to whom would become—in the next year—the subject of intense scrutiny and analysis, both in the justice system and the court of public opinion. Had Mangum portrayed the events accurately, or was her story total fiction? Was Levicy's medical examination of Mangum at the Duke Hospital thorough and definitive, or the self-fulfilling prophesy of her views on the mistreatment of women? Which version of Mangum's story were the Durham police interested in pursuing—the one in which she recanted her rape charge, or the one in which she insisted it had happened? And were the players telling the truth when they said nothing at all had happened to Mangum in the bathroom? One thing was soon apparent: everything related to what did or did not happen in that bathroom was going to take on an importance far beyond what anyone could have ever imagined. And no one could stop it from happening.

CHAPTER TWO

Frat Life

For much of the second half of the twentieth century, fraternities and "frat life" dominated the living and social scene on Duke's elegant West Campus. Frat houses—referred to as "sections"—lined the main quadrangle on the campus, and each fraternity section had constructed, not unlike wide lifeguard's chairs, large plywood benches several stories high in front of their entrances. Each bench was painted, and continuously repainted, with various designs and colors representing, more or less, the unique character of the fraternities. "Dorm benches provide more than outdoor sitting space for Duke students," Robert Bliwise, the longtime editor of *Duke* magazine, wrote in a November 1995 article. "They also stake out turf and define dorm identity." On most days, the "brothers" would bide their time sitting on their benches, hanging out, catching some sun, and feeling free to comment on everyone who walked by. Thus arose a continuous wave of quasi-intimidation that could follow a student as he or she walked the length of the residential half of the quad back to his or her dorm room. Needless to say, the "brothers'" commentary ratcheted up exponentially as women walked by or as the consumption of alcohol increased. There was nothing overtly nasty about the commentary as students passed the benches day after day, but it was nonetheless an unwanted annoyance added to the difficult process of adapting to a new and rigorous academic subculture.

During this period, university social life revolved around the West Campus fraternities. Often starting on Thursday nights and continuing into the early hours of a Sunday morning, the frats became the alcohol-fueled nerve center for what passed for entertainment at Duke. Although intimidating for those who were unfamiliar with fraternities or were not members of the fraternity hosting the party, the parties were generally an amusing way to meet new people and try to cope with the numerous stresses of college life. While hardly unique to Duke, this scenario—played out week after week—was unlikely to be the healthiest way, either physically or emotionally, for young adults to figure out how to relate to one another socially.

In the fall of 1995, after almost two years of study, then-president Nannerl "Nan" Keohane set out to change the dominant influence fraternities had on the *gestalt* of Duke. She decreed that Duke's East Campus would be turned into a residential community devoted solely to incoming freshmen. She also turned West Campus into a collection of "quads" that were a mixture of living arrangements, rather than one dominated by the fraternities. "If you go into any quad," Dean Sue Wasiolek told Bliwise in 1995, "the hope is that you will find a fraternity, maybe a selective house, maybe a single-sex residence and a coed residence, so that you see a balance."

Another key aspect of Keohane's efforts to transform the influence of fraternities at Duke was to implement a new policy regarding the consumption of alcohol on campus. Ever since President Ronald Reagan signed into law, in July 1984, a bill requiring states to increase the legal age to twenty-one, college campuses across the country had been forced to grapple with the growing problem that although social life on campus revolved around drinking alcohol, most of the people on campus doing the drinking were below the legal drinking age. In September 1986, North Carolina raised its legal drinking age to twenty-one. Of course, just because the law of the land had changed, few people were foolish enough to think that those under twenty-one were not drinking. "Underage drinking had once been an extracurricular activity the Duke administration treated with a wink and a smile," Mike Pressler, the varsity lacrosse coach, observed.

But Keohane tried to change that dynamic. She banned alcohol from East Campus, since by definition there would be no freshman twenty-one or older. She allowed student groups to sponsor keg parties only if a university-approved bartender were dispensing the beer to students whose IDs had been checked and who were at least twenty-one. This policy effectively banned keg parties from West Campus. The student groups were also charged inflated prices for the beer in an effort to dissuade students from purchasing it. Along with Keohane's new drinking policy, the school's Interfraternity Council adopted a new alcohol policy that limited fraternities to a "bring-your-own-bottle" policy, effectively eliminating keg parties. And not only at Duke. The national organizations of the local fraternities were quickly starting to require that their local chapters comply with the laws of land, including the new legal-drinking-age law. Failure to comply could mean the end of the local frat house through withdrawal of its charter. Fraternities had "for too many years harbored the legal liability and financial burdens of the social scene at Duke University," Lex Wolf, then the president of the Interfraternity Council, wrote in a *Chronicle* column in 1995. The Interfraternity Council also imposed sanctions on frats that violated the drinking policies, which could result in fines against individual members and a suspension of social privileges.

Wolf noted in his column that the problem was not just a legal one. It was also health-related. He observed that thirty-four students had been taken to the Duke Hospital emergency room in the previous year because of alcohol-related accidents, and that violations related to alcohol were also continuing to increase. Some traced the increase in drunkenness on Duke's campus to the back-to-back national championships won by the Duke men's basketball team in 1991 and 1992. The celebration after the 1992 championship game was particularly rambunctious. "As an alumnus, it did not make me happy to tell people to not come to campus because it was too dangerous," Lew Wardell, a member of the Duke class of 1975 and then the assistant director of Duke's public safety effort, told Bliwise for his article in *Duke* magazine. "And in large part it was dangerous because of the unbelievable drunkenness of the crowd."

In 1994, Wardell's office toured a number of in-progress on-campus parties. "The anecdotal evidence was unbelievable," he said. "We're talking about criminality, deviance, and extraordinary personal threat just because of the level of intoxication. I was a detective for eight years and worked in some of the worst areas of Durham, and I was seeing things on [the Duke] campus that I had never seen in those places—places where students are afraid to go." He was amazed there had not been an alcohol-related death on campus.

But there was no illusion that Duke's new policies toward drinking on campus would eliminate the problem. Wardell explained that the new policy was "still more liberal, more permissive" than that of many other universities. "What we've done is to take the first step," he told Bliwise, "which is to say that you don't learn how to responsibly drink when you can clamp your mouth on a beer keg and not let go until the keg is empty—which is what we were allowing up through last year."

Asked by Bliwise to gauge the response to the new alcohol policy, Wasiolek explained, "The social scene has changed. I'm drawing this conclusion not only from my own impressions, but also from what students have told me. I'm not saying that I support it or that I want to perpetuate it, but there was something about a keg of beer that naturally and very spontaneously and very conveniently and very effortlessly brought students together. And that is a part of the keg scene that I would somehow like to capture without all of the negative impact that we know that kegs brought."

Not surprisingly, the ban on alcohol on East Campus and the increased difficulty of finding it on West Campus prompted Duke students to party in the homes off East Campus, in Trinity Park, that seniors often rented together. Heather Young, a Duke senior, noted that one fraternity started having keg parties weekly at its off-campus house. "They don't want to get in trouble with Public Safety"—the Duke police—"and they don't want to start trouble with the University," she told the *Chronicle*. "It's just easier to have [parties] off-campus." But a number of neighbors in Trinity Park were unhappy about the growing number of parties and their drunken revelers. "The freshmen can come down here and go to parties and their [identification] won't be checked," explained Joan Austin, a Trinity Park resident, in March 1995. "There ought to be something that Duke can do to accept more responsibility." Others, though, noted that the tension between Duke students and the longtime residents of Trinity Park dated back at least twenty years, and the number of complaints had not risen since Keohane implemented the new drinking policy.

The *Chronicle* quickly realized that trouble loomed in this unintended consequence of the Keohane drinking policy. "Durham residents are beginning to experience the effects of the new alcohol policy, and they don't like what they see," the paper editorialized in March 1995. "But what they are experiencing is out of the University's control. Since the new alcohol policy went into effect, University students have slowly begun to move their parties to off-campus locations. As a result, people who live in surrounding areas, such as Trinity Park, feel the tension growing in their neighborhoods. They complain of underage drinking, excessive noise, and large numbers of students loitering in the area." The paper noted that while Joan Austin's idea that Duke should be held responsible for the behavior of students in off-campus housing was commendable, the reality was that the university's authority ended at the East Campus wall and that the best it could do was to notify the Durham police about the parties.

The paper urged students to take responsibility for their own behavior. "The issue now has become one of personal responsibility," it continued. "It is simply a matter of respect. Students living among non-University residents must learn to be respectful of their neighbors. Until residents stop complaining about loitering, underage drinking and excessive noise, students need to understand that they are not the only people living in these areas. Once a student moves off campus, the student's behavior translates into the image of the University. Consequently, the views of Durham residents toward the University are shaped by these students' behavior."

For the next year or so, students living off East Campus kept their raucous partying to a minimum, or to enough of a minimum to keep their neighbors from objecting publicly. But by the start of the 1997 school year, the student parties in Trinity Park were bothering neighbors again. To get students in the neighborhood to behave more responsibly, the neighborhood association sent letters to the parents of students living in the neighborhood houses where the police previously had been summoned to break up parties.

Then, in November 1999, the very thing that Lew Wardell had worried about—a student's death resulting from excessive alcohol consumption— occurred. Raheem Bath, a twenty-year-old junior from outside Philadelphia and a member of the Phi Kappa Psi fraternity, died two weeks after a night of heavy drinking. At the time, the papers reported that Bath's death resulted from pneumonia, or an infection in his lungs. What was not reported until much later was that Bath had drunk so much alcohol that he vomited and passed out. "He then inhaled the vomit, which can occur when excessive alcohol suppresses a person's gag reflex," said a March 2000 opinion column in Duke Today, a Duke blog. "The debris caused an overwhelming infection in his lungs that not even the best medicine could fight. It was just too late." Bath, a double major in electrical engineering and economics, had SAT scores of 1440 out of a possible 1600. "I don't want Duke to ever think this is something that's going to go away," Raheem's mother, Catherine, told the *Chronicle* in April 2001 when she visited Duke to give a speech more than a year after her son's death. "It's a problem that needs to be dealt with. I'd like to see Duke take a major part in that nationwide." When the *Raleigh News & Observer* spoke with Bath five years later, in April 2006, to get her take on whether anything had improved at Duke regarding excessive alcohol consumption on campus in the wake of her son's death, she said, "Six years ago, I asked Duke to step up and lead the way for other universities. They haven't really done that."

Then, in October 2010, senior Drew Everson fell down a stairwell in the student union building on East Campus and later died from his injuries. Months later, the autopsy report noted that Everson's blood-alcohol level had been 0.133. In North Carolina, 0.08 is considered legal intoxication. Everson had worked at Goldman Sachs in the summer before his death and had a bright future. Then, in September 2011, Matthew Grape, a senior from Wellesley, Massachusetts, was killed when the car he was a passenger in, driven by his friend Lee Royster, struck a tree near Duke's West Campus, rolled down an embankment, and flipped over. Royster, who sustained minor injuries, was later charged with driving while impaired. He was also indicted for felony death by vehicle.

The off-campus consumption of alcohol by Duke students was not only making life difficult for the longtime residents of Trinity Park, it also was affecting the social scene at Duke itself. As Keohane's 2004 report on the status of women at Duke made abundantly clear, the negative role that alcohol played in Duke's campus life was still not resolved. "Both men and women expressed dissatisfaction with the dating scene at Duke," the report said. "Students rarely go on formal dates but instead attend parties in large groups, followed by 'hook-ups'—unplanned sexual encounters typically fueled by alcohol. Men and women agreed the double standard persists: men gain status through sexual activity, while women lose status. Fraternities control the mainstream social scene to such an extent that women feel like they play by the men's rules. Social life is further complicated by a number of embedded hierarchies, from the widely understood ranking of Greek organizations to the opposite trajectories women and men take over four years, with women losing status in the campus environment while men gain status."

How students of color experienced these same dating and appearance issues was also briefly touched on in the report. Regarding dating, because of "their relative scarcity" at Duke, "African-American men hold power over their female counterparts, who vie for their attention." On the related topic of physical appearance and behavior, black students "expressed an insider/outsider perspective on these issues; they were aware of norms of dress and body size and felt somewhat constrained by them, but also recognized that their own communities had different standards and, in some cases, greater freedom."

On the issue of safety and "stranger rape," the women interviewed for the study feared it, of course, but considered it "an improbable event." A December 2001 incident—an alleged date rape involving a member of the Sigma Alpha Epsilon, or SAE, fraternity at Duke—brought together publicly for the first time the issue of excessive alcohol consumption with inappropriate and aggressive sexual behavior. It was also a vivid example of one of the unintended consequences of Keohane's stricter on-campus alcohol policies: drinking and partying at Duke seemed to be thriving in the off-campus homes shared by fraternity brothers who once upon a time would have lived in the frat sections on West Campus.

According to a civil lawsuit brought by Nora Kantor, then a Duke undergraduate and a member of the Delta Delta Delta sorority, a night of Christmastime partying in 2001 began at 203 Watts Street, a house off East Campus that, like 610 North Buchanan, fraternity brothers favored. Before dinner, Kantor and members of SAE started drinking shots of Goldschläger, a cinnamon-flavored schnapps liqueur. At Pop's restaurant in Durham, Kantor, along with a number of her girlfriends, as well as James Thompson, a senior and member of SAE, "engaged in more drinking." Then the students took a bus to a "big barn in a remote location" where the annual SAE Christmas formal was happening. According to Kantor's legal filing, the party was "characterized by widespread drunkenness and alcohol abuse," complete with two kegs of beer and a self-serve, open liquor bar. Nobody at the party was checking IDs for underage drinking.

Between 2:30 a.m. and 3 a.m., the group returned to 203 Watts, where drinking continued and the alleged date rape occurred. According to Kantor's lawsuit, Thompson "wrongfully seduced and debauched her . . . through persuasion, deception, enticement, and artifice." Kantor noted that, prior to the incident, she was "chaste, innocent, and virtuous" and that Duke's SAE fraternity was notorious for "incidents of acquaintance rape, alcohol violations, and other problems." Her suit added that "it was widely related among female students at Duke that the acronym 'SAE' stood for 'Sexual Assault Expected.'" She claimed that as a result of the incident, she "suffered from extreme psychological distress, left school before finishing her exams and did not do as well as she had hoped in her classes." She took a leave from Duke and continued her studies at Ohio State University. She said she brought the civil lawsuit against Thompson because she had experienced "a lot of physical and emotional pain" and wanted "closure."

For his part, Thompson disputed the facts of Kantor's story. In his own court filing, he denied that he was "very intoxicated," as Kantor had described him. He said he and Kantor had engaged in "voluntary, consensual sexual intercourse" and that when Kantor asked him to stop, he stopped. After the "incident," Kantor claimed, Thompson took her home to her dorm room, while he claimed that she "remained with him that night, sleeping with him in his bed." Kantor also charged the national chapter of SAE with negligence because of the incident. A lawyer for the national office replied that it was not responsible for "day-to-day activities" of a local chapter and that, in any event, Kantor had "failed to exercise due care and circumspection for her own safety . . . in the same manner as a reasonable and prudent person would act in similar circumstances to protect herself from harm."

Although the lawsuit was later settled—and the contents of the file sealed in June 2005—the Duke chapter of SAE disaffiliated from the national organization a month after the incident, because "pressure and sanctions" from the Duke administration and alumni "made it impossible for the group to continue its existence in a form its members were comfortable with." SAE lost its housing privileges at the end of the 2002 academic year and became Delta Phi Alpha, an off-campus social group. "I think it's really tough for fraternities to exist on a university campus in university housing," Will Brown, the former president of SAE, said just before the fraternity lost its on-campus housing. "If [punishments] become more and more strict, we could find more fraternities who get to the point where there's not that many benefits to living together and being liable for so much stuff."

The tension the higher drinking age created among Duke administrators, Duke students, and residents of Durham communities around East Campus escalated in the years following, as more fraternity brothers moved off campus in the aftermath of Keohane's crackdown on drinking on campus. On August 24, 2003, Bettie Crigler wrote to her Trinity Park neighbor Christopher McLaughlin about a drunken scene she had endured the night before. "Well over one hundred drunken students, many clearly underage, were in the street until after 2:00 a.m.," she wrote. "Just before midnight, I called 911. . . . At about 12:15 an officer arrived here to say he had asked the students to take the party inside and turn down the music, and said those who wouldn't fit in the houses would have to leave." But the officer asked for Crigler's understanding because the students had just returned from summer break and classes wouldn't begin until the following Monday. "Next time they would crack down," she says the officer told her. "Needless to say," she wrote, the partying did not end following the visit from the Durham police. "The excuse that 'kids will be kids' as we all know only makes the situation worse and more difficult to deal with for the rest of year," she continued. "It is only a matter of time until we have another death from fire or binge drinking, and I would be willing to bet that most likely it will be an underage drinker. I asked if anyone was carded and the officer said no, as that would take too many officers. It appears that there were many such parties in Trinity Park and nearby last night. I believe it is not only the responsibility of the police but also of Duke and the wealthy slumlords in our neighborhood who need to step up and do something."

Chris McLaughlin, a 1996 graduate of Duke Law School, was an administrator at the school. He was not happy about the partying, either, and thought it violated the zoning requirements of the neighborhood. "Each and every one of these party houses described in this weekend's postings blatantly violate the 'three non-related occupants' limitation that applies to our zoning district," he wrote his neighbors. "The landlords who profit from these houses, of course, have zero interest in enforcing this zoning regulation and depend on the non-enforcement of this law to continue reaping excessive profit from their houses (the aging seven-bedroom house next to mine rents for OVER $3,600 month—with seven unrelated students living there in violation of zoning regulations). Why doesn't the city enforce this explicit regulation?"

The neighbors' complaints reached the Durham Police Department, causing Ed Sarvis, a police captain and the District 2 commander, to write a letter on August 25 to the Trinity Park neighborhood residents that was clearly directed to the Duke students living there. "It is my understanding that loud parties took place . . . over the weekend," Sarvis wrote. "I want you to be aware of the impression you left on your neighbors. . . . Your argument may be that the problem was your guests and you had no control over their actions. Our feeling is that when you choose to host a party, you are responsible for the activity of the guests, and you will be held accountable."

Sarvis then proceeded to explicitly explain how the Durham police force would enforce city noise ordinances as well as those against underage drinking. "We have access to a list of the actual residents in each of these homes," he wrote, making clear that the next violation of a noise ordinance where there had been a previous infraction would result in criminal charges against the residents. "If the officers responding to the scene feel it is more appropriate, residents may be subject to an actual physical arrest and will be transported to the Durham County Jail for formal charging," he continued. As for underage drinking violations, Sarvis wrote, "Our officers will criminally charge each person determined to be in violation."

He was not shy about threatening the students and appealing to their presumed ambitions. "I should not have to remind you of the long-term problems you face by having a criminal record, regardless of how insignificant you may feel the offense is," he continued. "Furthermore, since you are considered adults in the eyes of the law once you turn eighteen years of age, any criminal charge you face is a matter of public record." He also made clear that the Duke administration and the Duke faculty—many of whom lived in the neighborhood—were now working closely with the Durham police and were united in their goal to stamp out the offensive behavior. "I cannot speak for the specific actions of Duke University," he wrote, "but I feel safe in saying that disciplinary action should be expected." He then made clear that he intended to inform the students' parents of any violations or criminal charges. "We firmly believe that most residents have parents who assist them in rent and tuition payments," he continued, again invoking an element of class warfare. "We believe that the persons paying those bills have a right to be informed. Perhaps they have a greater ability to modify behavior than either the North Carolina courts or Duke University." In closing, Sarvis urged the students to take responsibility for their own behavior.

The Duke administration also sent a letter of apology to the Trinity Park residents for the bad behavior of its students. On August 26, Larry Moneta, Duke's vice president for student affairs, wrote to the community, "You need to know that Duke administrators are very disturbed about the situation and have conferred extensively with city police and city officials to help ensure that there is not a repeat this weekend." He then trivialized the events of the past weekend. "While the partying is not totally inconsistent with the kind of behavior you normally see at the start of the year, we recognize that this weekend was excessive by all reports."

Moneta also conveyed a "long-term approach" to the problem that Duke had undertaken by working with the Durham Police Department to enact new state legislation that authorized the City of Durham to contract with the Duke Police Department to give it the "legal authority" to patrol off-campus, specifically in the areas off East Campus where Duke students were renting homes. He said the patrols would begin at the start of 2004. In the interim, he noted, "we have agreed to provide funds to the Durham Police Department to support overtime costs associated with their patrolling more intensively in the neighborhoods around East Campus for the next three to six weeks. This is something that Duke has done occasionally in the past, with good results."

On September 1, Mark Boyd, a Duke senior and the former president of Eta Prime (an off-campus fraternity that had once been Kappa Sigma before it left West Campus in the fall of 2002), wrote a long opinion column in the *Chronicle* urging the Duke administration to return keg parties to West Campus. Boyd explained that he lived in one of the houses off East Campus and spent his Sunday morning picking up the beer cans strewn around his front lawn by groups of students looking for parties in the neighborhood. "The safest form of college drinking is a keg party," he wrote, apparently giving little thought to the fact that the drinking age was still twenty-one. "Keg beer is weaker even than normal beer, and I challenge anyone to find me an example of someone going to the hospital because they drank too much beer of any kind." The problem was a long time coming, he wrote. "There were no kegs on West when

I was a freshman, so freshmen routinely took multiple shots of hard liquor on East because they knew booze could be hard to come by on West," he wrote. "This practice is still widespread, and it is not safe for anyone."

Throughout the fall, the Durham police kept up their "zero-tolerance" policy in the Trinity Park neighborhood. Some thirty citations were issued for violating the noise ordinance, and two students were arrested. Then, in January 2004, Durham announced a new plan, whereby officials would begin to inspect homes in neighborhoods across the city to make sure they were in compliance with various ordinances. The inspection teams were authorized to look for code violations and to issue citations accordingly. Trinity Park was the first neighborhood that the new inspectors decided to evaluate. According to press reports, Larry Moneta encouraged the students living in Trinity Park to cooperate with the inspectors. But people quickly came to realize that the inspections were just a cover for the city, with Duke's endorsement, to more closely monitor the disruptive partying in Trinity Park and to enforce the city codes against too many unrelated people living in one house.

The tension between the Duke students and the residents of Trinity Park continued into the start of the next school year. In late August 2004, as students trickled back to campus after summer vacation, the off-campus partying began. Some residents in Trinity Park tried to make peace with the students by going to their homes with "goody bags." Still, the partying continued. Joint teams of patrol cars from both the Duke and Durham police forces monitored the neighborhoods between 10 p.m. and 2 a.m. "Frustrated residents in neighborhoods near East Campus said they saw more students than ever before stream past their sidewalks to the houses unrestricted by Duke's on-campus [drinking] regulations," the *Chronicle* reported. "And as undergraduates stumbled by front porches, they made as much noise as the thumping basses of the stereo systems at the parties down the street." One party raged at the Sigma Nu fraternity, at 706 Buchanan Street, late into the night. The fraternity, known as "Halfway House," had hired bouncers to try to keep the party under control. "I don't think things are that different from last year," Jay McKenna, the frat's president, explained. "The police are still going to be out there, and we're still going to be doing what we want to do."

On the weekend of September 5, five Duke students were given citations by Durham police for serving alcohol to minors; they all conceded they were residents of 708 Buchanan, meaning their living arrangement violated Durham laws. "I and a good number of my neighbors in Trinity Heights and Trinity Park firmly believe that enforcing this ordinance with respect to student party houses that present problems year after year is not only reasonable but necessary if we are ever to take back our neighborhoods from the absentee landlords who care only about their bottom lines," Chris McLaughlin, the Duke Law School administrator, wrote to Frank Duke, the Durham city planning director.

At 2:21 a.m. on January 14, 2005, the Duke police responded to a call for assistance from the Durham police to help break up a party at 1111 Urban Street. Like a number of houses in Trinity Park, 1111 Urban Street was owned by Guy Solie, a 1967 Duke graduate, and rented out to students. Many of the homeowners in the neighborhood blamed Solie for renting to students, accepting violations of the city's living-arrangements codes, and of continuing to tolerate the ongoing disruptive behavior. The latest incident had continued to test the patience of the neighbors, and some of them started to lash out at Solie. "It is abundantly clear that for years you have succeeded in blowing smoke up our collective asses just long enough for you and your family to get the next rent check," Jim Manson had written on January 14. "Perhaps it's time for you to reevaluate and maybe even do a complete turnaround, stop artfully dodging the zoning ordinances, become responsible to the neighborhood in which you own property, and maybe even work to improve the homes, the situation with the tenants, and even the surrounding neighborhood. I challenge you to dig deep, find some honor and civic responsibility in yourself, and fix this situation."

A week later, Ed Sarvis, the Durham police officer in charge of District 2, wrote an e-mail to the community about the party on Urban Street that had so upset local residents. The title of Sarvis's e-mail was "These students are so arrogant." As for the inevitable future parties, Sarvis wrote to the neighbors: "Our response will be as consistent as it has been all year. We will hold the actual residents accountable for the noise that their guests make. Please continue to call 911 if you feel parties are too noisy." He reminded the residents that answering such calls might not be the department's first priority, depending on what else was happening in the city. He also told the residents that their testimony would be necessary in order to prosecute any students for bad behavior.

Unfortunately, none of these police or community efforts seemed to be making much of a difference to the Duke students, who kept right on partying. On Friday night, January 21, Durham police sergeant Dale Gunter reported that five students were given citations for noise violations, and that Durham police had ended a party at 704 North Buchanan. The next night, January 22, Durham police shut down one party after another in the Trinity Park neighborhood. One party in particular, at 508 North Buchanan—involving bikini-clad coeds wrestling in a kiddie pool filled with baby oil—made national news. "If you thought you saw out-of-control, drunk, scantily clad college students 'slipping thru the yards,' then you did!" Sergeant Gunter reported the next night. "Officers arrived to find about two hundred students inside the residence. Inside were several of America's future [leaders], reenacting a scene from the movie *Old School*, where females wrestle in a pool of lubricants. It was a slippery situation, with many folks falling on their bums before making their getaway." Durham police cited Duke student Nicholas Hunter Roberts for a noise violation and shut the party down around midnight, sending out into the cold evening "a few of the women who had no other clothing besides the bikinis they were wearing." Not only did the *Durham Morning Herald* write about the "kiddie-pool party"—putting the ongoing issue of partying in the neighborhood into context—but *USA Today* also picked up the story, just the kind of negative publicity that no university administrator would appreciate. Papers around the country printed the story.

In the wake of the baby-oil party, *Durham Morning Herald* editorial writers wondered what was the best description of Duke students: "Are they intelligent, high-achieving young people, future leaders of our nation, attending one of the top universities in the world? Or are they rude, thoughtless drunks, so contemptuous of the community that they hold wild bacchanals at all hours, making life miserable for their more sedate neighbors?" The problem, the editorial pointed out, was that some students were being tarred with both descriptions, and the latter one did not reflect positively on the university or its students. Where was the outrage? the paper wondered.

The number of incidents in the neighborhood was sobering. According to Durham police department records, between January 2001 and January 2005, the police received 229 "loud music/party" or "alcohol" violation calls at sixteen residences in the Trinity Park and Trinity Heights neighborhood. At 508 North Buchanan alone—the site of the baby-oil party and the home of Eta Prime—there were thirty-eight separate police responses in four years to complaints of loud music or alcohol abuse. Kevin Breaux, a junior and the president of Eta Prime, acknowledged that the baby-oil party had gotten out of hand. There would not likely be another party "of that magnitude," he told the *Chronicle*, because "there is no desire to cause that much attention." But he also argued that the police were starting to show signs of more aggressive reactions to parties that seemed out of line. He mentioned one incident, in 2004, when four police cars arrived to end a party of twelve students. "If there's a huge party and trash in the yards, that's a legitimate complaint," he said, acknowledging some degree of responsibility.

Billy Fennebresque, a Duke junior and a member of Delta Phi Alpha (which once had been SAE before disaffiliating from the university in 2002), said the police and the Trinity Park neighbors seemed to be especially focused on 203 Watts Street, where a number of his "brothers" lived. "We've had fraternity meetings at eight o'clock at night with just brothers, no girls, no alcohol," he said, "and the police will come and say, 'What are you guys doing?' because they been called for a noise ordinance." The targeting needed to stop, the students at Eta Prime and Delta Phi Alpha said. Members of on-campus fraternities "and sports teams like lacrosse and track also choose to live in groups off campus and throw parties," they told the *Chronicle*.

By this point, neighbors were getting tired of waiting to see if the Duke students could figure out a way to act less like adolescents and more like adults. On February 8, a group of twelve Trinity Park neighbors purchased options from Guy Solie to buy four of his homes on North Buchanan Boulevard—said to be in the 700 block of the street—where the most disturbances had occurred. The options did not come cheaply. Linda Wilson, a former elementary school teacher who signed the option for the group, said the options alone cost a "ton" and that she was urging her neighbors to dig deep into their savings accounts or home equity loans to help raise the money needed to buy the homes from Solie. "It's such a difficult problem," she said. "The kids want a place to party, the university doesn't want them on campus, we don't want them in the neighborhood."

For the remainder of the school year, the number of reported noise- and drinking-related incidents in the Trinity Park neighborhood seemed to subside. There was a report of a drunk, naked Duke student—wearing only a bandana—crossing several heavily trafficked streets in a disoriented manner, causing concern among a number of neighbors that an alcohol-related death might occur. There was also an incident involving a father and son who had been drinking heavily for most of the day and were causing a public disturbance with their quarreling. But efforts were also made to improve the relationship between Duke and Durham, whether through a general neighborhood cleanup afternoon or an April 1 charity contest in which Durham police officers, including Sergeant Gunter, and Duke administrators, such as John Burness, would take turns getting dunked in a tank of water on Duke's West Campus, with the proceeds of the event going to the Special Olympics of North Carolina.

Come August 2005, there was little question that Duke and Durham officials were hoping to avoid a repeat of the relentless confrontations that had plagued the relationship between students and their Trinity Park neighbors. On August 10—even before most students returned to campus—Ed Sarvis wrote a letter to Duke students living in Trinity Park that articulated the resentment (on both sides). With Duke's approval, his officers would pursue a "zero-tolerance" policy from the start of the school year. Durham police officers would respond rapidly to complaints from "permanent residents" in the neighborhood against Duke students and issue citations for noise and underage drinking violations. Arrests were not out of the question, either. But within a week's time, students off East Campus were already complaining that police were stopping too many parties. Billy Fennebresque, by then a senior living on Urban Street, noted that police had broken up three parties on a recent Wednesday night. "Standing on my porch, you could see four or five cops," he said. Dean Wasiolek continued to try to walk the fine line between understanding that underage drinking would occur and encouraging students to be responsible adults. "My hope is that students can continue to enjoy their lives off campus, have fun, have parties, but at the same time be responsible members of the community," she told the *Chronicle* in its perennial opening-of-school article about partying off campus. "I believe those two goals are compatible."

It quickly became apparent that there was going to be less tolerance than there had been in the past. In a premediated operation on Thursday, August 25—and then again two days later—known as the "Back-to-School Operation," the state's Alcohol Law Enforcement agency, working alongside the Durham police, began a series of "warrantless raids on Duke students' homes," according to the *Durham Herald-Sun*. They charged 194 people in and around Duke's campuses with 216 infractions: 159 charges for underage drinking, 13 charges of aiding and abetting those under twenty-one in their drinking, and 22 charges of possessing fake IDs.

In a separate incident at 1206 Markham Avenue, an off-campus fraternity house, police charged eighty-seven students, including twenty freshmen, with underage possession of alcohol, and another four people with aiding and abetting them. The raid at the house started after an undercover officer—posing as a Duke freshman—was invited into the house and "saw young revelers drinking from red plastic cups and sucking beer from a keg tap while being held upside down in a headstand," according to Phyllis Tranchese, the assistant district attorney who prosecuted the case. The agent then called for backup, and the police sealed the house for nearly three hours and refused to let students leave, even if they said they had not been drinking. Police gave students three options: admit their guilt, take a portable Breathalyzer test, or go to jail. They were not read their Miranda rights. It was an "unprecedented sting operation that looked more Hollywood than higher education," senior Adam Yoffie, a member of the fraternity, explained. "After cordoning off the house, more than a dozen officers engaged in a warrantless search of the entire premises. Refusing to let anyone leave, the officers remained at the site for more than three hours. Forget Miranda; students present said the officers not only strong-armed students into taking Breathalyzers"—including with reused exhalation tubes because police did not bring enough—"but also harassed many young females in attendance."

At 910 North Gregson Street, the story was the same, with forty-two people charged with drinking underage, and the six students who lived there with helping them to do so. The raids won plaudits from the community. "This was a great move to suppress the use of alcohol," wrote Wilkie Wilson, a Duke Medical Center research professor. But Yoffie expressed concern about the apparent violation of the students' civil rights during the raid and was especially aggrieved by the "Duke administration's failure to address diminishing social options at this University." For defense attorneys, the raids were nothing short of "unconstitutional" and a declared "war on Duke students."

The state alcohol agency did not solely pick on Duke students. Efforts had been under way at both the University of North Carolina in Chapel Hill, at NC State in Raleigh, and at North Carolina Central University in Durham to curtail underage drinking, but the Duke raids were the most flamboyant and offensive. Coincidentally, an article in the *New York Times* on September 1 catalogued similar problems between college students and their off-campus neighbors at the University of Colorado at Boulder; the University of Texas, Austin; and the University of Wisconsin, Madison. Like Duke, each of these college communities was dealing with the problem of the increasing size of the student body without the requisite on-campus dormitory space, and the resulting consequence of students moving into residential neighborhoods, crammed together in living arrangements that violated local ordinances.

On October 18, fifteen months into his tenure as Duke's ninth president, Dick Brodhead went to WUNC, the Chapel Hill National Public Radio affiliate, and spoke about, among other subjects, the ongoing clashes between Duke students, the Durham police, and the longtime residents of Trinity Park. It was the first time Brodhead had confronted the issue publicly. "It has received a very great deal of attention," Brodhead explained, "and the first thing I'd say about it is I have great regret for what the neighbors of these party houses have had to experience. They've been the victims of boorish behavior, and it's not something that any of us would want to live with or should expect anyone else to live with." But he also expressed his view that these were not the "typical" Duke students, nor was this a problem unique to Duke and Durham. "The problem of drinking in college, the problem of rowdiness in college—this is by no means a Duke problem," he continued. "You're not going to go to any college in this country where you're not going to have some variant of this experience. It's not an isolated issue for any one school. It's a problem that all of us face, and to some extent I suppose it's part of the freedom of our culture to have access to all these forms of pleasures. But, Lord knows, there are dangers associated with it, too, harm you can do to yourself, harm people can do to others when they drive."

The radio show's host, Melinda Penkava, cited the *behavior* of the Duke students toward their Trinity Park neighbors—being disrespectful and boisterous, peeing on their lawns—as more offensive than the drinking itself. "There is a special feature [to the problem at Duke]," Brodhead replied. "The drinking is not a special feature, or the challenge that it presents. That's something we have in common with every university in this city, this state, and this country. But the geography of Duke and Durham is curious, because right along the boundary of our East Campus is a very, very nice residential neighborhood that has some oversized houses that have been rented by student groups through the years. What that means is that the kind of behavior that might be boorish but not so troubling if it were on campus, there we have this friction with the neighbors—that's just a fact of life. We've taken this pretty seriously. I know before I arrived, and certainly since I arrived, we've had teams led by our dean of student affairs going out to these houses, sitting down with people and talking about these issues. We've stepped up the training about alcohol to where it's in our freshman orientation. We've taken a new degree of interest in police complaints against students in off-campus locations, and we're paying attention to that within our disciplinary process now."

One caller to the show—Betty, a resident of Trinity Park—asked Brodhead to comment on her perception that the students seemed to be drinking to excess on a regular basis and then causing trouble. Brodhead referred to a *New York Times* article about how beer companies encourage heavy drinking on college campuses by pushing drinking games, such as beer pong. "It's a challenge for everybody," he said, "and we can't make the problem go away by wishing it didn't exist. The only way that I know to do it is eventually to make people take this seriously, that they have to take responsibility for their own conduct; they have to behave in ways they're not ashamed of, in ways that aren't harmful to themselves and aren't harmful to others."

Another caller wondered if Duke hadn't contributed to the ongoing problems in Trinity Park by making it harder to drink on campus. Brodhead did not duck the question. Indeed, he noted that it was one of the key problems on college campuses across the country: When the drinking age is twenty-one, what is to be done in a large community where underage drinking is rampant? "This is a difficult issue for American universities," Brodhead conceded. "The drinking age in this country was made twenty-one some years ago, and it was written into the law that states can't get money to build highways unless they enforce that drinking age. The great mystery, as you know, is that no American college environment actually obeys that. Schools have to uphold it because it's the law, and if one upholds it ferociously, you don't stop drinking on campus; you only move it off campus, where another danger is added, namely that now driving is coupled with drinking. There is no simple solution to this in the current environment."

Brodhead explained how he been at a meeting of university presidents earlier in the week where the topic of making drinking legal again for eighteen-year-olds was a major concern. "Every university president I know wishes that the drinking age could be dropped to eighteen so that we could say to students, 'You can drink. We know you're going to anyway. You can drink, and we'll hold you responsible for keeping it in bounds, for doing it in a responsible way,'" he said. "If we can't allow it, we can't allow that space of education, and it tends to get moved off campus, with dangerous results." When Penkava likened that suggestion to legalizing drugs, Brodhead objected. "Let me remind you," he continued, "that during my adult lifetime, and yours as well, I believe, the drinking age was dropped when the point was made, during the Vietnam

War, that people who were old enough to be drafted weren't old enough to have a legal beer, and at that time the drinking age was dropped. Then, as you remember, it was put back up. . . . I'm not going to pretend that that's a trivially easy problem, because I do remember that when the drinking age was lowered, the number of traffic fatalities caused by drunk drivers went up. So the trouble is, the solution to half the problem aggravates the other half of the problem. It's not an easy thing."

Despite the happy talk from Brodhead on WUNC about ways to improve the relationship between Duke students and Durham residents, throughout the fall, Durham police officer Mark Gottlieb kept up his crusade against the Duke students in Trinity Park. During the early morning hours of Saturday, November 6, Durham police officers noticed two Duke students drinking beer from cans and walking on the sidewalk around 702 North Buchanan. They also noticed "numerous people" standing in the yard in front of the house. "Two nineteen-year-old males were stopped and identified for possession [of] open containers on the public right-of-way," Gottlieb informed the neighborhood group on November 7. "They stated they had gotten the beer from inside of 702 North Buchanan while attending a party." They were each charged with "possession of a malt beverage" and underage drinking. The police also charged two women, both residents of 702 North Buchanan, with "aiding and abetting, providing possession of malt beverages to persons under twenty-one years of age." The residents of the house were further warned to keep the noise level down.

On January 10, 2006, a neighbor of 610 North Buchanan Boulevard called 911, complaining of a "banging" noise emanating from the trash cans belonging to the house. Durham police officers Kevin Watts and E. C. Peterson were dispatched to investigate. They later testified that they could hear "music from two houses away as they approached" 610 North Buchanan. It was clear to them that a party was raging. When the officers went inside the house—without a warrant and without consent, defense attorneys noted—the music was so loud they had to ask that it be turned down so that they could have a conversation with lacrosse players David Evans and Dan Flannery. There was no evidence that the loud noise had come from the clanging trash cans. The officers also did not measure the decibel level of the noise in the house. Watts later testified that both Flannery and Evans were "polite and respectful" to him, but he nevertheless charged them with violating the city's noise law, since that was a "directive from [his] supervisor" when he was dispatched to the house.

Back in February 2005, a number of neighbors in Trinity Park had come up with the idea that they could curtail the student partying if they were somehow able to buy the rental homes from Guy Solie and then resell them to more family-oriented permanent residents. The notion, while clever, was a long shot. After all, where would they come up with the millions of dollars needed to buy the various Solie properties dotting Trinity Park? On February 27, 2006, Duke provided the answer. Through its Durham Realty affiliate, the university agreed to pay Trinity Properties, Solie's company, $3.7 million for twelve rental properties and three vacant lots in Trinity Park. Many of the Solie houses were rented to Duke students and were the locations of the ongoing offensive behavior, including both 203 Watts and 610 North Buchanan Street and many of the homes surrounding them. In its press release announcing the deal, Duke said it intended to allow the existing renters to stay in the homes through the remainder of the school year but would not rent the homes thereafter. The university would then modestly renovate—fumigate?—the homes and "sell them to any family or single person who will agree to invest in renovations and live in the houses."

Not surprisingly, the reaction from the neighbors was positive. "Our neighborhood will become more residential," said Eugene Brown, a Trinity Park resident and a member of the Durham City Council. "Duke will have fewer town-gown problems, and the city will increase its tax base when those houses are purchased and renovated by new homeowners." But Solie, for one, reiterated his view that the Duke students had been unfairly picked on by the Trinity Park neighbors. "Infrequently, people would have a party and bother the neighbors," he said. "I'm shocked at how poorly some of the students were treated. It's a two-way street."

While it was true that from time to time the Durham police treated the students shabbily—during the early morning raid at 203 Watts in particular— there was also little question that, through the ongoing partying, the Duke students displayed a callous disregard for the welfare of their Trinity Park neighbors. And the fall 2005 arrest statistics bore that out. "The neighbors are fed up with this behavior," Wilkie Wilson explained. "Finally, the university and the Durham police cooperated to suppress it."

By March 2006, the official policy of both Duke and Durham and their respective police forces was to once and for all get tough with the Duke student partying off campus in order to restore some measure of dignity to the Trinity Park neighborhood. The bad behavior had simply gone on for too long, and the Duke administration's policy of tacit acceptance while issuing public scoldings and hoping for the best was clearly not changing anyone's behavior. There was no more enthusiastic enforcer of the "zero-tolerance" policy in Trinity Park than Durham police officer Mark Gottlieb.

Forty-three years old at the time and the father of twins with a third child on the way, Gottlieb, an Ohio native, was described once as a "barrel-chested man" who "tends to walk with his shoulders back and chin up." Among his fellow officers, he was said to be "outspoken and sometimes headstrong." In the affidavit Gottlieb filed prior to the raid at 203 Watts, he described his edu-

cational background as attendance at a smattering of community colleges—
among them Durham, Wake, Davidson, and Guilford County Community
Colleges—as well as college-level law enforcement classes at the University of
South Carolina, which for some reason was listed as being in Reno, Nevada,
as well as a number of topic-specific classes involving how to be a paramedic
and how to handle "rape and sex-crime investigations." He wrote that he had
been a "Sworn Law Enforcement Officer" in North Carolina for sixteen years,
the last twelve of which were in Durham. Since May 2005, Gottlieb had been
assigned to Durham's District 2, which included the Trinity Park neighborhood, as a patrol supervisor.

For whatever reason—envy, jealousy, frustration with their haughty attitudes, following orders—Gottlieb seemed to have it in for the Duke students
living in Trinity Park. Between May 2005 and February 2006—when he was
taken off the beat and given a desk job in District 2, making him "on-call supervisor of investigations," he said—Gottlieb made twenty-eight arrests, twenty of
which, or 71 percent, were of Duke students. They included a quarterback
on the football team and a sister of one of the Duke lacrosse players. Of the
twenty Duke students arrested by Gottlieb during his nine or so months on the
beat, fifteen were taken to jail for noise violations and for allowing underage
drinking. Meanwhile, critics noted, Gottlieb did not arrest a Durham resident
for carrying a concealed .45-caliber gun. By contrast, Gottlieb's three fellow
supervising officers in District 2—John Shelton, Dale Gunter, and Paul Daye—
made sixty-four arrests during the same time period, only two of which were
Duke students, both of whom were taken to jail. Not surprisingly, Gottlieb had
his supporters in Trinity Park. "There were a lot of homeowners and taxpayers
who were calling the cops saying, 'Please come and make yourself seen,'" said
resident Ellen Dagenhart, who knew Gottlieb well. "Anyone who's seen kids
passed out in a puddle of vomit is certainly happy to see the police show up.
You can't blame Mark Gottlieb for that."

Gottlieb also had the support of his boss, Ed Sarvis, who later conceded that
Gottlieb was only doing what he had asked him to do. "I fully stand behind
the decision to make an actual, physical arrest," Sarvis told a reporter for the
Durham Morning Herald. "I sent every off-campus student in the Trinity Park
area a letter and warned them of this very thing. They knew to expect it. Maybe
they didn't like it, but they certainly can't say they weren't warned. They were
warned. . . . [Gottlieb] was doing his job, and doing what I asked him to do."

Whether or not the Duke students living in Trinity Park were part of some
Durham police officer's vendetta, they were, according to allegations in the
court cases that were to follow, aware of Gottlieb's often erratic behavior
toward them. Students reported that a police cruiser—with Gottlieb at the
wheel—would drive onto the sidewalks in Trinity Park to block their path.
Sometimes he would chase the students to arrest them or "fly into a raging

interrogation on the street in plain view of passersby." Other times, on the way to jail after an arrest, Gottlieb would appear to befriend the students, claiming that the arrest was for their own good. But sometimes he would continue to verbally abuse the students on the way to the jailhouse. Once he threatened to have a student deported because he—wrongly—believed the student was in the country improperly. He would threaten to put the students in jail with "crack whores" to show them "what life was really like."

In February 2006, Gottlieb's apparent bias against Duke undergrads living in Trinity Park caught the attention of the Duke administration, which authorized an investigation—soon to be known as the "Gottlieb Dossier"—of his manic behavior and disproportionate arrest record. "It was plainly obvious that Gottlieb perseverated over Duke students," according to defense claims. "His roster of arrests was filled with them[.] It was also plainly obvious that Gottlieb had an established pattern over time of enforcing the criminal law disproportionately with respect to Duke students in both charging decisions and in decisions to make a formal arrest in cases involving petty crimes. Simply put, Gottlieb habitually arrested Duke students in circumstances [in which] a 'permanent resident' would not be arrested." On February 16, the Gottlieb Dossier was given to John Burness, Duke's senior vice president for public affairs and government relations. According to defense attorneys, Burness then discussed the contents of the dossier with his fellow administrators, as well as with members of the Duke and Durham police forces. Sometime around March 6, Gottlieb was removed from his beat and given a desk job. He was replaced by John Shelton, who was one of the first responders to the call in the early morning hours of March 14 to the disturbance at 610 North Buchanan.

Despite his responsibility being taken away at the end of February, after the reports of the rape at 610 North Buchanan, Gottlieb could not resist getting involved in what appeared to be a potentially grave case involving rich white Duke students and the rape of a black stripper. By the next morning, he had wormed his way into the investigation—a development that would have enormous implications for everyone involved.

CHAPTER THREE

An Alleged Rape

Within hours of its occurrence, the case became a huge focus of the Durham police department, despite their supposedly having turned it over to the Duke police. At the 8 a.m. morning roll call on March 16, Gottlieb asked the other investigators in his district to coordinate with Benjamin Himan, his deputy, "to obtain as much information as possible during the day." Twenty minutes later, Gottlieb called Mangum, who said she could see Gottlieb and Himan at her home at 909 DaVinci in Durham "anytime this morning." At 8:44, Jason Bissey, the lacrosse players' next-door neighbor, called Gottlieb—supposedly in response to the message about the rape that Gottlieb had put on the neighborhood Yahoo! bulletin board—and reported that he had "heard men at the party yelling racial slurs at the women in the car as they were pulling off to leave." Bissey also told Gottlieb he was going to call the police "earlier in the evening but didn't" as "things" at the house "became rowdy." Gottlieb and his colleague Michele Soucie then drove to the Duke police headquarters and met with Sergeant Gary Smith. Smith gave Gottlieb the Duke police report about the incident and a computer disc containing photographs of each member of the Duke lacrosse team "for line up's [sic] if needed at a later time," Gottlieb wrote. The photographs, publicly available from websites such as GoDuke.com, were retrieved without notification to the students, which defense attorneys later argued should not have happened.

Himan, meanwhile, had also started his investigation. He called Mangum and left her a message. He mistakenly called the escort service looking for Mariecia Smith but was told she did not work there. He was told that she might be a contract employee, since that was the way the company worked with its escorts, but that in any event the information could not be shared. He also called Tara Levicy, the SANE nurse, and left her a message to call him. When she returned Himan's call she told him she could not legally release patient information but confirmed "there were signs consistent with a sexual assault during her test."

Later that morning, Gottlieb and Himan visited Mangum. She was home with her two young children. The detectives noted that she "had a very slow gate [sic] that was obviously painful while she was walking" and that her "facial expressions conveyed her pain as she ambulated." She held the back of the sofa as she walked, slowly, around the room. When she sat down on the sofa, she kept trying to position herself to keep her buttocks off it. When her posterior did touch the sofa, "she groaned and had a facial expression consistent with pain." She tried to comfort her children when they gathered around asking what had happened. She said she did not know how she would be able to tell them the story and "became emotional when describing her attack," Gottlieb wrote. "Tears ran down her face freely, and her nose began to run." Mangum told the officers that she attended North Carolina Central University and was "making a living as a stripper." She said she worked at Platinum Pleasures, a club in nearby Hillsborough, North Carolina, and had also started working at the Angels Escort Service, which called her and told her where to go to perform. She was a stripper, not a prostitute, she told the Durham police.

She then told Gottlieb and Himan what had happened to her thirty-six hours earlier. After being contacted by Angels and told to "go to a bachelor party" at 610 North Buchanan, she arrived "late," just before 11:30 on the night of March 13. She entered the house through the back door, met "Nikki"—the name Roberts had given her—and was handed a drink she believed was rum and Coke. She then was paid her $400 and went to the bathroom with Nikki for ten minutes, where they got ready to dance and discussed "how they would perform the act." At one point, Mangum said, she spilled her drink, by accident, into the sink and then began drinking Nikki's drink. As soon as they left the bathroom and began to dance, the men "became aggressive in their language and started to get very excited."

After Peter Lamade suggested sticking the broomstick "up into them," they stopped dancing some five minutes after starting, "fearing for their safety," Mangum said. They then went into the bathroom, found what they could of their belongings and went outside. That's when a guy named "Adam" came out to the Honda, was "very nice to them," apologized and convinced them to go back to the house and continue the show. She said she and Nikki were separated when they went back inside and Mangum was led back into the bathroom. She described it as the "master bathroom" with a floor-to-ceiling mirror and a blue rug.

There were three men waiting in the bathroom and one of them shut the door. She said that Adam said, "I'm sorry sweetheart, you can't leave." She then explained that the three men—"Adam," "Brett," and "Matt"—grabbed her, forced her down on all fours by the toilet and began to serially rape her. She said Brett was "behind her" and was the "first" to "sodomize and then to rape her."

After "Brett ejaculated," he said to the others, "I'm done, it's your turn." During the assault, the guys were yelling at her "Fuck this nigger bitch" and "Fucking nigger." She told the detectives that "Matt" was next to assault her and attempted "to put [it] in my ass" but she was in such pain by that point he started to "choke me from behind" because "I was screaming so loud." She said she could not breathe and tried to get him to take his arm away from around her throat so she could breathe again. During this process, she said four of her fake red fingernails broke off. Gottlieb wrote in his report that he looked at her right hand and noticed the four fingernails were missing. Matt then "penetrated her rectum," and "at the same time" Adam "became excited while he was masturbating" and then "pulled her up" and "stuck his penis around her lips and mouth." After Adam ejaculated on her face and mouth, she said she "spit the fluid out on the side of the toilet." At that point, Matt "penetrated her vaginally."

Mangum described her three alleged assailants as: first, a young white male with blond hair, "baby faced, tall and lean"; second, a white male of "medium" height, about 5'8", with "dark hair" and a "medium build"—Gottlieb noted she could be describing Himan—who had "red (rose-colored) cheeks"; and, third, a white male with a large build and dark hair who was more than six feet tall. Himan's handwritten notes had a different description of the men: Adam ("white male, short, red cheeks, fluffy hair, chubby face, brn"); Matt ("heavyset short haircut 260–270"); and Brett ("chubby"). She said that after the men raped her, one of them took her purse, removed the money from it and threw it back on the floor. She noted that she no longer had her purse, her phone, or one of her shoes. She also said that half of the money—$200—was for Nikki. After she was raped, she said, Matt "dragged her out of the house and placed her in the car" with Nikki.

She recalled that Nikki "drove her around for a little bit" before taking her to the Kroger supermarket parking lot, where she remembered meeting the police officers. She told the detectives that she had not taken a shower, used the bathroom, brushed her teeth, changed her clothes or had anything to eat or drink after the "attack." Reiterating that she was not a prostitute, she remembered having consensual sex "about a week ago before this interview" with one man she met while dancing at another party and that she had sex with him because she thought he was "nice" and said she received no money for that. She said she did not use drugs and that she had "very little" alcohol to drink that night, although she did recall becoming "fuzzy" when she started to dance at 610 North Buchanan even though she was "fine when she arrived there."

An hour or so into the conversation with Gottlieb and Himan, Mangum said she had "bruising" that was "beginning to show up from the assault." Gottlieb called a crime scene investigation (CSI) photographer to come to the house to take photographs of Mangum, which was done in private. According to Gottlieb, the CSI photographer noted that she had seen "the onset of new bruises present." In sum, Gottlieb recalled of that meeting with Mangum, "She looked extremely uncomfortable. She was having a difficult time ambulating. She was actually holding on to things. When she was sitting, she was sitting off-kilter so that her bottom or her buttocks was off the sofa. She was complaining of a lot of pain if she was sitting flat. She was having muscle tremors. Her legs were spasming. She was doing a lot of crying when she was describing acts that were purportedly performed against her will. When her kids would come into the room and ask for something and she would go to comfort them, she was very slow and appeared to be in a lot of pain just to comfort her children. So the appearance that she gave was consistent with what she was claiming happened."

At 1 p.m., Gottlieb returned to the police station. Himan set to work obtaining a search warrant to get a judge's authority to enter and search 610 North Buchanan. In the meantime, Gottlieb asked a colleague to photograph the house and to obtain a key from the landlord so that when the search warrant was ready, "we would not need to make forced entry to the home." It was not clear whether Gottlieb knew that Solie no longer owned the home, since it had recently been sold to Duke. Gottlieb asked a colleague to see if Angels, the escort service, could be located. He also asked Soucie to put together several photo lineups using the photographs of the Duke lacrosse players obtained from the Duke police "based on the potential suspect names ADAM, BRETT, and MATT." When Soucie was done, Gottlieb asked her to give the lineup to another officer, Richard Clayton, to show to Mangum to see if she could ID anyone. Soucie and Clayton had put together twenty-four photographs in four sets of six photos each, labeled A, B, C and D. They had put one suspect—Matt, Adam, or Brett—in each group of six photos and another picture of Matt in the fourth group of six photos. While Mangum looked at each photo, the police asked her, "Is this the person who sexually assaulted you?" Mangum did not recognize any of the players in the photos as her assailants, nor did she recognize any of the players whose first names were Adam, Matt, and Brett. She picked out four players as being at the party with 100 percent certainty and one player, Reade Seligmann, with 70 percent certainty as being there, but wasn't sure where she had seen each person at the party. "This is harder than I thought," Mangum told Soucie, according to her notes.

In his search warrant, Himan listed twelve items he wanted to procure from 610 North Buchanan, including DNA evidence—"hair, semen, blood, saliva"—from either the "suspects" or Mangum; the blue rug; Mangum's supposedly lost money, cell phone, pocketbook, fake fingernails, and shoe; as well as any photographs of the party or digital records of the crimes or events related to the crimes to be found on the suspects' computers. On the warrant, Himan listed the alleged crimes as first-degree forcible rape, first-degree kidnapping, first-degree forcible sexual offense, common law robbery, and felonious strangulation. To obtain the warrant, Himan had to establish "probable cause" for the magistrate.

Himan crafted a narrative based upon information obtained from Mangum earlier in the day. He also mentioned that on the night of the alleged incident, police had gone to 610 North Buchanan around 3 a.m., but no one would come to the door. He wrote that the police had noted a 1996 green Honda with Virginia license plates that was in the driveway and wanted permission to search that car as well as any others that were in the "curtilage" of the house.

At 6:55 p.m. on March 16, Durham magistrate Tammy Drew issued the search warrant for 610 North Buchanan. At 8:47 p.m., Gottlieb and Himan arrived at 610 North Buchanan. Himan knocked on the door of the house five times and each time announced that it was the Durham police with a search warrant and the residents should open the door. After about a minute, Himan used the key provided by the landlord to make a nonforced entry into the house. As the two policemen opened the door to the house, they were met by David Evans and Matt Zash, who had been asleep. Himan described Evans and Zash as "calm. I mean, as calm as you could be with a search warrant [for] your house. They were a little nervous." About thirty minutes later, Dan Flannery arrived home. The officers then cleared the home "for possible threats." Himan read the contents of the search warrant to Evans and Zash and left a copy for them. "Zash was just laid back sitting on the couch and so was Dave Evans," Himan recalled. But from the start, the three lacrosse players knew something was not right. "When I started to read the search warrant to them, they both stated that was not what happened and they both said she was lying," Himan wrote later. "They both stated they wanted to tell their side of the story." Himan noted that Flannery said the narrative in the search warrant was "bullshit" and was "not what happened at all." The players offered to tell Himan "their side of the story," but he told them that would best be done at the station house.

As Himan was reading the warrant, Gottlieb began looking around the front room of the house. "In plain view was money on the coffee table (twenty-dollar bills) and the victim's purse, phone and ID on a refrigerator in the southeast corner of the living room," Gottlieb wrote. Himan explained to the men they were not under arrest but that while the police were executing the search warrant, they would be limited in where they could go inside the house, although they were free to go outside the house. "They were polite and agreed to sit on the sofa," Gottlieb observed. When Himan asked whether they would be willing to go to the station and answer questions, they agreed to do so. Himan then asked Gottlieb to take Zash to the station to be interviewed.

Gottlieb asked if Mangum's "belongings" had been sitting atop the refrigerator the entire time. Zash responded that, no, he had "found them outside on the side of the house thrown everywhere the morning after the party [and] I picked them up and brought them inside the house to keep them safe." At that point, Gottlieb told Zash he would drive him to the police station but that he first wanted to pick up something to eat. Zash "politely agreed."

Gottlieb and Zash left 610 North Buchanan, with Zash sitting unhand-cuffed in the front seat of Gottlieb's cruiser. "He did allow me to do a pro-tective search of his person before he sat down inside of my vehicle for any weapon which might present harm to my person," Gottlieb wrote. Gottlieb drove to the Jimmy John's sub shop on Ninth Street and parked, leaving the car engine idling. Gottlieb told Zash to make himself comfortable in the car and suggested he listen to whatever music he felt like. The shop was closed. He returned to his car and found that Zash had tuned the radio to an easy-listening station. Without stopping again, Gottlieb drove to the District 2 sta-tion house. Investigator Soucie met Zash there and interviewed him about what had taken place at the party.

At 10:48 p.m., as Soucie was completing the oral interview, Gottlieb inter-rupted and asked Zash if he could give him a list of people at the party. Gott-lieb pulled out a lacrosse team roster—Zash confirmed, incorrectly, that only lacrosse players were at the party—and wrote down the names of thirty-three players who had been at the party, including himself, Flannery, and Evans. Zash then began his five-page handwritten statement about what had occurred that evening. He finished around 12:30 a.m. His statement reiterated the events as he recalled them from the evening and did not even remotely hint that anything like a rape had occurred. Indeed, he expressly denied that any "gang rape," as Mangum alleged, had taken place.

Just before eleven, Himan asked Gottlieb to go over a "non-custody" form with Flannery, an acknowledgment that someone is not under arrest and is voluntarily cooperating with police on an investigation. Flannery signed his form at 10:57 p.m. He then set about writing his own six-page statement about what happened that night at 610 North Buchanan. Like Zash, Flannery made no mention that anything like a rape had occurred. In his list of attendees at the party, he listed thirty-six people, three more than Zash. Gottlieb let Flan-nery know he was free to use the restroom, get something to eat, or use the phone. When Flannery told Gottlieb his cell phone did not work in the police station, Gottlieb encouraged Flannery to go outside. At one point, Flannery asked Gottlieb what he would do if he were in Flannery's position. "I told him it is important for him and his roommates to consult with their parents and keep them informed of the situation," Gottlieb recalled. "I told him he [and] they may want to consider speaking to an attorney also to get their input."

Around the same time, David Evans signed his noncustody form. After-ward, he set about writing his seven-page statement of what had occurred. Like his housemates, Evans made no mention of anything like a rape hav-ing occurred on the night of the party. Evans listed forty people at the party, including several neighbors and the names of some teammates who had left before the strippers arrived. He also noted that his teammate Kevin Mayer was at the party but had "passed out."

Just after midnight, Gottlieb suggested that Himan ask the three students if they would participate in a "suspect kit process" as a way to "rule them out as potential suspects." They all agreed to voluntarily go to Duke Hospital, where a nurse administered the kit. Each player voluntarily gave hair, blood, saliva, and pubic hair samples. Each also agreed to be photographed, and then signed the consent forms for the samples at around 2:25 a.m. Each voluntarily agreed to submit to a polygraph test, but Himan and Gottlieb declined their offers. Himan then drove the students back to 610 North Buchanan. It was just after 4 a.m. They had been together for more than seven hours.

While the three men were at Duke Hospital sharing samples of their DNA, Gottlieb went back to 610 North Buchanan to see how the search at the house was progressing. He spoke with the investigators at the scene and asked what type of evidence they had located. He then walked around the house "to see if there were any other clues present that could link the incident reported to this residence." In the rear center bedroom in the house, Gottlieb saw a photograph of one of the residents "at what appears to be a party (unrelated to this incident) drinking alcohol." He said the "interesting thing" about the photograph was how the "subject has red cheeks most likely due to alcohol consumption." He then concluded that the red cheeks of the student in the photograph "are consistent with the subject who the victim alleged attacked her."

The Durham police seized thirty separate items from 610 North Buchanan. Most of the confiscated items would be typical for any college student to own. There were laptop computers, a digital tape recorder, cell phones, several digital cameras, a web camera, some carrying cases, a PC card, and a Sony hard drive. The police also took a "large rectangle green bath rug," a small bath mat and a hand towel with initials, as well as a plastic bag with a wet paper towel inside, plus $160 in cash, a dishrag, and a bottle of K-Y jelly. They also grabbed a "makeup bag with ID" and "five fingernails," which presumably were the fake ones Mangum had been wearing that Zash had tossed into the garbage. With the items in hand and photographs taken, "the scene was secured," Gottlieb wrote at 1:14 a.m. Himan also later said that both Flannery and Evans had told them that another player at the party, Kevin Coleman, had taken pictures that night, including one of Mangum "passed out on the back porch." Himan asked Flannery and Evans to get him a copy of the pictures, and they told him they would.

At the same time that Himan and Gottlieb were searching 610 North Buchanan, their colleague R. D. Clayton returned to Mangum's house on DaVinci Street to see if she could identify the men who had raped her from a series of photographic arrays the Durham police had put together. Although Mangum did not know it, these were the photos that Gottlieb had obtained of the players. When Clayton arrived at Mangum's house, she invited him in. Although the room was not particularly well lit, they sat down on the couch in the living room and put the photographs on the coffee table in front of the couch. Clayton noticed that Mangum's two children were there, watching television. He asked Mangum to instruct the children to go to another room and to turn off the TV. "As she sat down on the couch," Clayton noted, "she made a facial expression that she was in pain." He asked Mangum if she was okay, and she said she was sore but would be fine with looking at the photos while seated on the couch.

Clayton had four folders with six photos in each folder, or a total of twenty-four different photographs. He instructed her to share whether she recognized any of the men in the photographs on a scale of one to ten, with a ten indicating she recognized the man 100 percent. Although she said she thought "the people in the photos looked alike," in the first photo array, Mangum recognized one man—Reade Seligmann—with a 70 percent probability, but was not sure whether she had seen him at the party. She did not identify him as an "attacker." In the second photo spread was one of the men she recognized with 100 percent certainty. In the third photo collection, she recognized two of the men with certainty, and in the fourth group, one of the men. The problem was that one of the men she identified with certainty—Brad Ross—had not been at the party, and she had never met him before. It took Mangum around four minutes to view the photo arrays. She also signed a standard form indicating she understood what the procedure was all about. Her failure to identify any of the men as her "attackers" apparently did not faze the Durham police.

Despite having the statements of Evans, Flannery, and Zash in hand—statements that clearly denied that anything like a rape had occurred—the next morning, at 10:15 a.m., Gottlieb publicly unleashed the rape narrative, without the slightest equivocation. On the District 2 digital bulletin board, Gottlieb wrote, "The Durham Police District 2 Criminal Investigations Violent Crimes Unit is conducting an investigation concerning a rape of a young woman by three males at 610 N. Buchanan that was reported on 3/14/06 in the early morning hours. The female arrived at the residence for a party close to 11:30 p.m. on Monday 3/13/2006 and left on Tuesday 3/14/2006 reportedly after midnight." He asked that "anyone in the area who saw or heard anything unusual" to contact Himan at his office.

Seven minutes after Gottlieb's missive landed on the community bulletin board, Susan Kauffman, a Duke administrator responsible for community relations, forwarded the headline "Rape Investigation in Trinity Park—610 N. Buchanan" to a group of fellow administrators, including Burness, Moneta, and Leonora Minai, who worked in the Office of Communication Services. To the end of the headline, Kauffman had attached seven question marks. Minai responded to Kauffman's e-mail at 10:25 a.m. with the question "Is the young woman a student?" Kauffman responded immediately: "I would think so, wouldn't you? A party on Buchanan? Maybe not. . . ." At 10:30, Minai responded, "If it is a student, we might want to consider an item on [the Duke police department's and the university's public information websites] because this is one of those Clery Act [requiring universities to disclose crime on or around their campuses] crimes that people want to know about, even if the incident occurred off campus." She wrote that she was going to check with the Duke police to see if the victim was a student.

At 11:02 a.m., Minai responded with the update that the "woman is not a student" and that "she is not affiliated with Duke in any way." That was the good news. The bad news was that "lacrosse players live in the house where this allegedly happened. There was allegedly a party at the house over the weekend and strippers might have been involved, and the alleged victim might be one of those strippers. These details have not been confirmed. What we know for sure is that the students live in the residence and that the woman is not affiliated with Duke." She signed off with the warning: "Be prepared . . . people might start asking questions since this is on the [community] site and 'party' is mentioned."

Keith Lawrence, the school's head of media relations, wondered if anyone had been in touch with the Durham police about whether the Duke students were suspects and whether they would be charged. "The word 'rape' and the word 'Duke' together are not good for public relations," Chris Kennedy recalled thinking when he saw the e-mail chain. Robert Dean, director of the Duke police department, weighed in. "Yes, Duke students who resides [sic] in the house are suspects," he wrote. "As far as whether charges will be filed is unknown at this time. Durham police continue to investigate."

Finally, at 11:50 a.m., Wasiolek explained the situation to the wider group. By then, she knew that the three Duke students living at 610 North Buchanan had voluntarily agreed to give DNA samples and that police had searched the house. "Here's the latest update on this situation," she wrote in an e-mail to her colleagues. "Most important is that the students who reside in this house have been fully cooperative and are concerned that their names will be in the press. Since they have not yet been officially charged with anything, they have asked that should the realty company (or anyone else at Duke) be asked for those names, that we not give them out since this is still just an investigation. Scott Selig [the Duke administrator in charge of the university's real estate] has called Allenton Realty and alerted them to this."

Unlike Gottlieb, Wasiolek was careful enough to at least raise some doubt about the nature of the incident and whether it had happened as Mangum described. "The Durham police are, in fact, investigating an alleged rape/kidnapping at 610 N. Buchanan," Wasiolek continued. "On Monday, March 13, two strippers were hired to perform at 610 N. Buchanan. About thirty men were in attendance, all members of the Duke lacrosse team. One of the strippers appeared to be on drugs. The men decided to pay the women early, and then asked them to leave. They refused, and the men paid them more.

The one stripper ended up passing out either on a porch or deck in the back of the house, and the men carried her to the other woman's car. At some point later, the passed-out woman interacted with Durham police at the Kroger on Hillsborough Road and made the allegations. I believe she was examined at Duke ER. Last night the house was searched. The men volunteered to engage in DNA testing and to take a lie detector test. I believe the DNA testing was done." Wasiolek let her colleagues know that both Mike Pressler, the varsity lacrosse coach, and Chris Kennedy, the senior associate athletic director, were "well aware of this situation" and that the three Duke students "have denied all allegations" but "they obviously admit to hiring the strippers."

Around the same time as the Duke administrators were sorting through what they knew about the incident, Flannery, Evans, and Zash met with Pressler and Kennedy, whose son had been a captain of the lacrosse team in 2005. "They told me broadly what had happened, that the police had come, they had searched the house," Kennedy recalled. "They had helped the police search the house . . . [then] they had gone downtown." He was surprised to learn that they had not told their parents or consulted an attorney. Ignoring Wasiolek's previous advice, Kennedy encouraged the three men to tell their parents what had transpired and to seek the advice of independent counsel. Evans, Flannery, and Zash called their parents from Kennedy's office. "Regardless of how inconsequential you think something is going to turn out, when a search warrant has been executed on your house, I would think that you would want, as a twenty-one-year-old college student . . . to consult somebody else's advice about that. . . . I told them, 'Go call your parents.' I was really angry at them."

Curiously, despite having advised the students not to tell their parents and not to seek legal advice, Wasiolek contacted one of the university's outside counsels, J. Wesley Covington, a Durham attorney and 1972 Duke graduate, then also advised Kennedy to tell the three lacrosse cocaptains to consult with him. Wasiolek later described Covington as a "wonderful lawyer" with "lots of experience in this kind of situation," even though he had little, if any, experience in criminal defense assignments. Nonetheless, Covington "had often been engaged by Duke to handle potentially embarrassing or controversial legal problems," according to court documents filed by the athletes' attorneys.

The next day, Evans, Zash, and Flannery met with Covington and told him their account of what had occurred. "Referring to his close relationship with Dean Wasiolek, Covington assured the cocaptains that he had dealt with similar matters in the past and that he would make the problem 'go away,'" according to court documents. He also "emphasized that they should not mention this matter to anyone" but he left it "unclear" whom he was representing in the case, although he was on Duke's payroll and was advocating Duke's recommended strategy that the players lay low and not engage a lawyer. What neither Kennedy nor the players knew at that time was that Covington's law license had been suspended in 2000 by the North Carolina State Bar for "ethical violations" (but was later reinstated) and that just weeks before the March 18 meeting he had been censured "for engaging in a conflict of interest, failing to provide his clients with adequate information to make informed decisions, permitting a third party who paid his fee to make decisions regarding the clients' representation, and thereby engaging in conduct prejudicial to the administration of justice." In any event, after meeting with Covington, the cocaptains told Kennedy things went well. For his part, Kennedy believed their account of the evening. He had known the three men for years. "I was confident that the allegations were, in fact, baseless," he said.

After Duke defeated archrival North Carolina, 11–8, in lacrosse on Saturday afternoon, Covington spoke with Evans's parents and told them that "his friends" in the Durham Police Department had told him that "everything would be okay." He also reiterated the idea that they should not hire an attorney—including him—and that they should keep silent about the alleged incident and the investigation. According to court documents later filed by attorneys for the athletes, "Covington was careful never to enter into a formal attorney-client relationship with most or all of the players or their parents, while repeatedly advising them and urging them to allow him to work on their behalf, and not to retain other counsel, while secretly acting on behalf of Duke and its administrators."

Late that Sunday night, under the headline "Off-East House Site of Reported Rape," the Duke *Chronicle* broke the story of Mangum's allegations. The paper had picked up on the story from Gottlieb's March 17 message placed on the neighborhood digital bulletin board. An updated version of the same story the next morning quoted Wasiolek. "From what I understand," she said, "the situation is under investigation by the Durham Police Department, and we will await that investigation." Moneta added that the university would take "appropriate measures" once the police investigation had been completed. Gottlieb told the paper that any man who attended the party would be "a viable suspect," but that no suspects had been identified and the residents of the house had cooperated with police. The report in the student newspaper, nearly a week after the alleged incident occurred, was the first time Brodhead, the Duke president, heard anything about it. After he read the story, Brodhead called Moneta, who assured him "the accusations were not credible and were unlikely to amount to anything." McFadyen remembered reading the *Chronicle* story before a class and talking to the male students around him: "What fucking dumb shit. We were all there. We know what happened."

That same morning, Bruce Thompson, father of the fourth lacrosse team cocaptain, Brett Thompson, spoke with Covington. Although Brett did not live at 610 North Buchanan and had not been contacted by the Durham police, he was no doubt concerned that Mangum had mentioned the name "Brett" in passing as one of her attackers. According to court documents filed by attorneys for the athletes, Covington told Bruce Thompson, "I do this all the time for Duke" and that because of his contacts with the Durham Police Department, "we're going to get this swept under the rug." He reiterated his advice that Thompson not hire a lawyer. When Thompson pressed Covington about who his client was in the matter, Covington replied he was not representing "anyone" but was rather "the unofficial legal adviser to everyone."

While this conversation was unfolding, Himan called Pressler, the lacrosse coach, and left him a message. When the two men spoke that afternoon, Himan set up a time with Pressler for the lacrosse players to be interviewed in generally the same way that Himan and Gottlieb had interviewed Evans, Flannery, and Zash. According to Gottlieb, "Himan was working with people at Duke to get the players to come in under the radar, sit down and talk with us if they wanted to." Himan then spoke with Duke police officer Greg Stotsenberg, who confirmed that Pressler would voluntarily make the players available during practice time—"to ensure everyone will be there," Gottlieb wrote—to speak with the Durham police, to be photographed, and to give DNA samples. "None of the subjects would be required to participate if they did not want to," Gottlieb allowed. The DNA swiping session was set for March 22. Gottlieb elaborated on the thinking behind getting the players to voluntarily share what they knew about the incident: "The coach from Duke wanted to assist us in this matter also because he wanted to help get things cleared up," he explained in a later deposition. "So a day was planned where the coach said he was going to make the players go. We said we didn't want the players to be made to go, but we wanted to have the opportunity to talk with them. He said, 'No problem. We'll do it during a practice time.'"

Gottlieb also spoke with a crime scene investigation officer, who said that given the number of DNA samples to be taken from the players, CSI would only do "a buccal swabbing"—rubbing a Q-tip on the inside of a person's cheek—and Gottlieb agreed that procedure made sense.

Himan, meanwhile, contacted the Angels Escort Service and spoke to Tammy Rose, who told him that the request for the dancers on the evening of March 13 had actually been a referral from another agency, and that the dancer "Nikki" was really Kim Roberts. Rose gave Himan Roberts's phone number. Around ten that morning, Himan called Roberts at home. She confirmed that she had been dancing at 610 North Buchanan on March 13. She said she knew she would be hearing from the police about an alleged "incident" at the party and that she had heard that Mangum claimed to have been sexually assaulted. Roberts said she had been with Mangum throughout the evening, except for five minutes toward the end when she would not leave the house. She dismissed the rape allegation as a "crock," implying there was no way it could have happened during the five minutes the two women were not together. "She was with her the whole time," Himan recalled Roberts telling him. "She was never alone. Time less than five minutes. She was being very evasive on the phone [and] didn't want to answer any questions." Since she seemed uncomfortable, Himan asked her to come to the police station. Roberts agreed to come the next day.

That same day, March 20, the Durham District Attorney's Office—led by Mike Nifong—appeared to get involved in the case for the first time when, under Nifong's signature, the office requested a subpoena to obtain the rape kit documentation that Levicy had produced at Duke Hospital the night of the alleged incident. (Nifong later explained that his signature on the rape kit subpoena was just a computer spitting out a standard document with his name at the bottom; he had no idea what had happened or how the investigation was proceeding until the afternoon of March 23.)

At 9 a.m. the next morning, on Himan's behalf, Gottlieb went to the Durham County courthouse and picked up the subpoena and then went to Duke Hospital and served it on Levicy. She took Gottlieb to the "secure custody file room" and gave him a copy of her SANE report and the accompanying photographs. When Gottlieb asked Levicy about her examination of Mangum, she said that Mangum had been "very apprehensive" around the police officers who had brought her to the emergency room, and that even after the officers had left, it took her fifteen or twenty minutes "to calm down and open up." She remained relatively calm except for the few moments when Levicy went down the hall to get a wheelchair, at which time Mangum "began to scream hysterically" and Levicy had to run back to the examination room to "reassure her she was not going to be hurt."

From then on, Levicy told Gottlieb, for the next "6–7 hour time period they were together," Mangum never changed her story about being raped. Gottlieb asked Levicy if the exam revealed actions consistent with "blunt-force trauma," and she replied that it did. "It was so painful for the victim to have the speculum inserted vaginally," Levicy told Gottlieb, "that it took an extended period of time" to conduct the exam.

Roberts, who had agreed to meet Himan at 1 p.m. that day to give her statement to the Durham police, did not show up. After waiting two hours for her to appear, Himan asked Gottlieb and Clayton to go to the address of Roberts's boyfriend in Durham to see if they could find her. But she was no longer staying at that address, and her boyfriend's brother suggested the officers stop by his mother's house on East Cornwallis Road.

While Gottlieb was trying to locate Roberts, Himan spoke with Brian Taylor, a friend of Mangum's who had driven her to the party at 610 North Buchanan on March 13. Taylor told Himan that Mangum had had three beers with her when she arrived at his house to be driven to the party but drank only about half of one beer. "He states there were no drugs, and he does not know her to take any drugs," Himan recorded. Taylor told Himan he had known Mangum for about eighteen months and that they were just friends, nothing more. After she took a shower at his place, he drove Mangum to the party at around 10:40 p.m.

On the evening of March 21, Mangum arrived at the Durham police station to meet with Himan. According to Himan, Mangum wanted to know when she could get her "property" back, including the cell phone, pocketbook, and money she claimed had been stolen from her. Himan asked her for a "better description" of her attackers, but she said she was "unable to remember anything further" about them. Himan asked her if she had been drinking prior to the party and she mentioned that she had had one beer—a twenty-four-ounce bottle—that she drank prior to leaving for the party at 10:40 p.m. They also had a discussion about whether Mangum had had sex prior to the party, and she told Himan that she had had sex a week before the party with her boyfriend, Matthew Murchison, and that she had danced for a couple—a man and a woman—in a hotel room and had used a vibrator. She did not mention that she had had sex with someone for whom she had danced.

Just before 7 a.m. the next morning, Gottlieb stopped at East Cornwallis Road to see the mother of Roberts's boyfriend. But she did not want to give out her son's telephone number or address. Instead, she promised that either her son or Roberts would contact Gottlieb "within a couple of hours." About an hour later, Roberts called Gottlieb and said she would stop by to see Himan around noon.

Around the same time, Himan received the news from Andrew Peterson, a lawyer working with Covington, that the lacrosse players would no longer be available that afternoon, as originally planned, to voluntarily meet with the Durham police—during which time, unbeknownst to the players, the police intended to get DNA samples from them by swabbing their cheeks. Late the day before, another Durham attorney, Robert Ekstrand, had heard that the players intended to meet with the Durham police voluntarily and without representation. Ekstrand, a graduate of Duke Law School, was so appalled that Covington and the Duke administrators had recommended that the players keep quiet about the alleged incident, not tell their parents, and not retain independent counsel that he set about calling as many of the parents of the lacrosse players as he could find by telephone, even though it was late at night. Many of the parents with whom Ekstrand spoke with that night were hearing about the party and the alleged rape charges for the first time, since the students had followed the advice of Wasiolek and Pressler about not telling their parents. Needless to say, the parents were shocked.

Larry Lamade—the father of student Peter Lamade, who had suggested that Mangum use a broomstick during the dance—was particularly outraged. "This is a travesty," the elder Lamade said soon thereafter. "These boys are

being lynched, and the university's throwing them under the bus." A for-
mer general counsel for the Navy during the second Reagan administration,
Lamade was a partner at Akin Gump, the powerful Washington law firm.
Like Peter, Larry Lamade had graduated from the Landon School in suburban Maryland, a lacrosse hot spot and a Duke feeder school. Peter's brother,
Ted, played lacrosse at the University of Virginia and the University of Geor-
gia. After hearing from Ekstrand late on the night of March 21, Lamade called
Pressler the next morning and told him the lacrosse players could not meet
with the Durham police until all the parents had been notified and given an
opportunity to hire lawyers. Pressler told Lamade to speak with Covington.
When Lamade met with Covington that day, he demanded to know whom
Covington represented. "I'm not really representing anyone," Covington told
Lamade. "I'm here to kind of fix this. And I'm advising Duke." Lamade, irri-
tated, insisted that Covington cancel the meeting he had arranged for the stu-
dents with the Durham Police Department. At the last minute, Peterson, on
Covington's behalf, e-mailed Gottlieb that the meeting was off for March 22.
They agreed to reschedule it for March 29.

Later that afternoon, Covington met with Lamade and Tricia Dowd,
another parent, and again urged the players to agree to have "uncounseled
interviews" with Gottlieb. "On the day it was supposed to happen, Investigator
Himan and I got information that they were not going to show up," Gottlieb
remembered. "And this had roughly been a week to a week and a half after the
rape. We knew that one of the players"—David Evans—"reportedly had been
scratched during the altercation, or the alleged attack. And a week and a half
is pushing the amount of time for a wound to heal. And the attorneys wanted
to make it another week before the players could come in. . . . And we felt if
there was a possibility of getting any evidence, meaning the scratch, something
would have to be done immediately."

Despite the unexpected setback, Gottlieb and Himan continued their
investigation. On March 22, Roberts came to the Durham police station and
met with the two officers. Himan led the interview while Gottlieb "sat in on
and assisted with the interview" of Roberts, whom he referred to as "Nikki."
By then, Gottlieb and Himan had realized that by traveling out of the state—
to visit her sick father—Roberts had violated the terms of her probation for
the 2001 conviction of embezzling $25,000 from a photo-finishing company
where she had once worked keeping payroll records. Before serving her with
the warrant for her arrest—and then keeping her in jail for two hours until she
posted $25,000 bail—Gottlieb and Himan listened again to her story about
what had happened on March 13. Himan took notes from the conversation
and Roberts wrote a seven-page statement.

In her new statements, Roberts no longer claimed Mangum's rape allegation was a "crock" and that she and Mangum had been together for all but five

minutes on March 13. These were facts that had given credence to her original statement that Mangum could not have been raped without Roberts knowing about it. Roberts now noted that she "forgot to mention" in her original statement that the "first time Precious came to the car, she left because she felt there was more money to be made" from the lacrosse players still inside the house and returned to the party. "It was after then that the boys helped her to the car," she continued. "The[y] carried her by throwing her arms over their shoulders and assisting her walking to the car—I can't remember if only one boy helped or two." Himan later remembered that both Roberts and Mangum said the other dancer had insisted they go back into the house and try to make more money. "We were just trying to figure out who was actually telling the truth about who wanted to make more money." He said he knew at that point that either Mangum or Roberts was not telling the truth about what had happened that night.

Meanwhile, attorneys for the Duke students would later argue that at this moment the Durham police engaged in "witness tampering" by "offering her [Roberts] a deal" on her probation violation. This was in exchange for altering her story about what had happened that night and involved "writing a false addendum" to "create a fictional window of opportunity" where it would have been plausible for Mangum to have been raped without Roberts's knowledge. In any event, soon after Roberts finished her written statement, around 4 p.m., she was arrested and spent her brief time in jail for violating the terms of her probation.

Given the Duke players' decision not to meet with Himan and Gottlieb, Gottlieb got the idea about seeking a "nontestimonial order," or NTO, from a Durham judge that would require the members of the Duke lacrosse team to meet with the police and give DNA evidence samples. In other words, if the Duke students would not voluntarily give their DNA evidence, the Durham police would ask a judge to order them to do so. Gottlieb spoke with Toni Smith, a Durham police attorney, and told her he planned to seek an NTO. "The bottom line was," Gottlieb later recalled, "anyone who was at the party, based on statements that were given, could have been a potential suspect. . . . In order to get a nontestimonial, we have to have reasonable grounds to believe that someone could be a potential suspect."

Himan went to see Tracey Cline, a Durham assistant district attorney, and discussed the case. He told her the police wanted to seek a judge's support for issuing an NTO and gave a number of reasons, including the deluge of misinformation the police had received from the Duke students such as "aliases," "different names," "different teams" like "baseball" and "track" and the statement that they were "grad students." There was too much confusion, Himan believed. Indeed, he later wrote, the "whole atmosphere of confusion and the exigent circumstances of the healing of the wounds of the suspect that the victim possibly scratched" had led police to seek the NTO as quickly as possible. Cline agreed with Himan and suggested they seek "upper torso pictures," "current mug shots," and "cheek swabbings" from the students. Cline asked Himan to draft the NTO for the DA's office to submit to a Durham judge the next morning.

From 7 p.m. until just before 2 a.m., Himan and Gottlieb worked together to draft the NTO. Their claims were devastating and betrayed no lack of certainty about what they believed had happened. The two Durham police officers sought a judge's authority to require forty-six Duke lacrosse players—the entire team except for the one black player who was at the party—to appear on March 23, at 4 p.m., at the Durham Police Department Forensic Unit. There, they were to provide photographs of their torsos and upper extremities, to show "potential injuries" to the suspects that might have occurred "during the alleged offenses"; to provide "mug shot photographs" for "lineups"; and, to provide "swabbings of the mouth" for DNA evidence that could show "a link between the victim and the suspects." The mug shots would give evidence of the "suspects' current hairstyles, complection [sic] and body mass" for lineups to be used to "identify the suspects." The upper body photographs would give police "documentation of injuries consistent with the assault that will be lost if not discovered and documented immediately"—the point that Himan had made to Cline. The DNA swabbings would "prove a link between the suspects and the victim in this case." Gottlieb and Himan listed the names, dates of birth, and local Duke addresses for each of the forty-six players. David Saacks, the assistant district attorney who signed the NTO, claimed that the evidence taken from the players would help to establish their role in the alleged crimes of first-degree forcible rape, first-degree kidnapping, first-degree forcible sexual offense, common law robbery and felonious strangulation.

In order to establish probable cause for issuing the NTO, the police officers recounted the story of how at 1:22 a.m. on March 14, Durham police officers "were called to the Kroger" on Hillsborough Street where "the victim," a twenty-seven-year-old black female, told police she had been "raped and sexually assaulted" at 610 North Buchanan, even though Mangum had not told the police who found her in the Kroger parking lot that she had been raped. She had made that allegation later. In the NTO application, Gottlieb and Himan recounted Mangum's story. Gottlieb and Himan further noted that when 610 North Buchanan was searched on March 16, pursuant to the warrant, Mangum's "red polished fingernails were recovered inside consistent to her version of the attack" in which she "claimed she was clawing at one of the suspect's arms in an attempt to breathe while being strangled" and the "nails broke off." Gottlieb also noted that one of Mangum's fake fingernails was found perched on the keyboard of one of the computers in the house "like a trophy," despite Zash having claimed that he had thrown them into the garbage.

As for the names of the forty-six lacrosse team players that were to be brought in to the police forensics lab for pictures and DNA testing, they had been selected because all but five had been listed by Evans, Flannery, and Zash as having attended the party, and because the three cocaptains had told the police "they knew everyone there" and "there were no strangers who showed up at the event." As a result, Gottlieb and Himan included the names of "all of the white male Duke lacrosse team members," since "they were all aware of the party and could have been present." Furthermore, the police officers wrote, "the suspects used one another's names to disguise their own identities and create an atmosphere where confusion would become a factor in this event should problems arise in the future where any actions or conduct would be questioned." The DNA evidence would "immediately rule out any innocent persons," the men wrote, "and show conclusive evidence as to who the suspect(s) are in the alleged"—the only time the word was used in the NTO application—"violent attack upon this victim." The DNA evidence needed to be collected as soon as possible because many of the men who attended the party were seniors and lived out of state, "making it difficult if not impossible to collect the DNA evidence in the future when necessary."

The next morning, March 23, Himan submitted the NTO request to Saacks, the Durham ADA, who then presented it to Ronald Stephens, a Durham superior court judge. Himan soon reported to Gottlieb that Judge Stephens had signed the application for the NTO and the players should be informed, through their attorneys, about the need to show up at 4 p.m. at the forensics lab for pictures and DNA testing. Gottlieb then contacted Andy Peterson at Covington's law office and told him about the order. Chris Kennedy was standing at the front of the room when the NTO was read to the lacrosse players. "They were confused," he recalled. "They were concerned. [It] just sort of dropped out of the sky on them. But I didn't see any evidence of anybody being worried about the DNA testing itself." The players were concerned the police might "misinterpret" the scratches and bruises on their bodies from playing lacrosse. A few hours later, Peterson e-mailed Gottlieb that Wes Covington would be present at the forensics lab and that the students would also be available for questioning on March 29 at 3 p.m. At 3:21 p.m. on March 23, Himan told Gottlieb he had the signed NTO in hand and then headed over to the forensics lab in order to meet the forty-six students as they started to arrive forty minutes later.

By this time, not surprisingly, the media had gotten word of the NTO—"tipped off" was how one defense attorney described it—and the procession of Duke lacrosse players that were to appear at the forensics lab. The accusation of rape by a poor black stripper against three unidentified white, presumably well-off Duke lacrosse players was, understandably, like catnip to the local media. "Within a brief time period the press showed up and began filming and taking photographs," Gottlieb observed while at the forensics lab. "I asked everyone to come inside and set up security for the players to assist in protecting their privacy." Gottlieb asked patrolling officers to come to the forensics lab and "stand by the gate and the parking lot to ensure that no one who was unauthorized could make entry." The Duke students arrived at the forensics lab in "carpool" groups, and each group of students was processed separately. "Due to this security, the press left about halfway through the event," Gottlieb reported.

Attorneys Covington, Peterson, and Ekstrand attended the forensics session. According to Gottlieb, Ekstrand "made it a point to state he represented every athlete present," although several of the students went out of their way to say Ekstrand did not represent them. As the students arrived in the processing room, they were asked to sign in. From there, Himan or Officer Clayton would verify their identification by looking at the GoDuke website to see if their names and pictures matched the information that the lacrosse team had provided to the website. After each student's identification had been verified, he was photographed and swabbed, then dismissed. Gottlieb's version of the DNA collection made it sound antiseptic and clinical, but it was actually a humiliating experience for the Duke lacrosse players.

At first, according to Ryan McFadyen, the players did not think it was a big deal. "We were so convinced that, like, nothing happened," he recalled. "'Let's go give it.' The cops were like, 'You give it and nothing matches, it'll be over.' Okay, well, nothing is gonna match. Take our DNA. Just take what you need." He said the police took a mouth swab, some of his hair, and fingernail clippings. "Initially I remember sitting at that lab in downtown Durham," McFadyen said, "[with] them being, like, 'Listen, the witness isn't credible. We know what is alleged didn't happen. This is all just to cover your bases. You guys will be fine.' They were so calming and cooperative, going, 'Hey, it'll work out. Don't worry, guys. It's all right. We got it.' Then they're trying to come around and just talk to you like a friend, 'Hey, man, let's talk about what happened.'" Since Mangum had said in her complaint, according to McFadyen, that she had "viciously" scratched her attacker, the police were also looking for evidence of scratches on the players' bodies. They stripped down to their boxers. "We all got frickin' basically naked and they took pictures of our body," he said. "I mean, we're lacrosse players. We're young, twenty-year-old guys. We're covered in bruises. We're scratched up. I remember Reade [Seligmann] had a—because we beat the shit out of him in practice— had a bruise down his arm. 'Oh my god,' they said, 'take a picture of this,' and they're documenting his arm. We're giving all this information to prove that we're innocent."

At about the same time that the parade of Duke students had arrived at the forensics lab for DNA testing, Durham district attorney Mike Nifong walked out one of the two doors to his corner office at the Durham courthouse into a small area defined by the usual array of office machines—a copier, a shredder, "and things like that," he remembered. He wanted to use the copy machine. That's when he saw a copy—or it might have been the original, he was not sure—of the NTO that his deputy Saacks had authorized and Judge Stephens had signed that morning. "I saw a nontestimonial order with a lot of names on it, which I had never seen before," he said. "And so I picked it up and looked at it and saw what it was. It was a nontestimonial order essentially for the Duke lacrosse team, and it involved a sexual assault, and I immediately sought out Mr. Saacks, because his signature was on it, to find out what was going on. . . . Frankly, I had never seen a nontestimonial order before this case that named more than one person. This was one reason that it struck me as being so unusual when I saw it on the copy machine, because I had never seen anything with forty-six people named."

Nifong continued, "Because of the nature of what was in the nontestimonial order, I thought that this was likely to be something that would—when it became public, as I knew it would, since the nontestimonial would have to be returned—would likely garner significant media attention. Although, in retrospect, I would have to say I never expected it would garner the attention that it did." After speaking with Saacks, Nifong began to think to himself that this was a case in which he might have to get personally involved. "I was certainly aware that we were in the middle of an election [for district attorney]," he recalled. "I expected that this was a case that the media was going to have some interest in, and for that reason I figured that I was likely going to be asked about the case. . . . And so, I said, 'Well, I probably need to be the person involved with the case.'"

After speaking with Saacks, and beginning to ponder his direct involvement in the evolving case, Nifong called the police department to see if he could reach Captain Jeff Lamb or Gottlieb or Himan. But since it was after 4:30 in the afternoon, the main switchboard was turned off. Nifong would have to wait until the next day to speak with Captain Lamb. He did recall being slightly annoyed with the language in the NTO Saacks had allowed Gottlieb and Himan to write about how the DNA testing would prove who was, or was not, involved in the alleged incident. He would have written the language, he said, in a way that would have hedged the DA's bets a bit more. "I don't know that Mr. Saacks had ever dealt with a rape case," Nifong said. "And he's a very bright man. He's a wonderful chief assistant, but I'm not sure that that language would have been the language I would have allowed to remain in a nontestimonial." At around 7 p.m., after nearly three hours, the last of the forty-six students had been processed and was out the door. Nifong asked that the results of the DNA testing be expedited by the state lab, with the hope that they would be available in a few days. From what little he knew, he was worried that with the end of the school year coming up, the students would return home—outside of Durham—making the task of getting their cooperation more challenging.

The photographing and testing of the forty-six white Duke lacrosse team members was big news. "It was too delicious a story," Daniel Okrent, a former *New York Times* public editor, told the *American Journalism Review*. "It conformed too well to too many preconceived notions of too many in the press: white over black, rich over poor, athletes over nonathletes, men over women, educated over noneducated. Wow. That's a package of sins that really fits the preconceptions of a lot of us." The *Raleigh News & Observer* blazed the story on its front page the next morning under the headline "DNA Tests Ordered for Duke Athletes." The paper quoted the NTO as well as the search warrant and reported that "police think at least three of the men could be responsible for the sexual assault, beating, robbery and near-strangulation of one of two women who had an appointment to dance" at the party on the evening of March 13 at 610 North Buchanan. The paper also noted that no one had been charged as of late Thursday in the incident and that, according to Gottlieb, "alcohol was involved."

The *News & Observer* interviewed Joe Alleva, the Duke athletic director, in Atlanta, where he was attending the men's basketball team's third game in the annual NCAA tournament. (Number 1–seeded Duke lost to number 4–seeded LSU, 62–54). Alleva said the lacrosse team, which had been a finalist in the NCAA tournament the year before, would continue its season. "It's just an unfortunate situation," he said. "We're just going to have to let the legal process work out." The Raleigh reporters also interviewed local attorneys, who said they found disturbing the Durham police department's decision to bring forty-six players into the forensic lab to be tested. "On its face, without learning more, it could be really problematic when you have some sweeping unscrutinized searches," said John Fitzpatrick, a Durham criminal defense attorney. Added Alex Charns, another criminal defense attorney, "I can't imagine a scenario where this would be reasonable to do . . . so early in the investigation. It seems unusual, it seems overbroad, and it seems frightening that they're invading the privacy of so many people."

The paper also recounted the scene at the forensics lab. Gottlieb was mentioned as standing inside the lab as "carloads of young men" rolled up to the lab. He declined to comment when asked by the *News & Observer*. Ekstrand was seen standing outside the lab building holding a briefcase. "Don't answer any questions," Ekstrand told the Duke students as they entered the building. He would not comment when asked if he represented the students. One of Ekstrand's assistants told the players as they arrived for testing to "cover their faces, wear hats, and pull their jackets up to conceal their identities." In the back of one of the players' cars was the recent issue of *Inside Lacrosse* magazine. "Everyone's talking about Duke," the cover read, coincidentally.

The *Chronicle* played the story on its front page the next morning and updated it on its website throughout the day. The paper quoted a statement from John Burness, the senior vice president for public affairs and government relations, confirming the police investigation: "Duke University is monitoring the situation and cooperating with officials, as are the students." He said the team would continue to play its games as scheduled, including the one on Saturday against Georgetown. The players were at practice on Friday and, according to Coach Pressler, were in "good spirits" following an "emotional loss" to Cornell the previous Tuesday. "All our focus is on trying to beat the Hoyas now," Pressler said. "They are very mature young men."

That Friday morning, Nifong was able to reach Captain Lamb. Nifong said he indicated that he would like to be kept abreast of any developments in the matter and, if the police needed any further advice in the case, to come directly to him. "I decided that it was probably going to be a case that would get enough attention that I probably needed to handle it," he said. "I just said that all the other inquiries, rather than come over here and just talk to the first DA that's available, just talk to me about it." While the local news media was reporting the events at the forensics lab, Lamb told Gottlieb that Nifong had decided to take control of the prosecution of the case against the Duke students "in the event that criminal charges are sought." Lamb told Gottlieb that he and Himan should continue with their investigation but that they should "go through" Nifong "for any directions as to how to conduct matters" in the case. He also instructed Gottlieb to keep him informed as the case developed. For his part, Nifong didn't recall being so definitive about his role in the investigation of the case. "I never would have said that we were going to be running the case," he said. "I may have said that I would probably be the prosecutor if the case were prosecuted."

Regardless of the precise semantics, many observers believed that it was highly unusual for Nifong, as district attorney, to take effective control of both the investigation and prosecution of the case. "The police let Nifong usurp the chain of command, and this is unforgivable," defense attorney Jim Cooney observed later. "The police work for the chief, who works for the city manager, who works for the city council. The police do not work for the DA." But his critics also thought they understood why he did it: by March 2006, Nifong was "trailing badly" in the polls behind his chief opponent, Freda Black, in the upcoming May Democratic primary race for district attorney. (There was effectively no Republican opposition in November, so the winner of the Democratic primary would likely be the overall winner.) But there was animosity between Black and Nifong. It stemmed from Nifong's decision to fire Black the previous year shortly after he was named interim district attorney in April 2005 by North Carolina governor Mike Easley following the appointment of Jim Hardin, the previous district attorney, as a superior court judge. If Black won, she was certain to return the favor to Nifong and fire him just two years before he would qualify for the maximum in monthly pension payments. Nifong's critics believe he personally took control of the Duke lacrosse case to increase his visibility at a crucial moment when his political career was floundering. (Needless to say, Nifong disagreed completely with this assertion.) The case would be worth "a million dollars of free advertisements," his former campaign manager later quoted him as saying. That much was true.

Born September 14, 1950, in Wilmington, North Carolina, Mike Nifong was the oldest of the four children of Julius Lee Nifong, whom everyone called Bill, and Shirley Mae Smith. Both of his parents graduated from Duke, where they met after both transferred from local colleges. Nifong's grandfather had been a Methodist minister and received his religious training at Duke. Bill Nifong worked for the Alcohol and Tobacco Tax, or ATT, division of the Internal Revenue Service, the precursor to what today is known as the ATF, the Alcohol, Tobacco, Firearms, and Explosives division of the IRS. Shirley Nifong, who had been a nursing student at Duke, was a stay-at-home mother. Shortly after Nifong's brother Tim was born in December 1952, the Nifongs moved to Rockingham, North Carolina, for Bill's job. He worked in the alcohol enforcement division and was known as "a revenuer," charged with finding illegal alcohol stills, destroying them, gathering evidence against their perpetrators, and testifying in court as needed. The operators of the stills were selling what was known in ATT jargon as "nontax-paid whiskey." "They would determine the locations of stills, and then they would go do surveillance on these locations to try to see some activity and, if possible, arrest the people that were involved," Nifong said. His father would spend days at a time in the field, tracking down illegal stills—often at night—and chopping them into pieces with an ax. A few times, when Nifong was older, he went back into the woods with his father to see the still he had chopped up the night before. During the daylight, his father would affix dynamite to the broken stills and blow them to smithereens. "That was a lot of fun, because you'd set the dynamite charges and then you'd run through the woods and set the fuse off," he said. "Then you'd wait. And there'd be this big boom and stuff would fly up out of the trees."

After attending a private kindergarten in Rockingham, Nifong enrolled in first grade at the segregated L. J. Bell Elementary School. He taught himself to read when he was three years old. He spent six weeks in first grade before being advanced into the second grade. After his sixth-grade year at L. J. Bell, his father was promoted to Wilmington area supervisor of the ATT, and the Nifongs moved back to Wilmington, to the upscale Forest Hills section. Nifong attended both junior high and high school there. Every Sunday, the family attended a Methodist church in Wilmington, and grace was said before every meal. His parents were both Republicans. One of the reasons Bill

Nifong voted for Nixon for president instead of Kennedy in 1960 was because he considered Kennedy to be the son of a bootlegger "who had gotten rich during Prohibition by cheating." When Nifong discovered, at an early age, that his maternal grandparents were Democrats, he cried. "Everything didn't fit together the way I had expected," he said of that moment. Other than that minor blip, the Nifongs seemed the picture of the harmonious, white, Southern, 1950s American family.

Nifong was a Cub Scout and loved sports, with a special interest in football, even though he was relatively small for his age, especially compared to his peers. But he would think nothing of tackling the bigger kids. "A certain fearlessness born of ignorance can enable you to accomplish things sometimes," he said. "I saw myself as a football player even though I was very small."

He also was taught by his father to endure excruciating pain. For instance, when he went to the dentist, he never had Novocain or anesthesia. "I'm sitting in the chair, I'm gripping the arms for all I'm worth, I'm sure my knuckles were white," he remembered. "I got tears streaming down my cheeks, but I sat there and took it. And I think that part of that was just to prove to myself that I was able to do that pain. Until about ten years ago, I had never used any type of anesthesia for dental work." He also figured out quickly that as a white male growing up in the South, sooner or later he was going to get in a fight about something. "When there was a dispute between people and you disagreed about what was going to happen, there were certain disputes that could only be settled physically," he said. "And boys were going to get into fights. It didn't have to happen a whole lot. And the reasons differed. . . . But if you were somebody that got picked on, then you were either going to have a life of getting picked on or at some point you were going to have to fight."

It was from being forced to stand his ground that Nifong developed a lifelong disdain for bullies. And he learned from his father that pain—physical or emotional—had to be endured. "If you got hurt, you don't cry, be a man about it," he said. "It's not so bad. It's physical pain. If somebody beat you up, well, you should have fought better. He wasn't one of those people who was going to go hire a lawyer and go after the family, the people down the street. He said no, that's what happens. That's part of growing up. You are going to be in some fights that you are going to lose."

Nifong spent the summer between his sophomore and junior years in high school in Winston-Salem at the prestigious Governor's School, an experimental education program started by North Carolina governor Terry Sanford (later a Duke president) for the best and brightest high school students in the state. An IQ of at least 125 was a minimum requirement. Nifong was fourteen years old; it was his first summer away from home. In the morning he studied chemistry, and in the afternoon he studied philosophy, logic, and the great works of literature. Even though his Wilmington high school began to be integrated when Nifong was in ninth grade, there were few black students. At the Governor's School there were many blacks, as well as other ethnic students.

It was an eye-opener for Nifong. When he lived in Rockingham, he went to the "white" school and did not even know the name of the school the black students attended. "The only African-Americans that I saw were people like janitors at the school or the sexton at the church," he said. Back then, "people of color" were not called "African-Americans," he said. "They were called colored—not people of color, but colored people. They were called Negroes. And 'Negro' rhymes with 'hero'; that is something I heard at an NAACP dinner one time, and I thought, 'What a great thing.' I wish somebody had told me that when I was little. But anyway, obviously a lot of people did not pronounce it 'Negro'; they would say 'Nigro,' and that was obviously also often used in another form, the infamous N-word. . . . I remember my father telling me that that was not a word that was ever to be used, because it was disrespectful. And I don't recall him ever using that word in my presence. He was not a liberal man, and I would imagine that his attitudes on a lot of racial matters would probably have been pretty conservative. But I have not heard anything generally disrespectful to people of another race in the home. I don't think anybody would have considered us liberals. I do remember in the early 1960s when the Freedom Riders were going down to Mississippi and places like that that he thought that was a bad idea, and when some of them were killed he said that that was something that they should have anticipated and there would have been a lot of danger in that. He didn't express sympathy with the people who were doing that—he was a federal law enforcement officer."

His tenth-grade history teacher encouraged Nifong to explore—as a sociological phenomenon—some of North Carolina's more unseemly—and racist—organizations, such as the John Birch Society and the White Citizens' Council. He went to a meeting of the White Citizens' Council, which was known for its virulent opposition to integration, and interviewed the head of the John Birch Society. At the White Citizens' Council meeting, he noted that the participants were "a group of older, not necessarily very well-educated white people who were probably scared to death of what was going on." They could not pronounce the words "apathy" and "inevitable" correctly. "I remember thinking—and I was a fourteen-year-old tenth grader—'What a bunch of dummies,' which is a very arrogant way of looking at things." Looking back, he said he should have been more understanding of what they were experiencing. "It's like everything else: if you live in a society that is pretty much designed for people like you, it's a great situation to be in," he said. "And of course that society was white males. As a matter of fact, most of America, if you think about it, was designed to benefit white males, because we are a country that was founded with the idea that white males with property made the decisions. If you were female or not white or didn't own property, then your opinion didn't count. So white males with property have always fared very well, and if you are a white male with property, you probably don't think about that not being such a great plan. Here we had these people who were really seeing the end of the world that they knew and didn't have a response to it other than 'We need to stop these people who are going to take away what we have.' It was never like, 'Boy, they really have a point. What we have is not right. Everybody could have this. And it doesn't threaten us to bring other people up to our level. What threatens us is making other people, forcing other people to not have things that we have.'"

When Nifong was a junior in high school, his father was diagnosed with bone cancer. He thinks that it resulted from when his father, then a senior at Duke, had tonsilitis. Back then, tonsils were irradiated, which got rid of the tonsils effectively but occasionally led to cancers elsewhere in the body. Nifong said he thinks his father's bone cancer began in his thymus and metastasized. "He went to Duke for chemotherapy and was treated on and off for a while," he recalled. "But he just kept getting worse. And of course he was in a lot of pain. He refused to take pain medications for a lot of that because he didn't want to become addicted to them, because he was figuring on beating the cancer and being fine. . . . But it was not a good time, and for somebody who had been so fit and healthy and active all his life, it got to the point where he couldn't walk without assistance. And he spent most of his day lying in bed. And of course he was wasting away. It was painful. It was very painful. He didn't look like what I remembered my father looking like. And he insisted on being strong and stoic about everything. So when his death finally did come, I remember that he'd been hospitalized up at Duke and my mother had come up to spend time with him, and she'd go back and forth. He was hospitalized after Christmas of 1966. I remember I woke up one morning and she was kneeling beside my bed, and she told me that he passed away." It was January 1967. Nifong was in his final semester of high school. After his father's death, his mother had to return to work. She became the office manager for a group of surgeons in Wilmington; she never returned to nursing.

His parents expected Nifong to go to Duke. "I was raised a Duke man," he said. He would occasionally go with his father to Duke football and basketball games. When he was a senior in high school, it was just assumed he would apply only to Duke, get in, and go there. "I had really good grades, had very good SAT scores," he said. "There wasn't much question that I would get in. But I'd applied for the Angier B. Duke scholarship. At the time they gave forty nationwide. And ten of those were for people in the states of North and South Carolina." As a favor to his tenth-grade history teacher—a UNC graduate— Nifong also decided to apply to UNC. In the fall of his senior year, Nifong had interviews at both schools with the people who decide on the scholarships. "The impression that I had from the interview at Duke was that what they were in essence telling me was 'We are a really great school,'" he said. "'We're a really fine school, and you would do well for yourself to come here.'" He believed he would be admitted with a full scholarship. As a result, for Carolina, he was just going through the motions. "I really didn't have an interest in going there," he said.

In the end, Nifong was admitted both to Duke, on an Angier B. Duke scholarship, and to Carolina, on a Herbert Worth Jackson scholarship. The UNC scholarship was equal to 90 percent of the tuition cost per semester, while Duke's scholarship covered 67 percent of a semester's tuition. It would have cost Nifong $1,000 more per year to go to Duke than to UNC. "One thousand dollars was a lot more in 1967 than it is now," he said. "But my situation was that we were a one-income family. My father had died, so the only income that we would have would be from Social Security and stuff like that and some life insurance. And there were three other children after me." He thought Duke had made a mistake in its calculations. He wrote a letter to the admissions office asking for reconsideration. He said he got a "terse" letter back explaining the calculations that led to the scholarship offer. Nifong said the letter showed that Duke had miscalculated but would not admit it. "I didn't know what to do, because I really didn't want to go to Carolina," he said. "But now I wasn't sure that I wanted to go to Duke anymore, either." His guidance teacher told him to relax; the right decision would come to him.

In the spring of his senior year, Nifong decided to go to UNC. He felt more comfortable there. He said it was the first decision he made as an adult. "If my father had not died, if my father had been alive, there's no question that I would have gone to Duke," he said. "I would never have been allowed to consider the option of going to Carolina." By then, he had also decided to be a lawyer. At UNC, he majored in political science. He ended up graduating Phi Beta Kappa. He did not join a fraternity. "It just seemed kind of frivolous," he said. "When I was in school, the people I knew who were in fraternities, particularly as pledges, were subjected to a lot of drinking games and stuff like that. They'd tell me about being forced to drink until they threw up and things, and I thought, 'Well, that's not really something that I need to pay somebody money to do. If I really wanted to, I could do that on my own, but I'm not inclined.'"

Part of the reason fraternities seemed frivolous to Nifong was because of the growing concern at UNC and elsewhere about American participation in the Vietnam War. What had focused the minds of many men on college campuses about the war was the draft. Nifong was no exception. To figure out in what order young men should be drafted, there was a lottery, with birth dates drawn randomly. "I had gone out to eat dinner with some friends and came back in and it had already started," Nifong recalled. "There were a bunch of people sitting around, watching TV in the dorm common area. I said, 'Has anybody heard September 14?' and everybody started laughing. My birthday was the first one drawn. I was at that point number one, the first contest that I ever won, if you want to look at it that way. . . . You don't know how to react. The first reaction is disbelief. I guess you go through the five stages of grieving." For Nifong, understandably, it was no laughing matter.

Even before September 14 had been selected first in the draft, Nifong had decided he wanted no part of fighting in Vietnam. He had told the draft board in Wilmington that he wanted to apply for "conscientious objector," or CO, status. The board told him his status as a student was better protection from being drafted then the "conscientious objector" status and that so long as he remained a student, there was little need to apply for it. But Nifong wanted the status anyway and filed an application. He also asked people to write recommendations on his behalf, with the understanding that nothing would be considered until he lost his student deferment a year later. At some point, Nifong had to get a physical, in Fayetteville. He got on a bus filled with young men from many different socioeconomic backgrounds. He rememberd one fellow—a towering black man—who desperately wanted to go to Vietnam and fight. "He was a mountain," Nifong said. "I mean, he was just really an obviously fit man who really wanted to go into the service, an African-American who really wanted to go. They rejected him because he had flat feet. He was crushed. I mean, he just couldn't believe that he wasn't gonna get to go. Then you had all these people who were physically able to go who were trying to think of anything that would get them out of it."

Nifong passed his physical. The local recruiters in Wilmington were trying to get him to enlist. They would call his home, speak with his mother, and make their pitch. She told them that her oldest son did not want to enlist and had applied for CO status. And to Nifong's surprise, the draft board awarded him CO status. He remembered the local recruiter couldn't believe it when his mother told him that her son was a conscientious objector. "I was a CO, which meant that I was not subject to military service, but I was subject to being called for alternate civilian service," he said. "So it was quite likely, since my draft status was what it was—I was number one—that I was gonna be called for some sort of alternate service for two years somewhere in the United States." He decided to try to find a job that would satisfy the requirement that he participate in some sort of service capacity, and eventually got offered a job teaching middle school math and boys' physical education in Southport, North Carolina, south of Wilmington. "I had to learn how to be a teacher and teach all at the same time," he said. At $600 per month pre-tax, it was his first paying job. He paid his mother $100 a month for room and board. He taught at Southport for nine months.

The following year he got married and moved back to Wilmington. (He has a daughter, Sarah, from this first marriage.) He got a job as the assistant manager of a paint store, at $400 per month, three blocks away from his apartment.

He did that for a few months, then was offered a job by the NC Department of Social Services as a social worker, also in Wilmington. One time, after taking away a woman's children, he went to her house and was confronted by her boyfriend and his rifle. He said Nifong could not enter the house. "I just ignored him like he wasn't there," he said. "That night he shot up the neighbor's house. I never had any idea. He was trying to intimidate me with a rifle."

In 1975, Nifong decamped to UNC for law school. From the start, Nifong said he knew he wanted to be a litigator. Like many a child of the sixties, Nifong had fallen under the spell of *Perry Mason*. "*Perry Mason* was the show to watch, because *Perry Mason* wasn't about a fancy lawyer getting a guilty guy off," he said. "It was about justice. He was always getting innocent guys off, because there had been sloppy work somewhere along the line, or because things just looked bad. But he never got guilty guys off. . . . So it was really about doing the right thing." During his first mock-trial class, he was smitten. "It was exactly what I wanted to do," he said. "I loved it."

He applied for positions in the District Attorney's Office in Durham, Raleigh, and Greensboro. Dan Edwards, a Duke graduate and the former mayor of Durham, was the district attorney when Nifong applied for a job in his office. But there was no opening. "Nobody wanted to hire me," he said. "I made them an offer they couldn't refuse. I said, 'If you'll put me in a courtroom, I'll work for nothing.'" Edwards agreed to that deal. Nifong started work in October 1978. His office was the courtroom. "On November 8, Dan came into the courtroom and said, 'I found you some money. We're going to be able to pay you,'" Nifong remembered. "They paid me on a per diem basis, no benefits, nothing. It worked out to $11,200 a year." He had been making $10,000 working for Social Services. The following April 1, Ron Stephens—then an assistant DA—announced he was leaving to go into private practice. Edwards came to see Nifong. "I've got some bad news for you," Edwards told him. He could no longer pay Nifong on a per diem basis.

"I've also got some good news for you," Edwards said.

"What's that?" Nifong wondered.

"I'm going to hire you full-time," the district attorney told him.

"I basically became Ron Stephens's replacement," Nifong said. He got a raise to $14,500 a year. "I was on the way, because now I had a full-time job with the DA's office. My dreams were coming true."

By June, he had also maneuvered himself out of district court—where he had started—into being a prosecutor in superior court. He competed for the job against a couple of other prosecutors in the office, with each taking a week-long stint in the role. In Nifong's first case—a speeding case—the defendant represented himself. When the the defendant took the stand, the first words out of his mouth were "I'm not saying that I wasn't speeding." Nifong won the case, and was so confident that he would win the competition for the spot, he just moved his belongings out of his district court office into an office in superior court.

Between October 1978 and April 2005—nearly twenty-seven years—Nifong worked for three district atttorneys: Dan Edwards, Ron Stephens, and Jim Hardin. Nifong never kept a record of his wins and losses—although he won most of his trials—because, over time, he came to realize that only the less clear-cut cases go to trial. "The best cases that you have are almost always going to be pled, because if you have that strong a case, the defendant is going to get hammered at trial and knows that, and so he's trying to work out the best deal that he can because it means less prison time for him," he explained. "So the cases that you end up trying are the cases that have problems. The problem may be a victim who has a less-than-attractive past. It may be that your witnesses are not cooperating or that your witnesses themselves have questions about their veracity." Durham had many drug-related crimes, particularly robberies. "We got to the point where most of the victims of robberies were drug dealers," he said. "And the reason that the drug dealers were being selected as victims of robberies were, one, they always had money or drugs or both, and two, most of them weren't gonna tell the police. . . . So if you say, 'Well, we're not gonna try these cases because these people are not the kinds of people that we want to protect,' then what you're doing is you're sanctioning a species of crime that can have all kinds of unintended consequences for innocent people and all. You're just saying, 'Okay, go ahead and rob the drug dealers.' Where do you draw the line? You've got to draw the line somewhere. You've got to say, 'We can't have this going on.' So I always thought that you had to look at the case and if you had a victim who was not very sympathetic, but the case was a case that needed to be prosecuted for one reason or another, either because of the injury being unusually severe or because there were other factors in the case that made it important for the community's sake, that you deal with those kinds of cases, that you prosecute those cases. And if you prosecute them, you've got to try to do the best you can to win them, because you don't do anything but waste the court's time and money if you try a case that you either don't want to win or don't try to win."

Nifong, ever the competitor, always wanted to win the cases that made it to trial. "It's only when people realize," he said, "that you're willing to fight, that you're willing to do this, even if it's not necessarily the most advantageous situation for you, that they realize, 'We can't just bully this person into doing what we want to do. We've got to be ready to go. If we say this is for trial, we've got to be ready to go try the case.'"

Nifong recalled, "There was a case where an infant had been literally stomped to death by a caregiver who was a teenager, who was inappropriate— I mean should never have been left with a child in the first place, but basically just lost it. . . . The child ended up dying. I helped Dan Edwards do the probable-cause hearing in juvenile court for this teenager who was charged with this murder. Afterward he took me to lunch in Chapel Hill. He had two beers before lunch and three martinis with lunch. . . . For Dan, that would not be enough to make him appreciably impaired or intoxicated. He certainly didn't appear any different. But I'd never seen anything like that in terms of a lunch." Nifong also believed that Edwards's personal style—somewhat condescending and always reminding you that he had done you a favor—didn't make him many friends in the law enforcement community, particularly among the police. "One night Dan left Mr. Harvey's Bistro," Nifong said, "after having been drinking, and was pulled over in his brown Porsche with the DA14 tag— not something that is very subtle—and they got him for DWI. Now he insisted that he was set up, that they didn't really have probable cause to make an arrest or reasonable suspicion to stop him or anything like that, but the fact of the matter is when that happens to you, you're stuck, and that happened to a surprising number of elected district attorneys in North Carolina in that period of time. There are two others I can think of right offhand, and there were probably more than that. But the consequence of that happening was almost always that you lost your next election, and I think that was certainly a factor in Dan losing to Ron."

Even though Nifong worked for Edwards, he thought Stephens was the better choice to be Durham's district attorney, and voted for him. "Dan had been good to me," Nifong said. "Everything that he'd ever done for me had been helpful, but it kind of wasn't about me. It was about Durham, and I lived in Durham and was raising a family in Durham. It just seemed to me that what I needed to do was what was best for the community." When Stephens won, it dawned on him that maybe Stephens would not keep him on. "He brought me in and sat me down and kind of looked at me," Nifong recalled. "He wasn't really smiling or anything, and he said, 'Well, I guess I don't really need to talk to you.' I didn't know for sure what he meant, but at that point he said something like, 'Obviously I'm going to keep you,' and I felt a great weight had been lifted." He was thirty-two years old.

Stephens eventually asked Nifong to be his chief assistant—a job that required him to be in charge of scheduling court cases—while continuing to be a leading prosecutor of felonies. "My reputation with the police department was that I was the most accomplished and most vigorous prosecutor, that I would take it in the courtroom and I would do a good job with it," he said. "All of a sudden I had armed robberies, I had felony assaults, I had all kinds of cases that, just by virtue of how long I'd been in the office, would not normally have been assigned. But I was getting those cases and I was trying them and I was winning them, and that was great. Obviously, I loved that." One thing Nifong said he decided during the time that Ron Stephens was the Durham district attorney was that he did not want the DA's job himself. It was too political. It was too administrative. It paid more money, yes, but it took him away from the courtroom, which was his first love.

After Stephens became a superior court judge in January 1993, Jim Hardin was named to replace him. Nifong continued to be the chief assistant and a hard-charging prosecutor. Nifong always prided himself on turning over evidence to the defense even before that became the law of the land in North Carolina. Hardin was less sure about Nifong's approach, and the two men would often discuss the strategy. But he eventually came around to Nifong's way of thinking.

Nifong tried his first rape case around 1980. The case was handed to the newbie by another prosecutor, in part because no one else wanted to try it. Nifong was game. It was what Nifong called an "acquaintance" rape, in which the two parties knew each other and, oddly, the victim was physically larger than the defendant. "It was a classic he-said, she-said kind of case," Nifong recalled. And the jury quickly found for the defendant. Nifong accepted his loss even though he believed the victim had been raped. He also learned something about rape prosecutions. "A rape case may be the only major criminal offense—and by 'major' I mean really serious crime—that you can literally try with one witness," he said. "If you think of everything else, you can't try a murder case with one witness, because for one thing the victim is not going to be able to testify about anything. So you have to either have witnesses who saw what happened [or] you can have lots of forensic evidence and things like that. . . . But so often, when you think about the circumstances in which a rape is going to occur, it's never going to occur in a crowded theater. It's never going to occur in a church while the services are going on. It's always going to be between two people who are alone somewhere by themselves, and that's the reason that it's taking place there. That spot has been chosen for that reason. You're not always going to have forensic evidence. You may, but the thing is, if you have a victim who can testify that the very specific act that constitutes a rape . . . which is, of course, the forcible insertion of the penis into the vagina—and that's the only act that constitutes a rape—without the victim's consent and with the use of sufficient force to overcome whatever resistance she makes. There is usually only one person who can testify about that . . . usually it's just going to be her. . . . By the design of nature, the vagina is accommodating to the penis, so the entry of the penis into the vagina is not normally going to cause trauma. It can, and it depends on the circumstances, but that in and of itself, it's not like sticking an object into another orifice that was not designed to receive it. . . . If she is believed with respect to that, then there is nothing else that you need to do to prove the case. That is sufficient not only to go to the jury but also to convict the defendant if the jury finds it convincing beyond a reasonable doubt. If they believe that one witness, they can convict. And so anytime that you have a case where the victim believably says this has occurred to her, you have a case that is worthy of being tried. Not necessarily a case you can win, but a case that is worthy of consideration for trial."

He also learned that trying a rape case can be an emotional roller coaster. "Trying a rape case is one of the hardest things to do, because I think the victim who cooperates in a rape prosecution is pretty much putting everything into your hands," he explained. "She's been through a significant trauma, and she's probably getting ready to go through another significant trauma"—the trial—"[and] after it's all over, you really want her to think that you did the best that you could for her. But you're not going to be able to change anything. And unlike a homicide prosecution—a successful homicide prosecution doesn't bring the victim back, obviously—but a successful homicide prosecution allows some closure for the family. I'm not sure that a successful rape prosecution really allows closure for the victim, because the trauma of what happened is not something that is going to be cured by somebody saying, 'Yes, what happened to you is wrong, and we want the man who did this to you to be punished.' It's better than having somebody consider it and either saying 'I don't believe you' or saying 'Well, I'm not going to do anything significant to this man' after the jury has been convinced. That obviously is something that would be hard to accept, but you're not going to fix it. So having a living victim can sometimes put more pressure on you, because there is a life that's going to continue to exist that you're having a big impact on, and what you do is going to have another impact, and you're not sure what it's going to be."

Nifong had prosecuted eleven rape cases before he stumbled upon the nontestimonial order about the alleged rape in the house at 610 North Buchanan on his office copy machine. Of the eight cases in the middle, he had won six of them and two resulted in mistrials. One of the rape cases, in the early 1980s, involved an eighty-one-year-old woman—a Duke professor—and one of the first successful uses of DNA testing in North Carolina. The single woman was at home in Durham when the man broke into her house through a window and raped her. "There were no suspects," he recalled. "All she was able to say was that the person who had attacked her was a young black male. The investigation had gotten to a point—there was forensic evidence that was collected from her by way of a rape kit, but there was nothing to compare it with," rendering the DNA evidence of little use until the database got larger and there was a chance a match could be found.

After the incident, the professor went and lived with some friends, but her neighbors were asked to keep an eye on her place. A few weeks later, a neighbor called the police when they noticed a young black man trying to break into the professor's house, coincidentally through the same window as had been broken into prior to the rape. "When the police arrived, they found a young black male crouching in the bushes underneath the window," Nifong said. "The window had not been opened, and he had not been able to get inside.

They placed him under arrest, and because, to my recollection, it was the very same window that was entered previously, they obtained samples from him and the DNA test was conducted. This was the first time that I had seen that. The victim was unable to identify him physically because it was dark, and because of the circumstances in which she observed him she was able just to say something relative about his size and his age and race. So without DNA there really wouldn't have been a case, but the DNA was done and was conclusive that he was the assailant. As a result of that, he came into court and entered a plea of guilty, and we did not have to go through the trial."

Nifong was surprised that he lost his final rape case before the Duke lacrosse incident. In that case, after two women friends had gone to a nightclub together in Durham and as the hour became late, one of the two women wanted to leave and the other one didn't. "The victim"—a petite white woman—"left on her own, on foot, with the idea, I guess, of going somewhere and calling a cab or something," Nifong recalled. "She walked several blocks and came to a convenience store and went in and asked to use the telephone." The only person in the store was the store manager—a big black man. "She was obviously intoxicated," Nifong said. "She asked to use the phone. She apparently tried to make some calls, wasn't able to reach anybody, and to make a long story short, she ended up being taken to a closet—I guess it was a storage closet—within the establishment, where I think mostly cleaning items were stored, and she had sex with the cashier or store manager on the floor of the storage room, on a piece of cardboard that he'd put down on the floor for that purpose."

The victim then left the store and called the police and explained that the black man at the store had raped her. She said that initially he was helpful to her but then he turned aggressive, showing her he had a gun and forcing her into the closet. "She said that the encounter was by force and against her will," Nifong said. "She reported this to the police, and this particular situation is one that, sadly, I've seen on more than one occasion, and that is that the police officer who arrives is not particularly sympathetic to the victim and the crime that's being reported. The officer, whom I will not name, felt that he was dealing with a hysterical white female. The officer was a black male—I'll just put that in. He could tell that she was drunk. He didn't have a lot of empathy, I suppose, with her situation."

The police officer went to the convenience store and saw the store manager, but did not find a gun. He also searched the manager's car and found no gun. "The absence of the gun was apparently a concern of the jury in the course of this, because the victim said that the presence of the gun was what caused her to go along with the demands as opposed to fighting back, although the gun was never pointed at her, and he never said, 'I'm going to shoot you,'" Nifong said. "The fact that the gun was present carried the implicit threat of all that, and that was what she was concerned about."

There was another peculiar twist in the case, too. It turned out that the two women were roommates and lovers. The victim, in fact, had been a lesbian her whole life and had no interest in having sex with a man. She had tried it once and decided heterosexual sex was not for her. "I thought that that was certainly a circumstance that made it less likely that she would have sex with somebody," Nifong continued. "The defense theory was that she was mad at the girlfriend and that she did this to get back at her." The jury acquitted the store manager. "There is no such thing as a case that you can't lose," he said. "You never have a case that you tried where there's no possibility of a not-guilty verdict. But in the first place I felt that the victim was an excellent witness, and I think that she was a very appealing person, both when I spoke with her prior to all this and then in the courtroom. I thought that she came across as very honest." Here was the lesson he learned from the case: "The thing about the case that I think really stuck with me was how important it is for the first officer to arrive on a scene—and it's not just with rape cases, but certainly it's especially true with rape cases or sexual assault cases—how important it is that the officer who arrives on the scene has some understanding and appreciation of the kind of crime that he or she is investigating, and does not immediately discount the victim's story," Nifong said. "It is that officer who determines what the course of the investigation thereafter will be. The case may end up being assigned to an investigator who can come back at a later date and presumably try to fill in some of the holes in the investigation up to that point. But it's always the case that the failure to seize, to take control of evidence at a certain early time often means that that evidence will never be collected." When that officer's initial skepticism is combined with a traumatized victim, who may not be thinking or speaking clearly, the entire case can get off to a bad start from which it may never recover. "The problem, of course, is that you've got somebody who's excited, who's upset, who may be suffering from a post-traumatic stress reaction from something; someone who, in other words, is not necessarily capable of giving that kind of comprehensive interview speaking with someone who doesn't know anything about the circumstances," he said. "And so what may be obvious to the victim who is talking about this is not at all obvious to somebody who didn't witness any of this. So something is said and he writes something down that is his interpretation, but it's not at all what the other person meant, and that's not discovered until somebody goes over that statement later, and then it becomes 'Oh, somebody's changing the story.'"

By 1999, when he was nearly forty-nine years old, Nifong had been in the DA's office for twenty years and, during that time, had gained a reputation for being a behind-the-scenes, hard-nosed but fair prosecutor. He pushed himself hard, and at times was viewed as arrogant, but there was little doubt that a high-degree of self-confidence was a prerequisite for the job. In court, he felt invincible. "I felt like I was going in there, and there wasn't going to be anything that was going to be able to stop me," he said. "That I was that good. That I was that prepared. I was ready. Give me your best shot, because it's not going to be good enough. And most of the time I was right."

For years, Nifong's second wife, Cy Gurney, had pushed him to get a physical exam. He resisted her request, most likely because he had no health problems—beyond the usual indigestion and heartburn—and continued to keep in decent shape. He coached Little League and had a weight-training regimen that he mostly observed. In any event, he eventually acceded to his wife's request and went to see the family physician. Among other tests, the doctor gave him a PSA (prostate-specific antigen) test, which usually is not administered to those under fifty. "I talked to him several days later," Nifong recalled, "and he said, 'Well, everything looks great, except there's a problem with one of your tests. Your PSA came back elevated.'" His PSA was at 16, on a scale where a score of 4 was considered high.

Three weeks later, Nifong had another PSA exam. This time his score was 25, an increase of more than 50 percent. The doctor suggested that he might have prostate cancer and he needed to undergo a biopsy. This was an extremely unpleasant procedure—done without anesthetic—involving a tube inserted in a most unpleasant place. The test showed that Nifong did have prostate cancer.

Nifong was treated at Duke Hospital. He asked his doctor there which option would be the better choice. She recommended that he get his prostate removed surgically. He had the surgery, and to Nifong's dismay, the cancer had spread beyond the prostate. His next option was radiation.

He was sick for another seven weeks. At that point, Nifong appeared cancer-free. But he no longer felt invincible. He no longer had the "fire in the belly" to prosecute cases. He was more concerned, understandably, about his own mortality. "After this it was just like my perspective changed," he said. "It seemed like I wanted to be around for my son [his child with Gurney]. I wanted to spend time with him. I totally just stopped lifting weights and stuff. It was kind of like, what's the point?" He was borderline depressed. "I certainly wasn't despondent," he said. "I think that I had maybe a flat affect about certain things. I was maybe less enthusiastic. I don't remember any real problems with sleeping that weren't caused by some specific physical symptom."

He ended up beating the cancer. But even some of his friends believed the disease took its toll on his once-impenetrable professional façade. "He ended up in traffic court, which is boring and frustrating and routine and miserable," explained Chapel Hill attorney Ann Petersen. "Whether he viewed it as the cancer causing it, or the cancer taking away his ability to be in felony court, where he felt he was doing something worthwhile, I think he felt like the cancer had more or less killed him, even if he was still alive. I mean, you could tell. He was angry, and I can appreciate that, because when you get something like cancer and you have to worry every day whether it's going to come back, you are angry. Different people deal with it in different ways, and I think Mike internalized it, and he wasn't happy there, and you could tell he wasn't happy there. . . . There was no question in my mind that the cancer changed Mike's personality. Now, he was probably not an easy person even before that, and he wasn't, from what I understand—I didn't know him well when he was in felony court—but he wasn't an angry person, and he wasn't sharp and unhappy with other people. He was intense, and people who are intense sometimes can say things or do things that don't always sound friendly and nice, but it was different in district court. And because I've been there"—she had been diagnosed with cancer as well—"I truly believe that he felt he was going to die and was going through the motions, and he was angry about it. I think that what happened is, once he got to the point where he became the DA and he could then get back into what he loved to do, it sort of brought him back to life."

After being away from the office for around eight weeks, Nifong returned. But his lingering physical ailments—such as feeling the need to go to the bathroom and having to go immediately—made it impractical for him to remain as a courtroom prosecutor. Instead, he took over the job of revamping Durham's traffic violations process, which had been criticized during Hardin's terms in office for allowing repeat offenders to cut lenient deals with the state prosecutors. "Everybody assumes that the DA's office is about murders, rapes, drug violations, stuff like that, but more than half of the cases that the DA deals with every year are traffic violations," Nifong said. For nearly the next six years, Nifong prosecuted traffic violations in the morning and did other administrative duties in the afternoon. He once proclaimed, "My name is Mike Nifong, and I'm the chief asshole of the Durham County District Attorney's Office."

Over the years, Nifong had any number of cases that involved Duke students. Prior to the lacrosse case, though, one in particular stood out for him. Out of the blue, in September 1998, he got a call from a man who was in tears. The man had three children who had gone to Duke. His youngest child—a daughter—was still a student there. She was living in a dorm on campus, and in her hallway a couple of boys had decided it would be great fun to fill empty two-liter plastic soda bottles with "corrosive acid" and aluminum foil, according to a Duke *Chronicle* article, shake the mixture up, and then roll the bottle up and down the dorm hallway. "The idea was you don't want to be the guy [around] when the thing finally explodes," Nifong recalled. "She opens her door just as the bottle gets to her door and it explodes, showering her with acid. So she has burns. And the guy calls me in tears and he says, 'Look, I've had two kids at Duke. I know how things go at Duke. I know how things happen at Duke. They're going to make this go away. Nothing will ever happen to these guys. I've spent X amount of money sending three kids to Duke. I don't want them to get away with this.' I said, 'Sir, I will make you a promise right now. I will not allow this case to be dismissed without somebody talking to me.'"

Nifong made a notation on the case file: "Do not do anything with this case without talking to me." About three weeks later, he overheard a conversation in Hardin's office, next door to his own. "Usually when he's talking about stuff, he leaves his doors open," Nifong recalled. "Always did. So I hear him talking about a case, and I realize that he's talking about this case, and I walk in, and he's in there with John Burness"—Duke's senior vice president for public affairs and government relations—"and somebody else."

Nifong walked into Hardin's office. "Jim, are ya'll talking about this case?" Nifong wondered.

"Yeah," Hardin replied.

"Well, did you see my note on the back of the file about not doing anything about it without talking to me?" Nifong said. "I had a conversation with the victim's father and he was in tears, and he asked that nothing be done with this case without consulting him."

"He's on board with this," Hardin replied. "He signed off on this."

Nifong remembered, "They paid him off. They paid him a shitload of money. I tried to call him. He wouldn't pick up my calls. . . . I was willing to go to the wall for him, and then he backed out on me. That's the kind of stuff you deal with. There is a perception that Duke gets stuff 'cause it's Duke. I think that perception is overstated. I don't think that's as true as many people believe it to be. But, like most things people believe, there is a kernel of truth in there somewhere that got people thinking that way to begin with. I tried not to let that be the case. I tried for everybody to be treated the same."

By any objective measure, with years of criminal prosecutions under his belt—and an enviable winning percentage—Nifong was seemingly well prepared to handle the prosecution of Mangum's charges against members of the Duke lacrosse team.

CHAPTER FOUR

Conflagration

At the same time that Nifong was taking over the prosecution of the Duke students, Pressler and the four cocaptains of the lacrosse team met with Duke senior administrators Tallman Trask, Joe Alleva, and Chris Kennedy. At the meeting, Trask asked the four students to tell him everything that had happened at the March 13 party, even though he and the other Duke administrators were well aware by then that at least three of the four cocaptains—Evans, Flannery, and Zash—had specifically denied that anything like what Mangum had alleged had actually occurred.

Regardless of their previous statements, Trask wanted to hear again from the students. According to a complaint later filed by lawyers for the lacrosse players, when they replied they had been advised by legal counsel not to speak, Trask became angry and demanded to speak with Covington. When the students said this legal advice had come to them from Ekstrand, not Covington (even though it had also come from Covington), Trask told the students that anything they told him would be protected by "student-administrator privilege," although there was no such legal privilege. Based on Trask's representation, the students shared with him and the other Duke administrators their story of what had happened, including admitting to underage drinking and to hiring the strippers but once again denying emphatically that a rape had occurred. Alleva and Trask told the players they believed them and urged them to not worry about the allegations and instead said to focus on the game against Georgetown the next day. "I was in a similar situation when I was your age," Flannery recalled Trask telling him as he was leaving the meeting. "I got through it and so will you. Go beat Georgetown." Kennedy recalled that Trask told the players "he would be amazed or astounded if there was anything to the allegations" and said as "punishment" he would make the lacrosse team clean up the Duke-owned homes in Trinity Park.

At a regularly scheduled faculty meeting that same day, Brodhead got an earful from a group of professors who demanded that the lacrosse players talk to police—such a meeting had been scheduled for March 29—and that the lacrosse team be disbanded. Additionally, one lacrosse player—Peter Lamade—was "subjected to in-class harassment by his professor before his peers," according to court filings by attorneys for the athletes. There was no question that by then Mangum, the Durham police, and Nifong's office had formulated the narrative that three of the lacrosse players were guilty of rape and it didn't take long for that story to filter out into the Durham community and to the Duke faculty, administration, and students. Doubts about the players' culpability were few and far between, and no one seemed to be giving any credence to the statements from Evans, Flannery, and Zash or from Duke police officer R. L. Day that cast doubt on the veracity of what Mangum had reported happened.

That night, WRAL, the local TV station, was full of the story. The station reported the DNA testing of the forty-six students in "hopes of finding at least three men suspected of the rape and beating of a woman hired to dance at a party." Durham police spokesman David Addison said of the process of taking DNA samples from the forty-six students, "We are not going to bypass them because of a small inconvenience. . . . You are looking at one victim brutally raped. If that was someone else's daughter, child, I don't think forty-six [tests] would be a large enough number to figure out exactly who did it." Duke spokesman John Burness also appeared on camera. "Duke University is monitoring the situation and cooperating with officials, as are the students," he said. "If what is alleged is true, it's deplorable. It's very disturbing at one level, but at the same time, until police complete their investigation, we really don't know what happened." Although Burness did not mention it on TV, he had met that day with Duke police chief Robert Dean and so knew of Dean's belief that Mangum's claim did not seem credible. Burness also had been made aware of Officer Day's report that questioned the validity of Mangum's claim. Regardless of this mitigating evidence, the central narrative that the students were guilty continued to be pushed along. "When I saw Addison quoted," Burness recalled, "I had one of those 'holy shit' moments. It was a stunning statement. When the police and the DA make that strong a claim, with no ambiguity, you think that they must have something."

On Saturday morning, March 25, the *News & Observer* published a front-page story with the headline "Dancer Gives Details of Ordeal," which quoted Mangum—though not by name. Mangum had been inside her parents' Durham home while her two children played outside in the yard. She had a gym bag slung over her shoulder as she walked down from the home's screened-in porch. That's when the paper's reporter met her and told her, for the first time, that reports of her allegations had made it into the newspaper. "She put a hand over her mouth and gasped," the paper reported. "Tears welled up in her eyes." She said she had decided to report the incident "because many men don't believe forcing a woman to have sex is a big deal."

The party on March 13 was the first time, she said, she had danced provocatively for a group. She told the story of how she and the other dancer started to leave "as the men became aggressive" but were coaxed back inside the house after several of the men apologized. "That's when the woman was pulled into the bathroom and raped and sodomized, police said," the newspaper allowed, in broaching the delicate topic of what had happened. Mangum said at first she was not going to tell the police what had taken place, but decided she had no choice when she thought about what keeping silent would mean to her young daughter and to her father. "My father came to see me in the hospital," she said. "I knew that if I didn't report it that he would have that hurt look forever, knowing that someone hurt his baby and got away with it." She then pulled her young son close to her. "I'm just trying to get on with my life," she told the paper.

That life had not been an easy one. Born in Durham, Crystal Mangum was the youngest of three children and had been raised in a working-class neighborhood. She graduated from Durham's Hillside High School in 1996. Her yearbook photo showed a girl with chin-length black braids and dark brown eyes. "Her lips are pursed in a shy smile," the News & Observer explained. One classmate, Frederica Thomas, remembered Mangum as reserved. "She usually kept to herself," she said. "She was quiet. . . . When I saw her, she was usually with her sister," who was one year older than Mangum and also attended NCCU.

On August 18, 1996, Mangum reported to police in Creedmoor, North Carolina—about fifteen miles from Durham—that in June 1993, when she was fourteen, she had been gang-raped by three men in a house on Hillsborough Street. "Suspects did for a continual time rape and beat victim about her person," said a report filed by Lieutenant B. G. Bishop. She gave Bishop the names of three men who had allegedly gang-raped her and the addresses of two of the men. She also said that at least two of the men were black. Bishop "advised" Mangum to "write a chronological ordered statement of the incidents and occurrances that had taken place and return the statement for investigative purposes." But she never did that, the men were never charged, and the matter was dropped.

Mangum had wanted to follow her older sister to NCCU but instead met and fell in love with a man fourteen years older. In the fall of 1996, Mangum enlisted in the Navy for two years of active duty followed by six years of reserve duty. Wanting to see the world, she moved to Virginia Beach, Virginia, to begin her active duty the following summer. The Navy sent her to school in Dam Neck, Virginia, to be trained for her job operating radios and navigation equipment.

In 1997, Mangum, then nineteen years old, got married. Her husband, Kenneth McNeill, was illiterate, but she taught him how to read. Eventually, he was able to fill out his own job application form. "She never downed me for that," McNeill told a local reporter. "She loved me for who I was." The newlyweds moved to Concord, California, where Mangum was assigned to the USS Mount Hood, an ammunition ship. She was away at sea for weeks, and the marriage became strained. "She was young," her former husband said. They fell behind in paying their bills, and Mangum suggested to him that she could get a job dancing to earn extra cash. She would have to dance nearly naked, but it was quick money. He said she visited one club but decided she wasn't ready to do that work. "I couldn't fault a woman for taking care of her family and trying to pay the bills," he said. (She later accused McNeill of trying to kill her.)

During this time, Mangum met and fell in love with another sailor—a white man named Ryan—who would later become the father of her two children. Mangum and McNeill separated, then divorced, as the new relationship took hold. Six months later, Mangum was discharged from the Navy, although the Navy would not say why she left. Her first child was born less than nine months later, suggesting that her relationship with the other sailor had reached a point where the Navy thought it best to dismiss her. Soon after the birth of her second child with the sailor, they split up. In 2003, a Durham court ordered the children's father to pay about $400 a month in child support as well as another $2,700 in public assistance to the children, according to court records. Back in Durham, Mangum worked to support her children, including on an assembly line in a computer factory and in various sales jobs.

In June 2002, when she was twenty-three, Mangum had her first brush with the Durham police. The trouble started when Mangum went to the Diamond Girls Club, on Angier Avenue in Durham, and "tried out" as a lap dancer at the club by giving lap dances to a few men. She did not get the job, though, because the manager, Larry Jones, said Mangum was "acting funny." She did one more lap dance for Abdul Rahim, a thirty-year-old taxi driver. She asked him for a ride home. "As she was feeling him up and putting her hands in his pockets, she removed the keys to his taxi cab without him knowing," according to the police report. "He told her he would drive her home but needed to use the restroom first." While Rahim was in the bathroom, Mangum stole his taxi, a blue Chevrolet Caprice. He called 911 to report his stolen car, and then he and another patron tried to follow her as she drove away. A sheriff's deputy responded to the call and saw Mangum driving the stolen Chevy near the club, on the wrong side of the road and without headlights. She crossed back to the right side of the road, then off it onto the shoulder, "turning up dirt," according to the police report. Mangum sped up to pass the officer and he gave chase. She ran a stop sign and drove across the grassy median onto the shoulder on the other side of the road. She then drove back to the other side of the road, then drove onto US 70 in Durham at seventy miles per hour in a fifty-five-mile-per-hour zone. She drove down the center of the highway. "I continued to pursue, and the suspect still refused to stop," Officer Carroll continued. "Still traveling at 70 MPH in a 55 zone." She kept driving the wrong way on the road and ended up in a dead end, where she tried to drive the taxi through a fence. "She was unable to, and it appeared that she was not going to go any further," he wrote.

The sheriff's deputy cornered Mangum in the cul-de-sac, got out of his car and told her to turn off the taxi's engine. But she laughed and backed up the car into the woods. "It appeared that she was stuck," he wrote. But Mangum then drove forward again, nearly hitting the officer. "I jumped out of the way to the right and she missed me," Carroll continued. She then "struck" the right rear quarter of the cruiser, which had flashers, headlights, blue rotating lights, and sirens on. Carroll ran up alongside the taxicab and tried to smash the door window with his flashlight but was unsuccessful. Mangum then returned to Brier Creek Parkway into oncoming traffic and almost hit another sheriff's deputy. That deputy then took up the pursuit of Mangum and finally caught her—after a few more twists and turns—when the taxi got a flat tire. She was taken into custody and put in the back of his cruiser. She kept trying to lie down in the back of the cruiser but Carroll told her to sit up. She was administered two "alcosensor" tests, one at 1:21 a.m. and another six minutes later. They both registered Mangum's blood alcohol level at 0.19, more than twice the legal limit. She then "passed out and was unresponsive." An EMS unit was summoned and took Mangum to the Duke Hospital emergency room.

Ultimately, Mangum pleaded guilty to four misdemeanors: larceny, speeding to elude arrest, assault on a government official, and DWI. She served three consecutive weekends in jail and was then placed on two years' probation. She paid restitution and court costs and served out her probation period without further incidents.

After the drunk-driving debacle, Mangum was eager to clean up her act. She got a job in a nursing home, like her older sister. In June 2004, she changed jobs to work at Ellison's Rest Home in Durham. After two weeks of work, she wanted to get paid but didn't get her paycheck because her employee file was incomplete, lacking her criminal records. She called the police. At the rest home, a "Ms. Ellison" told the police she would pay Mangum once her criminal record had been obtained and provided to her employer. But she soon left the rest home job. Still, her father said, her criminal record did not prevent her from getting odd jobs, although he said he did not know she was working for an escort service while she attended NCCU.

The *News & Observer* article about Mangum also quoted Durham police spokesman David Addison, who for the first time broached what would soon become an overarching theme of the saga: to wit, that for some reason the Duke lacrosse players were not cooperating with police and had entered into a pact of *omertà* to keep the damning truth from getting out. "We're asking someone from the lacrosse team to step forward," Addison said. "We will be relentless in finding out who committed this crime." The paper reported that "authorities"—none was specifically mentioned—"vowed to crack the team's wall of solidarity." Addison reiterated the "seriousness of the accusations": first-degree rape, kidnapping, assault by strangulation, and robbery. Art Chase, the Duke sports information director, said that Pressler and the athletics department had spoken with the cocaptains about the incident and Duke did not plan to do its own investigation. "I think they'll let the judicial system run its course," he said.

That same Saturday morning, Brodhead convened the first of what seemed to be a crisis committee of sorts at his home near the Duke campus, a beautiful, Gothic-style mansion just off West Campus. Paul Haagen, chairman of Duke's Academic Council, was there, along with Wasiolek, Trask, Alleva, Burness, and a Duke attorney, Kate Hendricks. Burness, later reported that the Duke administrators decided they "needed to send a signal that they took seriously what happened in that house." They canceled the next two lacrosse games, including the one scheduled that day against Georgetown. Protesters had already assembled in the rain outside of Duke's Koskinen Stadium, holding makeshift signs that read, "Don't be a fan of rapists." Added Francis Conlin, a Durham resident, who was protesting at the lacrosse stadium, "I was dismayed at the thought that the lacrosse team was trying to put this behind them and move forward. I am fully aware a crime was committed by someone. It is too bad the rest of the team won't fess up." At 11 a.m., ninety minutes before game time, and with the Georgetown team already in their uniforms, Alleva told Pressler of Brodhead's decision to forfeit the game against Georgetown and the one on Tuesday against Mount Saint Mary's. "See ya," he told the players as he was leaving, which they found so insulting they would later joke about it.

"I remember that being a real chilling moment, like, 'Holy crap, this is getting serious,'" McFadyen recalled. "Our game just got canceled. I mean, Georgetown was on the field warming up. They had taken a bus, driven five hours, spent the night. . . . And suddenly Duke had to go, 'Hey, sorry. We're gonna cancel the game. . . .' It got canceled, and . . . we still didn't think anything of it because we knew that nothing had happened."

Following the announcement of the forfeited games, Brodhead made his first public announcement about the alleged incident. His statement seemed cautious but scornful of the players and their behavior. "Physical coercion and sexual assault are unacceptable in any setting and have no place at Duke," he wrote. "The criminal allegations against three members of our men's lacrosse team, if verified, will warrant very serious penalties. The facts are not yet established, however, and there are very different versions of the central events. No charges have been filed, and in our system of law, people are presumed innocent until proven guilty. We also know that many members of the team, including some who were asked to provide DNA samples, did not attend the party. I urge everyone to cooperate to the fullest with the police inquiry while we wait to learn the truth. Whatever that inquiry may show, it is already clear that many students acted in a manner inappropriate to a Duke team member in participating in the March 13 party."

When the parents of the lacrosse players, who expected to see a game played against Georgetown, discovered that it had been canceled at the last minute, they demanded—and got—a meeting with Alleva and Kennedy. "The parents were upset and angry," Kennedy recalled. He noted that a number of them were "fairly accomplished, prominent lawyers"; they demanded answers about Wes Covington and why the two games were canceled. "They were interested in knowing if every team that had a party would have their games canceled," Kennedy said. They demanded that Wasiolek, Moneta, Trask, and Brodhead show up and answer their questions. Brodhead did not attend the meeting, even though he was on campus that morning and had made the decision to cancel the Georgetown game. Kennedy recalled that Wasiolek was having a hard time defending the decision to cancel the two games "as compared to when other teams have had parties." Kennedy, who left the meeting before Moneta and Trask arrived, said the parents were upset by the "equity" of the decision and that by "canceling the games" the Duke administration was "sending the message that they believed in the guilt of the players." He said that in light of the *News & Observer* article about Mangum's "ordeal," the parents had a good point. "I thought that that would send the message that that was, in fact, an accurate account of what had happened," he said. He also said Brodhead's statement was "unfortunately constructed" and left the impression in readers' minds that there was substance to the allegations.

Shortly after Brodhead released his statement, Burness wrote an e-mail to the Duke board of trustees, filling them in that Trask was "inclined to believe the players" and that the players had hired an attorney "who, for perhaps understandable reasons, has urged them not to say anything. While that may be a sound legal strategy, it leaves them vulnerable to the woman's version of events filling a vacuum and the students appearing to be uncooperative. . . . The situation is further complicated by the behavior of the lacrosse team over many years, which, for those predisposed to be angry with them, presumes their guilt. . . . We simply do not know what happened, which is why the [police] investigation is so important."

That night, some 175 "incensed community members" showed up in front of both 610 North Buchanan and 1103 Urban Street, another lacrosse house around the corner, for a "candlelight vigil" to protest the alleged crimes. The group, which included neighbors, students, and Duke employees, repeated the word "shame" and sang "This Little Light of Mine" and "Amazing Grace" in "solidarity for a stripper, who was allegedly raped, sodomized, and strangled by three white men." Said neighbor Janene Tompkins, "This is to let her know that we're with her. If anyone could come and take a piece of her grief, we would." At 610 North Buchanan, there were no lights on at the house and it appeared that the three lacrosse cocaptains were not home. At 1103 Urban, as soon as the protest began the lights in the house were turned off, but protesters could still see people inside. "The students need to realize they live in a community, and people are going to talk back if they do something that is disrespectful to women," explained Faulkner Fox, a lecturing fellow in the Duke English department and one of the organizers of the protest. Another protester, Betty Greene, criticized Duke's slow-footed response to the incident. "I find Duke's behavior deplorable," she said. "They took so long to respond, and when they did, it was sort of wishy-washy."

The next morning, Sunday, at 9 a.m. another group of around 150 protesters were again out in front of 610 North Buchanan for a protest they called, "Wake-up Call Against Sexual Assault." With the sun shining brightly, the group were banging pots and pans on a continuous basis, which a reporter from WRAL pointed out was an act of protest with origins in the poor barrios of Latin America among women concerned about ongoing domestic violence. "There is a sense that Duke students need to be protected from Durham, but rapes are happening off East Campus at the hands of Duke students," said Manju Rajendran, an organizer of the event. She added, into a bullhorn: "This is a wake-up call to challenge sexual assault and racial violence. We're trying to break the silence. . . . Women have a right to dignity and respect." The protesters carried signs that read "You can't rape and run," "It's Sunday morning, time to confess" and "Real men tell the truth," and then taped the signs to the outside of the house.

From their demonstration in front of 610 North Buchanan, about sixty of the protesters walked around the corner to Markham Avenue, where Duke provost Peter Lange lived. After about ten minutes of hearing pot-banging and chanting, Lange, a brilliant leprechaun of a man, came out of his house wearing a Duke T-shirt and a baseball cap, a far cry from his usual attire of businessman's pinstripes. In response to questions and statements hurled in his direction by protesters, Lange said, "This is an extremely serious crime, if it happened. We don't know the facts of what happened in the house. We have allegations. . . . The only people who have the means to discover what happened in that house are the police." When this statement was met with howls of protest, Lange said, "We obviously have a difference of opinion. No large institution behaves in a way the community always wants it to." One demonstrator complained to Lange that the problems in the neighborhood had been of a long-term nature and for too long the university had ignored them. "I believe we've been doing a lot," he said. "There is always more work to be done."

Later that afternoon, Burness told the *Chronicle* that while he had not spoken with any of the players directly, he knew that there were "two different versions of what went on at the party" and that "some people who have talked to the players have suggested it would be very much to their advantage to get their side of the story out in one way or another." But despite the statements that Evans, Flannery, and Zash had made to police and their ongoing denial in their conversations with Alleva, Kennedy, Trask, and Wasiolek—and presumably Brodhead—that any rape had occurred, this part of the narrative did not seem to be finding a home in the media coverage. The truth was nobody, it seemed, was willing to believe that version of events—not yet, anyway. In a conversation with the student newspaper, Provost Lange broached for the first time the notion that the rest of the lacrosse season might be canceled. He said, though, that if the allegations proved to be false, he would not support canceling the remainder of the season simply because the team had engaged in underage drinking and had hired strippers.

On the television news that night, Lange declined to speculate whether a crime had occurred. "Do I know that those crimes happened in a way that would allow me to take a position on that? No," he said. "That's why we have the police. That's why the police have the means to undertake steps to investigate the crime that Duke could never have." But in the same report, Durham police spokesman Addison was convinced there had been a crime and he wanted someone at the party to come forward and share what happened. "That brutal assault, that brutal rape that occurred within that house, cannot be explained by anyone," he said.

On the evening of what became known as the "Potbanger Protest" in front of 610 North Buchanan, Father Joseph Vetter, Duke's Catholic chaplain, delivered a homily about the alleged lacrosse team incident in Duke's magnificent Gothic cathedral. Vetter did not seem to have much doubt about what had happened on the evening of March 13. "All of us are very much aware of what is going on at Duke this week," he said. "How Duke is in the news in an unfavorable way." He said he had noticed the protest on Buchanan Boulevard as he was going to mass earlier in the day. "We don't yet fully know what happened, and no one is guilty until . . . everybody's innocent until they're proven guilty," he said. "But it seems pretty apparent that something was going on there that was pretty bad the other night and at the least it involved a bunch of guys getting together and getting drunk. That's not too hard to believe because that happens around here a lot . . . and apparently they hired an exotic dancer to come in and strip for them, two exotic dancers to come in and strip for them, and I know that's not very uncommon, either. . . . It just becomes kind of part of the culture . . . and when we get caught up in patterns like that, sometimes it really gets out of control."

That same night, fresh from leading the protest in front of 610 North Buchanan, Sam Hummel, the first environmental sustainability coordinator at Duke, sent a more secular message around, urging the Duke community to continue the protests on Monday "in response to [the] recent rape." Hummel urged people to gather in front of the Allen Building—the administration building—on West Campus to educate "the larger Duke community about the sexual assault that occurred two weeks ago in a house just off East Campus that is rented by Duke students. The event will be audience-input oriented with the intention of compiling concerns the community feels must be addressed." There would be an "open-mic session" followed by "small-group discussions." Hummel intended to distribute "fact sheets" about what happened—even though very few people knew actually what happened—and "large posters" will be used "to collect comments from the community."

Hummel's inspiration to organize the Allen Building protest came because a "number of folks" he met at the Sunday morning rally were "interested in organizing in a continuous way that will build pressure until *real* long-term change is achieved," he posted on a Yahoo! bulletin board, Durham Responds. "We talked about planning an ongoing response to the March 13 sexual assault that addresses root-cause issues such as racism, sexism, misogyny, alcohol culture, paternalism, economic exploitation, athlete impunity, and Duke's [lack of] accountability to the community." He urged those interested to meet at a local coffee shop, but warned any men who wanted to attend to "please be mindful of the energy you bring and space you take up in the conversation. Keep in mind that assertion of male domination and violence, even in a well-intended response, is part and parcel of this whole thing."

Jack Bury, a Duke senior, expressed outrage about the incident and much of his thinking reflected the sentiments about the growing "bad-boy" culture among many Duke athletes that Peter Wood had expressed in his 2004 letter to the Duke administration. "Duke University's observable culture of athletic impunity, whereby student athletes are allowed some vague extrajudicial status if they commit a wrong in the name of a unified, successful and hyper-confident team, is, I think, no more conspicuously displayed than in head lacrosse coach Mike Pressler's recent response to the alleged rape by members of his team," Bury wrote. He wanted Pressler to resign and the team to forfeit the entire 2006 season. "The behavior of the team as a whole, at present, prior to any individual arrests or convictions, is undoubtedly enough to warrant the removal of its privilege of representing Duke before the country," he continued. "At present writing, I'm personally ashamed of being a Duke student. My conscience is clouded even with whatever fourth degree of separation I might have with some of these players." At the Allen Building rally, "our demands must be CLEAR: PRESSLER MUST GO! THE 2006 MEN'S LACROSSE SEASON MUST BE FORFEITED. PERIOD. IN ITS ENTIRETY. PERIOD. THEY WILL NOT REPRESENT DUKE. PERIOD."

By Monday morning, the editorial writers were in full dudgeon. The irony of the situation was that, months before, the week had been declared "Sexual Assault Prevention Week" on campus, and few were missing the opportunity to rub salt in the wound. "The entire Duke community should be ashamed and outraged by the alleged events that occurred at the lacrosse party [on]

March 13," senior Nina Ehrlich wrote to the *Chronicle*. "Student athletes have
the privilege of representing our University on and off the field, and if allegations of a gang rape, robbery, and assault are proven true, the Duke men's
lacrosse team has truly shamed our school. . . . In the meantime, may the
community respond with outrage and demand the highest level of integrity
from the administration, the coaches and the players involved in the alleged
incident."

Under the headline "Holding Our Breath," the editors of the *Chronicle*
urged caution. "Getting the story straight is the most important thing the team
can do right now, because there will not be a second chance to do so," the editors wrote. "But when the events of that night fully come to light, when the
DNA results come in today, and if there are found to be perpetrators among
the forty-seven men on the lacrosse roster, then the University must do all in
its power to distance itself from these abominable alleged acts."

The editors also recognized that whether the charge of rape held up,
the admitted behavior—underage drinking, hiring strippers, hurling racial
epithets—give "the University, the community and the nation reason to
doubt the team's virtue." The paper continued, "Neighbors on Buchanan overheard racial slurs shouted at the victim, hardly lending the scene an innocuous,
college-party-gone-wild air. . . . It's an embarassment to the entire University.
The cost is almost unfathomable—town-gown relations could plummet to
all-time lows, even after years of effort and service-based work to engender
mutual trust and respect. The caricature of a Duke student as a spoiled-brat,
hard-partying Caucasian—hardly an accurate representation of the student
body—is only further corroborated. . . . To our peer schools up North and
across the globe, we are still mired in the Civil Rights Movement. For a university supposedly espousing advanced thinking and open minds, we don't
seem to be walking the walk. From a public relations standpoint, yes, this is
a disaster of monumental proportions. But from a moral and ethical standpoint, the University cannot help break the fall of the perpetrators if their
'alleged actions' become simply 'their actions.'"

But the harshest condemnation, by far, came from Ruth Sheehan, a columnist for the *News & Observer*. Sheehan was merciless in accusing the students
of erecting a "Wall of Silence" and standing behind it. "Members of the Duke
men's lacrosse team: . . . Whatever happened in the bathroom at the stripper party gone terribly terribly bad, you know who was involved," she wrote.
"Every one of you does. And one of you needs to come forward and tell the
police. Do not be afraid of retribution on the team. Do not be persuaded that
somehow this 'happened' to one or more 'good guys.' If what the strippers say
is true—that one of them was raped, sodomized, beaten and strangled—the
guys responsible are not 'good.' This seems an elementary statement, I know.

"But," she continued, "I can see loyal team members sitting around convincing themselves that it would be disloyal to turn on their teammates—why, the guys who were involved were just a little 'over the top.' In real life, they're funny. They call their mothers once a week. They share class notes with friends. They attend church. On this night, they were just a little too drunk, a little too 'worked up.' It was a scene straight out of *I Am Charlotte Simmons*, by Tom Wolfe. Indicative of the times. The alleged racial epithets slung at the strippers, who were black? Those were just . . . jokes. Ditto for the ugly remarks overheard by a neighbor: 'Thank your grandpa for my cotton shirt.' Har, har. After all, these guys are not just Duke students, but student athletes. The collegiate dream. And the women? They were . . . strippers, for Pete's sake. I can see the team going down this path, justifying its silence, and it makes me sick."

By this time, what Duke had shut down was the roster—names, pictures and other information—about the lacrosse players and removed it from the school's GoDuke.com website. Meanwhile, some Duke alumni living in Durham were anxious to make sure that the news of the alleged assault reached Duke alumni around the country who may not have been following closely the situation at their alma mater. Claudia Horwitz, a Duke public policy alumna who was the founder of Stone Circles, a center for spiritual life and strategic action located on seventy bucolic acres in Mebane, North Carolina, with an office in Durham, urged out-of-town alumni to contact the Duke administration as soon as possible. "Just as I was beginning to be a fan of Brodhead's he has been way too silent on this issue, giving only a brief statement of little consequence," she wrote. "Tell him you are paying attention, that you give a shit, that your relationship to Duke is impacted by this incident and how the administration handles it." She urged people to write to Burness, the Duke head of public relations.

She attended the rally of more than two hundred people that morning at the Allen Building. "It was pretty amazing," she reported. "A very good crowd, lots of press showed up again. And students are speaking out. . . . People are disgusted, angry and sad; at the same time they are also incredibly savvy about the intersection of so many issues that are revealing themselves through this tragedy. Peace."

Senior Tiana Mack, who attended the West Campus rally, said that the incident was "a matter of white privilege. When I read what was going on, it made me think about Jim Crow. . . . If these culprits get away with it, it will prove to me that Duke does not honor the black woman's body." Students wore T-shirts emblazoned with phrases such as "Men's Lacrosse? Not fine by me" and "Men's Lax, Come Clean." Fumed Meenaksi Chivukula, a junior from Massachusetts, "I am outraged that there's a silence. . . . I am outraged that legal rights are used to quiet this issue." Another senior, Jay McKenna, said that although he knew some of the members of the lacrosse team, "the fact that this wall of silence has been constructed only adds to the mystery, which adds to the speculation." But

another student, sophomore Darby McEvoy, was concerned that there was a
rush to judgment under way. "Rape is a very heavy, heavy charge to be accused
of," he said. "I'll change my mind the day the DNA tests come back, but right
now it's one person's word versus another."

Community leaders also expressed their growing concerns. "If it were black
students accused of that, everyone would be in jail," Charlie Dixon, a deacon
at the Church of Apostolic Revival in Durham, told the *News & Observer*. "If
it would have been a Duke University student who allegedly got raped by a
sports team from NC Central University, all heck would have broken loose."
Brodhead spoke with Durham mayor Bill Bell on Sunday night. On Monday, Bell shared his thoughts with the paper. "I'm concerned about the code
of silence that continues to prevail," he said, even though the investigation
was ongoing. While he said he was glad that Duke officials had forfeited two
lacrosse games, he urged them to go further. "I think it would send a strong
message to the community if they canceled the whole season," he said.

Toward the end of the protest, students started wondering if anyone from
the Duke administration would emerge from the Allen Building and address
the crowd. Both Wasiolek and Moneta watched part of the demonstration, but
Wasiolek told the *Chronicle* it was not the right venue for her to speak because
any comments she made would be construed as official university thinking.
Julia Lewis, a reporter for WRAL, at one point asked to speak with Brodhead
to get his reaction but was told that he was not in his office and then was told
that he was out of town. "We saw him a few minutes later walking across the
quad," Lewis explained.

While the protest was gathering steam in front of the Allen Building,
Durham police officers Gottlieb and Himan were in a training class at the
police department. While in the class, David Addison "summonsed" Gottlieb
to step outside so that Addison could show Gottlieb a "disturbing message"—
Ryan McFadyen's *American Psycho* e-mail—that "was written in a manner that
indicated the possibility that two or more people may have conspired to kill
someone," according to Gottlieb. In reviewing the e-mail, what stood out for
Gottlieb was "the use of a double period (..) at the end of a sentence." According to Gottlieb, Ryan McFadyen, a member of the Duke lacrosse team, sent the
e-mail just before 2 a.m. in the early morning hours of March 14, some ninety
minutes after the party at 610 North Buchanan had ended. As sordid as what
did or did not happen in the house on the night of March 13 was, it seemed
that the incident was about to get a whole lot more unseemly.

Gottlieb and Himan took McFadyen's e-mail very seriously. Ten minutes
after each officer reviewed the e-mail, they went together to see Nifong at the
Durham courthouse. Nifong recalled the meeting lasted about thirty minutes.
This was to be the briefing that he had requested the previous Friday. He had
read the NTO, but no other evidence that had been gathered in the case by

Gottlieb and Himan. "Most of the information that they shared with me at that time was already in the nontestimonial order," he said. "There was also an additional e-mail that had apparently been sent by one of the lacrosse players to other members of the lacrosse team that had come to the attention of the police department by way of Crimestoppers."

Nifong said he knew by the March 27 meeting that Zash, Flannery, and Evans, in their statements—which he had not yet seen—had denied that any sexual assault had occurred at the house. But, he continued, "it was my impression that the officers did not believe that they had been totally truthful in their responses." Nifong continued, "For one thing, the impression that I got from the officers was that they definitely believed that a sexual assault had taken place. . . . The one thing that struck us—and I don't know necessarily that it was on this date—but certainly one thing that struck us all early on is there had been kind of a history of parties in that neighborhood where there was drinking and loud noise, and things like that. . . . One thing that struck me very early on about this, and I believe also struck the officers, was that the response time from when the 911 call came in until the time the officer got there was less than five minutes. And when the officer arrived, there was nobody in the house. There were no lights on. There was no sign of any activity. There were no people on the street. And I think it certainly struck me, and I believe it struck everybody, as very unusual that everybody would have cleared away from that scene so quickly in this case."

It turned out there were different recollections of what happened at the March 27 meeting. There was Nifong's. There was Gottlieb's. There was Himan's. And there was a version later put together by defense attorneys. At issue, of course, was how Nifong thought about the events of March 13 and what he intended to do about them. Himan recalled, "We went over what took place and what our interviews with Crystal were. He had mentioned there were some discrepencies in the beginning" of how many men she had alleged raped her—"and there was some explanation of possibly why there were discrepencies. That is when we also, I believe, discussed her being possibly drugged. And the photo arrays, I think." Himan said the three men also spoke about Mangum's credibility and whether the police investigators thought she was telling the truth, since there were so many holes in her story. Himan shared his opinion with Nifong. "Talking with Crystal, I mean, she looked like she was in pain," he said. "When we went and interviewed her, she was wincing. She could barely sit down. She could barely walk. And from the story that she was telling us, it looked like she was telling the truth." Also during that meeting, according to defense attorneys, "Nifong acknowledged to Gottlieb and Himan that the Duke lacrosse case would be a very hard case to win in court and said 'You know, we're fucked.'" Himan later explained what he thought Nifong meant by this statement. "There really wasn't an investigation in the beginning;

there was nothing done in the beginning, basically," he said. "I think he was trying to tell us that it was going to be a hard case to prove." Himan elaborated: "There was no search warrant at the house. No one had talked to the players that night. His words were, 'You know, we're fucked.' And that's when he started asking Sergeant Gottlieb how many rape investigations he had done."

Nifong concurred that the "we're fucked" comment referred to the fact that the police had waited three days before getting a search warrant to investigate the house and the crime scene. "The three days passing," Nifong said. "That's where we were fucked. I didn't mean by that that the whole case was fucked. . . . If somehow people had put this together that night, and had gone over there with a search warrant when there was nobody at home, nothing had been cleaned up, then you'd know exactly what you were dealing with, and that could actually have been to the benefit of the people who lived in the house. I mean, there's no way of knowing. It could've been to their detriment or their benefit, but we clearly would've had a more complete picture of what was going on had that happened. By the passage of the three days—and, of course, the fact that they cleaned stuff up and all that—if you'd gone over there, for instance, that night and you'd documented that you found the cell phone and the shoe and the money in the living room and not outside under the window, then that story would've never been told. They would've had to come up with something different."

At that meeting, according to court documents filed by attorneys for the athletes, "Gottlieb and Himan discussed with Nifong a number of weaknesses in the case, including that Ms. Mangum had made inconsistent statements to the police and had changed her story several times; that the other dancer who was present at the party during the alleged attack disputed Ms. Mangum's story of an alleged assault; that Ms. Mangum had already viewed two photo arrays and had not identified any alleged attackers; and that the three team captains had voluntarily cooperated with police and had denied that the alleged attack occurred."

Nifong said he did not recall any discussion of the inconsistencies in Mangum's versions of events in the immediate aftermath of the alleged incident. Nor did he recall any discussion of Roberts's version of events or that she thought, initially, that Mangum's story of being raped was "a crock." He said he did not get Roberts's statement that day. He said he did not know then that Roberts and Mangum had each said the other had talked about going back into the house to try to "make more money." He did concede that, sometime after April 3, he became aware that "there were discrepencies between what Ms. [Roberts] and Ms. Mangum had said," and there were "discrepencies between things in officers' reports reporting what Ms. Mangum had said upon direct questioning or what they overheard was said." He did not recall speaking about photo arrays. "My initial attempt was not to prepare the case for prosecution," he said, "but to learn as much as I could about the case because I knew that I was going to be asked questions just because of the fact that anything that occurs in Durham that involves a Duke team and criminal charges is going to get some attention."

As of March 27, and his briefing with Gottlieb and Himan, Nifong said, even though there were not yet any suspects in the case, he believed "that a sexual assault had taken place in the bathroom, based on what had been told to me by the officers, and based on what had been reported by the SANE nurse, and there didn't seem to be any point raised by any of the officers"— Shelton aside—"that something didn't add up about this. Sometimes you have a situation where an officer will express reservations about what a witness has said, and that's an indication that you need to look a little further. I never got any of that in this particular case." Nifong added that at that point he just knew that the attacker, or attackers, was "a Caucasian," but "I don't know that it would be fair to say that we had reached any conclusions about whether or not it was a lacrosse player. We did not believe that the young men who lived in the house had been completely straightforward about what they told police in the first part."

The three men, Himan recounted, turned their attention to the McFadyen e-mail that had come through a Crimestoppers website that allows citizens to anonymously share potentially relevant evidence in a case. (The McFadyen e-mail had originally been forwarded by an unknown sender with the e-mail address Dukeblues44@gmail.com to Durham police captain Fritz LaVarge, who forwarded it to Crimestoppers. No one has ever been able to figure out who or what Dukeblues44 was, although online the consensus seems to be that it was an e-mail address created by Sam Hummel, the Duke environmental coordinator and an IT specialist.) Based on reading the e-mail, and their fear—whether well-placed or not—that it suggested an intent to carry out a serious crime, Nifong authorized Gottlieb and Himan to do the work required to obtain a warrant to search McFadyen's dorm room at Duke. This was an unprecedented step of bringing the case onto Duke's West Campus itself and beyond the confines of a Durham neighborhood off East Campus. Even though Mangum had previously ruled out McFadyen as one of her attackers, with Nifong's blessing the police officers returned to the station to draft the warrant.

That same day, Julia Lewis, the WRAL-TV reporter, went to the lacrosse stadium to get video of the team practicing despite the forfeiture of the two games against Georgetown and Saint Mary's. The upcoming Saturday away game against Ohio State University was still on the docket. She knew by then that Nifong expected the DNA results to be returned in a week or so. There was little doubt Nifong and the community wanted the matter resolved as quickly as possible. She then went over to the Durham courthouse to see if she could speak to Nifong. It was around 12:45. He had heard from his receptionist that, as he had anticipated, members of the news media wanted to talk to him about the NTO.

Nifong, as it turned out, was about to go on a media spree. Lewis spoke with Nifong in his office and discovered the Duke lacrosse case would be the first case he personally would prosecute since he had been diagnosed with prostate cancer in 1999; it was a chance for him to show the community he had recovered his mojo. Nifong told Lewis that the matter was "a statement case." He explained, "This is a rape that also has overtones of racial animus and that is something that this community can just not tolerate." Lewis subsequently reported that "police sources" and Nifong had confirmed to her that Mangum's rape kit had revealed her "body was traumatized." It was a leak that gave further credence to the tidal wave of public opinion that a rape had occurred at 610 North Buchanan. Nifong lamented that nobody at the party had stopped the rape. "There is a good chance," he said, "if someone had spoken up and said 'You can't do this, what are you thinking about?' these events might never have happened."

Meanwhile, Nifong told the *Chronicle* that while it was "not especially common to take such a large sample" of DNA pursuant to the NTO, it was also "not common to have a well-defined group of people in the suspect pool. Here, we were able to identify assailants as Caucasian members of the lacrosse team." The student paper also confirmed that Bob Ekstrand was representing "virtually all" of the lacrosse players, but beyond that he would not say much. That left it to Tom Loflin, another Durham attorney, to question the validity of any of the DNA evidence obtained through the NTO. "You've got a fishing expedition where forty-six people—without individualized suspicion focusing on any one of them—are being subjected to a very extreme violation of privacy," he said. "Not everyone in that pool was at the party. Should they hit a home run with any of these samples, then that person is going to have a very, very strong motion to suppress the evidence. Any lawyer worth his salt is going to tell them not to talk to the police or the press or anybody until this case shakes out."

Indeed, by then, Nifong had made a host of public statements about the case, most of which made clear he believed a rape had occurred and three unknown Duke lacrosse players were to blame. He told the Associated Press on March 27, "The circumstances of the rape indicated a deep racial motivation for some of the things that were done. [That] makes a crime that is by its nature one of the most offensive and invasive even more so." He told ABC, "The contempt that was shown for the victim, based on her race, was totally abhorrent. It adds another layer of reprehensibleness [*sic*] to a crime that is already reprehensible." To a reporter at the *Durham Herald-Sun*, he said, "Every rape is a serious case. But some speak to the community in a different manner. This is one of them." On MSNBC, echoing what he had told Lewis in his office, he said, "Well, this is the type of case that, because of the—on top of the rape—which is already an abhorrent crime enough, you have the additional racial animus and the hostility that seems totally out of place for this community in this day and age. And I felt this was a case that we needed to make a statement [about], as a community, that we would not tolerate this kind of behavior here in Durham. And I felt that the best way to make the statement was to take this case myself."

Bob Ekstrand, the Durham attorney then representing a group of the players, was increasingly concerned about Nifong's public statements and how they might be influencing opinion about what had happened. He set up an appointment for March 28 at 12:30 p.m. to see the district attorney. The meeting started cordially enough. Ekstrand asked Nifong how he intended to make decisions in the case and urged him to wait for the results of the DNA tests before seeking any indictments. Nifong became offended by Ekstrand's suggestions and abruptly ended the meeting. Ekstrand later recalled Nifong's words as he left: "If you've come here to ask me questions instead of telling me what you know about who did it, then we don't have anything to talk about. You're wasting my time. You tell all your clients I will remember their lack of cooperation at sentencing. I hope you know if they didn't do it, they are all aiders and abettors, and that carries the same punishment as rape." Needless to say, Ekstrand was taken aback by Nifong's comments.

Meanwhile, the effort to secure a search warrant based on McFadyen's e-mail continued. Critics of Nifong and Gottlieb—of which there are many—pointed out that the e-mail, while in poor taste, was nothing more than a satirical reference to *American Psycho*. The subsequent replies McFadyen received back from his friends after sending out the e-mail reflected that they understood the cultural reference to the book and the movie, but apparently the subtle reference to an American literary enfant terrible was lost on Nifong and Gottlieb, and they set about doing what they could to get the McFadyen e-mail into a public document in the middle of a media frenzy. "They knew that Ryan's e-mail, stripped of its context and held out to be evidence of a 'conspiracy to commit murder,' would explode into nuclear dimensions," explained McFadyen's attorney, Bob Ekstrand, and was a deliberate attempt by the prosecutor and his investigators to "evinc[e] a malicious, evil motive animating the intentional violation of Ryan's Fourth and Fourteenth Amendment rights to be free from government searches without probable cause." There was no "probable cause" to search McFadyen's room, Ekstrand argued, because McFadyen had already been excluded as a possible suspect by the descriptions Mangum had previously given of her alleged attackers. Still, the officers pressed on.

Since Himan and Gottlieb would again be in front of Judge Ronald Stephens, who four days earlier had approved the NTO that required the forty-six lacrosse players—including McFadyen—to show up at the forensics lab and provide DNA evidence, the two officers simply tweaked the original narrative used in the NTO document. To the original five crimes that the officers believed had been committed, they added a new, sixth crime—conspiracy to commit murder—in order to justify the request for a search warrant for McFadyen's dorm room. In addition to including the e-mail in the search warrant application, Himan and Gottlieb added the additional random supposed fact that at the party at 610 North Buchanan "players also used numbers when calling for one another across the room [—] again to hide their identities." The officers helpfully pointed out that "41"—McFadyen's sign-off in the e-mail— "is the jersey number for Ryan McFadyen, a member of the Duke lacrosse team."

According to the search warrant application, the officers hoped to find in McFadyen's dorm room "any clothing related to the suspect and the victim from the night of the attack"; any documents identifying the suspects; documents showing that McFadyen lived in the dorm room; Mangum's white shoe—which had been left behind at 610 North Buchanan, actually; photographs or video or digital recordings of the party; $340, in $20 bills; e-mails "that have sentences punctuated with two periods"; a Duke lacrosse jersey with the number 41 on it; and any and all computer files, discs, and equipment that might provide evidence of the crimes. Nifong and his officers also wanted copies of all of McFadyen's e-mails on the Duke server, and asked the judge to order the keeper of those digital files at Duke to turn them over as evidence. They also wanted to search McFadyen's white 1998 GMC Yukon, which was in a parking lot near the Edens dormitory.

Judge Stephens granted Nifong and the officers the search warrant they were seeking but—importantly—ordered it sealed indefinitely, meaning that it could not be made public at that moment. At 5:35 p.m., Gottlieb let the Durham police communications office know that they were going to search a dormitory room at Duke pursuant to the search warrant. An officer from the Duke police force accompanied the Durham police officers to McFadyen's room. The search began at 6:01 p.m.

Gottlieb and Himan led the search, along with four other officers; at least one, Sergeant Smith, was a member of the Duke police force. After knocking on the door and announcing he was a police officer, Himan served the search warrant on John Brad Ross, McFadyen's roommate and a fellow lacrosse player. Gottlieb observed that Ross was "polite and cooperative" and listened attentively as Himan told him he was not under arrest and was free to leave the dorm room. Ross went into the hallway. After Himan asked Ross if he knew "anything about what happened," he told the officers he was not at the March 13 party and "had a document" showing that he was in Raleigh with his girlfriend—a student at NC State—that night and "could provide names of people" who saw him in Raleigh "if it was necessary." Asked further about McFadyen's e-mail, Ross said it was "a team e-mail" but did not know anything about it.

Gottlieb started looking through the garbage can in the room and asked Ross if it was okay by him if the contents could be put outside in the trash can in the hall when he was done looking at it. While in their reports Gottlieb and Himan described a calm scene, there was at least one other perspective. According to a court document filed by Ekstrand, on McFadyen's behalf, "Gottlieb, in particular, was in a rage" and the "officers destroyed furniture, and needlessly threw clothes, papers, cords, and books everywhere." Ekstrand wrote that Gottlieb's behavior was consistent with his ongoing, hostile demeanor toward Duke students during the past years.

Soon, Ross told Gottlieb he felt he should contact his attorney and placed a call to Ekstrand. Ekstrand arrived a few minutes later and asked to see the search warrant that had been given to Ross. Ekstrand questioned the validity of Judge Stephens's signature, even after being shown the original document. The search proceeded, but Gottlieb left before it was concluded. Before he left Edens 2C, he noted that inside the room were a "number of hand-drawn penises on the wall with team members' nicknames, jersey numbers and questionable racial/ethnic things written on same." He noted there was also a "hangman's noose" on a light fixture and some hard copies of e-mails "with the same markings" as the March 14 e-mail that McFadyen had sent around after the party.

At 7:15, McFadyen returned to his room to find the search still under way. In many ways, McFadyen seemed like a typical Duke student-athlete: tall, strapping, handsome, with an unmistakable presence when he entered a room. Bright but not overly bookish or intellectual, he had grown up in central New Jersey and attended the Delbarton School, a Catholic school for boys. He played lacrosse at Delbarton, where he was good but not a standout, making the second, all-county team. His father was a home builder, and McFadyen worked for him during the summers when he was growing up. "My dad is blue-collar, old-school," he said. "I don't think he has ever said 'I love you' to me four or five times, but he's not a guy who will say it casually. But still, he shows his affection in other ways and I know that."

McFadyen was the oldest of four children, with three younger sisters. His mother was very strong-willed. "You know," he explained, "'No means no' and 'Respect women' and certain things like that that were just—not in those words, but things that just kind of brought me up to, I think, be a more respectful person than maybe other people. So I knew that was an advantage, seeing how some of my peers acted in high school, and I was thankful for it." His parents had been married for thirty years. "I'm very fortunate in the fact that I had that dynamic growing up," he said. "I always told my dad, if I had a brother, I'd probably be in the NFL, but I had three sisters, which has also been a good thing, because I understand women and I'm in touch with my emotions more than most guys."

McFadyen was, indeed, very emotional when he arrived back at Edens from the Duke library. "I look at my room and it's like, 'What the—' It looks like a fire," he said, recalling the flashing police lights. "It was, like, wavy. It looked like there was a flame. What the hell is going on in my room?" He walked upstairs and saw four police officers in the hallway outside his room and another three cops in his room. "They're just tearing through everything," he said. "Tearing it apart. It was an intimidation. . . . I walk in. They don't have a copy of the search warrant for me. I'm like, 'What? Are you kidding me?' I walk in there, 'Sir, you need to get out. You need to get out of this room.' There's one cop up in my—I was lofted up—digging through my sheets. They're throwing shit on the ground. They're going through all this stuff and antagonizing me." They told him they had a search warrant. "Let me see the damn warrant," he told them. "Let me see it."

He continued, "I'm fucking freaking out, 'cause this is to the point to where now they're coming in and invading my personal property. They don't have a warrant. Eventually they were able to produce one. Someone comes and gives me one. Flipping through pages, I see my name: 'What the fuck is this? Are you kidding me?' Then I see the charge—conspiracy to commit murder. My fucking heart drops. I'm like, 'Are you fucking kidding me? You really think—?' [The police told me], 'Sir, we have to take every threat credible. We have to take it seriously.' Rightfully so. I guess that's the way to handle things. But I was just like, 'This is a fucking joke. It's a reference to a fucking movie. Are you kidding me?' It's just my single e-mail, singled out, nothing following it, nothing preceding it, and that's it." Ekstrand's paralegal, Stefanie Sparks, a former lacrosse player at Duke, was there. She told McFadyen to just cooperate with the police. "I was like 'I'm just gonna sit here and be quiet,'" he said. "'Keep going through my shit. I've got nothing to hide.'"

The police then asked McFadyen to take them to his car. "Get in our Durham cop car and take us to your vehicle," they told him. "I'm like, 'I'll walk you there.' . . . In the meantime, they had one of the cops talking, 'If you don't get us to the vehicle, we will find it. We will seize it. I will forcibly gain entry to it,' threatening me. I'm like, 'Dude, relax. I'll take you to my car. I have nothing to hide. You guys are just blatantly trying to scare me.' Then they're tearing through my car and I'm off to the side. Stef has to take a phone call. A cop walks up to me [and encourages McFadyen to cooperate with the investigation into what happened at 610 North Buchanan] and I'm like, 'Are you fucking kidding me, bro?' I'm like, 'Nothing fucking happened. Fuck you. This is unbelievable.' I was so rattled."

Having calmed down a bit, later that night McFadyen was doing his laundry. "I remember calling my parents," he said. "I think it was the first time I even brought up that there was an investigation, that we'd given DNA or anything like that: 'Yeah, I just got home. My room was being searched. I'm being investigated for conspiracy to commit murder.' I remember just saying that, like, 'Holy shit.' How do you tell your parents that? They don't know. I remember saying that word and my heart dropping, just being like, 'Listen, listen. It's all bullshit. They're just trying to scare me into saying something happened that didn't.' I could just tell. They wanted me to be like, 'There was a rape.' There wasn't. I had nothing to hide." He told his parents everything. "I tell them about the DNA," he said. "I tell them about the party. But remember, all the other stuff, all the background that gets filled in since then, I didn't know. So it's just like, 'Someone accused us of rape. The police say she's not credible. But now they're searching my room.'"

He told them about the e-mail he had written. "I mean, I was nineteen years old," he said. "I was a boy on a sports team. . . . It wasn't like I was gonna skin a couple of strippers with some of my teammates. It was a joke. They said, 'In hindsight, maybe you shouldn't have sent it.' Okay, great, yeah. But how am I supposed to know that? How was I supposed to know those accusations would come from that night? I didn't. That was really hard because my mom knows me and she didn't raise a group of boys. She raised me. My parents did a great job raising me, and I'm not someone who would ever say something like that to a woman to degrade them in any way. It was just—she understood. . . . I don't even remember what they said. I just remember saying, 'Listen, it's not a big deal. . . . They were just trying to scare me. It's fine.' I went about my day. . . . I went about school like nothing had happened. I put my room back together and I went to sleep that night."

Himan told the story of executing the search warrant on McFadyen's room and car a bit differently. He said McFadyen was read the contents of the search warrant in front of Ekstrand's paralegal. McFadyen told Himan he did not want him "looking in his vehicle" and said he did not know where he had last parked it. Himan called Gottlieb, who had left by then, and told him McFadyen had arrived back in the room but would not tell him where his car was parked. Himan asked Gottlieb to speak with McFadyen. Gottlieb told McFadyen they would find his SUV with or without his help, and if that meant they had to break into the car to search it—per the search warrant—that is exactly what they intended to do. "It is not our intention to destroy belongings," Gottlieb told McFadyen. "However, we intend to carry out the order and will take the necessary steps to do so." Gottlieb said it was up to McFadyen whether he wanted the investigators to enter his car in a "nonforceful manner or not."

That was good enough for McFadyen, according to Himan, who then gave Himan the keys to his car and told him where to find it in the parking lot. Inside the car, Himan found a $20 bill, a disposable camera, and a piece of paper with the words "suckie, suckie $5" written on it. In addition, the police officers also confiscated from McFadyen's dorm room: a copy of the e-mail; a poster with the words "the shaker" on it; $40 in the form of two $20 bills; a Kingston computer memory card; a Toshiba laptop; a Dell laptop; an external hard drive; some storage DVDs; some papers with penis drawings; and a Duke backpack with McFadyen's number, 41, on it.

At this point, very few people knew that the police had McFadyen's e-mail or that his room had been searched as a result of it. He went about his life at Duke as normally as he could. But that meant enduring nearly instantaneous judgments about what had happened on the night of March 13. A week or so after the alleged incident at 610 North Buchanan, he was in his history of labor relations class along with other lacrosse players. At the start of the class, the professor, Reeve Huston, decided to address the allegations. "He got up one day," McFadyen said. "He was my adviser, so I knew him on a personal level. He got up and said, 'I just want to take the first couple minutes of class to discuss a few items that are hot in the news. I want to talk about the alleged Duke rape case.' There were about eight lacrosse players in a class of about fifteen people. . . . We're like, 'Okay.' So he was like, 'Three things are identified to be fact. One, there was definitely intercourse that night. Two, a condom was most likely used as cited by . . .' and went on." Casey Carroll, a lacrosse player in the class who was not at the March 13 party, decided he had heard enough. "I remember Casey just getting up in the middle of class and just walking out," McFadyen said. "He said, 'I'm not gonna sit here and have you berate me with what you've established to be facts.' We all just kind of got up and followed suit."

Another time, he remembered seeing a friend, Jacinta Green, at Alpine Bagels in the Duke cafeteria. "She slapped me in front of a lot of people and screamed at me over the alleged rape," he said. "We were great friends." Despite the controversy about the incident, McFadyen used to proudly walk around campus wearing a "Duke Lacrosse" T-shirt. He recalled, "I was like, 'Nothing to hide here. I'm proud of who we are. We didn't do anything wrong.' I was trying to take a stab at that." Green came up to McFadyen at the bagel store and started yelling at him in front of everyone. "How could you let your teammates do this?" she screamed. "How could you let them do this?" She then slapped him. "I'm just like, 'Jacinta, you're wrong and you'll see,' and just walked away," McFadyen recalled.

While the officers were conducting the search of McFadyen's room, Angela Ashby, the Durham police forensic manager, collected the DNA evidence previously obtained from Mangum—including the sexual assault evidence kit; her clothes, including her panties; a blood stain; and smears from her mouth, rectum and vagina—plus the buccal swabs taken previously from forty-six of the forty-seven team members and brought it to the North Carolina State Bureau of Investigation laboratory in Raleigh. Roy Cooper, the state attorney general, asked the forensics lab to expedite the examination. So ordered, Rachael Winn, a forensics biologist, starting closely examining the Mangum rape kit for evidence of semen, blood, and saliva to figure out what needed to be sent to a DNA lab for further testing. According to a court filing, that same day Winn concluded that DNA testing would be "futile," since "there was no semen. There was no saliva. There was no blood. There was nothing to test." That same day—March 27—Winn reported her preliminary findings in a conversation with Nifong.

The next day, Winn spoke with Himan and told him that the lab had examined the rape kit as well as Mangum's clothing and found no evidence of blood, semen or saliva and would soon be wrapping up its investigation unless the Durham police had more evidence to share. Himan informed Nifong that the SBI lab test results were going to come back negative for any DNA match between Mangum's rape kit, her clothing, and any of the DNA taken from the Duke lacrosse players.

Theoretically, the lack of matching DNA evidence that Winn reported to Nifong and Himan might have ended the matter then and there. While that outcome would have been plenty embarrassing to Nifong in light of his decision to prosecute the case himself, his reelection campaign and his many public statements about how damaging the alleged rape of Mangum had been to her—of course—and to the precarious relationship between Duke and Durham, it was an early enough moment in the saga when the damage could have been contained.

Instead, Nifong doubled down. He asked Himan to inform Angela Ashby to tell Winn not to end the SBI investigation; the Durham police would find more evidence and send it over to Winn as soon as possible. On March 29, Ashby sent more evidence to Winn for DNA testing: a "large blue rug" from "bathroom A" at 610 North Buchanan; a green rug from "bathroom B"; a white bath towel from the hallway near "bathroom A"; and a Band-Aid and plastic bag from the rear steps of the house. Ashby also sent over swabs from the various bathrooms, a rag in the wastebasket from the one of the bathrooms, cuttings from the various towels found in the bathrooms as well as "five false fingernails"—presumably Mangum's—from the trash can in "bathroom B." On March 30, the Durham police sent still more evidence Winn's way, including Mangum's cosmetic bag, two more fake fingernails, liquid foundation, a cell phone, and a driver's license. Also sent to Winn were the "evidence collection" kits from Zash, Flannery, and Evans. An ultraviolet light examination of some of the towels from the house's bathrooms showed evidence of semen, but unless Mangum's DNA was also on the towels, not much of a conclusion could be drawn that something like a rape had occurred in the bathroom. "It was the forensic equivalent of a 'Hail Mary,'" according to Ekstrand. On the evening of March 28, at 10:40 p.m., Himan visited Mangum and told her that the DNA tests had come back negative. He discussed with her, according to Ekstrand, "the obvious consequences that fact had upon the viability of the case."

Although Himan's notes about the case are often incredibly detailed, he made no mention of his discussions on March 28 with Winn (about the lab results), with Nifong (about what to do about the lab results) or with Mangum (about what the lack of conclusive DNA evidence meant for the validity of her allegations against the Duke lacrosse players). Instead, on March 28, Himan wrote about his conversation with William Blake Boehmler, one of two Duke students (the other being Brent Saeli) who had been at the March 13 party but were not on the lacrosse team. Boehmler told Himan that when the two women started to dance, "none of them looked impaired." There was then "an argument," he told Himan, and "someone mentioned something about a pimp." He got scared—he was on probation and shouldn't have been at the party—and left soon thereafter. (That same day Nifong told the *Durham Herald-Sun* that everyone at the alleged rape scene was a member of the lacrosse team. "We don't know who the assailants are, but we know they came from this group.")

Gottlieb made no mention of any of the discussions with Winn and Nifong in his case notes, either. He did mention that he went with Himan to Boehmler's house at 1107 Urban Avenue and that Boehmler voluntarily agreed to come to the police station and answer questions. And Nifong made no public disclosure about what he heard from Winn and Himan about the DNA evidence.

In fact, despite knowing the nature of Winn's findings and the North Carolina Rules of Professional Conduct that required prosecutors to "refrain from making extrajudicial comments that have a substantial likelihood of heightening public condemnation of the accused," Nifong kept up his relentless public assault on the lacrosse players. "The information that I have does lead me to conclude that a rape did occur," Nifong told a local television reporter on March 27. "I'm making a statement to the Durham community and, as a citizen of Durham, I am making a statement for the Durham community. This is not the kind of activity we condone and it must be dealt with quickly and harshly."

He told other reporters the DNA evidence would "reveal who the attackers" were and that they would be charged as soon as the lab report came back. He told a local radio talk show host that the DNA evidence would be "bulletproof." He told MSNBC that the DNA evidence "will enable us to definitely establish who the perpetrators of this offense were." He said he would consider also charging those players at the party who stood around and did not stop the attack. "There's a good chance, if someone had spoken up and said, 'You can't do this,' it might not have happened." To another local television reporter, he said, "My guess is that some of this stone wall of silence that we have seen may tend to crumble once charges start to come out" in the wake of the results of the DNA testing.

Nifong had a strategy in mind for making his bold public statements. "One of the reasons that we did what we did the first week in terms of trying to publicize what occurred is the officers believed there were members of the team who really wanted to talk to them, but didn't feel like they could violate the team's wall of silence," Nifong said in subsequent interviews. "We were hoping that if we could get some separation and stuff—I actually thought, and this was probably very naïve of me—that parents might tell their kids that if they know something about this, they ought to do that because that's what my father would have done and that's what I would have done if my son were involved." In his effort to penetrate the supposed "wall of silence," Nifong had, early on, contacted a local Durham bar where Duke lacrosse players often hung out. The bar owner was a retired Duke public safety officer. "I knew that he had a lot of strong ties to the lacrosse community and to the Duke athletic community through that," he said. During the first week of the case, Nifong remembered calling him. "Joe, I'm dealing with all this kind of stuff and nobody's talking," Nifong told him. "Do you still have any sources of information that might know what's going on?"

"I'm not as involved as I used to be," Joe responded, "but I still know some people who are. Let me see what I can find out and get back with you."

A week later, he called Nifong back. "I never seen anything like this before," Joe said. "Everything is shut down. Nobody's talking at all. I've never seen a situation involving anything over here where nobody's talking. But that's it. Nobody's saying anything. I don't know why. I don't know what's behind it, but nobody's talking about this at all."

This notion that the players on the lacrosse team were suddenly clamming up and keeping to themselves the real story of what had happened was quickly gaining traction among not only prosecutors, like Nifong, but also among Duke administrators and the media. "I think the students would be well advised to come forward; they have chosen not to," Duke provost Peter Lange told the ABC affiliate in Raleigh the same day that Nifong made his comment about the "stone wall of silence." Unfortunately, it was not exactly true that the players were stonewalling about what had happened. Zash, Flannery, and Evans had given detailed statements about the party and what transpired there and had given freely of their DNA to police investigators. They also offered to take lie detector tests, an offer that was not accepted. The cocaptains of the team had met with Duke administrators and stated repeatedly that no rape had occurred. The forty-six white members of the lacrosse team had also given DNA samples to investigators.

And it was hardly unusual for a defense attorney to tell a client to keep quiet. "Attorneys advise [clients] not to talk to police even if they're totally innocent, because of the possibility that things you might say even if you're totally innocent in the case might be viewed differently by the person hearing them than you meant them," UNC law professor Kenneth Broun, who wasn't involved in the case, told the *Herald-Sun*. "That's pretty standard operating procedure."

Joe Cheshire, a Raleigh attorney representing David Evans, reached out to Nifong on the afternoon of March 29 to try to arrange a meeting. But Nifong refused to meet with Cheshire, prompting the defense attorney to write a pointed letter to the prosecutor. "You and I have known each other a long time," Cheshire wrote Nifong on March 30, "and I do not mind telling you I was amazed at that response. In thirty-three years, I have never seen such a request denied by a prosecutor, nor in such a manner." According to Cheshire's letter, Nifong suggested that Cheshire call the Durham police and have David Evans "charged with a crime" before Nifong "would have a conversation with me on a topic you have demonstrated no reluctance to discuss with myriad local and national news reporters over the last several days." Bill Cotter, another defense attorney, later explained, "I don't think anyone in the police department would expect that we would go around the district attorney to speak to the police department." He added that defense attorneys started to believe the investigation in the case was designed to prove Mangum's allegations rather than to figure out what actually happened. "While this was progressing, we were getting the idea that people were cheating," he said.

For his part, Nifong said that was an inaccurate portrayal of his position, which was that "if their clients wished to talk about a crime, the people to talk to about the crime would be the police department, because I wasn't the investigator, and they were investigating the case." He said, furthermore, that his experience with Cheshire "has been that the amount of cordiality that he shows is directly proportional to whether you give him what he asks for, but there are a lot of lawyers like that." He also said, "I do not recall any situation in my twenty-nine years in the DA's office where somebody who had not been charged with any offense, I ever sat down with an attorney who represented that person to discuss with him whether or not that person was going to be indicted." He said he was also careful never to put himself in a position where he had had a conversation that would end up making him a witness. "Obviously what happens when you sit down is they tell you that they didn't do it, and [they are] seeking to make you, or whoever you have taking the statement, a witness to the fact that they didn't do it, and that's not going to be very helpful."

In the letter, Cheshire then quoted verbatim from Nifong's public comments in previous days to the *New York Times*, the *News & Observer*, and WRAL. He was upset that, "in essence, before the first charge in this matter has been brought against the first person, your reported public comments have announced the criminal guilt of potentially dozens of people for committing a racially motivated gang rape, effectively saying they are *equally* guilty as principals or aiders-and-abettors. The comments have inaccurately suggested that no one has cooperated with law enforcement, when you know that at least three of them, including my client, submitted to the search of the alleged crime scene and, *without asking for lawyers*, gave lengthy oral and written statements to law enforcement." Cheshire believed that Nifong's comments had "greatly prejudiced" any future court proceeding, jeopardizing its fairness, and he could not understand why he was so willing to talk to the media about the case but not "to someone who has a judicial interest in the matter"—i.e., him. "Because this behavior is not typical of the Mike Nifong I thought I knew," he concluded, "I have left open the possibility that you have been misquoted by the media and that we somehow misperceived your response to our meeting request. . . . Sadly and unfortunately, that has created an atmosphere of trying these matters in the media, rather than a court of law, and that could have been—and should have been—avoided."

Nifong never met with Cheshire. The one decision that the team seemed to make together—based on the advice of their lawyers—was to cancel both the March 22 and the rescheduled March 29 meetings between the players and police investigators, where individual players were to give statements about what had happened on the evening of March 13. Somehow the media repeatedly translated this decision—which should have fallen into the category of exercising their legal rights—as "police said team members have refused to cooperate with their investigation."

Indeed, in short order, the local media were hanging on every word being uttered about the case by Nifong, by Duke administrators, and—soon—by Duke faculty members. On March 28, the *Durham Herald-Sun* editorialized, with several inaccuracies: "When police officers arrived at the house with a search warrant on March 16, none of the players would cooperate with the investigation. Later, under threat of further penalty, forty-six members of the team were DNA-tested by police. . . . There's no question the student-athletes were probably guilty of all the usual offenses—underage drinking, loud partying, obnoxious behavior. . . . We agree that the alleged crime isn't the only outrage. It's also outrageous that not a single person who was in the house felt compelled to step forward and tell the truth about what happened."

In a 1,500-word front-page article, the paper reported that the players' DNA samples had been sent to the SBI lab in Raleigh and would be available as early as the following week—"lightening speed" for a "chronically backlogged" agency. Nifong reiterated that he would personally prosecute the case. He said the "racial aspect" of the alleged crime was "particularly abhorrent," especially the reports of racial epithets being hurled as the two dancers were leaving the party and the allegations by Mangum that her attackers were white and had sodomized, beaten, kicked, and strangled her.

Nifong also defended his decision to send DNA samples from only the forty-six white players on the Duke lacrosse team and to limit his investigation to these men. But, in the same article, Tom Loflin, a Durham attorney not affil-iated with the case, said Nifong's "broad DNA sampling" was a "dragnet fish-ing expedition" that is "mammothly unconstitutional." He questioned Nifong's tactics. "It's sad because they're invading the privacy of a whole lot of innocent people," he said. "Even if everybody at the party was a lacrosse player"—which Nifong knew not to be the case—"it doesn't give you suspicion against all of them." He predicted that in the end a judge would not allow the DNA evidence into any trial. "If they match any DNA," he said, "the defendant is going to have a wonderful motion to suppress evidence. I don't think they'll be able to use any DNA evidence even if they hit a home run with it."

Another Durham attorney, Bill Thomas, who had been hired by lacrosse cocaptain Brett Thompson and his family, said Thompson and other players had been "forthcoming and have given detailed statements to the Duke admin-istration" but that he would be remiss if he didn't strongly advise Thompson not to speak with police. He sensed that the DNA evidence was not all that Nifong had made it out to be. "I think the results of the DNA tests will be quite enlightening," he said. "There simply is no corroborated evidence at this point that anything happened to give rise to any liability—civil or criminal—with the possible exception of alcohol violations. Right now, you have a lot of innocent people under a cloud of suspicion. But once all the evidence is in, we believe it will be clear to the public that there was no merit to these allegations."

But Thomas's coolheaded—albeit biased—thinking was not having much of an impact on the wider Duke community. As the Allen Building protest continued on Monday, there was both shock about the rape allegations and caution about what the correct response should be. "This crime affects every Duke student," one student said, "male, female, black, white, purple, brown." Added another: "I am a woman, so I am disgusted. But above that, I am a human being, so I am disgusted." Duke junior Brian Hanson told the *Durham Herald-Sun*, "Most people are just waiting to see it play out, waiting until some of the players come clean." He said he was not surprised by the allegations against the lacrosse team because it had a reputation around campus of "being its own fraternity, like a frat straight out of a movie."

Duke alumna Jill Hopman had observed some of that fraternal behavior on the previous Saturday night when she ran into a group of about twenty members of the lacrosse team at Charlie's Pub and Grill on Ninth Street in Durham, not far from 610 North Buchanan. The guys were drinking shots and bellowing, "Duke lacrosse! Duke lacrosse!" She overheard some talk about the rape allegation. "They were saying things like 'This is ruining our sea-son.'" Although she said she understood the need for "blowing off steam," she thought their behavior would have been more circumspect under the circum-stances. "They need to act like they're under a microscope, because they are," she said.

As with any ongoing criminal investigation, there was plenty of information about what had, and had not, happened at 610 North Buchanan on March 13 that Nifong, Gottlieb, and Himan had in their possession—for example, the preliminary word about the DNA testing, the transcript of the 911 call, the police document used to get the judge to require DNA testing from the players—but in the absence of its public availability, the news media began doing some digging on its own. The *News & Observer* checked court records and figured out that fifteen of the forty-seven Duke lacrosse players previously had been charged with misdemeanors—drunken behavior, underage drinking, and public urination—and that the charges had been dropped through agreements with prosecutors, known as deferred prosecution agreements, as long as the players stayed out of trouble. For instance, on August 25, 2005, David Evans had been cited for "possessing a can of beer in the passenger area of a car" and was also cited on January 10 for a "noise ordinance violation." He was given a deferred prosecution agreement, with a review scheduled for August 2006. Evans's housemate at 610 North Buchanan, Dan Flannery, had also been cited on January 10 for a "noise violation," with a court date scheduled for April 18. Ned Crotty, nineteen, had been cited for "public urination" on August 27 and was given a deferred prosecution agreement with a review scheduled for July 14. Matt Danowski, twenty, was cited on September 3 for "underage possession of a malt beverage," but was found not guilty by a judge.

The paper also had got its hands on the March 23 nontestimonial identification order that described Himan's version of what had happened in the house on March 13. Released publicly for the first time was the allegation that "when the woman and another dancer began their routines . . . one of the men watching held up a broomstick and threatened to sexually assault the women." Based on the NTO, the paper further reported that "the women were told that the men at the party were members of the baseball or track teams, apparently to hide their identities" and that "after the broomstick threat, the women left but were followed out by a man who persuaded them to return. . . . That's when, the woman said, three men pushed her into a bathroom and began the assault, which she said lasted for thirty minutes. She lost four fingernails as she scratched at one of the men who was strangling her." The paper sought the reaction of Duke officials to the NTO description. "In direct conversations with the captains, there was absolute denial of the criminal allegations," Burness responded.

On the morning of March 28, the four cocaptains of the lacrosse team met with Brodhead in his Allen Building office. They "expressed sincere regret over the lapse in judgment in having the party on March 13, which has caused so much anguish for the Duke community and shame to our families and ourselves," according to a statement the team captains issued later that day. They told Brodhead "unequivocally that any allegation that a sexual assault or rape occurred is totally and transparently false" and added, "The team has cooperated with the police in their investigation. We have provided authorities with DNA samples. The understanding is that the results of the DNA testing will be available sometime next week. The DNA results will demonstrate that these allegations are absolutely false." Brodhead later recalled of the meeting, from which Pressler was excluded at the last minute despite having pushed for it to happen, "The main thing I told the students was, 'Tell the truth, whatever it is. It's not going to get any better by telling some portion of it now and some portion of it later. Tell the truth.' I also said that they were telling me things that the world had not heard them say, and I urged them to state their case more fully. . . . These kids expressed significant contrition to me. They were mortified—they were mortified by the shame they had caused to themselves, their teammates, their families, their university. They mentioned all these things at the same time that they fervently denied the rape charge. And I said to them, 'Whatever it is that is true, you should acknowledge, and you should find a way to do it as quickly and as fully as you can, and then draw the line between that and what you didn't do.'"

After the meeting with Brodhead, the captains informed Alleva, the athletic director, and Brodhead that they wanted to suspend future games until the results of the DNA tests were available and, they believed, exonerated the team.

The voluntary suspension of games was said to be "rare," and would have "serious implications" for a team that was ranked second in the nation before the events of the night of March 13 and that had played for a national title the previous year, losing to Johns Hopkins in the final game. In lacrosse, unlike other high-profile college sports such as basketball and football, playing the sport professionally is not considered a realistic future career path, considering the grueling lifestyle and minimal pay. Athletes devoted themselves to practice year after year for the chance to play for the NCAA championship. That was especially true for the Duke lacrosse players, whose team had come so close to winning it all so many times and was a perennial contender for the crown without yet having won it. Suspending the future games would virtually assure that the 2006 season was going to be a washout, an especially tough penalty for the seniors on the team. "It was supposed to be Duke's year," the *New York Times* allowed. They had lost the national title the year before by a single goal. The team was returning most of its starters, including everyone from its "high-scoring attack" unit. "Duke was a preseason favorite to win a national title," the *Times* reported.

That same afternoon, the Durham police released the transcript of Roberts's 911 call from 12:53 a.m. in the early morning of March 14—though Roberts was not identified as the caller or as one of the two dancers at the party. The police also released the second 911 call, at 1:22 a.m. from the Kroger security guard, explaining how "drunk" and "intoxicated" the alleged victim—Mangum—was and how she refused to "exit" Roberts's vehicle.

By the time Brodhead and Alleva met with some forty members of the local and national media that night in the Old Trinity Room of the West Union Building—the first time Brodhead had met with reporters since the story broke—confusion reigned about what was alleged to have happened on the night of March 13. Dressed formally in a navy blue suit and navy tie decorated with Duke insignia, Brodhead read from a prepared statement before he answered questions. Brodhead bears more than a striking resemblance to comedian Wally Cox, in his *Hollywood Squares* days, albeit without the humor. He started by explaining that the rationale behind forfeiting the previous two lacrosse games was based upon the acknowledged facts of what had happened March 13. "A majority of the team members attended the party, which included underage drinking and the hiring of private party dancers," he said. "This conduct was wholly inappropriate to the values of our athletics program and the university. Forfeiting two games was a substantial penalty for a team that hoped to compete for the national championship. Director Alleva made clear that this move was not a punishment for pending allegations that team members deny and that remain unresolved."

The question Brodhead attempted to answer at the press conference was what to do next. "This afternoon the captains of the Duke lacrosse team notified Mr. Alleva and me that the team wished to suspend competitive play until the DNA results come back," he said. "I met with the captains this morning and they expressed regret for their errors of judgment and the embarrassment they had caused themselves, their families, the athletic department, and the university. They repeated their denial of the criminal allegations that have been widely reported against three of the players." He said he and Alleva agreed that the suspension of play was the right course of action and that he appreciated "the importance of their taking responsibility for their conduct." With the approval of the trustees, he decided to suspend the lacrosse games until the legal situation was clarified.

His logic was simple. "Physical coercion and sexual assault are unacceptable in any setting and will not be tolerated at Duke," he said. "As none of us would choose to be the object of such conduct, so none of us has the right to subject another person to such behavior. Since they run counter to such fundamental values, the claims against our players, if verified, will warrant very serious penalties, both from the university and in the courts. The university community is based on mutual respect among all its members and for those in the larger community. We are all obliged to live up to these values to create the world where we all can thrive.

"I feel these things deeply," he continued, "but there is another principle at stake as well. The facts of the March 13 episode remain unclear and there are very different accounts of the central events. No one has been charged by the police, and we know that many members of the lacrosse team, including some who were asked to provide DNA samples, did not attend the party. To determine responsibility, we need to learn the full truth as quickly as possible. While I have urged and do urge everyone to cooperate with this inquiry, unavoidably, we have to look to the Durham police to take the lead in the investigation."

Duke's decision to stand aside and let the Durham police investigate the allegations had infuriated many of the lawyers representing the players, and Brodhead attempted to explain why. The lawyers believed the Duke police force did have the authority to investigate what happened but Brodhead disputed that assertion. "Duke does not have the power to compel testimony from citizens of this city, and it lacks access to warrants, DNA records, and other confidential information," he said. "I have confidence in the authorities to find the truth and to take whatever legal steps are necessary in the best interests of the community. While we await the results of the investigation, I remind everyone that under our system of law, people are presumed innocent until proven guilty."

In the question-and-answer session that followed, Brodhead elaborated on the unusual and difficult challenges both he and the university faced as a result of the incident. He said that within twenty-four hours of its occurrence, his staff was working to figure out precisely what had happened. And he said that Dean Wasiolek had urged the students to speak honestly to the police.

But he also said his information about what had happened was limited. "One thing that I hope you will understand is that a lot of this story is known to the police and it isn't known to us," he said. "Even now, we have no idea on the basis of what evidence did they seek the DNA samples, for instance. What this means is that our understanding of the story has been a very partial understanding, and it's only been as we've learned certain things, very obliquely and indirectly from the police, that we've understood a different magnitude of the event."

He elaborated on his meeting earlier in the day with the lacrosse cocaptains. He did so with some reluctance, because, he said, the conversations that occur in his office are meant to be confidential. (Indeed, attorneys for the cocaptains claimed Brodhead promised them confidentiality.) But this was a case with extenuating circumstances, requiring a modicum of unusual disclosure. "We looked each other in the eye," he said. "This is a story in which we're all participants. They were eager to express their contrition for what they acknowledged they had done and for its consequences. At the same time, they were equally eager to deny to me—and they did so most sincerely—that the further and larger charges have any validity to them."

Why, then, had the players involved been so cryptic in their denials of what had been alleged? Why not shout their innocence from the proverbial rooftops? "What can I say to you?" Brodhead answered. "I met with the students today and I urged on them the notion that they should come forward. I was pleased to the extent that they have in their statement given some account. All I can tell you is I have to assume that they have legal counsel, and that legal counsel has foreseen complexities associated with speaking out. It's not for me to know the situation or to judge it."

Still, he wished their proclamation of innocence had been more "broadly heard," since "they are students of mine as much as anyone else at this place is a student of mine. But it's a painful situation to be in a room and not know whether someone is innocent, and thus a victim, of a charge that does them unfair ill, or the perpetrator."

Alleva spoke about the players' high moral character. "These are really outstanding student-athletes," he said. "Over the years, we have 100 percent graduation rate of our lacrosse players. We have over thirty of them on the ACC honor roll for academic achievement. They're outstanding student-athletes and they're wonderful young men. As I said earlier, unfortunately, they're young men, and sometimes young men make bad decisions, make some bad judgments, and that's what this whole incident is about, is making a bad judgment."

Brodhead was asked about his reaction to the days of protest about the incident. "How can I be surprised at the outrage?" he said. "As I have said all through my remarks, if the things alleged are verified, they're outrageous. . . . At the same time, it's extremely important for us to remember that an allegation is not the same thing as a conviction, and what makes it so hard for us all now is to know how to balance the outrage we properly and inevitably feel, and a category of that, with the fact that we have to suspend our judgment because the facts are so uncertain."

He was asked about the other misdemeanor legal infractions racked up previously by a third of the team. "Do you want to know what my life is like?" he said. "I come down every morning, and before I read the national papers, I read the Durham and the Raleigh papers, and I do freshly remember opening my *News & Observer* and seeing an article about other charges against the players. When I turned inside, it turned out that those charges involved bad behavior, but I think at a fairly low grade and familiar sort of bad behavior. I'm not going to pretend that we haven't had charges before, over time, against members of the lacrosse team, and they have all been dealt with in our usual fashions. But the charges have been like drunk and disorderly behavior, or noisiness. Once there was a vandalism charge. But I promise you, there is not a history of behavior associated with this team that connects with the things that are alleged at this point. It's just a quantum leap in the chart." Still, Brodhead conceded, underage drinking remained a problem at Duke and at colleges and universities across the country. "Many, many things in university life are aggravated by the presence of alcohol," he said. "If you talk to anybody at any university, you will learn the truth of that. At the same time, the presence of alcohol doesn't guarantee that really bad things happen thereafter, although it can make the road easier, nor does it prove in this case that such things did happen."

The one question that stumped him came from a local television reporter who asked Brodhead about the nasty racial overtones found in Roberts's 911 call. The contents had just been aired on the station's six o'clock news after the tape was leaked by the Durham police to the media in an effort, some said, to interject another element of racism into the firestorm. It was another example of how quickly events were unfolding. "Pardon me," Brodhead said. "These are tapes from the night of the party? This is the first I've ever heard of this."

Was there a culture of racism on the Duke lacrosse team or on Duke sports teams generally? "I have heard such things said," Brodhead replied. "Things that have been reported in the paper have raised the question. . . . I'm a recent arrival in this town, and one of the things that actually makes it quite friendly here in Durham is it's a place that has a very lively African-American community. I'm happy to have friends in significant parts of my life in connection with both of them. It's the nature of race that any place where race is a fact—if you tell me that there's a place where race is an utterly unproblematic phenomenon, I'll tell you that you're from a different planet than the one I live on. Right? Any place where race is a fact, things follow from it—and those things have a certain history here, to be sure. But what I've to say is, I have a group called the President's Council on Black Affairs made up of faculty, students, administrators, graduate students, all kinds of people. We have the liveliest discussions, very frank, no-holds-barred discussions about what their experience on this campus is like, and I'd have to say, I think that such people feel themselves to be valued members of this place, and I'll tell you, if you ask me about it, they certainly are valued by me."

Alleva then answered the question about racial bias on the lacrosse team. "I've been in Duke athletics for twenty-six years," he said. "I've seen no evidence of any racial problems with the lacrosse team, or, frankly, any of our teams, so I haven't seen any evidence of that."

After Brodhead left the press conference, about one hundred students confronted him outside of the West Union building demanding answers, according to the *Chronicle*, "and a stronger response from the school's administration." It was the fifth demonstration about the rape allegation in four days in and around Duke's campus and Brodhead promised the protesters he would answer more questions the next morning at the school's Mary Lou Williams Center for Black Culture, where students and community activists would gather to formulate their reaction to what had occurred at 610 North Buchanan. "I promise you, you will see this university respond with great and appropriate seriousness once the truth is established," he said. "I want this resolved as quickly as you do." Brodhead's words did little to assuage the growing concerns on campus. The administration "is making us agitated, nervous and upset," sophomore Simone Randolph said. "Since they've taken such a quiet stance on it, we're not confident that they're going to do the right thing." Added Bridgette Howard, a sophomore from Baltimore, "How are you going to protect us from these lacrosse players?"

That same night, in part because of Brodhead's press conference, the national media began clueing in to the story. Nifong appeared on the MSNBC show *The Abrams Report*, with Dan Abrams, a 1988 Duke graduate and son of Floyd Abrams, the First Amendment lawyer. After explaining that his office was still awaiting the results of the DNA testing that might or might not confirm the rape allegation, Nifong nonetheless told Abrams that he was certain a rape had occurred. "The circumstances of the case are not suggestive of the alternate explanation that has been suggested by some of the members of the situation," he said. "There is evidence of trauma in the victim's vaginal area that was noted when she was examined by a nurse at the hospital. And her general demeanor was suggestive of the fact that she had been through a traumatic situation." Abrams pressed Nifong on what he meant by the alternate explanation. "So that there is no sexual activity at all is the alternate explanation?" Abrams asked.

"That would be the alternate story," Nifong said.

In the brief interview, Abrams and Nifong discussed the possibility that Nifong would bring charges against the other men at the party who may have known the rape was allegedly occurring but did nothing to stop it. Abrams also asked Nifong if he was satisfied with Duke's response to the incident and he said the university "had done nothing to interfere with the investigation."

NPR broadcast a segment about the incident that evening, which was followed by a story in the *New York Times* the next day under the headline "Rape Allegation Against Athletes Is Roiling Duke." After recounting what was known about the incident and the decision to suspend the lacrosse team's season while the allegations were being investigated, the paper interviewed Nifong. "The thing that most of us found so abhorrent, and the reason I decided to take it over myself, was the combination gang-like rape activity accompanied by the racial slurs and general racial hostility," he said. "There are three people who went into the bathroom with the young lady, and whether the other people there knew what was going on at the time, they do now and have not come forward. I'm disappointed that no one has been enough of a man to come forward. And if they would have spoken up at the time, this may never have happened."

The paper also quoted from the statement of the team captains that "we have provided authorities with DNA samples. The understanding is that the results of the DNA testing will be available sometime next week. The DNA results will demonstrate that these allegations are absolutely false." And then the two reporters writing the story concluded in their own words, "The incident has cast an unflattering light on a university that has a track record for success and integrity in athletics rivaled only by its highly regarded academics."

Nifong's sudden media visibility also had political repercussions. Jackie Brown, Nifong's campaign manager for the upcoming election for district attorney, was on vacation at her home at North Topsail Beach, on the coast of North Carolina, in late March, when she received a phone call from Nifong telling her he would be mentioned in a few news stories involving something about Duke lacrosse. "Hold it," she said to him, "Do you have any idea what this could do to your campaign, good or bad?" Nifong responded that he had not thought about that. Brown told him to "keep quiet" until they had figured out what the effect might be. When she hung up the phone, she turned on her television set and saw Nifong giving one interview after another to the cable news channels. The next morning, she packed up and headed back to Durham. She needed to speak with Nifong in person.

Before Nifong called Brown in the fall of 2005 to see if she would be willing to be his campaign manager, she had never heard of him. In part, this was because of Nifong's relatively low profile and in part because back in April 2005, when Governor Mike Easley appointed Nifong to fill the remainer of Jim Hardin's term, Easley believed Nifong had promised not to seek his own full term as Durham district attorney in 2006. When Brown agreed to meet Nifong on January 2, 2006, for lunch to suss out the viability of his candidacy, his wife, Cy Gurney, was with him. Brown remembered Nifong's first words to her: "He said, 'I really don't want this job; I was the last one on the list. I just need three years and seven months for retirement. You won't have to worry about running another campaign for me.'" Did Nifong really want the job? Brown wondered. "I know nothing about politics," he told her. "That's why I need you to be campaign manager."

That first conversation with Nifong filled Brown's head as she drove back to Durham, starting at dawn the next morning. When she got to Nifong's office, she noticed that the courthouse was surrounded by television trucks and reporters were lined up waiting to see him. When Brown saw the media scrum, she was appalled. She tried calling Nifong on his cell phone, but he didn't answer. Finally, she cornered him as he was going to the men's room. "What are you doing?" she asked. "Why don't you answer my calls?" He told her, she recalled, that the television crews had told him to turn off his cell phone during the interviews.

"You don't have any idea what the impact is going to be on your campaign," she told him.

"I'm getting a million dollars of free advertisements," Brown said Nifong told him. With that, she said, "I left and didn't say another word."

Nifong remembered the conversation with Brown differently. After she told him it might damage his campaign to speak so openly with media about the lacrosse case, he said he told her, "The two things were not related, that I was speaking to the media about something that was part of the job, that was not part of the campaign, and that what I was doing had nothing to do with the campaign and it wasn't an appropriate area for her concern." Had he made the comment about the media attention being worth a million dollars in advertising? "I'm pretty sure that I never made any comment like that to her," he said.

That day, Brodhead met with a large group of students at the Mary Lou Williams Center. Many of the students had spent the night preparing for Brodhead's visit, and a group calling itself Concerned Citizens at Duke University had distributed a statement claiming that "the university is cultivating and sustaining a culture of privilege and silence that allows inappropriate behavior to plague the campus." Brodhead listened to the concerns and maintained his previously articulated view that the lacrosse players should be assumed to be innocent until proven guilty. "We can't promise you there will never be instances of disgusting and disturbing things," he said. He asked students to learn from such controversies. He urged the gathered students not to rush to judgment. "If you were at a university where the president meted out punishment based on what he reads in the newspaper, it would be a pretty dangerous place," he said. "We are not a perfect community, but we are a community where we take these issues seriously."

Afterward, Brodhead returned to his office and listened to the 911 tape of Roberts's call that he had been asked about at the press conference the previous evening. "I have now had the opportunity to listen to the tape," Brodhead then wrote in a statement. "It is disgusting. Racism and its hateful language have no place in this community. I am sorry the woman and her friend were subjected to such abuse."

At about the same time, a flyer produced by the Durham police began circulating around the Duke campus in the form of an old-fashioned "Wanted" poster. The clear message was that anyone with information about what had happened at 610 North Buchanan on the evening of March 13 should contact the police and share that information. The words "Please Come Forward" appeared in large type above mug shots of forty-three of the forty-seven members of the Duke lacrosse team taken from the team's website before those pictures were taken down, Alleva said, for the protection of the players.

The poster, printed at a Duke printing facility with the knowledge of Duke officials, became known as the Vigilante Poster. "Each and every one of those young men who were present at this party categorically deny that any assault of any description took place," attorney Bill Thomas told the *News & Observer* after seeing the flyers. "The entire Duke lacrosse team looks forward to the results of the DNA test in order to clear their names." That afternoon, the lacrosse team returned to the practice field at Koskinen Stadium "knowing that their season was in limbo and that their character was under scrutiny," the *New York Times* wrote. Campus police patrolled the practice on foot, on mountain bikes, and in SUVs. The media assembled as well, and for thirty minutes were allowed to take photographs of the players in their uniforms before they were eventually shooed away.

That night, more than a thousand students, faculty members, administrators, and Durham residents marched across Duke—starting at the Marketplace on East Campus and ending more than a mile later at the Duke Chapel on West Campus—in a Take Back the Night protest that was part of the ongoing Sexual Assault Prevention Week. The protesters distributed printed chants and the names and pictures of the lacrosse players as well as the phone numbers for police officers to be contacted. During speeches and the reading of poetry, some people defaced the players' pictures. As they marched from East to West, they chanted, "Out of the dorms, into the streets, we won't be raped, we won't be beat." One student wore a sign taped to his T-shirt: "It isn't what Duke has, but what it lax." Malbert Smith, a Duke alumnus living in Chapel Hill, attended the rally because he expected Duke to handle the situation differently. "For us to say it's basically boorish behavior, I'm offended by that," he said. "I'm offended by the fact that the lacrosse team is still practicing."

The Duke campus has been the site of many student protests over the years—from a takeover of the Allen Building during the Vietnam War to demonstrations about the role of the Reagan administration in the Iran-Contra scandal to the outrage that filled the campus after four members of the Communist Workers Party—three of whom had ties to Duke—were shot and killed (a fifth died later) in November 1979 by members of the Ku Klux Klan while marching in Greensboro, North Carolina, to protect their civil rights. In recent years, Duke students have pitched tents (and lived in them for weeks) to participate in the Occupy Wall Street movement and have organized rallies to protest Apple's use of gold in its iPhones mined, using oppressive means, from the Congo. In truth, unlike students at many campuses across the country, Duke's undergraduates have long enjoyed a good and vocal demonstration. "There's a culture of rape at Duke," one student told *USA Today*, "so we're hoping this will get them to speak up."

The protesters were angry. "[The alleged incident] exemplifies what goes on every day," said senior Lara Pomerantz. "It's important to have dialogue . . . because we live in a culture that doesn't talk about it." In the crowd, a reporter from the *Chronicle* found Ryan McFadyen, the lacrosse player whose dorm room had just been searched by police, although that fact had not been released publicly. "I completely support this event and this entire week," he said. "It's just sad that the allegations we are accused of happened to fall when they did." The paper reported later that day that the Durham police had searched "a dorm room on campus" on Monday after obtaining a search warrant. (Incredibly, Nifong told the *Chronicle* he was unaware that a dorm room—McFadyen's—had been searched. He did offer his view that he remained convinced that a sexual assualt had occurred. "The statements that [the team] make are inconsistent with the physical evidence in this case," he said. "They don't want to admit the enormity of what they've done.")

McFadyen went back to his dorm and turned on the television to watch ESPN, along with his teammates Collin Finnerty, Kevin Mayer, and a couple of others. The media coverage of the alleged incident had exploded by then, of course. "All of a sudden I'm quoted on ESPN," he said. "It's like, 'Sophomore Ryan McFadyen said it's unfortunate these incidents occurred while attending Take Back the Night.' And I was like, 'Are you kidding me?' The kid who I casually knew from a class had been recording our conversation. He worked for the *Chronicle* and had recorded our conversation without me knowing, and had taken a quote that was innocent: 'It's unfortunate this happened, but I'm just here supporting this event.'" He and his teammates were in disbelief. "We're kind of looking at each other like, 'Holy fuck,'" McFadyen said. "That's when we were like, 'Wow.'" He realized at that moment that something had changed. "It's like anything you say can and will be used against you," he said. "You can say anything. Forty different guys telling the story, someone's gonna put in two discrepancies, or some guys aren't gonna remember something the right way. You can run this wherever you want."

In an editorial, the *Chronicle* generally lauded Brodhead's performance at his press conference. Suspending the lacrosse season sent the right message about the seriousness of the allegations while his note of caution about jumping too quickly to conclusions about what had happened was an important reminder about the students' legal right to due process. The racial slurs on the 911 tapes were another matter, though. "In protests and on these pages, some students claim the administration has a reputation for sweeping racial issues under the rug," the editors wrote. "Even if the pending allegations of rape are proven false, and even if the team is completely exonerated, some feel the racial slurs and the culture of racial insensitivity they suggest will both go unaddressed." The *New York Times*, meanwhile, interviewed Reverend Luke Travers, headmaster at the Delbarton School in Morristown, New Jersey, where five players on the Duke lacrosse team had attended high school. (Some twenty-six of the forty-seven players attended New York, New Jersey, and Connecticut high schools.) "These are wonderful boys from wonderful families," Travers said. "We're all worried for them." The paper also spoke with Philip Seligmann, the father of player Reade Seligmann, outside his home in Essex Fells, New Jersey. "It's unfortunate, but it will all be resolved positively very shortly."

For Brodhead, this was an intense period of damage control. The media had virtually staked out the entry to West Campus with one remote television broadcast truck after another clogging the road. A siege seemed to be brewing. Amina Turner, executive director of the state NAACP, said the leaders of her organization wanted to meet with the Duke president. "Our concern is because of the confluence or race, class and gender to make sure it doesn't become another 'boys-will-be-boys' situation," she told the News & Observer, prompting Brodhead to meet the next day with Reverend William Barber, president of the North Carolina Conference of the NAACP. He met with Bill Bell, the Durham mayor, with NCCU chancellor James Ammons, with local pastors as well as the leaders of the Durham Committee of Black People, with the Trinity College board of advisers, and then with some 230 members of the Duke faculty to discuss the allegations. After Brodhead's meeting with Ammons, the NCCU chancellor told the Durham Morning Herald, "I thought that it was a very good beginning to, first of all, share our feelings about the seriousness of these allegations and our stand against sexual violence against women, racial discrimination and racial hate, and to share our concern about the young lady who was obviously traumatized by these alleged acts and to find a way to be respectful of the legal process, to let it play out and not rush to judgment."

Brodhead also sent an e-mail to Duke alumni. "As painful as these times are," he wrote, "the test of a school is not preventing bad things from ever happening, but in addressing them in an honest and forthright way. In my meetings with students, faculty, and administrators, I believe Duke is doing just that." To the parents of Duke undergraduates, he wrote, "This is a difficult time at Duke. Allegations have been made that, if verified, will justify all of our outrage and call for very severe penalties. On the other hand, we need to remember that allegation is not the same thing as conviction, and that we must not prejudge until the facts are established. The Durham police will have our full cooperation in expediting their investigation. I would gladly have spared your sons and daughters this experience. But painful as these days are, times of strain can also be times of education. We will be working as always to assure the welfare of our students, and we'll be struggling to make this an occasion where we can all grow in wisdom."

CHAPTER FIVE

The New Duke

The conflagration engulfing Duke had been foreseen, at least by Duke history professor Peter Wood, who had written the June 2004 letter to Robert Thompson, the dean of students. Not only had Wood taught a number of the lacrosse players over the years but he also had serious chops on the subject of the consequences of high-pressure college athletics on the academic careers of student-athletes and on the universities that place too high a priority on them.

For starters, his grandfather, William Barry Wood, a cotton broker in Boston, played varsity baseball and football at Harvard, Class of 1902. His father, William Barry Wood Jr., known as Barry, or Will to his close friends, was one of the most famous student-athletes of the first half of the twentieth century. Born in Milton, Massachusetts, in May 1910, Barry Wood was a standout at Milton Academy for both his athletic and academic prowess. From Milton, Barry Wood enrolled at Harvard, where he "burst on that national scene for his skill as a quarterback and his ranking as a tennis player," according to the *Times*. At six feet two inches tall and 175 pounds, he may have been the perfect human physical specimen. As a freshman in Harvard's class of 1932, Wood was the captain of the freshman football team, played on both the baseball and hockey teams and was the freshman class president. He also went to the semifinals of the Massachusetts state tennis tournament and was the highest-ranked student-athlete in his class. In his junior year, Wood was elected captain of the football team. He was class president and president of the student council. That same year, he was elected to Phi Beta Kappa. Harvard also awarded him the Francis H. Burr Scholarship in his junior year, an award given to the student deemed the most outstanding leader, student, and athlete.

In October 1931, the *Times* wrote an extensive profile of Wood, "Harvard's Scholar-Athlete." The writer, Robert Kelley, seemed shocked that Wood seemed so much more like a scholar than an athlete. In recounting the outstanding football game Wood played against Army—where Wood led Harvard to a 14–13 victory after being behind 13–0, and made two crucial game-saving defensive plays (these were the days when players played on both sides of the line)—Kelley observed, "As captain, Wood is apparently rounding off well a career that is among the most remarkable of any athlete who has ever played in an Eastern college." *Time* magazine put Wood on the cover of its November 23, 1931, issue, crouching in his uniform, holding a football. After the 1931 season, Wood was named an All-American, the last Harvard quarterback to receive that honor. (He was elected to the College Football Hall of Fame in 1980, the only Harvard quarterback ever inducted.)

After earning his medical degree at Johns Hopkins, Wood began an illustrious medical career as a physician, researcher, and teacher. His professional accomplishments were every bit as impressive as his academic and athletic ones. He moved to St. Louis and, at thirty-two, became one of the youngest chairmen ever of the medical department at Washington University. He was also in charge of the school's hospital. In 1955, he returned to Johns Hopkins as the head of the hospital and a vice president of the university.

Widely acclaimed as a superb teacher, he also became well-known for the efficacy of his scientific research. In 1943, along with other physicians, he wrote a paper about the benefits of penicillin. He was the first to describe the idea of phagocytosis, the process by which white blood cells fight disease. He was also renowned for his discovery of pyrogen, a substance that can contribute to the causes of a fever. In 1959, Wood took over the department of microbiology at Johns Hopkins, a position he held at the time of his death in 1971 from a heart attack. He was sixty years old.

Following in such huge paternal footsteps would not be easy for any son, but Peter Wood managed to do it, in his own outspoken way. He grew up in Owings Mills, Maryland, and attended the Gilman School in Baltimore, the nation's oldest private, all-boys day school, founded in 1897. Gilman was also a bastion of lacrosse, with many of its top graduates recruited to play the sport in college, including by Duke. After graduating in 1960, Wood attended Harvard, where he lived in Eliot House. Like his father, Peter Wood excelled in both athletics and academics. His chosen sport—lacrosse—had only been played competitively at Harvard since 1961, and Wood himself began playing the game in the spring of 1962. As a junior, despite suffering a painful shoulder separation, the six-foot-tall Wood was the team's fifth leading scorer, and only one other midfielder, a senior, scored more than Wood's fourteen during the 1963 season. In May 1963, Wood was elected the varsity lacrosse team's captain.

In the fall of his senior year, Wood was named a Rhodes scholar, along with five other of his Harvard classmates, making Harvard by far the school with the most Rhodes scholars in 1964. He was also a Harvard Prize Fellow and wrote his senior thesis about the relationship between the Puritans and the Indians. By then, he had begun dating Ann Watson, an undergraduate at Radcliffe. She graduated summa cum laude in 1964 and was a member of Phi Beta Kappa. Wood graduated Harvard magna cum laude. They went off together to Oxford, where Wood also played lacrosse. The couple got engaged in the summer of 1965 and married in September in Bernardsville, New Jersey.

After Oxford, where he received a master's degree in 1966, the Woods returned to Harvard. Peter enrolled in the PhD program in American history. In September 1969, Wood was named the senior tutor at Eliot House, a position of great authority at Harvard. The senior tutor in each house advises students on course choices, graduate schools, fellowships, and careers and writes letters of recommendation for students.

Wood's PhD thesis was a groundbreaking examination of enslaved blacks in the pre-Revolutionary-era American South. In the thesis, Wood showed how the slaves in South Carolina, who worked in the rice fields, were recruited specifically from the western coast of Africa for the skills they had developed in the cultivating, growing, and harvesting of rice. The slaves also knew how to build dams and irrigation systems with proficiency. Wood's thesis revealed that the slaves were imported to the New World not only for their labor but also for their skill, and were the key to enriching the local plantation owners, who had figured out how to build thriving businesses on their backs.

Harvard awarded Wood his PhD in 1972. In 1973, Knopf published his thesis as *Black Majority: Negroes in Colonial South Carolina from 1670 Through the Stono Rebellion*. The book won the American Historical Association's 1974 Albert J. Beveridge Award, and was a finalist for the National Book Award in the history category.

In 1975, Wood was a hot property. Duke scooped him up at a time when the school's history department was becoming one of the most intellectually dynamic and highly regarded in the country. Along the way, Wood divorced Anne and met and married Elizabeth Fenn, a 1981 Duke graduate and historian who abandoned Duke housing in her senior year and lived in a $300 teepee in the middle of a tobacco field on the outskirts of Durham. (Fenn was also an expert auto mechanic.) Peter Wood became a core member of a department that also included celebrated historians Larry Goodwin, William Chafe, Jack Cell, Charles Maier, and Ron Witt.

Duke, too, was on the rise, and nothing seared that impression into the minds of the nation's elites more than the November 18, 1984, cover of the *New York Times Magazine*. Under the headline "Hot Colleges and How They Get That Way," the cover photograph showed some Duke students in school sweatshirts walking on the quad in front of Duke's Gothic chapel. Ironically, the story itself, written by Michael Winerip, gave much more space to other schools— among them Brown University and the University of Virginia—than it did to Duke. The lead, though, featured a prep school student who wanted to go to Vanderbilt but was wondering what to do because her father was really pushing Virginia and Duke. He'd heard those two schools were "hot," and according to Winerip, "'hot' seems to be getting more important all the time when it comes to picking a college. It is much on the minds of bright high school seniors and their parents these days, with decisions from top colleges on early admissions only a month away." The article noted, though, that students were fickle and schools were trendy. While Duke was popular in wealthy Greenwich, Connecticut, it was of less interest to students at the more parochial Boston Latin School, in Boston. And, yes, while applications to Duke had risen by one-third since 1979, they had also risen by that much—and more—at other schools, such as Northwestern and West Point.

Even the space Winerip gave to observations by Duke president Terry Sanford, the highly regarded former governor of North Carolina (and a future senator from the state), about why Duke had become so popular seemed especially superficial. Sanford said Duke was appealing because of its emphasis on a liberal arts education and because "there is a hotline that runs from the college students to their high school buddies."

Sanford had been hired at Duke in 1969 "to transform Duke into a national institution," according to Daniel Golden in *The Price of Admission*, his 2006 book about elite college admissions, "and the *Times*'s coverage seemed to be powerful evidence that he had delivered on that commitment." But Golden wasn't buying what Sanford was trying to sell to the magazine about why Duke had become so "hot." It had nothing to do with the liberal arts education, Golden wrote, but rather Sanford's vision of "outrageous ambition" for the school and his policy of recruiting students from wealthy suburbs (like Greenwich and Bethesda) and the children of rich and powerful families, "including the daughter of the newspaper's publisher"—Cynthia Fox Sulzberger, a 1986 Duke graduate—"and the son of the editor in chief of the *Times*'s magazine." Alex Klein, the son of Edward Klein, then the magazine's editor, was applying to Duke when the story came out but went to Brown instead. Golden noted in his book that none of these potential conflicts was mentioned in the article but concluded that the *Times*'s publisher had no role in the selection of the cover photo, although Klein admitted he wanted the Duke shot for the cover. (In his book, Golden also accused Duke of cultivating "wealthy non-alumni by giving breaks to their children who fall below its rigid admissions standards," and noted that "their grateful fathers and mothers joined Duke's parent fundraising group, which year after year led all universities nationwide in unrestricted gifts to its annual fund from non-alumni parents." Golden then told the story of one Baron Maurice Jeffrey Locke de Rothschild, who had been admitted to Duke in the late 1980s and who "cut quite a figure" on campus, driving "expensive cars," buying champagne for frat parties, and "boasting" about his "famed European banking relatives." The young Baron de Rothschild turned out to be the considerably less blue-blooded Mauro Cortez Jr. from El Paso, Texas. In 1991, Cortez was sentenced to three years in prison for bank fraud.)

Regardless of these not-insignificant points, all anyone seemed to remember was that Duke *was* on the cover and was the hottest school around. Applications to Duke—and its popularity—soared. Then, in 1986, the Duke men's soccer team won the school's first national championship of any kind, and when five years later, in 1991, Krzyzewski's basketball team won its first national championship after years of getting close and being in four Final Fours in a row, suddenly Duke had a new message to share with prospective undergraduates: like Stanford, not only were the academics at Duke top-notch but so, too, were the athletics. Duke was a place where student-athletes could thrive and excel. Few other top schools could offer that same powerful combination. In a 2011 deposition, Chris Kennedy, the associate athletic director, described the kind of citizens that Duke has been trying to create with its emphasis on top-notch athletics and academics. "When that person goes through this experience at the highest level of college athletics and the highest level of college academics, they emerge at the other end of that with a degree, but also with a sense of themselves that's changed, and a sense that if I can do this, I can do anything," he said. "This has been a vastly empowering experience, and I think that's been true for a hundred years. . . . Five years after you graduate, you don't remember the score of the Clemson game in your junior year, and you don't remember the physics problems or equations that you studied so hard for that exam. The actual details aren't as important as the preparation and the commitment and the dedication and the hard work that goes into mastering them." When Duke won its second national basketball championship in 1992, a rare repeat—only UCLA under John Wooden had pulled that off before, but in a "different" era for college basketball—the message of Duke exceptionalism was reinforced.

And then Krzyzewski did it again in 2001. The women's golf team won five national championships, and the women's tennis team won one. Duke had become the collegiate version of the New York Yankees, "an easy place to hate," in the words of Peter Boyer in the *New Yorker*. By 2005, Duke was ranked among the top five schools for athletic success, with twenty-six varsity teams. Duke's annual athletic budget was close to $50 million. "If you were starting from scratch at Duke, no one would have imagined an athletics program where the budget is almost fifty million dollars," observed Orin Starn, a Duke professor of sports anthropology. "This huge outlay of expenses and energy and visibility of sports is just clearly out of proportion with what it should be. Yes, athletics has a place in college education, but not this sort of massive space that it's taking."

After Coach K's back-to-back national championships, Duke seemed to be sitting on top of the world. "Duke students are the happiest in the nation," the Princeton Review's 1992 *Student Access Guide to the Best Colleges* proclaimed. "And why not? They attend one of the best universities in the nation . . . have access to incredible resources, inhabit a beautiful campus, and, best of all, don't work all that much harder than their peers at much less prestigious universities." After elaborating on this theme a bit, the guide then observed that

"Durham is not popular with the students . . . That hardly matters, though, since students are quite happy to spend all their time on campus. Fraternities and sororities are quite popular and host lots of parties; their challenging studies not withstanding, Duke students can always find time for a few brews . . . 'work hard and play hard.'"

Lisa Birnbach—author of the famous *Preppy Handbook*—offered her own observations the same year. She noted that the "best things" about Duke were its "relaxed and easy-going atmosphere" where the students "are intelligent and friendly. . . . Dukies study hard and work hard." The "worst things" were "too many rich, snobby and fake people" who "are very cliquish." The social life, Birnbach wrote, "is centered around fraternity kegs" and is limited unless you just want "to get drunk and get laid every weekend."

None of this social disfunctionality at Duke was lost on President Keith Brodie. Just before Thanksgiving, in 1992, Brodie asked William Willimon, the dean of the chapel and a professor of Christian ministry, to meet with him in his office along with a few other senior administrators. "They told me they had become increasingly concerned about student life at Duke—alcohol, residential life, safety, social activities, sports—particularly as student life helped or hindered the academic mission of the university," Willimon recalled. Brodie asked him to venture forth onto the campus, talk to and listen to students, gather insights into the relationship between the academic side of the undergraduate experience and the social side and then report back. For the next four months, in his spare time, Willimon met with and observed students, especially after five o'clock and on weekends. He conducted some two hundred hours of interviews with students. Others who heard about his assignment sought him out to share their thoughts. He spent several nights riding around with the Duke police force. Other nights, he attended keg parties, listening and observing. One night, Willimon found himself, at 2 a.m., watching in amazement as a bonfire made from the wooden benches collected from in front of a frat house raged nearly out of control in one of the quadrangles on West Campus.

As Willimon was beginning his extracurricular assignment, he attended the annual Founders Day celebration in the Duke Chapel. There, he listened, rapt and amazed, as Reynolds Price, the legendary novelist and Duke professor, delivered a blistering attack on the devolving behavior of the students. James Buchanan Duke had founded the school in order to train future leaders, educated "along sane and practical lines" by professors noted for their "character, ability, and vision." (Duke's complete thought, as found in the indenture to the Duke endowment, was "I have selected Duke University as one of the principal objects of this trust because I recognize that education, when conducted along sane and practical as opposed to dogmatic and theoretical lines, is next to religion the greatest civilizing influence." He further insisted that should the university "not be operated in [a] manner calculated to achieve the results intended," funds from the endowment could be withheld).

Price had become concerned that the founder's vision was clouding over. In his classes, Price increasingly found "the stunned or blank faces of students who exhibit a minimum of preparation or willingness for what I think of as the high delight and life-enduring pleasure of serious conversation in the classroom and elsewhere." He asked the audience to consider the prospect of standing at the West Campus bus stop "at noon rush hour" or "roam the reading rooms of the libraries in the midst of term and the panic of exams" or "eat lunch in a dining hall and note the subjects of conversation and words employed in student discussion . . ." According to Price, one phrase would be heard repeatedly: "I can't believe how drunk I was last night." Willimon wondered, "Had we at the university wandered as far afield as Price charged?"

The next day, Willimon was speaking with a student who recalled that when he first arrived at Duke, "I quickly found, my freshman year, that this place had some definite ideas about the picture of the 'good' Duke student. I found myself caught up in the fraternity rush scene, the keg scene. I changed my wardrobe [and] my hairstyle to suit the image I was trying to adopt." But when he went home for Thanksgiving, a thought dawned on him. "The conversation was better around my family dinner table at home than any conversation I had all semester at Duke!" He continued: "I took a look at myself, what I had become . . . I decided then and there that I would have to move off campus if I were to have the intellectual life that I wanted." Then the student told Willimon something that he would never forget. "Duke students say, 'We work hard and we play hard' but do we say we *think hard*?" He wondered, "Are we really developing for ourselves the critical thinking skills we need?" Willimon noted that while, in the early 1960s, Duke was once referred to as the "Gothic Rockpile," it had now become known as the "Gothic Wonderland." What were the implications of that change?

In his fifty-three-page April 1993 report to Brodie, *We Work Hard, We Play Hard*, Willimon noted that the rituals of assimilation into the Duke culture began nearly immediately upon a student's arrival on campus and seemed to include a palpable "anti-intellectualism." One evening he met with a dozen Angier B. Duke scholars, a select group of freshman remarkable for their brilliance. He said he was "surprised" by the "level of discontent" among them, chiefly because the campus gestalt seemed to be disdainful of intellectual pursuits. Observed one student, "Try bringing up a book you've read or a great lecture you've just heard in class, and other students will tell you, 'Keep it in class. My brain's meter is not running now.'" Willimon introduced the idea that "sometimes . . . the University gives scholarships not only to those people who represent who we are, but also to those who represent who we want to be." True enough, the students told Willimon, but despite an "energetic and expensive recruiting process," the school seemed to put little additional effort into making these special students feel welcome. He was shocked to discover that more than half of them had filled out applications to transfer to other schools. "I was impressed with their deep level of disastisfaction, their sense of a certain betrayal and victimization by 'false advertising,'" Willimon observed. He noted that many black students and science students felt similarly. He noted that the athletic facilities were closed at nights and on weekends when they should rather be in full swing. He noted that the dining facilities should be places that encouraged languishing over discussions rather than food-service efficiency.

There was something about the DNA of the school that did not make some students feel welcome. "Students do not walk into a vacuum when they arrive as new members of the university community," he wrote. "They are subtly but powerfully initiated into a distinct culture. I have come to the reluctant conclusion that this student culture mitigates against serious and sustained intellectual engagement by the students. . . . The 'We work hard, we play hard' mentality thus fosters a rather rowdy, carefree, anti-intellectual image of the 'perfect' Duke student. Seen in its best light, this means that Duke students are known for their exuberance, their enthusiasm at basketball games, and their general love of life. At its worst, it means that our students are engaged in activities which not only do not contribute to the academic mission of the university, but actually work against the mission by trivializing the time they spend here."

He discovered, too, that the Duke faculty had little engagement with students beyond the classroom. For reasons of convenience, self-interest, or structure—there was no place for professors to live on West Campus, for instance—Duke teachers pretty much abandoned the students after certain hours of the day. "I believe that we teach people to learn how to think," Willimon wrote, "to learn how to stand on their own two feet, to take hold of their lives, not by stepping back from them, not by leaving them to their own devices, but rather through engaging them, through intense encounters with other people. . . . We have structured the University in such a way that the chances of our [professors and students] ever becoming friends with one another are slim. Detachment seems to be the ruling mode."

Then there was the pervasive role of alcohol at Duke. "The 'work hard, play hard' ethos permeates the students' image of themselves," Willimon discovered. "Yet I am uncertain if we know how to play hard. 'We know how to *drink* hard,' charged one sophomore, a woman who admitted to being totally repulsed by the dominant social scene, 'but do we really know social skills?'" He found that nearly a decade after federal law made drinking under the age of twenty-one illegal, alcohol abuse was the number one health issue at Duke and the number one safety issue. Willimon found that students accepted the keg party scene because, socially, it was the path of least resistance. Much to his dismay, he noted that beer advertising revenue underwrote the cost of many collegiate athletic programs, sending a very mixed message to undergraduates and university administrators. "If one were devising an environment to produce alcoholics, one could do no better than Duke's West Campus on a weekend," Roy Matthew, the director of Duke's Alcohol Treatment Center, told Willimon. "All of the factors that contribute to the development of alcoholics—availability, social pressure to overindulge, no social restraints against overindulging, etc.—are there on a Saturday night."

He concluded that alcohol abuse at Duke might be related to a lack of alternatives to heavy drinking. "When it comes to the party scene, the fraternities are clearly in control," Willimon wrote. "They have the organizational structure, the financing and the commitment to pay for the kegs and the bands so their concept of social life dominates the scene." He was particularly critical of the social scene offered to freshmen. He urged his audience to remember that Duke, first and foremost, was an educational institution. "Training in the wise use of alcohol is an educational matter," he wrote. "Tragically, the effects of early alcohol abuse, like being infected with the HIV virus, do not show up until years later. When students' alcohol abuse patterns bear fruit, they are alumni."

Willimon searched for answers. One Monday, after the usual "weekend of carrousing and vandalizing" on campus, he walked into a "damage control" meeting of the Student Affairs Committee. One of the assistant deans remarked to Willimon about how serious the drinking problem had become. "Can't something be done about this?" Willimon said. "Don't you think it is a shame that these people come to us with such potential and then waste themselves with alcohol?"

"But what can we do?" another dean chimed in. "After all, *we are not their parents.*"

"No, we are not their parents," Willimon replied, "but could we at least try being their older brothers and sisters? Could we possibly be their friends?" This is the kind of idealistic question that Willimon suspected often got a response along the lines of "Well, I think it is important that we give them their freedom. Freedom is developmentally important at this age. We show our faith in our students by treating them like adults, by relying on them to make mature, responsible decisions for themselves." Willimon believed that attitude was unrealistic and an abdication. "Leaving them to themselves," he wrote, "they become the willing victims of the most totalitarian form of government ever devised, namely, submission to their peers, obeisance to people who are just like them. This is neither freedom nor maturity." He argued that the backgrounds of the majority of Duke students—mostly wealthy and mostly elite—rendered them less experienced in caring for themselves. "If the university were filled with students who grew up on the streets of Harlem or the South Side of Chicago, then perhaps we could trust them to look out for themselves," he continued. "After all, they had had so much experience looking after themselves before they arrived here. Unfortunately . . . few of our students grew up on the South Side of Chicago. Most of them have come from privileged homes where there was a relatively high degree of parental supervision and determination of their lives. To bring such people to a university, wave a magic wand over their lives, and tell them that they are magically transformed into mature responsible adults is ridiculous."

Willimon wrote of the need for faculty and administrators to work together with students to help design an even more substantive, meaningful experience for Duke undergraduates. "All of us, in long collusion, have failed to exert a sustained and serious attempt to nurture the literal heart of a great university," Reynolds Price said in his Founders' Day speech. He said the university must nurture "an environment that is suited for and continuously encouraging to the more or less constant discussion of serious matters" and "an atmosphere that awards itself a steady supply of human beings (students, faculty, and other staff) who are fitted to converse with one another on serious matters or are willing to learn how." Willimon argued that Duke had failed—by 1993, anyway—to achieve Price's vision. "We have tried to have a university without arguing about what a university is, what we want out of ourselves, who we expect our students to grow up to be, what we expect them to give to the world," he wrote. "James B. Duke was quite clear that the only reason he could think of for a university was to produce people who would influence the world for good. We should spend more time thinking about what is the best possible way to live in this community and then we should unashamedly ask students to conform to this best way."

Eight years later, another Duke president, Nan Keohane, asked Willimon to reprise his study. He noted that Keohane had made some important changes to campus life—in part in reaction to his earlier study—including requiring all freshman to live on East Campus, breaking up the stranglehold of fraternities in the best housing on West Campus and building two state-of-the-art athletic facilities and keeping them open around the clock. The so-called Thursday kegs were banned in 1993, "and our alcohol policies have been under almost continual review and revision since then," Willimon wrote. James Clack, a student affairs administrator, wrote the incoming freshmen in August 2000, "You are coming to a great university where you can expect a great education, an exciting and enjoyable social life, and the making of friendships that will last a lifetime. Don't mess up this opportunity by giving in to pressures to become a dangerous drinker. . . . If you want to major in alcohol, please go elsewhere."

Not surprisingly, though, alcohol remained a problem. Some 41 percent of students said they engaged in "binge" drinking, just below the national average of 44 percent. In the first two months of the 2000 school year—Duke's seventy-fifth anniversary—eighteen students were admitted to the emergency room with alcohol-related problems, thirteen of whom were freshmen. Despite the drinking age being twenty-one, some 74 percent of "drinking violations" at Duke in 1999 were committed by freshmen. Drunk-driving incidents on campus were five times higher in 1999 than the year before. Clack told the *Chronicle* he faced each weekend "with a certain amount of dread."

Part of the reason drinking remained a problem—not that anyone had any delusions that it could be eliminated—was that the university continued to send "mixed messages" and "conflicting signals" to students. "That which is prohibited on East Campus is condoned on West," Willimon wrote. "We say we do not want underage drinking, but we distribute cups to [freshmen] before basketball games, knowing that they are engaging in underage drinking." There still were parties in dormitories—where obviously students under twenty-one were drinking—with few repercussions. "The students who abuse alcohol really feel that they can get away with anything," one resident adviser told Willimon. "I understand the amnesty provision"—where, incredibly, students admitted to the emergency room with alcohol sickness were not disciplined—"but it's a bit strange that if you get sort of drunk, you can be punished. But if you get dead, dangerously drunk, you will receive amnesty." An administrator observed that the alcohol rules made sense in the abstract but were "a farce in their application."

He noted that one engineering professor encouraged his freshmen students to attend a keg party. "Come meet other engineers and get wasted," he told them.

"But we're freshmen," a student replied. "We can't drink."

"Don't most of you have fake IDs?" he wondered.

One late Saturday night in September 2000, two student affairs deans were wandering the campus. "Students were traveling from party to party carrying cups, open cans, and bottles of beverages," they reported. "We noted cans and broken bottles on the ground. The stench of spilled beer (and in some locations urine) . . . a drug exchange (marijuana) which was observed . . . we observed intoxicated students plus a drinking game in a room. . . . Overall we are very concerned about the environment we observed on West Campus: specifically, the number of students engaging in high-risk behavior; the safety hazards from large numbers of students in areas not designated to accommodate them; the level of intoxication; and the lack of any controls . . ."

However, Willimon noted that some progress had been made: there were now "breakage fees" and a required cleanup by students of excessive messes following parties (which used to be left for the predominantly black janitor crews). Compared to his 1993 survey, there were "fewer parties, an absence of kegs, and less visible rowdiness," he wrote. "The amount and availability of alcohol have been reduced." He observed, though, that there seemed to be a corresponding increase in off-campus parties, particularly in rented homes off East Campus. "I am uncertain whether or not this is a positive development," he continued. "On the one hand I find the off-campus party locations, such as the restaurants that students rent after hours, to be attractive and safe places for parties, far better than the grim, dangerously overcrowded common rooms. On the other hand, I share some students' concerns that we are simply watching as our problems move 'out of sight and out of mind' as more parties move off campus."

The changes at Duke in eight years—some obvious, some hard to discern—led many around the campus to lament the loss of the fun "Old Duke" and the emergence of the staid "New Duke": politically correct, dry, and "ridden with rules." Students, Willimon found, thought the school's administration was "taking them somewhere new that they do not want to go, recreating Duke into the image of some college in the Northeast that Duke is not." But the changes on campus made in reaction to his 1993 report came, in large part, in response to demands from the students themselves. "The 'we work hard, we play hard' mentality, so highly touted by some, meant a limited, alcohol-and-fraternity-dominated social scene to others, particularly many women and ethnic minority students," Willimon wrote. "Increasing numbers of our students wanted changes to be made." He sensed a change of sentiment generally in the incoming class of 2004, credit for which he rightly gave to the admissions office, which has the ability to annually remake the character of the campus. The new class seemed "less pessimistic about their prospects after Duke," he wrote, "less cynical about the system, not overly troubled by the future, though somewhat disengaged from their world"—this was a year before September 11—"at times a bit too pleased by the status quo. Whoever they are, they are different from their predecessors."

Willimon then delivered his sermon. "Our great purpose is not the accumulation of knowledge but erudition," he wrote. "We are called as a university to the task of developing people, of increasing the wisdom of a new generation, of pioneering those new forms of community for which our society yearns. The university is more than a place where people get their needs met or have their desires fulfilled. We are also a community that cultivates needs worth having and that transforms our desires. We were meant to be a locus for transformation, a privileged place where talented young adults become considerably more interesting human beings than they would have been if they had been left to their own devices. . . . A university as good as Duke aspires to be must always be attacking itself, must be forever criticizing itself because it is that place where one generation tells another what it knows in order that the next generation may create a better world than the one in which we presently live. . . . The issue is, how can Duke be true to its originating purpose of leadership in undergraduate residential, liberal education? Let Duke be Duke, let the

New Duke be the best of the Old Duke: young, brash, outrageously ambitious, bold to lead, forever renewing, ceaselessly committed to the high vocation that is given to us in our time and place."

Willimon's elegant articulation of the dynamic changes and shifting priorities then facing Duke—and many other colleges and universities across the country—was precisely what Wood was, in his own way, describing in his prescient letter in June 2004 to Thompson, where he feared that "the play-hard cohort was poisoning the campus culture" at Duke, and that "lacrosse players were at the heart of the problem."

Needless to say, Brodhead's appointment as Duke's president was the logical continuation of the university's ambition to be counted prominently among the nation's top schools. But the idea that the fastidious Brodhead, in his first two years as a university president, would have to serve as a bit player in the national drama about whether or not Mike Krzyzewski would stay at Duke and then confront allegations that three members of the lacrosse team had sodomized, strangled, and raped a black stripper inside their home could not have been further away from his intellectual bent and more foreign to his finely honed character. Brodhead would face a challenge unlike nearly any he had faced before in his life.

Born in Dayton, Ohio, in April 1947, Brodhead moved with his family to Fairfield, Connecticut, in 1953 and attended public schools. At age thirteen, he enrolled at Phillips Academy in Andover, Massachusetts, one of the world's most elite and prestigious private high schools. One of his classmates was George W. Bush. At Andover, Brodhead was "studious, outgoing, with a wonderful wit and sense of humor," remembered Jock Reynolds, who was in the class of 1963. "And kind—as long as I've known Dick, he's been a kind and considerate person. He never was the sort of person who wielded his considerable intellect and academic accomplishments over other people." After graduating from Andover in 1964, Brodhead was off to Yale, where he stayed for the next forty years.

As a Yale freshman, Brodhead was accepted into the highly selective "Directed Studies" program, an interdisciplinary study of Western civilization featuring three yearlong courses—literature, philosophy, and historical and political thought—in which students read the "central texts of the Western tradition" from antiquity to the twentieth century. In his sophomore year, Brodhead took a class on American literature from the legendary professor Richard Warrington Baldwin Lewis, a decision that influenced Brodhead to pursue English as his major course of study. He also studied with Harold Bloom. But he had to get a job to help him afford the Yale tuition, since that year his father lost his job. From then on, Brodhead worked in New Haven to help defray the cost of his education, which Yale also supported with a scholarship. "I had some sense of what it's like to have your education be able to continue because your university has a commitment to you that picks up where your family has a lapse," he said many years later.

Toward the end of his junior year, Brodhead was one of sixteen students tapped to join the Manuscript Society—one of Yale's secret societies—this one being dedicated to finding those particularly gifted intellectuals for membership. (Other members of Manuscript include Anderson Cooper, David Gergen, and Jodie Foster.) George W. Bush, who, like Brodhead, went from Andover to Yale, once recalled about his classmate, "I remember him as a young scholar, a bright lad, a hard worker. We both put a lot of time in at the Sterling Library, in the reading room, where they have those big leather couches. We had a mutual understanding—Dick wouldn't read aloud, and I wouldn't snore." In 1968, Brodhead graduated summa cum laude from Yale, with a degree in English with "exceptional distinction." By then, he said, he had developed "a strong sense of calling" to become a university professor.

That fall, while many of his brethren were either off to war or protesting against it, Brodhead enrolled in Yale's PhD program in English. This was a difficult time for Brodhead, whose intellectual petri dish narrowed considerably as a graduate student, much to his frustration. "I would say that my first two months in graduate school were the hardest time in my life," he once told a fourth-year PhD student at Duke. "In the US, undergraduate school gives you a whole life. There is intellectual life, social life, plenty of extracurricular activities, all those things. And then when I went to graduate school, all of a sudden, I had only one subject to study, and only one dimension of my life. I found that transition hard. . . . In your undergraduate days, it can be enough just to be a very good student. But when I went to graduate school, being a good student was not enough anymore. You had to make personal contributions to your field, and to have ideas of your own. It was a period of strain before I began to feel mental independence." He decided to become an "Americanist," and studied the novels of American writers. "English literature, and especially poetry, was in the ascendan[cy], so the choice of American and fiction was, as one might say, a minor personal rebellion," he explained.

Somehow, in the middle of studying for and writing his dissertation, "Polysensuum: Hawthorne, Melville, and the Form of the Novel," Brodhead also managed to get a master's degree in philosophy from Yale in 1970. That was the same year he met and married Cindy Degnan, who had grown up in Lockport, New York, and attended Syracuse University. They became acquainted when Degnan also enrolled in the English PhD program at Yale. She found him quirky and brilliant. She soon fell in love with him and his Volkswagen Bug convertible.

Brodhead wrote his 462-page dissertation in near-record time. By 1972, doctorate in hand, Brodhead began climbing the rungs of the Yale academic ladder. For his first five years at Yale, he was an assistant professor of English. The Brodheads spent 1977 in England on sabbatical. When they returned to New Haven, Brodhead was promoted to be an associate professor of English. In 1979, the Yale chapter of Phi Beta Kappa named Brodhead the recipient of the William Clyde DeVane Medal for Outstanding Scholarship and Teaching, one of its highest honors.

Although Brodhead won tenure in 1980, he had been worried he might not, given Yale's predilection for preferring scholars educated elsewhere. He had offers from other schools. Indeed, with one in hand he went to see Howard Lamar, then the dean of Yale College. "We had a very frank talk," Lamar recalled. "And I said that he must ride this one out. In fact, I believe I said, 'One day you will be chairman of the English department,' which expressed my own faith that he was going to get tenure and promotion. Well, he listened to that, I guess, because he stayed. And just within two years or so after that, he was on his way." In response to a Valentine's Day wish by one student that she could be late for Brodhead's class, the *Yale Daily News* took up his defense in February 1980 by urging Yale to give him tenure. "If the University continues to effectively ignore teaching ability as a criteria for tenure, Brodhead probably won't be around to be late for." (A few months later, the paper wondered whether he would still be around in the fall.) "Brodhead's reading list is almost as entertaining as his lectures, both of which are top-notch," the paper wrote.

In April 1980, he was one of the 120 or so Yale faculty members who signed a public letter against the reinstatement of the draft, then under consideration by President Jimmy Carter. "Selective service is selective servitude," was one line of the letter. "It capitalizes on existing social inequities by disproportionately conscripting minorities and the poor." He also participated in the student sit-ins against the draft. These protests did not hinder his rise at Yale. After gaining tenure, he wasted little time before he started publicly criticizing Yale's tenure process for internal candidates. Brodhead was only the third junior faculty member in the English department to have gotten tenure since 1969. "I can think of maybe one other university that has . . . so dismal a record at promoting people from the inside," he said in April 1981. Brodhead did become a full professor, but not until 1985.

During the summers of many of these years, he taught aspiring teachers at the Bread Loaf School of English in Middlebury, Vermont. "I was very happy," he said. In 1990, he became the Bird White Housum Professor of English at Yale, a chair he held for five years before being named the A. Bartlett Giamatti Professor of English, in honor of the late president of Yale. Teaching was always his first love. In 1991, Brodhead oversaw an external review of Duke's English department when it was "roiled by internal conflict," thanks in large part to the unconventional thinking of Professor Stanley Fish, who arrived at Duke with great fanfare in 1986 along with his "outsized ego, a Jaguar, and postmodernism."

During his years as an English professor at Yale, Brodhead wrote or edited more than a dozen books on Nathaniel Hawthorne, Herman Melville, Charles W. Chesnutt, William Faulkner, Harriet Beecher Stowe, Louisa May Alcott, Richard Wright, and Eudora Welty. The University of Chicago Press published his PhD thesis in 1976. Ten years later, the Oxford University Press published Brodhead's *The School of Hawthorne*, which his publisher described as "a detailed account of Hawthorne's life in American letters, showing how authors as various as Melville, Howells, James, and Faulkner have learned from Hawthorne's model while at the same time changing the terms in which he has been read." The book was dense and highly intellectual. In 1993, the University of Chicago Press published Brodhead's *Culture of Letters: Scenes of Reading and Writing in Nineteenth-Century America*.

Brodhead got his second whiff of North Carolina during the early 1990s when he took on the task of editing, for Duke University Press, the journals of Charles Chesnutt, a celebrated writer who, although born in Cleveland in 1858, worked to "free persons of color" from Fayetteville, North Carolina. After the Civil War, the Chesnutts returned to Fayetteville, where Charles's parents ran a grocery store, which later failed. Although Chesnutt described himself as "seven-eighths white"—and certainly physically appeared to be—he identified as black and became one of the most highly regarded early chroniclers of the experience of blacks in America in the period after the Civil War and before the Roaring Twenties, a period, according to Brodhead, that Chesnutt himself called "Post-bellum, Pre-Harlem."

Chesnutt's journal, Brodhead realized, "gives the most comprehensive record we have of the educational resources that became available to African-Americans in the wake of Emancipation." Chesnutt not only "taught himself Latin, French, and German in his spare time" but also, at age twenty-two, was named the head of a state-funded school to train future teachers. "But," Brodhead continued, "while Chesnutt's journal documents an unsurpassable love of learning, it also chronicles the pains of inequality. When Chesnutt eventually met someone who could listen to him read Latin verse aloud and confirm that he had got the pronunciation right, it was a moment of swelling pride for this self-taught prodigy but also of stinging hurt, another reminder of everything he had been denied. Chesnutt writes: 'It was like discharging the matter from an old sore.'"

Brodhead edited Chesnutt's revealing and introspective journals—in which, for instance, he shared the depths of the ongoing prejudice against blacks, writing that he had no white friends, and that "any man who feels himself too good to sit at table with me" could not be considered his friend. He also edited and wrote the introduction to what he termed the "unexpurgated" version of Chesnutt's *The Conjure Woman and Other Conjure Tales*, first published in 1899 to great acclaim.

Nearly a century after its initial publication, Brodhead determined *Conjure Woman* to be a book that "has increasingly been recognized as a literary creation of remarkable interest and power" that "has a place in the line of distinguished short-story collections that runs from Washington Irving's *Sketch Book* and Nathaniel Hawthorne's *Mosses from an Old Manse* to many more modern instances, making its own ingenious contribution to a well-established formal tradition." He observed that *Conjure Woman* presented "a fiction of black folk life," rich in dialect and "cool mastery" of "this form's conventions." But Brodhead also wrote about how struck he was by the way the book had been originally conceived and published—a travesty of late nineteenth-century literary biases that he himself sought to rectify in the 1993 publication: "What we have in *The Conjure Woman* is a work partly proposed by an author but also in significant part imagined by a publisher, then written by the author to the publisher's specifications," he wrote. The publisher then "chose the volume's contents from the batch of tales Chesnutt submitted."

Brodhead reassembled the stories chosen by the publisher to be included in the original publication of *The Conjure Woman* with those Chesnutt had first submitted for publication. Finally together again, the new edition, Brodhead wrote, "gives an extraordinarily vivid picture of the conditions that enabled and restricted African-American literary aspiration in late nineteenth-century America—the conditions Chesnutt worked through, in and against."

Brodhead's writing is lucid, witty, tight, and highly informed by his extensive knowledge of late nineteenth-century American novelists who had a far easier time being published—and accepted—than did Chesnutt. One gets the sense that Brodhead reveled in the opportunity to reassemble the various pieces of *The Conjure Woman* into an entirely new and complete work of fiction that provided readers for the first time with a full picture of what Chesnutt was thinking. It's as if Brodhead were a literary archaeologist sharing his findings with the world. "Whatever version of these stories we end up preferring," he concluded, "there will be no escaping the fact that it is a collaborative product—the result of the cooperation and competing pressures brought to bear by the author, his first publisher and his later readers, ourselves included. But this outcome is, in the spirit of *The Conjure Woman*, a work that suggests that cultural events always have more than one party to them and unfold through the actions of competing interests."

In 1988, Brodhead was named chair of the Yale English department, a position he held for five years. In 1993, at age forty-five, Brodhead was again promoted, this time to the hugely prestigious position of dean of Yale College, a post he held for the next eleven years after being reappointed two more times. He was only the second dean of the college in the previous fifty years to have graduated from Yale. The Yale faculty seemed utterly infatuated with him. "It grows increasingly clear that he will enter the history books as one of the legendary deans of Yale College," one faculty member wrote to Richard Levin, Yale's president. "His performance is brilliant. Students love him, the faculty trust[s] him, the alumni are in awe of him. He represents the College and the University as we wish they could always be represented . . ." Added another, Brodhead "is to articulation what Michael Jordan was to basketball, and can handle difficult situations with dignity, grace, and good judgment." Thomas T. Whitaker, a colleague of Brodhead's in the English department, described him as a man with "an unusual combination of educational vision, eloquence, and tact—qualities that are especially important at this moment in Yale's history."

Brodhead once said he never aspired to be an administrator. "It never occurred to me . . . ," he explained. "I knew some people did those jobs, but I just never thought about it, and I didn't know why they would want to do that." He wrote that being part of a university's administration was "a temporary crossing over from the realm of education proper into the enabling realm of arrangement." But with these appointments, a new world of learning opened to him. "I learned about different disciplines," he said. "I learned about the economics of universities. I learned about admissions policy and its challenges, and a hundred other aspects of running a university. I used to have a passive vision of administrative work: someone has to do the 'dirty work'! But when I became an administrator, I found it was a powerful source of education. In American universities, as long as you are in a single department or laboratory, it is very hard to get a sense of how the whole organization works. What the challenge is about."

Not surprisingly, during Brodhead's eleven years as dean of Yale College, he managed to offend some people. Two incidents during his tenure stand out for giving plenty of ammunition to his critics. The first, in 1994, involved his steadfast opposition to GESO, the Graduate Employees and Students Organization, and its efforts to unionize the hundreds of graduate students at Yale who taught the university's undergraduates for nearly minimum wage. Some had argued that Yale deliberately relied on graduate students—and paid them poorly—in order to rationalize the status quo system under which tenured professors were very well compensated. GESO's idea was to organize the graduate students in order to force the university to pay them more. Brodhead, as dean, was naturally opposed to the unionization effort, supposedly because at Yale, GESO was affiliated with another union, the Hotel Employees and Restaurant Employees International Union, and the administration did not want to negotiate topics such as class size or teacher pay with hotel and restaurant employees. (Apparently, Yale would have been willing to do so with another unaffiliated union.)

One of GESO's leaders at Yale had been one of Brodhead's graduate students. In February 1994, she was one of four signatories of a letter to Perry Bass, a wealthy Yale alumnus, informing him that the tutors for the writing class Daily Themes, underwritten by the Bass family, had been "downsized"—reduced in number to ten from twenty—while the student enrollment had been cut to seventy-five from one hundred. What's more, they wrote, "tutors now teach seven students for the same pay that last year's Graduate School Dean (former Yale President Richard Levin) recommended for teaching *four* students. All this to save approximately $20,000 per year."

In July 1995, Brodhead wrote a letter of "recommendation" about the graduate student for her "dossier" in which he was critical of her and her union-organizing activities. At first, he praised the papers she had written for him as a student, but when it came to her involvement with GESO, he was far less satisfied. She was "a poor listener on the subject" of the union organizing and "has on at least one occasion . . . shown poor judgment in the choice of means." He concluded that the graduate student and GESO leader "will bring civic intelligence and concern about communal life to her future job." Cary Nelson, a professor of English at the University of Illinois and an outspoken activist for higher education reform, wrote in his 1997 book *Manifesto of a Tenured Radical* that Brodhead's letter damned the student with faint praise and would surely make it more difficult for her to get hired. "She is bright but ruthless," Nelson wrote of the message he felt Brodhead's letter conveyed, "and will not listen to reason when her political beliefs and 'concern about communal life' are at issue."

Nelson had met the student, too, when he spoke up in support of GESO at a forum at Yale in 1994. He found her "witty" and "reflective." He did not recognize the woman Brodhead had portrayed. "But perhaps Brodhead can no longer see her that way," he continued. "A genial fellow who has functioned well within Yale's paternalistic hierarchy, his seminars are popular and he has helped many students with their dissertations over the years. But the combination of his deanship and the union's affront to Yale's pecking order have been too much for him." Brodhead's letter criticized the student for contacting Perry Bass—although she did not write the letter and was merely one of its signatories—and the cumulative effect of Brodhead's assessment, according to Nelson, "would be to eliminate her from consideration from almost any job for which she applied." Nelson found Brodhead's criticism of the letter written to Bass and the alumni hard to stomach. "Why anyone would get exercised about either of these letters is hard to guess," he wrote. "They are certainly not rabble-rousing; they seem a responsible effort to get donors and alumni involved in supporting full funding for 'Daily Themes,' nothing more. They make no threats and ask no threats of their addressees."

The second incident that gave Brodhead's critics pause was his handling of a tragedy that struck Yale on the evening of December 4, 1998. That night, senior Suzanne Jovin was stabbed and left to die in a prosperous New Haven neighborhood, exactly one mile from the center of the Yale campus. To many at Yale, the murder of Jovin evoked the painful memory of another murder, some seven years before, of Christian Prince, a nineteen-year-old freshman athlete on the varsity lacrosse team and a fourth-generation Yalie, as he was walking home from a local bar. James Fleming, then seventeen, a New Haven native, allegedly shot Prince in the heart shortly after he robbed Prince of his wallet, containing $46.

The Jovin case seemed like a replay of the Prince murder, only even more complex. There was no obvious suspect, and the DNA evidence found on Jovin's body, under her fingernails from the struggle, was not much help in finding one. Within a few days of the murder, the local media publicly fingered James Van de Velde, an adjunct political science professor and Jovin's senior thesis adviser, as the police department's leading suspect. There was apparently no forensic evidence linking Van de Velde to the crime (or anyone else, for that matter), and his apartment was a half mile from the crime scene. The police spoke with Van de Velde but did not take him up on his offer to allow them to search his apartment, take a DNA sample from him, or give him a polygraph test. The police dusted his Jeep for fingerprints but found none belonging to Jovan. Later tests would show that Van de Velde's DNA was not found under Jovin's fingernails.

After the New Haven police named Van de Velde as being "among a pool of suspects" and the only one mentioned by name, Brodhead decided to cancel Van de Velde's spring lecture class. "The cancellation of the course doesn't follow from a judgment or a prejudgment of his hypothetical involvement in the Jovin case," Brodhead said at the time. At the end of the academic year, Brodhead allowed Van de Velde's contract with the university to lapse—even though his supporters said he was consistently one of the most admired and well-reviewed teachers—and he left Yale shortly thereafter. "The situation has been so extraordinarily perplexing," Brodhead told *Vanity Fair* in August 1999. "Someone has been murdered; no one knows who did it months after the fact. Allegations have been put in motion. . . . There is a confirmation by the police that he is a suspect, but then there is no arrest."

The Jovin murder remains unresolved. After Brodhead did not renew his contract at Yale in 1999, as a result of the negative publicity surrounding his alleged involvement in the Jovin murder—it certainly would have been problematic to have a murder suspect teaching at the university—Van de Velde was also forced out of a journalism program he was enrolled in at Quinnipiac University. In 2001, he sued Quinnipiac; three years later, he settled the lawsuit for $80,000. Also in 2001, he sued the New Haven Police Department for violating his civil rights relating to the Jovin case. In 2003, he added Yale as a defendant, including both Levin and Brodhead. Although the lawsuit against the defendants was dismissed in March 2004, the same federal judge reinstated the lawsuit on December 11, 2007. Needless to say, Van de Velde's academic career was over. He became a counterterrorism expert at Booz Allen Hamilton, the consulting firm, in Washington.

In June 2013, Van de Velde settled his lawsuit against Yale and the New Haven police. "The case is another example of the awful damage that can occur when authorities make a rush to judgment and ignore the facts," his lawyer said. "There was zero evidence connecting him with the crime. We brought this lawsuit to vindicate his good name, and the settlement of this lawsuit gives him the vindication he deserves."

Brodhead got much better marks for his response to another tragedy at Yale, this one involving the January 2003 deaths of a group of four fraternity brothers driving back to New Haven from New York City on Interstate 95 North. The four brothers, plus another five students, were driving together in an SUV on the slick, icy road during the early morning of January 17 when, around 5:20 a.m., the SUV smashed into a tractor-trailer truck that had jackknifed. All four of the students killed were members of the Delta Kappa Epsilon fraternity and had been in New York for a fraternity event. A National Transportation Safety Board investigation determined that icy road conditions, among other problems, helped cause the crash. Alcohol was said not to be a factor. All four of the victims were athletes: one was on the Yale football team, two were on the Yale baseball team, and one was a former varsity lacrosse player at Hotchkiss and played golf, squash, and paddle tennis at Yale.

On the evening after the tragedy, Brodhead organized a vigil for grieving students at the Payne Whitney gym on campus. Years later, those in attendance still recalled Brodhead's comments that night. "He brought the undergraduates together in the gym, and he just looked at them and said, 'In all my years at Yale, this is the darkest day I can remember,'" recalled Peter Salovey, who replaced Brodhead as dean of Yale College. "It was clear that he was feeling much of what they were feeling. And it was comforting to the students to see that this was a difficult situation for their dean, that he was trying to do the best he could, and that they should, too. He was reaching out to other people, and they should reach out, too."

Brodhead also seemed to win praise for his comprehensive review of the Yale undergraduate curriculum, completed in April 2003 after a sixteen-month study. He led the committee working to revise the curriculum and wrote the final report, which was the first time since 1972 that Yale had evaluated what and how it teaches its undergraduates. While the recommendations that Brodhead and his colleagues made were fairly sweeping—for instance, increasing the number of faculty at Yale, improving the science and arts literacy of Yale undergraduates, and widening Yale's interactions globally—there was no mistaking Brodhead's elegant prose in defense of a liberal arts education. "Liberal arts education aims to train a broadly based, highly disciplined intelligence without specifying in advance what that intelligence will be used for," he wrote.

"In many parts of the world, a student's entry into higher education coincides with the choice of a field or profession, and the function of education is to provide training for this profession.

"A liberal arts approach differs from that model in at least three ways," he continued. "First, it regards college as a phase of exploration, a place for the exercise of curiosity and the discovery of new interests and abilities, not the development of interests fully determined in advance. Second, though it permits (even requires) a measure of focus, liberal arts education aims at a significant breadth of preparation, storing the mind with various knowledge and training it in various modes of inquiry rather than building strength in one form alone. Third and most fundamentally, liberal arts education does not aim to train a student in the particulars of a given career. Instead its goal is to develop deep skills that people can bring to bear in whatever work they eventually choose." To Susan Hockfield, Yale's provost at the time (and later the president of MIT), Brodhead's herding of the cats that resulted in his eighty-six-page *Report on Yale College Education* was "just remarkable" and an example of "being able to persuade people to go in a direction they might not have seen."

Revamping the undergraduate curriculum would be Brodhead's lasting legacy to Yale. On the morning of December 12, 2003, the Yale community woke up to the news, sent via e-mail, that after forty years Brodhead would be leaving Yale for Duke, to become the school's ninth president. Since July 2003, when Duke president Nan Keohane announced she was retiring, a nineteen-member committee—comprising faculty, students, and alumni—had been searching for a new president. Robert Steel, a Durham native and a 1973 Duke graduate, was both vice chairman of the university's board of trustees and chairman of the search committee. The committee considered two hundred candidates and winnowed that list down to ten people whom it chose to interview. Steel said Brodhead stood out, even on the short list. "You didn't have to be Dick Tracy to find Dick Brodhead," Steel explained. Steel, then a senior partner at Goldman Sachs with an impressive Rolodex, heard about Brodhead from a member of the Duke community whose daughter Brodhead had taught at Yale.

Steel and the committee vice chair, Sara Beale, had their first meeting with Brodhead at a small restaurant off Interstate 95 in Connecticut. "Steel knew something about the Ivy League . . . and he believed that the rich and venerable old schools were a bit sclerotic," Peter Boyer wrote in the *New Yorker* years later. "Duke was young and willing to take risks, and, as Steel would say, 'We're in a hurry.'" At the restaurant, Steel, Beale, and Brodhead discussed ways in which Duke and Yale were similar—their size, their balance between teaching and research, and their professional schools—and how Duke and Yale were very different. Whereas, like the rest of the Ivy League, Yale had long before abandoned any hope of competing on a national scale in athletics, Duke had no intention of giving up that ambition, and without compromising academic standards to do so. "It is an audacious proposition—only two other private institutions, Stanford and Northwestern, even try it—and the undertaking alone attests to Duke's vigor and its idea of itself," Boyer wrote. "Duke's basketball coach, Mike Krzyzewski . . . [who] has won three national championships with smart, disciplined players, exemplified the ideal. 'Is that something you want to be part of?' Steel asked."

Brodhead was the unanimous choice of the Duke board of trustees. According to Cindy Brodhead, her husband could have left Yale many times previously but never considered a move seriously until the Duke offer came around. While Yale was stunned by his departure, it could not have been totally unexpected. After all, both he and Levin were about the same age and the chance of Brodhead succeeding Levin at Yale was minimal. Still, it rankled. Observed one Yale undergrad: "It was like Dean Brodhead was married to Yale—and now we learn that he's leaving us for someone younger and more athletic."

At the morning press conference at Duke announcing his appointment, held in the elegant Rare Book Room in Duke's Perkins Library, Brodhead emphasized how unique an opportunity he had been offered. "I have had other tempting invitations in the past to consider leaving Yale but I have always declined," he said. "Duke is a special place, however, and its allure in the end was overwhelming. I know I'm facing an immense amount of new learning and challenge, but I expect that to be a pleasure as well. I am looking forward to becoming both a Blue Devil and a part of the vibrant Durham community." He said he was not only captivated by the school's reputation but also by its potential as a relatively young university with a future that could still be shaped. "I am tremendously excited to join a university that has already established itself in the top rank of institutions, yet is still so up-and-coming," he said. "Duke is a school with a taste for excellence, the energy and optimism to aspire to it, the dynamism and lightness of foot to actually make required changes, and the ability to avoid complacency in the face of accomplishment."

Top Duke officials expressed their unqualified support for Brodhead and hoped he would take the school to the next level. "Dick is a scholar with a deep commitment to undergraduate and graduate education, a proven and effective administrator and fund-raiser who understands how research universities work, and an eloquent spokesman about the central role of higher education in American life," said Peter Nicholas, the chairman of Duke's board of trustees and a billionaire businessman. "Duke's trustees are confident that the qualities that have led Dick Brodhead to be so revered in New Haven will also serve him well as our next president."

The consensus seemed to be that in her successful eleven-year tenure at Duke, Keohane had bequeathed Brodhead a school that had never been in better shape. She had just finished a multibillion-dollar fund-raising campaign that had increased the school's endowment to $2.5 billion from the less than $700 million it had been when she took over in 1993. She also oversaw the creation of Building on Excellence, Duke's version of Brodhead's revamp of Yale's undergraduate curriculum, which set out the university's plan for the future as well as an ambitious building program involving the construction of forty new buildings on campus. Keohane also made significant changes to Duke's undergraduate life by moving incoming freshman to a campus of their own and by deemphasizing, to the extent it was possible, the outsized influence of the fraternities and sororities on Duke's social life. The expectation was that Brodhead would have to focus on the evolving relationship between Duke's medical center and the university's health system as well as on how a proposed plan to revamp the school's so-called central campus—a hodge-podge of unimpressive student housing—would be integrated into Duke's West and East Campuses.

Keohane told the *Times* she hoped Brodhead would also elevate in importance the way women were treated at Duke. She worried that women still felt the need to primp for men and were not yet fully comfortable standing up for themselves as equal members of the Duke ecosystem—or so argued a report, published in September 2003, about the experience of women at the university as undergraduates, graduates, alumnae, employees, and even as members of the board of trustees. By and large, the report touched on many of the issues women face across America: making sure they have the same opportunities for equal pay and advancement as men, making sure that their efforts to balance family life and work life are not penalized, making sure they are not discriminated against because of their gender or sexual orientation, and that they are not the focus of predatory sexual behavior. "We were trying to figure out what it's like to be a woman at Duke," Keohane told the *New York Times* about the yearlong study.

But the headlines the report garnered, including those in the *Times* and other national media, centered on the fairly shocking—by early twenty-first-century American standards at one of the nation's best universities, anyway—description of the way many undergraduate women at Duke felt they had to behave. "Undergraduates described a social environment characterized by what one sophomore called 'effortless perfection': the expectation that one would be smart, accomplished, fit, beautiful, and popular, and that all this would happen without visible effort," the report claimed, noting that the university's frat culture reinforced these feelings. "This environment enforces fairly stringent norms on undergraduate women, who feel pressure to wear fashionable (and often impractical) clothes and shoes, to diet and exercise excessively and to hide their intelligence in order to succeed with their male peers. Being 'cute' trumps being smart for women in the social environment." Quite an indictment, in 2003, of one of the nation's top schools. The report noted that some men felt similar pressures but were more easily able to dismiss them and act the way they wanted to act.

There was plenty of reaction to the report around campus. Concerned about the feeling of "effortless perfection," on November 20 a group of students created Comfort Day, where students were encouraged to dress "for comfort, not fashion," followed by a panel discussion of "work/life balance" issues. Another group of students started a "speed dating" service on campus to combat the perceived lack of dating opportunities at Duke. Mary Adkins, a Duke senior, directed a play, *All of the Above*, a series of monologues written and performed by Duke women "ruminating on body, identity, and self." Of course, the *Chronicle* was filled with stories, op-eds, editorials, and letters about the report and the issues raised by it. But not much changed as a result.

Even though Brodhead was not to start officially at Duke until July 1, he began his reeducation almost immediately upon being selected in December. In January 2004, he commuted regularly between New Haven and Durham, hoping to absorb as much as he could, as quickly as he could, about the school. He made the trip three days a week. He oversaw the appointment of new senior-level administrators and began to focus on one of his favorite topics: how to improve undergraduate education at the school and make the cost of it affordable to every student. "I have been pretty deeply enmeshed in the business of my new home, certainly since late February," Brodhead explained. "In truth, this thing I went through in the last few months was called a transition, and that's exactly what it was. And that's to say that I was an outsider at the beginning who didn't know very many people here, and I had a lot to learn about every aspect of Duke. People took the time and trouble to help me to an amazing extent and by March I'd say that I began to know quite a number of people here more than a little."

Then, by July, he dealt with the crisis involving Krzyzewski, narrowly avoiding disaster in the process. By the middle of September, the time had come for Brodhead to deliver his inaugural address at the Duke Chapel, in front of a crowd estimated at 1,500 people. It was classic Brodhead: witty, literate, self-deprecating, and inspiring. But he was careful to stay away from two of the most sensitive topics circulating around the Duke campus: the issues of gender inequality raised a year earlier by the Women's Initiative report and, of course, the schooling Krzyzewski had delivered to him about the power structure at the university. Instead, Brodhead used soaring rhetoric to deliver a speech of impressive oratory. He likened the decision to carve Duke's impressive West Campus from what had been "thick, unbroken woods" in the 1920s to Thomas Sutpen in William Faulkner's classic *Absolom! Absolom!*, who, according to Brodhead, wrested "his baronial estate from the uncleared forests and swamps of northern Mississippi." According to Faulkner, Sutpen set to "dragging house and formal gardens out of the soundless Nothing and clapping them down like cards upon a table, the *Be Sutpen's Hundred* like the oldtime *Be light*." (Brodhead acknowledged the analogy was slightly flawed in that the Duke family had considerable help building the university; Sutpen worked alone.)

He spoke about new interdisciplinary initiatives, a new physical building program "surpassed only by that of the 1920s and 1930s" when the bulk of the school was built, and the need to continue building a world-class faculty of "scholar-teacher[s]" who "enliven inquiry in their field but retain a sense of a larger picture, the larger questions their specially trained powers could help engage; people, too, who will keep asking new questions and engaging colleagues in flexible and opportunistic combinations to help them toward an answer."

But the thrust of his speech emphasized another of his major themes: to make sure the first-rate education that schools like Duke and Yale offer students is not reserved solely for society's elites but rather is available to all that aspire to it, regardless of an ability to pay. "It was not so long ago that schools and universities (the best not least) played a role in reinforcing received social hierarchies, assuring that to those who had, much was given, while denying others the best means to advancement, a first-class education," he said. "The namesakes of this school were far more enlightened than many of their time, but Duke remained racially segregated until the 1960s, and the first African-American undergraduates and medical students at Duke (I've met members of both groups) are people my exact age. (I myself attended a college that excluded women until 1969.) Through the work of men and women, many of them still alive, the high places of American education have been reconstructed from sites of exclusion and inequality into scenes of access and opportunity, but it's not time to stop that labor now.

"Nowadays the danger is that colleges and universities will exclude not in the crude old-fashioned way, by category of social identity, but more invisibly, by cost," Brodhead continued. "The figure for tuition, room, and board for an undergraduate at Duke approaches $40,000 a year. Mention of this figure provokes a predictable spasm of outrage from the American public, but for all the polemics that may soon be mounted on the issue, the problem of private college cost is not trivially easy. In the last generation and indeed in the last decade, America's selective colleges have offered a more and more super-enriched experience to students, and every component—state-of-the-art labs, the most up-to-date information technology, instruction in more and more foreign languages, the widest array of extracurricular activities—comes at considerable expense. But the problem can't be solved by simple-minded cutting. Rich or poor, the students a school like Duke wants would never be attracted to a no-frills university or the academic equivalent of a generic drug. Just for that reason, however, universities must do everything they can to mitigate the problem of cost for those who can't pay the full fare, and to advertise the availability of aid to those who might miss such opportunities out of ignorance."

To conclude, Brodhead referenced a Talmudic thought from a Rabbi Tarfon in the *Pirke Avot*, shared with him by Bart Giamatti, the former Yale president and the man whose named chair at Yale Brodhead had held: "You are not required to complete the work; but neither are you free to desist from it." Brodhead interpreted the rabbi's words for his audience. "What is the work?" he asked. "It can only be the great work given us as humans, making a better world wherever we happen to find ourselves with whatever tools we have at hand. Why are we not required to complete the work? Because we never could: if that work could be completed, others would have done it already and we would be spared the struggle. But why, if we cannot complete it, can we also not be allowed to give it up? Because that would be cowardly and would leave an imperfect world in even more desperate shape than it needs to be." His predecessors did not complete the work of building Duke and neither would he, Brodhead concluded: "This is the work of a great university: the struggle to expand the domain of knowledge; the struggle to share that knowledge through education; and the struggle to put that knowledge to profound human use. On this the day of our union, I know that whatever I will do will be accomplished with your partnership and help. Others have given us this great place. Let's see what we can build together."

But despite the lofty and well-meaning rhetoric about building Duke into the future, by the end of March 2006, Brodhead was far more focused on defending the university against a minute-by-minute firestorm of negative media attention as well as ferocious criticism from within the very faculty he had been hired to inspire, improve, and lead. Some of Brodhead's fiercest critics believe that his late afternoon March 30 meeting with the Duke faculty proved to be another important turning point in the lacrosse saga. For nearly two weeks, the Duke campus had been in an uproar over the allegations about what had occurred on the night of March 13 at the house off East Campus, and Brodhead was trying to calm an increasingly angry group of professors, many of whom were tenured. Although minutes of other meetings of Duke's Academic Council exist, for some unexplained reason, there is no official record of what was said, and by whom, at the impromptu meeting. There have, however, been some contemporaneous and reconstructed accounts of what occurred. According to K. C. Johnson, a professor at Brooklyn College who blogged eighteen months later about the meeting, "Brodhead appears to have been cowed by extremists within his faculty," while noting that "it's worth remembering that this case began just over a year after Larry Summers lost a vote of no-confidence in Harvard's Faculty Council" and later resigned as president. The unsubtle message from Johnson, whose 2007 book about the

lacrosse incident makes clear his disdain for Brodhead's handling of the incident, was that Brodhead had little choice but to follow the lead set by Duke's
faculty—or risk being dispatched in a way similar to how Summers had been
at Harvard.

According to Johnson, "The president urged caution and asked faculty to
wait for the facts to come in. But the assembled professors, around 10 percent
of the arts and sciences faculty, responded with vitriolic attacks against the
team. One speaker claimed that Duke, as an institution, tolerated drinking and
rape, and the lacrosse incident reflected a University problem from the top
down. Another suggested punishing the team by suspending lacrosse for three
years and then making it a club sport. A third asserted that the team embodied
the 'assertion of class privilege' by all Duke students. A fourth called on the
University to do something to help the 'victim.'"

Johnson wrote that "three professors overpowered the meeting": Houston
Baker, a professor of African-American literature, who "stated as a fact that
African-American women had been 'harmed' by the lacrosse players and
claimed that students in his mostly white, female class were terrified of the
lack of an administration response." There was Wahneema Lubiano, an associate professor of African and African-American studies, who "alleged favorit-
ism by Duke toward the team and demanded a counter-statement from Duke
denouncing the players." And there was Peter Wood. According to Johnson,
Wood said "the team was out of control, and demanded a hard line against the
athletic director, coach, and team." Wood's comments were met with "robust
applause."

On April 5, the executive committee of the Academic Council issued a
statement about the March 30 meeting in order "to convey some of the intensity and cogency of faculty responses" not only to the events on the night of
March 13 but also to "the host of related concerns about the undergraduate
experience at our school that this episode has made especially and painfully
evident." The leadership of the Academic Council wrote that the Duke faculty
expected the "members of the lacrosse team to cooperate fully with the investigation insofar as their constitutional rights against self-incrimination allow"
and urged "all" Duke officials to "exert themselves" to facilitate the ongoing
investigation. While conceding that the university should not interfere with
the police investigation, "it is the sense of the faculty that we have reached the
point where a critical mass of information and witness[es] concerning lacrosse
team behavior compels a comprehensive inquiry into the program, its culture,
its staff, and its effects on the daily lives of our students and our neighbors." To
conduct the investigation, a committee chaired by Duke law school professor
James Coleman was appointed with the expectation that the report would be
available around May 1.

The leaders of the Duke faculty were also concerned about the broader

issues raised by the March 13 incident. "Across college campuses, already volatile issues of race, gender, and class privilege intersect negatively with the powerful social reaches of sports culture and alcohol use on campus," the executive
council wrote. There was both "collective reflection" and "collective anguish"
among Duke faculty members. "The anguish comes from faculty who already
felt too familiar, by experience and by expertise, with the taxing terms and
conditions of campus life for many segments of our student body," the statement continued. "The anguish came also from faculty for whom this occasion
brought forth formerly unknown details of student experience outside the
classroom, creating a new sense of both urgency and uncertainty about how
best to fulfill the educational mission of our institution in its broadest sense."

Houston Baker, the English professor, was not content to keep the
"anguish" he experienced as a result of the incident within the confines of the
Academic Council. He also wrote a letter—titled "Awaiting the Restoration
of Confidence"—to the Duke administration and released it publicly. Clearly
upset, Baker's letter broached the worst stereotypes about race, power, and
privilege that such an alleged incident inevitably raises and unleashed a tor-
rent of invective against the university's leaders:

> The alleged crimes of rape, sodomy, and strangulation of a black woman
> at a party populated in some measure by the Duke lacrosse team report-
> edly occurred on March 13. University administrators knew about the
> incident and had begun to respond internally within twenty-four hours.
> But Duke University citizens had no public word from our university
> leadership until President Richard Brodhead called a press conference
> on March 28. Two weeks of silent protectionism left all of us vulnera-
> bly ignorant of the facts. Receiving e-mails and telephone calls of con-
> cern from friends nationally and internationally, we have been deeply
> embarrassed by the silence that seems to surround this white, male ath-
> letic team's racist assaults (by words, certainly—deeds, possibly) in our
> community.
>
> It is virtually inconceivable that representatives of Duke University's
> Athletic Department would allow its lacrosse team to engage in regu-
> lar underage drinking and out-of-control bacchanalia. It is difficult to
> imagine a competently managed corporate setting in which such behav-
> ior would be tolerated (and swept under the rug), or where such a "team"
> would survive for more than a day before being tossed out on its ears by
> security. Moreover, in a forthrightly ethical setting with an avowed com-
> mitment to life-enhancing citizenship, such a violent and irresponsible
> group would scarcely be spirited away or sheltered under the protection
> of pious sentiments such as "deplorable"—a judgment that reminds us
> of Miss Ophelia in Harriet Beecher Stowe's *Uncle Tom's Cabin* saying that

slavery was "perfectly horrible." Such timorous piety and sentimental legalism, in the opinion of the author James Baldwin, constitutes duck-and-cover cowardice of the first order.

There is no rush to judgment here about the crime—neither the violent racial epithets reported in a 911 call to Durham police, nor the harms to body and soul allegedly perpetrated by white males at 610 Buchanan Boulevard. But there is a clear urgency about the erosion of any sense of confidence or safety for the rest of us who live and work at Duke University. The lacrosse team—fifteen of whom have faced misdemeanor charges for drunken misbehavior in the past three years—may well feel they can claim innocence and sport their disgraced jerseys on campus, safe under the cover of silent whiteness. But where is the black woman whom their violence and raucous witness injured for life? Will she ever sleep well again? And when will the others assaulted by racist epithets while passing 610 Buchanan ever forget that dark moment brought on them by a group of drunken Duke boys? Young, white, violent, drunken men among us—implicitly boosted by our athletic directors and administrators—have injured lives. There is scarcely any shame more egregious than one that wraps itself in the pious sentimentalism of liberal rhetoric as though such a wrap really constituted moral and ethical action.

Duke University's higher administration has engaged in precisely such a tepid and pious legalism with respect to the disaster of recent days: the actual harm to the body, soul, mind and spirit of black women who were in the company of Duke University lacrosse team members as far as any of us know. All of Duke athletics has now been drawn into the seamy domains of Colorado football and other college and university blind-eying of male athletes, veritably given license to rape, maraud, deploy hate speech and feel proud of themselves in the bargain.

Many citizens have weighed in, and one hopes all departments, programs, and concerned members of our university community will speak out forcefully for swift and considered corrective action.

Baker could have stopped his call to arms right there. But he was not nearly finished with his filleting of the powers-that-be at Duke:

But of course, it is not exclusively our academic administration that seems to have refused decisive and meaningful action. The most deafening silence—and, quite possibly, duplicity (which is to say, improbable denial)—has marked, in fact, Duke's Department of Athletics. Where was Joe Alleva before Tuesday's press conference called by President Brodhead? Where now is the commercial charisma of Coach K, who could certainly be out front condemning Duke athletes who call people out [by] name from the precincts of university-owned housing? Why aren't such stalwarts of Duke athletics publicly and courageously addressing the horrors that have occurred in their own domain? We remember the very first day of our new President's administration—how he and Coach K shared the media dais, and the basketball magnate was praised for his bold leadership. It all seems rather like an Indonesian shadow play at this moment of crisis. All a show.

What is precipitously teetering in the balance at this point, during weeks marked by inaction and duck-and-cover from our designated leaders, is, well, confidence.

It is very difficult to feel confidence in an administration that has not addressed in meaningful ways the horrors that have occurred to actual bodies, to the Durham community of which we are an integral part, and to our sense of being members of a proactive and caring community. Rather, gag orders and trembling liberal rhetorical spins seem to be behaviors du jour from our leaders.

There can be no confidence in an administration that believes suspending a lacrosse season and removing pictures of Duke lacrosse players from a web page is a dutifully moral response to abhorrent sexual assault, verbal racial violence and drunken white male privilege loosed among us.

How many mandates concerning safe, responsible campus citizenship must be transgressed by white athletes' violent racism before our university's offices of administration, athletics, security and publicity courageously declare: enough!

How many more people of color must fall victim to violent, white, male, athletic privilege before coaches who make Chevrolet and American Express commercials, athletic directors who engage in Miss Ophelia–style "perfectly horrible" rhetoric, higher administrators who are salaried at least in part to keep us safe, and publicists who are supposed not to praise Caesar but to damn the unconscionable . . . how many? Before they demonstrate that they don't just write books, pay lip service or boast of safe citizenship . . . but actually do step up morally, intellectually and bravely to assume responsibilities of leadership for such citizenship. How many?

How soon will confidence be restored to our university as a place where minds, souls and bodies can feel safe from agents, perpetrators and abettors of white privilege, irresponsibility, debauchery and violence?

Surely the answer to the question must come in the form of immediate dismissals of those principally responsible for the horrors of this spring moment at Duke. Coaches of the lacrosse team, the team itself and its players, and any other agents who silenced or lied about the real nature of events at 610 Buchanan on the evening of March 13, 2006. A day that, not even in a clichéd sense, will, indeed, always live in infamy for this university.

Five days later, Peter Lange, the Duke provost, responded publicly to Baker's letter. He needed time to cool off after receiving it. "I cannot tell you how disappointed, saddened and appalled I was to receive this letter from you," he wrote. "A form of prejudice—one felt so often by minorities, whether they be African-American, Jewish, or other—is the act of prejudgment: to presume that one knows something 'must' have been done by or done to someone because of his or her race, religion or other characteristic. In the United States our sad racial history is laced with such incidents, only fully brought to light in the recent past and undoubtedly there are uncounted numbers of such incidents not yet, or ever to be, known."

Lange acknowledged that perhaps the administration had been too slow to respond to the incident, incurring the disappointment of some. "But we will not rush to judgment nor will we take precipitous actions which, symbolically satisfying as they may be, assuage passions but do little to remedy the deeper problems. These problems will certainly be easier, but not easy, to understand than they will be to repair. The latter will take less rhetoric and more hard work, less quick judgment and more reasoned intervention, less playing to the crowd, than entering the hearts and lives of those whose education we are charged to promote and who we must treat as an integral part of the community we wish to restore and heal. Sadly, letters like yours do little to advance our common cause."

Such public acrimony, between a prominent Duke professor and the university's provost, seemed ineluctable proof that the Duke community was coming apart at the seams.

CHAPTER SIX

Forty-six DNA Swabs

A mid all the increasingly high-pitched protests in the media and on Duke's campus about what had happened on the evening of March 13, the Durham prosecutors and the Durham police investigating the incident were increasingly worried that the DNA evidence would not prove what Mangum said had happened and that Nifong had repeated—nearly continuously—in the media for more than a week. Nifong was not yet prepared to admit that "we're fucked," as police officers had suggested to him on the same day—March 27—he received the preliminary DNA results, but he seemed to hedge his bets.

Indeed, Nifong began to shift the narrative away from the importance of the DNA evidence to the importance of Levicy's rape examination in the early morning hours of March 14. What's more, after speaking with her at length, Nifong believed Levicy and was convinced she'd be a great witness at trial. "Tara Levicy described that whole evening and everything that she'd done and all that, and everything that she said was consistent with Crystal having been sexually assaulted," he said. "I thought that she would've made a really convincing witness, just based on my conversations with her. She would have every incentive to do this by the book, and I have no reason to think that she would do otherwise. It obviously was very much in the interest of the other side to discredit her, and I'm sure that part of the discrediting would have something to do with what they would call her relative inexperience, although, as she pointed out to me during our conversation, she actually had a lot more experience in these kinds of cases than the doctor that she was assisting."

He told the *New York Times* on March 29 that he "did not necessarily expect the DNA samples" to match those from Mangum's rape kit. "I would not be surprised if condoms were used," he said. Nifong later elaborated that although as of March 29 he "had no evidence that a condom was, in fact, used," he said he believed it was likely that "since rape is not a sexual act but an act of the exercise of power, that there would have been protection involved by anybody in the position of these young men who committed an assault involving the use of their penis on a female who was unknown to them and was employed as an exotic dancer." He told Rita Cosby of MSNBC that he believed "that a rape did occur . . . [because] the victim's demeanor and the fact that when she was examined by a nurse who was trained in sexual assault, there was swelling and pain in the areas that would have been affected by the rape." Nifong's tornadic media appearances were too much for Joseph Cheshire V, a Raleigh attorney who represented cocaptain David Evans. "The fact that the DA is out in public saying these boys are guilty is just extraordinary," Cheshire said. "I am absolutely convinced, and I think that everyone in that house will testify, that nothing like these allegations happened."

But Nifong kept talking to the media. He told Dan Abrams on MSNBC, "I am convinced that there was a rape. Yes, sir. . . . There is evidence of trauma in the victim's vaginal area that was noted when she was examined by a nurse at the hospital." He told the *News & Observer*, "How does DNA exonerate you? It's either a match or there's not a match. . . . If the only thing that we ever have in this case is DNA, then we wouldn't have a case." Nifong explained that his "purpose" in making these comments was not only to try to get members of the lacrosse team to come forward voluntarily but also to quell any local unrest. "We had allegations of an assault having been made by privileged members of one race against an unprivileged member of another race," he said. "That added a dimension to what I was having to deal with that was of great concern to me because we had another racial incident that was totally unrelated to this since I had been the DA involving the burning of crosses in the Durham community. And so when this first came to me, my real concern was that because of the nature of the allegations that were involved, there might be some unrest in the Durham community over how this case was handled. That was one of the reasons that I chose to handle this case myself. At the same time, I wanted to assure the members of the Durham community that these allegations we took very seriously, that it did appear that an assault had taken place, and that we would be acting on that basis to try to identify the assailants so that they could be brought to trial. . . . This was not something that we were going to sweep under the rug."

Attorneys for the lacrosse players believe this shift in tactics by Nifong began to take shape in the early afternoon of March 29, within a day or so of getting the preliminary results that the lab tests wouldn't likely be of much help to his cause. At 1 p.m. that day, Himan and Gottlieb were summoned to a meeting at the Durham police headquarters with the police "command staff," the Duke police "command staff" as well as the Durham city manager and the police department legal adviser. "Mr. Nifong was pleased with the investigation to date," Gottlieb wrote in his notes about the meeting, "and asked for us to attempt to make contact with the individuals on the team to try to see if any of them will speak to us concerning the case." Gottlieb told Nifong he would try to reach out the players.

Attorneys for the players believe that Nifong was also present for the first of what they called a "joint command" meeting to discuss the strategy and tactics of the case with both Duke and Durham officials. As opposed to the anodyne description of the first meeting in Gottlieb's notes—he later testified there were so many of these meetings that had he kept notes, his notebooks would be filled with nothing else—the players' attorneys believed that on March 29 the joint command discussed the fact that the state lab's test of Mangum's rape kit "contradicted" her "allegation of rape" and that Mangum's various descriptions of the players along with the two "identification procedures" ruled all forty-six white players out as suspects. "They had no suspects and no evidence that a rape had occurred," the attorneys wrote.

The attorneys also believed the joint command discussed the impact that the public release of Ryan McFadyen's e-mail would have on him personally, as well as the case generally, "and would almost certainly cause his immediate and irreparable vilification." As for Mangum's story, the attorneys believed the joint command was well aware that she had made the rape allegation as she became aware in the backseat of the patrol car that she faced the threat of "involuntary commitment" due to her symptoms of a "psychotic break with reality," and then "recanted her claim" of rape when the threat of being committed went away. They also believed that the joint command knew that Mangum's "medical evidence" was not "consistent" with a "violent gang rape" and the examination of her "was abandoned," indicating that the nurse doing the examination "did not believe Mangum's claims."

At the same time, the attorneys argued, the joint command was aware of the digital photographs that showed that none of the forty-seven lacrosse players had had an opportunity to commit the alleged crime. They also believed that both Brodhead and Nifong had refused their offer of producing the evidence that would exonerate their clients. Instead, they argued, the joint command "directed" Nifong and the police investigators "to act swiftly to charge, prosecute, and convict" the players. As a result, the team and many of its players "were further subjected to public humiliation and vilification and the universal condemnation of hundreds of millions of people around the world." They believed that the actions and statements already in the public realm by March 29 had stirred up so much "local racial animus" that they feared the "outrage they had fomented" would be turned against Duke and Durham officials "if there were no charges, no trial, and no convictions." The joint command predicted there would be "race riots" and that "Durham would burn" if charges were not brought against someone for what had allegedly happened at 610 North Buchanan. It was at that moment, the attorneys believed, that "all appearances of a legitimate investigation were abandoned."

On the morning of March 31, the *Durham Herald-Sun* ran a front-page interview with Mangum's father. He was not identified (nor was she, of course), other than to say that he and his wife "keep to themselves in their small home on a quiet street in southern Durham." The paper also reported that he was a retired moving van driver and had a good opinion of Duke and Duke Medical

Center, where he had been treated for a bad back. He worried that his daughter would not be treated fairly by the justice system. He said she had stopped by her parents' house the day after the alleged attack. "I asked her what had happened, and she said it was a long story, and she left," he said. "I knew somebody beat her because you could look at her face and tell that her face was swollen. It was all around her eyes, and her jaw was swollen. She tried to get out of the car but she couldn't walk." He said he was surprised to learn of his daughter's part-time job as a stripper. "She told me she was working on the weekends," he said. "She didn't tell me what she was working at." He also said his daughter was "halfway nervous, scared. She doesn't really know who to talk to."

The same day, during the lunch hour, Gottlieb and Himan again met with Nifong to discuss putting together a photographic lineup of the lacrosse players using the new mug shot–style photographs taken along with their DNA a week earlier. Normally, an alleged victim would be shown a cross section of photographs of people from the community so that she could possibly identify her attacker. But because Mangum was so specific about who her attackers were, Nifong decided to just group the lacrosse players together in one presentation to see if she recognized her attackers. "If in fact she could recall, just let us know how she recalled seeing them from that night, what they were doing and any type of interactions she may have had or observed with a particular individual," Gottlieb wrote, logically, in his notes.

In the face of such an extraordinary media maelstrom and conflicting accounts of events, it was not surprising that people did not know where the truth lay or how to react. "Accounts of the incident have sparked outrage about elitism, racism, and sexual violence," Boston Cote, a Duke senior, wrote in an opinion column in the *Chronicle*. "And while the situation is intrinsically heated and divisive, it seems as though widespread speculation has taken the place of a critical response to hard evidence." In the absence of the facts, she feared there had already been a dangerous rush to judgment: the team had been condemned for its "wall of silence"; Mangum had been "faulted" for her "bad career decisions" and then blamed for "her own violation"; and the university administration had been criticized for "not doing more" to punish the lacrosse players, including keeping them off the practice fields and out of classes. "These unwarranted suppositions and condemnations are downright shameful," she wrote. "In the absence of more information, this campus has a responsibility to accord every alleged victim of assault dignity and has an obligation to respect the rights of the accused." She defended the players' constitutional right to due process. "To those who demand that the players in attendance feed the public more details, I am appalled," she wrote. "It should be obvious to any rational American citizen that coercing public disclosure of 'facts' unequivocally undermines the constitutional rights of the accused."

On March 31, when the wounds were still fresh and the information vacuum still expanding, a particularly arresting commentary came from Duke historian William Chafe, a former dean of the faculty of arts and sciences. Writing in the *Chronicle*, Chafe focused on how the incident at 610 North Buchanan again raised the specter of the sordid American history of the relationship between white men and black women. "Racism has always constituted the original sin of our democracy," Chafe wrote. "Slavery, and then Jim Crow, systematically contradicted our commitment to the equality of all citizens. Race also stood as a primary source of power for those whites with privilege." Women were equally poorly treated throughout much of American history, Chafe observed. "Sex and race have always interacted in a vicious chemistry of power, privilege and control," he wrote. "Whether or not a rape took place (and this is an issue that needs to be assessed objectively and with full fairness to everyone), there is no question that racial epithets were hurled at black people. Nor is there any question that white students hired a black woman from an escort service to perform an erotic dance. The intersection of racial antagonism and sexual exploitation is all too familiar." What kind of community did Duke want to be? Chafe wondered. Did Duke want to be a community of inclusion, embracing people of different ethnicities and backgrounds, or a community that replicated the patterns of "racial and sexual control" that for too long had been part of the country's history? "The choice is ours to make," Chafe concluded.

As the precise facts about what may or may not have happened remained unknown, it was perhaps inevitable for there to be the kind of soul-searching that Chafe's column encouraged. He was not alone. Selena Roberts, a sports columnist at the *New York Times*, wrote, in a particularly harsh column, that Duke was at the "intersection of entitlement and enablement," a place "virtuous on the outside, debauched on the inside. This is the home of Coach K's white-glove morality and Cameron Crazies' celebrated vulgarity," Roberts wrote, referring to Duke students' antics during home basketball games at Cameron Indoor Stadium. Something had happened on the night of March 13, she wrote, but allowed that the captains might be right that the allegations were baseless. Still, she wondered, "why is it so hard to gather the facts?"

Roberts lamented the failure of the team to denounce the various assertions that the victim was "raped, robbed, strangled and was the victim of a hate crime," figuring that their silence was the result of a culture of silence among athletes, drug dealers, and gang members that put team above all and relegated "snitching" to the thing "men fear most." She made no mention of the fact that the three captains had offered to take polygraph tests, had given clear and complete statements to the police that nothing even remotely like what Mangum suggested had happened, and that there was a legitimate legal strategy to keeping the players' public comments to a minimum at this particular moment. "Whatever the root, there is a common thread: a desire for teammates to exploit the vulnerable without heeding a conscience," she wrote.

She was openly critical of Coach Pressler's decision to have the players resume practice the day after they submitted their DNA evidence to the police, calling his decision to concentrate on beating the Hoyas as evidence of his "warped priorities." Even the protests across Durham and Duke in the previous days, while "heartening," might also be "hypocritical." How many of the protesters were also Cameron Crazies who had been known to berate opposing players accused of sex crimes with taunts of "Did you send her flowers?" Then she turned her wrath on Brodhead. "Has President Brodhead reveled in the Crazies' witty ability to belittle villains in an environment that only serves to nurture the entitlement of his own athletes?" she asked. "Does President Brodhead dare to confront the culture behind the lacrosse team's code of silence or would he fear being ridiculed as a snitch?" (Six days later, the *Times* ran a correction. Roberts's column had "misstated the nature of the players' cooperation with the authorities. The police in Durham, NC, said that although most team members had not voluntarily submitted to police interviews and DNA tests, the three residents of the house where the accuser said the incident occurred had done so.") Himan was so excited by Roberts's column that he sent an e-mail to some friends: "The media has scooped this case up and made it a very popular story. . . . Its [*sic*] not every day you make the *NY Times*."

That same afternoon, Nifong spoke with George Smith at ESPN and made his most pointed comments about his intention to bring charges—including "first-degree forcible rape," "first-degree kidnapping," and "first-degree sexual offense"—against three still-unknown lacrosse players. A conviction on these charges could result in a minimum prison sentence of between sixteen and twenty years for each player. "Under North Carolina law, the only felony more serious than that is first-degree murder," he told Smith. "These crimes are actually punishable at a higher level than second-degree murder." Nifong told Smith he believed a crime had been committed at 610 North Buchanan. If the DNA evidence came back negative—as Nifong knew that it had—he told Smith that the case would still be prosecuted, in the same way that thousands of rape cases had been prosecuted (many successfully) in the hundreds of years before DNA sampling was available to law enforcement officials.

Meanwhile, the players' attorneys were busy trying to counteract Nifong's media onslaught. In a press conference held in Raleigh, they questioned the authenticity of the first 911 call and attacked Mangum's account of what happened. They predicted that the DNA results would clear their clients. Kerry Sutton, a lawyer for Matt Zash, told the *Times* that Zash had cooperated with police by giving them a lengthy statement and by offering to take a polygraph test. "They told him it takes too long to set up, it's too much trouble, and it's not admissible in court," Sutton said. Attorney Bill Thomas, representing Brett Thompson, disputed the idea that there was a wall of silence the players were hiding behind. "Everyone asks why these young men have not come forward," he said. "It's because no one was in the bathroom with the complainant. No one was alone with her. This didn't happen. They have no information to come forward with."

Another attorney, Butch Williams, who represented Dan Flannery, questioned the "inconsistencies" in Roberts's 911 call. At one point she said the two women were driving by 610 North Buchanan, and then she said they were walking by the house. "Three times she gives the exact address of the house," Williams told the media, "and there are no address numbers to see, especially at night. It seems too pat to me." He said there was no house number at all, merely a "faded imprint" of a number near the base of the front door of the house. "There are a number of discrepancies that point to a contrived situation—maybe," he continued. "I can't speak to speculation" about why the caller may have fabricated a story, "but once you tell one lie, you've got to tell another and another and another. You get caught up in a web of lies."

The *Durham Herald-Sun* asked Nifong about the attorneys' charge about the inconsistencies in the 911 call. But he declined to answer questions. "I don't see it as an issue that would affect the way I prosecute this case," he said. "Right now, I'm just trying to get into a position where we can charge somebody or conclude that no one will be charged."

As part of the *Times*'s increasingly blanket coverage of the story, the paper's Rick Lyman tackled the long-simmering issue of the strained relationship between Duke and Durham, a city of around 230,000 people, according to the 2010 census, 41 percent of whom were black and 42 percent of whom were white. Obviously, Mangum's allegations, if true, were a serious setback for the modest progress that the two communities had made over the years. But, true or not, there was still the fact that the ongoing migration of Duke students to rental homes in the Trinity Park neighborhood off East Campus—and their occasional hard-partying antics—had been a source of much anger and frustration in the neighborhood.

Lyman cited a Princeton Review study of 361 colleges and universities and the relationship they had with their surrounding communities. Duke ranked fifth worst in the category of "strained town-gown relations" and sixth in "having little interaction between students of different socioeconomic classes and racial groups." One explanation Lyman offered for these statistics was that "Duke is an especially elite and privileged institution in a culturally diverse and economically struggling city that already carries the harsh history of race relations in the South." And he mentioned Tom Wolfe's 2004 novel *I Am Charlotte Simmons*, about a "hard-partying college" that was likely Duke, where Wolfe's daughter, Alexandra, had graduated in 2002 and where Wolfe was the commencement speaker that year.

Lyman spoke with Durham mayor Bill Bell, who found Duke's ranking in the Princeton Review study a little hard to believe, but acknowledged that the partying in Trinity Park had irritated the city's relationship with Duke. He said he did not believe "the lacrosse team accusation will set back progress." The next day he held the first of a series of meetings between city officials, black residents, and the leaders of local universities. The *Los Angeles Times* also wrote about how the alleged incident was dredging up a history of bad blood between Durham and Duke. "There's a wonderful line from *I, Claudius*: 'Let all of the poisons that lurk in the mud out,'" John Burness told the paper. "There are people at Duke who work here now whose fathers and mothers and uncles and aunts worked here when it was a segregated institution. [Duke became integrated in 1963; Yale allowed black students to enroll in the 1850s.] Imagine the stories they must have brought home. And now all of that is coming back."

Brodhead seemed keenly aware of the challenges he faced leading Duke through the crisis, given the university's checkered history when it came to race. "To any present member of this community, it's almost inconceivable that Duke ever could have maintained a policy of racial exclusion," Brodhead said in a March 2012 speech to the university's faculty about Duke's legacy of race relations. "The school we see around us is so manifestly and exuberantly diverse, and the interaction of talent from all backgrounds is so clearly the precondition for the stimulation we experience here every day, that it's hard to fathom that Duke ever could have *been* otherwise, let alone that it could have been *wished* otherwise. But racial discrimination was once the official practice of this school, as it was of the surrounding region and, de facto, much of this land."

There was some progress to report: black enrollment at Duke stood at 10.8 percent of the student body in 2004, up from 5.1 percent of the student body in 1980. Some 35 percent of undergraduate students at Duke were minorities. And, in 1996, Duke created the Duke-Durham Neighborhood Partnership to help support poor neighborhoods near Duke in obtaining medical care, affordable housing, mentoring, and tutoring. The partnership raised $12 million for the local neighborhoods. Venis Wilder, a twenty-one-year-old senior from Plantation, Florida, was one Duke student who had participated in the Neighborhood Partnership program. She had witnessed improvement in the relationship between Duke and Durham during her years at the school but worried the lacrosse incident would set back that progress. "People in the community and on campus are both watching to see what disciplinary action, what stance, the university is going to take," she told Lyman. "Is this going to be a team with rich white men who get away with assaulting a black woman? People are really watching to see how Duke is going to respond."

On April 1, the *Times* ran yet another story about how few around Duke were surprised "that trouble had found the lacrosse team, a clubby, hard-partying outfit with roots in the elite prep schools of the Northeast." The team's defenders allowed that the players were easy targets because of their relatively privileged upbringings and status on campus; its critics believed the players "operated with a sense of entitlement that stood out" even at Duke "and surely brought the trouble on themselves."

The *Times* interviewed Peter Wood, who explained that the lacrosse players "stood out for their aggression" on campus in part because of the nature of the game itself, which was invented by Native Americans and played by them with a gusto that bordered on violence. The modern-day, less animalistic version of the game was especially favored by white prep-schoolers from towns in Maryland, New Jersey, Connecticut, and Long Island. "The football players here are often rural white boys with baseball caps or hardworking black students who are proud to be at Duke," he said. "Basketball players are held at a higher level and are more tightly controlled. Too often, there seems to be a surliness about some lacrosse players' individual demeanor. They seem hostile, and there is a group mentality." Wood said that for many years, when he taught lacrosse players at Duke, they were keenly interested in the history of the game. As he had written in his letter two years earlier, he told the *Times* he did not quite know why attitudes among the lacrosse players had changed when it came to academics. "It's gotten noticeably worse in the last four or five years," he said. "They've gotten more aggressive." He recounted the story he had told Dean Thompson about how, before the Virginia lacrosse game two years before, a number of the players had told him they intended to skip his class because Pressler, the coach, had scheduled an extra practice to try to improve the level of play before the big game. He told the players he would not give them permission to miss his class, and then he complained to the athletic department. They skipped his class anyway. "To me, that is beyond the pale," Wood said. "You don't do that at Duke."

After reading Wood's comments in the *New York Times*, Mary Semans, the great-granddaughter of Washington Duke, the great-niece of James B. Duke, and a major Duke philanthropist, wrote to Wood that "it was so good to see your remarks in the paper. There is something wrong! As Houston Baker said— the racial feelings weren't that stressful eight years ago. What has happened?"

Around the same time, Wood sent a letter to Kathleen Smith, a Duke biology professor and the chair of the Duke athletic council, informing her that the last time he taught his course in Native American history, two years earlier, there were six members of the lacrosse team in the class, including both Matt Zash and Dave Evans, two of the three cocaptains who lived at 610 North Buchanan. Something had changed. "I am all too familiar with the particular blend of strength, privilege, and boorishness that unfortunately has been associated with the lacrosse subculture nationally from time to time," he wrote. "But this seemed out of place at Duke, for it was occasionally tinged with defiance, belligerence, and even antisocial racism. Why else would one student write at the end of the semester, 'I wish all the Indians had died, and then we wouldn't have to study them'?" He worried about the "groupthink" among the lacrosse players. "When these players approached me, it was generally as a delegation with a [single] spokesman," he continued. "Younger players seemed to defer to older leaders." He explained to Smith that he did not know what to do about what he was seeing. "In retrospect, I wish I had pursued my unease more forcefully," he wrote, "though I had little sense of the right direction to turn. Since that time, I have learned of other professors having similar experiences with the same group of students, and I have heard plenty of confirmation from undergraduate remarks regarding the unsavory reputation of the team in social matters on and around campus."

Another time, after Wood shared his famous June 2004 letter about the lacrosse players in his class with Susan Thorne, an associate professor of history at Duke, she wrote him to say how "wonderfully eloquent, if chilling" it was. She told Wood that she had taught eight members of the lacrosse team over the years and seemed quite concerned that she may unwittingly have failed to pick up on the subtle indications of their alleged bad behavior. "I am clearly no judge of character," she wrote. "I was totally blind to any warning signs." She said that before she heard about what supposedly happened on the night of March 13, she just generally felt sorry for the lacrosse players. "They are academically underprepared to a much greater degree than athletes from any other sport I've had in class. . . . I vainly gave them moral credit for taking my classes, which are intensely antiracist. When I read the racist remark most quoted—thanking the girl's grandfather for the cotton shirt—I felt a dreadful certainty that whoever said it [had taken] my class, History 113B: Europe's Colonial Encounter." She informed Wood about some of the class discussions regarding how the West's wealth was a result of past and present "exploitation of the poor at home and abroad." When she heard about the racist remark, she said it "turned everything we learned about the West's debt to the rest into an insulting taunt. I don't know if I'm more heartbroken or nauseated by that. . . . All that said, I still feel sorry for them. . . . As a redneck friend of mine remarked about all this, these kids have no idea what all the fuss is about. A street kid would know. But these kids think it was all just a case of bad judgment, a party out of hand. But of course that's how their obnoxious behavior has been treated in the past—and how this was treated by Duke for about a week after the party was reported."

With the DNA results looking to be inconclusive, at best, from Nifong's perspective, he continued to use the media's seemingly insatiable demand for his attention to spin the story in ways that would bolster Mangum's (and his own) case. This tactic was hardly unprecedented in American jurisprudence on either side of a case. But the extent of Nifong's blanketing of the airwaves—

especially as he was facing an election in May—made the district attorney the object of much criticism. "He'll say whatever he wants to say in public," attorney Joe Cheshire told the *News & Observer*, "but he won't say in public what the evidence is."

But Nifong was unfazed. "How am I trying this case in the media?" he asked a Durham reporter. "We have not identified anybody as a suspect. The only reason we are investigating the lacrosse team is because the lacrosse team themselves said they were present at this house party. I haven't called anyone who said, 'Would you like to interview me and write a story about this?'" Nifong said reporters were "swarming him" rather than "the other way around," making it difficult for him to get other work done.

As for the DNA tests, he told the *Durham Herald-Sun*, he might not make the results public when they became available in the next week or so and that, in any event, the tests were not the "be-all and end-all" of a potential rape case against the players. He also reiterated his view that charges against three players would be possible even if there were no DNA evidence, since the "victim's identification of her alleged attackers could suffice."

As for his suggestion, posited a few days earlier, that maybe the players had used condoms during the assault—containing their DNA and then tossing it away—the fact that police had waited sixty-four hours between the time Mangum made her rape allegation—2:50 a.m. on March 14—and the time the search warrant was issued for the house on March 16—at 6:55 p.m.—could have resulted in additional missed evidence. "Obviously, any delay would have given an opportunity for somebody to clean up if they were inclined to do so, or felt there was something they didn't want left behind," Nifong told the *News & Observer*. The fact that there was no evidence that condoms were used—assuming there was even an assault—didn't seem to prevent Nifong from continuing his public ruminations about where the case might be headed.

He told the Durham paper it was best to wait for the DNA evidence—such as it was—before bringing charges. "Suppose somebody was able to identify one assailant but said there were three assailants," he said. "One might want to wait for evidence to determine who the others were. That would seem preferable to charging one person and leaving the other cases hanging. It is my desire to know exactly what evidence I have to present at trial before I decide who will be charged with what." He also said it was proper to ask for DNA samples from the forty-six white players on the team. "They have pointed the fingers at themselves," he continued. "They have told us the only ones in that house were members of the lacrosse team"—a statement he knew by then to be inaccurate, since the Durham police had already questioned several Duke students who were at the party but were not on the lacrosse team.

On April 1, Nifong's argument that Levicy's examination might prove to be evidence enough that a rape had occurred in the early morning of March 14 received an unexpected boost from Levicy's boss, Theresa Arico. Like Levicy, Arico was a sexual assault nurse examiner at Duke. In an interview with the *Durham Herald-Sun*, she decribed the job as a process of conducting both physical exainations and interviews with alleged rape victims. She had no doubt Mangum had been raped, although it was not her responsibility to render that opinion—a responsibility belonging to the State Bureau of Investigation after it tested the DNA. "You can say with a high degree of certainty that there was a certain amount of blunt force trauma present to create injury," she said. "I can reasonably say these injuries are consistent with the story she told." Arico's public ratification of Levicy's examination of Mangum proved particularly damning, as attorneys for the athletes were quick to point out. "Arico knew or had reason to know that Levicy's representations to police and prosecutors were false and misleading," according to their court filings. "Yet she attempted to bolster Levicy's credibility to the police and to the public with intentional or reckless disregard for the truth."

Later on the afternoon of March 31, Gottlieb had a visit at the District 2 police station from two Duke police officers. They gave Gottlieb reports about employees at Duke who were being "harassed due to this case," a mini-outbreak of incidents where students and employees of the university were being verbally hassled by random people in Durham just because they were affiliated with Duke.

The Duke officers also gave a Gottlieb a "key-card report" for the lacrosse players on the evening of March 13. The report was the copy of the digital record of when they left and returned to their dorm rooms on that evening. No supboena had been obtained for the key-card information that the Duke officers gave to Gottlieb. (Some felt that this information could not have been supplied even with a subpoena and in any event was not only a violation of the university's privacy policy but also a clear violation of the Family Education Records and Privacy Act.)

Gottlieb later testified about the importance of both the key-card records and the SANE records to his investigation. "We ha[d] the time cards, per se . . . ," he said. "Each student has a magnetic card that if they go in the parking lot or dorm room or buy food, whatever, they use that card, it leaves an electronic stamp. And we have a document showing that [a player] arrived back to the dorm at the [same] time as the people who we knew were at the party. So we were able to put together information to at least corroborate, one, he was there; two, he met the description; three, she was able to show them the SANE nurse's report was consistent with a sexual assault. So we have something to work with for an indictment."

By nine o'clock that evening, there was genuine concern around the campus about unconfirmed reports of a drive-by shooting at 610 North Buchanan. Duke officials were so worried that Larry Moneta sent students a late-night e-mail message. "I write to inform you of a rumor I've just learned," Moneta wrote. "I don't have a way of validating the credibility of the rumor, as it came to us thirdhand from the Durham Police to various members of the Duke community. What we've heard is threats of 'drive-by shooting' of the lacrosse house in the Trinity Park area." He wrote that while he was not aware of any shooting at 610 North Buchanan, there was "a gang-related shooting that took place this afternoon on Sedgefield Street in Walltown (several blocks from Trinity Park). We are assured by Durham Police that this is not related to Duke in any way." But there was also a report "that passengers in a car yelled at Duke students in houses on Buchanan Street."

Moneta made no mention of the reports of "harassment" directed at Coach Pressler or the lacrosse players. Nor did he mention the physical assault against seniors Morgan Gieseke and Basil Camu, who were at the Cook-Out restaurant on Hillsborough Road, in Durham, at 3 a.m. early Friday morning when they were blocked from leaving the drive-through at the restaurant by the car in front of them, which would not leave. A group of men approached their car. "All of a sudden we heard all this screaming," Gieseke told the *Chronicle*. "The people were saying, 'This is Central territory,'" a reference to the area in Durham around North Carolina Central University, where Mangum was a student. Gieseke said the men, who appeared to be in their twenties, told them, "Duke kids aren't welcome here because they're all rapists" and "We don't want Duke kids here at Cook-Out because they're going to rape our women." When Camu put his head out of the window to hear what the men were saying, one of them "punched him in the back of the head," Gieseke told the paper, knocking him unconscious for a brief time. When he recovered and they left the parking area, the car that had blocked them in continued to follow them.

Moneta was fearful about sending the e-mail. "I share this information with great discomfort," he continued. "I neither want to create any sense of hysteria for the Duke and Trinity Park communities nor withhold the existence of this information. We've spoken with several of the students who live in those houses and many have chosen to stay elsewhere tonight." Moneta said there would be increased patrols by the Duke and Durham police in the neighborhoods around Duke's East Campus. "Unfortunately, tensions are very high right now and may not abate for a while," he continued. "I would anticipate further rumors and conflicting information and we'll do our very best to keep you informed."

There was no longer any question that the fallout from Mangum's accusations of the Duke lacrosse players was reverberating around the community. People were getting very upset. The public commentary was starting to boil and, according to the *News & Observer*, "the story seemed to get worse with each new detail." In a small measure of protest, Bonnie Belk, a Duke alumnus from Rockville, Maryland, and a former twenty-year university employee, returned the Duke sweatshirts she had bought for her three children. "I never thought I would feel as embarrassed and ashamed as I feel seeing Duke high-lighted on the evening news and front pages of our nation's newspapers," she wrote in a letter. As for the Duke sweatshirts, Belk concluded, "they are now defective" and "cannot be worn without subjecting the wearer to ridicule or worse." (Ironically, in the same way that years later wearing a hoodie in public became a symbol of solidarity with Trayvon Martin, the seventeen-year-old African-American fatally shot in Florida by George Zimmerman, supposedly in self-defense, people throughout the country, without any affiliation with Duke whatsoever, began wearing Duke lacrosse T-shirts and sweatshirts out of both sympathy for the players and as an act of protest against a seeming rush to judgment. Others wore the emblazoned jerseys to—grotesquely—align themselves with the alleged acts of violence and racism.)

Duke alumni were also getting peeved about the increasingly negative por-trayal of the university by the media. "Those guys have really ticked me off and embarrassed me," said Donald Van Dyke, who had played lacrosse at Duke and graduated in 1978. "I wore that jersey and they're wearing it now." Mal-bert Smith and his wife, Alisa, both went to Duke and their daughter was then a Duke undergraduate. They lived in Chapel Hill but their allegiance to Duke was clear. "Duke has always been very dear to me," Malbert told the *News & Observer*. "I'm an Iron Duke"—a reference to the steadfast supporters of Duke sports—"[and] in my work, I travel all over the country, and people know how I feel about Duke. They're calling me up now, asking me what in the world is going on." An "ex-Dukie" had taped a poster to a tree outside Brodhead's Allen Building office: "To many for whom Durham is really home, Duke's silence following what the men's lacrosse team did is just the latest sad chapter in Duke-Durham relations. Shame on Duke!"

But alumnus Graham Watkins urged caution. "It is remarkable the way the local news media, at least some Durham residents and at least some Duke stu-dents have already tried and convicted the lacrosse players," he wrote. "You do realize, folks, that there is at least a tiny possibility that this didn't happen exactly the way the presumed victim says it did?"

Another neighbor sent around a blog post by David Steele, who wondered why a culture of exceptions for the Duke lacrosse players had been allowed to fester for so long. Duke administrators "have to wonder," Steele wrote, "if this all could have been avoided had someone cracked down long before. . . . Everything about this, in fact, points to a culture—one of permissiveness about everything the athletes do, from drinking to rowdiness to disrespecting women to, most of all, expecting to get away with it because of who they are. Entitlement is at the heart of the issue and at the heart of the fury this inci-dent and its handling has inspired. It's not just about college athletes getting in trouble; it's about lacrosse players. It's a sport of privilege played by children of privilege and supported by families of privilege. The university involved is one of privilege."

Steele, writing from Baltimore—one of the hotbeds of lacrosse mania in the country—saw a link between the alleged incident and the so-called lax bro culture of the sport that celebrates bad-boy behavior. "Too many people who are close to the sport see this as a symptom of the lacrosse culture for it not to be taken seriously," he continued. "If any group of people should understand that, it should be those close to the game here—if not just because this is the epicenter of the sport, then because this also was the epicenter of what probably was the worst team-related incident before the one at Duke."

Steele recounted an incident five years earlier at St. Paul's School outside of Baltimore, where in the spring of 2001 the school canceled the top-ranked boys' lacrosse season after some two dozen players were discovered to have watched a videotape made by one of their teammates of him having sex with a fifteen-year-old girl. "That should give some sense of how ingrained the sort of mind-set that leads to situations like that one at Duke can be," he wrote. He quoted Mitch Whiteley, then the coach of the team, who said, "I'd put these kids up against anybody, and yet, look at what they did. . . . I never considered myself old-fashioned, but when you consider what is acceptable behavior to these kids—boys and girls across the board—it's mind-boggling." It took eight days for St. Paul's to cancel the lacrosse team's season. "The time that has elapsed since Duke officials first heard about the alleged rape at the players' house is fifteen days and counting," Steele continued. "Even the phrasing of the season suspension announcement seems to allow for the team to return to action if or when the investigation ends. Also, while there has been an apology by the players and school to the community at large, none has been offered, at least publicly, to the accuser. This can happen when you're convinced that no matter what you've done and who you've done it to, you haven't done anything wrong."

The story of what happened—or didn't happen—was quickly transcending the existing tropes between Durham and Duke—which many in the community still referred to as "the Plantation," in an unsubtle reference to the stereotypes about the agrarian South—and becoming something else altogether: a referendum on decades of perceived racial, social, and economic injustice in America. "The situation is mushrooming way beyond the central issue of just the lacrosse players," Stacy Murphy, a Duke graduate living in Trinity Park, told the *New York Times*. "When you have this kind of incident, and the public outrage that goes with it, people on the fringe might do something rash. I'm afraid for the students, because it's clear that tensions are at a crazy level." Would this be yet another time when the rich white boys got away with vile behavior toward a defenseless, working-class single black mother, or could the incident be a new inflection point in the ongoing struggle for justice and equality? "If she was a white woman raped by black students, the whites would be in an uproar and things would be much more out of hand," Felita Judd, who lived in Mangum's neighborhood across town, told the *Times*. "But now we're mad because this woman is being treated as a low-class person. The players? They are treated like high class, and they are being protected because they have money."

One thing was clear: the existing stereotypes were tough to overcome. There had always been "an air" about "Dukies," Maya Jackson, a twenty-three-year-old sociology major at North Carolina Central, told the Associated Press on April 1. "Some of them came off as snooty," she said. Rayone Bland, a black divinity student at Duke, concurred with Jackson: "There is really a sense of 'I'm entitled to do what I want to do,'" she said. Added Jeannine Carpenter, a Duke PhD candidate in linguistics, "There's a stereotype of white Duke privilege that can't always be denied. I think that there's always historical truth in stereotypes. Whether it's present-day or not is definitely a question."

Inevitably, the high-profile Duke basketball players got dragged into the fray. Not only was the NCAA tournament under way—the men lost to LSU in the Sweet Sixteen; the women were in the Final Four in Boston—but also, as had been the case for years at Duke, basketball—particularly men's basketball—was the school's flagship athletic brand, and of course Coach K was the most powerful person on campus. He remained silent about the events of March 13. But the Associated Press found J. J. Redick, the star of the men's team, at the Final Four in Indianapolis and asked him what he thought about the allegations. After referring to the incident as "surreal," he said, "It's really just a sad situation. I'm actually close with some of the guys on the team, a few of the seniors. They are all great guys, and whether it happened or not, it's just unfortunate that this incident has become such a big deal. But it should be a big deal if it did happen."

The *New York Times*'s sports columnist Harvey Araton wondered why the women on the varsity basketball team, six of whom were black, had remained silent about the lacrosse incident. "Here at the women's Final Four, the men's lacrosse scandal that has rocked Duke University down to its proud preppie roots would remain a subject not open to the student-athletes from the women's basketball program with a perfect graduation rate." He blamed both the NCAA, which enforced the "unofficial gag order" that it places on athletes competing in the tournament and on the Duke sports information staff that did not think it fair to have the women basketball players talk about the controversy, especially on the eve of their Final Four semifinal game. But Araton persisted and eventually spoke with two of the players in the locker room after the official NCAA press conference where they were gagged.

Lindsey Harding, a guard, said the alleged incident had no impact on her or the team. "Maybe I'm just focused on what I'm doing in terms of basketball," she said, "but you didn't really see any of that." Mistie Williams, a forward and the daughter of Chubby Checker, "twisted" away from Araton's questions. "We haven't paid any attention to it," she told him. "It's not really important to us at this point." Why hadn't these student-athletes realized there was a bigger question at stake? Araton wondered. "Too bad they weren't encouraged to express themselves," he wrote, "to do what supposedly comes with the higher-learning territory. Too bad they were made mute, like the lacrosse players in the Blue Devils' wall of silence, which serves only to insulate athletes and convince the reprobates among them that they can get away with whatever. . . . Important questions have been raised by recent events at Duke that young, engaging people in the process of being educated should be encouraged to answer. Student-athletes included."

There was also the view—espoused by Peter Wood, among others—that some Duke coaches had been too willing to overlook the bad behavior of their athletes. "Coaches have a lot of leverage to manage behavior," explained Michael Palmer, Duke's director of community affairs. "In this case, it doesn't appear that that's been maximized." Palmer's opaque comment was the first from inside the Duke administration to suggest that perhaps Mike Pressler, the lacrosse coach, had been too lax in his oversight of the team. Another Duke professor, Herbert Kitschelt, not only wanted the lacrosse coaches suspended but also a "blue-ribbon panel" convened to investigate the university's lacrosse program. "To date," he wrote Brodhead in a letter, "the university's public communications have taken a narrow and legalistic direction. While it is appropriate and necessary for Duke University to acknowledge the legal rights of students who may ultimately be charged with crimes, it is equally important to restate and reaffirm the university's commitment to our core values as a learning community."

Suddenly, everything seemed open to questioning. Bob Ashley, the editor of the *Durham Herald-Sun*, wrote of his "deep concern that our society's infatuation with athletic corruption has spawned a cocoon of perceived untouchableness around many athletes. Like many stereotypes, it is deeply unfair to many athletes, but it is grounded in enough reality to trigger a 'here they go again' outrage when college—or high school—athletes step over the line. Some athletes reinforce this anger by an indifference to public dismay that reflects arrogance and entitlement."

On Sunday, April 2, the Reverend Sam Wells, dean of the Duke Chapel, put aside his planned sermon and spoke from the pulpit about the main topic that seemed to be on everyone's mind: the lacrosse team allegations. Wells had come to Duke the year before after holding various religious positions within the Church of England. Wells's principal message in his sermon was that the events that may or may not have occurred on the evening of March 13 were not particular to Duke but rather were symptomatic of problems across society. He made the further point that while universities may seem like mini city-states unto themselves, with sui generis rules, customs, and wealth, they cannot operate outside of society as a whole. He then laid down his view of the "law" of a university, one that he believed was rarely articulated but no less important as a result. "Learning and discovery require imagination, and that imagination is formed by disciplines of loving attention to detail; rigorous but generous dialogue with a wide range of voices; deep but undaunted respect for traditions and those that uphold them; earnest searching for goodness, truth, and beauty; and constant vigilance in regard to the social significance and embodiment of knowledge," he said. "Such disciplines train our desire."

He said if he were a Duke undergraduate he would be especially confused about how to develop intimacy with others. "Student culture is often described as 'work hard, play hard'"—a reference to William Willimon's 1993 report to then Duke president Keith Brodie—"but who says in what sense a personal relationship is part of the 'play'? I'd like to suggest that what I'm calling the 'law' of the university—loving attention, generous dialogue, deep respect, beauty, and social benefit—may have something to offer to the conduct of visceral, intimate, and physical relationships—the conventional realm of desire. The last week has exposed the reality that sexual practices are an area where some male students are accustomed to manipulating, exploiting, and terrorizing women all the time—and that this has been accepted by many as a given."

That Sunday, the *Durham Herald-Sun* tracked down William Willimon, then a bishop of the North Alabama Conference of the United Methodist Church. What did the former dean of the Duke Chapel and the author of two studies about Duke's campus culture think about the ongoing challenges of excessive drinking on (and off) campus? What did he think of the rape allegations? "It's sad," he said of the alleged incident, "because Duke has tried to be up-front in dealing with some of these challenges. In my thinking, Duke was really a leader in trying to grapple with [student alcohol abuse and related behavior]." He noted that after he wrote his two reports, other college administrators contacted him and said, "Duke is amazing for putting these issues out on the table. Our administration is in denial and suppression."

He said that Duke's athletes generally impressed him with their discipline. "It seemed like the athletes had much more interaction with grown-ups through their coaches than the average Duke student," he said. Willimon noted that while the *Chronicle* "condemned" his studies, some one hundred students surprised him and asked for copies of them. "Many of them said one of the greatest disappointments of their college years was that they thought you went to college to have great arguments and discussions, and then they got here and found out that it was about getting drunk and getting laid," he said.

While Wells was urging the Duke community to search its soul, the media was busy searching for Crystal Mangum. The *New York Times* reported on April 3 that the "local college student who accused several [Duke lacrosse players of] sexually assaulting her at a party"—Mangum still had not been identified by the press, even though they knew who she was and where she lived—had "temporarily" moved out of her Durham home because "the news media attention has overwhelmed her." Mangum was staying with friends. "She's very scared of everyone right now and doesn't trust no one," Mangum's mother told the *New York Times.* "She's even afraid to come here and stay with us because reporters might show up looking for her. She's so nervous about talking about what happened." Mangum's older brother added, "It's terrible that she was in the wrong place at the wrong time. Now it's hard for her to be normal and live her life." He said she also had been staying away from her classes at NCCU for fear she would be recognized on campus and around Durham as "the woman involved in the Duke scandal."

While Mangum's whereabouts may have been a mystery to the news media, Mark Gottlieb, the principal Durham police investigator, knew exactly where she was. At 8 a.m. on April 4, he spoke with her and arranged for her to come to the Durham police station to take a look at Himan's PowerPoint presentation of the Duke lacrosse players that he had finished the day before.

In order to record his conversation with Mangum, Gottlieb set up a colleague's laptop computer, to which he attached a full-size monitor. Using this setup, he could show Mangum pictures of the lacrosse players believed to be at the March 13 party while Ashley Ashby, the forensic investigator, could photograph Mangum's facial and body reactions in real time as she looked at each player's picture. Gottlieb's idea was that members of a prospective grand jury, as well as defense attorneys and prosecutors, could see not only the pictures of the players but also Mangum's simultaneous reaction to them. (This was, of course, Mangum's third try at identifying her attackers from a group exclusively comprising white Duke lacrosse players.)

At 11:25 a.m., Mangum arrived at the District 2 police station. Gottlieb explained to Mangum that an unidentified picture of a player would appear on the computer screen for one minute and then she could simply tell Gottlieb whether she recognized the face from the party. After the picture flashed on the laptop, there would be a blank screen that followed—like a touch of sherbet to cleanse her palate between courses—before the next photo would appear. While Gottlieb and Mangum were going through the forty-six pictures, other officers from the precinct would be taking notes, recording the session, and timing the intervals between pictures. "I explained to her it was very important not to say anyone was present at the party if they were not, or say they were if she could not recall they were present," Gottlieb recorded. "I also told her it was important to tell us if she recalled seeing a particular individual at the party and to let us know how she recalled seeing them from that night, what they were doing, and any type of interactions she may have had or observed with a particular individual. She agreed."

Up first was the picture of Matt Zash, one of the three lacrosse cocaptains who lived at 610 North Buchanan and had given his DNA and a statement to the police that first night. Mangum did not recognize him from his picture as having attended the party. The first player she recognized—image three—was William Wolcott because, according to Mangum he was "sitting on the couch in front of the television." The next picture—Matthew Wilson—Mangum thought might have been "Brett," one of the "guys that assaulted me." But she wasn't sure.

Image five was of David Evans, another of the three cocaptains that lived at 610 North Buchanan and who had cooperated with police the first night. Mangum told Gottlieb about Evans, "He looks like one of the guys who assaulted me, sort [of]." Gottlieb asked Mangum how sure she was that Evans was one of the men who attacked her. "He looks just like him without the mustache," Mangum said. She had never before mentioned that one of her attackers had a mustache. This was news to Gottlieb, who asked her about it, and Mangum said yes, the person who attacked her had had a mustache. "Percentagewise, what is the likelihood that this is one of the gentleman who assaulted you?" Gottlieb asked.

"About ninety percent," Mangum replied.

After looking at image seven—a picture of Reade Seligmann—Mangum said, "He looks like one of the guys who assaulted me." Again Gottlieb asked Mangum how sure she was. "One hundred percent," she said.

"You're one hundred percent sure," Gottlieb said. "Okay."

"Yes," Mangum replied.

Gottlieb asked her what Seligmann had done to assault her and she replied, "He was the one that was standing in front of me . . . um . . . that made me perform oral sex on him." Anything else? "That was it," she said. Gottlieb then repeated Mangum's findings for investigator Clayton, who was sitting in on the session. Player John B. Ross, image nine, Mangum recognized as being at the party but not as one of her attackers. "He was standing outside, talking to the other dancer," she said. Player Adam Langley, image eleven, was also at the party, Mangum said, in the master bedroom watching television, where she and Roberts had danced. What was he doing? Gottlieb asked. "Just drinking," she replied. She also told Gottlieb she recognized Glen Nick ("Just drinking") and Erik Henkelman ("He had on some brown shorts, khaki shorts.")

As for Dan Flannery—image seventeen—another of the three cocaptains who lived at 610 North Buchanan and had cooperated with police the first night, Mangum said she recognized him as the "one who gave me $400" but remembered nothing else about him. As for Peter Lamade—image twenty—the player who had made the comment to Mangum about putting the broomstick in her vagina, she said she did recognize him as "sitting in the kitchen" and "um, making a drink." Mangum recognized John Walsh from outside the house, where he had been "talking." At first she thought she recognized Chris Loftus—image twenty-six—from "sitting down" in the living room, but then corrected herself and said she remembered him from "the master bedroom" but nothing more. She recognized Ben Koesterer—image thirty-one—from "sitting in the front row" while she was dancing.

Tony McDevitt—image thirty-four—was in the master bedroom "sitting on the couch, watching television." She said he was the player who "made the broomstick comment." When Gottlieb asked her what that "broomstick comment" referred to, she said, "He said, um, he was going to stick broomsticks up [our] asses." He did not do anything else, she said. Mangum recognized Josh Coveleski—image thirty-seven—from the master bedroom, where he was "just yelling and screaming" the words "Yeah!" and "Whooo!" Mangum also recognized Kyle Dowd, because, like Coveleski, he was yelling in the master bedroom, "Let's see some more action!" Image thirty-nine was of Ryan McFadyen but Mangum had no recollection of his being at the party.

Then there was Collin Finnerty, image forty. "He is the guy who assaulted me," Mangum told Gottlieb.

"What did he do?" he asked her.

"He put his penis in my anus and my vagina," Mangum replied. Gottlieb noted parenthetically, "The victim's eyes were pooling with tears."

"Was he the first or second one to do that?" Gottlieb wondered.

"The second one," she replied, and also said Finnerty had not been the one to "strangle her." After looking at the next image, which she did not recognize, Gottlieb asked Mangum if she needed a tissue. "I can see you're crying," he said. Mangum responded that she was fine.

Going back briefly to the picture of Finnerty, Gottlieb asked Mangum how sure she was that Finnerty had put his "penis in your anus"? She replied, "One hundred percent." Mangum recognized none of the last five players. Afterward, Gottlieb turned the video monitor that had been facing Mangum around so that both monitors were facing the camera that the forensics unit was using to tape the interview. He played the presentation again for the people in the room so that they could see that the "screens are showing the same presentation at the same time." In short order, Mangum had fingered Reade Seligmann, David Evans, and Collin Finnerty as the three men who had sexually assaulted her on the evening of March 13.

This was a most curious turn of events. Mangum recognized seventeen of the forty-six lacrosse players, eleven of whom she had not recognized at all in the two earlier identification sessions. During the earlier sessions, she said she recognized four of the players with 100 percent certainty. Now she recognized only one of those four players, Brad Ross, Ryan McFadyen's roommate. Of course, as Ross had let Gottlieb and Himan know during the still-undisclosed search of his and McFadyen's room, Ross had been in Raleigh the night of the party visiting his girlfriend. Mangum also identified Chris Loftus as "sitting in the master bedroom" but, according to the key-card reports that Gottlieb had obtained from Duke a few days earlier, Chris Loftus was actually in his dorm room on the evening of March 13, from 10:59 p.m. on. (McFadyen said Dan Loftus, Chris's brother, was at the party, well past 11 p.m.) To add to the confusion, she recognized players on April 4 whom she had not recognized earlier and recognized players during the two earlier sessions that she no longer recognized on April 4.

By this time, the Durham police had obtained several photographs from the party and, defense attorneys later claimed, showed them to Mangum before the April 4 session in order to aid her memory of who had been at the party and what they looked like. In any event, Mangum now recognized Erik Henkelman and his brown or khaki shorts, when two weeks earlier—a week after the party—she did not recognize him at all. She also recognized William Wolcott as sitting on the couch in front of the television but had not recognized him previously. She now recognized Peter Lamade as sitting in the kitchen, mixing a drink, but she had not recognized him previously. Lamade, Henkelman, and Wolcott were in the photographs that the Durham police had in their possession by April 4.

As for Seligmann, Evans, and Finnerty, there were also inconsistencies between what Mangum recalled about them in the previous sessions and the April 4 session. For instance, a picture of Finnerty was not included in the two previous March identification sessions because Gottlieb and Himan had determined from Mangum's previous descriptions of her attackers that the tall and thin Finnerty did not fit the bill. On April 4, she identified Finnerty with 100 percent certainty as being one of her rapists. She also now identified Evans with "90 percent certainty" as one of her attackers, but in both of the previous two sessions, she had not recognized him at all. As for Seligmann, she now recognized him with 100 percent certainty, but in March had said he was familiar to her with only "70 percent certainty." None of the men she identified as her attackers matched the descriptions she gave Gottlieb and Himan during her March 16 interview with them. But Gottlieb's superior, Michael Ripberger, remembered that Gottlieb had told him, after Mangum saw the faces of Seligmann, Finnerty, and Evans on April 4, "that the expressions on her face changed dramatically when she made the identifications of those persons."

Then there was the unorthodox identification procedure that Nifong and Gottlieb used with Mangum on April 4, which defense attorneys later contended was improper and violated their clients' rights to due process; Nifong and the police maintained that it was just designed to help Mangum remember. The Durham police regulations were designed to "protect against both negligent and malicious misidentifications." But, according to defense attorneys, the April 4 procedure should have used "an independent administrator." Instead, Gottlieb administered the examination, and obviously was anything but independent. Gottlieb's procedure also did not use any "true fillers," or photographs of men who were not Duke lacrosse players, as a way to make sure Mangum's recollections of the March 13 evening were reliable. (Gottlieb's position remained that the April 4 session was not a "photographic array" because there was no suspect at that point, and so the regulations were not relevant.) In the three identification sessions, Durham police showed Mangum eighty-two pictures—some more than once—every one of which was of a white Duke lacrosse player. The combination of these omissions, according to court filings by defense attorneys, made the April 4 identification session the "criminal justice equivalent of a game of Russian roulette. There were three bullets in Nifong's chambers, and they would randomly strike three party attendees. All players were in roughly equal jeopardy of false indictment and further persecution."

Another defense attorney referred to the procedure as a "multiple choice test with no wrong answers"—an observation that was true except for the fact that by April 4, the key-card information that Gottlieb had in hand informed him of who among the lacrosse players was actually at the party at 610 North Buchanan and who was not. Defense attorneys believed that had Mangum recognized as one of her attackers a player who was not at the party—ever—that would seriously damage the case Nifong and the Durham police were trying to assemble. "It was essential," defense attorneys stated, for the Durham prosecutors "not to indict any players who could readily prove that they had not even attended the party. The information Duke illicitly provided through the key-card reports was critical to ensure that Mangum did not select a 'wrong answer' from the photo lineup." They believed Gottlieb and his colleagues "coached" Mangum both "prior to and during the photo identification process," which is why she identified three men as her "attackers" who police knew for certain were at the party. Needless to say, if defense attorneys were correct, the students' civil rights would have been horrifically violated.

Soon after completing the session with Mangum, Gottlieb and police investigator Michelle Soucie met with Nifong to review "the results of the presentation," as Gottlieb wrote in the notes he reconstructed after the fact, without elaboration. At the same meeting, Nifong gave Gottlieb a copy of a letter he had received the day before from Kate Hendricks, deputy general counsel at Duke. In her letter Hendricks informed Nifong that several lacrosse team captains had met with Duke administration officials about what had occurred at the March 13 party. "These administrators are very willing to provide the information to you and your investigators," she wrote. "Please be assured that a court order will not be necessary." She suggested that Nifong's "investigators" contact her or a Duke police officer to arrange for the "interviews with any Duke personnel who received firsthand accounts of the incident from the players."

After Gottlieb and Soucie left Nifong's office, Durham attorney Bill Thomas—representing cocaptain Brett Thompson—stopped by to see Nifong. Thomas and Nifong had known each other for years, since Nifong began his career as a Durham prosecutor. When Nifong had announced his candidacy for district attorney in January, Thomas was one of the first attorneys to write him a check—for $1,000—to support the campaign. After having spoken with Thompson, Thomas was convinced no crime had occurred at 610 North Buchanan on the night of March 13. He was worried the Durham Police Department might be misleading Nifong with faulty evidence. Thomas urged his friend to proceed slowly and carefully. He offered to share Thompson's version of events with Nifong. But Nifong was not interested in Thomas's advice. "He said that he had personally interviewed her [Mangum] and had spoke with her at length about this case, and that he fully believed every word she said about the incident," Thomas recalled, "and that he knew a lot more about the case than I did, and that he was going to proceed as he saw fit." Thomas remembered Nifong being "smug" and "self-assured" and in no mood to listen. "I had twenty-seven years of experience with him," he said, "and he was looking me in the eye. He said he had interviewed her, he discussed the details of the case, he believed her and that my view of her as perhaps being a call girl working for an escort service, running around making things up for financial gain, was absolutely false. . . . He went on to say what a wonderful person she was. He said she was fully believable. She was intelligent, articulate . . . and telling a convincing story about what happened." Nifong would later tell a Durham judge that he had never interviewed Mangum, contradicting Thomas's recollection of the April 4 meeting.

No doubt part of Nifong's confidence in Mangum's story came from the fact that years earlier, in 1992, Nifong had successfully prosecuted the man who had murdered one of Mangum's uncles, who owned a small grocery store in Durham. The uncle was killed during the robbery. The case took three years and won Nifong the trust of Mangum's family. "People had confidence in him that he would do us right because he had prosecuted that case," explained Delois Burnette, a longtime friend of the Mangum family.

After Thomas left his office, Nifong called Michelle Soucie, the police investigator, and asked her to determine what Mangum had done the day before the March 13 party "so we can show that she did not receive trauma prior to [the] incident—with witnesses." Soucie immediately set about that task.

Left out of Gottlieb's notes from the April 4 meeting with Nifong was the very important fact that Nifong had received that day, in a conference call, the "final results" of the SBI lab's DNA tests on the lacrosse players. He had known for days, of course, that the DNA results were unlikely to provide the evidence of rape. But, on April 4, the findings were definitively conveyed to Nifong: there was no match between the DNA samples taken from the forty-six Duke players and any DNA "on or within Mangum's clothing, body or belongings," according to legal documents.

That might have been the end of the case. Things might have returned to normal, or close to it, at Duke and in Durham. After all, without the DNA evidence linking the Duke players to a rape and an assault of Mangum, how could Nifong possibly make a case that would stand up in court, before a jury? Certainly, had the SBI's DNA results been made public on April 4, when they were definitively known, the reaction from nearly every constituency in the case—the students, their attorneys, the Duke administration, even likely the skeptics in and around Duke and Durham—would have demanded an end to the investigation. They might also have demanded Nifong's scalp for being so continuously and outspokenly contemptuous of the players, their alleged behavior, and their civil rights. The public release of the DNA evidence on April 4—or its sharing with defense attorneys who had a right to know it and who would then have made it public—would likely have also doomed Nifong's reelection effort, the vote for which was still a month away. Both of his Democratic challengers for the job—former assistant DA and Nifong nemesis Freda Black and Keith Bishop—already were questioning whether Nifong had "politicized" the case in order to dispel criticism that the DA's office was too slow in prosecuting crime.

But Nifong was not ready to concede that he did not have the evidence to support the rape charges. Even though he told the media the SBI had not finished its DNA testing, by April 4 he was already armed with the knowledge that the DNA evidence would not support the case he was making. He had been saying for days that he did not intend to rely on the DNA evidence anyway. Instead, there was the evidence—Nifong had claimed repeatedly—of rape found by Tara Levicy, the SANE nurse, and there was Mangum's identification of the three players earlier that day. Nifong was on a mission.

Indeed, the legal hijinks and media histrionics were about to ratchet up to an entirely new level, leaving in their wake nearly inconceivable carnage.

After Nifong shared the SBI DNA results with Gottlieb and Soucie, and after receiving a recommendation from Mike Budzinski at the SBI lab, he directed Soucie to arrange for a new set of DNA tests to be conducted by a private lab in Burlington, North Carolina—DNA Security, Inc., or DSI, as it was known. At his suggestion, Soucie called Brian Meehan, a PhD in marine science and a specialist in DNA analysis and testing who had founded DSI in 1998. Meehan had aggressively been marketing his services to sheriffs, police departments, and district attorneys. Meehan claimed DSI could do more detailed DNA analysis than the state lab at a lower cost. That was good enough for Nifong.

Nifong hired DSI to retest the evidence in the lacrosse case, including the forty-six DNA swabs taken from the white Duke lacrosse players and the DNA swabs taken from Mangum. Meehan agreed to do the testing, and cut his fee in order to "be involved in the high-profile rape investigation." To transfer the evidence from the SBI to Meehan's lab, Nifong needed a court order.

The next day, Nifong secretly filed a motion with Judge Stephens. The new tests were "believed to be material and relevant to an ongoing criminal investigation," the motion stated. Had Nifong's motion—or Stephens's court order approving the transfer—been made public contemporaneously, the resulting outcry might well have forced an end to the case. But both Nifong's motion and the judge's order were sealed. In his motion, Nifong informed Judge Stephens that "various items of evidence seized and collected in this case, including a standard rape kit from the victim and cheek swabbings from the group containing the suspects" were submitted to the SBI for testing. He noted that "the tests conducted by the SBI laboratory failed to reveal the presence of semen on swabs from the rape kit or the victim's underwear," and that "in cases without semen present, it is sometimes possible to extract useful DNA samples for comparison purposes using a technique known as Y STR," which isolates cells containing a Y chromosome from the sample provided. A Y chromosome necessarily must have been "contributed by a male person," David Saacks, Nifong's assistant district attorney, wrote to Judge Stephens. "The SBI laboratory is not equipped to conduct Y STR DNA analysis."

Saacks further asserted that DSI had agreed to undertake the tests in "an expedited manner" and that "no other reasonable means exist to obtain this information from another source." The new tests and their analysis would be "in the best interest of the enforcement of the law and administration of justice." Within hours of the motion's submission, Judge Stephens signed the order as requested. The next day the SBI transferred the DNA materials to DSI in Burlington, and the new DNA testing commenced. The results of these new DNA tests would have repercussions that no one at the time could have anticipated.

CHAPTER SEVEN

A Sudden Resignation

While Nifong was quietly building his rape and assault case against three Duke lacrosse players, he also decided to dramatically curtail his media appearances—not because of the criticism he had been getting for seeming to try the case so publicly before any charges had been filed, but simply because it was taking too much of his time. He said he had spent forty hours in the previous few days answering reporters' questions and had given some seventy interviews about the case, ten times more than he had been asked to give in death-penalty murder cases. He wanted a break.

Despite Nifong's intentional strategy to blanket the airwaves during those first weeks after he took over the case, he said he initially misjudged the media's interest. "When I first learned of this assault and the circumstances under which it allegedly occurred, I expected that it would receive some media attention," he told the *Durham Herald-Sun*, ironically. "Unfortunately, I greatly underestimated both the breadth and the depth of the media interest that would ensue."

Meanwhile, on Duke's campus, Brodhead continued his efforts to try to reduce the tension that the alleged rape had caused. He met with two student groups—the undergraduate InterCommunity Council and the Graduate and Professional Student Council, for graduate students—and explained that everyone remained on high alert. "Everybody understands the capacity of this event to rip this place apart and reactivate tensions with very long-running histories," he told the graduate students. "Everyone I've talked to who's lived in this city in a substantial way understands how very dangerous that would be." He urged students to learn from the incident, no matter how it turned out. "Even if the most serious of these things come to pass, it will be in our power to write a better history," he continued. He also reminded the graduate students of the importance of due process. "The business of a presumption of innocence is not just some abstract thing that people in law schools care about," he said. "It is actually the safeguard that allows us all to live our lives."

The students wanted to know why Duke had turned over the investigation to the Durham police instead of doing its own investigation. He said the university did not have access to the same information as the police and warned that tampering with what the police were doing could backfire against the school. "If we were to conduct our own separate, parallel investigation, there's all kinds of ways that could interfere—without meaning to—with the police investigation," he continued, sounding very much like he had been briefed by legal counsel. He reiterated that once the police concluded their investigation, the university would respond "appropriately and seriously" if the lacrosse players were in fact culpable. He said he had been in contact with the leaders of the Durham community and was not terribly concerned that the situation was spiraling out of control. "This is not exactly the place where never is heard a discouraging word, and the deer and the antelope play," he said, implying that there had often been trouble between Duke and Durham.

That night more than 250 people from around Durham held a candlelight vigil at North Carolina Central University. In her coverage of the gathering, Juliet Macur of the *New York Times* appropriately noted the many differences between Duke and NCCU. Although only three miles apart, NCCU was a historically black college on Durham's landlocked south side without Duke's "landscaped lawns" and lacrosse team. Annual tuition and housing cost around $9,500 at NCCU, compared to $44,000 at Duke. "The issues of race and class could not be avoided [at the rally]," Macur wrote, "considering the glaring differences between the universities, both of them steeped in tradition, that share this city." But there were some tenuous ties, such as an auditorium at NCCU provided by Benjamin Duke in 1938 and an occasional football game between the two schools (in 2009 and again in 2012).

But what the schools did have in common was not on the rally's agenda. The gathering was designed to show support for Mangum—who was not at the rally and whose name was still not known—as a twenty-seven-year-old NCCU student and single mother. "We want the woman to know that we're not going to let this issue just slide by," said Renee Clark, the president of the student government association at NCCU. "We're not going to let Duke keep sweeping this under the rug just because they want to save their lacrosse season. . . . Things get hushed up pretty quickly at Duke . . . because they have money and can lawyer up pretty quickly. How many lawyers do the lacrosse players have? It's like the O. J. Simpson dream team. Here, we couldn't afford that, and if the situation was opposite, our players would be in jail right now." Other NCCU students agreed. "We really want to show our support for our fellow Eagle [the nickname given to NCCU students], especially as she's being portrayed as someone who deserved it because she's an exotic dancer," said Jazmine Godbold, a NCCU sophomore from Charlotte. "We want to show her that we know it wasn't her fault, that she didn't deserve this, that we support her. Regardless of what her job was, no person deserves to be raped."

After making sure his colleague, Michele Soucie, was arranging for the new DNA tests, Gottlieb had two new assignments of his own to get under way.

A few members of the Durham city council were starting to hear from the community about the alleged rape at 610 North Buchanan and at least one city council member, Howard Clement, believed the council should make a public statement about it. "I don't think it is appropriate for the city council to just sit by quietly and witness the flow of events in this great city that has, to my regret, attracted nationwide attention," Clement told his fellow council members. "In my twenty-three years of being on the city council, I have never witnessed anything like what is happening in this city [today]. . . . I think we have an obligation to have a response. To sit by idly would be a gross dereliction of our responsibility." While his fellow council members did not respond to Clement's entreaty, the Durham city manager wanted to make sure he had a clear understanding of the time line of events surrounding the rape allegations. Accordingly, Gottlieb's boss asked him to prepare the time line and have it ready by noon on April 5 so that the city manager could share it with the council.

That same afternoon, Gottlieb also organized an old-fashioned "canvass" of the neighborhood around 610 North Buchanan, whereby police officers talked to residents at each of the neighborhood's homes to see if any useful new information related to the alleged incident could be learned. Police visited homes to the north and south of 610 North Buchanan and also on Watts Street, which runs parallel to North Buchanan. They asked questions of the neighbors and passed out Himan's card and urged people to call him if they had anything to report. They used a simple flyer with a Durham Police Department logo stating that at around 11 p.m. on the evening of March 13 the "Duke University lacrosse team solicited a local escort service for entertainment," adding that the "victim" was paid to dance at 610 North Buchanan, where the team was hosting a party. At the party, the flyer noted without qualification, the "victim" was "sodomized, raped, assaulted and robbed." The "horrific crime sent shock waves throughout our community." The police wrote that they needed help in solving this case.

In accord with his new strategy of keeping a lower public profile, Nifong refrained from giving media interviews during the first week of April. But that did not keep the press from getting seemingly obscure pieces of information about the Duke lacrosse players that would prove, in short order, to be particularly damning. For instance, on April 4, Juliet Macur reported in the *New York Times* that lacrosse player Collin Finnerty, then nineteen, and two of his high school lacrosse teammates at Chaminade High School on Long Island had been arrested the previous November 5 in Washington, DC. At 2:30 a.m. that day, Jeffrey O. Bloxsom told police that Finnerty and his friends had "punched him in the face and body" because "he told them to stop calling him gay and other derogatory names." He said the three men had "without provocation attacked him, busting his lip and bruising his chin." Finnerty's attorney, Steven McCool, declined to allow Finnerty to speak to Macur but said, "The assault was a minor scuffle and is in no way related to any inappropriate comment. If this was anything more than a minor assault, the US attorney would have brought appropriate charges." The story revealed that in order to eliminate the assault charge against him, Finnerty had entered a "diversion program" that required him to perform twenty-five hours of community service and to stay out of trouble.

A story in the *New York Times* about Finnerty and a gay-bashing incident six months earlier was unlikely to have been a mere coincidence. More likely, Macur was tipped off not only that Finnerty had been involved in the alleged assault in Georgetown but also that Mangum had fingered him as one of her alleged attackers.

Nifong's decision not to release the DNA results from the state lab also caused a stir, especially since he had earlier indicated the results would prove that he was right when he said he was "convinced that there was a rape." By law, though, the DNA results had to be given to the students tested or to their attorneys, who would likely release them publicly, especially if they showed there was no DNA evidence of a rape. At least one defense attorney, Kerry Sutton, doubted Nifong would prevent the release of the DNA evidence, even if he were not the one to release it. "I can't imagine that Mr. Nifong would have any interest in delaying the process of allowing these young men to get their lives back in order when the DNA tests come back and show they were not involved in any sexual assault," she said.

The *Chronicle*'s editors, meanwhile, found Nifong's "inconsistency" to be "maddening." "If his intention all along was to keep the results to himself for the time being, why would he whet the public's appetite with his statements of limitless confidence?" the editors wondered. "Perhaps he should have taken a 'wait and see' stance from the beginning. Now his community is on edge." The paper, insightfully, wondered whether the coercive way in which Nifong obtained the DNA evidence might make it inadmissible in a courtroom. Its editors also thought that Nifong's decision to personally prosecute the case even though he had not tried a case in five years—while also being in the middle of a contested reelection campaign—smacked of "political opportunism." "That Nifong has conducted himself with so little professionalism as of late might mean he is not the person for this extremely important job," the editors wrote.

Instead of using DNA evidence to make his case, Nifong reiterated that he would rely instead on Mangum's personal identification of the men who had allegedly raped her. He alone knew she had made her latest attempt at identifying her assailants on April 4. Indeed, defense attorneys told the media that had Mangum been able to positively identify her attackers, "they already would have been arrested without DNA evidence." One defense lawyer, speaking anonymously, told the *Durham Herald-Sun* that Nifong had told him "he had not received reports of such an identification," even though officers Gottlieb and Soucie had briefed Nifong within minutes of the conclusion of Mangum's identification session on April 4.

There was no question that a shift in prosecutorial strategy was under way. And, as if on cue, on the evening of April 3, Mangum's father—without revealing his identity—gave his first national television interview on the *Rita Cosby Live and Direct* show on MSNBC. "She's a well-spoken girl," he told Rita. "And she'd take care of her kids. She'd go to school. She's just a good child. I mean, she's my baby girl." He said she was the mother of two children, ages five and seven. "She believes in God and she don't believe in doing anything wrong," he said.

Mangum's father did not know she had been performing as an "exotic dancer" to make extra money for herself and her children. "No, I didn't," he said. "No, I didn't. I mean, that's where she was going when she said she was going to work, but she didn't ever tell me what kind of work she was doing." He said his daughter called him from Duke Hospital at around 8 a.m. on the morning of March 14. "Well, she said, 'Dad, it's something bad happened.' And I said, 'What was it?' She said, 'Well, I'll have to talk to you later about that. I've got to go.'" When Mangum's boyfriend bought her to her father's house a few days later, "she was in a lot of pain, and her face was swolled up," he told the audience. "She had bruises on her eyes. And she just looked awful, and you look at her, you could tell she had been beaten up. . . . She looked like she had been in a fight. I don't know if you've ever seen the boxers on TV. She looked like she had been in a real good fight and lost." She told him her leg also was hurt badly. "She said, 'My leg is hurting real bad. . . . I think it was thrown out of joint,'" he said. "As a matter of fact, she told me the doctor had tried to put it back in, in the joint."

Turns out, he had seen his daughter on March 12, the day before the alleged incident. She had no bruises then, and they were talking and laughing. Two days later "she was a whole lot different," he said. "She wasn't the same person." Mangum told her father that "she had got raped by three men. They had took her pocketbook, her cellular phone, and her money and all the stuff she had." What was his reaction? Cosby asked. "I just—I couldn't concentrate on anything," he said. "It was just a terrible feeling. A person would have to go through it to know, you know, exactly how it feels. It's hard to explain. I didn't want to believe it. And at the same time, I knew it was true." He said the assailants made "racial slurs" while they were "beating her." He said the scene inside the house made her daughter feel like "she thought she was going to die. She said she thought they were going to kill her. . . . She didn't know if she was going to get out of there alive or not." She told him that when she reached for her cell phone to call 911, her alleged assailants took it away from her. "She said they told her she wasn't going to call nobody," he said.

Cosby asked Mangum's father if her daughter was able to identify the three men who allegedly raped her. "She said she did," he said. "She ID'd them to [the police]." Positively? Cosby asked. "Yes," he said. No doubt it was those three men? she inquired. "No doubt in her mind," he replied. "She said she know their face." Was it possible that his daughter had engaged in consensual sex? "No, I don't think she would have," he said. "I think she only went there to dance, and that was it." And what would the DNA evidence show? "I think it will show that they did rape her," he replied. He said he was 100 percent certain of that fact. "I believe she was raped," he said. "I believe she was beaten and raped."

At around noon on April 5, Gottlieb got a tip that there might have been a second rape involving Duke lacrosse players from a few years earlier "that may add light to this case," but that that assault was unrelated to Mangum's allegations. According to Gottlieb's case notes, the mother of a former Duke student informed Durham police that her daughter was attending a lacrosse team party at a house in Trinity Park, off East Campus, when she became drunk. The mother told police that team members "surrounded" her daughter and then "gang-raped her." She said her daughter did not want to report the incident "even now" and had been "in and out of treatment for the traumatic experience." The mother also reported that her daughter had dropped out of Duke and "never returned." Gottlieb noted that he asked a colleague to track down more information about the alleged incident, specifically if there was a rape kit related to it and whether the daughter had received any medical treatment at the time. For the moment, news of this new allegation involving Duke lacrosse players would be kept quiet.

But what had been made public—and prompted the ongoing avalanche of negative media coverage—was beginning to test the resolve of the Duke administrators. At 10 a.m. on the morning of April 5, Joe Alleva, the athletic director, and Chris Kennedy, the associate athletic director, asked Pressler to meet at Alleva's office at Cameron Indoor Stadium. Alleva had bad news for Pressler. "The situation has gotten out of hand," Alleva told him, "and they must cancel the season immediately." Pressler was shocked. "You promised the players to their face there would be no more forfeiture of games unless charges were brought," Pressler responded. "What new [thing] has happened? Joe, you told the players and the parents you believed their story, you believed in them, you believed they were telling the truth. It's all about the truth. We must stand for the truth."

Looking right at Pressler, Alleva replied, "It's not about the truth anymore. It's about the integrity of the university. It's about the faculty, the city, the NAACP, the protesters, and the other interest groups." Pressler was "dumbfounded" and told Alleva that if he was worried about the players' safety, the school should "hire a thousand security guards." He told Alleva that if a similar problem were occurring in the football or the basketball program, "that is exactly what he would do." But lacrosse, he said, was "expendable." "We are educators first and foremost," Pressler told his boss. "Now we are saying to the players the truth only matters when it is convenient." Pressler pleaded with Alleva not to cancel the season. "Joe, the DNA results are imminent, and you know there will be no match," he said. "Just wait a few more days and we will have verification of what we all believe. Just a few more days."

There was silence in the room while Alleva considered what his lacrosse coach had said. In the end, Alleva acceded to Pressler's request. "Okay, we will wait," he said. "You can continue to practice and prepare to go to Ohio State on Saturday." Pressler left Cameron Indoor Stadium and walked into the spring air. He called his wife. "I felt like we had won a stay of execution," he told her. That feeling would dissipate quickly.

Moments after Gottlieb received word of the new rape allegation, Durham court officials unsealed the warrant that had authorized the March 27 search of Ryan McFadyen's dorm room. Not only was the fact that police had searched McFadyen's room now public but so also was McFadyen's toxic e-mail. Why Judge Stephens chose this moment to unseal the warrant, and at whose request he did it, was not known. In short order, after people digested McFadyen's e-mail, all hell broke loose. According to Brodhead, John Burness, Duke's director of communications, found McFadyen's e-mail that morning on the website of the *News & Observer* and "came bounding through my door and handed me something from the [*News & Observer*] website," Brodhead said. "And that's where I first read this e-mail, and I have to say when I read it, I was sickened. I found it repulsive, that's all I can say."

That morning, McFadyen went to his Spanish class and then headed to the library to write a five-page history paper due later that night. "I was leaving the Spanish class on East Campus, walking to the library to finish a paper before practice, and I get a call, a phone call from a number that I don't recognize," he remembered. "I used to always answer. Someone is calling me. They must mean to call me. . . . So I answer it and it's Mrs. Tkac. Chris Tkac's mom, Chris and Joe Tkac, two of my teammates, both younger. It's their mother. I know Mrs. Tkac casually. She's not good family friends with us. It's not like she's from Jersey. She's from Maryland. 'Hey, Mrs. Tkac, what's up?' She's like, 'Well, your e-mail has been on—your search warrant has been unsealed. Your e-mail is public. The next couple weeks are gonna be really tough for you. I just want to say I love you, and if you need anything, please don't hesitate to call.'"

McFadyen thanked her and said he had no idea that the search warrant had been unsealed. "I had been in class and I was walking to the library," he said. "It was the middle of the quad on East Campus. In between that call and me getting to the library, I had five other calls. I remember one of them was Bob Ekstrand. One of them was Coach Pressler. One of them was KJ Sauer [a senior on the team]. KJ was going to Bob's office to meet with the captains. All the seniors were there. Coach Pressler was there." Ekstrand told him that his e-mail had gone viral. "We need to prepare a statement," Ekstrand told McFadyen, who then went to the library and pounded out on his computer a passionate defense of his actions. McFadyen remembered the draft, which he did not save, went something like: "This is Mike Nifong's attempt to scare me into accusing all my teammates of rape and nothing happened." He said he "went on to rip apart Mike Nifong, say that it was a joke and that was it. But it was really poorly worded and just not the way you go about it." After he finished the draft, he spoke with Sauer, who told McFadyen he would meet him on a street corner on East Campus and drive him to Ekstrand's office. "He picks me up, drives me over," McFadyen said.

At noon, standing in front of the Duke Chapel, a television reporter read from the warrant and the e-mail without mentioning—or likely knowing about—the *American Psycho* reference. After watching the broadcast, Pressler said his first instinct was to find McFadyen. "I was worried about his well-being," he said. "I was worried that they had shown his picture and in the craziness that something could happen to him." He said he had repeatedly called McFadyen's cell phone without reaching him. Finally, according to Pressler, at 1 p.m. he heard from McFadyen, who was at Ekstrand's office. He was safe but scared. Pressler immediately went to Ekstrand's office to see his player. "He started to explain the e-mail," Pressler recalled, "but I let him know it wasn't important. His well-being was the priority." They agreed McFadyen should stay put at his attorney's office for the time being.

When McFadyen walked into Ekstrand's office, he saw Pressler talking to his lawyer. "Coach Pressler was emotional," he remembered. "And I'm just like, 'If my e-mail is making something more serious, I quit. I'm off the team. I quit. Just cut me off. I don't need to be associated with the program.' I had no idea what was going on in terms of how the media was covering it. I was just like, 'Sacrifice me.' I remember him being like, 'No, it's fine.'" They talked a bit more and then Pressler left. (Alleva had summoned him back to campus.) Ekstrand turned on the TV and pulled up the stories about McFadyen on the Internet. "Things got real serious," Ekstrand told him. "We're gonna keep you at Stef's apartment for this afternoon. We'll get you some food. Just hang out there until we figure out what's going on." Ekstrand also asked to see McFadyen's draft of a statement about the e-mail. "I read this thing out, and [Ekstrand's] like, 'No, we're not reading that,'" McFadyen said. "I didn't know anything about how to handle yourself in terms of media. I didn't realize how significant it was at that point still."

Stefanie Sparks took McFadyen back to her apartment. "That's when I got my first time to watch TV and see what was going on in the news, and this is when the Duke rape case was on every channel twenty-four hours a day," he said. "Dan Abrams [on MSNBC] was just starting to get involved with it. I hid out there for the day." He could not believe what he was watching on TV about himself. "Holy shit," he said. "I'm seeing people tearing me apart on TV, taking every word I wrote, taking my e-mail verbatim and taking it literally, and then: 'What a sick, twisted individual, misogynistic, racist.' It was every kind of unappealing stereotype you could imagine, any unappealing generalization you could make about somebody. That's what they were saying about me. It all started from a frickin' joke. It was a joke. It was an e-mail that I wrote within two seconds and it was never meant to be—you know, it was just like, 'Oh my god.'"

McFadyen explained the context for the e-mail. "That e-mail is one of a string of e-mails that start on the first day when a new team is assembled and we have our team e-mail chain—no coaches. E-mails cover everything from 'Hey, practice has changed to this time' to 'Hey, we're all gonna meet at this house before we go out' to 'Hey, we're doing a party for whoever' or 'Hey, everyone wear your blue shorts for practice today'—everything, just amongst the guys," he said. "And it's a lot of ripping each other back and forth, especially at that time, when guys began to have e-mail on their phones. It's constant 'cause everyone is just, like, boom, and you send something to forty guys and you don't think about it. So that was me. I was just making a joke about that night. I sent it off and that was it." Of course, he had been asked a thousand times why he sent the e-mail. "Well, had I known it was gonna be published in the New York Times, maybe I would have rephrased it or I would have cited my sources, or maybe I would have said, 'Oh, by the way, there's no way I plan to act on this e-mail and there was no assault,'" he said.

Referring to his e-mail, he continued, "It was 'Let me make a joke.' And if you had gone back, if I had that e-mail chain for the year, there would be plenty of e-mails that, when taken out of context, can be read as offensive. It was locker-room talk. It was digital locker-room talk, you know. This is something that kids now, six years later, it's known. [But back then,] if you send something in text or you send off an e-mail, the way you treat it is boom, boom, boom. You don't think about it. But now people have to understand that's not the way it is. It's etched in that digital medium for a life. I could send something to God knows who and the FBI could be stalking me for twenty years. But in 2006 that mentality hadn't set in yet. So for us, this e-mail chain was just fooling around. You know, you say things and it comes and it goes."

He said he did not even remember sitting down in the early morning of March 14 and sending the e-mail, that's how casual and unpremeditated it was for him. Indeed, he explained, the whole afternoon and evening were unremarkable. "Somebody said, 'Let's drink some beers. Let's order some food.

Let's have some girls dance for us. No big deal. Let's go to a bar. Let's call it a night.' What happened was everybody chipped in twenty bucks. The girls danced for five minutes. They took all our money. They didn't dance. It was five minutes of dancing and this girl is, like, passed out on the floor. And I just remember seeing Dan Flannery carry her out. I'm like, 'Jesus Christ, what a mess. This girl is high on something.' It was kind of like a casual night. That e-mail was just one of a lot I had sent that year. I thought of myself as a funnier kid on the team. I made a lot of jokes and I definitely still do that with some e-mail chains. Obviously now I second-guess everything. . . . I was making a joke, and I happened to make a dark-humor joke referencing a movie about a serial killer who kills strippers and homeless people and prostitutes, and that tied in perfectly to the story line of the mostly white lacrosse team raping a poor black girl from Durham."

McFadyen's hours at Sparks's apartment in Durham were nothing if not chaotic. He spoke with his mother. "I was a frickin' mess while watching the media coverage," he said. His father got on a plane and flew to Raleigh. "I'm coming down to get you," he told him. Ekstrand said he needed to hire his own attorney and recommended Glen Bachman, whom the family quickly hired. "I didn't know who he was. Ekstrand recommended him to my parents, and I said, 'Yeah, sure. Let's hire him,'" he recalled. "He was my lawyer that night." McFadyen spoke with Sue Wasiolek, the dean of students. He said he doesn't recall the precise conversation but remembered it was something along the lines of what he had told Pressler when he saw him in Ekstrand's office. "I'm not an idiot," he said. "I know what's going on. The same way I said to Coach P, 'I quit. I'm off the team. Just cut me away.' I remember just being like, 'Holy shit, they're tarnishing Duke. They're tarnishing my team. They're tarnishing my coach.' I don't know if I was exactly crying, but I was just being so overwhelmed with 'I don't know what to do. I'm really sorry. What can I do to help? I don't want this to affect anything,' not having a clue in terms of long-term [consequences]," he said. "I know after the fact she was like, 'We'd like you to sign this document, just so we can say that we've put you on interim suspension. You didn't do anything wrong. It's only temporary,' whatever, whatever." He said Wasiolek told him he was being suspended, in part, for his own protection because people were protesting outside of his dormitory. But he e-mailed a dormmate to find out if that was true, and she e-mailed back that no one was protesting outside of Edens.

Not surprisingly, in the wake of the tense discussion earlier that morning between Alleva and Pressler—before McFadyen's e-mail saw the light of day—Alleva wanted to see Pressler immediately. After visiting with McFadyen at Ekstrand's office, Pressler returned to see Alleva around 1:30 p.m. There were no pleasantries this time. "Alleva immediately said the e-mail was very bad," Pressler wrote in his diary. "He said our season was immediately canceled and

I had to resign by 4:30 p.m. that day or take an interim suspension until a committee report on the program was furnished to the president—which is the investigation of the program." Alleva told him Brodhead would be holding a press conference at 4:30 that afternoon to announce the end of the lacrosse season and Pressler's resignation. "It was a kick in the gut," Pressler recalled. "I asked Joe who was firing me, him or Brodhead? He hesitated and said, 'I am firing you.' In my mind, I thought, 'Even at the very end he can't tell me the truth.'"

Pressler reminded Alleva for the second time that day that he had told the players he believed their story that no rape had occurred on the evening of March 13. "Joe, if I knew this was true and my players had not turned themselves in, I would have turned them in to the police immediately," he told Alleva. "I would have offered my resignation, and I would have encouraged you to end the program. I would have done so in a New York minute. But with the *same zeal*, I am telling you they didn't do it. They didn't touch that person." His comments fell on deaf ears. "Joe Alleva wasn't hearing a word I said," Pressler recalled.

He left Alleva's office—"my head was spinning"—and returned to his own. He called his wife and asked her to fax him his new contract—a three-year deal he had negotiated soon after leading the team to the championship game the previous season, with a car allowance and a "substantial raise." A multiyear contract for the coach of a "nonrevenue" sport at Duke—other than basketball or football—was unprecedented. At the time of the contract extension, Alleva had told Pressler, "Mike, as long as I'm athletic director, you're my lacrosse coach." The Presslers were so relieved by Alleva's unequivocal endorsement that they had built an addition to their Durham home.

Since Brodhead was announcing his "resignation" at 4:30 p.m., he had ninety minutes to somehow come to an agreement with Alleva about the financial terms of his departure from the university. He also wanted the lacrosse players to hear from him directly that he had been fired. He called a team meeting for 4:30 p.m. "No questions asked," he remembered. "Everyone knew this was the low point."

After discussing the situation with his lawyer, Pressler went back to see Alleva and told him what he thought he was owed under his contract. "Okay, I think we can do this," Alleva told him. He then called over to Allen Building to get the needed approval. Twenty minutes later, Pressler was back in Alleva's office. "Mike, you are not going to be happy with this," Alleva told him. "They are not going to give you what you asked for, what we agreed upon. The university counsel has said we can fire you with cause."

Pressler blew up. "What?" he yelled at Alleva. "What cause? What did I do?"

"This is about your players and their past disciplinary problems," the athletic director replied, a reference to the fifteen players who had been cited in prior years for underage drinking, public urination, and being too rowdy.

"Joe, that's bullshit and you know it," Pressler responded. "You knew all of those incidents two years ago. We dealt with those. You also know that the majority of those problems I was never aware of because the dean of students' office did not make me aware of them. Joe, you are holding me accountable for things I didn't know. You know that, and I know that." Alleva sat silently. But Pressler concluded quickly he had little choice but to "resign" and take the severance offered, even if it was well below what he was contractually entitled to receive as head lacrosse coach. If he waited out the report and the "interim suspension," it was quite possible he would be fired for cause at that point and then get nothing. "With a wife and children, I couldn't risk being fired with cause, and having no severance and no benefits," he wrote later. "But maybe the part of this that bothers me the most is that after sixteen years building a program for Duke, sixteen very loyal years, I was being given an hour and a half to decide my future."

Alleva then further offended Pressler by asking him if he preferred if Alleva tell the team about Pressler's firing. "Are you fucking kidding me?" Pressler thought to himself. "If he goes over there with me, this guy will not make it out of that room alive." Incredibly, while Pressler was dealing in real time with his own horrific fate, he found the time to counsel Chris Kennedy, who was also thinking of resigning as a result of the conflagration. Pressler talked him out of it. "It would have been a mistake," Kennedy recalled four years later. "It would have been a reaction as impetuous as forcing [Pressler] to resign. But I've been at this university . . . thirty-five years, virtually my entire professional career. . . . I believe completely in what the university stands for and in its goals and missions. My life is intertwined with the place. I met my wife here. We were married in York Chapel. My children were born in Duke Hospital. They're both Duke graduates, and I felt that this place that I had given so much to and stood for so much that I believed in was abandoning those beliefs in the way it was acting. And that was not intolerable, but it was close to it." He said, though, by not resigning he appeared to be condoning what was going on, which he did not find palatable. "The university was not supporting the students as well as it could have," he said. He conceded that while he had "sympathy" for the tough decision-making that needed to occur amid the "chaos," still, "so many segments of the university had abandoned those kids, and abandoned them when they needed support the most, and they didn't get much support from any quarter."

As he headed out of Cameron yet again to where the players were meeting in the Murray Building, Pressler noticed reporters and photographers streaming toward him as he headed to what he described as "the worst meeting of my life," more difficult even than eulogizing his younger brother, who had died suddenly three years earlier of a heart attack at age forty-one.

As he walked into the room, he saw his assistant coaches and told them what was happening. Every player but McFadyen was present. As usual, the seniors were sitting in the front row, the juniors behind them, and then the sophomores and freshmen. Pressler looked right at them. "Gentlemen, our darkest hour has arrived," he told them. He could see the emotion suddenly descending over the players. "The season has been canceled and I am resigning, effective immediately, as the head men's lacrosse coach at Duke." According to Pressler, "mass hysteria broke out," with nearly everybody overcome with emotion and crying. The players were shocked. "We walked in that day thinking we are going for another meeting," defenseman Tony McDevitt recalled. "Coach looked exhausted. He did his best to stay strong. He was at a loss for words." Pressler continued to try to explain what had happened. "You are not responsible for this," he continued. "You did not do this. It is not Ryan McFadyen's fault. It is the administration that did this to us. It is the prosecutor who did this to us. We have paid our price for that evening of March 13; all that has occurred after that is not your fault, guys. You didn't get me fired. You didn't cancel the season."

Pressler was not certain the players even heard what he said because of how emotional the scene became. "Gentlemen," he concluded, "someday we will have our day. Someday I will tell the world the truth. I promise you all the lies, all the myths, all the injustice, will be made right. Someday we will tell the world the truth. I promise you." The players begged Pressler not to resign, "missing that the choice was not his," he explained later. They asked him questions, many of which he could not answer. "The pendulum of emotion swung from fear to anger, from pain to guilt," he continued. He thought they blamed themselves for his firing, despite Pressler's efforts to assure them otherwise. On the other hand, what other logical conclusion was there? "Stick together and always stand up for the truth," he told the players one last time before they headed out into the media scrum. Some were on their cell phones; others provided comfort to one another. An unidentified woman asked the media to leave the players alone.

"I remember leaving the meeting, tears in my eyes," McDevitt said later, "because I was watching a guy I looked up to in so many ways and a guy who took a chance on me, my coach, a friend, a mentor, everything. And everything has just been taken from him." He called his mother at work. "I remember telling her this is so wrong, what happened to this poor guy," he continued. "That was the climax of the disaster. It was April 5. It couldn't get worse than that day." Added Dan Flannery, the cocaptain who had made the call to arrange for the strippers on the night of March 13, "Sometimes you ask yourself what you learn from people. I don't have to ask what I learned from Coach Pressler. He showed more class, more strength, more dignity, than anyone in this whole situation. I can confidently say that the meeting on April 5, when Coach resigned, that was the worst meeting of my life and will be the worst meeting of my life. Duke took his livelihood away for something we did. And he was a complete stand-up man. I will keep that the rest of my life."

Other reactions to Pressler's resignation varied. "I think it's extremely appropriate that the coach resigned and that the season was canceled," Peter Wood told the Durham paper. "Given the new evidence that emerged"— McFadyen's e-mail and the unsealing of the warrant—"further steps are going to have to be taken. The university will have to decide about men's lacrosse in the coming years and about the status of other officials at Duke." A week earlier, Pressler had called Joe Breschi, the Ohio State University lacrosse coach, and told him the Duke team would not be coming to the April 1 game. "You could just tell he was in a tough spot," Breschi said after Pressler's resignation. "It's a tough situation, something you wouldn't wish on your program or any program. The kids, they're your responsibility. You preach every day about every situation, and every weekend you tell them to be safe and be careful and to take care of each other. That's all you can do. . . . He has to be considered one of the premier coaches out there. It's just an unfortunate and sad situation." Observed Pressler, "The kids weren't responsible for what happened. They were responsible for poor judgment, immaturity, and stupid behavior. But that's why we have adults to sort it out . . .politicians and administrators, who have experience dealing with issues like this. In this case nothing fit, and all they needed to do was wait for the DNA. You couldn't make up a scenario more unfair." Chris Kennedy was not consulted about the decision, but he would not have done it. "I thought it was impulsive and reactive rather than well thought out," he said.

As part of his 4:30 p.m. press conference, Brodhead also announced that McFadyen had received an "interim suspension" from Duke—after signing a permission form allowing Brodhead to make that fact public—and was no longer on campus. Brodhead also canceled the remainder of the lacrosse season "effective immediately" and announced that Pressler had submitted his resignation to athletic director Joe Alleva, also "effective immediately." He "again" urged "anyone with information pertinent to the events of March 13 to cooperate with the authorities."

Alleva issued a statement that Pressler had "offered" his resignation earlier in the afternoon "and I accepted it." He added, "I fully support President Brodhead's decision to cancel the remainder of the season as well as his outrage at the latest developments involving the men's lacrosse program. I believe this is in the best interests of the program, the department of athletics, and the university." Alleva helpfully pointed out that Pressler had spent sixteen years at Duke and had a 153–82 record as the lacrosse coach, including the team's 2005 first-ever appearance in the NCAA national championship game. He was named the 2005 National Coach of the Year. Canceling the 2006 lacrosse season meant the end of the not-unreasonable chance the team had of becoming national champions.

• • •

McFadyen called his teammate Kevin Mayer. "Kevin, can you get me an over-night bag?" he told him. "Go into my room and grab some contacts, a pair of clothes, some shoes. Just put it in a bag."

"How long are you leaving for, a day or two?" Mayer asked.

"I'll be back within a week," he told Mayer. "This is nothing big."

He was wrong, of course. "April 5, 2006," McFadyen said. "I wanted to get that tattooed on my body, because that moment has changed my life forever. I think about it every day. I got Coach Pressler fired. I'm responsible for my teammates having the season canceled. I take responsibility. Over a year, over two years, I've told Coach Pressler. He said, 'It's not your fault.' I still get teary thinking about it right now. Think about it. Everything was just kind of going along. The rape case was gaining momentum. Nothing happened. Then it was like, 'Holy shit.'"

After making his announcements, Brodhead invited CNN and other members of the national news media into his office to discuss McFadyen's suspension. "In the normal course of things, we could not tell you anything about any individual student or their disciplinary history because of federal privacy laws," he said on CNN. "In this case, the student has waived his rights to privacy, and so we did make known today that this student is under what we call 'interim suspension'; that means he has withdrawn from school. He is not a student here at the moment." Brodhead said McFadyen would still have "access to the whole disciplinary process" at Duke in "the normal course"—whatever that meant—but that he would not be enrolled while he "goes through it." To another television interviewer who wondered "what it was about that e-mail" that made Duke suspend McFadyen, Brodhead said, "In the climate we're in where such grave things are in question, anyone who reads that e-mail . . . it's sick."

McFadyen's new attorney, Glen Bachman, said in a statement that "while the language of the e-mail is vile . . . the e-mail itself is perfectly consistent with the boys' unequivocal assertion that no sexual assault took place that evening. The time stamp on the delivery of the e-mail is 1:58 a.m., shortly after the party, which is further evidence of a lack of a guilty mind." Added defense attorney Bill Thomas, "This is a first-degree rape investigation . . . not about e-mails sent between college students that are in poor taste. . . . This one e-mail, while it is certainly disturbing, is not a reflection that a crime occurred. It is clearly aimed at inflaming the community and has no relevance to the real issues."

The stunned McFadyen sat silently while his father mapped out a possible future game plan. "Let's get on the horn," John McFadyen told his son. "Let's start getting in touch with other college coaches. Obviously you're not going to graduate from Duke." Ryan wondered if he could ever go back to Duke and what his friends and classmates would think of him. Would he always be "the kid who wrote this completely repulsive e-mail," who "must be a sociopath" and "unstable"? But he was also frustrated. "I had never had a chance to speak my side of the story," he said. "Nobody ever gave me an opportunity to explain myself." He spent the car ride and much of the night thinking about his father's advice. "I had to turn my phone off that night," he remembered. "I got a bunch of calls and e-mails from people and texts, a lot of very supportive friends, all supportive. We drive through the night. We get home, like, 6 a.m. the next day."

By the time they arrived back in New Jersey, a horde of television trucks and newspaper photographers was lined up in front of their house. "There's big news trucks outside the house, but they can't come up to the property, can't go on the property," Ryan said. "We live up the hill a little bit. We go around the barn. We pull into the house, walk up, and my three sisters and my mom all are pretty teary-eyed watching the news. I remember, the news flashes this picture of me and reads the e-mail, and then changes to something else. The news anchor was just like, 'What a sick, twisted kid. This kid's parents must really be ashamed,' or something like that. And I'm with my parents and all my little sisters are there. I just remember it being like the heaviest moment of the whole entire experience."

By the next morning, McFadyen had a plan. "Listen," he told his family. "I'm coming back to Duke. I'm going to graduate from this university." But it was going to be a long slog. While his sisters went off to school, McFadyen remained hidden inside his house. He sought out old friends. "I reached out to [my high school] Delbarton, obviously, and tried to see if, you know . . . and they're like, 'We think you should kind of stay away at this point,'" he said. "Thanks a lot. They said, 'We're supportive, but it's best if you don't come here. There're news reporters here. We don't need to feel like we're being watched.' So that was like a couple of days. So my being gone for a couple of days turned into a couple of weeks, then to a couple of months." While Delbarton wanted nothing to do with McFadyen, he did hear from Finn Wentworth, a local real estate investor and one of the founders of the YES Network. McFadyen used to play basketball with Wentworth's son. "Let's see if we can get you working, just keep you busy so you're not sitting at home, dwelling on this," Wentworth told him. "I understand the importance of that."

While if for no other reason than his own safety McFadyen needed to leave Durham—with more than a little encouragement from Brodhead and his fellow administrators—what was less explicable was the utterly nonchalant reaction the same administrators had to a far more threatening message conveyed to Pressler, the lacrosse coach, and his family in the days prior to his dismissal on April 5. On March 27, just before 2 p.m., Chauncey Nartey, a Duke junior who had been born in Liberia but raised in Ghana, sent Pressler two e-mails that "nearly sent him spiraling out of control," he would later explain. The first said, "Some things are more important than winning a few games. End the season until the alleged rapists are found! You'll be a much better coach for it." While presumptuous, Nartey's first e-mail was typical of the "fifty million" Pressler received that "presumed his lacrosse players were guilty." The second e-mail, sent minutes later, was more personal. "What if Janet Lynn were next?' Nartey wrote, referring to Pressler's teenage daughter. Understandably upset, Pressler turned the e-mails over to his attorney, who told him that he could have Nartey arrested. His wife, Sue, filed a report with the Durham police about Nartey's apparent e-mail threat.

But the police decided not to pursue the matter, and Pressler opted not to push for Nartey's arrest. Instead, he asked Larry Moneta, the dean of students, to "deal with it." To Pressler's "outrage," though, Moneta gave Nartey a "slap on the wrist" and told him "Chauncey, don't do it again. Okay? And you should write the coach an apology."

With the pressure of the Duke administration ratcheting up exponentially in the wake of the release of McFadyen's e-mail, as well as the accompanying warrant that revealed publicly for the first time new details about what allegedly happened at 610 North Buchanan, Brodhead issued a lengthy, hard-hitting, and articulate statement about the ongoing controversy that seemed to be overtaking the university. Brodhead tried to walk the very fine line between not utterly condemning the students for a still-unproven incident while demonstrating a sufficient level of anger over the admitted bad-boy behavior and the possibility that more serious charges were brewing. The allegations against the lacrosse team "have deeply troubled me and everyone else at this university and our surrounding city," he wrote. "We can't be surprised at the outpouring of outrage. Rape is the substitution of raw power for love, brutality for tenderness, and dehumanization for intimacy. It is also the crudest assertion of inequality, a way to show that the strong are superior to the weak and can rightfully use them as the objects of their pleasure. When reports of racial abuse are added to the mix, the evil is compounded, reviving memories of the systemic racial oppression we had hoped to have left behind us."

If the allegations proved true, Brodhead continued, "what happened would be a deep violation of fundamental ethical principles and among the most serious crimes known to the legal system. Such conduct is completely unacceptable within the university and in our society at large. If the truth of the allegations is upheld, it will call for severe punishment from the courts and from Duke's disciplinary system." He then offered his sternest defense of permitting the legal process to run its course before drawing conclusions. "Reaching certainty without evidence or process is a double wrong in a university because it opens the door to injustice and violates our commitment to truth," he concluded.

That didn't mean that Duke intended to sit idly by and do nothing. Brod-head asked Professor James Coleman, at the Duke law school and a member of the athletic council, in charge of oversight of Duke athletics, to chair a com-mittee that would investigate and report back by May 1 "persistent problems involving the men's lacrosse team, including racist language, a pattern of alco-hol abuse, and disorderly behavior" that were "quite separate from the criminal allegations." Professor Paul Haagen, chairman of the academic council, told the *New York Times*, "I think everything's got to be on the table." Brodhead also wanted an investigation into the response of his administration to the rape alle-gations. "I have heard a good deal of criticism of the Duke administration for being slow to respond," he wrote, adding that he had explained why it took so long: "We learned the full magnitude of the allegations only gradually, as police and other information was reported in the media, and indeed it appears it took the police themselves some time to understand the nature of the case." Nev-ertheless, to address this concern, he asked two respected outsiders—William Bowen, the former president of Princeton and the president of the Andrew Mellon Foundation, and Julius Chambers, a former chancellor at NCCU—to investigate the matter and to report back by May 15.

He also asked for an examination into the way "Duke deals with problems of student behavior" and created a Campus Culture Initiative to study whether the considerable freedom students enjoyed at Duke was matched "with a com-mensurate sense of responsibility." There was no "quick fix," he wrote, but he hoped the group would figure out a way to promote "a more responsible approach to the culture of campus drinking, a major factor in Duke's recent crisis and the source of much bad college conduct throughout the United States." (One of the students appointed to the Campus Culture Initiative was Chauncey Nartey, the student who had sent the seemingly threatening e-mail to Pressler. Nartey was also given an award, at his graduation in 2007, for his distinguished leadership while a Duke student.)

Brodhead also created a "presidential council" to give him and the board of trustees guidance. He asked Roy Bostock, chairman of the Partnership for a Drug-Free America and later chairman of the board of Yahoo!, Inc., and Wil-helmina Reuben-Cook, the provost and vice president of academic affairs of the University of the District of Columbia, to chair the council. "This group will be made up of wise figures from within the university community, from the larger Duke family, from the national higher education community and from the City of Durham." He also said he would remain in close contact with Durham mayor Bill Bell and NCCU chancellor James Ammons "to seize the moment to do what I can to strengthen what is in many respects, but surely not all, a positive relationship between our university and our city." But, he warned, "I guess one of the best ways to describe this is we have the potential for a perfect storm."

Brodhead knew this was a serious moment. "Nobody wishes trouble [on] one's house, and I regret the trouble this incident has brought to Duke and Durham," he concluded. "But when trouble arrives, it's the test of a community and its leaders to deal with it honestly, act accordingly, and learn from it. This is a deeply emotional time as well as a rare opportunity for education—for our students, faculty, administrators, and members of our community. Let's move forward with a serious commitment to make progress on the many complex issues that confront us now."

Brodhead, meanwhile, had the full support of the Duke board of trustees. "The very first thing is how do we make sure this doesn't escalate into other acts of violence around campus," explained one board member. "Canceling the season was an easy one, because if you think about the things that could happen, now these lacrosse players who have been accused of this go out wearing helmets, and the next thing you know, there's a whole Black Panther gang coming from across the street, shooting them and shooting spectators. You'd sit there and say, 'What were these morons thinking? Putting these guys out on a field, in the midst of e-mails saying we're going to kill these guys and do this kind of stuff?' Remember, this wasn't that long after the Virginia Tech shootings [in which a crazed gunman killed thirty-two people and wounded seventeen others in two separate attacks]. So the main thought was 'How do we make sure this doesn't escalate into some acts of violence that will really be bad?' Early on, accusations of white boys raping a black woman, and the black community saying this can't happen, your first thought is the first and foremost thing you've got to make happen is no escalation of violence."

Firing Pressler was more an issue of holding the team's leader responsible for ongoing, unacceptable behavior. "This is now on the front page of every paper, this is what this team did, this was your job as a coach to control your team," the board member continued. "There's got to be consequences. . . . First of all, there is some evidence that this was not the first time this kind of activity came to people's attention and the coach knew about it. He didn't go out of his way to stop it. He made that decision. There's a standard you have to be held to, and I think this is lost in the whole shuffle of this thing, the whole ridiculousness of the DA and all the other stuff. I said this a lot when we were talking to [lawyers] at the time. I said, 'What's going to get lost in the shuffle is now it's going to look like the whole team were these poor, innocent kids.' They weren't. Three kids were being railroaded for something they didn't do. That's bad. But the rest of the team saying they were mistreated and this was all blown out of proportion I think is just dead wrong. In a way, I wish what this had been is this party happened and it got broken up by the cops, but it was on the front page because something happened, because then there would be no innocent victims for this team and you'd have to say, 'What do we do with a team where this is on the front page? If that was the only headline, what should we have done?' I still would've canceled the season and still would've gotten rid of the coach."

By the time Pressler made it home after the final meeting with his players, a myriad of television trucks and reporters were already camped out on his front lawn. To help her handle the media onslaught, Sue Pressler called her best friend, Debbie Savarino, Coach K's daughter. "When Sue called," Savarino recalled, "I could barely even recognize her voice, she was so shaken. All she said was 'Well, it's over.'" Soon, coaches from other teams started assembling at the Presslers', as did neighbors and friends. It became like an "Irish wake," Pressler recalled. Sue Pressler's various phones were ringing off the hook. Savarino quickly took over the job of answering them and taking notes about who had called and what they wanted. At one point, Savarino picked up the phone and heard, "Hello, this is Larry King calling. . . . I wanted to know if I could speak with Mike Pressler." Savarino told him no.

"Well, we are live" on CNN, King said.

"That's great," Savarino replied. "But I am sorry, he's unavailable right now; may I take a message for him?" Then Barbara Walters called. "It was craziness," Savarino recalled. "I filled up two pages, single-spaced, on a yellow legal pad." The two women discussed whom Sue would be willing to speak with from the media, if not Larry King or Barbara Walters. "Oprah," she said. "If Oprah calls . . ." But Oprah didn't call.

When Pressler walked past the cameras and journalists into the house, he saw Savarino, whom he always called Debbie K. "Debbie K, I took a hard one today," he told her.

As tears welled up in her eyes, she replied, "Yes, you did. *Yes, you did.*" She recalled, "And this man, this big, burly, bearded hunter-man, was hugging me in his kitchen and was crying. It was awful."

Coach K was walking through Dulles Airport when he saw the news about Pressler on the CNN crawl. "I thought that they'd either found incredibly incriminating evidence or jumped to a conclusion," he recalled. "Mike shouldn't have been fired, especially at that moment. The way it was handled and the timing made it seem like he was the reason all this occurred." Krzyzewski said Pressler was a "loyal friend" and a "hard-charger." He added, "Mike's a man, and he's handled this like a man." In private, though, Coach K was unhappy that Duke had fired his friend. A Duke board member saw Krzyzewski around this time and told him, "Mike, this whole thing is, about five years from now, when people look back, did Duke emerge stronger, or was this the thing that sent Duke down? That's what this is all about. Did Duke figure out how to come through this, get itself together, learn some lessons and move on and become stronger than ever, or is Duke written about, five years from now, as the school that was on the rise before this scandal? That's the same thing that Penn State is going to face [after the Paterno scandal], and that's the same thing that Rutgers is going to face [after firing Mike Rice, its men's basketball coach] . . . You've got to think of these things in the construct of when people look back. Everybody has their moments: Did you rise above it or did you let it be the crushing blow? He said, 'You know, I really agree with that, but the president handled things wrong.' So I said, 'Mike, so if that's the measurement five years from now, it means none of us are going back and rerunning the play. You sitting here telling me what we could have done or what Brodhead could've done is kind of like me telling you, "Why the hell did you let Calhoun run that?" [A reference to a play run by Connecticut basketball coach Jim Calhoun that sunk Duke in the 1999 NCAA championship game.] Are we going back and playing the 1999 championship game again? Look, as far as I'm concerned, there are two kinds of people left: those who want to help us move on, and those who want to sit here and talk about the past. You've got to tell me which team you're on, because I've got to tell the board.' Mike, being Mike, sort of said, 'I totally get it,' and that was it. He said, 'I'm going to meet with Brodhead and I'm going to stand side by side.' So Mike turned on a dime, because that's how Mike is."

Another board member recalled how Krzyzewski complained that Alleva was a weak athletic director. "We chose Alleva because we didn't want anyone that challenged Coach K," the board member said. "I met with Coach K, and he told me Alleva was kind of weak. I said, 'Fuck you. He's in the job because you wanted a weak pussy in the job, so now you're telling me that you've got a weak person in the job. You chose a weak person. You're the reason why. You've got no right to whine about him being weak because you put him there so you could basically be the puppeteer.' And he said, 'Well, there's some truth to that,' and I like Mike a lot."

The next day, Pressler's attorney, Edward Falcone, issued a statement defending Pressler and his stewardship of the lacrosse team. "Coach Pressler is no more guarantor of the behavior of eighteen- to twenty-one-year-olds than are parents of children that age," he said, raising the specter of the in loco parentis idea that Willimon had wrestled with in his two studies of the Duke social scene. Falcone said that during Pressler's sixteen years as the lacrosse coach, he had worked hard to try "to develop young men who are a credit to Duke University, both off and on the field." He noted that Pressler's play-ers had a 100 percent graduation rate, had been heavily involved in commu-nity service projects in Durham and, during the past five years, had had 146 players on the conference's academic honor roll, "seventy-four more than the next closest school." The allegations against his players were "very difficult" for Duke, the lacrosse program, and for Pressler personally. In the end, Fal-cone said, Pressler "felt that it was in the mutual best interests of himself and Duke University to resign," but that "resignation should not be construed as an indication that he has done anything wrong. He has done nothing wrong."

• • •

The combination of the rape allegation, the McFadyen e-mail, the firing of
Pressler, the cancellation of the lacrosse season that promised the possibility of a
national championship, and the vitriol flying on all sides further plunged Duke's
campus into turmoil, aided and abetted in nearly every way by the relentless
attention of the national media. The *Chronicle* editorialized that, whether "in
jest or in earnest," McFadyen's e-mail was "cause for concern as is our current
state—sans lacrosse coach, sans lacrosse season, sans spotless reputation."

Armed with the perfunctory time line of events put together by the Durham
police, the members of the Durham city council also weighed in on the controversy that was engulfing the city. Council member Mike Woodard, a member of the Duke class of 1981 and a Duke employee, called the allegations
against the players "abhorrent and disgusting" but criticized the media for its
coverage of the unfolding events. "These parachute journalists who drop in to
find a titillating story for the twenty-four-hour news cycle do Durham a dis-
service," he said. "Every day in the community, thousands of people are working to build bridges. . . . My sincere and fervent prayer is that in the difficult
weeks and months ahead we don't burn these bridges."

Standing in front of the Durham County Judicial Building, in downtown
Durham, a group of about ten North Carolina civil rights leaders made a plea
for justice to be properly administered. "We are in the midst of a community and legal crisis," explained Reverend William J. Barber II, the president
of the state conference of the NAACP. He said the release of the McFadyen
e-mail "raises the stakes" before adding, "How we handle this will determine
what kind of community we are. As this process unfolds, it should be done in
a transparent manner so the whole community will feel confident that justice is being served without regard to racial, economic or social status." Tracy
Egharevba, a Duke senior and president of the campus NAACP, did not criticize the Duke administration's handling of the matter. "But I do feel, as a student at Duke, that this incident has brought to light the racial issues of campus
that have been in existence before I came onto campus. We have to find a way
to integrate race relations, different cultures, and to include tolerance in the
Duke code. In answer to a question, Barber said, "What all of us need to recognize at the end of the day [is that] the biblical wisdom must be applied in this
situation: only the truth is gonna set you free."

To get insight into the effect the alleged incident was having on campus, the *New York Times*'s Karen Arenson interviewed Robert Thompson Jr.,
dean of the undergraduate College of Arts and Sciences (and the recipient of
Peter Wood's 2004 warning letter). "This event served as a lightening rod," he
said, for complex issues of race, sex, violence, privilege, and elitism that had
been simmering at Duke for decades. "It tapped into underlying feelings that
existed." He said that whatever Duke had been doing to try to address these

issues in the past had been insufficient and "needs to be doubled and tripled." Peter Lange, Duke's provost, seemed worried that much of what he had witnessed in his twenty-five years at the school might unravel. "I only hope that after we get through this that we can restore and expand the real character and reputation of the institution," he said.

Arenson observed that "Duke was for decades a bastion of Southern privilege" but for years had been trying to change that image by recruiting students and faculty from around the world. In 2006, Duke had 19,358 applicants and admitted 19 percent. In 1984, 91 percent of the freshman class was white, while the incoming class that started at Duke in September 2005 was 20 percent Asian American, 10 percent black, and 7 percent Latino. Between 1994 and 2004, Duke doubled the number of black professors to about eighty, still only 3.5 percent of the faculty.

But, she discovered, there had been concerns about the behavior of the lacrosse team, in particular, as early as the previous December when Brodhead, Lange, and Tallman Trask met to analyze what could "go wrong on campus" and how they would handle it. Athletics was an area of possible concern to the administrators. "I think the thing we were most worried about was that something could happen in athletics," Trask told the *Times*. "We didn't know what or how. But Duke athletics are on a pedestal, and the higher you climb, the faster you fall." He said the fifteen violations for "misbehaving" that the lacrosse players had received in the previous three years had been "a kind of red flag." Trask said he had pulled all their disciplinary records a year before and discovered the charges for public urination and for holding an open container of alcohol. "In hindsight, do I wish I had done more?" he wondered. "It is a stretch to get from their previous boorish behavior to gang rape." Brodhead added, though, "The notion that this kind of behavior is confined to athletes is just not so."

Arenson spoke with William Bowen, who Brodhead had just enlisted to investigate the lacrosse program at Duke, for his thoughts about big-time college athletics. "If you recruit aggressively, as Duke does in lacrosse, then you are going to end up with a group of students who are there primarily to play their sport," he said. "That's their focus. That is why they were recruited, why they were admitted. Then if you allow them to hang out together, to live together, you get a group of people largely cut off from the values of campus." She also quoted two students, Shawn Brenhouse, a "white junior from Montreal," and Taiesha Abrams, "a black freshman from Brooklyn." Both students said they had witnessed no "racial tension on campus." But Abrams cited a friend—a black student—who noticed that when he walked around, "white women look at him and are scared." "If racism is a problem," she said, "then we need to act on it; both races need to work together to change Duke."

Arenson's article mentioned, in passing, a full-page advertisement that had appeared that day in the *Chronicle*, taken out by faculty members primarily from the department of African and African-American Studies—but also from other undergraduate departments—that referred to the alleged incident as a "social disaster." Before long, the ad—appearing under the headline "What Does a Social Disaster Sound Like?" and signed by eighty-eight Duke faculty members, who collectively became known as the "Group of 88"— touched off yet another conflagration at the school. Much of the content of the ad was taken from both a March 29 forum, sponsored by the African and African-American studies departments, and from a North Carolina *Independent* article of the same date in which black women at Duke expressed their frustration with the misogynist and racist attitudes found at the school among some white students.

Danielle Terrazas Williams, a first-year student in Duke's PhD program in history, commented to the *Independent* about the alleged incident at 610 North Buchanan: "This is not a different experience for us here at Duke University. We go to class with racist classmates. We go to gym with people who are racists. That's not special for us. . . . That's part of the experience of going to a predominantly white school." Audrey Christopher, a recent Duke graduate on her way to Harvard Law School, told stories about how she and her black woman friends were treated when they went to parties at the white fraternities. "I remember once meeting someone at one of the quad parties: it was me and another black female friend, and these white guys immediately told us how they liked hanging out with black girls because white girls are sheltered and we're more free, and how they wanted to see us dance and immediately assumed that because we were black girls no one sheltered us and we weren't naïve and innocent. That was the implication [that the women would be willing to have sex with them]. I would say that if you were there, it would have come across as more than an implication. At first we thought we were just chatting with . . . *people*, and then they said that, and so we just left." Asked about her reaction to being treated that way, Christopher said, "This is something that I have cried over. It's happened quite frequently; actually, too frequently. Way too frequently. And it's really upsetting when it's a classmate. It's not some random guy on the quad, it's not some random guy at a club. It's someone you work and go to school with and who you respected up until they propositioned you, or they grabbed you in front of everyone at the party. . . . As a black female, you go to a party, you're expected to dance, you're expected to be sexually provocative. You [are expected to] want to be touched, to be grabbed, to be fondled."

Danielle Williams said the behavior of the white guys at the frat parties was "as if they're reenacting a rap video or something. As if we're there to be their video ho, basically. We can't just be regular students here. We can't just go to a party and enjoy ourselves."

"And just dance with your friends," Christopher added.

"No, it can't be just that," Williams continued. "It always has to be something more. And you wonder why there aren't a lot of black people at white parties, why we self-segregate."

"You go to a party," Christopher continued, "you get grabbed, you get propositioned, and then you start to question yourself: 'Did I give him some reason to think that I wanted to hook up with him in the bathroom?' Stuff like that. And there is no reason. There's no reason unless I said, 'I want to hook up with you in the bathroom'; there's no reason to make that assumption. But it happens all the time."

Christopher and Williams recalled a letter to the *Chronicle*, in December 2003, from Duke junior Paul Musselwhite, who argued that affirmative action was detrimental to the student population, especially to some minority students whose SAT scores were found to be some two hundred points lower than their peers' and yet were still admitted to the university. "Having a group of clearly identifiable students that are part of an educational cohort that is considerably lower than the general population of the school is bound to lead to ghettos, socially and academically," he wrote. "Making academic excellence, as opposed to academic competence, a universal standard will encourage beneficial interaction. The end of affirmative action would allow students to interact with each other as true peers, and thus increase the chances for racial mixing. Try ending institutionalized discrimination before killing frats and selective living groups."

They still remembered Musselwhite's provocative letter. "When people got offended, all you heard was 'Black students just complain all the time, all you do is complain and self-segregate,'" Christopher said. "And whenever we try to explain why we're offended, it's pushed back on us. Just the phrase 'self-segregation': the blame is always put on us. . . . And from somebody who doesn't self-segregate, for somebody who is in lots of different groups, I understand. I've known people to say, 'Oh, calm down, racism is funny.' That quote exactly! And I was like, 'You only think it's funny because you don't have to deal with it.' This was at a game night, we were playing Taboo or something. And I realized why Duke is as divided as it is. Who wants to sit there and have to listen to stuff like that and be the only one in the room who speaks up and realizes that that's inappropriate to say?"

Their anger was palpable. And the Group of 88's ad showcased it. "Regardless of the results of the police investigation, what is apparent every day now is the anger and fear of many students who know themselves to be objects of racism and sexism, who see illuminated in this moment's extraordinary spotlight what they live with every day. They know it isn't just Duke, it isn't just everybody and it isn't just individuals making this disaster." And then, in big, bold type: "But it is a disaster nonetheless."

The sponsors of the ad, which was conceived by Karla F. C. Holloway, a professor of English and African-American studies, and composed by her colleague Wahneema Lubiano, wanted to move the debate beyond what may or may not have happened on the evening of March 13. Lubiano knew that the ad would be controversial. But she recalled that many of her students felt discriminated against on campus, and she had been offended by a "blackface" picture of one of the lacrosse players that appeared on Facebook after the March 13 incident. She later told *ESPN The Magazine* that she knew "some would see the ad as a stake through the collective heart of the lacrosse team. But if the black faculty couldn't speak for black students now, could it ever?" The ad concluded: "The students know that the disaster didn't begin on March 13 and won't end with what the police say or what the court decides. Like all disasters, this one has a history. And what lies beneath what we're hearing from our students are questions about the future. . . . We're turning up the volume in a moment when some of the most vulnerable among us are being asked to quiet down while we wait. To the students speaking individually and to the protesters making collective noise, thank you for not waiting and for making yourselves heard." Among the more prominent signatories of the ad were Professor Houston Baker, the author of the hugely inflammatory "open letter" to the Duke community; William Chafe, the respected professor of history and dean of the faculty of arts and sciences at Duke; and Ariel Dorfman, the world-famous Chilean novelist and playwright and, since 1985, a Duke professor. (Peter Wood did not sign.)

Not surprisingly, the ad proved extremely polarizing, upsetting many Duke students, who perceived that a meaningful chunk of the undergraduate faculty had chosen to condemn publicly their classmates before law enforcement officials had made their case and justice had been meted out. "When our peers are accused of heinous acts, we should be the first to demand they be given the presumption of innocence—their immutable right," Duke junior Stephen Miller wrote in the *Chronicle* in reaction to the Group of 88. "Instead, from day one, many immediately presumed the lacrosse players' guilt and called for their punishment. . . . Not only have many already convicted the lacrosse players, but they have also diffused that conviction across the entire team. Being a white, male lacrosse player was all it took. Protesters and community leaders have claimed the alleged rape speaks to the larger ingrained prejudice of Duke students and the University's administration. But in reality, the only widespread prejudice we have seen is the prejudice that has allowed a single unproven allegation to condemn and defame an entire community."

Miller was particularly struck that the Group of 88's ad repeated the charge that "the situation would be handled differently were the accused not a bunch of white lacrosse players." He called the ad "absurd" in that it "levied the untrue and indefensible charge that Duke is filled with racists." He wrote that, "to understand this behavior, one must realize that for many members of the political left, the belief in a racist society is an article of faith—beyond all reason, question of rational discussion.... As profoundly disturbing as this entire situation has been, I hope it will at least illustrate for many the frightening lengths, against any and all evidence to the contrary, to which people are willing to go to confirm and propel their own worldview."

Several of the lacrosse players also weighed in on the Group of 88 ad. Kyle Dowd's mother, Tricia Dowd, wrote a letter to the Group of 88, in response to the ad, toward the end of 2006. She received an e-mail reply from Houston Baker, the English and African-American studies professor. "LIES!" Baker wrote. "You are just a provacateur [sic] on a happy New Year's Eve trying to get credit for a scummy bunch of white males! You know you are in search of sympaathy [sic] for young white guys who beat up a gay man in Georgetown, get drunk in Durham and lived like 'a bunch of farm animals' near campus. I really hope whoever sent this stupid farce of an e-mail rots in . . . umhappy [sic] new year to you . . . and forgive me if your [sic] really are, quite sadly, mother of a 'farm animal.'"

Kyle Dowd had firsthand knowledge of how at least one of the professors in the Group of 88—political scientist Kim Curtis—seemed to hold a grudge against the Duke lacrosse team that spring. Dowd and another lacrosse player were students in Curtis's class, Politics and Literature. Before the scandal broke, Dowd and his parents alleged in a later civil lawsuit against Duke and Curtis, Dowd and his fellow lacrosse player were earning passing grades in Curtis's class. The grade in the class was to be determined by three papers— each counting for 25 percent of the grade—plus class participation, making up the final 25 percent. On the first two papers, Dowd, who had transferred the previous year to Duke from Johns Hopkins University—which also has one of the premier lacrosse programs in the country—received grades of C+ and C–.

On May 1, Dowd turned in his final paper for the course. Four days later, he found out Curtis had given him a failing grade on both the paper and the class. Even though he had a GPA of 3.3 (out of a possible 4.0) and had received a grade below C only one other time, he was now in danger of not being able to graduate on May 14. He had to "suffer the indignity of calling his parents and telling them he did not believe he was going to graduate," according to the lawsuit. He also had a job waiting for him at Goldman Sachs, in New York, which began in July but only if he graduated from Duke in May. Dowd immediately sent off an e-mail to Curtis to talk about the grade, to see what her rationale could possibly be and to see if maybe she did not receive his final paper for some reason. On May 7, Curtis e-mailed him back. "I did receive your final paper and gave it an F. I also gave you a failing grade for [p]articipation, since you did not attend nearly the entire last month of class," she wrote. "I am currently out of town and will return on Wednesday when I will be available to discuss this with you." Dowd had missed six of the thirty classes; one was an excused absence for a lacrosse game, and four of the other five resulted from having to meet with lawyers pending the criminal investigation into what happened at 610 North Buchanan. Dowd had let Curtis know he would be missing from class for legal reasons, and she never raised an objection with him about these absences.

On May 6, Dowd sent an e-mail to Michael Munger, the administrator in the political science department who he believed was responsible for "grade appeals." On May 7, Munger wrote him back. "We are not going to meet," he wrote. "There are no grade appeals. Instructors assign grades, and that is all there is to it." On May 10, Curtis met with Dowd and explained that she had given him an F on the paper because he "had made strong statements in the paper without backing them up." As for class participation, she told him he had received an F because "he was not there" and "had dropped the ball." She also said that only two students in the class—Dowd and his lacrosse colleague—had received an F on the final paper. At the end of the meeting, Curtis refused to change the grade. Dowd then pursued his appeal to the senior Duke administration. During her conversation with Duke administrators, Curtis explained she had given Dowd an F on the final paper because he "had confused characters from the book" that the paper was about—a different reason from the one she had given Dowd in their meeting.

Soon thereafter, Dowd prevailed, sort of. Duke kept his grade in Curtis's class unchanged, at an F, but allowed him to graduate on May 14 after it decided that Dowd had enough credits from his two years at Johns Hopkins that could be applied to Duke. After Dowd graduated, he continued to appeal the failing grade in Curtis's class. On July 17, Duke decided that a "calculation error" had been made and changed the grade from an F to a D. The school notified the Dowds by e-mail on August 8.

On April 7, the day after the Group of 88 ad appeared, Robert Steel, chairman of Duke's board of trustees, made his first public announcement about the alleged incident. While praising Brodhead for his "responsible leadership at a time when the facts are not clear and emotions run high," he also noted, with considerable regret, "how the current situation has cast a cloud over the many wonderful people who [make up] our campus and the larger community of Durham." But his central message was patience. There was simply no choice but to await the determination of the facts of the incident and he urged "full cooperation with the police investigation"—a pointed reference to the growing sense that the lacrosse players were hiding behind a "wall of silence" and had not been fully forthcoming to the police about what had transpired at the house. "As President Brodhead has consistently stated, the crimes alleged are grave and, if verified, will warrant severe punishment from both the criminal justice system and Duke's student judicial process." But he also recognized that the accused students had rights, too. "Simultaneously, we must protect the rights of students who have maintained their innocence and [who have] not been charged with any crime." He also applauded Brodhead's efforts, while awaiting Nifong's next move, to "address broader issues" on campus involving the "social culture" of students and "difficult questions" involving race and Duke's relationship with Durham, Steel's hometown. "When all the facts are in, Duke will be judged by how it responded to the challenges before us," he concluded.

CHAPTER EIGHT

A Dark Day for Duke

While the Duke campus slipped further and further into turmoil—and, some would say, civil war—the Durham police continued to check off the boxes in their ongoing investigation of the alleged incident. What they quickly discovered was that Crystal Mangum had been actively moving around the Durham area. In the late afternoon of April 6, Officer Gottlieb interviewed Jarriel L. Johnson, who had driven Mangum occasionally to dancing gigs around town. He did not drive Mangum to 610 North Buchanan on the night of March 13—he had a prior engagement—but he had driven her to a job two nights earlier at a Holiday Inn Express in Raleigh. After she finished dancing, Johnson drove her back to her mother's house in Durham.

Gottlieb asked Johnson if he had ever had sex with Mangum. Why, yes, Johnson explained, as a matter of fact, they had been together on March 9. Johnson said he and Mangum "had oral and vaginal sexual relations" but that "he did not ejaculate and did not wear a condom." He told Gottlieb he had never had "anal sexual relations with Crystal." Gottlieb asked Johnson if he was aware that Mangum had been "sexually or physically assaulted in the past while working." He responded with an emphatic no. He also told Gottlieb that he did not think Mangum had suffered any injury prior to the evening of March 13. "She did not look or act as if she was injured," Johnson said.

In Johnson's handwritten statement to Durham police, he laid out the events as he recalled them. The timing of these events is not particularly clear. But, according to Johnson, for much of the day and night of March 10 he drove Mangum around Raleigh, Durham, and Hillsborough for jobs. Sometime before midnight on March 10, Johnson drove Mangum to the Platinum Club, in Hillsborough, where she danced occasionally. He remained in the car while she danced. "Around 2 a.m., I go inside to find her," he recalled. "She asks if we can stay for about another hour. We leave at 4:30 when the club closes. She then tells me that she has a job at the Millennium Hotel [in Durham]. We get there at 5:15 a.m., where she goes in and I remain in the car. At about 6:15 a.m., she returns and I drive her back to her parents' home." From there, Johnson returned to his parents' home in Raleigh and went to sleep.

At around 2 p.m. on March 11, Mangum called Johnson and asked him if he could drive her that night, beginning around 4 p.m. She later changed the pickup time to about 5:30 p.m. because her boyfriend, Matthew Murchison, was coming by her parents' house to bring her something. Once Murchison had left, Mangum called Johnson and asked him to pick her up. "Her daughter lets me in," he continued. "I sit there and play with her kids while Crystal is getting ready. Once she is ready, we leave and ride around for about half an hour. We then go over to Forest Hills Park and sit and talk." She then asked Johnson to drive her to Raleigh "to find this guy she met" but she couldn't find him. "We decide to get a hotel room and wait to see if he calls," Johnson wrote. "This is about 9 p.m. or so. We go to get something to eat at a Chinese place over on Wake Forest Road. Once we get our food we take it back to the hotel and eat. After eating we get into bed and watch TV. While watching TV we engage in sexual intercourse." Johnson left Mangum at midnight and asked her to call him the next morning to pick her up.

The next morning, Johnson drove to the hotel in Raleigh to get Mangum. "When I arrive, she is with an older gentleman that she says wants to see her perform," he recalled. "I go back down and wait in my car until I see the man come out. After I see him leave, I go to the room and help Crystal gather her things. We then head over to my parents' house and hang out for about twenty minutes." They then went to a car wash, and while Johnson was washing his car, Mangum was talking on her phone. Johnson told Mangum he was going to take her home, but on the way there the two of them got into a spat, during which Mangum demanded to get out of his car and then refused to get back in. Eventually, she got back into Johnson's car. "We went back to my parents' house, where we talked it out," he continued. "We sat on the couch for a little while and then went to my bedroom. While there, we talked and she knocked over her drink, which spilled on my phone." He then took her back to her parents' home. That night, Johnson noticed that his phone wasn't working properly. "I called Crystal and told her that it was messed up. At that time she told me that she had a bachelor party [at 610 North Buchanan] to work that night, and asked if I could drive. I agreed. Later on that night, I couldn't get my phone to work and called her to let her know that it wasn't working and I wouldn't be able to take her." Mangum told Johnson that that was okay and that Brian Taylor would drive her to the house off East Campus. At around 1:30 a.m., according to Johnson, he got a call from "Tammy" at Mangum's escort service, asking if he had driven Mangum earlier that night. He told her he had not, and Tammy hung up. "I tried calling Crystal for the next couple of days and didn't hear from her until Thursday," he wrote.

Also on the night of April 6, around six o'clock, Mangum gave a five-page handwritten statement to the police about what had happened to her on the night of March 13 and morning of March 14:

On Monday, March 13, after doing my nails and my hair, I received a call from Tammy, the owner of Angels escort service. Tammy stated that "there will be a bachelors party at 11 p.m. tonight, there will be a group of guys and the guy's name is Dan Flannagahn. The address is 610 N. Buchanan Blvd." She [said] that that Melissa could call back later, closer to the time of the appointment to give the directions. I then get dressed, and my father took me to Brian's house. When I arrived at Brian's, it was about 9:30–10p.m. At Brian's house I had two 22 ounce Ice house beers, and I took a shower. Brian and I left his house (at the Bridges of Southpoint) about 10:30, Melissa called around 10:15 to give us directions. She gave directions several times because Brian and I kept getting lost.

I arrived at the party at 11:20 p.m. When I arrived I saw about 10 guys surrounding Nikki in the backyard, and they were all holding drinks including Nikki. Nikki and I greeted each other. When we started hugging the guys started screaming "yeah."

Nikki and i talked for about 5 minutes. She asked me my name and I asked hers. After we exchanged names we began talking about our routine, and how we were going to dance. We both agreed that this was our first time doing a bachelor party. The guys (called Dan and Brett) showed us to the bathroom. We went into the bathroom and shut the door. "Dan" knocked on the door and asked if we wanted a drink. We said yes. He gave us a drink and we continued to talk. Two of the guys started to push their way into the bathroom while Nikki and I were talking. He said "What's the problem[?] get out here now" There were about 15 guys outside the door screaming "come on show us something" "Let's see some action." Once Nikki and I came out. We began to dance (attempted to) when a guy said that he was going to stick a broom stick up our asses. When he said that, the other guys (about 30) started yelling "Let's fuck these black bitches," Nikki and I started crying. I told Dan that I needed my money and I started to get dressed so that we could leave. We ran out to the car screaming and crying. Dan and Adam followed us to the car and Dan appoligized to Nikki. At that point Nikki told me that they were sorry and that they were going to give us $1200 if we stayed. Nikki and I got out of the car and went back into the house.

As soon as we got back into the house they were more excited and angry. They were screaming "We are going to fuck ya, black bitches. We are going to stick broomsticks up your asses." Nikki and I started to leave again, and three guys grabbed Nikki, and "Bret," "Adam," and Matt grabbed me they separated us at the Master bedroom door, while we tried to hold on to each other. Brett, Adam and Matt took me into the bathroom while, the other guys were watching television, and they closed the door slightly. Matt grabbed me and looked at me, he said "sweetheart, you can't leave." He grabbed the back of my neck and said "I'm going to kill you nigger bitch if you don't shut up." They were all scream[ing] "we are going to fuck this nigger bitch."

They started kicking me in my behind, and my back. Matt stood behind me and bent me over onto my knees and Adam stood in front of me. Adam said I can't do this, I'm getting married, and Matt and Brett said "yes, you can do it." Matt started having sex with me in my vagina and he got frustrated because he said he couldn't cum. He had sex with me for about 2 minutes in my vagina. He then placed his penis in my anus for about 3 minutes. He said "I'm done" come on try some, Adam. Adam said I can't do it. Brett said I will. So Brett got behind me while Matt held my legs. When Brett had sex with me in my vagina, he stopped after about 5 minutes, then he put his penis in my anus for about 2 minutes. When Brett said that he was done, Adam said he was done also. Matt hit me in my face while Dan and Brett kicked me and called me "nigger Bitch." I heard Nikki on the other side of the door and when Adam opened the door, she rushed in and helped Adam to get me dressed. They dragged me out to the car because my legs would not move.

Nikki said "What happened girl, did they hurt you." I said yes, and she said that she would get help for me. She wanted to take me to Raleigh and drop me off. but I told her to take me home. She said that she would call the police. She took me to Kroger on Hillsborough Rd. to call the police. She tried to get me out of her car before the police arrived, but I was afraid to get out. When the police came, she pulled me back into the car, and the police took me to the hospital from Kroger parking lot.

I would like to add that Adam ejaculated in my mouth and I spit it out onto the floor, part of it fell onto the floor after he pulled his penis out.

While the Durham police continued their investigation, most people were awaiting the DNA test results from the state lab in Raleigh. (No one outside of Nifong's inner circle was aware that he had sent more samples to the other, private lab). Nifong had been promising for more than a week that the results would be available any day. He had also been saying that the results were not likely to be positive and that, in any event, his prosecution would go forward regardless. The players' attorneys, understandably, were anxious to get the DNA results and promised to release them publicly if they exonerated their clients, as they expected they would.

Where were the test results? As of late Friday afternoon, April 7, an SBI lab spokesman told the media she did not know when the results would be shared with defense attorneys, who presumably would then make them public. The delay was "frustrating," defense attorney Kerry Sutton said: "My client [Matt

Zash] is waiting eagerly to be able to set his life straight, as well as the rest of the team. We're confident that the DNA is going to help them achieve that." Also fueling the nervousness of the defense attorneys were the comments made by Mangum's father that he believed his daughter had identified her attackers to the police. The "cloud of suspicion" above the forty-six students was "a very delicate and difficult situation for everybody," Kenneth Broun, a UNC law professor, told the Durham paper. The results of the DNA evidence, Broun continued, would not be clear-cut, no matter what was revealed. "DNA analysis is not as much of a science as folks make it out to be," he said. "There's a lot of judgment in it that experts do, and different experts may have different opinions as to whether there's a match. It all ain't necessarily so." He added, though, that "the presence of DNA evidence certainly would be relevant to show that a particular person had been at the scene [but] it wouldn't tell you the particular circumstances."

That afternoon, Nifong gave another long—live—interview to Dan Abrams at MSNBC. Since everyone was still awaiting the DNA results from the state lab, Abrams asked Nifong if he still believed the tests would "show conclusive evidence" about who the alleged perpetrators of the attack were. "Well, you have to understand how DNA is used," Nifong said outside the Durham courthouse. "Obviously the first step that is involved in DNA testing is determining whether or not there is any DNA evidence that is left with the victim that does not belong to her, and so the initial tests are to determine whether or not DNA foreign to the victim can be detected on the samples that are taken from her body. Now, if there is no DNA left, then there is obviously nothing to compare. For instance, if a condom were used, then we might expect that there would not be any DNA evidence recovered from, say, a vaginal swab."

Wouldn't the victim have told you, Abrams asked Nifong, whether the players had used condoms during the attack? (In fact, she said no condom had been used.) "Well, if you are being forced to have sex against your will, you may not necessarily notice whether or not somebody behind you is using a condom," he replied. "This was not a consensual sex situation. This was a struggle, wherein she was struggling just to be able to breathe. So I'm not sure that she would really have much way of knowing whether a condom was being used. . . . Now, obviously if there is a DNA match, then that's very strong evidence, but the absence of DNA doesn't necessarily mean anything other than no DNA was left behind." This theme—the "absence of evidence is not evidence of absence"—would be one Nifong would return to repeatedly throughout the case and in the years afterward.

Abrams then asked Nifong about the statements from Kerry Sutton, Matt Zash's attorney, about her frustration that Nifong would not meet with her to discuss Zash and his apparent lack of involvement in the alleged crime and the idea that a "wall of silence" persisted despite the fact that Zash, Evans, and

Flannery had voluntarily given statements to the police on the night of the party. "Well, you need to understand that Mr. Zash is one of the three young men who actually rented the 610 Buchanan address where this assault took place," he said. "And those three young men did come down pursuant to an invitation from the police department; they did make written statements. They listed the other people who were present. They did voluntarily consent to having suspect kits taken. So, in that sense, those three young men were in fact cooperative. Now, if they made statements that were not true during the course of this, then obviously to the extent that the statements were not true, that would not be cooperative." Did Nifong know of any statements the three men had made that were not true? "Well, they denied that a sexual assault took place inside that residence, and the position that the state is taking is that that is not a true statement, and I would go on to say that none of the other members of the team, other than these three, have made statements to the police," he said.

Abrams then asked Nifong if the police had uncovered any evidence on the players' skin of marks left by the victim during her struggle to break free of them. After all, she had claimed that the thrashing around was sufficient to break off her fake fingernails in the process. "That's a possibility," Nifong replied, "and certainly we did investigate that particular possibility. But let me point out that the evidence that she would present with respect to that particular situation is that she was grabbed from behind. So that, in essence, somebody had an arm around her like this"—and here, on national television, Nifong simulated being in a choke hold—"which she then had to struggle with in order to be able to breathe, and it was in the course of that struggle that the fingernails—the artificial fingernails—broke off. Now, as you can see from my arm, if I were wearing a shirt, a long-sleeve shirt or a jacket of some sort, even if there were enough force used to press down, to break my skin through the clothing, there might not be any way that anything from my arm could get onto those fingernails. So again, whether or not there would be any evidence would depend on exactly the situation. Were the fingernails actually in contact with the skin or were they in contact with clothing?"

In the absence of the DNA evidence and Nifong's sudden decision to duck most—but not all—publicity, the players' attorneys and prominent writers and columnists began filling the media void. The North Carolina State Bar's rules of conduct permitted attorneys to make public comments about their clients as long as they didn't "have a substantial likelihood of materially prejudicing" a proceeding. Lawyers were also permitted to talk about documents placed in the public record, such as the unsealed search warrants. "I've never seen a case being tried so early, and based on such inconclusive evidence, being tried in the media," said Pete Anderson, a Charlotte lawyer representing one player. "It is clear that [Nifong] has made conclusions that a rape has occurred. Who could possibly, even it's narrowed down to two or three [people], get a fair trial?" He thought that Nifong was motivated by his reelection campaign. Added Jim Cooney, another Charlotte attorney not then involved in the case, "When the DA says there was a sexual assault and she was beaten up, the opinion of the public is formed fairly quickly. The best the defense lawyers can do is blunt the damage and get people to pause and think a little. . . . No matter how flat the pancake, there are always two sides."

Another defense attorney, Bill Thomas, leaked to the Durham paper that he had "time-stamped" photographs—using a camera that had been "tested and calibrated to guarantee the accuracy of its time stamps"—that contradicted Mangum's claim that she was raped, beaten, and strangled by three lacrosse players. Thomas, who wouldn't share the photographs with the paper, suggested they were taken by someone at the party who was not on the lacrosse team. Thomas told the *Herald-Sun* that Mangum "had a big smile on her face" when she tried to reenter the house at 610 North Buchanan. Thomas said that shortly after the smiling picture was taken, Mangum "fell down at the back door of the house" and stayed on the ground "for quite some time." He also said the photos showed that when Mangum arrived at the house, her face and legs were already "severely bruised" and that she had "cuts" on her legs, knees, and feet. The photos show "there is no way she was assaulted at all, much less in the manner she described," Thomas said. He told the *New York Times*, "These photographs cast serious doubt on allegations made by law enforcement and the University."

Joe Cheshire, who was representing Dave Evans, and Kerry Sutton, who was representing Matt Zash, told the local papers that the photographs "depict cuts and bruises visible on the woman's body" as she began to dance and that a twenty-seven-minute gap between the times on the photos corresponded to when the two women had locked themselves in the bathroom. Cheshire told the *News & Observer* that a photograph taken of Mangum after she came out of the bathroom showed her to be "smiling" and "wearing a negligee" that "shows no signs of damage or violence." Sutton told the *Chronicle*, "These photos are real. We have them, and we will release them if it's appropriate. As we've said all along, this is a completely atypical way for a case to progress. We have a lot of evidence that wouldn't have come out yet, as does the state—and we don't even have a case yet."

Thomas, too, said he was looking forward to getting the results of the DNA tests. "It's unfortunate that these young men have been vilified by the press, the community, and the university they attend," he said. "It's a real miscarriage of justice for them to be convicted in the public's mind before everything is known. It is unfair. The allegations against them don't contain a kernel of truth."

Meanwhile, Gottlieb, the Durham police investigator, was still seeking evidence from the community. He renewed his request for information on the Trinity Park digital bulletin board and reminded people that "Durham Crimestoppers will pay cash for any information leading to the arrest and conviction of any suspects." Another community member, Kelly, wondered why there had been so little reaction to this news. "What????" he wrote. "No thread 10–12 messages deep about this? Perhaps because it does not fit in with the Master Plan to brand Duke the source of all evil?" Replied Berry McDonald, "I for one will be glad to say that any comments I have made about the lacrosse team obviously being involved in behavior that was embarrassing to themselves, and to Duke, the night of March 13 were wrong if the evidence shows that to be the case. Are [you] prepared to be an adult and do the same if evidence proves otherwise?" "Absolutely," Kelly replied. "That's the point I'm trying to make . . . that Duke has been vilified beyond all imagination, based on not one ounce of proof. Good thing this isn't Salem." Terri then added to the discussion about the lacrosse players living in the neighborhood: "A long history of bad behavior (drunkenness, violence, verbal abuse of neighbors, to name just a few things) by a subset of the lacrosse team unfortunately has made it easy for many people to believe that it's possible (and I stress, possible) that members of this same group committed a serious crime. Regarding the pictures—they may or may not be legit. In this day and age, it's possible to fake just about anything. But here's what I wonder: Why would someone take pictures of a person who is clearly in need of medical help? That seems inhumane and perverse."

Readers of the Sunday *News & Observer* on April 9 were greeted with a front-page headline that the Duke lacrosse team "has swaggered for years." Since 1999, the paper discovered, forty-one of the Duke lacrosse players—about 31 percent of the players who had been on the team in the previous seven years—had been "charged with a variety of rowdy and drunken acts," including an incident of "speeding down I-40 while drunk." By contrast, the paper revealed, only two players on the twenty-seven-man soccer team roster and four on the twenty-two-player baseball team had been "arrested in connection with underage alcohol offenses." Former baseball players said they also invited "dancers" to team parties and were capable of "loutish behavior." The previous charges against the lacrosse team were minor, alcohol-fueled misdemeanors that were quickly settled or dispensed with, the paper reported. "But taken as a body of work," it continued, "the charges track the noisy passage of a championship lacrosse team with a reputation for a swaggering sense of entitlement and privilege. They underscore the hard-drinking image of the Duke lacrosse team—which some residents say is a super-sized version of the university's elitist, party-hearty ethos."

On the same day, the *New York Times*, as part of its increasingly blanket coverage of the lacrosse story, published two opinion pieces: one by its columnist David Brooks and the other by bestselling novelist Allan Gurganus, a resident of Hillsborough, North Carolina, just outside of Durham, and an occasional Duke professor. Neither piece was particularly straightforward but both men raised serious questions about Duke's campus culture of privilege and elitism and how it could possibly have produced anything like the events that allegedly occurred on the night of March 13. Brooks started by invoking Tom Wolfe. "All great scandals occur twice, first as Tom Wolfe novels, then as real-life events that nightmarishly mimic them," he wrote. "And so after *I Am Charlotte Simmons*, it was perhaps inevitable that Duke University would have to endure a mini–social explosion involving athletic thugs, resentful townies, nervous administrators, male predators, aggrieved professors, binge drinking and lust gone wild."

Brooks's main point was that the language of how an alleged incident such as might have occurred at 610 North Buchanan had changed dramatically over the years, from being evidence of individual "morality and character" flaws to being evidence of sociological wreckage, a "clash between classes, races and sexes." In the old days, McFadyen's e-mail would be an example of how he had "crashed through several moral guardrails" and that "his character had been corroded by shock jocks and raunch culture and that he'd entered a nihilistic moral universe where young men entertain each other with bravura displays of immoralism. A community so degraded, you might surmise, is not a long way from actual sexual assault." Brooks's heavy message seemed to be that the Duke case was further evidence that young people no longer adhered to the "old code of obsolete chivalry" and were no longer sure what constituted respectable behavior.

Using his novelist's gift, Gurganus was even more damning. While the players were "innocent until proven guilty, yes . . . everybody has an opinion. Certainly here, where Topic A—ACC basketball—just ended with Duke and North Carolina falling short, March Madness takes on new meaning." He noted that lacrosse was "our Eden's first team sport" where the "Cherokees called it 'the little brother of war,'" "swore it offered superb battle training" and "bred loyalty among players, a solidarity demonstrated by the code of silence among Duke's party attendees." Up north, he wrote, "this story must seem like yet another involving Southern frat boys run wild, besmirching the great-granddaughters of their own ancestral slaves. But Duke's lacrosse team is largely recruited from Northeastern prep schools." He noted that McFadyen, "who showed such lively interest in peeling skin off his next stripper, has a white SUV with New Jersey plates." For good measure, he reminded readers that "though Duke is in Durham, NC, whose namesake family made its billions in tobacco"—and lived in New Jersey, he could have thrown in—"most of Duke's students hail from elsewhere. The university's popularity as an alternative to the Ivy League has been refined in recent years. Students fondly call the campus the Gothic Wonderland. This Disney reference acknowledges the incongruity of its gray-stone Oxbridge architecture, constructed in the 1930s as a wishful invocation of Europe: real culture, faux antiquity. It could not, like Chapel Hill's eighteenth-century campus, be built of native brick. Why? The tobacco warehouses visible from the Duke campus are all brick."

After sharing his North Carolina bona fides, paying homage to the good works found at Duke and in Durham, with Duke's help, and regretting the impulse to make this incident stand for the behavior of the community as a whole, Gurganus noted that "like all universities," Duke "lives and dies by attracting top students. That means convincing college-shopping high schoolers that Duke is sexy and fun. (I still find it hard to believe that anyone would choose a college based on how well its basketball team played the previous year; but, about so many things, I seem to be the last to understand.) Lacrosse is a draw. Glamorous boarding-school sports are magnets for the attractive, competitive, and wealthy young people that increasingly define Duke's student body." He wrote that unlike the Ivy League, Duke does provide athletic scholarships and that "talent has its privileges, especially in lacrosse, the bailiwick of Abercrombie allure." One such perk was for the team captains to be allowed to live in a house, "close to campus but far from adult supervision." The "Animal House" at 610 North Buchanan was "notorious," he wrote, and explained how friends of his "painstakingly restored an old home" in the neighborhood but sold it immediately after "Duke planted a sports team next door."

He claimed that young male lacrosse players take on the characteristics of their sport. "One early explorer, after witnessing an Indian game involving hundreds of stick-wielding players, wrote, 'Almost everything short of murder is allowable.'" At Duke, the lacrosse team was known on campus as the "Meatheads," and when a group of them went to a local restaurant on the night of March 12—the night before the notorious party at 610 North Buchanan— and were chanting team slogans (while drinking), "no one quite dared confront them. Though they pass as ordinary citizens—unlike the pituitary cases found among basketball stars—they're still guys of serious, strenuous bulk." He cited his Hillsborough neighbor Peter Wood's 2004 letter and wondered, since Wood never got a response from Robert Thompson, "what administrator is going to risk driving away a winning team from a winning university? How soon Boys Will Be Boys become Administrators Who Administrate in Defense of Such Boys. This lacrosse season, until rape accusations ended it, featured six wins and two losses. Code for 'Leave them alone.'"

Reaching his crescendo, Gurganus then asked the question on many people's minds. "When the children of privilege feel vividly alive only while victimizing, even torturing, we must all ask why," he concluded. "This question is first personal, then goes ethical, soon national. Boys eighteen to twenty-five are natural warriors: bodies have wildly outgrown reason, the sexual imperative outranks everything. They are insurance risks. They need (and crave) true leadership, genuine order. But left alone, granted absolute power, their deeds can terrify. The imperative to win, and damn all collateral costs, is not particular to Durham—and it is killing us. Why is there no one to admire?"

In truth, like Brooks and Gurganus, columnists and other observers of the social scene had long been wondering about what tobacco baron James B. Duke had in mind when he decided to create the $80 million Duke endowment—made up mostly of his stock in the Duke Power Company—with the mandate to, among other things, provide for the founding of Duke University with a gift of 42 percent of the annual interest income on the first $40 million, 10 percent of the annual interest income on the second $40 million plus a flat $10 million for what became the Duke medical school. First, in 1892, Washington Duke, James's father, gave $180,000 to what was Trinity College, in Randolph County, to move the school to an abandoned racetrack in Durham and create what is now known as Duke's East Campus, off which the house at 610 North Buchanan sat. Eventually, James "Buck" Duke's endowment contributed another $19 million to build Duke's West Campus on five thousand forested acres just outside of downtown Durham. To design the new campus, Duke hired the famed Philadelphia architect Horace Trumbauer, who, the *New Yorker* once observed, "had put mansion roofs over the heads of the ruling class during the Gilded Age." Trumbauer's vision was to create a Gothic Revival tableau in the esteemed style of Oxford and Cambridge universities, "and the spectacular sandstone result was hardly intended to mute any inference of privilege," the magazine intoned. The Duke Chapel was completed in 1935. "The late Buck Duke's immediate aim in pouring out his millions to transform an obscure Methodist College in a North Carolina mill town into the university which now bears his name was simplicity itself," the Charlotte columnist W. J. Cash wrote in the September 1933 edition of the *American Mercury*, the magazine of H. L. Mencken. "What he wanted was a Babbitt factory—a mill for grinding out go-get-'em boys in the wholesale and undeviating fashion in which his Chesterfield plant across the way ground out cigarettes."

As Duke had himself, Cash noted that Duke was focused on educating men with a "practical" education as opposed to a "theoretical" one, just as Duke himself had oriented his businesses around making immense amounts of profit. But Cash noted that the Trinity College that Duke inherited contained impressive strands of "Liberalism" in its DNA, which could not be ignored. He gave the example of a Trinity history professor, John Spencer Bassett, who, in 1903, wrote an article in *South Atlantic Quarterly*, in which he proclaimed that "[Booker T.] Washington is a great and good man, a Christian statesman and, take him all in all, the greatest man, save General [Robert E.] Lee, born in the South in a hundred years." Editorial writers screamed for Bassett's head, students withdrew from the college and the meager financial support the college did receive was choked off until Bassett resigned. But he refused to leave the school and the Trinity administration more or less supported him. "Then the trustees came down with blood in their collective eye, and it began to look as if the jig was up," Cash wrote. "But the president of the college in those days was old John C. Kilgo, afterwards to become, under the inscrutable will of God, a Southern Methodist bishop. A proud, forceful egotist, he had no intention of being dictated to, regardless of the issue, by anybody. With lightning in his eyes, he told the trustees that if Bassett went he went, too, and thundered: 'Coercion of liberty in all times has been a miserable failure. . . . Bury liberty here and with it the college is buried.'"

With Kilgo's support, the faculty found its collective spine and declared that by supporting Bassett "this college has now the opportunity to show that its campus is undeniably one spot on Southern soil where men's minds are free." Every member of the Trinity faculty tendered his resignation, effective immediately upon the departure of Bassett. After a debate that raged on the board until 3 a.m., the trustees voted eighteen to seven to keep Bassett around, and then issued the proclamation: "The search for truth should be unhampered. . . . A reasonable freedom of opinion is to a college the very breath of life; and any official throttling of the private judgment of its teachers would destroy their influence, and place upon the college an enduring stigma." This strand of Duke's DNA was preserved in amber the following May when President Theodore Roosevelt gave the commencement address. "I know of no other college which has so nobly set forth, as the object of its being, the principles to which every college should be devoted."

Still, as Cash drily noted, old traditions die hard. "Plainly enough, to take such a college, to take it with its native wishy-washiness reinforced by the paralyzing influence of old Buck's reactionary intentions, and transform it into a great university with a clear-cut personality of any kind, above all to transform it into a great Liberal university, was a task of considerable magnitude." He observed, though, that under the leadership of great men, the school was slowly transformed into a respectable university, albeit as of 1933 there was still some ground to cover. "Maybe this is one of the reasons why the student body yet remains one of the most inert in the country," he wrote. "Among the 2,000 undergraduates there is almost nothing of that concern with social and economic questions, that 'great argument about it and about' which has been fevering most American colleges of any importance since the advent of the Blight. The prevailing *mores* are Philistine and by no means passively so. Not only does the student body as a whole hold Mr. Wallace Wade (Mr. Wade is a high-powered gentleman who used to turn out very high-powered football teams at Alabama till Duke lured him away with $18,000 a year) for its chief hero and look forward to the day when he shall take a Duke team to the Rose Bowl as Ultima Thule"—which did indeed happen one time only, in 1942, when Duke hosted and played (and lost) the Rose Bowl in Wallace Wade Stadium—"it insists that everybody on the campus shall share the same view—and declines pointedly to tolerate dissent. My own researches indicate that David Cornell De Jong, a fellow in English, was only telling the truth when he reported in the university magazine for March 1932 that to be caught "voluntarily reading anything above the level of *Liberty,* or willingly taking any interest in any intellectual matter, is an offense against the Duke *esprit de corps* which is not uncommonly punished by outright physical violence."

But times do change, and Duke students, by and large, had found their voice and were no longer shy about protesting. Later on April 9, around 2 p.m., a group of about fifty people—local residents, students, and members of the Church of the Apostolic Revival in Durham—gathered in front of 610 North Buchanan to protest the perceived injustice of how the alleged rapists at Duke had not been arrested. "[We are here] not in an antagonistic spirit," Apostle John Bennett, the leader of the church, told the assembled group, many of whom had just come from church services, as well as the local and national media television cameras. "We are not gathered in the name of race, but in the name of justice." Bennett said the "crucial question" was why had the suspects "not been arrested? Why does one"—referring to McFadyen, who was, in fact, not a suspect—"get to go to his New Jersey home? . . . Why do we allow the accused to roam our streets freely?" He added, "If truth be told, if it was another ethnic group they would have been charged and a high bond set." He wanted to know why the alleged Duke perpetrators were being treated differently than he suspected a black man would be. Until justice was served, he said, the house at 610 North Buchanan would remain a symbol of a system that "caters to and protects the rich." But, again, that view was not universal. David Krauss, a Duke senior who was at the protest, said, "There is a lot of misunderstanding of the Duke community. The light that Duke has been portrayed in is categorically incorrect. Nobody is doing stories about the good of the Duke-Durham Initiative because that doesn't make good news." As to whether the campus was racially divided, he said, "The first time I heard about the idea that Duke was a 'plantation' of the South was in a newspaper, so that must say something."

   A *Newsweek* article released that Sunday, written by Susannah Meadows, a 1995 Duke graduate, and Evan Thomas, was one of the first nationally to raise doubts about Nifong's assertions. "On the night of March 13, members of the Duke University lacrosse team, at the time ranked second in the nation, crowded into a small house rented by three of their captains to watch two exotic dancers perform," they wrote. "What happened next is very much a matter of dispute. There are at least two different scenarios, with vastly different implications for everyone involved." Meadows and Thomas then described the facts of the case, as found in Gottlieb's affidavit, and how Nifong "publicly criticized" the players for failing to testify about the alleged rape. "There is, however, possibly a different side to the story—a chapter from another Tom Wolfe novel, *The Bonfire of the Vanities*, a tale of a prosecutor exploiting racial tensions with a trumped-up charge." *Newsweek* quoted Joe Cheshire, who said Nifong had "unfairly tried the players in the media" as part of his reelection strategy, since one of his principal opponents was a woman. "The real story," Cheshire said, "is how he pandered to the public to stir up race and class division."

Meadows and Thomas wrote that if Zash, Flannery, and Evans had "anything to hide" after the party at their house on the night of March 13, "they didn't act like it." The journalists pointed out how the three men voluntarily went down to the police station to give their statements, without lawyers, and how their offer to take lie detector tests "was rebuffed by police." *Newsweek* also asserted that the players' families dismissed the cliché that the Duke teammates were "privileged louts" and explained that two of the players were sons of retired New York City firefighters who were involved in the September 11 attacks.

Late that same Sunday night, Brodhead sent around an e-mail to Larry Moneta and Joe Alleva. "Friends," he wrote, "a difficult question is, how can we support our lacrosse players at a devastatingly hard time without seeming to lend aid and comfort to their version of the story? We can't do anything to side with them, or even, if they are exonerated, to imply that they have behaved with honor. The central admin[istration] can't, nor can Athletics. On the other hand, they have human needs. [Does] either of you have a bright idea?" Early the next morning—1:05 a.m.—Moneta responded. "Ironically," he wrote Brodhead and Alleva, "we have been supporting them throughout. We have worked with them on housing and counseling needs and have ensured that faculty treat them fairly"—the incident in which a professor would fail player Kyle Dowd was still a few weeks away. "The dilemma, of course, is with public acknowledgment of our support without feeding the 'cover-up' allegations. . . . I assume that the coach [Pressler] is no longer communicating with the players (at least I hope not)? Is someone in Athletics maintaining contact with the players? With their parents? Sue [Wasiolek] has been fielding dozens of calls from their parents. . . . I've had just a few. We should be clear on point position with the players and parents especially when this thing breaks one way or another. I'll follow up with Joe tomorrow."

With the Duke campus on high alert awaiting the results of the DNA testing and with story after story appearing in the media, including an article in the newest *Sports Illustrated*, just before 1 p.m. on April 10, Nifong, joined by officers Gottlieb and Himan, drove to Burlington and met with Brian Meehan and Richard Clark from DNA Securities. Unlike the players and their attorneys,

Nifong, Gottlieb, and Himan already knew the results of the state lab DNA tests and were eager to hear the results of Meehan's supposedly more sophisticated tests of the players' DNA and that of Mangum.

During the previous three days, DNA Securities had tested the items in Mangum's rape kit. Defense attorneys later stated unequivocally that at that meeting Meehan informed Nifong, Gottlieb, and Himan that his lab had concluded "that the rape kit provided decisive evidence of Mangum's sexual activity with at least four males around March 13—*none* of whom was a Duke lacrosse player." (A subsequent investigation by the North Carolina State Bar confirmed the defense attorneys' account of the meeting.) According to defense attorneys, Nifong, Gottlieb, and Himan decided not to take any notes of the meeting—that was clear from the officers' diaries—and agreed not to release Meehan's findings publicly or to the defense attorneys.

At 4 p.m., the State Bureau of Investigation faxed the results of its DNA tests to Nifong's office and also made them available to the police and defense attorneys. Nifong said in a statement that it would be "inappropriate" for him to release the results but that defense attorneys were "free" to do so. Like Nifong, the defense attorneys chose not to release the results, either. But at a press conference at around 6 p.m. on the steps of the Durham County Courthouse, a group of them announced the findings.

Reading from a prepared statement, Wade Smith, who represented Collin Finnerty and was the dean of the North Carolina defense bar—he had represented Army officer and doctor Jeffrey McDonald in the infamous 1979 *Fatal Vision* case about the murder of McDonald's family—said, "No DNA material from any young man tested was present on the body of the complaining woman. Not present within her body. Not present on the surface of her body and not present on any of her belongings. Not present on any of the articles or materials she had with her, including her clothing. No DNA from any young man tested was found anywhere on or about the body of this woman." He then turned his attention to Nifong. "The prosecutor in this county asked for these tests," he said. "It was an extraordinary procedure, and he asked for these tests saying that he believed they would assist in clearing the innocent. We hope now, with this long-awaited test and these results, that Mr. Nifong will announce that he is not going to pursue this case further. There was no sexual assault in this case, and we hope with these announcements and with this carefully prepared test and these results that perhaps this community could begin to heal."

Smith then turned the microphone over to Joe Cheshire, who represented David Evans. "There is no evidence other than the word of this one complaining person that any rape or sexual assault took place in that house on that evening," Cheshire said. "It's not here today. It won't be here tomorrow. It won't be here next year. No rape or sexual assault happened in that home and this DNA report shows that loud and clear." What about the DNA evidence on Mangum's broken fake fingernails? Cheshire was asked. "There is no DNA evidence that shows that any of the boys were touched by her fingernails," he replied misleadingly. He was asked whether the lacrosse players he had spoken with were surprised by the DNA results. "None of the boys in that home that night are at all surprised in any way, shape or form because when you know you haven't done anything wrong, you don't worry about a test result," he said. "It is simply an impossibility, reading the report, that we have seen [that a] a rape or sexual assault happened in that home that evening."

Were the allegations a hoax? "I think it is a false accusation," he said, "that has been made for some reason against these boys and I think that it has been used to hurt their lives forever and to tear this community apart. As Mr. Smith said, it is time for all the healing to start and I hope that will happen." But Cheshire was willing to concede that there had been bad-boy behavior in the house. "None of us standing up here are saying that there aren't proper social and moral issues that have come out of this whole [episode] that aren't appropriate for discussion," he said. "There are. But unfortunately, people have meshed those things with the sexual assault and tried to make them all the same."

When reporters asked about the photographic evidence that defense attorneys had alluded to but had not yet released publicly, a third attorney, Bill Thomas, answered, "The photographs are very consistent with the statements from all of the young men. They have said consistently that a sexual assault did not occur. These photographs corroborate the statements of all forty-six of these young men without question. It is very clear that the victim in this case came to the house with injuries on her, and also very clear that less than thirty minutes later she was outside the door and the door was locked." Thomas said the allegations had been "an absolute nightmare for these young men as well as their families." He conveyed the pain suffered by the "crying mother of my client who doesn't sleep at night and has difficulty eating" and his client "who tosses and turns" at night and whose "life is upside down [and] who really can't believe this happened to him."

But one of the lingering questions was what if the three men had used condoms, which might well not leave a DNA trace on (or in, as the lawyers liked to say) the victim. "It's very important for you all to understand that if you go back and read all the pleadings and search warrant applications for DNA [testing] and the statements attributed to the accuser here, there's no mention of a condom," Cheshire said. "The only time a condom has ever been mentioned is by the DA. When people started coming out and saying there won't be any DNA, all of a sudden that's the first and only time you've heard something about a condom. That's awfully important but it is absolutely true. The experts will tell you, if there was a condom used, they would still be able to pick up DNA, latex, lubricant and all other types of things to show that—and that's not here."

The final question of the press conference was whether there was any DNA evidence found on any of the towels in the bathroom where the rape allegedly took place. Cheshire's answer, though factually correct, did raise some unanswered questions. "There was DNA found from two of the boys on a towel and on the floor," he said. "But you need to remember that none of that matches up with her in any way, shape, or form and that the bathroom where this DNA was found happened to be the bathroom that the two boys [used regularly]. Any expert and any person in the world will tell you that your [own] DNA is in your bathroom."

It was a virtuoso performance. After the press conference, as Cheshire was walking on the street, he reiterated to a television interviewer that the photographs of Mangum showed that she had had serious injuries as she arrived at the house at 610 North Buchanan. He said he had no idea where she had been before she arrived at the house on the evening of March 13 and that exotic dancing was "a rough business."

But not everyone was convinced, especially Nifong. He was furious that the defense attorneys had spoken publicly and conclusively about a confidential DNA report that they knew could not be released to the press and that Nifong would not be able to comment about, either. "I'm always offended when somebody publicly says things that are not true, that I'm not in a position to call them on," he said, years later. "They knew as well as I did that neither side could release that report. It would be a specific ethical violation. But they knew that I couldn't say, 'Oh, really? Did you read the report? Why don't you see what it really says?' They did that, knowing that they wouldn't get called on it. Defense attorneys do that all the time. They play by a different set of rules because they can get away with it. Nobody ever disciplines somebody for going too far in trying to help their client. It doesn't make any difference. If you do it in court, in front of the judge, he might find you in contempt, but all these things that you do outside the courtroom, that are really improper, they don't do anything to you for that, because that's just zealous representation. But when it's done publicly like that, it's an attempt to keep one side from getting a fair trial, and that side is me. I wouldn't say that that made me dig in my heels. It pissed me off, but I had already pretty much decided that I wasn't going to let them railroad me."

At a candidate's forum that night in Durham—the primary election was twenty-three days away—Nifong said he would continue his investigation regardless of the state lab DNA results. (He made no mention of the results he had received earlier that day from the Burlington lab.) "I'm not saying it's over," he said at the forum. "If that's what they expect, they will be sadly disappointed. They can say anything they want, but I'm still in the middle of my investigation. I believe a sexual assault took place."

A statement released by John Burness on behalf of Brodhead was also surprisingly cautious and ambiguous, given the results of the DNA tests. "As both President Brodhead and I have said repeatedly over the past few weeks," he wrote, "we have to have confidence that the police investigation will ultimately reveal the truth. While the criminal allegations in this case are extremely serious, it is important to remember that no one has been charged and that in our system of law people are presumed innocent until proven guilty."

Tom Clark, a resident of Alabama Avenue in Durham, found Burness's cryptic statement after the release of the DNA results to be particularly offensive. "Despite 'Duke bashing' charges I'm sure I'll get, I do have to say that this statement is a great example of the clumsy, purely self-interested, pure strategic calculation that has characterized Duke's performance as a community leader in the last few years," he wrote. "By leaving out any expression of feeling for the community trauma that has occurred—that Duke presumably still claims it will take some responsibility for with the study groups it has organized, and that must be dealt with no matter what the outcome of the legal battle—the statement functions as virtually an outright declaration that if there is no rape, there is no problem—all we have to do is wait for the police to reveal the truth. Instead, we get a reminder, a small lecture, really, about the most well-known legal principle in the country. What might have been helpful, and certainly more graceful, is the needed lecture about the fact that while the DNA tests could have all but convicted someone, they did not and could not exonerate anyone."

That night, Mangum's father, Travis, gave an interview to a Raleigh television station. "I think my daughter told me the truth about what happened," he said. "I support her. I got a lot of trust in the DA and I feel like he's gonna do the right thing." Added Mangum's mother to the *News & Observer*, "I don't have a reaction because I know it happened. They must have tampered with [the results] or something."

James Coleman, the Duke law professor leading the university's investigation of the lacrosse team, said caution was needed. "Just as there was a rush to judgment to convict, now there is a rush to judgment to acquit," he told a local television reporter. "But there still are allegations out there. The DA has to decide if a crime has occurred. If so, he has to file charges. There has to be a trial and a verdict. So until that aspect of it is completed, I think all of this is still up in the air." Still, Coleman was very critical of Nifong. "What the DA did was regrettable and so unprofessional," he told the *Chronicle*. "The public was left so confused. . . . He got way ahead of himself." He said that Nifong had used the whole episode as a "photo opportunity."

A few hours after the players' defense attorneys announced the results of the DNA evidence, Mangum called Himan. She told him she was depressed about "what has been going on" and that she hoped "it would be easier." Mangum told Himan she wanted to talk with someone but she didn't want that person "to think she was crazy." Himan gave her the number of Amy Wilkinson, a rape crisis counselor at the Durham Crisis Response Center.

Mangum wasn't the only one confused by the DNA results. Students at both Duke and NCCU had trouble making sense of them, too. At NCCU, the reaction seemed to be that the "racist system" had worked against their classmate. "If it was a black man, do you think they would have waited for DNA tests, or that the DNA tests would have played a valuable part in the evidence?" wondered senior Donald Parker. Ashley Lofton, a freshman, said, "Someone is lying, obviously." And Shirika Brammell said she was "surprised and shocked" by the test results. "I was expecting some DNA to be found with the fingernails," she said. Tiffany Evans said of the negative results, "It doesn't mean nothing happened. It just means nothing was left behind." At Duke, there was a degree of relief. "I thought at the beginning, people were quick to judge," said Kristian Hinson, a freshman. "'Innocent until proven guilty'—I think everybody forgot about that." Durham mayor Bell, though, said it was still too soon to put the alleged incident to rest. "I've consistently said that they were allegations and we need to let the process go through the legal [steps] that we need to go through," he cautioned. "I think we still need to do that." But Bell's city council colleague, Eugene Brown, was less sanguine than the mayor about where the case was heading. "There are no winners in this," he told the *Los Angeles Times*. "We are all losers. The community has become so polarized that, in the end, the truth might not matter."

In the aftermath of the release of the DNA evidence, CNN's Nancy Grace was chomping at the bit. "Tonight, breaking news, a major blow tonight to the state," she yelped. "DNA results in the Duke University lacrosse team rape scandal are in, and, according to the defense, no DNA—not no DNA match, but no DNA whatsoever. Was there a multiple rape, as [Mangum] said? The DA has publicly stated she did have vaginal trauma. Did the perpetrators use condoms? Also tonight, the defense claims photos show the student turned stripper was injured when she got to the party. Could that be true?" Larry Kobilinsky, a forensic scientist, said that it was possible that a condom could have been used but that most condoms have lubricants on them and that the DNA tests are able to search for that lubricant. Without finding that lubricant, he said, he thought it was unlikely condoms were used. Radio reporter Kevin Miller said the defense attorneys said there was no trace of the lubricant and that no condom had been used. "Right now, this ace in the hole for the prosecutor turned out to be a joker," Kobilinsky said.

Grace then brought Wendy Murphy, a former federal prosecutor, into the discussion. "Now, you and I have prosecuted long enough to have prosecuted rape cases, serious rape cases, before we had DNA, all right?" she asked. "I didn't have

DNA in my original rape prosecutions. We didn't have it to use it. I mean, it may have been there, but we didn't have that technology. But, Wendy, listen, when you put together vaginal trauma—the district attorney has point-blank stated in the *Herald-Sun* there in [Durham] that there is vaginal trauma. We know that there was bruising around her neck. We know that she was found dazed and confused in a Kroger parking lot. We know that she basically ran out of this house and left behind her pocketbook with money, cell phone, her car keys in it—"

"And a shoe," Murphy interjected.

"A shoe," Grace continued. "What do you think, Wendy?"

"Look, I think the most telling thing we can say about what the defense [press conference] meant today, the most telling statement is what they didn't do, Nancy," Murphy said. "They didn't just turn over the [DNA] results. . . . About ninety percent of rape cases involve no DNA at all, even with the available technology. And frankly, that towel, the towel in the bathroom, the deafening silence from the defense attorneys about what was found on the towel in the bathroom—how do you explain that? . . . [T]he reason there was no DNA found in her body is because they finished the act, if I could be polite for a second here—they finished the act outside of her body, on the towel. That's damning evidence!"

Added Murphy, "Look, I think the real key here is that these guys, like so many rapists—and I'm going to say it because, at this point, she's entitled to the respect that she is a crime victim. These guys watch *CSI*, and they know it's a really bad idea to ejaculate on or in the victim. And maybe what she said, which makes her particularly credible, is 'These guys didn't ejaculate on or inside of my body,' which means she deserves extra credibility because no one's suggesting that she lied about whether there would be DNA found on her person. . . . Why do we live in a culture [in which] people are so willing to assume women are masochistic enough to not only do all the things you describe but [also] strangle themselves and tear their own vaginas to make, what, a false claim look good? We would let women be perceived as hysterical masochists rather than believe that if it walks like a duck and quacks like a duck, it's a duck? Can we use a little bit of common sense here? Forget respect and disrespect for a minute! How about common sense and decency? A DA who was not born yesterday has said, after two weeks of investigation, 'I believe this woman was brutally raped and attacked.' And now, because of DNA—which never tells the whole story, ever—somehow, we're going to just abandon the case and celebrate the boys as, you know, having had a bad night?"

The next morning at a panel discussion at NCCU, along with Mayor Bell, a Durham councilman and representatives of student government at both NCCU and Duke, Nifong dismissed the idea that he intended to drop the case. "I hope that you will understand by the fact that I am here this morning that my presence here means that this case is not going away," he said, to applause from the predominantly black audience of around five hundred people. "I read the comments in the paper this morning from the attorneys and I saw a comment from an NCCU student, Tiffany Evans." He asked if she was in the audience. "Ms. Evans actually made a lot more sense than all those attorneys. Her comment is about the absence of DNA: 'It doesn't mean nothing happened. It just means nothing was left behind,' which is the case in seventy-five percent to eighty percent of all sexual assaults. DNA results can often be helpful, but, you know, I've been doing this a long time and for most of the years we've been doing this, we didn't have DNA. We had to deal with sexual assault cases the good, old-fashioned way—witnesses got on the stand and told what happened to them. . . . The fact is, this case is proceeding the way a case should proceed. I am trying to determine exactly what the evidence is that we have to proceed on and to assemble that evidence before anyone is charged. But as I said earlier, I assure you by my presence here this case is not over."

The NCCU students' anger was palpable. At one point early on, Shawn Cunningham, an NCCU senior, said he was especially dismayed by two different groups of people, neither of which was the Duke lacrosse team, for which he had little sympathy. First, he was upset with those people at NCCU who were blaming the victim for what had happened. "No one, male or female, heterosexual or homosexual, deserves to be assaulted, sodomized, raped, abused or beaten," he said, "and anyone who takes the position that this is her fault, shame on you." Second, he ripped the media. "The press has disrespected this young lady," he said. "You have minimalized my sister to a stripper and an exotic dancer. She walks this campus every day, going to class and trying to provide for her family. You don't identify her as a mother. You don't identify her as a student. You don't identify her as a woman." Cunningham said that in addition to the 80 percent of rape cases in which no DNA is left behind, 80 percent of women who have been sexually assaulted do not report the attack. "You have the audacity to put this woman up to ridicule," he continued. "That's why women don't report—fear of humiliation, fear of retaliation, fear that the victim is going to be blamed. I wouldn't report, either!"

One questioner wanted to know if Nifong's actions in the case—including taking it on in the first place—were motivated by his reelection campaign. "As a DA, you do not get to choose what crimes occur or when they occur," he said. "You have to deal with the situation as it exists. This is not about an election; this is about doing justice."

Then, after Danielle Little, a junior criminal studies major, asked Nifong about different kinds of DNA tests, Nifong casually broke the news that his office had ordered another set of DNA tests aside from the one performed by the state lab. "You are absolutely correct," he told Little. "There are many kinds of DNA tests that can be done, and it might surprise you . . . to know that we're still waiting for results of some DNA tests that have not been done."

While that statement brought applause from the audience, the next questioner blasted Nifong for not already arresting the Duke students suspected of raping Mangum. If the situation were reversed, the student said, and a group of black students were accused of raping a white woman, the suspects would already be in custody. It was hard to argue with that logic. But Nifong took exception to the question. "Certainly I have heard the criticism from many people that if the situation were reversed, if this were a white girl and the focus was on the NCCU basketball team, they would all be in jail right now," he said. "I understand that that is a sentiment in the community from some people, but I just want you to know that that is not the way I conduct business. It never has been. I have been in the DA's office for more than twenty-seven and a half years, and I challenge you to find a single incident, which is well documented. I have over three hundred jury trials. My position on this is very clear. There has never been a case under me [in which] the decision was made based on race."

Nifong later said he had never before experienced the kinetic energy that he felt in the NCCU auditorium that day. "Of every place I've ever been in my life, I would have to say that that was the most—and the only way I can describe it—electric atmosphere," he said. "It was so charged. It was almost like you were about to be hit by lightning. I have never experienced that kind of, I would say, dangerous energy. I've never been in a situation that had so much potential for something bad to happen if things went badly."

The next day, Nifong called Brodhead for the first time. "I just called him and said, 'This is Mike Nifong. I'm just calling to let you know that I'm aware of what you're dealing with. I think you've dealt with it very appropriately so far, and if you have any concerns that you want to discuss, feel free to call me.'"

"It was a very short conversation," Nifong said later. "He seemed uncomfortable, but I didn't know exactly why. See, at that time, I wasn't really aware of some of the inside conversations that had taken place within the Duke administration before that. I found out about them after the fact. So he may have had hostile feelings toward me just because he had been told that nothing was going to happen. Who knows?"

In the wake of the release of the DNA evidence, Selena Roberts, the *Times* sports columnist, wrote a devastating piece about the lack of accountability for athletes' behavior at college campuses across the country. Duke was Exhibit A, along with the University of Colorado at Boulder, "where sex, alcohol, and marijuana were used as recruiting currency," and the University of Vermont, where the hockey team "forced freshmen to binge drink and walk naked while holding each other's genitals." Roberts asked rhetorically, "What is the lifespan of a perverse subculture? It's the longevity of institutional denial minus the instant of a public disclosure. Once unseemly details find light—as in TV camera lights—there is a mad scramble to purge the lapsed caretakers."

But nipping problems in the bud "means never have a paper trail," Roberts wrote, "and this is Duke's problem." In addition to the ongoing investigation into what had happened at 610 North Buchanan, there was also "the outing of a high-minded institution running in the red on accountability. . . . Now they are under the lights. Now they act, fretting over the atmosphere of degradation, over the symptoms of misogyny. . . . Duke officials can't be the conscience of every athlete, but they can confront them with repercussions, with a new paradigm of acceptable behavior, with a fresh discussion on race, gender, and respect." Roberts's solution? Alleva should resign. "His department, his burden," she concluded. "Sometimes purging is the only route to reclamation."

The lack of DNA evidence left the editors of the *Durham Herald-Sun* confused about what to believe had really happened at 610 North Buchanan. "Even some of the people willing to believe the worst about the Duke lacrosse team are now having a hard time believing the rape allegation," they wrote. "But even in the wake of the compelling DNA evidence, those who would echo team members' attorneys and declare the case shut would be smart to wait and see what District Attorney Mike Nifong has up his sleeve."

Duke student Jordan Koss shared the Durham paper's view that the lacrosse team was "out of control." In an opinion piece in the *Chronicle*, Koss wrote that his fellow students deserved some of the blame for what had happened on March 13. "The elevation of athletes into the sexual stratosphere gives these individuals the idea that they have more behavioral freedom around women," he wrote. "Many Duke girls say they suddenly find a guy more attractive when they find out he is an athlete. . . . I personally have listened to several girls recount which sports they've 'covered.' . . . Of all Duke athletes, the [lacrosse players'] heads might have been the most inflated because of a dedicated female following referred to as 'The Lacrosstitutes.' Rape or no rape, Duke students have played a part in making athletes believe they are on a pedestal when it comes to women."

After Nifong's appearance at NCCU, reporters were especially curious about the news he had dropped that Mangum had supposedly identified her attackers the previous week and that additional DNA tests were under way at a new, unidentified lab. But without Nifong elaborating on his comments, defense attorneys were quick to fill the void. Bill Thomas said it was "quite unusual" for a DA to withhold this information from defense attorneys. "It's amazing to me that now this woman says she can identify someone," he told the Durham paper. "Why hasn't this information been revealed before?" Lawyer Kerry Sutton was confused about Nifong's announcement that Mangum had identified her attackers. "Mr. Nifong told me last week that no identification had been made," he said. "If this woman has made an identification since then, I'd have to question whether she is now identifying someone who allegedly attacked her four weeks ago or if she is merely identifying certain young men who she has seen plastered all over the international media in incessant press reports over the last two weeks." Echoing Sutton, Thomas told the *News & Observer*, "I would find it astounding that now . . . is the first time she can ID one of these men. And of course this is after pictures of them have been plastered on national TV for the last two weeks." He also reiterated that the still-unreleased contemporaneous photographs did not back up Mangum's story.

To bolster the defense's legal firepower, that same day a group calling itself the Committee for Fairness to Duke Families—relatives and supporters of the lacrosse players—hired Robert Bennett, the well-known Washington trial lawyer at Skadden Arps. Bennett had been President Clinton's personal lawyer in the lawsuit involving Paula Jones, and also represented former *New York Times* reporter Judith Miller in a case involving her refusal to testify before a grand jury investigating the leaking of the name of CIA operative Valerie Plame. Bennett would not be representing individual players, only the collective group of parents and friends. "They need advice on how to handle the situation," he told the *News & Observer*. Defense attorney Wade Smith told the *New York Times* he was not aware of what Bennett would actually be doing for the Duke families but hoped his involvement would soon be moot. "I still have great hope that we would persuade the prosecutor not to go forward with the case," Smith said, although he added that if Nifong did take the case before a grand jury, an indictment would be inevitable. "Grand juries pretty much do what the prosecutor tells them to do." (In North Carolina, although they bring the case to the grand jury, prosecutors don't actually appear before it; that role is left to the police.)

Nifong had no time for reporters—or defense attorneys—after the NCCU forum because he was on his way to a scheduled meeting with Mangum at his office with officers Gottlieb and Himan. In their conversation on the way to the meeting, Mangum told Gottlieb that her two children were having "emotional problems" both at home and at school because of "this event." As Himan had done the day before for Mangum, Gottlieb suggested the Duke Center for Child and Family Health, a local resource center, could assist Mangum and her children. At 2 p.m., Nifong, Mangum, and the officers met to talk about the prosecution of the case. "Mr. Nifong introduced himself," Gottlieb recalled. "Ms. Mangum was what I would consider very nervous and very cautious around him. He explained basically how the procedures went for a court case. He explained to her that at some point he and Tracey Cline—an assistant DA—would meet with her and basically get more information and basically asked if she had any questions." Gottlieb said Mangum "was acting very traumatized that day, very guarded around him. She was okay with me. She was talking with me. I think she trusted me. But this was the first time she met him." Nifong was trying to make her feel comfortable, Gottlieb recalled, and to convey that, "We're here, we're looking at this stuff; if we go to court, this is what's going to happen. Are you comfortable with that?" Mangum said yes.

Nifong informed the group he intended to seek indictments against Duke lacrosse players Reade Seligmann and Collin Finnerty—both of whom Mangum had identified a week earlier as being among her alleged attackers. When Himan heard that Nifong was hoping to indict Seligmann and Finnerty, he could not quite believe it. "I think I made the response 'With what?'" Himan recalled. "We didn't have them at the party, so it was a big concern for me to go forward with the indictments if we didn't know they were there. . . . I didn't want to indict someone who shouldn't be indicted." He said he had made numerous attempts to contact the players' attorneys, but they would not call him back. "And if the lawyers weren't going to let us talk to someone, I understand that," Himan recalled. "But I just wanted to make sure that we tried to lift every stone that we could, every possible avenue that we could get information, we tried."

Himan raised his concerns about the likely Seligmann indictment with Gottlieb. Recalled Gottlieb, "The concerns that were raised were basically this: with Mr. Finnerty, we were able to show that he was at the party and that she had indentified him. And we had the time cards per se. . . . We had a document showing that he arrived back at the dorm at the [same] time as the people who we knew were at the party. So we were able to put together information to at least corroborate, one, he was there; two, he met the description; three, she was able to show that the SANE nurse's report was consistent with a sexual assault. So we had something to work with there for an indictment. With Mr. Seligmann, we never had anything to tie him to the party directly. Meaning, when we asked the players—I had asked the two about the list [of people at the party], the two that I asked never placed him at the party, and the third guy never placed him at the party. And, yes, he met the physical description. But strictly looking at a picture and saying, 'That's the man that raped me,' Ben was very concerned. We knew that he came in close to the same time that the other players came in. So it wasn't out of the question that he was at the party. But, again, we had nothing that we could say we knew for a fact he was at the party."

There was then a conference call among Nifong, Gottlieb, and more senior police officials in which the police discussed "their concerns" with seeking indictments of Seligmann in particular, because the police were not sure he was even at the party. (It turned out he was, of course.) "I got them in a room with me where we got on the telephone to Mr. Nifong," Gottlieb recalled, "and I explained what the concerns were. And he said, 'If we believe the statements of Ms. Mangum as far as Mr. Finnerty, along with the information we had for Mr. Finnerty, then we should believe the information on Mr. Seligmann.'"

That was Nifong's mantra. And he decided to proceed with seeking the indictments. Nifong asked superior court judge Ronald Stephens for an unusual order sealing what he presumed would be the forthcoming indictments of Seligmann and Finnerty and further requesting that nobody disclose "the finding of the bills on indictment" or the "proceeding leading to that finding" until both men had been arrested. Nifong's argument in defense of the motion was that neither Seligmann, a sophomore from Essex Fells, New Jersey, nor Finnerty, a sophomore from Garden City, New York, had had "long-term ties to the Durham community" and that the "severity of the punishment" they faced because of crimes they were to be charged with created "a substantial risk" that they would "attempt to flee the jurisdiction" of the court if they "learned that an indictment had been returned against" them. "We wanted to give the defendants an opportunity to turn themselves in," Nifong recalled. "We felt that if we just sent the indictments to the grand jury, then obviously the media . . . would be on the indictments before the players had been notified that they had been indicted, and we wanted to be able to notify them after the indictment that they had been indicted to give them an opportunity to choose how they would present themselves to the court."

Nifong's motion stated that both players were to be charged with two class B1 felonies and one class C felony, which together carried a minimum prison sentence of between twelve and fifteen years. Stephens approved Nifong's motions on April 13 and ordered the bills of indictment sealed until it was necessary to open them "for the issuance and execution of an order of arrest." As for why Nifong was pushing to go to the grand jury on April 17, Himan recalled hearing, "It was coming near the end of graduation, and some of these guys lived outside of North Carolina."

Knowing that he intended to seek indictments against Seligmann and Finnerty—and that his chances were good that a grand jury would give him what he sought, given the old saying (coined by Sol Wachtler, a former New York State judge) that a grand jury would indict a ham sandwich if asked— that night, filled with vim and vigor, Nifong attended a candidates' forum at the Durham County Courthouse, along with Freda Black and Keith Bishop. Incredibly, the forum was being broadcast on national television—on cable— no doubt accounting for the increase in the level of political grandstanding. (Nifong was quick to point out that the full quotation about the "ham sandwich" and a grand jury is "a grand jury would indict a ham sandwich in the death of a pig" and noted that "gives it a whole different context.")

Asked why she was running to be district attorney, Black was especially critical of Nifong and his handling of the lacrosse case. "When I began my campaign last July," she said, "I decided I would go into the community and find out what regular people had to say about Durham, about Durham's government, about Durham's District Attorney's Office, and about the problems in our community."

She found that in addition to concerns about gang violence, drugs, and violent crime, people in Durham did not seem to trust their elected officials and worried that their voices were not being heard. That was bad enough, she said, but now, in the wake of the lacrosse case, Durham had become the focus of intense—and negative—national media attention brought on by Nifong and his prosecution of the case. "When you consider our present situation, just look right outside the courthouse," she said. "Look here in this court-room. The media has taken over Durham County again, this time in a nega-tive light. There has been increased tension. Now, the press hasn't caused all of the increased tension, although I do believe that they've caused some of it."

She blamed Nifong. "Perhaps he thought that he landed a case that would save his prosecutorial career," she said. "He gave many statements, he gave many interviews, and only when he began to reap what he sowed did he back off from that type of conduct. The problem for us in Durham is that now the damage has already been done, and I suggest to you the worst part of it is that some of the damage is most likely irreparable. We have daily protests on TV. We have angry citizens. Durham has been portrayed in a negative light nationally. The people I've talked to—and believe it or not, I've had hundreds of phone calls in the last two weeks, from all across the nation—the people I've talked to basically say, in their belief, that this case was mishandled from its inception."

Later during the forum, a woman in the audience asked the candidates if they would have handled the lacrosse case differently. Black, not surprisingly, said she would, even as she conceded she did not have nearly the insight into the details of the case as did Nifong. "But what I do know is that premature information that is either leaked or told to the public can jeopardize a case," she said. "When you speak publicly about a matter, a pending case, you are talking to your potential jury pool, not knowing who the twelve people might be that would sit in a jury box later. You have to be very careful about what information you publicly disseminate in any case." She was also worried that Nifong's comments could mean the lacrosse players might not be able to get a fair trial in Durham County, forcing their lawyers to push for a change of venue. "If you want a jury of your peers, it needs to be a jury of your peers from our county, from Durham County," she said. "I believe if the case had been handled differently, we would have less tension than what we have right now. We also would have less of what's outside the courthouse right now. We wouldn't be on national TV."

When it was his turn to answer the question, Nifong pushed back at Black and Bishop. "Well, I'm not going to surprise anybody here," he said. "I would not change anything about the way that the current district attorney has han-dled the situation. I have handled the situation the way the situation should have been handled. I appreciate the fact that Ms. Black acknowledges that I'm the only person up here who knows what the facts of the case are and I also appreciate the fact that it's very difficult for anybody to respond to questions about how you'd do something differently when you don't know what it is—although Mr. Bishop, the other night at a Democratic Party forum, said if he were the DA, everybody would already be in jail. He didn't say who. He said everybody. I guess if you arrest everybody, it's a lot easier. I guess you'd just put everybody in jail and sort it out later—and there was pressure put on me to do just exactly that. There was also pressure put on me to do nothing, to say, 'Well, you know, her profession was not really the most honorable in the world,' and 'We really don't have the strongest case in the world if there's no DNA, so let's forget about it.'"

Then Nifong—standing at this point—made a most emphatic defense of his handling of the lacrosse case. "Well, ladies and gentlemen, that's not doing your job," he continued. "If I did that, then you should vote against me. I would vote against me if I'd done that, because that's not what this job is about. The reason that I took this case is because this case says something about Durham that I'm not going to let be said. I am not going to allow Durham's view in the minds of the world to be a bunch of lacrosse players at Duke raping a black girl from Durham."

As he had done the day before, Nifong left the Durham courthouse under a police escort without answering any additional questions.

The next day, defense attorney Bill Thomas arranged for another meeting with Nifong to try to get him to slow down on his march toward the grand jury. Thomas arranged for two attorneys to join him who he hoped would help persuade Nifong: James "Butch" Williams Jr., a respected Durham attorney, and Wade Smith. Thomas was clever enough not to invite Joe Cheshire, a Durham lawyer whom Nifong detested and used to refer to as "Joseph Blount Cheshire the Fifth," which was Cheshire's full name, of course, but, said with Nifong's sneer, made the point that Cheshire thought he was special. In any event, Thomas, Williams, and Smith did not know that two days earlier Nifong had filed his motion with Judge Stephens that he intended to seek the indictments of Seligmann and Finnerty. At the meeting, Wade Smith did most of the talking and conveyed a simple message: "Please slow down," he told Nifong. He said the defense lawyers would open their files to Nifong and share what they had discovered from their clients. According to Thomas, Nifong put his hands over his ears. "Gentlemen, I know a lot more about this case than any of you do," Nifong told them, "and I'm going to proceed as I see fit." The meeting lasted less than ten minutes. As the attorneys were leaving, Nifong grew visibly angry. "And by the way," he told them, "you can tell that fucker Cheshire that . . ."

"Don't even go there," Williams interjected. "We don't want to hear about Joe."

As the lawyers walked out of Nifong's office, they were convinced "there was no talking with Nifong," or slowing him down, either.

• • •

The next meeting of the Durham County grand jury was Monday, April 17, and Nifong had left little doubt in the minds of the defense attorneys that he was going to seek at least one indictment that day. They remained highly skeptical that any charges would stick, but there was nothing they could do to prevent Nifong from seeking the indictments. What they didn't know was that Nifong had already received Judge Stephens's backing to keep the expected indictments of Seligmann and Finnerty sealed until they could be arrested in what would amount to nothing less than a massive media event. "It is very unclear what [Nifong's] intentions are other than he intends to charge someone," attorney Bill Thomas told the *Durham Herald-Sun* for a front-page story on the morning of April 13. "Based on his public comments, I am assuming he is submitting this case to the grand jury as quickly as he can, and seeking one or more indictments when he does."

Thomas said he had been surprised to learn from Nifong—at the NCCU forum—that Mangum had identified her attackers. That was news to him. He also wondered why he had not received from Nifong a copy of Mangum's identification report. Instead, he got from a Nifong a letter saying the report would be ready the week of April 17. As for the news that Nifong was seeking a second set of DNA tests, Thomas said he welcomed the tests. "That's not unusual at all," he said. "[Nifong] has not disclosed the nature of the tests, but these young men are glad these tests are being conducted. They are in favor of all scientific and DNA tests which can be conducted because they know that these tests will clear them."

The next day, Gottlieb spoke with Sergeant Gary Smith, of the Duke police force, about getting Duke's permission for Gottlieb and Himan to return to the Edens dormitory to talk to several of the lacrosse players—just days before Nifong was to seek an indictment of one or more of their teammates. This was part of police efforts to gather information about who was or was not at the party—and to make sure Nifong was not about to seek an indictment for someone—Seligmann—who was not even at the party. The two officers did not contact the players' attorneys before speaking with Gary Smith, nor did they read anyone their Miranda rights before speaking with them.

Thirty minutes later, Gottlieb and Himan knocked on the door of Michael Young, a midfielder from Long Island. Young invited the officers in "and made room on his sofa for us." They talked about how Young, who had given DNA evidence along with the other forty-five white players, had been with his girlfriend on the night of March 13 and was not at the party. They talked about other players who were also likely not at the party and they discussed McFadyen's e-mail and how that had been a "team e-mail."

Four minutes later, they went to see Rob Schroeder, also in Edens. He told them he did not want to answer their questions. But he agreed to listen. He let the officers into his room. They asked him if he knew anyone who was not at the party. Schroeder answered that the only one he knew was not there was Chris Loftus. He did not want to answer any more questions, and Gottlieb and Himan left his room. They then knocked on Reade Seligmann's door, but there was no answer.

As the officers were leaving Edens, Himan noticed Zack Greer coming up the stairs. He asked Greer if they could talk for "two minutes," and Greer said he would listen but not answer. Himan asked him if he could tell them who was not at the party. "No comment," Greer told Himan. "Thank you." Greer walked away. From Edens, the two officers went to HH dorm to speak with Bo Carrington and Rob Wellington. Himan knocked on their dorm room door and was told to come in. He told the two players he wanted to talk about who was not at the party, but Carrington said he needed to speak with his attorney before he could speak with the two officers. Wellington gave a similar response. Before leaving the campus, the officers gave Carrington and Wellington their contact information.

When the players' attorneys discovered that the police had visited their clients without a search warrant and without contacting them first, they were incensed. They said it was a "last-ditch attempt" by the police "not to embarrass themselves" by indicting a player who was not at the party. Bob Ekstrand, who represented thirty-two of the forty-six players who had had their DNA tested, said Gottlieb and Himan waited outside Edens until a woman used her card key to enter. "Then," he told the Durham paper, "they stuck a foot in the door and sneaked in behind her," since they did not have a search warrant. "The clear gist of what they were looking for was to find out who was at the party and who wasn't," he said. "That's really odd, given that the accuser claims to have identified two people. The accuser maybe picked someone out of the photo lineup who wasn't even in the state at the time."

Joe Cheshire agreed with Ekstrand. "It seems awfully interesting that they would be doing something like that two days before [the meeting of the grand jury]," he said. "They don't have a case, and they're trying to fit a round peg into a square hole." Added Bill Thomas, "It is illegal, unconstitutional, and reprehensible. It will be the subject of court action. . . . [The questioning] is a clear sign they have little if any confidence in the information they will present to the grand jury as early as Monday."

But Aaron Graves, Duke's vice president for campus security and safety, defended the police visit. "They were there as part of the ongoing police investigation, and they notified the Duke Police Department ahead of time," he said in a statement. "No search warrants were executed. The purpose of the visit was to conduct interviews. We do not know who they interviewed during the hour and fifteen minutes they were in the Edens Residence Hall. Duke reiterates its earlier statements that it is cooperating fully with the police investigation and urges anyone with information pertinent to the events of March 13 to cooperate with the authorities. Any further questions about this should be directed to the Durham Police Department." Mayor Bell said the detectives' visit to Edens "wasn't any more than their usual knock and talk," although it clearly was more than that.

Defense attorneys took this moment to share with a reporter from the *Durham Herald-Sun* the photographs they had that purportedly showed Mangum at different times during the evening of March 13. The attorneys let the reporter look at the photographs but not publish them. According to the paper, the pictures revealed the following progression of events:

11:02 p.m. The players are shown sitting around 610 North Buchanan, holding beer cups in their hands, waiting for the dancers to arrive.

12:00 a.m. Mangum "is sprawled on her stomach on the floor," the paper reported, "as a second dancer stands over her." The players are "watching the show" but "not grabbing or attempting to touch the women." Meanwhile, "bruises are clearly visible" on Mangum's "legs and thighs."

12:01:16 Roberts is "lying on her back on the floor" with Mangum "kneeling over her."

12:03:57 The dancers leave the room after four minutes of dancing. Mangum "clearly" leaves behind one of her shoes.

12:10:39 One of the players is passed-out drunk on the floor, his head leaning against a sofa, and a "crushed beer can" is at his side.

12:30:12 Mangum is on the back porch of the house. She has only one shoe on, "appears to smile" and is trying to get back inside.

12:31:26 Mangum "appears to be stumbling down" the back steps.

12:37:58 A series of photos, according to the paper, starting at this time show Mangum "lying on her left side" on the back porch, "seemingly passed out or asleep." There were "pink splotches" on the "wrought-iron" railing beside her that defense attorneys said were from "nail polish" Mangum "applied" in the bathroom between 12:10 and 12:30. The attorneys argued that Mangum was "manicuring her nails" during the "only time a rape could have occurred in the house."

12:41 Mangum is being helped into Roberts's car.

At 12:53 a.m., Roberts called the 911 dispatchers about the racial slurs, and at 1:22 a.m. police responded to a 911 call from the Kroger supermarket parking lot.

The police also released a copy of a tape of the call that Officer John Shelton made to the police dispatcher in the early hours of March 14 about seeing Mangum in the Kroger parking lot. Shelton can be heard telling the dispatcher that the woman was "1056 and unconscious," using police code for an intoxicated pedestrian. The dispatcher asked if an ambulance was needed and Shelton said, "Nah, she's breathing and appears to be fine. She's not in distress. She's just passed-out drunk." Defense attorneys took the release of the tape as more good news for their clients. The call was consistent with "what I have seen of the photo evidence before," attorney Kerry Sutton said, which showed Mangum was "way beyond where you would put somebody behind the wheel of a car." Added Butch Williams, "Not only did the tape say she was passed out, but it mentions nothing about any signs of physical trauma."

Interviewing the lacrosse players without their lawyers' consent—and without the Duke police giving the students a heads-up that police were heading their way—and releasing tapes of police conversations and amateur photographs from the night of the alleged rape had the feel of the same kind of last-minute jockeying and spin that accompanies a presidential election. And, of course, there was more. Reprising a meeting first held March 30 at Duke, NCCU chancellor Ammons met on April 14 with Brodhead and Durham mayor Bell, along with local black leaders, to continue the ongoing discussion about how to reduce the tension in the community brought on by the alleged incident on March 13. At a press conference after the meeting, Bell said the group discussed the obvious issues of sexism, racism, and bad behavior the incident raised. But he said the problems were not unique to Durham. "If you go into any town, any state, across the nation, you'll find the same type of issues, even on college campuses," he said. "What we're dealing with is a national issue. It also happens you guys have come in and made it a Durham issue." Ammons was critical of the portrait of Durham the national news media was busy painting. "Justice is served in the courtroom, not in the media or in the hands of individuals," he said.

Brodhead, the only white face at the front of the room, seemed less than thrilled to be there. "I'm the newcomer to this town," he said, "and I want to say the events that have made us so newsworthy in recent weeks have highlighted strains in this city, and all of us are committed to addressing those strains and using this incident as an occasion to move this community forward. But if they've highlighted strains, they've also highlighted a tradition of neighborliness and collaboration."

At one point, amid the happy talk of working together to reduce the tension in the community, a reporter asked Brodhead about the breaking news that Gottlieb and Himan had entered Edens dormitory the previous afternoon without the knowledge of defense attorneys. Brodhead visibly stiffened and noted that his fate in the ongoing drama was always being the last to know basic facts, a veiled reference to not knowing about McFadyen's e-mail until after the warrant containing it had been unsealed and released publicly. He was clearly not happy. "I am aware that police attempted to enter these rooms, and now I am about to leave this news conference to learn the whole story," he said. He was off to address a group of new students admitted to the Duke class of 2011, which prompted a reporter to ask whether the ongoing scandal had damaged the school's reputation.

When angered, the usually soft-spoken Brodhead tensed and spoke even more pointedly than he normally did. "Pardon me for saying that both Duke and NCCU are wonderful institutions with long histories and anyone who wants to know their character is probably going to want to look past the news of the last two days," he responded. "We are taking these things very seriously. We want to draw what benefit we can for the future education of our students as students and as members of this town. But I do want to say [that] a person who wants to judge a school for their kids had [also] better look at the faculty, the quality of the teaching, and all the resources."

Adding to the growing carnival-like atmosphere in Durham were the persistent rumors that Reverend Al Sharpton, the civil rights activist, would soon show up in town. Sharpton, who had run unsuccessfully for president in 2004, was perhaps best known then—before he became the host of his own television show on MSNBC—for, as the Durham paper put it, his "fiery rhetoric" and his association with the 1987 case in New York involving a young black woman named Tawana Brawley. Then fifteen years old, Brawley alleged that six white men had assaulted and raped her. "She was found lying in a garbage bag, smeared with feces, with racial epithets written on her body in charcoal," the Durham newspaper reported. But the Brawley case was a hoax, and Sharpton, by taking up her cause in a very public way, made himself the subject of ridicule, as well as putting himself on the wrong side of a $345,000 defamation-of-character judgment against him brought by a New York prosecutor.

The rumor was that Sharpton would appear alongside Deacon James Scales, of the Church of the Apostolic Revival, during Scales's (by then) weekly Sunday prayer vigil in front of 610 North Buchanan. "His office contacted us," Scales told the *News & Observer*. "We did not ask him to come. That's not to say anything negative, but this is a Durham issue. To the best of our knowledge, he is not coming." Eddie Harris, spokesman for Sharpton, said that while there had "been race-baiting" in the lacrosse case, making it a natural place for Sharpton to make an appearance, the reverend would not come to Durham unless asked. "At no time do we ever get involved unless the family invites us," he said.

Not to be outdone, Reverend Jesse Jackson, of the Rainbow PUSH Coalition in Chicago, announced that he wanted to pay the tuition costs for Mangum at NCCU. He wanted her to finish college "so she will never again, in an act of desperation, have to expose her body," he said. "She should never again have to stoop that low to survive. That happens to all too many women." He wanted to meet with Mangum in person when she was "strong enough" to do so and he said his offer to her was good "regardless of the outcome of the case." Mangum's mother said of Jackson's offer that she thought it would make her daughter happy. (Mangum later said Jackson never followed through with her on his offer, though her mother reportedly spoke to him again.)

It was all almost too delicious as theater, unless, like the Duke lacrosse players, Crystal Mangum, Dick Brodhead, and Mike Nifong, this was really happening and dramatically altering the courses of their lives.

The weekend before Nifong was to seek indictments brought the editorial writers out of the woodwork. The *Los Angeles Times* published an opinion piece by Michael Skube, a former Pulitzer Prize–winning columnist at the *News & Observer*. He recounted the dynamic engulfing Durham and Duke and concluded that the "picture was clear: Prep schools. Privilege. Power. And with that the three gears of academic epistemology—race, class, and gender—were fully synchronized." Skube worried that "left unsaid" was that "many people" had a "psychological and moral investment in the lacrosse players' guilt." The lacrosse players "were suburb-bred athletes who grew up playing a sport most Americans have never seen. If the white and privileged Duke lacrosse players were not culpable, only two possibilities remain: She had been assaulted by someone else, or the hospital workers were mistaken and she was not assaulted at all." That raised the specter of the Tawana Brawley case, of course, and Skube's hope that the "level of discourse in Durham" had not—yet—sunk to that level. "Even so, with more than a month having passed since the woman first accused the lacrosse players, suspicions of a rush to judgment are not abating," he wrote. "To the contrary, they are building."

He understood why the players were an unsympathetic bunch, what with the arrogance and the many previous run-ins with the law (he did not seem to be aware of Mangum's previous run-ins with the law). "Then there is the question of Duke itself," he concluded. "It is not an easy university to love. Few universities do as much to enroll minority students, and yet its public face is one of arrogance and elitism. Surrounded on most sides by down-at-the-heels black neighborhoods, the school sits like a fortress amid privation, its faux Gothic architecture all but declaring wealth and entitlement." By contrast, there was NCCU and Mangum, whom the media continuously referred to as "an exotic dancer," prompting the students at NCCU to wonder why. "The point in rebuttal seems almost too obvious," Skube wrote. "She did not show up at the lacrosse players' house to study voting behavior. She showed up to dance. None of this, it goes without saying, indicts her. But nothing yet indicts the players, either. They may well be louts and cads. Whether any of them is a rapist is quite another matter, and one whose seriousness demands something more than pep rally assertions and the willingness to believe they must be."

• • •

At 11:45 a.m., on April 17, Himan and Gottlieb met with the grand jury. In his notes, Himan simply stated he was there, without elaboration. He later said he had spoken with Nifong prior to going to the grand jury. "He asked me to bring up basically my whole case file," Himan recalled. Gottlieb wrote that he testified before the grand jury concerning the "involvement" of Duke sophomores Reade Seligmann and Collin Finnerty in the case. He wrote in his notes, "After Inv. Himan and I completed our testimony, we were notified a true bill was voted on. We met with District Attorney M. Nifong and briefed him." Around 2 p.m. the indictments were handed down and sealed. (The last time an indictment had been sealed in Durham was in 1997 for Broadus Crabtree, a veteran police officer accused of murdering a prostitute.)

According to the six "true bills" signed by jury foreman Charles A. Harris, at least twelve members of the eighteen-member grand jury had indicted both Seligmann and Finnerty on three charges each of first-degree forcible rape, first-degree sexual offense, and first-degree kidnapping. With regard to the rape charge, the grand jury found that both Seligmann and Finnerty "unlawfully, willfully, and feloniously did ravish and carnally know Crystal Mangum, by force and against her will. At the time of the offense, the defendant was aided and abetted by one or more other persons." As for the kidnapping, the two men were charged with "unlawfully confining" Mangum, "restraining her and removing her from one place to another, without her consent, and for the purposes of terrorizing her and facilitating the commission of the felonies of rape and sexual offense. Crystal Mangum was sexually assaulted and was not released in a safe place."

According to Gottlieb, when the indictment was brought before Judge Stephens, he decided Seligmann and Finnerty would be allowed to turn themselves in to be arrested the next morning at 5 a.m. at the Durham County Jail. The judge set bail at $400,000 for each player. Afterward, around 3:30 p.m., Gottlieb made a call to get a status report on Finnerty's case file from the Georgetown case and was told that the US attorney preferred that Nifong himself request the information. Gottlieb called Nifong and passed along that decision.

Meanwhile, more than fifty local and national journalists and television reporters staked out the sixth floor of the courthouse from dawn until dusk, waiting for information about the indictments. At one point, Nifong emerged from a bathroom. "It would be nice to figure out a way to give me back my anonymity," he said. "I no longer get to go anywhere in my community without people knowing who I am."

At another point that morning, a local television station ran an interview with Kim Roberts, the other dancer at the March 13 party. Roberts had been silent for weeks. But now she was talking. When Mangum arrived at the party, Roberts said, "she looked absolutely fine." But by the time they left together, "she was definitely a totally different woman than when I first met her. She was definitely under some sort of substance." She also expressed her view that Mangum had been raped, a change from her initial statement to police that she did not think anything happened in the bathroom that night. "I can't imagine that a woman would do that to herself if she didn't feel like it was worth doing it," she said. "And the only reason it would be worth doing it is if she was raped. So I have no reason to believe she was lying."

Although her identity was obscured, Roberts had said something similar that weekend on MSNBC. The idea that she had originally rejected the notion that a rape had occurred was "out-and-out lies," she said, perpetrated by defense attorneys. "It's making me believe more and more every single day, every single news story that I hear coming from them, that they have something to hide and they're scared of what's to come. . . . I think it's quite possible that something really terrible had happened to her," she said.

Two days later, Roberts e-mailed Ronn Torossian, the CEO of 5W, a public relations firm, seeking his help. Under the subject "duke lacrosse scandal," Roberts wrote: "Although I am no celebrity and just an average citizen, I've found myself in the center of one of the biggest stories in the country. I'm worried about letting this opportunity pass me by without making the best of it and was wondering if you had any advice as to how to spin this to my advantage. I am determined not to let any negative publicity about my life overtake me. I'm so confused as to who to talk to for relevant advice, and I hope that you can return my e-mail." Indeed, Roberts's obsession with making conflicting public statements about what she thought may or may not have happened on the night of March 13 became a problem for Nifong. At one point he told Mark Simeon, her attorney, that "it would be nice if she wouldn't keep making statements—I understand that he didn't have any real control over that—because every time that she made a statement . . . everything seemed to change. And we got to the point actually that we're not intending to call Ms. Pittman [as Roberts was also known] as a witness because she had made so many statements during the course of this."

Early on the afternoon of April 17—his mother's birthday—Seligmann was watching the movie *Capote* with his roommate Jay Jennison and their teammate Rob Wellington. His father, Philip, a private investor, and Jay's father were with them. They were together at the offices of Seligmann's Durham lawyer, Julian Mack. They knew the indictments, if any, would be handed down, but Seligmann was unconcerned: he knew he hadn't done anything wrong and had already left 610 North Buchanan by the time of the alleged incident. After two o'clock, Mack told him that two players had been indicted but that the indictments had been sealed. "I didn't know what that meant, but I didn't think that had any bearing on me," Seligmann recalled, "and they said they weren't going to release who it was. It was sort of a difficult situation, because I sort of wanted to know who it was. . . . I feel terrible for whoever it is but I hope it's not me."

After a while Wellington and Jennison left, and Seligmann stayed behind to talk with Mack about Mack's legal fees. They were joking around. "He's sitting across the table from me," Seligmann recalled, "and all of a sudden his secretary comes in and says, 'Julian, Mike Nifong is on the phone.' My first reaction was 'Oh, my God, it's one of those two'"—meaning Wellington or Jennison. "For some reason, you never think it's going to be you. . . . He picks up the phone and briefly glances up at me, and you can see his face, the coloring in his face was changing." The Seligmanns—father and son—just stared at each other. "You get that feeling in your stomach, that hit, and you don't even know what to do," he said. "You don't want to believe it, but you want to know. He asked us to stand in the other room. . . . We're standing in there and we're just circling, and the room felt like it was spinning. Julian comes in and says, 'She picked you.' I mean, my dad just fell to the floor, and I just sat on the ground and said, 'My life is over.'" After he got over the initial shock—how long it took, he can't recall—he decided to fight the charges: "Wait, I have everything to prove," he told himself.

When the two men were able to pick themselves—literally—up off the floor, they embraced. "Julian didn't even know what to say," Seligmann said. "The first thing I thought about was 'How am I going to tell my mom?' Right away, my dad said he had to go, and we had to start putting together alibi information, because we never thought it was ever going to be me, so I never worried about it." Seligmann then called the headmaster at the Delbarton School, the all-boys Catholic school he had graduated from two years before in Morristown, New Jersey, and asked him to go be with his mother, who was then watching his two twin younger brothers playing in a lacrosse game at the school. She was walking across the lacrosse field when her cell phone rang.

"Mom, I need you to be stronger than you have ever been in your entire life," he told his mother. Seligmann paused and then slowly told his mother, "Mom, she chose me."

He heard his mother gasp. "The life was sucked right out of her," he said. "And then I tried to calm her down and I just told her everything was going to be all right, and that we would prove this didn't happen, and she didn't need me to tell her that."

"The world started spinning," Kathy Seligmann recalled. She sprinted toward her car. When she got there, she collapsed into the arms of Father Luke Travers, the Delbarton headmaster. She then drove the fifteen miles back to the Seligmann home—a two-story, ivy-covered brick colonial with black shutters that the New York Times said was valued at $1.3 million—in Essex Fells, New Jersey.

4

When Seligmann's youngest brother saw the news on the television about Reade, he cried: "Mom, why are they doing this?" Kathy Seligmann said, "To see this happen to your eldest son, and to see your youngest son's reaction, is just heartbreaking." But Reade Seligmann never once cried or showed any fear, his mother said. "Even when he stepped out of the police car, he kept his head up high," she said. "He holds this family together. I would just like him to have his life back."

Nifong told Julian Mack that the news of the indictment had to remain confidential. If it leaked to the press, he told the lawyer, then he would come to Duke's campus, pull the boys out of class and arrest them publicly. They would lose the "privilege" of turning themselves in early the next morning at the Durham jail. "We were told that we [had] to go turn ourselves in for something that we didn't do," Seligmann said.

He went back to his room at Duke to pick up some things—he was going to have to leave school after being arrested—and found his roommate there with his girlfriend. "I had to put a smile on my face," he said. "I had to joke around with them and pretend everything was okay." Seligmann's girlfriend of more than two years had been calling him throughout the day, wanting to know who had been indicted. "I never told her, because I was told I wasn't allowed," he said. Eventually, he found her sitting in a friend's room. Initially, she was angry at Seligmann.

"Why didn't you call me?" she asked. "What have you been doing all day? I've been so worried." Seligmann took her outside the dorm. He remembered she was wrapped in a blanket to keep warm.

He told her what had happened. "She picked me," he said. "She just collapsed. I literally had to carry my girlfriend, and it was a long walk from one of the quads all the way down to my dad's car, and put her in the car."

That night, Seligmann and his father stayed at a hotel. He spent a few sleepless hours there before leaving at 4 a.m to turn himself in.

Collin Finnerty, meanwhile, had spent the weekend—Easter Weekend—at home in Garden City, New York, on Long Island. The Dutch colonial house was in a cul-de-sac next to the Garden City Golf Club and was said to be worth more than $2 million. The Finnertys also owned a $4.3 million summer home in West Hampton Beach, with a tennis court and a motorboat. His father, Kevin, was a very successful Wall Street banker, first at Bear Stearns, where he became a senior managing director and the head of mortgage-backed securities, and then at both UBS and what became JPMorgan Chase & Co. Finnerty was the middle of five children, with two older brothers and two younger sisters. His mother, Mary Ellen, described him not only as "a big boy with a big heart" but also as "private," "shy," "sensitive," and "religious." She said Collin was always athletic, played a variety of sports, and once he settled on playing lacrosse, his "dream was to attend Duke and play lacrosse there." She said that the family was thrilled when that happened in 2004 after he graduated from Chaminade High School.

She said the allegations against the players were "extremely difficult" to absorb, at first. "It was devastating to hear the way they were falsely described in the media," she said. "But it was hard to avoid. It was everywhere you turned. Everywhere you looked. It was an incredibly difficult time for every Duke lacrosse parent."

Somehow during the course of the Easter weekend, the Finnertys began to get the idea that Collin was on a "short list" of players who might be indicted. "We knew he was one of the boys to possibly be indicted, but we didn't know how long that list was," Mary Ellen Finnerty said. Finnerty's attorney, Bill Cotter, told the family to leave Garden City and move into a hotel in New York City. "We knew it was a sealed indictment," she said, "but we didn't know what the manner of turning Collin in would be so we didn't want it to happen at our house with other children there." Collin, his girlfriend, and his parents then headed into New York City.

By Monday morning, the Finnertys got the word from Cotter that Collin was going to be indicted. That afternoon, the lawyer called back with the news that Collin had in fact been indicted. Collin "let out a cry that I'll never forget," his mother remembered. "He howled and he just collapsed on the bed. I just went to him and held him and we all cried." She said they were "blown away" by the news and wondered how it could possibly have happened. "There was nothing to place him there," she said. "We were blown away but nevertheless we knew we had truth on our side and we had to be resolute to fight. We were now in the fight of our lives."

Mary Ellen Finnerty said she had been a parent for twenty-six years. "And I have to say this was far and away the hardest moment of mothering that I've ever had," she said. The news was especially hard on the two younger girls. "How do you explain to a ten-year-old that her brother has just been indicted for rape?" she said. "How do you explain that crime alone to a ten-year-old?" His sixteen-year-old sister, like everyone, was "just overwhelmed with grief" but the family "rallied to support their brother. The way we [went] through it was just to stick together as a family and we did everything we could to support him through this nightmare we were all living." Kevin Finnerty echoed his wife's observations. "The charges were extremely serious, and we viewed it as a life-and-death situation, and it was beyond painful," he told *Newsday*. Before long, Finnerty was on a plane from New York to Durham to turn himself in.

For other parents of the team's players, the weekend was equally miserable. "That Easter weekend was one of the worst moments of my life," Larry Lamade remembered. "Nifong had indicated that he was going to indict at least three lacrosse players the week after Easter. All the lacrosse families knew the allegations were false, but all had to retain attorneys. We felt like the men on the USS

Indianapolis in World War II after their ship was sunk. They bobbed hopelessly in the waters of the Pacific for days while the sharks indiscriminately picked them off. It was a Kafkaesque moment."

Word began to leak that two players had been indicted, but their names were not released. "Two young men have been charged with crimes they did not commit," attorney Bob Ekstrand said. "This is a tragedy. For the two young men, an ordeal lies ahead. They do not face it alone. They face it with the love of family and friends and strengthened by the truth. They are both innocent."

At 5 p.m., Duke's John Burness released a statement about the status of the grand jury deliberations. "We are aware that the district attorney made a presentation to the grand jury today, but we have no knowledge about the contents of his presentation, and no information about the grand jury's deliberations has been released," he said. "At this point we remain unclear about the precise status of this case and we must simply wait for news of today's proceedings. Until we have greater clarity it would be inappropriate to comment further." That night, Burness appeared on *ABC World News*. He looked tired and puffy. It had not been an easy month. "One of the prices of Duke's success, because of our reputation, because of our excellence, because of our openness, is that people will come after you in a situation like this," he said on national television. The network then showed a clip from the Easter Sunday protest in front of 610 North Buchanan. "Are there two sets of laws?" the speaker wondered, "one for the rich elite and then one for the poor community?" What was Burness's biggest disappointment with the news media's coverage of the alleged incident? the network asked. Fighting back tears, Burness replied, "Very easy: the portrayal of our students generally. These are great kids. These are great kids. That's all I can say." The piece ended by pointing out that the next day would be a dark one for Duke.

And it began at precisely 4:54 a.m. That's when both Seligmann, dressed in a yellow shirt, and Finnerty, dressed in a blue blazer, arrived at the Durham County Jail in the backseat of a sheriff's deputy's cruiser. Both were handcuffed. The cruiser pulled into a secured area behind the building. Camera crews were waiting. Seligmann remembered being blinded by the camera lights as he got out of the car. He was calm. "Maybe it was because I was so detached from the situation," he remembered.

The two men were escorted into the building, where they were served with the indictments, "processed"—photographed and fingerprinted—and each given a $400,000 cash bond, meaning the two men had to post the money in the form of a cashier's check if they were to be released. "Both men were polite and cooperative," Gottlieb recalled. "Both were obviously nervous and requested not to sign their booking sheets." Seligmann remembered putting his fingers on the futuristic fingerprint machine and thinking to himself, "Hey this is kind of cool." Then he remembered why he was there and snapped back to reality. He was put into a small, one-person cell while his father went off to arrange for the bail to be paid. Seligmann was in the cell for about ninety minutes, and remembered passing the time by reading the Spanish scribbles on the wall of the cell. Ironically, he was about to miss his Spanish exam. He remembered one phrase on the wall: *Ayúdame*, which means "Help me" in Spanish.

Seligmann's family borrowed the money for his bail "from a friend," Seligmann said later. "We couldn't pay that." He left the jail shortly before 7:15 a.m. and was met immediately by the media scrum as he made his way into the family's Ford Explorer. They ran a red light in their hurry to get away. The media also showed up at his house in New Jersey, having moved down the street from where they had staked out Ryan McFadyen's home. "The day I was indicted, my mom and my brothers had to pack up and drive to a friend's house because they parked big trucks—all the trucks that you see outside with satellite dishes and whatnot—on our front yard," he said. "From what I heard from our neighbors, I heard they were just going after every single person they could. I even believe one reporter got hit by a car, trying to get an interview. Probably deserved it. I mean, it was just everywhere you went."

It took the Finnerty family a few hours longer to get the $400,000 bail, forcing Collin to sit inside the Durham jail and wait until the bank opened. At around 9:30 a.m., Kevin Finnerty arrived with two lawyers, and together they escorted Collin Finnerty to the Durham courthouse for a "routine first appearance." He sat "stonefaced" next to his father. "They were surrounded by dozens of cameras while Judge Stephens conducted a sentencing hearing for a convicted child molester whose teenage victim testified how much he had hurt her and how much she hated him," the *New York Times* reported. Five minutes later, Nifong stood in the courtroom and called Seligmann and Finnerty to the defense table. Finnerty was released after signing a form waiving court-appointed counsel and after Cotter told Judge Stephens that Finnerty understood the charges against him. Seligmann was not there; he was represented by his attorney, who was told Seligmann would have to return and sign the same paper that Finnerty had. The next court appearance date for both players was May 15.

The defense lawyers quickly went on the offensive. "The grand jury only heard one side of the story," Cotter told reporters when he arrived with Kevin Finnerty to post the bond for his son. "They almost always indict. We're surprised anybody got indicted, quite frankly. The next jury will hear the entire story, which includes our evidence. We're confident these young men will be found to be innocent." Kirk Osborn, a lawyer from Chapel Hill brought in to represent Seligmann, said, "This kid is just an honorable kid, never done anything wrong in his life. He is absolutely innocent and we intend to show that sooner rather than later." He added, "It's hard to put into words the unfairness and miscarriage of justice that this indictment is."

Another defense attorney, Bill Thomas, said neither Seligmann nor Finnerty had had any contact with Mangum on the evening of March 13. Thomas said "multiple witnesses and a commercial transaction" indicated Seligmann wasn't at the party at the time of the alleged rape. And defense attorney Bob Ekstrand said neither Seligmann nor Finnerty was at the party "at the relevant time." Kerry Sutton, whose clients were not indicted, said, "Before yesterday I had never even heard Mr. Seligmann's name mentioned. That was completely out of the blue." She added, with obvious delight, "The state's going to be shocked. We were hoping [Mangum] would pick men that we knew were not there, and she did. Now we're ready for war. . . . The state has put itself in a situation that is going to be hard to get out of."

Although Osborn would not discuss with reporters Seligmann's alibi, the *Durham Herald-Sun* reported that after making three cell phone calls between 12:07 a.m. and 12:11 a.m., Seligmann called a cab at 12:14 a.m. and reported (incorrectly) that he was picked up at 610 North Buchanan at 12:19 a.m. The paper also reported that at 12:24 a.m. there was a photograph of Seligmann at a local bank ATM withdrawing cash. The alleged rape supposedly occurred between 12:10 a.m. and 12:30 a.m. "Once I left the party, Rob Wellington and I had decided to go to Cook-Out for some food," Seligmann explained later, "and I needed to get some money. I had taken a taxi to the Wachovia. . . . We went to Wachovia, and then I took out the money, and I guess we went down, that was probably whatever road we went to, to get to Cook-Out." At 12:25 a.m., Seligmann made a call out of state to his girlfriend. After getting his food at the drive-through at the Cook-Out, Seligmann and Wellington went back to Edens dormitory, using Seligmann's identification card at 12:46 a.m. to get in. "I remember those two guys starting enjoying their food inside my car, but I'm glad I end up with a nice tip and fare $25," the cabdriver said in an affidavit. If these documents were genuine, it seemed that it would be very difficult to believe that at the same time he was calling a cab and getting a late-night meal at the Cook-Out, Seligmann could also have been raping Mangum. (A Charlotte lawyer told the Durham paper that Finnerty also had an alibi.)

Others were equally stunned by the indictments. Duke sophomore Aaina Agarwal, who lived down the hall from Finnerty, said, "Collin is literally one of the most kind and gentle people I've ever met"—ignoring as many people had that afternoon that Finnerty had been involved in the gay-bating case in Georgetown. Hamish Russell, a sophomore and a member of the club lacrosse team, said he knew both Seligmann and his girlfriend very well. "There is no way that this even happened if this is the guy that the stripper is 'one hundred percent sure' about."

For his part, Ryan McFadyen was at once relieved that Mangum had not picked him—"She's basically picking out of a hat who raped me," he said—and then dumbfounded that she believed Seligmann and Finnerty had raped her.

"Then it happens to be Reade and Collin," he said. "Reade, a kid I've known since I was in middle school, I went to high school with, went to Duke together, a friend, but Collin, a really good friend and just a terrific, terrific guy. It was 'No way' no matter who it was, but it's just like, 'Are you kidding me?' I remember when we found out who it was. I remember, like, five times my dad was crying in front of me. My dad and I were just bawling our eyes out."

But there was another perspective, voiced by those concerned about Mangum. "In light of the indictments in the Duke lacrosse team case, we have to exercise patience as this situation unfolds," NCCU chancellor James Ammons said in a statement. "There are many sensitive issues surrounding this incident. Considering all the media scrutiny, this is a very intense time for the victim, NCCU, Duke University, and the City of Durham. Our hearts continue to go out to the young lady as she goes through this process. We will continue to do everything we can to support her." A couple of blocks from the courthouse, Durham community leaders convened to further show their support for Mangum. The indictments are "not the final proof of guilt," said William Barber, the president of the state chapter of the NACCP, "but it is an indication, based on the initial evidence, that something happened." He said the NAACP was putting together a team of "the best legal minds" to ensure that civil rights would not be violated.

Nifong would not talk about the indictments or the evidence he had compiled that led to them. But, in a public statement, he made it clear that at his suggestion, Judge Stephens had sealed the bills of indictment, which forbid any disclosure of them until the defendants were arrested. "Those arrests occurred earlier this morning, and each defendant was placed under a secured bond of $400,000," Nifong said in his statement. He also wrote that a third indictment was imminent. "It had been my hope to charge all three of the assailants at the same time, but the evidence available to me at this moment does not permit that," Nifong said in a statement. "Investigation into the identity of the third assailant will continue in the hope that he can also be identified with certainty. It is important that we not only bring the assailants to justice, but also that we lift the cloud of suspicion from those team members who were not involved with the assault." He concluded that since the cases were "now active and pending," he would make "no more public statements about the matter other than those made in open court."

The next grand jury meeting was scheduled for May 1, the day before the primary election.

CHAPTER NINE

Unanswered Questions

For its part, the Duke administration moved cautiously in the wake of the two indictments. In a statement, Larry Moneta reminded the curious that federal privacy laws prevented the school from releasing any information about the students. He also mentioned that it was "the university's practice" to suspend students on an interim basis who have been "charged with a felony or when the student's presence on the campus may create an unsafe situation." Brodhead was less overtly legalistic in his comments but clearly struggled to find the right mix of words.

"Today the case has taken a new turn: the grand jury handed down indictments against two students who have since been arrested," he said. "District Attorney Nifong will now have an opportunity to present his case, and we will learn on what basis he has pressed his charges. We also move from unfocused speculation about forty-six members of the team to the court of law where the guilt or innocence of the individuals charged will be established. It is worth reminding ourselves that in our system of laws, a person is presumed innocent until proven guilty. Many lives have been touched by this case. It has brought pain and suffering to all involved, and it deeply challenges our ability to balance judgment with compassion. As the legal process unfolds, we must hope that it brings a speedy resolution and that the truth of the events is fully clarified. In the meantime, we have important work to do. The Duke and Durham communities must restore the bonds this episode has strained and learn whatever lessons it affords. Building upon the progress that has been made over the past decades, we must work to create a community that assures respect and dignity for all."

Barely any time had passed for Duke, its students, faculty, and administrators to absorb the impact of the indictments before Gottlieb and Himan were again on West Campus looking for more evidence to build their case against the two sophomores. Just after lunch on April 18, the two officers were talking about their concern that useful evidence might be lurking in the dorm rooms of both Seligmann and Finnerty in Edens. Some two hours later, warrants had been drafted that would allow them to gather evidence from the two rooms.

Search warrants in hand, at 5:35 p.m., Himan and Gottlieb "briefed" outside of Edens with officers from the Duke police. Duke issued passkeys for the officers in case the rooms weren't open. Gottlieb searched Finnerty's room, while Himan searched Seligmann's. Just before 6 p.m., Gottlieb, along with a Duke police officer and another Durham investigator, arrived at room 203. "A soft entry was made using the key," Gottlieb noted. "No one was home." He noticed there were no computers in the room, "only evidence"—Internet access wires—"that they were recently there."

Gottlieb read the search warrant "to the vacant room." About ten minutes later, Finnerty's roommate, Rob Schroeder, arrived back in his room. He was on his cell phone speaking with someone from his family, but Gottlieb "went ahead and read the search warrant to him also." Gottlieb observed that while he was searching the room, Schroeder "chose to sit on his sofa." Gottlieb found a letter to Finnerty from his girlfriend, Jessica, a student at Boston College, from the previous September. In the letter, Gottlieb wrote, "she discussed how good it was to visit, and she thanked him for allowing her to use his ATM card as usual while she was there." There was also a copy of the *New York Times* article about his legal problems in Washington, DC. When Gottlieb found a copy of Finnerty's dorm room lease, he asked his colleague to photograph it.

Meanwhile, Himan found no one home at 301 Edens after knocking and saying, "Durham Police Department." He was let into the room by a Duke official and started his search after reading the search warrant to the empty room. At 6:17 p.m., Seligmann's roommate, Jay Jennison, returned. Himan described him as "visibly nervous" and said he asked to see Himan's search warrant. Himan asked him who he was. He said he was Jay Jennison and that "I live here." Himan then asked for his identification. By then Jennison had called Julian Mack, Seligmann's attorney, and Himan spoke to him and explained to him what he was there to collect. There was some confusion—and not a little irritation—about the dividing line between Jennison's side of the room and Seligmann's. Once that was resolved, the police officers stopped searching Jennison's belongings, focusing instead on what remained of Seligmann's stuff.

At around 6:45 p.m., Gottlieb met Himan in Seligmann's room. Jennison was there along with his attorney, Bob Ekstrand. Himan needed Gottlieb's help in determining how to handle the apparent fact that Jennison's printer was on the floor next to his bed, but the owner's manual for the printer was in Seligmann's desk drawer. Himan wanted to know if he should seize the owner's manual. Gottlieb asked Jennison who owned the printer, causing Ekstrand to pull Jennison aside, confer with him for a minute, and answer for his client that the printer was Jennison's. Why was the owner's manual in Seligmann's desk drawer? This caused Ekstrand to confer again with his client. Jennison said the manual was his. The manual was then photographed while Gottlieb told Himan that "we could charge" Jennison later "for lying if we discovered he was making something up [or] possibly hiding evidence, and have something to hold over him at a later time." While Gottlieb was looking for the suddenly controversial printer manual, he discovered an application for the Ku Klux Klan in Seligmann's drawer. He asked Himan about it and he told Gottlieb he believed Seligmann was in an African-American studies class, which explained why he had the document. Not taking any chances, though, Gottlieb told Himan to seize the KKK application "just in case there was something else to it." Gottlieb left the room while Himan reviewed the seized inventory with Jennison and Ekstrand. (Twelve items were taken from Seligmann's room, including the KKK application, a picture of Seligmann with "a white female with blond hair," a picture of "four white males," an iPod Mini and a bunch of computer cables.)

Defense attorneys weren't wasting any time, either, in continuing to put serious doubts in people's minds about the likelihood that either Seligmann or Finnerty had committed the crimes. Cotter told reporters that Finnerty would be pleading not guilty. "I don't think there is any chance in hell that there will be a guilty plea," he said. "I can't tell you about [others], but my client's case is either going to be dismissed by the DA or go to trial." Joe Cheshire told the *New York Times* that, like Seligmann, Finnerty also had a "clear alibi," although he would not specify what that alibi was, and Cotter did not return the paper's calls by press time.

Meanwhile, Seligmann's lawyer, Kirk Osborn, was more than happy to talk to the *Times* about the particulars of his client's alibi, which had been previously leaked. The *Times* noted that Julian Mack, Seligmann's first lawyer, also corroborated Osborn's time line for Seligmann's alibi. "There's no way Reade could have done this," Osborn said.

By then the cabdriver, Moez Mostafa, had already appeared on *Good Morning America* and MSNBC. He said of Seligmann and Wellington, in his accented English, "They were just joking and laughing inside my car, and everything just fine." He first spoke to the Durham paper after Phillip Seligmann visited with him. "I didn't want to get involved," he told the paper, "but when his father came and said it was a really serious situation, I talked to them." He said he remembered Seligmann and Wellington because not only had they paid $25 for an $18 ride but also "because I wait for them a long time and they make my car smell, that's the only reason I have that in mind." He told MSNBC he was sure he drove Seligmann. "Yeah, I know [his] face that time," he said, "and I recognize him and I still remember his face." Mostafa also told MSNBC that he went back to 610 North Buchanan an hour later to pick up another player, who he remembered "said in a loud voice, 'She just a stripper.'" He said he obviously did not know what had happened inside the house. "When I look back," he continued, "he look like he mad at the stripper. Or the stripper, she going to call the police and she just a stripper. . . . It look to me like somebody get hurt. But what kind of harm . . . I have no idea."

Osborn told the *Times* that he was hopeful, based on Seligmann's alibi, that Nifong would drop the case. But when he went to see the district attorney to share the documentation about the alibi with him, Nifong refused to meet with him. "I've known the guy for twenty-five years," he said. "I went over and thought surely he'd listen to me on it. And he sent some messenger out who said: 'I saw you on the TV saying your client was absolutely innocent, so what do we have to talk about?' He wouldn't even see me himself." But Nifong said, in an interview, that it made perfect sense for him not to see Osborn. "My recollection is that he made some comment about his client was innocent, or something along those lines," he recalled. "So I asked the kind of smart-ass rhetorical question, if I may say it that way, 'You know, since you've told the media that your client is innocent, what is it that you want to say to me?' I believe that was transmitted to him [by Nifong's assistant] and after that he apparently left the office. When I went out to see who was there to see me, he was no longer there."

But Nifong said that Osborn and many of the other defense attorneys were naïve to think he would drop the case. "That's the defense strategy," he said. "See, [defense attorney] Bill Cotter told me this at one point. They were having a defense meeting, and they were all talking about what we're going to do to keep this case from coming to trial, and he said, 'I know Mike Nifong. If he says the case is going to trial, he intends to take the case to trial. Sitting around here and thinking about how you're going to talk him out of taking the case to trial is not what we need to be doing. We need to be getting ready for trial because he says he wants to try this case.'"

The indictment of the two players brought yet another round of editorial soul-searching. "At a time when the wrists of two of our own have met the steel of handcuffs," the *Chronicle*'s editors wrote, "the environment of our campus is changing. For weeks now, students and administrators alike have asserted the importance of waiting—waiting for the DNA evidence, waiting for indictments, waiting for more news." But now, "in some ways, our wait is over," the editors continued. "We have names to attach to the allegations—names of two of the alleged perpetrators and names of several colorful personalities surrounding this case. After all, even Jesse Jackson has weighed in. The most vocal of community and campus backlashers presumed the players' guilt. They drew on testimony regarding the team's reputation as a racist and misogynist group as proof of their assertion. The team's past—its individual members' prior arrests, its presence at tailgates, and its racial homogeneity—was and is fodder for the press." But, the paper warned, "finding a culture of off-campus partying does not mean Duke breeds felonious offenders," and it noted that while students had started wearing T-shirts that read simply "Innocent" and banners—"We Support Duke Lacrosse"—had started hanging from dorm-room windows, "now that we have names, we have to be more careful."

DeWayne Wickham, a columnist for *USA Today*, viewed the indictments through the prism of history, always a useful guide in interpreting unfolding events. "Not the history of the white family that once made Durham the heart of America's tobacco industry and gave its name to Duke University," Wickham wrote. "Nor the history of the stretch of Parrish Street that housed so many successful black businesss in the early twentieth century that it came to be called 'Black Wall Street.'" What he was focused on was the more recent history—no surprise—of Tawana Brawley as well as the forgotten history, three years later, "drawn from the debauchery" of six white St. John's University students—five of whom were on the New York City school's lacrosse team—who "sexually abused" a black woman student.

After recounting the details of the case to the point of the indictments, he continued, "In Brawley's case, the ugly truth was that the black teen made up her rape story. Her hoax—and the inflammatory support she received from Reverend Al Sharpton—hangs over the Duke case like a badly mildewed rug. Some defenders of the lacrosse players point to Brawley as evidence that their accuser must be lying, too." But then he reminded his readers about the St. John's case. "Early in that case, one of the defendants copped a plea and testified against the three defendants to be tried," he wrote. "Even so, all three were acquitted. Some of the jurors doubted the woman's rape charge because she didn't report it to the police right away. Others questioned how much of what happened she could really remember because she admitted accepting an alcohol-laced drink from one of the men." Months later, one of the St. John's students admitted in a plea bargain agreement with prosecutors that the woman's story of "sexual abuse" was true. "I don't know how the Durham case will turn out," Wickham concluded, "but I do know this: race plus sex remains an explosive mixture in this nation's legal system—and in the court of public opinion."

Mike Lopresti, also at *USA Today*, thought that with the indictments and the two men being led in handcuffs into the Durham police station, the case had reached, to borrow from Winston Churchill, the "end of the beginning." As a result, he hoped things would calm down. "This does not seem easy at the moment in Durham, where the tensions have bubbled for weeks, like soup on a stove," he wrote. "Now everyone waits for the next headline, or update, or revelation by an unnamed source." A few weeks earlier, he wrote, people had spoken of lacrosse with the same enthusiasm they reserved for water polo and field hockey. "Now the sport, or at least some of its participants, has become a national flashpoint," he continued. "A litmus test. A cause. . . . It is race. It is sex. It is class. It is gender. Enough inflammable material there to start an inferno. The alleged victim is a college student working as an exotic dancer to make ends meet. One of the alleged perpetrators comes from a big house next to a golf course. It is almost as if life made them adversaries, long before the party that night, and now forces everyone else to choose sides."

Lopresti worried about the men and women on the jury who would hear the evidence in the case and have to render a verdict. It wouldn't be easy for them. "Some cases involving accused athletes, you knew, would not be able to hold society's weight before they even began," he continued. "O. J. Simpson. Kobe Bryant. Mike Tyson. Trials swallowed up whole by celebrity or race or notoriety or twenty-four-hour media attention. Or all of the above. I am not sure we ever found out what really happened with any of them. Here comes another. It would be nice to believe that when all this is over, the facts will be clear, the decision acceptable to nearly all. Not likely. The public will be fed a buffet of dirty laundry about both sides. The athletes had been louts long before this. Or not. The lady was really drunk. Or not. The public will believe what it wants and ignore the rest. It will not be about evidence. It will be about perspective."

Scoop Jackson, a columnist at ESPN.com, placed the blame for what was alleged to have happened squarely on the shoulders of Brodhead, Alleva, Pressler, and the Duke board of trustees. After discussing the swirling controversy wrought by the incident and the indictments, he worried, "All the while, the most troubling issue remains buried. Lost in the sensationalistic aspects of the rich men/poor woman, white men/black woman, guilty men/lying woman angle of what will be the biggest sports-related story of 2006 is the disturbing thought that this could have been avoided had three men employed some form of authoritative competence. Duke president Richard Brodhead, athletics director Joe Alleva, and recently resigned lacrosse coach Mike Pressler remain unguilty. Not enough criticism has been pointed in their direction or at the board of trustees at Duke for their roles in allowing the culture for the alleged assault to exist. No one wants to identify them at the scene of the crime before the crime was committed. No one wants to deal with the fact that the players on Duke's lacrosse team are not solely responsible for what happened at 610 North Buchanan five Mondays ago. . . . The fact that the administration allowed this team to behave in the worst interest of the university and still apparently not be held accountable for *any* of its actions leading up to the alleged rape of a woman is beyond irresponsible—it should be punishable by law. But it won't be. Society doesn't roll like that. Especially against the elite."

If the incessant self-examination and public flagellation was making Duke seem a lot less fun than it used to be, well, maybe that was the appropriate response to the indictments. "If our students did what was alleged, it is appalling to the worst degree," Brodhead said during a visit to the Durham Chamber of Commerce on April 20. "If they didn't do it, whatever they did is bad enough." It was one of his harshest public criticisms of the lacrosse players and one that would be long remembered. "One of the things that have pained me about this episode—one of the greatest ones—is all the publicity that this has brought, unwished to Duke University and, indeed, Durham," he continued. Brodhead was especially miffed by the clichéd portrayal of Durham as a "backward, poor Southern town" and Duke as an "uncaring, elite, wealthy university." Chris Kennedy, the associate athletic director, found Brodhead's comment—"whatever they did is bad enough"—to be "incredibly indiscreet," especially for a university president, and that "Brodhead believed they were guilty."

Despite the ongoing efforts of Brodhead, Ammons, and Bell to bring together Durham's diverse communities, if only briefly to grapple with the immediate fissures caused by the lacrosse case, tensions still ran high around town. Not only was there the looming matter of the second set of DNA results, but there was the impending indictment of a third Duke lacrosse player. The *News & Observer* described the "corrosive worry" among the players that another "one of their own could still face formal charges" and noted the growing anger at Nifong for causing them so much distress. "This has upset lots of people's lives, and it will continue to do so," Chuck Sherwood, the father of Devon Sherwood, the only black player on the lacrosse team, told the paper. "This is a bad thing, one way or another, whether the players are telling a lie or the accuser is a telling a lie. This has turned everything upside down."

Duke had already given permission for about a dozen members of the team—freshmen and sophomores—to talk to other schools about transferring. "Looking at coming back to Duke next year . . . isn't just a lacrosse issue," Chris Kennedy, senior associate athletic director, told *USA Today*. "They have to be wondering, 'What's my position in the student body going to be? Is it going to be like it was before? Would I be more comfortable, lacrosse or no lacrosse, somewhere else, where I could wear the shirt and everybody's [not] looking at [me]?' It used to be you'd say, 'I play lacrosse at Duke,' and there was a double wow. You went to Duke. And you played lacrosse there. Now there's a different kind of wow."

The prospect of yet another indictment was also weighing heavily on the team. "Even though my son was never implicated, he's part of the team and feels the stress and strain as well," continued Sherwood, who, like his son, had played lacrosse at Duke. "He's feeling a lot of a different kind of pressure than the rest of the team. There's a feeling that because he is an African-American, he should have stepped forward and told what he knows or stepped in and stopped this." Bill Cotter, Finnerty's attorney, said, "I can't tell you the pressure and the anxiety and the fear and the terror that all these families have lived under for the last several weeks." Rob Bordley, the lacrosse coach at Landon, had spoken with four players—Landon graduates—and their parents in recent weeks (although not with David Evans, one of the three cocaptains and residents at 610 North Buchanan) to see if he could get a sense of the truth of what had happened. Bordley also "buttonholed" one of the players. "Look me in the eye," he said to him. "Could there have been a conspiracy of silence?"

"No way," came the reply.

There was also growing pressure on Joe Alleva, the Duke athletic director, who during his nine years at the helm of Duke athletics—some believed—had been insufficiently attentive to the deteriorating behavior of many of the lacrosse players. But he remained confident that the lacrosse program would not be terminated in the wake of James Coleman's report. "Our lacrosse team has had a really good history," he told *USA Today*. "[Players] have good GPAs. They graduate. So I don't believe this committee is going to find anything so dramatically bad that the recommendation will be to end the program." Ending the program, he continued, "would be an injustice to all those alums who've played here . . . and helped create a really solid program." He also said he was not worried for his own job. "All I can do is what I think is right," Alleva said. "I've always tried to build relationships with people on campus, and I think they know what kind of person I am. . . . I think I feel as secure as I can be, given the situation." He said he believed the university's athletic programs would bounce back "better and stronger" from the challenge posed by Mangum's allegations, despite the efforts of some professors who saw the problems in the lacrosse program as "their opening" to push for deemphasizing athletics at Duke, except for basketball and football.

Meanwhile, Gottlieb and Himan pressed forward with their investigation of the case. Now that two indictments had been handed up by the grand jury, and another one was expected soon, the police had to produce the evidence that Nifong could then use to convince a jury of their peers to convict the men. On April 19, at 4 p.m., Himan spoke with DNA Securities, in Burlington, and discovered "there was some new information regarding the [DNA] tests." That "new information" turned out to be the fact that the DNA found on Mangum's fake fingernails could belong to David Evans. "They said they were still doing some tests on it and they would be able to tell us pretty soon," Himan recalled. He reported this news to Gottlieb and they, along with Nifong, agreed to go to Burlington again on April 21 to get the update in person.

That same day, after receiving a random tip, Gottlieb spoke with Dr. Nikolas P. Lemos, the chief forensic toxicologist at the San Francisco medical examiner's office. The idea that the lacrosse players had slipped some form of Mickey Finn into Mangum's drink—explaining why she went so quickly from being relatively sober to falling-down drunk—had been floating around the case and Gottlieb appeared to want to determine if it was true. They "discussed the possibility of [Mangum] being given an unknown drug" at the party on March 13 because, while she "was able to recall events," she also had "the onset of impairment in a rather fast manner." Lemos told Gottlieb he "specialized in testing hair for drugs" and that the test was effective as long as a hair sample was taken from the victim between thirty and ninety days after the "ingestion of the drug." According to Gottlieb, Lemos told him that, depending on the drug ingested, he "could tell when it was ingested and approximately how much entered the system." Lemos explained further how the test would work, how it "was started [in] France," that results had been published, and that it was commonplace at this point. He also told Gottlieb how much the testing would cost. Gottlieb thanked him and said he needed to review the details of the procedure with Nifong. Eventually, Mangum's hair samples were sent to Lemos's lab for drug testing. There was no evidence that Mangum had taken drugs.

That night, several hundred Duke students and faculty gathered inside the Duke Chapel for a conversation about how the scandal was affecting the school and how the campus culture could be changed. There was much discussion of Preeti Aroon's column in the *Chronicle* about how Duke had replaced a "culture of character" with a "culture of crassness." There was talk of changes to the curriculum, to the living arrangements, and to the permissiveness toward alcohol on campus. Dinushika Mohottige, a Duke senior, said the lacrosse incident had forced the community "to stop and think about white privilege" and to curtail the "us" and "them" mentality between Duke and Durham. Brodhead said the pain of the past few weeks had raised difficult questions about behavior on college campuses that was not unique to Duke. "This is the moment for us to look at all this and say, 'Is that really what we had in mind for ourselves?'" But he also wished more students had been there. "The median age of the audience as I look out is older than I'd hoped it would be," he said.

On April 21, Nifong, Gottlieb, and Himan returned to DNA Securities to hear the results of the new DNA tests. The officers' notes from the meeting provide little insight into what was discussed. "Information was not definite," Himan wrote, "but analysis had been done on [Mangum's plastic] fingernails['] DNA and had come back with a mixture DNA that had been isolated by the Y-chromosome." Himan later elaborated on what transpired at the meeting. It was all about the "DNA underneath the fingernails," he said, "[and] how easily DNA could be transferred. . . . I think that's what basically we were trying to get at, is how easily DNA could be transferred from that; since we knew Matt Zash had picked up the fingernails, why didn't his DNA show up on the fingernails also?"

According to the defense attorneys, it was at that meeting that DNA Securities formally reported to Nifong and the police officers that "DNA from four males was found on the items in the rape kit" but that none of the DNA found belonged to a Duke lacrosse player. "Every single one of the lacrosse players, including the two who had already been indicted, had been eliminated with 100 percent certainty as a possible source for this DNA," the defense attorneys concluded. Furthermore, they wrote, participants in the meeting had agreed there would be no notes taken about what occurred there, and that DNA Securities would produce a written report of its findings but the report "would omit crucial exculpatory findings of DSI's testing, including the fact that none of the players' DNA profiles matched or were consistent with any of the DNA found on the rape kit items."

For his part, Himan confirmed that Meehan had told them about how Mangum's "underwear or anal swabbing" revealed "another source," a "very, very weak source, possibly like an old source" of DNA that was "possibly a week" earlier that "did not match any of the lacrosse players," and that "there was no match [to the Duke players] from the sexual assault kit." There was no discussion of what that result could potentially mean for Mangum's allegations of a sexual assault against the Duke lacrosse players. But on the car ride back to Durham, Himan recalled, Nifong said he intended to seek an indictment of David Evans at the next meeting of the grand jury.

"It was based on a couple of things," Himan said. "Crystal was ninety percent sure that David Evans was her third attacker. And we knew that she had broken fingernails on someone and that she said she had scratched someone. And now that DNA . . . is coming back to David Evans. So, I mean, it was an assumption that that is where he got that from." Gottlieb remembered, "The victim stated that she was being choked or strangled. She stated that she had to fight to breathe. While she was fighting she said she grabbed the man, was fighting to get away, and that is when one of her fingernails broke off. And what wound up happening was the person"—David Evans—"that she indentified in the photo presentation as being one of the attackers, or a possible attacker at a ninety percent likelihood, actually had a scratch on his arm consistent to the DNA found under the fingernail." The next day, Nifong told reporters—he got cornered at a campaign event—the second batch of DNA tests would not be available until at least May 15.

While the three men were in Burlington, the readers of the *News & Observer* digested the latest pronouncements from the various actors in the drama. The paper reported that Mangum's mother said "It has been a rough few days," since defense attorneys started questioning nearly every aspect of her daughter's story. But, she added, "an outpouring of support from people far and wide" had helped ease their pain. She said Reverend Jesse Jackson had called her on both Wednesday and Thursday nights—presumably following up on his offer to pay the balance of Mangum's tuition at NCCU until she graduated—but that Mangum might not need his money because she had recently earned her own scholarship at the school by compiling a 3.0 grade point average. Susan Taylor, the editorial director of *Essence* magazine, also spoke with Mangum's mother and cousin—much to Mangum's consternation, because she said she believed her cousin was just trying to exploit the situation for her own benefit. The cousin told Taylor that Mangum was staying in a different place every night. She said Mangum had almost decided not to report the incident. "She was at the point where she felt like she just wanted to make it go away," Taylor reported. "But she just realized, once she had a minute to get herself together, that she has to do this. She doesn't want to be a victim any longer." (Of course this made no sense, since Mangum reported that she had been raped during the early hours of March 14.)

Also, in an affidavit, lacrosse player Rob Wellington confirmed Seligmann's version of events about what had happened on the night of March 13. After Mangum and Roberts stopped dancing, Wellington said, he "left the residence through the back door and talked to Reade. As I went out the back door, I did not see or hear anything unusual. Once outside, I saw Reade, who appeared normal in all respects. We were both tired from playing golf that afternoon, and we had practice the next day. In addition, the dancers had stopped dancing and were obviously impaired when they left the main living room. Reade said he had just called a cab and asked if I wanted to leave with him. We walked down the alley to Watts Street, took a left and walked to the corner of Watts Street and Urban Avenue (about a block from 610 North Buchanan Blvd.) to wait for the cab." He wrote that the "plan" was to go to the Cook-Out, get some food and go back to their respective dorm rooms. He then recounted the trip to the Wachovia ATM, the Cook-Out and back to Duke's West Campus. He swiped into his dorm at 12:49 a.m. and swore in the affidavit he was with Seligmann from the time he left through the back door of 610 North Buchanan until the time they went to their respective dorm rooms.

Interestingly, Wellington did not say he had been with Seligmann inside the house just prior to seeing him outside and getting the taxi. Wellington also added, helpfully, "It was a strict policy of the Duke lacrosse team that no member could have a mustache." This was a curious comment. When Mangum first identified David Evans as one of her attackers, she said she thought he had a mustache, and when she saw his picture again during the photographic lineup without the mustache, she said she still recognized him as one of her attackers but noted he no longer had a mustache. How would Wellington know about this conversation? (For his part, Nifong said he believed Mangum mistakenly said Evans had a mustache when he was actually just sporting a few days of stubble.)

Meanwhile, Kim Roberts told the Associated Press—as she had told others in recent days—that at first she doubted Mangum's story of being raped at 610 North Buchanan but now she was no longer sure. "I was not in the bathroom when it happened," she said, "so I can't say a rape occurred—and I never will," she said. But, she continued, "in all honesty, I think they're guilty. And I can't say which ones are guilty . . . but somebody did something besides underage drinking. That's my honest-to-God impression." Asked about the two indicted players, Roberts said she did not remember Seligmann's face, but she did recall Finnerty—the "little skinny one," she said—because "I was looking him right in the eyes." She confirmed Mangum's story about the threats the players made about sodomizing the women with a broomstick and how the men felt they got ripped off because the dancing ended so quickly after it had started. But she defended that decision. "They ripped themselves off when they started hollering about a broomstick," she said.

Roberts said Mangum was "sober" when she arrived at the house, but by the time they left the party, Mangum was "too incoherent to tell her where she lived, let alone that she had been raped." Tears welled up in her eyes. "I didn't do enough," she said. "I didn't do enough. I didn't do enough." She conceded that she had contacted a public relations firm in New York to help her figure out a way to profit from her newfound notoriety. "Why shouldn't I profit from [the rape case]?" she asked. "I didn't ask to be in this position. . . . I would like to feed my daughter." (Defense attorneys made much of the fact that on the same day Seligmann and Finnerty were indicted, a judge agreed to change Roberts's bonding agreement to save her 15 percent; Nifong signed off on the new deal. Roberts, of course, could have been an important witness for the prosecution at trial.)

She said since she knew what it was like "to sit in jail," she would never knowingly make a false accusation. "If the boys are innocent, sorry, fellas," she said. "Sorry you had to go through this." On the other hand, she noted, the players had the best attorneys "money can buy" and so "if they're innocent, they will not go to jail." But "if the truth is on their side, why are they support-ing it with so many lies?" She knew the defense attorneys would play rough but she seemed prepared for the looming fight. "Don't forget that they called me a damn nigger," she said. "[Mangum] was passed out in the car. She doesn't know what she was called. I was called that. I can never forget that."

Questions were also raised about the effect Finnerty's arrest would have on the deal he had reached on March 23—the day the white Duke lacrosse players were asked to provide DNA evidence—involving his use of gay slurs against Jeffrey Bloxsom outside a Georgetown bar at 2:30 a.m. on the previ-ous November 5. The media wanted to know whether Ben Curtis, the fed-eral prosecutor handling the case, would ask the judge to terminate the deal. "Unlike prosecutors down in North Carolina," Curtis said, "we don't comment on pending cases."

Curtis's jab at Nifong for his ongoing public commentary about the lacrosse case was not an isolated one. There was a growing sense in North Carolina—albeit among defense lawyers and "legal experts"—that Nifong "may have crossed ethical lines" by being so outspoken. On April 21, he addressed that narrow issue with the *News & Observer*. "In terms of what I said, no, I wouldn't say I regret anything I've said," he allowed. "I think what I have learned, basi-cally, is that if you cooperate with the media out of a sense of duty to public truth, you make yourself a victim."

The paper reminded its readers that Nifong had made his first public com-ments about the case on March 27 and "in the following weeks, Nifong granted dozens of media interviews, including several that were nationally televised."

Nifong had called the players "a bunch of hooligans" and remained emphatically convinced that Mangum was raped based on the medical evidence and her eyewitness account. The racial slurs, he said, made an "extremely reprehensible attack even more reprehensible."

The national media's fascination with the case continued to ratchet up. That weekend, the May 1 edition of *Newsweek* began to appear on newsstands. The lacrosse case was on the cover, under the headline "Sex, Lies & Duke" and a tagline, "Two indicted athletes, a rape charge and a university in crisis. Who's telling the truth?" Along with the unpleasant mug shots of Seligmann and Finnerty, there was also a color picture of Finnerty in his full Duke lacrosse regalia, holding his lacrosse stick. Inside was a ten-page spread, again written by Susannah Meadows and Evan Thomas. "What Happened at Duke?" the headline inside blared. This was not going to be good—for anybody. "Racial tension, class conflict and allegations of sexual violence are perfect ingredients for a media circus," the article began, accurately enough. There were the requisite *South Park* and Mike Nifong T-shirts being sold on eBay. Rush Limbaugh was quoted from his talk show wondering when Reverend Al Sharpton "would arrive on the scene to play the Tawana Brawley card [after] the lacrosse team supposedly, you know, raped some, uh, hos." Jon Stewart was making fun of Geraldo Rivera for "gravely and fatuously intoning" that "it is not always the nuns that get raped. Sometimes it's the strippers that get raped."

The writers observed that "from the beginning, the case has provided a tawdry real-world blend of true crime, high life and low manners, for the likes of novelists John Grisham and Tom Wolfe. Raunchy rich kids. Town-gown conflict. Raw racial politics. A bedeviling forensic puzzle. But the denouement may be tragic for everyone involved, and the only sure outcome is the iron law of unintended consequences. The story has freakish turns, but it is also the product of a widespread college-age culture that proud parents do not wish to examine too closely: future Masters of the Universe who sometimes behave like thugs."

Newsweek had obtained copies of the time-stamped photos taken at the party, which tended to contradict Mangum's version of what had happened on the night of March 13. Meanwhile, *Newsweek* bought into Seligmann's alibi, reporting that he made at least eight cell phone calls between 12:05 and 12:24 and that he and Wellington, "laughing and joking," were picked up by the taxi at 12:19. Then it was on to the ATM, the Cook-Out, and back to Edens at 12:46 a.m. "In other words, it would seem Seligmann must have committed a sex crime in less than two minutes or while he was on the phone," Meadows and Thomas wrote. As for Finnerty's alibi, they wrote, "Defense lawyers were broadly hinting [that he] left the party before the dance even began" and, in any event, that "both men's lawyers maintain their clients are innocent." (The

New York Times, meanwhile, reported that Finnerty's lawyer said Finnerty was "at a restaurant several blocks away when the women were dancing.")

Of course, Roberts spoke to *Newsweek,* too. This time, she recalled how the players at the party gave her and Mangum "mixed drinks." Mangum drank hers but Roberts didn't. After Mangum spilled half her drink, she then drank Roberts's. Roberts said Mangum arrived sober, but when the dancing began around midnight, "she started stumbling. When I think back on it, she had a glassy look in her eyes." She said she gave Mangum a look that said, "C'mon girl, what's going on?" but "got no response." Roberts said the dance lasted "about ten minutes," while the defense attorneys said "it lasted only about three minutes."

The magazine duly noted that Roberts at first did not think Mangum had been raped but then changed her mind. "She is careful to say that her version of events has not changed," *Newsweek* wrote, "just her opinion of what might have happened when the woman was out of her sight." But, Meadows and Thomas wrote pointedly, Roberts probably had some motivation for her change of heart. Quickly mentioned were her efforts to hire a New York PR firm, her unabashed desire to profit from her fifteen minutes of fame, and the two hours she spent in jail on March 22 for violating her probation.

But the magazine also fleshed out how Roberts got Nifong to go along with her request to waive the 15 percent bail-bond fee. It seems that after she posted her $25,000 bond to get out of jail on March 22, she hired Mark Simeon, a politically connected lawyer. In 2002, Simeon had run for Durham district attorney but lost to Nifong's boss and mentor, Jim Hardin. Simeon, who is black, told *Newsweek* that he and Nifong did not get along. But when Hardin was appointed a state judge in 2005 under the condition that Nifong succeed him as district attorney, the seeds of a reconciliation between Simeon and Nifong were sewn. Soon after Nifong decided to run for district attorney in February 2006, he reached out to Simeon, seeking his support. According to *Newsweek,* on March 28—the day after Nifong first spoke out about the case and urged the players to come forward and reveal what had happened at the house—Simeon said he would support Nifong for district attorney. Simeon invited Nifong to speak at his church, Ebenezer Missionary Baptist, and introduced him, on April 9, to the black parishioners as a "good prosecutor" who had also recently become a "good man." He also gave Nifong fashion advice: Lose the plaid shirts and wear black suits, light shirts, and power ties. "Women like power," he told Nifong.

Simeon also recommended Nifong to the Durham Committee on the Affairs of Black People—a powerful political force in Durham—and urged the committee to throw its weight behind Nifong. Given that the population of Durham was around 45 percent black, the support of the black community would be essential for Nifong to defeat his opponents Freda Black, who was white, and Keith Bishop, who was black. On April 16—a week after Simeon endorsed Nifong at church—Simeon asked Nifong to support Roberts's request to waive the bail-bond fees. Nifong supported Simeon's motion and the judge agreed. It may have been a minor sum of money—although $3,750 was not inconsequential for Roberts—and a tempest in a teapot, but the relationship between Simeon and Nifong threw a monkey wrench into Nifong's perceived armor of integrity and righteous indignation. (At a campaign event at Joe and Jo's Downtown Restaurant and Pub on Saturday, April 22, Nifong said Roberts had received no special treatment. "It's consistent with local bonding policy," he said.) Beyond Simeon's relationship with Nifong, the splashy headlines, the four-color photographs, and the major play, the *Newsweek* story didn't break much new ground.

Nor, for that matter, did the lengthy story the *New York Times* ran on April 23, although it did have the virtue of putting in one place many of the purported facts about what had supposedly happened in the house. Unlike the *Newsweek* version, the *Times* did include Mangum's version of events—quoting from a leaked copy of the April 4 photo identification session Mangum had with the Durham police—including how she was pulled into the bathroom by "two men," who then "locked the door" and told her, "Sweetheart, you can't leave." That's when, she told police, Seligmann "forced her to perform oral sex," Finnerty "raped and sodomized her," and an unknown third suspect "strangled her." On the other hand, the paper reported that Seligmann's attorney said that "taxi and bank receipts and dormitory access records prove that Mr. Seligmann could not have raped the woman."

It was really quite a conundrum. What the hell happened in that bathroom in the early morning hours of March 14? "To all but some of the people at the party, the truth of what happened that night to one of the dancers, who accused three white players of raping her in a bathroom, is a mystery," the paper reported. Added Renee Clark, the student government president at NCCU, "Everyone around here has strong feelings about this, one way or the other. But you can't be sure. If you weren't there in the bathroom with the players and that woman, you really don't know what happened, do you?"

Byron Calame, the *Times*'s ombudsman, then assessed the *Times*'s coverage to date, noting that it began with a front-page story on March 29 and continued with more than twenty stories on the topic since. He wrote that he had received a dozen "thoughtful messages" from readers about the paper's coverage, most of whom "complained of unfairness to Duke and the lacrosse players." Calame wrote that in his opinion the coverage had been "basically fair" and the paper deserved a "decent grade" so far. He then quoted sports editor Tom Jolly. "I'm very comfortable with our coverage," Jolly said. "From the beginning, we've felt this story had two main elements: one was the allegation of rape; the other was the general behavior of a high-level sports team at a prestigious university." Putting the first story on the front page was "controversial" but "warranted," Calame continued. "Even if the sexual assault charges should completely collapse, the allegations of racial slurs and other questionable behavior by members of a top-ranked athletic team that have been brought to light raise important issues of race and class . . ."

The Duke supporters had complained to him about the attention the paper gave to Nifong's "criticisms" that the players had refused to tell Durham investigators what had happened at the party. Calame, too, seemed concerned about fairness after he learned that the three cocaptains had voluntarily given statements to the police and had offered to take lie detector tests, an offer that was declined. But since "the players have volunteered little eyewitness information," he became less sympathetic to the charges of unfairness and more inclined to support the view of Selena Roberts, the *Times*'s sports columnist, that there was a "code of silence." He also wondered why the paper gave so much space—550 words—to Finnerty's assault on Bloxsom in Washington but did not publish Mangum's past criminal record, having deemed it not "germane" to the lacrosse case. He suggested giving space to Mangum's past, just as the paper had to Finnerty's. He also had a final thought: "Covering the legal proceedings that seem likely to focus on the extremely serious charges of sexual assault and kidnapping is vital. But the paper needs to keep an eye on the allegations and reports about the racial insults voiced by various players, and on the lacrosse team's seemingly flawed culture. If the rape and kidnapping charges do not hold up, the story doesn't end. The *Times* should be prepared to continue covering what is done about the racial-insult allegations, given the prominence of the team and the university."

Neither the *Times* nor *Newsweek* (nor the local papers) used Mangum's name in print. But her name was starting to leak anyway. On April 8, a writer using the pseudonym "OakOak" on FreeRepublic.com revealed Mangum's name ("Call her 'Mangum,'" he wrote), and on April 16, "Thomas," writing on StandYourGround.com, mentioned her full name. On the afternoon of April 21, Mangum's name was broadcast nationally on the *Tom Leykis* radio show. Matt Drudge mentioned Mangum's name on his radio show on April 23. Meanwhile, Dan Abrams, on his April 19 TV show, showed the pictures of Mangum and Roberts taken on the evening of March 13 at the house.

Abrams said the photographs, which he had received from the defense, were not only in proper sequence but were also accurate from a time perspective, a fact that he verified by blowing up one of the photographs to show the watch of one of the players showing the same time. He said both sides seemed to agree that at 12:04 a.m. the dancing stopped after the dancers and the players had a disagreement. "This is where the stories diverge," he said. "The accuser says she went out to her car before she was coaxed back into the house, then taken into the bathroom and brutally raped." He then discussed the alibis presented by the attorneys for Seligmann and Finnerty.

Naturally, Abrams opened the discussion up to his panel of former district attorneys and lawyers. He asked Yale Galanter, a criminal defense attorney from North Carolina, if he thought the defense lawyers expected Nifong to drop the case, given the new evidence from the time-stamped photos and the apparent alibis of Seligmann and Finnerty. "I think they're hopeful that the DA will see the light and dismiss these charges before a full-scale litigation takes place, but I got to tell you, Dan, I've spoken to them; they are not hopeful," he said. "They think they can go in basically with a busload full of nuns who will swear by these boys and give them alibis. They still don't think Mr. Nifong will drop these charges."

David Freedman, another criminal defense attorney from North Carolina who would later represent Nifong, said he believed Nifong had mishandled the case. "You had a district attorney coming out and making potentially unethical statements, saying he believed a crime occurred, which he should not do," he said. "He should not be commenting on the evidence. He took an adversarial position from the start." But Susan Filan, an MSNBC legal analyst and a former prosecutor for the state of Connecticut, was less willing to see the new evidence entirely the way the defense suggested. "I'm very, very unclear about the time line in this case to begin with," she said. "I don't exactly know when this is alleged to have happened. I don't know whether her idea of thirty minutes is really only seven minutes, because sometimes when something so horrible is happening to you, it feels like it's a much longer time than it actually is." As for the time-stamped photograph of Seligmann at the ATM, she said, "If that's true, if he's actually got a photo of himself outside a bank and that cannot be disputed, period, of course that's important, but I'm not sure that this assault didn't take place before 12:24 and he left afterwards, so that in and of itself doesn't exonerate and doesn't exculpate him."

Abrams asked Filan about the picture, taken at 12:30 a.m., that showed Mangum outside the house with "a demure smile" on her face. She couldn't have just been raped and been smiling, Abrams suggested. "But some people have started to speculate, and this comes from the other woman that was there with her," Filan said. "She says that she was completely sober and fine when she went in. She saw her have something to drink and she seemed completely intoxicated when she came out, suggesting perhaps that it was a date-rape drug. That would give her that silly little grin on her face. So it's not clear from that alone that something untoward didn't happen to her." But, Abrams continued, hadn't Roberts said she was not with Mangum when the attack allegedly happened and that she did not, at first, believe a rape had occurred? "She's saying, 'I don't think she would make this up. I don't think she would put herself [through all this],'" Filan continued. "She's also said, 'I do think something could have happened to her.' She's not an eyewitness. She's not an ear witness. She wasn't in that bathroom with her. That's a shame, but most rapes don't have eyewitnesses."

"Look," Abrams said, "I don't think anyone on this panel would disagree that something might have happened to her. Yale, would you agree that something might have happened to her?"

"Oh, something absolutely happened," Galanter replied. "The only question is, when did it occur?"

"No," Filan countered, "but she's saying something happened to her in that house with those boys, not that it happened afterwards, which is what you guys are positing based on the photographs, based on the time line, based on this potential alibi defense. And I want to go back to something that was said earlier. The DA's job here isn't to decide whether he personally believes her or not. That's why we have juries. If he's got a complainant, he finds her credible, he thinks he can go forward, [then] he has a duty to go forward."

This latest round of media sparring occurred against the backdrop of alumni reunion weekend at Duke—usually a time for much revelry, camaraderie, and school spirit. A record number of alumni—3,500—registered for the event. Not surprisingly, the cloud of the ongoing scandal hung over the festivities. (For pure symbolism, it was hard to beat the spring downpour during the weekend that forced everyone under umbrellas or into tents and buildings.) As usual, the media was lurking around every corner of the campus, trying to guage the reaction of the thousands of Duke graduates to the scandal at their university. Alumni had been warned the media would be allowed on campus during the reunion (but alumni would be under no obligation to speak to them).

Dick Perry, back for his fiftieth reunion with his wife, whom he met on the steps of the chapel, said, "I've never been more proud to be a Duke alum." Bonnie Birkel was slightly less effusive. "Although right now there is all sorts of bad press, the sign of a great university is to deal with it," she said. Michael Rose, a 1986 graduate, wondered why the lacrosse team's appearance in the 2005 NCAA final "received one-ten-thousandth of the coverage that this has." LaShawn Williams, a 2001 graduate, almost did not come back for her fifth reunion because of the controversy. "This is not what I wanted to remember," she said. However, she continued, the controversy provided yet another opening for Duke to come to grips with its uneven history of race relations and with the city of Durham. "I think this is a tipping point," she said. "Where it goes from here is up to Duke."

At one point during his "State of the University" speech on Saturday before about one hundred alumni, Brodhead stopped and decided to take questions—often thinly disguised as speeches—from the audience about the scandal, the indictment of the two players, and the endless media coverage. "It was convenient to throw the lacrosse team overboard along with their coach," said Joe Baden, Class of 1970. Would the university have done the same thing to Coach K? Baden asked Brodhead rhetorically. "I don't think they would have," he said. Had the players been suspended? another alumnus wanted to know. (Of course they had, but federal privacy laws prevented the university from confirming that fact publicly.) "We really asked ourselves, on the matter of interim suspension, 'How do we do these things?'" Brodhead answered. "The custom of this place—I assure you it is the custom of many places—on indictment for a felony . . . that's the way to go with it, and that's the way we did it this time."

Then Brodhead got an expected question on the deluge of media coverage about the incident and the university. "I am very happy to have that question, and I am very happy to have it be the question to conclude," Brodhead said. "The other questions were fun, but we all have this question in our minds. If you haven't enjoyed the media, imagine how I feel." Not surprisingly, Brodhead's insights were both poignant and lucid, especially since his answer was extemporaneous. "All I want to tell you about this," he continued, "is that one of the really, really disturbing things about this episode has been to discover that the media—including the most respected forms of the media—if you go back to the early stories, they are all written in the key of hysteria, they are all written to inspire hysteria, and they teach the lesson that hysteria breeds extraordinary mental simplifications: every student at Duke was filthy rich, right? At a school where more than forty percent of the students are on financial aid, and the average grant from the university is $25,000 of financial aid. Every student at Duke is a white preppy, right? And every person in Durham is a penniless black person. You know, there are such people at Duke, and there are such people in Durham—and it's important to remember it—but the truth is, it just teaches you that in the world of passion is the world where people just reach for any old stereotype.

"I've been very troubled by this, of course, and I'll just tell you one thing," he continued. "I have had so many conversations in the last month, but the one that I think touched me most profoundly was [with] the head of the NAACP in this state, who came to my office and who said to me, 'If you ever want someone to come and stand by you and talk about the damage that can be done by prejudging, by judging people because of a group they belong to and some theory you have of that group rather than actual evidence, you come to me,' he said. And actually there has been so much prejudgment in this case. It has been a powerful lesson in how deep the passions of prejudice run, all kinds of prejudice—prejudices against athletes, prejudices against the South have been very, very visible in the Northern media all through this. . . . Nothing has pained me more about this episode than the notion that people don't want to say where they went to college, because that name is now a source of embarrassment. If you are ever in a situation where you find yourself in that light, you've just got to turn that around. You've got to walk up and say some true thing about this place that is a source of pride and, Lord knows, there are many. And you know what? At the end of the day, this place will be known as it is. It will be known for what it is. And I hope this will be a better place after this episode. But it won't be an altogether different place. It will be known for the excellence that characterizes us now. And that's all of our work, to bring that day about." The alumni gave Brodhead a standing ovation.

Nightline, ABC's evening magazine show, was on campus for the weekend and listened in while Brodhead addressed the alumni concern. The show found, and interviewed on camera, three members of the 1956 Duke lacrosse team, back for their fiftieth reunion. Originally the 1956 team—the winningest lacrosse team in Duke history—was to appear on the field, at halftime, during the Saturday lacrosse game, but—obviously—that did not occur. The three alumni were not upset by the fact that they couldn't meet the 2006 team on the field. Rather, according to Marvin Botnick, the "fact that Duke is being characterized as a bad institution hurts, and the fact that there might have been some unwarranted actions, that hurts." Added Dick Saunders: "In the 1950s, we had a code of conduct, and even though it was legal to drink at that time, we didn't drink at that time. We couldn't vote. We could go to war and we could drink. How things have changed." For Mike Harrington, the incident showed "a lack of commitment by this team, which was picked number one in the country preseason. . . . The fact that they had a party showed a lack of commitment to me."

Among the many unanswered questions was how the scandal would affect Duke admissions and the future of the lacrosse program. The good news, if there were any, was that more high school seniors had applied to Duke for admission—19,358—for the class entering in August 2006, and a smaller percentage were admitted—3,778, or around 19 percent—than at any time previously in the school's history. About 1,665 students were expected to be part of the new freshman class. A typical response to the situation came from Tim Winchester, whose daughter Rachael, from Lexington, Kentucky, had been admitted to Duke. He said the family decided the issue was irrelevant and focused instead on the school's academics. "I don't for a minute think there are roving bands of rabid lacrosse players," Tim Winchester told the Associated Press. "We just decided, if this was where she wanted to come, this shouldn't hold her back."

There seemed to be less clarity, though, about the future of the lacrosse team. Much depended on the findings of James Coleman's May 1 report on the team and its culture. It was possible that the lacrosse program at Duke would be extinguished in the wake of the scandal. "The biggest obstacle will be the content of that report and the culture of lacrosse and if the president and the board of trustees feel like it is the right thing to continue the sport or not," Joe Alleva told the *Chronicle* on April 24. "Assuming we have lacrosse next year and in the future, it'll definitely set it back, although I believe we'll have a tremendously strong nucleus of kids coming back." He said the entire junior class of lacrosse players—the top-ranked recruiting class in the country—had agreed to return to Duke for senior year "no matter what."

The school had already told the team's existing players they could explore transfer options and released incoming recruits from their commitment letters. But everyone seemed to be proceeding cautiously. "These kids have extremely strong convictions about who they are," said John Danowksi, the father of junior Matt Danowski and the lacrosse coach at Hofstra University on Long Island. "They love the university, they love each other and they want to finish what they started." Zach Greer, a sophomore who had led the nation in scoring in 2005 (with fifty-seven goals) "expressed interest" in transferring to Syracuse. But Daryl Gross, the Syracuse athletic director, said any transfer students would be evaluated on a case-by-case basis. "We don't want to raid Duke; they're entitled to their players," he said. "This is far bigger than lacrosse players." (Greer ended up staying at Duke.) Several Duke lacrosse players also contacted Johns Hopkins, another perennial lacrosse powerhouse, but nothing transpired there, either.

Alleva conceded the incident had "cast a cloud over the athletic department" but had "not tarnished our reputation. We have outstanding coaches and outstanding student-athletes, and we have this great university. It has given us a black eye for right now but we'll come back from this stronger." As for his own future, Alleva remained sanguine that he would be at Duke. "I've been here for thirty years," he repeated, "and I think people at the university know what I stand for and know what kind of a good athletic department we have."

Pressler, meanwhile, remained secluded in his Durham home during May and June, still stunned by the turn of events. "It was surreal, bizarre," he remembered. "I kept thinking it couldn't be true. I was worried about the future of the boys, of the program." He followed the latest developments of the case on television and online. He applied for three coaching jobs and couldn't even get an interview. "I felt like I was blackballed," he said. He was getting increasingly depressed as the summer wore on. "I'm a jogger, but I couldn't even jog," he said. "I had nothing in the tank. I was emotionally drained. I was very angry, very bitter and vengeful. I wanted to get even. It was chewing me up. I was very unpleasant to be around, and it was affecting my girls." His wife confronted him and told him he couldn't behave this way any longer. "Gradually, I came to understand that I was letting the accusers win," he said. His new routine was to look into the mirror and tell himself, "Do the right thing today, Mike."

Ever since Pressler had been fired and the season terminated, the two assistant coaches and Chris Kennedy had met regularly with the players, even though there were no organized team activities. Still, there were concerns that Duke wasn't doing enough for the lacrosse players. Late on the evening of April 23, Keating Crown, a former cocaptain of the lacrosse team at Duke under Pressler and a graduate of the Class of 2000, wrote an e-mail to Brodhead—with copies to Alleva, Provost Peter Lange, Wasiolek, and Tallman Trask—under the subject line "Alienated lacrosse players and coaches." Brodhead had to take Crown's e-mail more seriously than most. Not only was Crown the chair of young leadership giving at Duke, but his mother, Class of 1980, was on the board of trustees and the wife of Jim Crown, part of the billionaire Crown family from Chicago.

Keating Crown had also survived the September 11 attack. He was then an associate at the Aon Group, working on the hundredth floor of the South Tower. He began evacuating from the office shortly after the hijacked jet slammed into the North Tower at 8:46 a.m. Once he and his boss were sure the hundredth floor had been cleared, he walked down to the ninety-second floor and then took the elevator to the seventy-eighth floor. He was one of about two hundred other people waiting for the express elevator to take them to the lobby of the South Tower when the second plane hit at 9:03 a.m., crushing many of the floors between the seventy-eighth and eighty-fourth floors. Suddenly, all but twelve of the two hundred people Crown had been with were dead or doomed to die. "I was standing in the one square foot that allowed me to survive," he said later. The impact knocked him to the floor and broke his leg. Unable to see because of the smoke and unable to walk because of his broken leg, Crown still managed to crawl down seventy-eight flights of stairs to safety. "There's no question some of the training I did as an athlete at Duke, particularly under Coach Pressler, helped me turn that switch into a survival mode," Crown explained. "My thought was to do whatever I can to help myself and everyone who was with me."

His e-mail caught Brodhead's attention. "I have been careful not to say that I am confident the players are innocent, though certainly a large number of them are of the criminal charge," Brodhead wrote to Lange and one other Duke administrator early the next morning. "I continue to hear this message, and so does Bob Steel [chairman of the board of trustees], who will beat up on me about it again later today." He asked them for their suggestions for how to make the lacrosse players and their parents feel more embraced by the university at a difficult time. "Trouble is, by 'reach out' they mean something different from having a chat with Chris Kennedy or someone from CAPS [Duke's counseling and psychological services department]. I believe they want an acknowledgment of their innocence, and that's where we are stuck. Or maybe they just want someone to meet with them and show them a humane face? I have done that [with two] sets of parents in the last week and it went fine. I am mindful, here, that even Mr. Nifong spoke of wishing to lift the cloud of suspicion from those who will not be charged."

Lange responded to Brodhead about thirty minutes later. "My view is that the absence of contacts with the assistant coaches—if true—and low contact with the players is probably mistaken," he wrote. "I think Sue [Wasiolek], perhaps Larry [Moneta], and possibly [one other administrator] could seek them out and have a conversation that, without committing on the facts, offers support as they end the year and take their exams. We could also let them know that we are anxious for the case to be made definitive and hence the cloud over the noninvolved, whether all or some, to be lifted." Lange wondered if Brodhead was going to meet Duke's graduating seniors at his home, which would be an opportunity—possibly—to express his sympathy. "Now, here's for me the downside," Lange continued. "1) It is possible that the DA has so screwed up this case that the guilty will never be found so, even though there are some; 2) the biggest cloud is that there was some cover-up by some—that is, that some know more than they are saying. I know these are both obvious points but they need somehow to be kept in mind even as we do the support thing." Early that afternoon, Brodhead replied to Lange: "Well, that's it in a nutshell. I do think Sue . . . [could] do it—doubt they would welcome Larry—and perhaps Joe [Alleva] should do something? But they all need to be on-script, as far as what we're saying about the legal dimensions. Did you ever see that movie [*Primal Fear*] with Edward Norton and the Catholic elementary school?" (The movie, starring Norton and Richard Gere, was about an altar boy accused of murdering a prominent Catholic priest in Chicago.)

In a front-page article, *USA Today* wondered why the scandal at Duke had struck such a raw nerve with the national media when other, equally sordid scandals—such as the one at the University of Colorado in 2004 involving accusations of rape and sex parties—had not. It was a good question. The paper noted that new details about the case seemed to be leaking daily, providing constant fodder for the twenty-four-hour cable news channels. "This is very quickly becoming an inkblot test, not a legal proceeding," observed Dahlia Lithwick in the *Washington Post*. "We look to the facts to confirm our own preexisting suspicions about what inevitably happens between men and women, rich people and poor people, black people and white people." She continued, "The Duke lacrosse team's rape scandal cuts deeply into this country's most tender places: race and class and gender. It reaffirms the unspoken fear that black women/white men/poor people/privileged people/victims/defendants can't get a fair shake under our legal system. It will be chewed over, regurgitated and chewed over again by television pundits unafraid of venturing opinions in no way informed by the rapidly evolving public facts."

There was also the popular animus directed at Duke sports teams. For them, the lacrosse incident was manna from heaven. "How did people get to hate Duke?" wondered Sheldon Steinbach, the general counsel of the American Council on Education. "Too much success under Krzyzewski? I don't know. But there is a real animus pervading the media scene. . . . For the nation at large to be so obsessed with as yet unproven allegations is amazing." But Paul Haagen, the Duke law professor, seemed to understand the dynamics well. "Somebody makes an allegation against somebody in the physics department, people think, 'Okay, there's a terrible person in the physics department,'" he said. "Somebody makes an allegation against the lacrosse team, that's an allegation against Duke University. . . . Athletics is the most likely place to have a major scandal in a university, and the scandals roil you in ways that just about nothing else can."

That somehow the wealthy Duke defendants would hire the best lawyers to figure a way out of their legal morass was also a driving factor in the perverse level of interest in the story. "The idea of privileged, hedonistic stars running amok on campus . . . gives it that whole *Animal House* quality," observed Robert Thompson, a professor of communications at Syracuse University. He said the story "breached the cultural zeitgeist" the moment McFadyen's e-mail was released publicly. "[That was] the Hannibal Lecter element that really put it over the top," he said. "That, I think, put this story into a zone journalistically and culturally." Steinbach, from the American Council on Education, praised Brodhead's handling of a very difficult situation. "People keep saying, 'Duke ought to be doing more,'" he said. "I hear that on TV and I think, 'What more do you want them to do? Have summary executions on the main quad?'"

For Eugene Robinson, a Pulitzer Prize–winning columnist at the *Washington Post*, the scandal remained "murky, like many cases of alleged rape—especially cases of alleged rape in which the accused can afford top-shelf legal counsel." He asked a series of rhetorical questions that few people had bothered asking. "What's the deal with *any group* of college students thinking it's a perfectly normal thing to hire strippers for a party?" he wondered. "What do their parents say when they see that charge on the credit card bill? For that matter, what's the deal with a college student, whatever financial pressure she might be under, thinking that working at night as an outcall stripper is a perfectly acceptable—and safe—way to support herself? It's not blaming the victim to ask if she couldn't have made better choices." The answers would have to wait.

If there were any doubt that the two indicted players' defense attorneys intended to play judicial hardball with Nifong, or that this was going to be nothing less than a death match, it was probably dispelled quickly on the morning of Monday, April 24, when Kirk Osborn, Seligmann's counsel, filed a motion asking for Nifong to release Mangum's medical, criminal, and educational records. "The complaining witness has a history of criminal activity and behavior, which includes alcohol abuse, drug abuse, and dishonesty," Osborn wrote, "all conduct which indicate[s] mental, emotional, and/or physical problems, which affect her credibility as a witness." He also wanted the judge to hold a pretrial hearing to "determine if the complaining witness is even credible enough to provide reliable testimony," especially since the DNA evidence did not seem to link the players to a crime and the case seemed to rest solely upon Mangum's eyewitness account. "This lack of evidence," Osborn wrote, "heightens the need for impeaching material regarding the complaining witness." Osborn said he had a "right to know" of evidence that could reveal a "defect or deficiency of character or untruthfulness" in Mangum or any "prejudice, bias, motive, interest, and/or corruption" on the part of a potential witness.

On his blog, Malcolm Gladwell, the best-selling *New Yorker* writer, also questioned the validity of an eyewitness account of a crime, noting in particular how difficult such an assessment can be when the victim and the alleged assailants are from different races. "I don't have any opinion on the guilt or innocence of Duke lacrosse players charged with raping a exotic dancer," he wrote. "But I do think the incident affords a small opportunity to think about the value of eyewitness testimony." He noted that Mangum's review of the lacrosse team's photographs had led the prosecution to push for the ultimately successful indictment of Seligmann and Finnerty. "So far, the accuser's testimony is the most powerful fact in the prosecution's arsenal," Gladwell continued. "The question is: How much credence should we give that identification." He cited research that showed that someone was 1.4 times more likely to identify correctly an "own-race face" than a "different-race face" and 1.6 times more likely to misidentify a "different-race face." Concluded Gladwell, "The problem seems to be that when we encounter someone from a different group, we process them at the group level. We code the face in our memory under the category black or white, and not under the category of someone with, say, an oval face and brown eyes and a prominent chin. Race, in other words, trumps other visual features that would be more helpful in distinguishing one person from another." He wrote of his belief that because of this racial misidentification, there were likely "thousands" of black men in prison because of wrong identifications made by whites. "Now, in the Duke case," he wrote, "we have a black identification of white suspects. The shoe is on the other foot. It will be interesting to see whether the legal system is any more willing to acknowledge the real limitations of eyewitness identifications when it is suspects from the racial majority who are on the receiving end of the bias, not the other way around."

Then, in another twist illustrating the ongoing confusion about what was real and what wasn't, Krystal Brent Zook, an adjunct professor at Columbia and reporter for *Essence* magazine who had spent some twenty hours with Mangum's parents in Durham, reported that Mangum's mother, Mary, had told her about Mangum's claim to have been brutally gang-raped in June 1993—when she was fourteen years old—by her older then boyfriend and his two friends in a house in Creedmoor, North Carolina. Mangum had failed to report the crime until August 1996, and then—after being asked by police to put together a time line of events—dropped the allegation. Making matters more confusing, after Mangum's mother shared the story with Zook, she declined to discuss it further with the *News & Observer*. "I'm not going to tell you anything," she said.

Meanwhile, to add to the theater, Mangum's father, Travis, told the paper his daughter had not been sexually assaulted in 1993. "They didn't do anything to her," he said. All they did was hold her "against her will" after picking her up from school one day. She was "not sexually assaulted or injured in the encounter," he said, and she was returned home safely the same day.

Then, a day or so later, the Mangums' story changed again when a local television station reported that Mangum's parents both said Mangum "was attacked by the boy she was dating at the time and two of his friends" and that the three men "allegedly held her against her will in a house, raped her, and threatened to kill her." The Mangums said their daughter was "so frightened at the time that she decided not to press charges" and that she "lost a tremendous amount of weight the following week and became suicidal, blaming herself over what had happened, so they took her to see a psychiatrist."

Kenneth McNeill, Mangum's first husband, joined the media fray, too, when he told ABC News that he believed she had been raped in 1993. She had told him about the rape when they were engaged in 1996, and he said he encouraged her to file the report with the Creedmoor police to "help her overcome the trauma," he said. "I wanted them to pay for what they did." McNeill said that Mangum had told him that her then boyfriend was seven years older than she and was "controlling, jealous, and abusive. . . . He would beat her, and she would hide the bruises from her parents." On that June day in 1993, the boyfriend "offered up his young girlfriend's body to his friends," McNeill said. "He let his boys take turns."

Not surprisingly, the defense attorneys were not immediately sure how to react to the idea that Mangum had previously made a rape allegation and then dropped it. Bill Cotter, Finnerty's attorney, told NBC 17, a local television station, "That's the very first I've heard of that." But Bob Ekstrand was incredulous. Not suprisingly, he picked up on Travis Mangum's comments that the rape had not occurred. "This is absolutely stunning," he said, "insofar as this appears to be a false and fabricated allegation. This prosecution needs to end soon, and has lost all credibility." Joe Cheshire said, "It's awfully bothersome when both allegations of rape include three men. It gives one a lot of pause about her credibility. . . . This is a train off the track." John Fitzpatrick, a Durham defense lawyer not involved in the case, said of Mangum's 1993 rape allegation, "As a defense lawyer, that's something I would want to investigate completely to see if she's crying wolf. If she's crying wolf in 1996, then potentially she could be crying wolf in 2006."

For his part, Nifong would not comment on Mangum's 1993 rape allegation but said the case would continue. "The investigation in this case is not yet complete," he wrote in a statement. "All of the facts are not yet known, and many of the so-called facts that have been reported and commented on are simply wrong. For the sake of the victim, for the sake of the accused, for the sake of our system of justice, I encourage everyone to step back from this situation and allow that system to do its job." As for whether he would seek an indictment of the third player on May 1, the day before the district attorney primary vote, he said he would not. "Even I would think that would look political," he said.

For Mangum, as described in her 2008 autobiography, *The Last Dance for Grace*, her brutal gang rape in a house in Creedmoor was frighteningly real, and raised serious questions about the defense attorneys' willingness to impugn her integrity. According to Mangum, here is how the 1993 incident occurred: Mangum met "Frederick Thomas"—his real name, according to police records, was Floyd Taylor—when she was fourteen years old and a freshman at Hillside High School in Durham. It was a chance encounter at the end of the school day. She was walking home with her older sister. In any event, Mangum had let her sister get ahead of her, so she was walking alone when she approached a crosswalk. While Mangum was waiting for the light to change, a truck with four guys in the front seat slowed down as it was passing by and she heard them "whistling and making catcalls," which she assumed were directed at another girl.

That's when she heard Thomas ask, "Hey, what's up girl? Where are you going? Do you need a ride someplace?" Mangum remembered, "I stood there transfixed. I felt a grin come over my face." She was tempted to take a ride from the men because of the chemistry she was feeling, but she knew that riding with strange men was not something her parents would condone. "That's okay," Mangum told him.

Thomas looked her over some more. "Come closer and let me talk to you, girl," he said. Mangum remembered he had a "funny accent"—he was from the Caribbean—and she was drawn to him. "Something about him was seductive," Mangum recalled, "and I moved closer to the truck. All my inhibitions went away as the sensation of being noticed made me feel warm all over. I was completely trusting, as I gave no thought that he or the other men might have meant me harm. I was overwhelmed because no boy and certainly no man had ever looked so intensely at my body and into my eyes." Thomas asked Mangum for her phone number and she gave it to him. By the time she got home, Mangum was filled with a feeling of both trepidation—she had given her phone number to a total stranger—and delight—an older boy (albeit seven years older) had noticed her.

At 10 p.m., while she was in bed, the phone rang in the Mangum home. Crystal suspected it was Frederick. The rule in the house was that no one was to call for the Mangum children after 8 p.m. Mary Mangum answered the phone and starting peppering Thomas with questions about how he knew her daughter and had she told him about not calling the house after a certain hour? Without asking Mangum to explain, Mary Mangum handed the phone to her daughter. "I didn't know what to say," Mangum explained. "I had never had a conversation with a boy like this."

They spoke for the next two hours, mostly about sex. "Almost immediately, Frederick told me how much he wanted to lick me down there," Mangum recalled. "He wanted to taste me and show how good he could make me feel. I had no clue about oral sex, but he told me not to worry, he was an expert. He made every woman he was with feel good. He could do it for twenty-four hours straight and make me feel like a woman. He would teach me how to accept the pleasure of his tongue. There was no way to even imagine how it would feel to be with a man. I was a virgin and I tried to make my body feel the sensation he was talking about, but it didn't seem to make any sense. Why would he want to lick my private parts? He had just met me." She was not totally naïve about sex: she had heard people talking about it and she had felt the changes happening to her own body. "Perhaps if I let him rub his tongue against my vagina, it would feel good," she thought.

The next day, Thomas showed up in his purple Nissan outside Hillside High, waiting for Mangum. "He was taller and huskier than I imagined," she remembered. "I had only seen him sitting in the truck. He also looked much older." He hugged her. "My heart pounded uncontrollably, as I was both nervous and excited," she continued. "Almost immediately, he brought up his desire to perform oral sex on me. I stood there in silence and tried to let it pass without responding." He asked her to take a ride with him. Mangum knew it wasn't the wisest idea, but she could not resist.

Mangum got in the car with him. They drove to the house of his friend, Marquis. She sat on the couch next to Thomas. The room was filled with marijuana smoke and a bunch of other, older guys. "It was apparent that I was drawing a great deal of attention as the only girl present," she said. "It made me feel uncomfortable to see men staring at me." Thomas suddenly became jealous of Mangum, what with the other men around, and told everyone that she was his girlfriend. "I was so taken by the jealousy he was expressing that I failed to realize that being his girlfriend would be a terrible mistake," she recalled. "I felt special right at the time I should have been on guard." He gave her his new hat and a gold chain as a token of his affection and told her he wanted to take it slow and get to know her better.

They became boyfriend and girlfriend. He became "Fred" to her and would pick her up after school nearly every day. She learned from him that he lived with his mom and that he had been married before to a seventeen-year-old girl, whom he had gotten pregnant. When their son was born, the couple got divorced and his ex-wife took their house and child. He told Mangum he didn't want to talk about that, and she believed the story and that he had done the right thing by the woman. One day, after school, Mangum walked to the purple Nissan more slowly than usual, making a show of looking for something in her purse. She wanted her classmates to see Fred and make sure they knew he thought she was special and to make them a bit jealous that he was her boyfriend. They joked about it when Mangum got into the car. Fred kept talking away and eventually Mangum drifted off, staring out the window.

When the car stopped at a crosswalk, she realized she had not heard what he had been saying and apologized to him for daydreaming. But Thomas thought she was looking out the window at another man and became angry.

"What the hell were you looking at?" he asked. She repeated she was just daydreaming but Thomas didn't believe her.

"Don't lie to me!" he said.

"I'm not lying," she pleaded. "I really wasn't doing anything."

"Don't ever lie to me," he screamed at her, "violently hitting me with a crushing backhand blow to the face," she recalled. She began to sob. "Don't ever lie to me again, I mean it," he said. He soon apologized for hitting her. "Sometimes I get so jealous and I am afraid you might leave me," he told her. "I don't want to lose you."

She forgave him. "You don't have to be jealous about anything because I love you," Mangum told him. She realized, though, that a line had been crossed. "The deal was sealed," she recalled. "I had given in to Fred, and now was offering him comfort for battering me. I felt powerless again, just like I had before I met him." He tried to get her to have sex with him but she resisted his advances—she was fourteen and not ready to lose her virginity—and he backed off, although it was a close call.

A few weeks later, with things patched up between them, he asked her go with him to his mother's house. Mangum agreed. When they got to the house, she realized that his mother was not home. "Fred . . . paid special attention to me after we walked into the house," she recalled. "He brought me a drink, and we sat on the couch. He put his arm around me, and then we kissed. I had kissed him many times but never alone in a house."

Soon enough, he was on top of her. She asked him to stop. He wouldn't. "You know you want me, girl," he said. "You know it's going to be good, too. Don't you?"

"No, stop," she told him. She pushed back against him. But it was no use. He then raped her. "You like for me to go up in your guts?" he laughed. "I'm going to smear your blood on the walls so my boys can see it." Mangum recalled that he laughed the more she screamed. She was not sure how long the rape lasted, but when it was over, Thomas said he loved her. "What he done to me did not feel like love at all," she said. "This hurt." Within weeks, the situation went from bad to worse—much, much worse. Ever since Mangum had started dating Thomas—understandably—her already tenuous relationship with her parents had deteriorated. She was skipping school. Her grades were suffering. "My behavior was completely out of whack," she recalled. "For as much as I felt my family was mistreating me, I was only adding fuel to the fire by skipping school and letting Fred in my life." Meanwhile, Thomas had started treating her better, as part of his desire to get her to leave her family and move in with him at his mother's house. The whole plan was crazy: the fourteen-year-old Mangum would leave her family in Durham behind and move to Creedmoor with her twenty-one-year-old highly abusive boyfriend. Worse, he promised her that she could become part of his drug-dealing business. She could run the "street operation," he told her. All in all, the scheme was well beyond the pale of logic.

But Mangum agreed to it. One Friday, several weeks after Thomas had raped her, she decided to leave home for good. "The only place for me to go," she recalled, "would be Fred's house. I wanted to be with him forever." She called him and asked him to come fetch her. And that was that.

Some three weeks into her new life, living with Thomas and his mother, who was sickly and often in the hospital, "things were about to come crashing down again." One afternoon, Thomas got a phone call and three of his "acquaintances"—Sam, Lamont, and Terry—announced they were coming by the house in Creedmoor to see him. At first, Thomas tried to keep the three men outside. "Fred don't want us to come in because he doesn't want us to see the little bitch he got up in there!" Sam said.

Lamont added his view that "I ain't stud'n that girl!"

Thomas let them in, and the three men sat on the couch next to Mangum. They all started smoking large joints—Lamont called them "baseball bats" because they were so big. While they were getting high, they watched music videos on television and sat around doing nothing. Thomas then asked Mangum to go upstairs with him to the bedroom. "In a flash he grabbed me around the neck and pulled me close to him," she recalled. "He told me he wanted to have sex right then, but I protested." But Thomas didn't really care about Mangum's opinion. He slapped her across the face and pushed her "forcefully" onto the bed. She screamed and kept on screaming. Sam wandered to the bedroom and wondered why Thomas was hitting his girlfriend. But he told Sam to mind his own business and go back downstairs. "Just wait until they leave," he told Mangum. "When I go up in you, you will know it." They went back downstairs, and Sam gave Thomas some grief about hitting Mangum, which he denied doing. Eventually, the three men left.

As soon as the front door closed, Thomas looked at Mangum. "Are you ready for your beating?" he asked. Mangum dutifully went back upstairs and could barely get her clothes off before Thomas set upon her and brutally raped her. "Every thrust was deep and vicious," Mangum remembered. "He had promised that it would get better each time he 'made love to me,' but this hurt worse than the first time. He pounded harder and harder, the more he sensed I was hurting. When Fred ejaculated, he was finished. He never once tried to pleasure me in the way he explained in that first phone conversation. When he got up, I could see blood everywhere. The sheets were covered as well as my inner thighs. Had I waited for God to give me this?"

That evening, a few hours later, Mangum was on the couch downstairs in the living room when Sam, Lamont, and Terry returned to Thomas's house. An earlier dispute among the men and Thomas seemed to have been resolved. They started looking over Mangum in a provocative manner. "They began to talk about their past and their many sexual exploits," Mangum recalled. "I kept silent." Suddenly, Thomas announced that Mangum was cheating on him. "There was no way that could be true," she recalled. "I was trapped in Fred's mother's house in Creedmoor. It was just Fred's sick delusion and obsessive jealous streak . . ." The men "talked about me openly as if I wasn't there" and "commented on my body without regard to how it would make me feel," which was "like a piece of meat."

When one of her favorite songs starting playing, she got up and started dancing. Mangum had wanted to be a dancer, but she always believed her parents looked askance at the idea, and she received no positive reinforcement from her friends or teachers. In any event, on this night, she danced because she enjoyed it and it pleased Thomas, and the other men seemed to enjoy her dancing, too. "They would throw money at me while I performed, and it gave me my own money to put away," Mangum said. "It didn't occur to me that it was exploitative for a fourteen-year-old girl to be dancing for grown men, but they wanted to see me perform." The men talked openly about what it would be like to have sex with Mangum—she heard every word they said—but figured the hyper-jealous Thomas would never let another man touch her. She actually felt safe.

When the music finished, Thomas asked Mangum to go back upstairs. But she declined. She was still sore from earlier and did not want to relive that pain, so soon anyway. "Not a wise decision on my part," she recalled. "Fred slapped me again, but this time he did not care if anyone saw what he did. He demanded that I go up to the bedroom. I dutifully consented." Upstairs, Thomas yelled at Mangum and told her never to "embarrass him in front of his friends ever again." He told her to sit on the bed and not to move. He left the bedroom.

To Mangum's "surprise," Terry came into the room, sat down on the bed "and began to touch me as if we were alone." Mangum did not cry out, for fear that if Thomas heard her scream, she would get the beating of a lifetime. Instead, she just let Terry have his way with her. Then Lamont came into the room and asked Terry what was going on. But Terry did not answer. "He kept touching me all over and sucking my breast," she said. Lamont sat on the other side of her on the bed and pulled off Mangum's panties. "They both laid me back on the bed and I was still too frightened to protest," Mangum continued. "Terry removed his pants and started to penetrate me. Fred walked into the room. Lamont and Terry stopped for a moment as Fred walked toward us. Fred was smiling and laughing. Terry moved out of the way as Fred came closer. Fred drew back and hit me hard against my face. It wasn't a slap this time. He hit me hard and sent me reeling."

Observed Lamont: "That's a little freak you got, Fred. She likes it rough." Thomas slapped Mangum in the face several more times. He told her to be quiet because she had "brought this on" herself by not objecting earlier when they were talking about having sex with her. She had not spoken up earlier because she didn't want Thomas to be angry with her; now he was angry with her for not speaking up earlier. In any event, the decision had been made to rape her mercilessly. "Fred removed his clothes and the three of them were naked and eager to abuse me," she recalled. "Each of them took their turns on top of me. All pounding at my already damaged vagina. I couldn't feel anything anymore. I just lay there and cried. I wasn't able to scream. It would not have ended the torture. Each time it appeared to end, the rape continued . . . for almost eight hours. When they were finally finished, my hairline was soaked from my tears. I couldn't move and felt numb from the waist down."

After all that, Thomas slapped her again. "Did you think you were going to have sex with my friends and get away with it?" he asked her. "You're a nasty slut." Mangum was helpless against Thomas. "I touched my face," Mangum remembered, "and it felt like a water balloon about to burst. My eyes were swollen and puffy and my ears felt as if they were stuffed with cotton." She tried to get up and run away but was so disoriented, she just ended up rolling off the bed onto the floor. Thomas demanded, "Get up!" but when she couldn't, he began to kick her with "heavy blows" to the side of her body. "I could only moan and tell Fred that he was killing me," she recalled. She began thinking about her parents. Did they even know where she was? Did they care about her? "For the first time since I left, I wanted to be at home," she explained.

Eventually, she drifted off into a fitful sleep. She would wake up in pain. "The smell of the rape was still on me, and I needed to wash it away," she continued. She was starving and went downstairs to the kitchen to get something to eat. Thomas was sitting at the kitchen table, "smoking a cigar as if he didn't have a care in the world." She walked past him without saying a word. She was furious and hungry. "Cris, I'm really sorry about last night," he said to her. "You know, we were all high, and we want you to know that we didn't mean any of it. Cris, are you mad? I won't let you hang with us anymore. I'm afraid you might get hurt."

A few days later, Thomas took Mangum back to her parents' home. Although she did not tell anyone what had happened to her, she became increasingly depressed. "I was a difficult person to deal with and, frankly, it was hard for me to live with myself," she recalled. "I internalized the blame for what happened to me. Fred was excellent at manipulation, like most abusers. Carrying the burden of the shame for being involved in this kind of trauma left me in a perpetual state of depression for years." She "hit rock bottom" in December 1993. She couldn't eat. She lay in bed, crying, day and night. Her mother became increasingly worried about her and suspected "something had been done to me" because of the abuse she herself had suffered as a child. Her mother decided to take Mangum to the emergency room at Duke University Medical Center. "It was and still is a very sad day in memory," she remembered, without irony.

The doctors at Duke diagnosed Mangum with post-traumatic stress disorder. They determined that she should be institutionalized. She underwent two months of intensive therapy and medication at the John Umstead Psychiatric Hospital. Against her parents'—and doctors'—wishes, however, Mangum called Thomas as soon as she could. "I knew my family did not want me to have anything to do with him," she recalled, "but I went back to seeing him clandestinely as soon as I got out of the hospital. The good feelings I was having were only short-lived, as he became violent and abusive again. Getting out of the relationship with Fred this time wasn't just a matter of walking away. When I told Fred I could not continue on with him, he told me he would rather see me dead than be with another man. Coming from Fred, that was a serious concern. He had shown his capacity to be evil, and I believed he was capable of killing me. I regret that I ever met Fred."

But she kept dating him off and on after getting back from Umstead, although she was living at home again. Eventually she met another man, who was very much the opposite of Thomas: he was kind to her, took an interest in her, wasn't abusive in the slightest. "Our relationship was not conditioned on having sex," she said. Six months later, though, he "abruptly" broke up with Mangum. She was devastated but realized it was her own fault, at least to the extent that she was still suffering from the lessons she learned about relationships from Thomas. "I learned that relationships were about manipulation and who was in control," she said. "You just took what you could and too bad about the other person's feelings."

She was desperate to win her boyfriend back. She told him she would return to Thomas—whom he knew all about—if he didn't return to her. She told him she would kill herself. Nothing worked. So the night after the breakup, she decided to follow through on the suicide threat. Her father took her to the grocery store. She wanted to find some drugs that she could take to kill herself. She left the market with a bottle of aspirin. At 10 p.m., she locked herself in the bathroom and swallowed the sixty tablets in the bottle. She went to bed, thinking she would die. "Of course, I did not die as planned," she recalled, "but when I awoke, I shook violently."

She started to feel a bit better during the morning and went for a car ride with her father and sister. But during the ride, her symptoms returned. She became dizzy and confused and started writhing irrationally on the floor of the backseat of the car. Her father noticed her in the rearview mirror and asked her what was wrong. Eventually, she was able to convey to him that she had swallowed an entire bottle of aspirin. He thought she might die, which made Mangum fearful that she actually might.

Back she went to the Duke Medical Center emergency room. The doctors pumped her stomach and checked to make sure none of her internal organs were damaged. She stayed in the intensive care unit for two weeks and then spent another two weeks at Duke's psychiatric ward. "My mental health was a shambles," she said. (Mangum had a medical history of bipolar disorder, according to the UNC Hospital records.) Slowly but surely, her mental and physical health improved—although Mangum continued to battle depression—and somehow she managed to graduate from Hillside High School in June 1996. Soon thereafter, she got engaged to Kenneth McNeill, who was fourteen years older, and he was the one who encouraged her to file the police report in August 1996 about what Fred, Lamont, and Terry had done to her three years earlier. Her police report mentioned the three men by name, but when the report was released publicly—during the lacrosse case—the three men's names were blacked out. And of course the case was never pursued, in part because she did not put together the time line as requested by the Creedmoor police. While they did not have Mangum's full account available, the media and the defense attorneys in any event gave only cursory treatment to the story of Mangum's brutal first rape, dismissing it—mostly—as another example of her ability to embroider her life's narrative.

Meanwhile, on Tuesday, April 25, Finnerty was in court in Washington, DC, where he was forced to appear again related to the charges of punching Jeff Bloxsom the previous November. At the hearing, the judge reinstated the charges against Finnerty and ordered him and his two codefendants to adhere to a 9 p.m. to 6 a.m. curfew and to keep away from any place where alcohol was being served or consumed. The judge also ordered Finnerty to stand trial in Washington on July 10 on simple assault charges. If convicted on the charges, he faced a prison sentence of six months and a $1,000 fine. The judge said he would put Finnerty in jail or in a halfway house if the rape allegations were true. All in all, it had not been a good week for Collin Finnerty.

That same day, Nifong decided to reinstate the misdemeanor charges of violating a noise ordinance and underage drinking against David Evans. He was scheduled to appear in court in May to answer these charges. "[Evans] was one of the people who rented the house that was serving alcohol to underage people and hiring strippers," Nifong said. "In order to put somebody under deferred prosecution, the DA has to, under requirements of the statute, certify that he does not believe the person is likely to do any further criminal acts. Under the circumstances, it's hard for me to see how we could maintain that." Nifong's decision about Evans was a harbinger of things to come.

Nifong also said he was considering reinstating the misdemeanor charges against others among the sixteen lacrosse team members. "For a long time," Nifong said, "we have treated deferred prosecution as a right. It's a privilege." As to whether Mangum's 1996 accusation of rape against Fred, Lamont, and Terry would have a bearing on her accusations in the Duke case, Nifong said that it would never come up in court because of the state's shield law, which generally kept a woman's previous sexual history out of open court. A judge, however, could decide the information was relevant and then determine the terms under which the information would be released in court.

By April 25, Himan was increasingly concerned for Mangum's safety. Not only had she been "harrassed by three vehicles," but she was also "constantly being harrassed by the media." Himan contacted a number of statewide rape agencies and rape crisis centers and found a woman who agreed to find Mangum a safe place to live, away from the media and others looking to bother her.

It was also out of apparent concern for Mangum that a black nationalist organization, the New Black Panther Party for Self Defense, decided to descend on Durham for a rally near Duke's West Campus. Founded in Dallas in 1989, the New Black Panther Party "preaches self-determination for a black nation through revolutionary changes," such as freeing all incarcerated blacks and exempting blacks from military service. The Southern Poverty Law Center, a nonprofit civil rights organization based in Montgomery, Alabama, listed the New Black Panther Party, which had no affiliation with the original Black Panther Party, as a "racist, black separatist organization" with a penchant for bringing guns to its organized events. "The sister had death threats," Minister Na'jee Shaka Muhammad, the party's national field marshal, told the Durham paper. "The sister was afraid, she was talking about dropping the charges, she had no protection or security. . . . We'll do the escort and the security, going to court, whatever it takes." (The idea that the New Black Panther Party would provide security to Mangum was canceled the next day after Mangum's parents declined the offer. "To me they're just as bad as the Klansmen," her father said.)

The group handed out flyers advertising the May 1 rally, featuring pictures of Seligmann and Finnerty and the question "Had enough of disrespect and racism from Duke University?" The plan was to hold a press conference at the entrance to Duke's Chapel Drive, the road that leads to West Campus and the chapel, and then march to the lacrosse fields and then double back past 610 North Buchanan. "We as black men cannot sit idly by and allow white men to rape black women, regardless of what our sister (who by nature is a queen and a divine black woman) was doing," Malik Zulu Shabazz, the leader of the New Panthers, was quoted as saying in a press release announcing the event. He also said the purpose of the rally near Duke was to discuss the rape allegations "as well as hate literature, graffiti, and disrespect by Duke University students." Shabazz's "graffiti" reference related to an April 13 incident at Campus Crossing, a student apartment complex near NCCU, where someone wrote: "Duke Number 1 NCCU niggers last" in blue spray paint on a door and in a stairwell.

In an interview with the *News & Observer*, Shabazz said his organization was "conducting an independent investigation, and we intend to enter the campus and interview lacrosse players. We seek to ensure an adequate, strong, and vigorous prosecution." Asked about his followers bringing guns to campus, Shabazz apparently chuckled and said, "I don't know if I can comment on that." A spokesman for the Anti-Defamation League in New York called the party "a racist and anti-Semitic group. These guys come armed. They carry shotguns to demonstrations."

Once again Duke was in a tough situation. "As an institution we support free speech," John Burness explained to the *News & Observer*, "and we will treat them like any other group. But we do not permit weapons. We will take necessary steps to keep the campus safe." Burness told the *Durham Herald-Sun* that the school was trying to keep on an even keel. "We're doing the same things we always do," he said. "One of the main things is that Duke has earned its reputation over the years as a world-class institution because of our first-rate academics, as well as medical care and, yes, athletics." He said the university had faced adversity in the past—he cited the October 2004 Palestinian Solidarity Movement's teach-in, where Duke was criticized for allowing the group on campus but also praised for its promotion of free speech—and would likely again. "We'll take our lumps if they come," he said. He told the paper that Duke had hired a "consulting firm for advice" about its public relations strategy and ways to devise a "crisis communications plan." He said the firm was "highly reinforcing of our approach" to be open with the media and to allow it on campus.

Still, an on-campus demonstration by such an obviously divisive group as the New Panthers was the last thing Duke needed, especially on the first day of final exams. In an e-mail sent to the Duke community, Brodhead noted that the New Black Panther Party was known to carry guns. "Guns are not permitted on Duke's campus," he said. He said that the Duke police were in touch with the leaders of the party. "They informed Duke police that they have no intention of entering the campus to be disruptive in any way," he continued. "They also assured us they will not have guns." Brodhead seemed genuinely concerned that the situation was taking yet another turn for the worse. "This is a period of considerable stress for our students, especially following the already stressful events of the past several weeks," he wrote. "We will not let the safety of our campus be jeopardized, nor will we allow our students' lives to be disrupted." He stated that additional police officers would be assigned to monitor the protest. "Any attempted access by this group to our campus will be tightly restricted and no disruption of the university will be permitted," he continued. "Duke has gone through a difficult period. I am proud of the way this campus community has responded to the many tensions and pressures we have been facing. I wish our students well on their exams." But tensions between Duke and Durham were raised another notch after a Duke undergrad and a Duke graduate student were arrested for "vandalizing a lamppost" in Trinity Park, the neighborhood where the rape allegedly took place. "I have so many reactions," Larry Moneta wrote on the community's digital bulletin board, "I don't know where to begin: anger, sadness and embarrassment among them . . . I am truly sorry that this persists."

Next, Travis Mangum hit the airwaves. He told Fox News that he thought his daughter was having second thoughts about testifying in the lacrosse case. "Not right now, I don't think she would," he said. "She wouldn't want to." He told MSNBC she had "talked about" dropping the case because "she couldn't take it." But in an interview with the Durham paper, he reversed course and said he had not spoken to his daughter and hadn't discussed with her whether she intended to testify against the lacrosse players. He said his words had been misconstrued and he simply meant that, given all that his daughter had been through, she was not anxious to testify in the near future. "Later on, she would," he said, "but right now I don't think she would want to. Which I don't think she'll have to, so that's why I said that."

Of course, the idea that Mangum might not be willing to testify would be the end of Nifong's prosecution, a point he quickly acknowledged to Fox News. "Realistically, there's no way anybody can try a rape case without a victim," he said. "But I don't anticipate that that's going to be the issue. I anticipate that the victim will be there." And he noted that May 15 was shaping up to be a pivotal day in the case. That was his next chance to take his third indictment to the grand jury, since he did not want to go to the grand jury the day before the May 2 primary. It was also the date that both the second round of DNA test results were due back from the Burlington lab and the next preliminary court hearing was scheduled to take place in the case against Seligmann and Finnerty. "There will be an interesting confluence of events on the fifteenth,"

Nifong said. As for the third alleged rapist, defense lawyers leaked to the press that Mangum was only "90 percent sure" of her identification of him, primarily because they said she said the third attacker had had a mustache, but none of the players pictured in the photo lineup had any facial hair (in keeping with team rules.)

On the morning of April 28, Himan went to see Mangum to understand better what had happened to her in Creedmoor in 1993. At this point she provided a version of what she claimed had happened that was considerably different from what she would describe two years later in her book. Mangum told Himan she was dating Floyd Taylor and that she had run away from home. She told Himan that Taylor "used" her to "sell drugs." She would take the money to him. When Taylor was not at home, she said, "some men"—Larry James, Anthony James, and Sean Umpstead—would come to the house, and she would "have sex with them when Floyd was not around," then elaborated that the men "paid Floyd to come over and have sex with her." She told Himan that one day Taylor "confronted" her about having sex with the three men and she denied it. Taylor then asked the three men to come by the Creedmoor house. He asked them if they had been having sex with her; they said they had been.

Taylor then grabbed Mangum and, along with the two James brothers, they went into the bedroom together, where, she said, they "ran the train on her." Mangum said she was "very scared." Himan noticed her fear at recalling the scene even thirteen years later. "I could sense that she was becoming very emotional," he noted.

Three years after the alleged rape, after Mangum met Kenneth McNeill and they were engaged, she confided in him about what had happened at the house in Creedmoor. He urged her to report the incident "to get closure" and so that it would no longer be a secret. That's when she went to the Creedmoor police. She said the police told her that prosecuting the case against the men would be "a long process" and that at her age—she was then seventeen years old—it "would be mentally and physically tough and very hard on her." The Creedmoor police also told her that each of the three men was in jail—for other reasons—and was going to be there for "a significant time." When Mangum heard that her three assailants were in jail, she decided not to pursue the matter further. (The only Floyd Taylor listed in the North Carolina state prison records is a white fifty-year-old recidivist who has been in and out of prison since 1981. NBC 17, a local television station, tracked down one of the two James brothers on April 28, who denied having raped Mangum. He said he was thirteen years old at the time. He told the station he was just getting married and he "really [didn't] need this in his life right now.")

At a hastily called press conference on the morning of April 29, Nifong read from a prepared text and did not answer any questions. It was his first substantive public comment about the lacrosse case in weeks, and was prompted by the news of Mangum's previous allegations that three men had raped her in Creedmoor. Nifong reiterated that he doubted any jury in the Duke lacrosse case would hear about those allegations, primarily because North Carolina's Rape Shield Law would likely prevent it. "That law," he said, "makes the prior sexual behavior of the victim in a rape prosecution irrelevant unless it falls into one of four narrowly defined categories"—among them, whether the incidents are so similar as to create a pattern of behavior or whether the victim and the defendant or defendants had a prior relationship.

Predictably, the defense attorneys repeated their claim that Mangum's 1993 allegation was false and that she could not avoid being asked about it if the Duke matter ever went to trial. "This woman will have to testify," Joe Cheshire told MSNBC, "and it's valid to ask her if she's made any false accusations." Around this time, Linwood Wilson, an investigator working for Nifong on the case, suggested to Nifong that maybe Mangum should take a lie detector test about the Creedmoor incident. But Nifong told him, "I don't polygraph victims, especially sexual assault victims, and make those victims think I don't trust them or believe them."

Nifong also said he had received "hundreds" of letters, e-mails, and calls from across the country about the lacrosse case, including five from women who had been victims of sexual assaults but had decided not to report what occurred for fear of the backlash. "Two of those letters are from former Duke students who were sexually assaulted by other former Duke students," he said. "The common thread in these five situations is that each of these young women believed that the cost of the public scorn she would receive for reporting such an event outweighed the benefit to herself and to society of pursuing justice. Sadly, we are seeing exactly what they were talking about playing out in Durham today as people who know none of the facts are standing in line to offer their condemnation."

On Dan Abrams's MSNBC show that night, Yale Galanter, the defense attorney, thought Nifong's public statement was a political ploy. "He's planning an exit strategy, and what he's trying to do is get reelected," he said. "The only reason he gave that political rah-rah speech—'I'm helping all these unknown women . . . and I'm fighting the good cause, even though I'm getting slammed in the media every day, [and] please elect me'—this is a man who's running for reelection next week; he's hanging on by a thread, he's doing everything he can to get reelected, and he really is the captain of a sinking ship. Your program has brought to light the fact that Mike Nifong has probably indicted innocent men."

CHAPTER TEN

"Witch Hunts Go in Stages"

The beginning of May 2006 brought not only final exams to the Duke campus but also three internal reports—one on the lacrosse program, one on the Duke administration's response to the alleged incident at 610 North Buchanan, and one on the university's student judicial system—commissioned by Brodhead on April 5. Law professor James Coleman's May 1 report about the lacrosse team praised the team's academic and athletic prowess. It also found that the team members were especially bad actors once the drinking started. "Alcohol is the single greatest factor involved in the unacceptable behavior of Duke students in general and members of the lacrosse team specifically, both on and off campus," Coleman wrote on behalf of his seven-member committee. "Drunkenness is the cause of behaviors that represent a serious nuisance to the community and a source of significant personal danger for the student." Much of the report was given over to describing the history of the lacrosse team's role in encouraging a raucous party atmosphere at tailgating events before home football games.

Coleman found that the lacrosse team had been involved in more alcohol-related incidents than players on other Duke athletic teams, which seemed to be explained by the relatively large size of the team—forty-seven players— and by its "clannish" nature. Interestingly, while lacrosse players made up less than 1 percent of Duke undergraduates in the fall of 2005, 25 percent of disorderly conduct cases, 50 percent of noise ordinance cases and one-third of all open-container violations involved lacrosse players. "Duke Lacrosse has been described as having a 'clannish' or 'pack' culture that is distinct from other Duke athletic teams and organized groups on campus," the report found. "Like other athletic teams, the strict discipline of training and play enforces community for a significant amount of time both in season and out of season. Lacrosse transfers this community to life off the sports field more fully and more visibly than other Duke teams for a variety of reasons. They are a small enough unit (in contrast to football) to have remarkable social coherence and they are a large enough unit (in contrast to golf) to be socially prominent as a group. The lacrosse players' backgrounds contribute to that cohesiveness. The majority of the players come from middle-class suburban families (there are a few players from both very wealthy and working-class settings). Most members of the team are recruited from the Northeast: New York, New Jersey, and Maryland are the traditional centers of the sport; many of the players competed against one another in high school." (One former varsity golf player explained in an interview that his coach would specifically warn the golf team to stay away from lacrosse team parties.)

The report was fairly perfunctory—unsurprising given that the task force had had less than a month to do its work—and came to the predictable conclusion that despite the team's alcohol-related problems and the ongoing legal imbroglio, the lacrosse program should continue, starting again in the fall of 2006. "Although the pattern of misconduct in recent years by the lacrosse players is alarming, the evidence reviewed by the Committee does not warrant suspension of the sport at Duke University next year," Coleman concluded.

If the report were not read too closely, one could almost wonder what all the fuss was about. "By all accounts, the lacrosse players are a cohesive, hard-working, disciplined, and respectful athletic team," Coleman wrote. "Their behavior on trips is described as exemplary. Players clean the team bus before disembarking. Airline personnel have complimented them for their behavior. They observe curfews. They obey the team's no-alcohol rule before games"— which prohibited drinking forty-eight hours before a game. "They are respectful of people who serve the team, including bus drivers, airline personnel, trainers, the equipment manager, the team manager, and the groundskeeper. Finally, the lacrosse program has a 100 percent graduation rate. Alumni of the program apparently contribute to the community after college. We received letters of support for the team from two recently graduated former players who are presently serving in Iraq. A remarkable number of alumni are volunteer coaches for their local lacrosse teams. Many are employed in prestigious positions in business, law, and medicine"—indeed, there was a remarkable pipeline, detailed in the report, between the Duke lacrosse fields and prestigious jobs on Wall Street. "As evidenced by their support of the current team, alumni of the lacrosse program and their families are fiercely loyal to each other, to the lacrosse program, and to Duke." Explained A. B. "Buzzy" Krongard, who played lacrosse in the 1950s at Princeton and was a former CEO of Alex, Brown & Sons, the onetime Baltimore investment bank, "Coaches used to say, 'Give me four years, and you'll be working at Goldman Sachs.'" (Incredibly, Krongard also was the executive director of the Central Intelligence Agency, the third-ranking officer.)

As for when the Athletic Department would look for a new lacrosse coach, Chris Kennedy told the *Chronicle* that it was "premature" to think about that question. For his part, Coleman told the *Chronicle* that the lacrosse team's ongoing bad behavior was not a case of boys being boys, he said. "What was missing from the record that we see was any effort at all at responsibility. The conduct was repetitive; the conduct was excessive. The conduct occurred not only in the fall semester, but also in the spring during their season." Coleman told the *News & Observer* that the lacrosse team's "deplorable disciplinary record" reflects "the extent to which they let down those who trusted them, including their coach, their families and the university."

The second report—an examination of Duke's student "judicial process and practices" led by Duke professor Prasad Kasibhatla—concluded, as had the lacrosse report, that alcohol abuse was at the root of many of the on-campus and off-campus problems. After recounting the hundreds of alcohol-related disciplinary cases that the university's judicial system processes each year and the thirty to fifty annual alcohol-related medical emergencies, Kasibhatla wrote, "It is also clear that alcohol use and abuse is the major underlying factor in both off-campus and on-campus student misconduct. Conversations with the staff of the Women's Center reveal that alcohol is involved in 70 to 80 percent of the roughly sixty cases of sexual assault complaints that are received by the center per year. From an off-campus perspective, neighborhood residents and police are in broad agreement that alcohol abuse underlies most of the 'public nuisance' complaints against students. The same is true for misconduct in on-campus residences."

The Kasibhatla committee also found that the enforcement of Duke's alcohol policies was "inconsistent"—especially at tailgate parties and at the so-called Last Day of Classes party—and therefore "undermines the effectiveness" of the policy. In other words, like nearly every college and university in the country, Duke consistently turned a blind eye to the federal law that prohibits anyone under the age of twenty-one years old from drinking alcohol. "I think we're very serious about it," Kasibhatla told the *News & Observer*. "This needs to rise to the highest levels of the university administration."

Meanwhile, events in Durham seemed to be taking a new, more ominous turn. At 10:05 a.m. on May 1, about thirty members of the New Black Panthers for Self Defense and their entourage met in a parking lot off the road that connects Duke's East and West Campuses. They were surrounded by their colleagues—dressed in military fatigues, black boots, bulletproof vests, and berets with the group's logo on them—and they huddled together for thirty minutes or so. News helicopters hovered overhead and nearby was a scrum of about forty members of the press, Duke administrators, employees, and police officers. Only a few students were hanging around the scene, as most of them were taking exams. At 10:35, the group went to the traffic circle, one branch of which leads off to Chapel Drive, the elegant street that leads to the Chapel and West Campus. They shouted repeatedly, "What do we want? Justice. When do want it? Now."

For the next hour, the group presented its list of eight demands, among them that both Seligmann and Finnerty be sent to prison and that all of the students who were at the March 13 party be expelled from Duke. The New Panthers also wanted 610 North Buchanan to be converted into a rape crisis center. They called "for an end to sexual abuse and rape in general" and described Duke's history as one "riddled with slavery and racist oppression." Malik Zulu Shabazz, the group's national chairman, also introduced his "allies," including Victoria Peterson and Jackie Wagstaff, both of whom had been at the NCCU forum a few weeks earlier, and an NCCU student, "Sister Sasha." "The number one priority is the survivor," Sasha said. "We have to remember that a rape incident occurred."

At 11:30, the group ended its press conference and started moving toward the bluestone gate leading to West Campus. "We would like to humbly, silently walk through this campus," Shabazz said. "My understanding is that Duke has an open campus." But the New Panthers were met by a wall of Duke administrators and campus police officers and were denied entry. Robert Dean, the head of the Duke police, told Shabazz that it was exam week and that the students "were stressed-out enough" by that and didn't need the additional stress of seeing the New Panthers marching around campus. Being barred from West Campus prompted Peterson to proclaim, "The president of Duke University is denying the African-American community the opportunity to walk through campus. We want to the talk to the president. . . . He is no longer welcome at NCCU."

After being turned away, the group then marched past Ninth Street to 610 North Buchanan while chanting "Shame on Duke," "No Justice, No Peace," and "Black Power." In front of the house, Shabazz reiterated his call for Seligmann and Finnerty—who never lived there, of course—to serve time in prison. "This is a hate crime, and we want a conviction," he said. "We are mad and fired up. We demand justice, and we will have justice, one way or the other." Then Shabazz got more personal. "You are the shame of the Planet Earth today," he said of the lacrosse players. "You are a shame to yourselves and you are a shame to the University. You want peace for your final exams. You want to take your exams in peace. You have disturbed the peace of our community, and you have violated the peace of the system. Leave the system alone." He added that black women need to be protected from a white-male-dominated system of supremacy. The protest ended as it had begun, with a communal prayer, this time on the front lawn of 610 North Buchanan.

While the New Panthers were bringing their message of support for Mangum to the scene of the crime, Himan met with Mangum's then-current boyfriend, Matthew Murchison. Murchison said he had been dating Mangum for six years after meeting her at the manufacturing plant in Research Triangle Park. He told Himan he did not know much about what had happened to Mangum on the night of March 13 but that "it made him upset" to discuss it and also made Mangum "upset" when the topic was mentioned. He said he knew she had been dancing at various nightclubs in the area, including Satin Dolls in Garner, Platinum Pleasures in Hillsborough, and Diamond Girls in Durham. Murchison, who had a criminal record for repeated instances of drunk driving and had spent eighteen months in jail, told Himan that Mangum liked to drink beer "now and then" but he had not known her to use drugs. He said Mangum was upset by her portrayal in the media, specifically her constant desire for sex and the suggestion that she and Roberts "were working together to set the [lacrosse] guys up." As for the incident years earlier in Creedmoor, Murchison said he was aware of it, through his conversations with Mangum and because she had mentioned it in her diary, which he had come across one day and read. He offered to get the diary for Himan, but returned after a few minutes and said he could not find it. Murchison agreed to give the Durham police a DNA sample and was taken to the lab on Broadway. Afterward, Himan gave Murchison a ride back to Mangum's home at 909 DaVinci.

At 6 p.m., Shabazz, the New Panthers, and their followers held a town meeting at the St. Joseph's African Methodist Episcopal Church in Durham. They said they had come to Durham "to share their revolutionary message" and to defend Crystal Mangum. They criticized the way the media portrayed the New Panthers as violent thugs. "All they will tell you is that we're carrying guns," Minister Hashim Nzinga said. Added Yusuf Shabazz, a New Panthers spokesman, the organization would "use violent means" to increase the power of blacks and to create "New Africa," an independent territory. "Anytime a white man grabs a rifle and stands up for his liberty and his wife, he's a hero," Shabazz said. "We'll kill everybody in a household, we'll kill everybody on our block." He called whites "our four-hundred-year-old oppressors" and "devils" and demanded the release of every black prisoner from prison and an exemption from income taxes for black people.

Malik Shabazz said he had "talked at length" with Nifong by telephone. "I asked him to consider not coming," Nifong told the *News & Observer*, "because I didn't feel like his presence here would do anything but aggravate the situation." But Shabazz ignored Nifong's request and as he was leaving Durham he pledged to return until justice was served. "We'll be back," he said.

The *New York Times* decided to shine the spotlight that day on NCCU, Sister Sasha's school. "North Carolina Central University does not have a lacrosse team," William Yardley reported. "Students often cannot check out books from the main library, which is being renovated after a mold infestation. The business school is fighting to regain accreditation. Sixty percent of the students receive need-based financial aid. Eighty-one percent are black. Only 28 percent graduate after four years. Just three miles from Duke University and its master-planned marriage of Gothic elegance and academic excellence, North

Carolina Central, a rambling redbrick, historically black institution, is across the tracks, across the highway, across an immeasurable cultural divide. Or so goes the armchair anthropology."

But, the *Times* reported, the conventional wisdom also missed some significant changes under way at NCCU. Since 2000, the state of North Carolina had spent $121 million at NCCU for new science and law buildings—Governor Mike Easley, who was white, had graduated from NCCU Law School in 1975—and for new dormitories. Enrollment was 8,200 students, up from 5,400 in 2001, and NCCU was competing aggressively for minority students, even against Duke. "The story line of race, class, and cultural divide in the South that has framed the case may be compelling, but it is simplistic," Yardley continued. "So while Duke is under intense national scrutiny, North Carolina Central is seeking a delicate balance of supporting the accuser, improving its relationship with Duke and continuing to raise its profile."

On the other hand, there were differences between the two schools: NCCU's endowment was $22 million, compared to $3.8 billion for Duke; some 90 percent of NCCU students were born in North Carolina, compared to 13 percent at Duke; and the cost of one year at Duke was approaching $41,000, while at NCCU the cost for an in-state student was closer to $8,000 annually. "America by and large doesn't know who we are," NCCU chancellor Ammons told the *Times*. "They see this incident, but they don't know that we're one of the fastest-growing institutions in the state, with an historic law school, the first public liberal arts college for African-Americans, at the center of a biotechnology initiative that's going to change the economy."

NCCU began in 1910—as the National Religious Training School and Chautauqua—as a private school to prepare blacks for leadership roles in Durham. Fifteen years later, it became America's first state-supported liberal arts college for blacks. Even though blacks could not attend Duke until 1963, there was always a symbiotic—some would say exploitative—relationship between the Duke family's tobacco fortune, with its roots in Durham, and the surrounding community of blacks in Durham, many of whom worked in both the tobacco fields and Durham's cigarette factories. As Durham prospered—largely because of tobacco—more blacks moved into the middle class and enrolled at NCCU. There was a thriving community of black businessmen in Durham, too. In 1898, a group of them founded North Carolina Mutual—its tower is still a prominent feature of the Durham skyline—one of the largest and most successful minority-owned businesses in the country. In 1907, James Shepherd and some colleagues founded Mechanics and Farmers Bank in Durham; Shepherd then started NCCU.

On the same day of the New Panthers protest, May 1, the day before Nifong's primary vote, the defense attorneys for the two indicted players filed a motion to remove Nifong and the other prosecutors in his office from the case, claiming that his desire to be elected district attorney had clouded his judgment about whether to pursue charges against the Duke players. They asked that a special prosecutor be appointed. Seligmann's attorneys wrote that Nifong was "willing to prostitute the truth and fair prosecution for his personal gain in his hotly contested election" and "in his zeal to make national headlines and win a hotly contested primary." In an eighty-nine-page filing—which included cell phone records and photographs of Seligmann's actions on the night of March 13—the lawyers also accused Nifong of ignoring Seligmann's alibi, of helping to design an "illegal" identification procedure that encouraged Mangum to choose a Duke lacrosse player as her attacker, and of making inflammatory statements to the media that were designed to help his election chances at the expense of Seligmann and his reputation.

Nifong "ignored the actual facts" of the case, the lawyers wrote. "All this evidence shows that DA Nifong's rape case was a post-hoc shakedown." The Durham police guidelines require that someone not involved in a case run the lineup, and that for each suspect photograph there should be five "filler" photographs of people not involved in the case. Since that had not happened, Seligmann's lawyers wrote, "the lineup procedure was nothing more than a multiple choice test with no wrong answers, a pin-the-tail-on-the-donkey identification." The lawyers also requested that Seligmann's bail be reduced to $40,000, from $400,000, since the person who loaned Seligmann the money was "being deprived of the imputed income" from the use of the money while it was being kept in Durham. They also wanted half of the DNA samples that Seligmann provided to the Durham police so that they could do their own, independent test of the evidence and they wanted Mangum's identification of Seligmann thrown out as evidence.

For his part, Nifong dismissed the effort to get him removed. "Some people try cases in the media by filing motions that contain outrageous and false statements in the hopes that the media will report on those false statements as if they were true," he told the *News & Observer*. "If I were him, I wouldn't want to be trying a case against me, either. . . . The best comment I ever heard about Kirk [Osborn] was he was the best-dressed public defender in North Carolina." Nifong hadn't fully absorbed the contents of the filing by the time he spoke to the paper. "I just don't have as much time for reading fiction right now," he said.

Durham attorneys, who knew Nifong well, agreed that he was not one to politicize a case. "It's just outrageous and unfortunate that things have been spun this way," explained Sharon Thompson, a Durham attorney. "There may have been a few missteps, but Mike is not the kind of person where his whole motivation is to benefit his campaign." Brian Aus, another Durham attorney, said Nifong had shied away from politics during his long tenure in the District

Attorney's Office. "He is not a political figure," Aus said. "The only reason I can see that he's politically involved these days is because the governor appointed him to the job, and now he wants to keep it. But I don't believe there was any political idea regarding these indictments."

Other Durham attorneys—among them Bill Thomas and Butch Williams—had donated to Nifong's election campaign and supported him politically, even though they had clients on the Duke lacrosse team. "I have a campaign sign of his in my front yard," said Kerry Sutton, who was representing one of the players. "[But] I think he's made some decisions I would not have."

Part of the problem for Nifong, of course, was that new information about Seligmann and Finnerty—especially Seligmann's possible alibi—had come to light after the grand jury indictments. "And so a case that from the start had been ghastly to ponder became even messier," *Time* magazine observed on May 1. "The defense lawyers criticized Nifong for bringing the case before he did his homework. They accused him of trying the case in the media. And they whispered that politics was involved. Nifong, they said, was rushing things to show some progress on a case that is racially charged—black victim, white suspects—before May 2, when he seeks election against two Democratic rivals in a county that is 50 percent white and 40 percent African-American." But, one attorney friendly with Nifong said, "he is convinced from the evidence that he has made the right choices." And *Time* added, "Nifong has a reputation for fair play. He is a Little League umpire on the weekends, and even lawyers who may face him in this case say he is competitive but uncommonly decent in court. At a candidates' debate, he admitted it was unlikely that many in the audience had ever heard of him before a few weeks ago. They certainly have now." Like it or not, the May 2 vote had become a referendum not only on Nifong—a once obscure lifer in the Durham District Attorney's Office—but also on his handling of the lacrosse case, one of the more divisive prosecutions in the history of Durham County.

On primary day, May 2, with 45.2 percent of the vote, Nifong won a narrow victory over Freda Black, who had garnered 41.5 percent. (Bishop took the balance.) Nifong won 44 percent of the black vote, far more than Bishop, with 31 percent, and Black, with 25 percent. "It was obvious to me early on that we did really well in the predominantly black precincts," Nifong explained. "I would go through the black community before the election; people would stop me and say, 'Keep your head up. We're with you.' . . . But [the lacrosse case] cut both ways. It hurt me among conservative white voters. I expect if this issue had never come up, we would have ended up with the same outcome." Nifong had spent a mere $16,000 on the race—Black spent about $45,000—but his name recognition was nearly ubiquitous in Durham County, thanks to his prosecution of the lacrosse case. Although Nifong still had to await the outcome of the

November general election, the lack of a Republican Party challenger for the position made him the de facto winner of his own four-year term.

Nifong's election victory had one decisive outcome: the prosecution of the case against the two, and possibly three, Duke lacrosse players would continue for the foreseeable future.

Meanwhile, the soul-searching continued. For some, including professors and lacrosse coaches, the incident at Duke had provided a "teachable moment." Mark Anthony Neal, an associate professor of African-American studies at Duke who taught several lacrosse players, said, "It's a real-world example that everybody had to respond to. The kind of explosion you saw among students on the Duke campus to use the issue to talk about issues of sexuality and violence shows that these issues are right there at the surface for these kids." His class, on hip-hop culture, raised questions about misogyny, sexual violence, and the portrayal of black women. "A black woman's body circulates in popular culture in a different way because of hip-hop," he explained. "What role does popular culture play in sexualizing these women in certain ways that make the attitudes easier to have?" Jim Kirkley, the lacrosse coach at Riverside High, in Durham, used the incident to have a frank discussion with his players. "Look," he told them, "you have to have a broader picture of the possible implications of all your actions." But that message could be diluted quickly. "Unfortunately, kids are kids," he continued. "Kids rarely think it applies to them or that they're going to be the one in the car accident or the one getting caught."

Dom Starsia, the lacrosse coach at the University of Virginia, which had won the 2006 ACC lacrosse tournament with Duke not participating, said, "There's not a day that goes by that we don't talk about it. It feels like we're under a bright light. The whole 'play hard, party hard' mentality may not cut it anymore. They have to be mindful of their behavior twenty-four hours a day.... For all of us, it's just a new reckoning that we all have to be aware of." For John Danowski, the Hofstra coach and father of Duke's Matt Danowski, the incident made him realize how fragile the lacrosse ecosystem could be. "Every educator or coach realizes we're one phone call away from an eighteen-year-old making a bad decision and putting you in a position you can't get out of."

On May 3, Brodhead met with the lacrosse team. He gave them very little notice, perhaps out of fear that their parents would assemble quickly and chastise him. He remained unsympathetic. He recalled later what he told the players: "I said why I think it's inappropriate for boys in their late teens to have enough money to make a woman come take her clothes off and dance around for your pleasure. You wouldn't have your sister do it; you wouldn't have your girlfriend do it. It's demeaning. That's the source of the ill. Is this the worst thing in the history of the world? I know it's not, and so do you. But it doesn't mean I find it acceptable. When I was asked about this by the team, and a person there brought up the idea of the twenty-two other strippers [at Duke parties], I said, 'You can take a stick of dynamite into a house twenty-one times, but the time it blows up is the time you realize that wasn't such a good idea.'"

The initial failure of the Duke administration to recognize the severity of the allegations coming from the house at 610 North Buchanan was the focus of the third report, issued May 8, from William Bowen, the former president of Princeton University and of the Andrew Mellon Foundation, and Julius Chambers, the former chancellor of NCCU. It was far more pointed than the two previous internal reports. This might have been expected given that Bowen and Chambers were outsiders to the Duke community, although still in the higher-education club. "The Duke administration was much too slow in understanding and addressing the serious and highly sensitive issues raised by the rape allegations and associated events," the report concluded. "As one person put it, there was 'radio silence' for too long." The report noted that while "some members" of the Duke community interpreted the slow response as indifference or as a strand of a cover-up, Bowen and Chambers disagreed, especially after Brodhead's "widely applauded" April 5 letter to the community.

Bowen and Chambers also faulted the Duke athletic department, first for allowing the behavior of the lacrosse players to get increasingly out of hand, and second for underestimating the gravity of the accusations. They suggested that "clearer and firmer actions in earlier days" by Pressler and Aleva about the team's obvious pattern of rule violations "might well have reduced the likelihood that the party of March 13–14 would have unfolded as it did." The report cited Peter Wood, by name this time, and his 2004 warning as one example of how Duke officials could have heeded a call to take action before it was too late. The report also found Pressler's comment that his team was "focused on beating Georgetown," notwithstanding the "distractions" caused by the incident, to be "obtuse, at the minimum." Pressler's decision to keep practicing, which had Brodhead's support, "also angered some people," as did Aleva's comment that the lacrosse players were "wonderful young men" despite their string of infractions. "Another aggravation" came from the "widely noted presence of lacrosse players in a bar, cheering for Duke lacrosse." There was the sense that "increasingly, the lacrosse team was seen by at least some part of the Duke/Durham community as a manifestation of a white, elitist, arrogant subculture that was both indulged and self-indulgent. In the eyes of some faculty and others concerned with the intersecting issues of race, class, gender, and respect for other people, the athletic department, and Duke more generally, just didn't 'get it.'"

The Bowen report also sought to assess Brodhead's handling of the crisis. It noted that the first official statement from Duke, on March 24, came not from Brodhead but rather from Burness, the head of the school's communications office. "On the one hand," the report observed, "President Brodhead knew little at this time, and it may have seemed better for him to wait a bit to speak out; on the other hand, this handling of the first official Duke pronouncement, coming ten days after the incident, had the unfortunate effect of reinforcing the view of some that Duke cared mainly about PR matters and less about the core issues of values and behavior—and was trying to cover up the situation."

To Brodhead's credit, the report continued, once he did have many of the facts at hand, he acted decisively. He created his Crisis Management Team on March 25, a Saturday, and met with the group that day and often thereafter. He also made a forceful statement condemning what clearly did happen in the house on the night of March 13—underage drinking and the allegations of rape—while also walking the proverbial legal fine line about whether in fact a rape, sexual assault, and kidnapping had occurred.

The report made eight fairly obvious recommendations. There was one suggestion, though, that could have quickly upset the balance of power at Duke had it been taken seriously. "Take a large step back," Bowen and Chambers suggested, "and think freshly about the role of athletics, and especially the aggressive recruitment of scholarship athletes, in the context of Duke's academic mission; and perhaps provide regional if not national leadership in addressing questions that are by no means peculiar to Duke."

Brodhead said he read the report "with considerable interest," especially the report's "analysis of why the administration did not respond more swiftly to the incident and of how our work was complicated by the sporadic fashion in which information came to light. . . . The situation was one of rapidly changing circumstances and considerable uncertainty—indeed the events at the heart of the case remain in dispute to this day." He told the *News & Observer*, "All of us wish we had gotten onto this story earlier" and that he appreciated the "candid criticism" the report delivered.

The future of the lacrosse program was also left unclear, despite Coleman's recommendation. The previous week Brodhead had met with the lacrosse team for more than an hour. He reported to the media that he had told the team that, to continue at Duke, it would have to change. "I spoke very earnestly with them," he said. "I told them, if we resume, it will be on a very different basis than in the past. We are not going to tolerate the kind of behavior and we are not going to continue the culture." As for whether Alleva, the athletic director, would be held responsible, Brodhead said, "Certainly he does bear a measure of it, but not exclusively. In any university, there is a chain of command as well as a chain of responsibility."

Since the Bowen report made reference to Officer Day's early morning March 14 police report about the alleged incident at 610 North Buchanan, Duke made the unusual decision to release it publicly after first refusing to give it to reporters. This was the one-page report where Day noted that Mangum was black—the public document blacked out her name and the names of the residents of the off-campus house—and that she "claimed that she was raped by approximately twenty white males at 610 N. Buchanan Street" after having been "picked up" at the Kroger supermarket. But, Officer Day noted in the same brief report, "the victim changed her story several times, and eventually Durham police stated that charges would not exceed misdemeanor simple assault against the occupants of 610 N. Buchanan." He also noted that the Duke police had not filed any charges and that "no suspects have been identified at this time." Burness said the decision to release Day's report came after Duke had received numerous media requests for it. The release added—once again—to the growing confusion about what had really happened at 610 North Buchanan in the early morning hours of March 14 and whether the justice system in Durham would ever be able to figure it out.

Patrick Baker, the Durham city manager, did not react well to the release of Officer Day's statement and its inclusion in Bowen's report. He told the *News & Observer* that Day's observations were based on "what a campus police officer overheard a low-ranking Durham officer say on a cell phone" during the early morning hours of March 14 on a loading dock at Duke Hospital. "Their officer did not speak to our officer," Baker said. "He appears to have overheard half a conversation and didn't follow up." Baker "bristled at the implication that city officers did not believe" Mangum, the paper reported, and "classified" the matter as a sexual assault some thirty minutes after Mangum arrived at Duke Hospital. "Any assertion that the Durham Police Department didn't take this case seriously or indicated that it would blow over is completely contradicted by the facts and our actions." He added that he had never heard that Mangum had initially claimed to have been raped by twenty men or that she had changed her story. "I have no idea where that came from," he said. "I've had a lot of conversations with the investigators in this case and with officials at Duke, and at no time did anyone indicate the accuser changed her story. If that were true, I'm sure someone would have mentioned it to me." Baker was also upset that neither he nor any Durham police officials were interviewed for the Bowen report. "I find it odd [that] the state of mind of the whole Police Department appears to have been accepted with no effort to verify that was indeed the case." At a press conference, Duke police confirmed that Officer Day had merely reported what he overheard during the early morning hours of March 14, as opposed to being a direct participant in the investigation itself.

Meanwhile, some additional justice was meted out to David Evans, the twenty-three-year-old lacrosse team cocaptain. District court judge Ann McKown ruled on May 8 that Evans's participation in the March 13 party at his house had violated the terms of the deferred prosecution agreement he had been given as a result of an August 2005 violation of having an "open container" in the passenger seat of a car and a January 10 noise violation citation at 610 North Buchanan. The ruling meant that not only would charges proceed against Evans but they would also be reinstated for six other lacrosse players, also at the March 13 party, who had been charged previously and received deferred prosecution agreements. At the court hearing, Evans's attorney, Brad Bannon, argued that his client was being penalized because of his cooperation with police following the March 13 party. "It was Mr. Evans's good conduct in cooperation with police investigators that put us here today," he said. "During that entire deferred period he has done what he was asked to do. . . . Everything else, other than the party on March 14, has demonstrated absolutely good conduct." Not only did Judge McKown not buy Bannon's argument—she ordered Evans to pay a $100 fine for the open container violation and scheduled a May 23 hearing for the noise violation—but neither did Ashley Cannon, an assistant to Nifong. "The state gives deferred prosecutions as a favor to defendants who did not have records," she said. "We have substantial knowledge that on the night of March 13 there was not good conduct going on at the defendant's house."

The media could not get enough of even the tiniest scraps of the lacrosse story, a point noted by a columnist for the *Guardian*, a British newspaper. "Sure Iran and Iraq are important," David Epstein wrote, "but nothing seems to have captivated the American public lately quite like . . . drumroll, please . . . the Duke university lacrosse team." What Epstein couldn't quite figure out, though, was that despite the case seeming increasingly "flimsy" and the DNA evidence being negative, the case roared forward. Ruth Sheehan, the *News & Observer* columnist who had previously skewered the lacrosse players for the alleged "wall of silence" they had created, now seemed struck by the case's relentless ambiguity. "We want it to be neat," she wrote in May. "We want it tied up in a tidy package that tells the world, yes, this is what happened, and this is what it means. But life is seldom that cooperative." She wondered how to make sense of the cast of characters. Was Nifong "the sacrificial lamb in the case," the "grandstanding media hog" or proof that "any publicity is good publicity"? What could have possessed the "graduates of all-boys Catholic high schools" to hire strippers, to write a "sadistic e-mail (as a joke?)" and be accused of rape? And what about Mangum? Her story would have been easier to digest if she had simply been a single mother trying to put herself through college instead of an "exotic dancer who filed rape charges against three other men ten years ago." Sheehan continued, "We want the woman to be honorable, even though she worked for an escort service—or a hustler. We want her to have told a consistent story—even though some victims of rape do and say things that do not help their cases. We want Duke officials to be part of a conspiracy to cover up bad actions by athletes—or responsive leaders willing to make tough choices under extreme pressure. . . . We want this rape never to have occurred. And yet we want this woman not to have lied. . . . We want black and white in a universe of gray."

• • •

John Feinstein, the Duke alumnus and author of numerous books about college sports, unleashed a blistering attack on the Duke administration—especially Joe Alleva and Tallman Trask—for allowing the festering wound that was Duke lacrosse to go untreated for years despite knowledge of ongoing disreputable behavior. He started his diatribe by recalling the laments of other basketball coaches in the ACC who were jealous of Coach K. "As one coach eloquently puts it, 'the sainted fucking Coach K,'" Feinstein wrote. "Well, the boys needn't worry about Duke's pristine image anymore. It has been shattered, not by Krzyzewski or his high-profile basketball team, but by the school's lacrosse team, a group known before the last six weeks only by friends, family, and those who follow the niche sport (albeit a growing one) that is lacrosse. Now the entire world knows Duke has a lacrosse team. Specifically, the world knows it has a lacrosse team that has been guilty of immature, idiotic, out-of-control behavior for years. . . . Duke's handling of this disaster has been disastrous."

The fight for Duke's soul continued in a lengthy article, titled "A Spring of Sorrows," in—of all places—the *Duke* alumni magazine, which, under the direction of longtime leader Robert Bliwise, had rarely shied away from controversies on campus but also walked a fine line, as it is under the auspices of the Duke alumni association, and therefore beholden to the university's administration. After noting that Brodhead had created five committees to ponder what had happened and why, Bliwise wrote, "Controversy, not committee studies, turned the media focus on Duke. On a single day in late March, more than 550 news outlets featured some version of the story. . . . By mid-April, a Web search produced 2.3 million hits under the heading 'Duke Lacrosse Scandal.' There was nonstop coverage on television and radio networks and in newspapers and news magazines around the country . . ." And it was inevitable, Bliwise continued, that such overwhelming coverage would focus on the obvious dichotomy between black and white, rich and poor, privilege and striving, while overlooking "the deep complexities of reality."

Bliwise's contribution to attempting to reduce the "hysteria" was to try to step back from it and seek some perspective. He spoke with David Folkenflik, the media correspondent for National Public Radio who had previously covered Duke at the Durham paper. He had written about Duke's "work hard, play hard" ethic and wondered whether it was "undermining" the school's "intellectual life" as it continued to try to ascend into the very top rung of the nation's elite universities. "Duke is a place of privilege," Folkenflik said. "There are people in Durham who do not make as much money as it costs to attend Duke for one year. That's true of every major private university and its community. But Duke is not every university."

Folkenflik noted that Duke, like Stanford, was trying to do something very few universities in the country attempt: to marry top-notch academics with top-rated athletics. "Duke has not been shy about trading on that image," he said. Added Orin Starn, a cultural anthropology professor, Duke "wants to be absolutely committed to a first-rate intellectual climate, committed to students who have an array of engagement in campus life. Duke has struck this very uneasy balance between, on the one hand, wanting to be this top-notch university, and on the other hand wanting to be a big-time sports school." Starn was, of course, reiterating many of the points that Peter Wood had made years before. Wood told Bliwise that no one wanted Duke to become "a pretty good [academic] institution with really good sports teams. That would make us 'Cruise Ship Duke'—a fun place to be, a lot of sports, a lot of sex, a lot of movies, a lot of games—where people earn pretty good grades for doing pretty good work. We should be shooting much higher than that." Rather, he said, Duke needed to keep its focus on academics. "Years ago, a player told me that he had been instructed not to get too interested in his classes," Wood recalled. "Surely that's an exception, but I was amazed. At a strong university, academic work comes first. Duke has a chance to revive the real meaning of 'scholar-athlete.' I hope we can do it."

Bliwise spoke to Houston Baker, the Duke English professor whose "blistering" open letter in March had set the campus on a knife's edge. Had his ardor cooled in the intervening weeks? "Many of us are afraid," he said. "A great many of us are feeling helpless at this point. 'Traumatized' is not really too strong a word. I think the reputation of the university has been injured forever by this event. And I think that didn't have to be." After recounting his own experiences as a black student at Duke—including having to listen to a supposed joke on campus: "How do you stop black people from hanging out in your backyard? Hang one in the front"—Nick Shungu, a senior and a campus leader, was optimistic that the incident, however it turned out, would benefit Duke and Durham in the long term. "[This is] a period of empowerment," he told Bliwise. "This is really the first time I can remember that students are mobilized around an issue."

On May 8, Himan spoke with Nifong's investigator Linwood Wilson, who told Himan he had found "an outstanding warrant" against Mostafa, the Durham cabdriver, "that needed to be served." Himan offered to "take care" of finding and arresting Mostafa. The cabdriver, of course, had provided an exculpatory affidavit about Seligmann's whereabouts during the early morning hours of March 14; was arresting him a form of prosecutorial intimidation? On May 10, after first checking with Gottlieb—who told Himan to "do what the district attorney wants done"—Himan and a fellow officer, R. D. Clayton, set about arresting Mostafa on a "misdemeanor larceny" charge that was more than two years old. Himan and Mostafa met by Mostafa's apartment building. Himan told Mostafa, "We had a little problem that we needed to take care of" and then informed the cabdriver of the outstanding warrant for his arrest. Understandably, Mostafa wanted to know why he was being arrested, and Himan told him a security guard had accused him of stealing "five pocketbooks" from "Hecht's Department Store." Officer Clayton then arrested Mostafa, handcuffed him, and put him in the back of the police car. "The detective asked if I had anything new to say about the lacrosse case," Mostafa said later. "When I said no, they took me to the magistrate."

On September 2, 2003, Mostafa had picked up Lisa Faye Hawkins and her daughter from their home and taken them to the Northgate Mall in Durham. He waited while they shopped, and then drove them back home. A few days later, Mostafa got a call from a Hecht's security guard who said Hawkins had stolen the purses before getting back into the taxi. Mostafa cooperated with the security officer by sharing with him Hawkins's address and giving him a copy of his driver's license. "I am not responsible for what she did inside the store," he said. "I am just a taxi driver." Three months later, Hawkins pleaded guilty to larceny. Mostafa never heard another thing about the incident until Clayton arrested him. He spent five hours at the Durham County Jail until a friend bailed him out—to the tune of $700—and he was released. One of Seligmann's attorneys, Ernest Conner, said of Mostafa's arrest, "It appears to me they are trying to pressure a witness who supports our defendant's rock-solid alibi." He added that it was "highly unusual" for the police to arrest someone on a misdemeanor charge more than two years after the crime, especially when the actual perpetrator of the crime had already pleaded guilty.

But Nifong, in an increasingly rare public statement and still glowing from his election victory, said the police had "no ulterior motive" when they arrested Mostafa. "It came up in the context of we were collecting information on potential witnesses," he explained. He said the idea that the police tried to get more information from Mostafa about the lacrosse case before taking him to see the magistrate was preposterous. "I would be very surprised if the officers even thought about using that as an opportunity to ask him something," Nifong said. On August 30, a Durham judge found Mostafa not guilty of the abetting-a-shoplifting charge.

On May 11, word began leaking to the *Durham Herald-Sun* about the results of DNA Security's new round of DNA testing; it appeared the leak originated with either the Durham police or a prosecution eager to put the best spin possible on news that appeared not to help their case. "Tissue found under the fingernail of an exotic dancer who claimed she was raped at a Duke University lacrosse party may match a player who was there," the paper reported, according to its "well-placed" sources. "Scientists concluded it came from the same genetic pool and was 'consistent' with the bodily makeup of one of the forty-six lacrosse players who gave DNA samples for testing." The paper reported that the sample in question also "ruled out a possible match" with the other forty-five lacrosse players on the Duke team. "If accurate," the paper continued, "the fingernail tissue match would offer the first DNA evidence potentially linking the dancer and an alleged attacker" and "was consistent" with the "DNA pattern" of an unknown "third man" at the party—David Evans—whom Mangum had previously identified with "90 percent certainty." The paper also revealed that "a male pubic hair" from a white man "had been linked to the case" but since the hair "lacked a root, no identifiable DNA was obtained from it." Still, there remained the possibility the hair could be tested—using the mitochondrial DNA method—and that the DNA that it matched could have a high—but not a certain—degree of accuracy.

Brian Meehan, the author of the DNA report, had tested the "DNA from crime scene fingernail"—the fake nails that flew off Mangum's fingers during the alleged attack in the bathroom at 610 North Buchanan and that police investigators later recovered. Meehan had then compared it to the DNA of the various white Duke lacrosse players. He found possible DNA matches from both David Evans, the five-foot-ten-inch, 190-pound senior cocaptain from Bethesda, Maryland, who lived at 610 North Buchanan, and from Kevin Coleman, a six-foot-two-inch, 185-pound senior from Ridgewood, New Jersey. Both Evans and Coleman had attended private schools before enrolling at Duke: Evans was a graduate of the Landon School, in Maryland; Coleman had graduated from Delbarton, the same New Jersey private Catholic school that Seligmann and McFadyen had attended. According to Meehan's report, neither Evans nor Coleman could be "excluded as a contributor to this mixture profile." The DNA match was especially close for Coleman—according to Meehan, 99.99 percent of people other than Coleman would be excluded—while the match with Evans was less certain—only 98 percent of other people could be excluded. Curiously, Kevin Coleman's name had not previously surfaced as one of Mangum's potential attackers, probably because during Mangum's April 4 photo identification session, she said she had no recollection of seeing him during the evening or during the attack. (It turned out Coleman's DNA was found on one of Mangum's *unpainted* fake fingernails that was in her makeup kit, and it was not considered as evidence in the attack, since Mangum had been wearing *painted* fingernails.)

Meehan also did a DNA test on a "sperm fraction" found on a swab from Mangum's vagina and discovered that it did not match any of the DNA from the lacrosse players. Rather, the DNA found in her vagina matched nearly perfectly the DNA of Matthew Murchison, Mangum's longtime boyfriend, whom Mangum had told Durham police early on in the investigation she had had sex with in the days before the March 13 party. Although Meehan's report mentioned that DNA samples had been taken from Seligmann and Finnerty, the report made no mention of any match between their DNA and that found in, on or around Mangum.

But Meehan's ten-page report to Nifong turned out not to be the whole story. It "used a limited reporting formula," according to defense attorneys—allegedly agreed to by Nifong and Meehan, among others—that was designed only to report the matches between Mangum and Murchison on the one hand, and between Mangum and the forty-six white Duke lacrosse players tested on the other hand. "In other words, it intentionally omitted any reference to the four unidentified males whose DNA had been found in Mangum's panties and swabs," the defense claimed. "By deliberately suppressing some of the results of the DNA testing, this report violated industry standards, North Carolina law, and FBI standards." The DNA found on or in Mangum from the "four unidentified males"—but was not mentioned in Meehan's report—"corroborated witness statements that Mangum was having intercourse with multiple different partners in the hours and days before she arrived at 610 N. Buchanan," according to the defense.

Nifong shared Meehan's report with defense attorneys at around 5 p.m. on Friday. Evans's attorney, Joe Cheshire, phoned Nifong, hoping to speak with the district attorney about the results. He was told Nifong was in the office "stuffing envelopes," but Nifong did not return the call. After quickly digesting Meehan's report, Cheshire and Wade Smith, Finnerty's attorney, held a twenty-minute press conference in what looked like a conference room at one of their law firms. Cheshire said, "There is no conclusive match . . . that ties any of these young men to this woman who has made these false accusations. There is no conclusive match of DNA." As for the DNA on Mangum's vaginal swab, he said, "In other words, it appears this woman had sex with a male. It also appears with certainty it wasn't a Duke lacrosse player."

For his part, Smith wanted to make sure the media comprehended what was not in Meehan's report. "I just want to point out that two of these athletes have been indicted, processed, and faced the court and have dealt with the indictment now for some period of time," he said. "The first DNA report that came back indicated not a smattering, not a smattering, not a spiderweb of an indication that there was any DNA from these boys anywhere around this woman. Now this is the second time this has happened."

Cheshire, who represented Evans and often wore a bow tie, said there were "no conclusive DNA results" in Meehan's report and that "one of the things that really sticks in my craw is that things are reported as being as what they are not. . . . There is no certainty in these reports." But he conceded, there was some ambiguity. "Does it absolutely exclude all of the Duke lacrosse players with absolute certainty from this one fingernail? No. Does it say that any of the Duke lacrosse players' DNA is conclusively on this fingernail? No." But, he continued, "there was no rape in that house" and the "fingernail . . . means absolutely nothing. It's almost laughable what it means and how the district attorney, by leaking this, allowed someone to think that that fingernail has any import at all to this case. Let's wait and see on the fingernails and see if they match up to the way she describes that attack that took place. Let's concentrate on these types of things, not whether or not there can be some genetic material which could be transferred—as any expert can tell you—from swabs or anything else in a trash can or any other plastic object."

After explaining that someone had e-mailed him the message "You really are a fancy little dandy in that bow tie, aren't you?" Cheshire revealed that Meehan's report mentioned "one or two non-indicted lacrosse players" but would not confirm that one of them was his client, Evans, even though he knew. He also reiterated Smith's point that there was "nothing in the report that ties Reade Seligmann or Collin Finnerty to this woman or this place in any way, shape, or form." The last word belonged to Wade Smith, who said he was considering thanking Nifong for commissioning the DNA tests. "We could compliment Mr. Nifong," he said. "We could say, 'Thank you very much, Mr. Nifong, that Collin Finnerty had no contact with this woman.' That's two tests now. You could think of it in that way. For all the players, we would submit that this DNA test was a complete failure if the prosecutor intended to find something that was useful. But the guys who have been indicted already and endured that, their names are not mentioned in any way, and so they could say, 'Mr. Nifong, thank you for being doubly certain that there was absolutely nothing about us in these reports . . .'"

Not surprisingly, the newspaper accounts of the second set of DNA results, as filtered through the commentary of the defense attorneys, were sympathetic to the lacrosse players. The *Herald-Sun* reported Cheshire's assertion that of course Mangum's fingernails had the DNA of the home's residents on them because they placed the plastic fingernails in the trash when they cleaned up from the party. It would have been more surprising if their DNA were not found on the fingernails, Cheshire said. More important still, Cheshire continued, was that despite knowing the police were investigating an alleged rape, the players gave the plastic fingernails to the police as they were collecting evidence. "Is that consistent with someone who knowingly committed a rape?" he asked.

The Durham paper also reported that defense attorneys questioned one of Nifong's ongoing premises for continuing the prosecution of the case: to wit, that Tara Levicy, the SANE nurse, had discovered "vaginal trauma" in Mangum. "But after receiving the new test results Friday," the paper reported, "defense lawyers said the trauma presumably was inflicted by whoever left semen or other bodily fluids in the woman's body—not by any lacrosse players."

On the same day the second set of DNA results came back from Burlington, another opinion piece by Duke history professor William Chafe, a former dean of the faculty of arts and sciences, appeared in the *Chronicle of Higher Education*. Chafe described the interaction he had had with a few of his students, in his seminar on twentieth-century social movements, during a dinner held at his house at the end of the spring semester. "What should I do to learn how to relate to women and racial minorities without using all the assumptions I have grown up with about people who are different from me?" a white male asked. Another woman student remarked, "You know, we are all responsible for this, because we have not held accountable those who have committed sexual assaults on our campus." A third student, a freshman woman, wondered why, the previous fall, she had not spoken up when she walked into a frat party and saw a black female stripper performing and being taunted with racial epithets. "Why had she not done something about that earlier?" Chafe quoted her wondering. He wrote that these students were searching for a new way to behave on campus. "At the heart of the Duke problem is who we have been and who we wish to be," he wrote. "Whatever progress has been made in creating a more diverse environment and equitable residential life, Duke is still a college where 'work hard, play hard' is the dominant ethos. So we work intensely four days a week so that three days a week we can binge drink, party, and forget about the life of the mind."

Chafe's column prompted Stuart Rojstaczer, a retired associate professor at Duke, to challenge the idea that Duke students "work hard," and claimed that the average Duke student spent less than twenty-five hours a week in class or studying. "The paucity of work and lack of intellectual demands placed on Duke students are key reasons why the lacrosse team can claim [a] 100 percent graduation rate, yet still have time to both pursue the equivalent of a full-time job playing intercollegiate lacrosse and get into a whole lot of trouble drinking," he wrote. "It is not playing hard to hire strippers on university property, drink yourself into a stupor, and hurl racial slurs; it's playing stupid. It is not playing hard for students to end up in Duke's hospital for alcohol poisoning, as frequently happens; it's being self-destructive. It is not playing hard to sexually molest female students on the campus, as is reported to happen about ten times a year at Duke; it's criminal behavior."

In the days after the April 17 indictments and arrests of Seligmann and Finnerty, the speculation about who would be the third lacrosse player to be indicted seemed to focus on David Evans. Given that the investigations were meant to be confidential, it was not obvious how or why Evans's name kept popping up. Was it that Mangum identified him with "90 percent certainty" at the April 4 photographic lineup? Was it that his name had appeared in the latest DNA report? Why had the press made such a big deal out of Evans, in particular, being resentenced for his misdemeanors of making too much noise and drinking an opened beer? And why did Kevin Coleman's name not get leaked?

Whatever the reason for the suspicions about Evans, they were sufficiently real for Joe Cheshire, his attorney, to worry and look for ways to try to absolve his client. On April 21, four days after the indictments of his two teammates,

Evans agreed to take a lie-detector test at Cheshire's urging. "During the polygraph examination, Mr. Evans was cooperative and readily related the events that took place during the party," Robert Drdak, the director of CT&B Inc., the Charlotte-based company that administered the test, wrote to Cheshire the same day. "He stated that neither he nor anyone else at the party physically or sexually assaulted either of the two dancers. He advised that he has no direct knowledge of a sexual assault on the accusing dancer and neither observed nor heard anything during the party that would lead him to believe such an assault occurred." Drdak, a former longtime FBI agent, tested Evans using a "state-of-the-art" Lafayette 4000 computerized polygraph system. Drdak asked Evans five questions about the March 13 party and whether a sexual assault had taken place. Evans answered no to each question. Concluded Drdak, "Consistent and significant responses commonly associated with deception were not observed at the relevant questions, and a numerical evaluation of the data placed the final values well within the nondeceptive range. Therefore it is the opinion of the examiner that this examination strongly supports the truthfulness of Mr. Evans concerning the relevant questions . . ." (Lie-detector tests are not admissable as evidence in a criminal trial in any state.)

On April 28, Cheshire wrote Nifong a letter about the results of Evans's April 21 polygraph test. He reminded Nifong that Evans had offered to the Durham police on the night of March 16 to take a polygraph test, an offer the police declined. Cheshire continued, "That was the same night he assisted police in their execution of the search warrant at 610 North Buchanan Boulevard; voluntarily provided oral and written statements to the police without asking for a lawyer; voluntarily consented to police reviewing his instant messaging account; and voluntarily provided certain biological evidence to police to assist in their investigation."

Cheshire pleaded with Nifong not to indict Evans. "We continue to sincerely hope that you will refrain from proceeding against Dave in this matter," he wrote. "He has cooperated from the first moment of interaction with Duke officials and the Durham Police Department about this matter. He has passed a polygraph examination administered by someone with unassailable credentials. While the alleged victim reportedly identified him with 90 percent certainty as one of her assailants, she went on to give a detailed physical description that, we can prove, did not match David Evans on March 13, 2006." For one thing, Cheshire explained to Nifong that Evans had never had a mustache, and did not on the night of March 13. "There is no credible evidence, direct or indirect," Cheshire continued, "to establish David's guilt in connection to a physical or sexual assault of the alleged victim. That's because he did not assault her in any way, and we simply ask that you not ruin his life by authorizing charges against him in light of the facts as you know them." He made one additional request of Nifong. If he did decide to indict Evans,

Cheshire asked that he be treated the same as Seligmann and Finnerty—by being given a day or so to turn himself in to the police to be arrested and to have a $400,000 bail.

Nifong never replied to Cheshire's letter. Duke law professor Robinson Everett, a former chief judge of the US Court of Military Appeals, had his own suggestion for Nifong about polygraph tests: Give one to Mangum, and if she doesn't pass, use it as a cover to drop the indictments. If Mangum passed the test, Everett argued, Nifong could use the results to bolster his decision to bring the case to trial. If, though, the tests were inconclusive or if Mangum declined to take the test, he could likewise use those facts to bow out of the prosecution gracefully. Everett had made a clever suggestion. But Nifong had other plans, and besides, he had already said he did not use lie-detector tests for rape victims.

The weekend brought the board of trustees to Duke for a round of meetings and for the university's commencement. Its first order of business was to raise undergraduate tuition to $43,115 a year, an increase of 4.5 percent. The trustees, meeting at the Washington Duke Inn—a luxurious hotel complex near the campus golf course—also approved a $40 million addition for the university's business school, $30 million for the renovation of the campus library, and $10 million for the renovation of the building on East Campus that formerly housed the art museum. The trustees also reviewed an eighty-page strategic plan for Duke. And at a press conference after the meeting, Bob Steel, the board chairman, was asked, inevitably, about Brodhead's handling of the lacrosse case. Steel said Brodhead had been a "voice for reason" and said, "We're extremely appreciative of the leadership he's provided. It's been a challenging situation." Asked about the Bowen report's assertion of a sclerotic initial response to the incident, Steel said, "It appears we were slow to recognize the importance of the situation, and we were slow to move it up the authority channel." But, like Brodhead, Steel said the slow unfolding could be easily comprehended. "When you look at these things in hindsight, those of us who were watching this develop, things weren't clear," he said. "If I had a list of everything that was not true, that I was told, it would turn out to be longer than the list of things I was told that turned out to be true."

Meanwhile, a group of defense attorneys had a conference call to discuss the latest DNA findings, which had cost North Carolina taxpayers $22,850. Afterward, attorney Bill Thomas told a reporter that the semen from Murchison found in Mangum was "of recent origin" and resulted—illogically—from having sex "immediately prior to her being examined" by Levicy at Duke Hospital on the night of the alleged rape. "I think it is highly unlikely that the district attorney would seek an indictment based on this report," Thomas said. "It completely exonerates all members of the Duke lacrosse team. An attempt to indict based on this report would, in my opinion, be misguided." As others had, Thomas also questioned Mangum's credibility. "Her story is nothing short of ridiculous and certainly should not be the basis of an indictment," he said.

The next day, Sunday, was both Mother's Day and commencement day at Duke, with more than sixteen thousand visitors and more than four thousand undergraduate, graduate, and professional degrees bestowed at Wallace Wade Stadium. Honorary degrees were given to Steven Chu, a Nobel laureate (and future secretary of energy) and to Nina Totenberg, the longtime NPR legal affairs correspondent. Ninety-one-year-old historian John Hope Franklin, an emeritus Duke professor, gave the commencement address.

But there were reminders, too, of the ongoing controversy and legal process. For one, the Washington Duke Inn unceremoniously canceled the dinner celebration that the graduating seniors from the lacrosse team and their families had long planned for a private room at the hotel. The reason given for canceling the reservation, made a year in advance, was that it might not be a safe location for the lacrosse players and their families to be, given that it was within walking distance of West Campus. But by far the bigger source of anguish for the graduating lacrosse seniors and their families was the knowledge that—in all likelihood—one of them would be indicted the next day by a Durham County grand jury.

Collin Finnerty's parents were at the Duke graduation. Their second son, Kyle, was graduating. Originally it was to be a family celebration, but Collin's indictment a month earlier meant that he had to stay home in Long Island with his younger siblings. After the ceremony, the Finnerty parents and Kyle took a cab straight back to the airport. "We were guarded, talking about graduation, the weekend, and Kyle—nothing else," Kevin Finnerty recalled a few months later. "The black cabdriver drove us to the airport and got out to help with our stuff. Out of left field, the driver gives me a hug. And then he's crying, he's teary, he's shaking my hand with two of his hands. He's holding on to me. 'You don't know me,' he said, 'and I don't know you, but I am a parent, too. I want you to know that I am praying for you and your son.'"

For David Evans, a senior who had already accepted a job on Wall Street—in JPMorgan Chase's two-year analyst program—it was a very trying weekend. He did not attend his own graduation. He found out on Friday that he would be indicted on Monday. "I didn't want to cry," he said months later. "I was surrounded by all these people who were so happy. If you remember, it was Mother's Day. So this should have been one of the greatest days of my mom's life, the culmination of twenty-two or twenty-three years of schooling—all this work. She couldn't experience that. When I wanted to walk and get my diploma with all my friends, I couldn't. My dad had to go get it because there were so many people in the press who knew I was going to be indicted the next day. They wanted a picture of me with my diploma, and I never got to get it. I didn't want to give them the satisfaction of that photo."

At ten o'clock the next morning, Gottlieb and Himan appeared before the Durham County grand jury. "Went to the courthouse on grand jury," Himan wrote later in his case notes. "Gave probable cause for indictment of David Evans." Like Seligmann and Finnerty before him, the grand jury charged Evans, twenty-three, with rape, first-degree sexual offense, and kidnapping.

Tensions were running high that morning at the courthouse. According to the *News & Observer*, "in a profanity-laced tirade," Nifong told Kerry Sutton, one of Evans's attorneys, that he was "unhappy" with the attorneys' late-Friday news conference in which Cheshire accused an unnamed person in Nifong's office of leaking the DNA results to the media. Nifong apparently "stormed out of his office, blowing past reporters in the hallway" and into the judges' chambers, where he saw Sutton. He made "liberal use of profanity," according to the paper, "including the word mother[fucker]. Nifong told Sutton he would "do no more favors" for Cheshire, even though the two men had not spoken in weeks. "The comment and the swearing could be heard clearly across the sixth floor of the courthouse," the paper reported. Cheshire then tried again to speak with Nifong but was told he was unavailable.

Just before 2 p.m., Evans arrived at the county jail to turn himself in. But before doing so, he held a press conference, becoming the first of the three indicted Duke students to speak publicly about his legal predicament. He was flanked by the seven other graduating seniors on the lacrosse team, who stood behind him with "solemn, almost military bearing," according to one account, and dressed similarly in preppy khaki pants and button-down oxford-cloth shirts, as if they had just stepped out of a Brooks Brothers advertisement. Evans's parents—Rae, the chairman of a Washington lobbying firm, the chairwoman of the Ladies Professional Golf Association board of directors, and a former CBS, Inc., executive, and David, a partner at Reed Smith, the Washington law firm—accompanied him, too. His mother wore on the lapel of her elegant, off-white suit a large button with her son's photograph and the number from his lacrosse jersey. "I was like a piece of meat with sharks coming at me," Evans later recalled about the moment. "It was suffocating."

Evans looked literally like the proverbial deer in the headlights, but he still managed to make an impassioned defense of his behavior on the night of March 13. "My name is Dave Evans, and I'm the captain of the Duke University men's lacrosse team," he said. "I have to say that I'm very relieved to be the person who can come out and speak on behalf of my family and my team and let you know how we feel. First, I want to say that I am absolutely innocent of all the charges that have been brought against me today; that Reade Seligmann and Collin Finnerty are innocent of all the charges that were brought against them. These allegations are lies, fabricated, and they will be proven wrong."

He then recounted for the media what he had done when the police first came to 610 North Buchanan. "I fully cooperated," he said, "and have continued to cooperate with them. When they entered and started to read the search warrant, my roommates and I helped them find evidence for almost an hour, and told them that if they had any questions we would gladly answer, to show them nothing happened that night." He then explained that he went to the police station to give police "an uncounseled statement" because "I knew that I had done nothing wrong and did not feel that I needed an attorney. After going through photos of my teammates and identifying who was there, I then submitted, perfectly willingly, DNA samples to the police. I then turned over my e-mail account, my [instant messaging] account, any kind of information that they could have, to show that I had not communicated in any way that anything had happened, because it did not happen." He also explained he had offered to take a lie-detector test but that the police refused his offer.

He said he had tried repeatedly during the previous weeks, through his attorneys, to speak with Nifong. "All of my attempts have been denied," he said. "I've tried to provide him with exculpatory evidence, showing that this could not have happened. Those attempts have been denied. As a result of his apparent lack of interest in my story—the true story—and any evidence proving that my story is correct, I asked my lawyer to get me a polygraph." He then explained that he took the test, administered by an expert, and passed. "And I passed that polygraph for the same reason that I will be acquitted of all these charges: because I have done nothing wrong and I am telling the truth, and I have told the truth from day one."

He thanked his family, his friends, Pressler, and the Duke community that had supported the team. "Their support has given me the strength to come through this," he continued. "But the thing that gives me the most strength is knowing that I have truth behind me, and it will not faze me. If I can close, I have always taken pride in my name. I take pride in my name today, and I will gladly stand up to anything that comes up against me. I've never had my character questioned before. Anyone who's met me knows that this didn't happen, and I appreciate your support. As for my teammates, I love you all. The honor of being voted captain of all of you—the forty-six best guys you could ever meet—it's been the greatest honor of my life. If I can clear things up and say this one more time, I am innocent, Reade Seligmann is innocent, Collin Finnerty is innocent. Every member of the Duke University lacrosse team is innocent. You have all been told some fantastic lies, and I look forward [to] watching them unravel in the weeks to come as they already have in weeks past, and the truth will come out."

Evans did not answer questions from the media. But Cheshire then moved center stage to make a long statement and to answer questions. He provided additional insight into the case he would make on David Evans's behalf. He came out swinging. "David Evans was at the house that night," Cheshire continued. "He is a captain. He did live there. We will provide evidence from credible people—many credible people—that will show where David Evans was each and every minute of that evening, and [we] will prove, absolutely, unquestionably—just as Collin Finnerty will, just as Reade Seligmann will— that this rape not only did not happen, but it could not have happened. We have, again, presented that evidence to the District Attorney's Office, [which] has simply refused to listen to any of it on behalf of anyone." As for the second DNA test, which revealed DNA consistent with Evans's on one of Mangum's fake fingernails, Cheshire said, "Then we have the DNA evidence that came out, as you all know, last Friday, which does show no conclusive match to any Duke lacrosse player, but does show that they are unable to exclude a match on one plastic fingernail in the trash can which contained numerous items, as we will show you, of David Evans's DNA, that they cannot say absolutely that it wasn't Dave Evans. That, according to our expert, is about as weak a DNA analysis as you could ever have. I don't have to get into transference with you, but what I do want to get into [with] you about this fingernail is, you all just wait until you see the fingernail and match it up to this false accuser's statement. It will show you a tremendous amount.

"This is one of the saddest days for justice in the state of North Carolina," he said. "This case has been taken out to the news media before an investigation was finished, by a person seeking public office. Accusations against many, many young men were made before an investigation was completed. An investigation continued, and began, and two young men who could not have committed a rape were indicted, simply because a person in a lineup that is fatally flawed said that she identified them with no other reason, and now a third. This community has been torn apart, intentionally, on racial lines, on political lines, and these boys have been chopped up in the process. They are victims, their families are victims, this community is a victim, and our justice system is a victim. These boys not only will prove that they are not guilty, but they will prove, unquestionably, that they are innocent. There are many tough questions that need to be answered, ladies and gentlemen, but those tough questions don't need to be directed this way. They need to be directed that way"—pointing to Nifong's office across the street.

During the question-and-answer period, Cheshire did a respectable job of advocating for Evans's innocence. Why had Evans chosen to speak publicly? "He wanted to speak today because he wanted you to see him," Cheshire said. "He wanted you to look in his eyes. He wanted to tell you who he is, and he didn't want you to watch him running away, because Dave Evans, if you knew Dave Evans, who is a kid who became captain of the Duke lacrosse team, has as much talent as everybody else, who graduated yesterday from Duke with a very high-quality point average, who probably didn't have the mind of everybody else but who has the character and hard work and integrity to do that. He wanted you to see that and he wanted to tell you, and to tell everybody else here, that he's innocent, and that's what the truth is, and he's not afraid to do that." Was there any additional evidence that Cheshire was aware of that might have led Nifong to seek an indictment? "There's absolutely, as far as we know—and we know right much—no additional evidence, and that's what's so stunning about this indictment," he said. "I don't want to forget to remind you all, because in the DNA reporting, somehow some of you didn't quite understand how important it is that the single male source shows that this woman did have sex with a male, and the male is not a Duke lacrosse player. And yet, with that evidence, that being the only additional new evidence, Dave Evans is indicted. In other words, his only additional new evidence is she had sex with somebody other than Dave Evans, so Dave Evans gets indicted."

Victoria Petersen, a local activist, started to question Cheshire aggressively about why the predominantly white Duke lacrosse team had hired two black women to dance for them. "When your players saw two black women walking in the door, why didn't they say, 'Stop. Hold it. We don't want to do this,'" Petersen said. "Why did they allow those black women to stay there and dance and perform, and now we have a mess on our hands in this community? That young woman—now, I don't speak for her, but I am a black woman in this community—those young men should've never have done that. When they saw who they had, they should've closed the door and said, 'We're sorry. We made a mistake.'"

Cheshire, trying to keep his composure, responded, "Ma'am, I will agree with you about this: those young men should not have had that party that night, and they should not have asked women under that situation to come to their house, whether they were black, Asian, or white, and I will agree with you. I can discuss that with you, about respect, all along, and two black women coming to the house and all of a sudden all these people saying, 'Oh, no. We don't want you because you're black.' Maybe they had too much respect for that. Maybe they didn't want to do that, and I understand that. But I'd like to say this to you, as a black leader in this community, which I respect greatly: you may not know me but you can go back and look at my family. My family, of centuries in this state, has fought for the rights of African-American and other minorities. One of the saddest things that I've seen in this case is that some members of the minority community do not seem to be willing to give these boys a fair shake, and give them the presumption of innocence. And look, in fact, there have been quotes made by some North Carolina Central students that they don't even care if these boys are guilty or not guilty. They just hope they're convicted and go to prison. This should not be, and is not, a racial case. I believe it was made one."

From there, Evans entered the Durham County Detention Facility. He spoke casually with Brad Bannon, another of his attorneys, and with both Gottlieb and Himan. "David Evans seemed calm," Himan wrote, after he arrested him, "and did not appear nervous." Thirty minutes later, Evans was brought before Eric Van Vleet, a Durham County magistrate.

"Do you understand the charges brought against you?" Van Vleet asked.

"Yes, sir," Evans replied.

While Van Vleet sorted through some papers, he engaged Evans in small talk. To post bail, Evans slid a certified check for $400,000, from a local branch of SunTrust bank, through a slot in the side of a protective window to Van Vleet. "You understand you should have no contact with her or her family," Van Vleet told Evans, about Mangum, before sliding a receipt for the check to Evans. "You're free to go."

Nifong declined to meet with the press to discuss the Evans indictment. Instead he issued a statement that there would be no more indictments in the case.

Dan Abrams, the MSNBC legal anchor, and his guests were incredulous that Nifong would not meet with Evans or Seligmann or their lawyers. "I have never refused a defendant the opportunity to come and sit down and speak to me," explained Susan Filan, an MSNBC legal analyst and a former Connecticut state prosecutor. "I've had people accused of murder come and sit down and speak to me, stupid move, shouldn't have done it, they were there with their lawyer, helped me convict them, but if these guys are truly innocent and they want to sit down with [the DA], the DA should talk to him because he may get something in his bag of tricks that will help him. But if not, he should sit down and see what they've got."

Filan was amazed that Cheshire allowed Evans to speak publicly after being indicted. "The typical wisdom when you're defending somebody is don't say anything," she said. "If they believe so clearly that he's innocent, and he certainly states very clearly that he's innocent, what have you got to lose? I mean if that's really the truth and the truth is on his side, then it was a great move. . . . If these guys are innocent and their lives are being ruined because we've got somebody, [a] vigilante, out of control—that's the worst part of the power of being a prosecutor," she said. "The prosecutor at this stage is supposed to be a prosecutor and defense lawyer, because you've got justice in your hands, you're supposed to have the truth on your side, and you're supposed to do the right thing and that means you protect the innocent as well as accuse the guilty. You don't just go after somebody because you can."

For his part, Reade Seligmann was distraught that the results from the second DNA test had not deterred Nifong in the least. He couldn't believe it. "I felt that the first DNA test was pretty clear, but that a second DNA test, that would really show them," he recalled. "I mean, I had the alibi. There were two rounds of DNA that came back, and the way in which they were describing this attack, there would have to be some sort of DNA. It was just such a terrible, terrible attack that they said was happening, you would think that there would be some DNA. I thought, at that point, absolutely, this is going to be over, everything is going to be okay, and we're going to be fine." When he heard, at Cheshire's press conference, that semen had been found inside Mangum from an unidentified male who was not a Duke lacrosse player, he thought for sure Nifong would drop the charges. "When there was DNA from another male found in her, I remember being downstairs in the basement," he recalled. "I was at home. I remember coming up to my mom and saying, 'This is it. It's over. They're done. It's done.' I told all my friends to turn on the TV, to watch all the news. Or I believe there was a press conference that night [with] Mr. Cheshire. And when he announced it, I thought everyone was going to say, 'They're innocent. This has been a hoax.'" But it was not to be.

Part of the problem for Seligmann was that Nifong did not believe him or his alibi. Nifong had concluded that Seligmann's behavior after leaving the party was designed to *create* an alibi for him, and was not the same as an *actual* alibi. "Our initial assumption was that she was in the bathroom with three people the whole time, and that one of them had her behind, there was another person who was not in front of her—it was not clear exactly what that meant, where that person was; not holding her but not in front of her, either— and then Reade Seligmann was the one who was supposedly in front of her," he said in an interview. "If you read the statement, what she's saying is that they were trying to get Reade Seligmann to let her perform fellatio on him, and he was resisting. He was saying, 'I can't do that. I'm getting ready to get married. I can't do that.' She goes on in the statement to say that the person who is in front of her, she does perform fellatio on him and he ejaculates, calls for a towel, and the towel is thrown into the bathroom and he wipes himself off with that, and that all this other stuff is going on. Reade Seligmann leaves the bathroom, and then David Evans, who has been behind her, he steps in front of her and David Evans is the one that she performs fellatio on, that he calls for the towel, the towel is thrown in. Okay. Now, if she has never heard anything about semen on a towel—and she certainly hasn't heard it from anybody in my office, and I don't think that's ever been produced anywhere else—where does she get that idea? Where does she come up with that? The fact is that David Evans's semen on a towel was there, and that towel was one of the items of evidence that was collected.

"Now, while we're on this subject—because this seems like a good place to do it—let's assume that you are Reade Seligmann," he continued. "Let's assume that you've been present in this bathroom when this assault starts, and you're there, and they're trying to get you to do something, and you really don't want to do it, for whatever reason. I mean, you're in there with them, so you say, 'No. I'm not going to do this. I'm leaving.' What would you maybe do to distance yourself from that party? Call a taxi. Buchanan is a main drag along there. He didn't catch a cab on Buchanan. He walked through the block and came out on

Watts Street, so he was not on Buchanan at all. The cabdriver call came to the 1100 block of Watts Street, and on the record of where he was picked up by the cab, he was picked up one block over, on Watts Street. And then what do you do? You don't want to be picked up at the party, because you know that something bad is happening at this party, so you've got to go somewhere. Where are you going to go? Well, let's go to the ATM, because what do they have at ATMs? They take pictures. So we're not picked up at the party. We immediately go somewhere, so we show up at an ATM. Then we go to get some food. But what else do you have to do? You have to make sure that cabdriver doesn't forget you. The cabdriver says he got a $25 tip. . . ." (Actually, the cabdriver said he received a $7 tip on an $18 fare.)

It was a media madhouse outside the Durham County courthouse on the afternoon of May 18, the site of Reade Seligmann's first administrative hearing in the state's case against him. Media tents—filled with cameras and crews—were set up along the top of the courthouse steps. A bank of nine television cameras drew in groups of protesters who had no direct involvement in the case but were more than happy to take advantage of the national media's spotlight on Durham. Among them were representatives of the New Black Panther Party and Durham TRY (an acronym for Together for Resilient Youth, a group dedicated to eliminating underage drinking.) As Seligmann and his attorneys approached the courthouse, the New Panthers shouted at him, "Justice will be done, rapist." Wanda Boone, of Durham TRY, said, "Our contention is that if underage drinking is addressed and was addressed in this situation, it would not have occurred."

Seligmann remembered the scene well. "As we were walking, the Black Panthers started screaming out, it felt like from all different angles," he said. "I might be wrong, but I remember it that way. They kept saying, 'Justice will be done, rapist.' They said, 'You're going to get yours, rapist.' . . . I was trying my hardest to keep a straight face. In anything you do, you don't want to let the people know that they're getting to you. But I was terrified. I was completely terrified. I already told you I was Mister Flustered, so you can imagine what that kind of situation was doing to me. I don't know whether someone was going to hit me from behind or take a shot. I had no idea. I'd never been in a situation like that before in my life. Like I said before, like a gauntlet. We were just tucked into this pocket of media and Black Panthers, and people holding up signs saying things like 'Zero Tolerance' and all sorts of different signs. Finally, we were able to get to the doors."

Inside Judge Stephens's courtroom, the tension was equally high, especially between Nifong and Kirk Osborn, Seligmann's attorney. But there were also people there determined to heckle Seligmann. "That was my first experience seeing a courtroom, and it sort of looked different than I'd anticipated," Seligmann said. "We walked in and there were tons of people sitting in, I feel like

I remember them as pews. I might be wrong. When we walked in, I felt like I'd walked into a cafeteria or a gymnasium. There were people yelling. There were people shouting all different things, and I tried, once again, to ignore it. I felt like I was going to be real safe because once you walk in a courtroom, then you're safe. Then the sheriffs are going to take care of it. We sat down in the first or second row, and there was a guy behind me that kept leaning up. He leaned up to me and sort of screamed it out at me, he screamed out loud and he goes, 'I don't want to sit next to this piece-of-shit motherfucker.' He's screaming that out, and I didn't want to turn around. I didn't want to look at him. I didn't want to have to deal with him. There were people, comments coming all over. There were media people sitting in there. I don't even know who these other people were. This guy did not look like a reporter to me. I can't imagine that he would be. But someone in the back, in the back corner, had screamed out—and this was something, every single time I come to something like this, a public event like this, I'm still scared about something like this— but he said, 'You're a dead man walking.' I was doing my best to try to keep it together, but to hear someone behind you that you can't see—you can't see who it is. Finally, I think it started to settle down . . ."

The first order of business was to share with the judge the status of the discovery process, whereby documents and other information accumulated by the police and the prosecution would be shared with the defense. Nifong explained to Judge Stephens that just prior to the hearing he had turned over to Osborn some 1,278 "consecutively numbered pages" of "documentary evidence," including two VHS tapes and one CD-ROM containing photographs. Next, Osborn sought the judge's order to protect—and retrieve—the numerical data on Mangum's cell phone, in police custody, that Mangum had left behind at 610 North Buchanan on the night of the alleged attack.

Osborn also asked Judge Stephens to allow the proceedings—even though they were administrative in nature and the actual trial was more than likely some six to nine months away—to be recorded. "I'm going to allow your motion to record everything," the judge said, "because apparently, we're going to need everything recorded in this matter." Osborn asked that all of the police notes and files be preserved (approved) and that the defense have the opportunity to go to the police department and look through all the files (denied). The judge decided not to order Nifong to allow Osborn to "rummage through" police files, since he believed Nifong would make the files available in the ordinary course of business.

Another request from Osborn—to reduce Seligmann's bail from $400,000— the judge denied. Osborn argued that Seligmann's bond money was borrowed and the lender wanted some of the money back. Besides, Osborn argued, Seligmann "submitted what we think is a pretty clear alibi defense that's airtight. And we have a box of material from senators, congressmen, and friends that says he's not a flight risk." (Seligmann recalled seeing Nifong "smirk" and was "smiling to himself" when Osborn spoke about his alibi.) But the judge said the bond was within the guidelines for the alleged crime and was not inclined to change it. He said he would review the filings and decide at a later time whether to accede to Osborn's request.

And that was that. The court set another hearing for the week of June 19, prompting Osborn to see if perhaps the process could be speeded up. "We want a trial as fast as we can," he told Judge Stephens. "This young kid wants to go to school in the fall. And he can't until this is resolved." The judge was sympathetic, but said he could not assure Osborn a trial would take place before the fall.

While the legal and administrative process moved slowly throughout the stifling Durham summer, Evans, Seligmann and Finnerty attempted to move on with their lives as best they could. Although nine of the eleven seniors on the 2006 Duke lacrosse team secured jobs in finance, Evans's offer to work at JPMorgan Chase was rescinded after he was indicted.

For Seligmann and Finnerty, the summer of 2006 was far less normal. Seligmann left Duke with a 3.375 GPA, including a 3.5 GPA during his final semester. But after his April 17 arrest and arraignment, "I had to finish all of my classes over the summer, over the phone, and over the Internet, with all of my teachers," he remembered. "When I was arrested, there was only a couple of weeks left in the semester, and at the end of the semester it's mostly exam review, and in college, that's when you really start to hunker down, at the end of the semester. I had to pretty much do it on my own at the end there, and we just communicated through Duke, and my guidance counselor had to get in touch—it took about three months for me to get all the information to finish the finals up." Eventually, Seligmann got an internship working at Bear Stearns, the investment bank, in New York. But he missed his entire junior year of college. Finnerty spent the spring, summer, and fall of 2006 at his home on Long Island. He eventually took one class at a local university but, like Seligmann, he missed his junior year of college, too.

The Evans indictment and the Seligmann hearing launched a new round of editorials about the direction of the case (including a treatise by William Safire, the *New York Times*'s language columnist, on whether describing Mangum as an "exotic" dancer as opposed to an "erotic" dancer was misleading). The paper noted that there had been an extraordinary amount of talk about the case, first from Nifong—before he quieted down—and lately from defense attorneys. "Which is probably why the evidence seems to be piling up on the side of the players," the paper continued. And despite its sympathy for Evans and his dramatic speech—"on what should have been a proud and happy day"— his graduation from Duke—the editorial writer was left at a loss. "Unfortunately, one strong speech and claims of passing a polygraph test aren't proof of innocence," the paper continued. "Nor are many statements by defense attorneys that, unsurprisingly, portray the defendants as blameless and downplay anything damaging." But Nifong was not to be underestimated. "Nifong is a prosecutor with twenty-seven years of experience in Durham," the paper concluded. "As such, we imagine he knows when evidence supports an accusation and when it doesn't. We also imagine there is evidence he hasn't revealed yet."

But for journalist Stuart Taylor Jr., writing in the *National Journal*, the evidence was in, and he embraced it, albeit with a slight twist of caution. "My rogues' gallery does not (in all probability) include any Duke University lacrosse player," Taylor wrote on May 20. "That's because the available evidence leaves me about 85 percent confident that the three members who have been indicted on rape charges are innocent and that the accusation is a lie." Taylor reserved his considerable ire for the "more than ninety members" of the Duke faculty "who have prejudged the case," as well as for both Bowen and Chambers, who "went out their way to slime the lacrosse players" in their recent report, itself "a parody of race-obsessed political correctness." Much of the media, Taylor wrote, had "published grossly one-sided accounts of the case while stereotyping the lacrosse players as spoiled, brutish louts and glossing over the accuser's huge credibility problems."

Then there was Nifong. "He has shielded his evidence (if any) from public scrutiny while seeking to keep the rape charges hanging over the defendants by delaying any trial until next spring," Taylor wrote. He added that Nifong, and a Durham police officer, should be "under criminal investigation" for "possible intimidation" for arresting Mostafa, the Durham cabdriver. While Taylor conceded that he had not seen all the evidence, either, and was therefore prejudging the case, too, he was supremely confident that a miscarriage of justice was occurring. After launching a tirade against Bowen, Chambers, and Houston Baker while praising Coleman's report and one of his conclusions that the lacrosse players were actually good kids, he wondered how likely it would be that the players at 610 North Buchanan would have stuck to "an airtight cover-up" about a "gang rape" that occurred in "a small, crowded house" without a single one "heeding pleas from parents and lawyers to protect himself by fingering any guilty parties." He also wondered why guilty players would voluntarily offer to take lie-detector tests or hand over evidence—the fake fingernails—three days after the alleged rape. "Something is rotten at Duke . . . ," Taylor concluded. "I don't think it has much to do with lacrosse."

Others wondered what toll the Duke allegations would take on the sport's image. "The sport of lacrosse is taking a beating," Dom Starsia, the head coach of the Virginia Cavaliers, told Greg Garber, at ESPN.com. "For coaches and administrators, this is our absolute worst nightmare. The college game is such a fragile little animal anyway. If Duke doesn't bring the team back, I don't know where we're going to be." Added Yale lacrosse coach Andy Shay, "That's the prevailing fear among college coaches. When ninety-nine percent of the country's first exposure to lacrosse is this incident, well, first impressions are the most important thing. It's certainly not something that we're all proud of. It's not indicative of the culture, but it's the first thing people are pointing to." But Shay conceded the alleged incident could have happened at Yale, too. "It could have happened to any of us," he said. "It's scary. What we know has happened, it could have happened on any college campus, Division I, II, or III. It just so happened to happen at a phenomenal academic institution, the ivory tower."

One Ivy League varsity lacrosse player, speaking anonymously to Garber, said the boorish behavior of the Duke lacrosse players on the night of March 13—aside from the sexual assault allegations—did not strike him as all that unusual. "I've seen stuff like this with our team and other teams at my school," he said. "The problem is, when alcohol becomes involved—and it always does in college—it impairs judgment. You get forty juiced guys and two girls, and it's a time bomb." He continued, "From my experience, the 'play hard, party hard' label is true. But the whole deal is hard work. We're not taking Golf 101 at Florida State. You get up at nine in the morning and go lift, eat breakfast, go watch film, go to class all day, practice for three hours, get dinner, do your homework, and try to get to bed at a decent hour. In college, you're under constant pressure to hold your spot—on the lacrosse team and academically, too. And after a big win on Saturday, you're ready to blow off some steam. You're there with your teammates, and everyone wants to be part of the fun."

Starsia agreed that lacrosse players, like other college athletes, get rowdy. "Fearless or reckless," he said. "Yes, those are words that can both apply. They can be guilty of sowing wild oats a bit in college—that may be accurate. Lax has always had a 'play hard, party hard' description. I've always felt like lax guys are the most engaging guys in the whole world. Maybe they drink too much on weekends, but you can slap them around on Mondays—they will listen to you."

As other writers had previously done, Garber spoke with Steve Stenersen, the executive director of US Lacrosse, to get some perspective on the game and what had happened in Durham. "As in any tragedy, these circumstances will certainly be a catalyst for even greater reflection on the sport's healthy development," Stenersen explained. "I feel that the depiction of lacrosse in such a narrow way in the media as solely an elite, exclusive sport is not only inaccurate but almost irresponsible. Without dismissing the circumstances in Durham, it's our goal to more accurately depict where the sport is today." In fact, he said, lacrosse is the fastest-growing sport in the country. In 2005, some 200,000 athletes under the age of fifteen played lacrosse, double the number that had played the sport five years earlier. The number of people playing lacrosse had grown 10 percent each year for the previous decade. Nearly 45,000 people watched Johns Hopkins defeat Duke at the 2005 NCAA tournament final game. He said that whatever had happened at Duke was not representative of lacrosse programs across the country. "One culture does not define college men's lacrosse," Stenersen said. "I believe, honestly, that each program is different. There's a big difference between the lacrosse culture at Duke and what the overall culture is."

But there was no question that the ramifications of the Duke allegations were being felt far and wide in college athletic programs across the country. "Every coach in America has sat down with his kids and talked about this," explained Steve Koudelka, the lacrosse coach at Lafayette College. "I think, compared to the time I was in school—I graduated from college in 1993—there's a lot more education with these student-athletes. This is definitely worthy of talking about and using as an educational tool." Added A. Craig Brown, the vice chair of the US Lacrosse executive committee. "A huge lesson that comes out of this for all college athletes is that when you take on responsibility and privilege, what you do reflects on all of the involved institutions, in this case both Duke and lacrosse. Kids need to take more responsibility for the consequences of bad behavior. I'm sure none of them thought whatever they did that Monday night would have this effect. It's a recipe for disaster."

With no prospect that any additional lacrosse players would be indicted and with the students gone from Duke's campus for the summer, the case against Seligmann, Finnerty, and Evans moved into the Durham courts, beginning months of legal wrangling between defense lawyers and the increasingly isolated Nifong. The media, of course, kept up its nearly daily vigil. The immediate task for the defense was to sort through the 1,278 pages of documents and other data that Nifong had turned over to them to determine whether they believed any of it damaged their clients and to try to figure out what was missing from the pile so that they could begin asking Nifong for it. They wasted little time. "We've been through all the discovery," Kirk Osborn told the *News & Observer*. "We're not at all concerned with what we've seen." Osborn, though, wanted more information. In a motion, he argued that a "substantial portion" of police notes and interview summaries, as well as cell phone records and physical descriptions of the players who she said had attacked her, had not been turned over to defense attorneys by Nifong, who was obligated to turn over every piece of evidence he had to them.

Defense attorneys also noted that the evidence Nifong shared did not contain a "toxicology" report for drugs or alcohol on Mangum from the night of the alleged incident (although there was the hair test that showed no evidence that Mangum had taken drugs). The SANE nurse, Tara Levicy, who had examined Mangum on the night of the alleged incident indicated that no toxicology tests were performed. Mangum's level of inebriation on the night of March 13 had become one of the central questions of the case. The police reported that she was so drunk—"passed-out drunk," the police wrote—that she could not get out of Roberts's car at the Kroger supermarket, so they had to give her a dose of smelling salts and physically remove her from the car before transporting her to Durham Access. The photographs of Mangum from the party showed her seemingly passed out on the back steps of the house. Nifong had "hinted" to *Newsweek* that perhaps Mangum had been slipped a "date-rape" drug. Roberts, meanwhile, had said that Mangum was not drunk when she came to the party, although she did quaff down a few drinks in the bathroom before the dance started. And Brian Taylor, who drove Mangum to the party, told police she was not drunk when he dropped her off. "Either way—whether it was a date-rape drug or voluntary intoxication—it would affect the reliability of her identification," Mark Edwards, a lawyer not involved in the case, told the Durham paper.

The defense also sought to further impugn Mangum's credibility by claiming that a "forensic examination" of her found "no tearing, bleeding, or other injury associated with a sexual assault," only "swelling" in Mangum's vagina and "tenderness" in her breasts and lower right body. This finding contrasted with the various search warrants obtained by the Durham police that said Mangum had "suffered injuries consistent with being raped and sexually assaulted vaginally and anally. The defense also said that the documents Nifong turned over revealed that Mangum had told police she had had sex with three men in the same time period as the alleged rape, one of whom was her boyfriend and the other two drivers for the escort service. But Nifong wanted no part of confirming these reports. "There is no percentage whatsoever in me making any comments about this," he told the Durham paper.

The members of the Duke women's lacrosse team, playing in the Final Four against Northwestern in Boston on May 26, decided to render their own verdict in the case against their brethren. As a show of support to Seligmann, Finnerty, and Evans, the women decided to wear sweatbands on their arms and legs with the word "Innocent" emblazoned on them. "Obviously we want to win a national championship for ourselves," junior Leigh Jester told a reporter, "but definitely also for the university and the men's team. They don't really have a chance to play their season, which is a shame." In a further show of solidarity, Kerstin Kimel, the women's coach, invited Pressler to speak with her team after a practice earlier in the week. "I think his message was a little bit more believing in themselves and looking at the year we had in spite of the difficulties that Duke and the lacrosse program have seen," she explained. "Our kids have been a real pillar of strength. They haven't let this be a distraction; if anything they've used it to motivate." Kimel, whose team had an 18–2 record, hoped the appearance in the Final Four would "focus a positive light on Duke and on Duke lacrosse, both men and women." As for why the women's lacrosse players were allowed to express their opinion on the case but previously the women's basketball players—also playing in a Final Four in Boston—had not been permitted to make their views public, John Burness told the Durham paper, "They don't clear those things with us, ever. We're not sitting here looking over people's shoulders quite that much."

But the contradiction was a bit much for Harvey Araton, a *New York Times* sports columnist. "So let's review Duke's First Amendment performance at these consecutive Final Fours," he wrote on May 26. "A basketball team with a majority of African-American women was in effect censored, while the lacrosse gals, thirty of thirty-one of whom are white, are apparently free to martyr their male lax mates." (What was it about only one black athlete on each of Duke's men's and women's lacrosse teams?) Araton tried to check his outrage but it was a challenge. "We seem to have reached a strange, paradoxical time in college sports, with the canceling of the Duke men's lacrosse season and the Northwestern women's soccer season after that team was trapped in a web of hazing," he wrote. "Frankly, I'll believe these colleges are really serious about policing their prodigies when one of them pulls the plug on a misbehaving football or basketball team and all the revenue it generates. When behavioral codes intersect with the vexing subjects of sex, race and class on campuses like Duke's, there are still many more questions than answers. Today, if I could ask just one, it would be directed at the Duke basketball women. What do they think of those sweatbands the women's lacrosse team was planning to wear?"

In the end, the word "Innocent" proved too controversial. Instead, about ten of the players wore wristbands with the numbers 45, 13, and 6 written on them—the jersey numbers of Seligmann, Finnerty, and Evans.

While Harvey Araton used his latest column to record the backlash directed his way from loyal Dukies, his main purpose was to wonder—correctly—why Coach K, the veritable face of Duke University athletics, had not made any comment about what had happened to the Duke lacrosse program. Araton said Coach K "seems to have taken a television time-out" and his absence from the debate was particularly noteworthy because he was "typically a ubiquitous sermonizer on the choices young people make—from college to credit card to car." Coach K, Araton wrote, "has virtually gone underground" and has been "conspicuously absent from the national discourse and noticeably scarce around campus." Coach K had also not shared his thoughts with the incoming basketball recruits, including Gerald Henderson, the son of the former Celtics point guard of the same name. "Coach K is a smart guy," the elder Henderson told Araton. "He understands what's going on with the situation, how it could affect the program," and was right to keep silent until more of the facts were proven in court. "In staying quiet, the erudite Coach K has proved, like a great point guard dribbling out of the backcourt, to have the intuitive capacity to recognize and avoid a trap," Araton wrote. "This is the only position a basketball coach who has achieved fame for himself and a fortune for his family in large part by luring black talent can take if he intends to keep his program on its figurative pedestal." Araton complimented Coach K on his restraint. "Good for him for lowering his profile, for letting the system work, but isn't it interesting how self-interest is the greatest motivation for being a silent voice of reason?" Araton concluded. But it was a good question: Where was Coach K in all this?

Truth be told, more than two months after the alleged incident inside 610 North Buchanan and three indictments of Duke players on the charges of rape, sexual assault, and kidnapping, there was still very little clarity about what had really happened on the night of March 13. But, argued David Brooks in his *New York Times* column—the *Times* took the story to heart—whatever had occurred was not what people assumed originally. "Witch hunts go in stages," Brooks wrote. "First frenzy, when everybody damns the souls of people they don't know. Then confusion, as the first wave of contradictory facts comes in. Then deafening silence, as everybody studiously ignores the vicious slanders they uttered during the moment of maximum hysteria. . . . Now, with the distance of some time, a few things are clear. There may have been a rape that night, but it didn't grow out of culture of depravity, and it can't be explained by the sweeping sociological theories that were tossed about with such wild abandon a few weeks ago. . . . The members of the lacrosse team were male, mostly white and mostly members of the suburban bourgeois middle class (thirty-nine of fifty-four recent graduates went on to careers in finance). For many on the tenured left, bashing people like that is all that is left of their once-great activism. And maybe the saddest part of the whole reaction is not the rush to judgment at the start, but the unwillingness by so many to face the truth now that the more complicated reality has emerged."

But other columnists did not see the same set of facts the same way Brooks did. On May 24, under the headline, "The Duke Case's Cruel Truth," the *Washington Post*'s Lynne Duke wrote, "She was black, they were white, and race and sex were in the air." No matter what happened on the night of March 13 at 610 North Buchanan, she continued, "it appears at least that the disturbing historic script of the sexual abuse of black women was playing out inside that lacrosse team house party. . . . In the sordid but contested details of the case, African-American women have heard echoes of a history of some white men sexually abusing black women—and a stereotype of black women as hypersexual beings and thus fair game. . . . It was the kind of predatory behavior that found its way into modern culture in the old Rolling Stones song 'Brown Sugar.' And the stereotype of black women as highly sexed, like the lascivious Jezebel from slavery days, is a recurring image in music videos today. . . . Racial history still resonates, still touches a deep and tender nerve."

Lynne Duke spoke with Dorothy Height, the ninety-four-year-old president emeritus of the National Council of Negro Women. "I think there's a

tendency to downgrade black women, and to discount the fact that, no matter what they are there to do, they are not just animals to be used," Height
said. "Whatever she did, she was not there as a prostitute." Yet, Duke pointed
out, that's how the two women were being portrayed in the media. She noted
that Rush Limbaugh had called them "hos" and that Tucker Carlson, on his
TV show, called Mangum "a crypto-hooker." Duke also talked with economist
Julianne Malveaux, who was outraged by those characterizations and wondered why Levicy's physical examination of Mangum on the night of the party
had not convinced people. "Whatever else happened," Malveaux said, "this
woman has been violated somehow. Is there no sympathy?"

Duke's view was that black women were being persecuted left and right—
she cited the radio host who described Condoleezza Rice as a "coon" and
another radio host who described US representative Cynthia McKinney as a
"ghetto slut"—and she wrote that Mangum was the victim of "the tug of war
over the victim's image and credibility." Kim Gandy, a former prosecutor and
the president of the National Organization for Women, described the Duke
case as an example of the classic "nuts and sluts" defense, while Susan Estrich,
a rape victim and a professor at UNC, said it reminded her of the 1991 case
of William Kennedy Smith "where there was a very organized effort to cast
doubt on the victim." Duke noted that the lacrosse players were not spared
in the "game of image-battering," either, often being described as "privileged,
racist brutes prone to binge drinking, who preyed upon a troubled and struggling young woman." In closing, Duke couldn't figure out, if the players had
requested a Latina dancer and a white dancer, why after Roberts showed up—
they assumed she was the Latina because of her mixed-race heritage—and
then Mangum, who was obviously black, they proceeded with the evening's
festivities anyway. "It's yet another of the case's puzzles," she wrote.

Another of its mysteries was why—given the intense beacon focused on
the Duke lacrosse team—any player on the team would continue to do the
crazy things young adults do. And yet, on May 24, Matt Wilson, twenty-one,
was stopped in Chapel Hill for drunk driving. Police found Wilson, who had
already received a summons for public urination, driving erratically at 2:30 a.m.
They gave him a Breathalyzer test, which found his blood-alcohol level to be
0.21 percent, almost three times the legal limit. Police also found marijuana and
a glass pipe in his car. On June 1, he was charged with driving while impaired,
misdemeanor possession of marijuana, having drug paraphernalia, and running a red light. Wilson was released after he promised to appear in court on
August 1. He was suspended from the lacrosse team. "I was very disappointed,
as you can imagine," Brodhead said about Wilson. But Chris Kennedy didn't
think Wilson's suspension from the team was fair, especially in light of another
incident involving a Duke wrestler who was stopped for drunk driving and
"had a large knife in the car," but received only a one-match suspension.

• • •

One of the recommendations in Coleman's report was that Duke should rein-state the men's lacrosse program. Word began leaking to that effect, first in *Newsday*, on Long Island. The paper reported that Kevin Cassese, a 2003 Duke graduate, three-time all-American, and an assistant Duke lacrosse coach, would be named the interim head coach. Then came the additional confirmation that Max Quinzani, a Duke recruit from Duxbury, Massachusetts, had been "promised by the coaching staff there will be a team." Tony McDevitt, a rising senior on the team, said he hoped a decision would be announced soon. "There's no playbook," he said, "so I understand President Brodhead is taking his time, but obviously on our side we want to hear as soon as possible."

The *New York Times*'s Pete Thamel reported on June 3 that Dom Starsia, the Virginia coach, had spoken with a Duke official about the "logistics" of the program's return. "I couldn't be more pleased," he told the *Times*. "I'm sure there will be some parameters for them to return, but it's a step in the right direction for our sport. . . . What I'm guessing they're going to do is introduce a code of conduct that's been hammered out over the past few weeks. Duke is in a position where they can assume a leadership role and provide a model for lacrosse teams and college teams in general. . . . I think it's a fresh start for Duke and good news for the rest of us." Starsia said he had spoken with Pressler frequently during the past few weeks and that Pressler was in favor of restoring the program. "My own sense is that he comes out of this looking hirable," he said.

Starsia was right about the new code of conduct. The new "team standard" of conduct seemed nothing more than common sense and long overdue. Student-athletes were required to adhere to all the "rules and regulations" of the NCAA, the ACC, and Duke and were required to follow all "academic procedures." There was to be no gambling or hazing or disorderly conduct. No student twenty-one years old or older could "provide" alcohol to anyone under twenty-one and—per the laws of the state of North Carolina, the new standard was careful to point out—no athlete under twenty-one "may purchase, possess, or consume" alcoholic beverages. Meanwhile, "conduct that constitutes harassment on the basis of gender, race, or sexual orientation [was] prohibited" as was "disorderly conduct, violence, property damage, and theft." The lacrosse players were required to report any violations of the code within twenty-four hours of their occurrence to the head coach or to the athletic director, including violations occurring during a vacation. Punishments for violating the code were spelled out, depending on the number of infractions, with stricter penalties possible at the discretion of the head coach or athletic director. There was no question the new standards were tough. "While these guidelines stand as a deterrent, we recognize that the most productive changes we can make to our social culture are to root out the very actions that would precipitate a penalty," the code concluded. "It is our hope that the values of the mission statement will mold such character so as to make the code of conduct superfluous. We are collectively committed to writing a new beginning for Duke lacrosse. We look forward to bringing the pride of our past to a new responsibility for our future."

There was also a new lacrosse "mission statement" that could easily have appeared—reproduced down to the final letter—in a Norman Rockwell painting. The new goal of the lacrosse program was no longer to win games but "to develop student-athletes of character and integrity who will serve as positive members of the school community and the greater society." The program would "promote pride, unity, and confidence" and the players were to place "primacy on our academic endeavors, and recognize the importance of intellectual growth throughout our undergraduate careers." Furthermore, they were required to show "positive leadership" around campus "and display the courage necessary to advocate just causes in the face of public or social pressures" and to hold "ourselves responsible and accountable for our thoughts, feelings, and actions." The lacrosse players had to dedicate themselves to "family" and "community," with a new, enlightened attitude: "Regardless of the challenges faced, we embrace a commitment to always put forth our best effort," the mission statement concluded. "Our attitude will be defined by our strength of character and our constant pursuit of excellence on the field, in the classroom, and within the community. The pride and confidence we derive from our team activities will not deter us from recognizing the great privilege we have been presented as student-athletes at Duke."

At a 2 p.m. press conference on June 5, Brodhead—flanked by Bob Steel, the chairman of the board of trustees, and Dan Blue, a board member, along with Alleva and Kathleen Smith, the faculty liaison to the athletic department—announced what the college lacrosse community had figured out: he had decided both to reinstate the Duke lacrosse team and to take over, personally, the responsibility for overseeing the athletic program. Kevin Cassese, then twenty-five years old, would take over as interim coach while Alleva searched for a permanent head coach.

At the press conference that followed the announcement, Alleva made clear that Mike Pressler, the former coach, would not be considered a candidate for the job again. Brodhead made his first extensive public comments about him since his April 5 departure. If one didn't know better, one might suspect that Brodhead thought a mistake had been made when Duke pushed him out—or perhaps it was a way to give him a public endorsement so that he could find a new job and potentially reduce the university's legal exposure to him. "Mike Pressler is a lacrosse coach with an extraordinary record," he said. "He has been Coach of the Year. He has been offered the position of head coach in many of the finest programs in this country, and during this past episode, we've learned some important things about him. If we hadn't had those committee reports, not everybody would know of the efforts he had taken to exert oversight over his team. Not everyone would know that when his team played for the national championship last year, there were players who were not allowed to play because they were being disciplined by him at that time. I must say, too, I've never met a single person who thought that Coach Pressler knew, in advance, about the party on the thirteenth of March, or condoned it. During the past several weeks, many people who have played under this coach, current and past, have called me to express their admiration. That said, I think we've just understood all along—we've been through an event this spring of fairly major proportions—and it has been my view of this that we're not going to go back to the old program. If and when we started lacrosse, I always said, we're going to start a new history, and it's just really for the point of making a new start that we would need to have a new coach to take us to that start."

Not surprisingly, parents of the players on the team seemed pleased with Brodhead's decision to reinstate lacrosse at Duke. Six of the nine new recruits to the program had stuck with their commitment and none of the current players had transferred. It looked like their collective gamble to stay at Duke to play lacrosse had paid off. "We're very thankful and very happy," said Eric Heinsohn, the stepfather of Bo Carrington, a rising junior. "And we're very hopeful it will be a good thing all the way around." He noted that none of the juniors on the lacrosse team had transferred away from Duke, despite the controversy. "I think it says a lot about their commitment to the team and their commitment to wanting to take the team to another level both on and off the field," he said. George Jennison, the father of Jay, another rising junior, said "That was good news, allowing the boys to get back to the sport they love. My son—like the rest of them—he's thrilled about it . . . but foremost in everyone's mind is the defense of those three young men whom we all feel are innocent." Patricia Dowd, the mother of Kyle Dowd, who had just graduated and been drafted into a professional lacrosse league, and of Craig Dowd, who was thinking about matriculating at Duke, was still perplexed. "We're still working through all the emotional issues after what happened, and there's been no relief," she said. "It's been a very difficult time, and there will be no relief until those three boys are exonerated. We still don't know what we're going to do."

The next day, Alleva introduced Cassese to the media at Cameron Indoor Stadium, but first he sought to make public amends with Pressler, since there seemed to be a growing view that Duke had acted too hastily in removing him and that Brodhead and Alleva had piled on at the press conference by saying that Pressler would not be considered for his old job. "I have had the pleasure to know Mike for sixteen years," Alleva said. "He has been my friend. He's a great family man. He took over a lacrosse program here at Duke that wasn't very good and made it into a national contender. He's an excellent lacrosse coach and a man of fine character. At the time of his resignation, we all agreed that a change in the leadership of the program was in the best interest for everyone involved." He then wished Pressler well in his career.

Cassese, Alleva said, was the right man for the job at the moment, despite the presence of Jon Lantzy, who was an assistant coach and more senior. Lantzy would be leaving Duke. (He became the head lacrosse coach at Durham Academy.) Alleva said Cassese was "was an excellent student at Duke, a tremendous lacrosse player, and a wonderful citizen" and represented "everything positive about Duke lacrosse. Even though he was part of the program, he's also part of the solution." He said he didn't think Brodhead had taken much of a risk reinstating the lacrosse program. "These lacrosse kids have character and integrity and are willing to accept responsibility for their behaviors, and I think they've learned from what has transpired in the past," Alleva said. "I think you're going to see really good citizens from our lacrosse team." As for the self-reporting rules in the new code of conduct, Alleva said, "If they do not self-report within twenty-four hours, and we find out about it, they will face a much stiffer penalty than they would have had they reported." He also was optimistic he would find a top lacrosse coach to take the Duke job. "This job is one of the top five lacrosse jobs in the country, and I believe coaches in the lacrosse profession realize that and will be willing to accept the challenges at Duke University and what it faces in the future."

To the accompaniment of cheers, Cassese, recruited to Duke in 1999 from Port Jefferson, Long Island, then took the microphone and announced, unabashedly, "Duke Lacrosse is back." He said that while "it is no secret we have all been through some incredibly trying times," the previous day had been "a great day for our program." He commended Brodhead for his "very difficult and courageous decision" to reinstate the lacrosse program and said "it would have been a tragedy for all of us if our program was not allowed to continue." He said that as interim coach he would work "tirelessly" to "rebuild [the] bruised reputation" of the program. Cassese, who had played for the Rochester Rattlers of Major League Lacrosse and expected to compete on the US National Team during the summer, said he recognized "there have been behavioral issues involving team members in the past and these issues cannot continue." He did wade, briefly, into the legal morass of the three indicted players. He had coached all three and had played alongside Evans when he himself was a senior. "Based on what I know of David's character, I find it impossible to believe he could have done the things he is being accused of," Cassese said. "While I never had the opportunity to play alongside Reade Seligmann and Collin Finnerty, I will, as with David Evans, support them until there is evidence and a court decision that leads me to conclude otherwise."

Following his appointment the previous day, Cassese said he had gotten on the phone to the current players, as well as lacrosse alumni and potential recruits, to let them know the program was back. He also had spoken to coaches from opposing teams to begin to get the 2007 schedule in order. He was off to New York the next day for a recruiting trip that would take him to five states in five days, including the Long Island high school championships at Hofstra. He said he didn't think the allegations and negative press would hurt his recruiting prospects, despite three of nine recruits to Duke having—legally—backed out of their commitments to attend the university. "People want to come to Duke just as I did," he said. Of course, he was asked about being the interim coach at such a young age. He said he was not nervous in the least. "My family bleeds Duke blue," he said. "After I graduated, my parents would drive down here to watch a game even though I wasn't even playing. My fiancée is a former Duke women's tennis player. Her two younger sisters are going to be Duke students. Duke is in my veins." Casey Carroll, a senior defenseman, was at the press conference. "It's kind of a bittersweet thing," he told the *New York Times*. "We all are ecstatic on the one end that we get the opportunity to represent our school again. But in the back of our minds, there will always be Coach Pressler having to leave and what happened with Collin, Reade and Dave." Coach K was at the press conference, too, in the audience, and said nothing.

CHAPTER ELEVEN

Nifong Loses Control of the Narrative

Not everyone at Duke applauded Brodhead's decision to reinstate the lacrosse team. Orin Starn, a professor of cultural anthropology, told the *Durham Herald-Sun* he disagreed with the team's return. "This is not to say there are not many good kids on the team," he said. "But it's a problematic pattern of conduct that really, to me, does not justify reinstatement next year, and calls for all the facts of the case to be known and for the court case to be resolved before we go forward and think about having lacrosse again at Duke." He was not suggesting—as some on the Duke faculty had—that big-time athletics had no place at the school, but he was concerned about its growing emphasis. For the year ending October 2005, Duke athletics had generated $42 million in revenue, at a cost of around $40 million. Coach K's basketball program generated revenue of more than $12 million, with profits of around $4.6 million; Duke football, meanwhile, with revenue of roughly $7.7 million, had a net loss of $1.6 million. "My own feeling is that college sports has grown into a very big commercial entertainment business with literally billions of dollars at stake, [with] TV contracts and coaching salaries and recruiting, and I think it's wrong," Starn continued.

The *Chronicle*'s editors were perplexed by Brodhead's announcement. On the one hand, they wrote, reinstating the team was "both necessary and timely," but the "parameters for the reinstatement" were "ambiguously worded" and "leave something to be desired." The paper applauded Brodhead's decision to reinstate the team and his timing: "Any earlier, it would not have been able to conduct a comprehensive investigation . . . any later, the program would have had to climb an even steeper slope in order to get back on its feet."

Meanwhile, Nicholas Kristof, the heavyweight columnist at the *New York Times*, agreed with Brodhead that the alleged incident should be used for some "deep reflection," not just about "racism and sexism" but also "about the perniciousness of any kind of prejudice that reduces people—yes, even white jocks—to racial caricatures." Kristof noted in a June 11 column that the case had not been the "finest hour" for either academia or the news media. "Too many rushed to make the Duke case part of the three-hundred-year-old narrative of white men brutalizing black women," he wrote. "The narrative is real, but any incident needs to be examined on its own merits rather than simply glimpsed through the prisms of race and class."

He then walked through the "facts," at least as they were then known after weeks of defense attorneys' filings in Durham Superior Court and public briefings. According to Kristof, Nifong, not the lacrosse team, was the "real culprit." He cited his belief that Nifong's plethora of public statements in the opening weeks of the case "seem[ed] to violate the North Carolina rules of public conduct" and that Nifong had used the lacrosse case "as a campaign tool" in his successful three-way primary election, since he was "the lone white man on the ballot." He also criticized Duke professor Houston Baker—whom Kristof revealed was leaving Duke (for Vanderbilt)—for referring to an "abhorrent sexual assault, verbal racial violence, and drunken white male privilege loosed among us." Kristof concluded, "Look, we have a shameful history in this country of racial prejudice. One of the low points came in the 1930s when the Scottsboro Boys were pulled off a train in Alabama and charged with rape because of the lies of two white women. The crowds and the media began a witch hunt (one headline: 'Nine Black Fiends Committed Revolting Crime') because they could not see past the teenagers' skin color. So let's take a deep breath and step back. Black hobos shouldn't have been stereotyped then, and neither should white jocks today."

Not surprisingly, Kristof's column touched off a firestorm among *Times* readers—but may also have served as the catalyst to slowly turn the battleship of public opinion away from Nifong and Mangum and toward the three lacrosse players.

Just as Kristof had aggressively questioned Nifong's handling of the case, the *Washington Post* examined the ordeal from the perspective of the parents of the unindicted players. The article revealed to the general public that, for the Duke lacrosse team, going "to a strip club" was a "team spring tradition" that could not be accomplished in March 2006 because a number of the players younger than twenty-one did not have the proper identification, resulting in the decision to hold the party at 610 North Buchanan and invite the two "exotic dancers."

John Walsh, a health administrator from Bethesda and the father of Johnny Walsh, a rising Duke senior, said he had had no idea that hiring strippers was a team ritual. "You see it in New York," he said. "It's the preferred type of entertainment for Wall Street. I'm not advocating it. It's open for discussion. But it's not behavior that is totally deplorable." Tracy Tkac, from Gaithersburg, Maryland, and the mother of Chris Tkac, disagreed with Walsh. "Hiring a stripper is just as inappropriate as being a stripper," she said.

But the message the article conveyed was that the parents and their sons had been victimized. Tracy Tkac was appalled that Duke could have allowed her son's picture to be used in a wanted poster put up by police around campus and in Durham. She saw the poster one night while watching the news.

"The people that I entrusted my son's education to allowing those posters to go up on the walls of their private institution" was the worst moment, she explained. In Chevy Chase, Maryland, Sally and Robert Fogarty, the owner of a local Chevrolet dealership, stopped socializing after the news broke. "I could not risk hearing my friends express doubt over my son, because I was afraid the friendships would be ruined," Sally said. Observed John Walsh about the lacrosse players, "In a fell swoop—a lightning bolt—everything is taken from them." The parents of the players in Washington banded together, sent one another reassuring e-mails and discussed how to pay for their sons' legal defense. The worst part was remaining silent "as their sons were cast as thuggish, racist, elite jocks," the *Post* reported. "I *know* these boys," Walsh said. At one point, in early May, an online company offered for sale a motivational poster of Matt Danowski entitled "Teamwork" with the subtitle, "You drag her to the bathroom, I'll guard the door."

Days after the alleged incident, said the article, the parents started to hear about it from their sons, not from the police or the Duke administration. Chris Tkac called his mother and denied that anything had happened. She said she believed him but, still worried, called Sally Fogerty. "Oh, come on, Tracy, there is no way," Fogarty recalled saying. "The kids are not capable of this. I am not being naïve."

The parents realized "the gravity of the situation," the *Post* asserted, when the lacrosse match with Georgetown on March 25 was canceled an hour beforehand. The Georgetown team was already on the field warming up. A number of the Washington-area parents had driven down to Durham for the game and the chance to see their sons and take them out for an early dinner afterward. Tom Clute called his father, who was on his way to Durham. "My son was very upset," the elder Clute said. "He asked me to turn around and go home." Tkac was just outside Durham when her son called. She was so upset and so anxious to get to campus, she got a speeding ticket.

The parents spent the next six hours with Pressler and other school administrators hearing about the accusations. Tom Clute told his father he was so upset by the allegations that he asked the team captains point-blank if anything had happened. "The captain looked him the eye and said nothing happened," Clute recalled. Still, as the campus erupted in protest during the next few days and the national media put the university—and the allegations—in the spotlight, the parents themselves harbored doubts. "Even our close friends said, 'Something must have happened in that house,'" Walsh told the paper. The parents, too, seemed to be under the microscope. "Their affluence, their child-rearing, their world of private schools, the careful pipelines to success that they had laid for their sons, were scrutinized and judged," the *Post* reported. "They were pummeled daily with harsh caricatures of their kids." Of course, as the paper noted, the party had been "no cotillion," what with the strippers, the excessive drinking, and Landon graduate Peter Lamade's comment about using the broom-stick as a "sex toy." That, and the "now infamous" comment "Hey bitch, thank your grandpa for my nice cotton shirt," to say nothing of McFadyen's e-mail.

Walsh said these "tangential issues" clouded the fact that, in his opinion, no crime had occurred in the house. "I'm not saying these aren't important issues, but the fates of these boys' lives are being lost in the shuffle," he said. Walsh was the one who decided to ask his cousin, Bob Bennett, the powerful Washington attorney, to join the legal defense, albeit from behind the scenes. But there was nothing Bennett or any of the local North Carolina attorneys could do to stop Nifong from seeking the indictments of the three players. Evans's indictment was especially painful, given his Landon and Bethesda connections. Some were incredulous that Finnerty's Georgetown assault charge had been tied to what allegedly happened at 610 North Buchanan and had been blown out of proportion. "Look at this kid," Walsh said of Finnerty. "Does he look like a mean kid?" To which Chip Royer, Jeff Bloxsom's attorney, had the good sense to respond, "All I'll say is that as parents, we have an idealized version of our kids, and whether they live up to that idealized version can be a disappointment."

Like Kristof, Walsh put the blame on Nifong, whom he said was "using a troubled woman to further his political career." During the interview, Johnny Walsh walked through the living room wearing his blue-and-white Duke shorts. "Tall, tan, boyish and friendly," the *Post* reported, "he was packing to leave for a summer internship on Wall Street where he'll earn $14,000." In the fall, he'd be a senior and would play on the revived team. "But on this afternoon, it's almost time for the 1 o'clock start of the national championship lacrosse game between the University of Virginia and the University of Massachusetts," the paper concluded. "'We should have been there,' Johnny Walsh said."

A day later, in a lengthy article titled "Sex, Scandal, and Duke," by Janet Reitman, *Rolling Stone* dropped a new bombshell about Duke's over-the-top hook-up partying culture. Reitman had nothing to add, per se, about the lacrosse case; instead, she pulled back the curtain yet again on Duke's "work hard, play hard" culture, revealing how little it had changed, despite Willimon's updated study. The riveting article also showed that little had changed from the 2003 Duke Women's Initiative that described the "effortless perfection" expected of Duke women. Reitman's article made clear that, at Duke, while the frat boys reigned supreme, the "lax bros" were at the top of the frat-boy pile. Frankly, it was the last thing the fragile campus needed.

Reitman attended a frat party at a Durham bar, Shooters, at the end of April, a little more than a month after the alleged incident at 610 North Buchanan. She was there with "Sarah," a Duke junior. The occasion was a special event—a "foam party"—sponsored by Delta Tau Delta—one of Duke's "top" fraternities, she allowed, without explaining why—to celebrate new pledges, spring, and the fact that the women were wearing "halter tops" and "everyone is covered in bubbles" and was quite inebriated. She described the party as a "sweaty, alcohol-soaked bacchanalia that's a little like taking an enormous bubble bath with hundreds of strangers," where "everyone is drunk" and "tiny soap bubbles that have been shot through a thick rubber hose into a mesh tent outside the bar cling to dozens of dancing kids." The scene: "The girls, dressed in miniskirts, whip off their shirts to reveal bikini tops; the boys, who've come in ratty shorts, remove their shirts. Thus attired, they fall into one another, spilling drinks. They make out. A few of them dry hump while doing the grind. There is a metal go-go cage in which a group of Duke girls clad in tiny denim skirts and halters perform a modified pole dance, but no one seems to be watching. Bad techno-rap music pulses, the dance floor throbs."

Reitman located a group of lacrosse players "tucked in a corner of the bar," where those older than twenty-one were drinking shots. "There are maybe a dozen of them: big-shouldered, handsome guys in clean polo shirts, khaki shorts, and baseball caps," she wrote, while noting that neither Seligmann nor Finnerty, who had already been indicted, nor Evans, soon to be indicted, was there. "They are pounding beers, exchanging high fives, and throwing their arms around one another in brotherly, inebriated affection." They are known around Duke as "the laxers" and "tend to be the most desired and most confident guys on campus. They're fun. And they're hot. It's something that frustrates and often baffles other young men, particularly those who've had girlfriends stolen by these guys. But women understand. 'It's a BMOC thing,' Sarah says. She's undecided about the rape charges but is much more certain about the boys. 'They have it all—you want a part of that,' she says."

The other minor dabbling Reitman did into the rape allegations while she was on her reporting trip to Duke revealed less ambivalence about the situation than Sarah conveyed. The women she spoke with were "deeply concerned" for the lacrosse players whose "lives have been totally ruined." The allegations made no sense to many of them. "They don't need to stoop to that level in order to have sex with somebody," one junior told Reitman. She had met some Duke women who lived in the same Edens dormitory as Seligmann and Finnerty and had decided to hang banners from their windows that read: "WE SUPPORT DUKE LACROSSE: INNOCENT UNTIL PROVEN GUILTY." They also had T-shirts, halter tops, and baseball caps inscribed with the phrase and wore them proudly around campus.

There seemed to be the view that McFadyen, despite being a lacrosse player, had been particularly foolish in sending out his late-night e-mail, despite its supposed literary references. "He was just like this big, goofy kid—not great with girls or anything, that's the funny part," a woman Reitman named "Naomi" explained. "He was just a kind of meathead guy." "Anna" was less critical. "Am I some kind of stupid girl?" she asked. "I just saw that e-mail, as inexcusable as it was, as kind of a joke—I got it." Naomi told Reitman that many students believed hiring strippers was a bit of a "joke," despite the considerable fallout of the lacrosse team having done so on March 13. "I was like, wow, I didn't realize that there was that stigma," she said.

The word on 610 North Buchanan—it had once been known as the "crack house," for obvious reasons—was that it was reserved for the top of Duke's social pecking order, and if Reitman were right about the lacrosse players being at the top of it, then it would be hard to beat having three lacrosse cocaptains in residence at once. "Their parties had more intoxicated cute girls taken off into rooms and having one-night stands than most," explained Matt Sullivan, a fraternity brother at Eta Prime. "There wasn't any sexual assault going on at these parties. The girls were fine with it. Because it would be like, 'Ooh, it's a lax player. Look what I did—I scored.'" Still, he couldn't quite figure out why the laxers were so idolized, far more so than the basketball players. "I don't know where this sensibility comes from," he told Reitman. "Maybe it's just athlete glory, for girls. I don't know. . . . It doesn't make sense."

The lacrosse case was a sideshow for Reitman. Her real purpose was to sit back and watch the hook-up culture at Duke unfold before her. Her guides, Naomi and Anna, were two sophomores who liked to hang out at the new, modernist Nasher Museum of Art on campus. "Sometimes, girls will be like, 'I'm just horny and I want to have sex,'" Naomi explained. She found the attitude liberating. "It's our decision if we're going to allow ourselves to be subjected to negative treatment," she said. "It's all framed by the way girls behave." The museum had an outdoor café, which served "wilted lettuce" and "strawberry salads" and allowed the students to hang out, get a tan, and scope out the action. "The patio is buzzing with pretty girls in silky skirts or skinny jeans, flitting back and forth between tables as if it were their cafeteria," Reitman reported. "Most of these women are members of one of Duke's elite sororities—known as the 'Core Four,' home of the university's most popular and best-looking women."

At one point, a couple of young guys, "dressed identically in slouchy designer jeans and freshly pressed button-down shirts," sat down and ordered a carafe of white wine. Naomi and Anna recognized them immediately. "Those guys are in the center of the social scene," Anna told Reitman. She noted that the "leaner of the two, a good-looking member of a top fraternity" was the "kind of guy who can get laid twice in one night if he wanted to." And there was lots of sex going on at Duke—of the vaginal, anal, and oral varieties, you name it. "Everybody gives blow jobs now," Naomi told Reitman.

As seemed to be increasingly typical on many college campuses, there was no dating, just a "hook-up" scene. "I've never been asked out on a date in my entire life—not once," one "stunning brunette" explained. Nor had a guy bought her a drink. "I think that if anybody ever did that, I would ask him if he were on drugs," she said. Explained Reitman: "Rather, there's the casual one-night stand, usually bolstered by heavy drinking and followed the next morning by—well, nothing, usually. 'You'll hook up with a guy, and you know that nothing will come out of it,' says Anna. The best thing you can hope for, she says, 'is that you'll get to hook up with him again.' Some girls they know have managed to score a regular hook-up—meaning consistent sex—but others play the field, bouncing from one guy to the next. The vagaries of sex on campus have created a specific 'hook-up culture' at Duke. As one male student describes it, it 'exists in a whirlwind of drunkenness and horniness that lacks definition—which is what everyone likes about it, [because] it's just an environment of craziness and you don't have to worry about it until the next morning.' But this culture has its downsides, say some students. 'I think the ease of hooking up has, like, made people forget what they truly want,' says Naomi. 'People assume that there are two very distinct elements in a relationship, one emotional and one sexual, and they pretend like there are clean lines between them.'"

From the Nasher art museum, Reitman went with a few more coeds to the Washington Duke Inn—the "WaDuke," as it was affectionately known around campus—for a late afternoon lunch. "We come here every day of our lives, pretty much, and order ten-dollar martinis," "Allison" explained as she "nibbl[ed] a cheeseburger." Allison was a "raven-haired young woman" from New York City. "I always say going out should be, like, a fifth class," she said. "It's exhausting." According to a Duke professor Reitman interviewed, there were really two Dukes: "Day Duke," where the students go to classes and study "insanely hard" to "ace all of their papers and tests," and "Night Duke," replete with partying and hook-ups. It was exhausting, and the women Reitman was hanging with were very tired and very hungover.

But there also seemed to be that lingering different standard for the men and women at the university, harking back to the 2003 study. The men hang out and play video games—or so the women Reitman interviewed thought—while the women at Duke were at the library studying until 11 p.m. and bringing their books to the gym. "Reading on the treadmill with the highlighter—see, that's Duke in a nutshell," Allison explained. "You've got to do everything at once, and you've got to do it well. . . . If there's ever a time when I just sit around, I get horrible anxiety." Added "Kasey," "Girls will either be at the gym or doing something productive. They work so much harder—spending two hours at the gym trying to look good, and eating salmon." Kasey explained the women at Duke "have to be up"—perky, cute, witty, and fun—or else they won't get guys. "Because, like if you're a 'terrible,' no one will talk to you," Allison agreed.

She continued, "I have done things that are completely inconsistent with the type of person I am and what I value." She told Reitman that she had spent more than a year with a guy "in a high-profile fraternity" who would "go to a party with all of his friends and do whatever he wanted, but God forbid I ever went anywhere without him." She put up with his behavior because "When you're in a relationship with somebody, especially with somebody in the frat scene, you're lucky to be with him." The women at the WaDuke found that ironic, considering there was nothing so great about the guys. "I'll see this beautiful model-type girl walking with this little scrunchy five-foot-two guy, and it's like, Oh, she's so lucky that she got him," explained Kasey.

"I found myself falling into this thing," Allison continued. "It made me very uncomfortable and unhappy, because it's not a way to live. But if I didn't do these things and he broke up with me for some reason, two days from now he'd have somebody else. That's just how it works."

"You're just scared," concluded Kasey.

"If my mother ever knew," Allison said, "I mean, she would smack me across the face. I was not brought up in that kind of environment."

For further insight into the Duke social scene, Reitman turned to an anonymous on-campus blogger who posted a helpful "How-To Guide to Banging a Sorority Girl." The key, he wrote, was appreciating how insecure the girls were in the first place, as evidenced by the fact that they joined sororities. (Why joining fraternities wasn't evidence of the guys' insecurity was not addressed.) "Of course," the blogger wrote, "they don't realize that entering the sorority world is entering a world of intense scrutiny from all directions . . . which compounds their already existing lack of self-worth. In turn, these delightful young ladies deal with their massive insecurity by getting fucked by frat boys. Lucky for us guys, frat boys treat sorority girls like shit. As soon as Sally PiPhi thinks she has secured Johnny Soccer Player, Johnny is off boning Chrissy Tridelt. . . . All of this leads to unhappy, insecure girls all fighting to get rammed by someone of status." He then confirmed that the Delta Sigs—the "alpha males of the Greek system" because they "consistently attract the highest quality poontang"—and their parties, such as one named "World War III," were the apex of the Duke social scene. There were other notorious parties, too, including the "Playboy" party, the "Dress to get Lei'd" party, the "Snowjob" party, the "Presidents and Interns" party, and the "Secs and Execs" party.

While some frat guys seemed not to understand the magnetic pull of the lacrosse players, the Duke women had an instinctual feel for it. Not for nothing were they referred to around campus as the "Lacrosstitutes." "Sarah" explained the dynamic to Reitman on the patio of the Nasher Museum. "It's the way they carry themselves," she said. "Frat stars and athletes—those are the only ones that matter. I mean, honestly."

"And except for three of them, they're not that attractive," Allison sighed. "I can think of, like, three or four guys that I'd be like, 'He's hot.' But that's it." Added Kasey: "I think the girls here are so much better-looking, there are so many good-looking girls at this school." Just then, "as if on cue," Reitman reported, "a pair of gorgeous girls, one blonde, one brunette, show up dressed in tight jeans, pashmina shawls, gold jewelry, and pearls. Both seniors, they're graceful, poised, and seem to have the concept of 'effortless perfection' down. The two beauties left a few minutes later with the two guys who had been sitting nearby.

"Those guys?" said Sarah. "Total frat stars."

"Super-frat," gushed Allison. "Frat-tastic."

"And that guy," explained Kasey, referring to one wearing a baseball hat. "He gets so much ass."

Reitman observed, "It's fairly amazing, since neither boy seemed to exude any charisma."

"That's what we're saying!" the girls screamed.

"You see these girls and you're like, wow," concluded Allison. "And you see these guys and you're like . . ."—she looked up to see that the two guys had returned to the patio alone—"I mean, no. Just no," about the guy in the baseball hat. "But you see how he carries himself? Like, 'I'm the man.' I feel like in the real world, these guys would never be with these girls—they're way too beautiful. And way too intelligent."

Just as people were digesting the *Rolling Stone* article, along came *Vanity Fair*'s take, courtesy of the bestselling author of *Friday Night Lights*, Buzz Bissinger. In his article, Bissinger broke little new reporting ground, although he did interview Kim Roberts, who provided yet another version of the events of March 13.

He noted that the indictments of the three players had not done anyone any favors. "If the three suspects have been charged with a rape they did not commit, it's a hideous tragedy," Bissinger wrote. "If the accuser's claims are in fact true, it's a hideous tragedy. The damage done to Duke, which in roughly three decades has transformed itself from a finishing school for the southern elite into a world-class university, is incalculable. The damage done to the lacrosse team at Duke, which was in the NCAA championship last year and which, many felt, would win it all this year, has been incalculable."

The rise of Duke into the ranks of the nation's elite universities—it ranked third, according to *U.S. News & World Report*, after Harvard and Princeton— came at a cost, according to Bissinger, using somewhat overwrought language. "In spite of the transformation, the sense of immense wealth and privilege lingered," he continued. "There was a sense that the school was still a kind of plantation on the hill built by the tobacco fortunes of the Duke family in a city that was still rediscovering itself after the closure of the factories that had once produced such iconic brands as Chesterfield and Lucky Strike. There was also the lingering sense of a school where students, regardless of their academic credentials, still considered partying as something of a Duke birthright, what one professor dubbed 'Cruise Ship Duke.' The allegations of rape were called a perfect storm by many, as they brought issues of race and gender and town-gown friction and the role of athletics into glaring view. 'This is like Katrina in your own backyard,' said history professor Peter Wood."

Bissinger also captured the frustration Brodhead must have felt when he had to confront Coach K's threatened departure for Los Angeles, even before he had unpacked the boxes in his Allen Building office. "I thought it was humiliating that the president of the university, when we should be celebrating, thinking about plans for the university, is forced to play the role of supplicant begging the basketball coach to stay," Professor Orin Starn told *Vanity Fair.* "It revealed the lay of the land, that athletics is oversized at the university." Like Wood before him, Starn had been irritated to have fifteen athletes, out of a class of one hundred twenty-five students, tell him at the beginning of a semester they would have to miss something like ten classes because of practices and games. "The fact is, you can't be a real college student if you're missing a lot of class and too tired to do the work," he said.

Meanwhile, Kim Roberts told Bissinger a slightly different version of what had happened on the night of March 13. Defense attorneys had argued for weeks that Mangum was drunk upon arriving at 610 North Buchanan, based in part on a private conversation Roberts had with an attorney (whom she did not hire) in which she supposedly said that Mangum showed up at the party "loopy." She told Bissinger that Mangum was not drunk when she arrived at the house. In their first discussion, Roberts said Mangum was "absolutely fine." Only later would she become "completely incoherent," Bissinger wrote. "We talked," Roberts told Bissinger. "We joked a little bit. I told her I was new to this and really didn't know what I was doing. [She] told me that she danced at a club and was a little more experienced. She told me about her kids. . . . It was a regular normal conversation. Nothing that set alarm bells off in my head." Before they went inside, Roberts told Bissinger she sought assurance from the two cocaptains that they would continue to behave respectfully. "'Okay, you guys seem very respectful,'" Roberts told Bissinger she said to the lacrosse captains. "'If everybody acts as you are acting, I'm sure we'll have a fun time.'" She continued, "They completely assured me that everybody in there were good guys—'Everybody in there is respectful, and you will be fine and safe.' [I was] completely assured of that."

But things got off course rapidly. "They definitely were drunk and drinking," she said, and not just beer but also hard liquor. She noticed a large open bottle of Jack Daniels. A number of the guys were even younger than she thought. And then there was the feeling she got, quickly, that the players expected Roberts and Mangum to, as Bissinger put it, "fully degrade each other during the course of the performance." That led to the well-known version of events, in which the two women feared for their safety and Peter Lamade asked the dancers if they had brought "any toys"—meaning sex toys—with them, prompting Roberts to question his manhood, which further prompted Lamade to suggest she use a broomstick he just happened to have available instead. After that, the dancing stopped, Roberts explained, although she was reluctant to share too many more details with Bissinger because she knew she was going to be a witness in the trial.

With the next court hearing scheduled for June 22, defense attorneys spent the weeks before filing one motion after another designed to advance the defense of the three indicted players. Nifong, meanwhile, remained eerily silent. First, defense attorneys attached to a motion twenty-three pages of Mangum's medical records in a sealed envelope, but then quoted from Tara Levicy's report that Mangum had "diffuse edema of the vaginal walls"—another way of saying swelling—without specifying whether the swelling had resulted from a sexual assault, her menstrual cycle, or consensual sexual intercourse. (An assistant supervisor at the UNC Hospitals said SANE nurses usually do not make such distinctions.) The lawyers claimed the medical report showed no other injuries to Mangum other than her complaint of a general sense of "tenderness" on her body, as well as a nonbleeding scratch on her knee and a "laceration" to her heel. They wrote that cuts on her knee and heel as well as her swelling could be explained by her activities in the days before the March 13 party. And to make that case, the attorneys included the five-page statement from Jarriel Johnson, Mangum's driver, who described the various sex-related activities Mangum had engaged in in the days prior to March 13.

The defense attorneys also included Roberts's March 20 and 22 statements that she had been with Mangum the entire evening except for five minutes and that the suggestion that she had been raped was a "crock." (Of course, Roberts had subsequently changed her mind and was no longer certain what had happened.) Defense attorneys said that Judge Stephens had been "misled" because he was not made aware, first, of Roberts's statements; second, that Mangum had provided police and medical officials with contradicting statements; and third, that she had appeared intoxicated. Judge Stephens would not have "found probable cause" to sign the warrants had he been told the full story, they argued. The lawyers also asked Judge Stephens to suppress the evidence from the photo-identification lineups—in which Mangum identified Seligmann, Finnerty, and Evans—because, they claimed, the police procedure was unconstitutional, since it contained only pictures of Duke lacrosse players. Also unconstitutional: the DNA tests, especially the portion that could show Evans's DNA on one of Mangum's fake fingernails. Joseph Cheshire again called on Nifong to drop all the charges. "All the things that Mr. Nifong said in his press conferences, the vast majority of those things, except his opinions, have proven to be untrue," he told the *New York Times*.

Defense attorney Bob Ekstrand was particularly exercised by the subpoenas issued by Nifong on May 31 demanding that Duke turn over the home addresses of the forty-seven lacrosse players, as well as those of two other students, plus their campus electronic identity-card data records. The purpose was to track their whereabouts on the night of the alleged crime. Nifong "unilaterally subpoenaed federally protected confidential records," Ekstrand wrote in his filing, "without any authority whatsoever." Other defense attorneys joined Ekstrand in arguing to Judge Stephens that the subpoenas were unconstitutional.

The public scrutiny of Nifong continued unabated. On June 12, *New York Times* reporters Duff Wilson and Jonathan Glater wrote a piece calling into question his ongoing prosecution of the case. Now that the once-loquacious district attorney had stopped talking, they wondered what had happened to his initial certainty. "In the intervening months, the case has come to appear far less robust," they wrote. "Three players have been indicted, but evidence that has surfaced, much of it turned over to defense lawyers by prosecutors and then filed in court with defense motions, [has] thrown the woman's claims into doubt." With Nifong's recent vow of silence, "The result is a growing perception of a case in trouble," Wilson and Glater wrote.

The *Times* interviewed H. Wood Vann, a Durham lawyer who had represented Mangum after she stole the taxi and went on a drunken joyride. "I have no doubt Mike believes her," he said of Nifong and Mangum. "[But] at some point he's going to have to get to a tipping point. His case is going to hell in public opinion. He's suffering death by a thousand cuts." The paper reminded its readers that Nifong had previously said the judge would have to send the case to the jury if there was medical evidence of rape and if the victim was able to identify her assailants. "Each element has come under question, amid attacks on the woman's credibility and on the characterization of the medical evidence by the police," they wrote. "[And] some experts say the identification procedure was fatally flawed." Nifong's case was further weakened, according to Joe Cheshire, because the 1,278 pages of evidence that Nifong turned over to the defense on May 18 contained little, if any, actual evidence. "Out of those 1,300 pages," he said, "I'd be surprised if two hundred of them relate to this case at all."

The seeming lack of DNA and medical evidence was also becoming problematic, the *Times* wrote, as was the fact that Mangum had been sexually active in the days before the March 13 party. The time-stamped photos from March 13 plus Seligmann's alibi also complicated the case, as did the story of Mangum having previously been gang-raped and then failing to follow up on her initial report. "I'm not saying any of this is a silver bullet," Kerry Sutton told the *Times*, "but with all this combined, it's a silver mortar."

Why had Nifong not dropped the case? the paper wondered. Some thought Nifong was too stubborn. "He jumps to conclusions, makes up his mind and that's it," said Julian Mack, who had represented Seligmann for a time. "His personality is that he's very stubborn." Others thought the case had become too political. "He'd have hell to pay from the African-American community," Vann said. "They'd say, 'Give her her day in court. What do you have to lose? If you lose, at least the jury made the decision.' So he's kind of stuck."

The next day, James Coleman, the Duke law professor and author of one of the reports about the lacrosse program, called for Nifong to step aside from the lacrosse case and to ask Roy Cooper, the state attorney general, to appoint a special prosecutor. "I don't think he's showing detached judgment," Coleman told the *News & Observer*. "I personally have no confidence in him."

On June 14, officer Ben Himan met with the social worker, Mariecia Smith, at the Durham Crisis Center, and her attorney. Himan wanted to review with Smith the events of the early morning of March 14 when Mangum arrived at the Center. Smith told Himan that when Mangum arrived, "she appeared nervous and was shaking." Mangum told Smith that she called herself "Honey" and said she "did not want to go to jail." Smith said Mangum was wearing a red dress with something "white" over it and that she had "one white high heel." Mangum then "grabbed" Smith and "started crying." They then went to the assessment room, and when they were seated with the door closed behind them, Mangum told Smith "she was raped." She wrote down the names and ages of her children on a piece of paper, and Smith told the police officer who had transported Mangum to arrange for the Durham police to check on Mangum's children. Smith said she told Mangum that "once she had been raped," the proper place for her to go was Duke Hospital. Mangum told her "she did not [want] any men touching her." At first, Smith reported, Mangum did not want to go to Duke Hospital and said "no, no, no" and that she "was talking about her children and that was a big concern of her[s]." Smith said she then escorted Mangum back to the police car and put her in the backseat.

Himan asked Smith if she recalled whether Mangum had talked about what had happened at the house. Smith said Mangum had mentioned that she worked for "Angels Escort" and that "in the end she was crying" and "someone had taken her money [and] that she needed that money to feed her kids." There was mention that $400 had been "taken" from her and there was another $1,000 in the police car—although that was the first time anyone had mentioned that sum of money.

While Himan's investigation continued, defense attorneys had also begun to compare Nifong's statements about the evidence with what they found in the 1,300 or so pages of documents he turned over to them. There were contradictions. For instance, Nifong had said the alleged rapists may have used condoms, but Mangum told Levicy no condoms were used. Nifong had said that Mangum was choked during the attack and struggled to breathe, but she told Levicy she was not choked. They claimed Nifong said he read a medical report on March 29, when the time-stamps on the evidence showed the report was not printed until the next day. There was an increasing risk that the defense attorneys might decide to call Nifong as a witness in the case to explain these contradictions and others. If that were to happen, Nifong would have to recuse himself from the case, since he could not act as both a prosecutor and a witness. Defense attorneys pointed to Nifong's use of the words "hooligans" and "reprehensible" to describe the lacrosse players as evidence that Nifong had crossed the line. Again, James Coleman took the lead, publicly at least, in criticizing Nifong. "Either he knew what the facts were and misstated them, or he was making them up," Coleman told the *News & Observer*. "Whether he acted knowing they were false, or if he was reckless, it doesn't matter in the long run. This is the kind of stuff that causes the public to lose confidence in the justice system."

The media then tried to figure out what the implications might be of the contradictions between Nifong's statements and the evidence he shared with defense attorneys. "In the public view, it probably seems like this is a big deal and that the police were caught doing something wrong," Irving Joyner, a law professor at NCCU, told the Durham paper. "It plays well in the theater, so to speak. But at this point, I don't think it's all that strong. A lot will depend on the fortitude of Mike Nifong and his faith in his case. If he believes in what he is doing, it could go all the way." But Mike Godsey, a former New York City prosecutor, thought the contradictions had hurt Nifong. "These events are more bad news for the prosecution," he said, "but we still don't know what evidence they have. Nevertheless, as we learn more, the universe of the prosecution's possible evidence seems to shrink."

The lull in the legal action also gave members of the media, which had been covering the story intensely for months, a moment to pause and potentially reflect on the havoc the case had wreaked. The *News & Observer* focused on what had become of Evans, Seligmann, and Finnerty. Evans, his attorney Joe Cheshire told the paper, had lost his job offer with JPMorgan Chase. (Evans had spent a number of months working as a "senior analyst" at Cyren Call Communications in McLean, Virginia.) "Those are very hard jobs to come by and are only given to some of the best and brightest people in the country, so it was a real blow to him," Cheshire said, doing his best to evoke sympathy for the indicted player. "He's angry, and his life has been materially altered by these false accusations. But he knows he's innocent, and that makes it easier to deal with."

After a post-graduation beach trip with his parents, Evans and a group of his lacrosse buddies from Landon had a cookout at the home of the parents of one of his former Landon teammates. "David seems to be holding his own," Matt Ward, an attackman on UVA's national championship team, told the paper. "If I were in his situation, I'd be in a shell. But not Dave. He's a great spirit, a strong-minded guy. If anybody can weather something like this, it would be Dave." Added his former Landon coach, Rob Bordley, who was at the cookout, too, "With us, David was just David. . . . We joked, 'Let's get a picture with the felon—it'll be a keepsake.' I think, frankly, this is tougher on parents. Kids tend to be resilient. . . . I think it's good therapy to be some-place where they don't have to defend their child." Bordley did acknowledge the players' poor choices. "There was some regrettable behavior that's been acknowledged . . . that didn't reflect well upon these boys, the school, and the community," he said, while lauding Evans for speaking out at his May 15 press conference. "I suspect a lot of people who saw the press conference saw a very impressive young man," he said. "So I'm confident he's going to land on his feet. There will be job opportunities. I don't think he'll be twiddling his thumbs for the next six or nine months."

The attorneys for Seligmann and Finnerty were less sanguine. The combi-nation of the Georgetown assault and the Durham indictment, made it vir-tually impossible for Finnerty to get a summer job, his attorney Wade Smith e-mailed the paper. He was living at home, in Garden City, New York, with his parents but under a curfew applicable between 9 p.m. and 6 a.m. He was not permitted near any place where alcohol was served. Seligmann was also living at home, in Essex Fells, New Jersey, with his parents. He had asked Duke to allow him to finish his course and his exams from the spring semester but had not yet been allowed to do so because of the pending felony charges against him. He had begun training for the April 2007 Boston Marathon. "Reade is funny; he's so goal-oriented," Edward Abbot, a family friend and the town's mayor, told the *News & Observer*. "He's a very confident young man and believes he's going to be fully exonerated." But Seligmann was lonely. "I'm sit-ting here talking to my imaginary friends," he related to a Duke friend. Selig-mann's attorney, Kirk Osborn, said he feared for Seligmann's safety ever since the May 18 hearing when onlookers shouted, "'Here comes the rapist and the rapist's attorney.' It was just so offensive."

The paper also reported that the parents of the players had started an e-mail network to stay connected and had created a fund to pay the legal fees of those less financially secure. To raise money, the parents were selling royal blue plastic wristbands embossed with "Duke Lacrosse 2006" on the front and, on the back: "Innocent #6, #13, #45," the lacrosse jersey numbers for Evans, Finnerty, and Seligmann. The Landon senior class wore the wrist-bands during its June graduation. "This has been a tragedy that I guess has to go down as a lesson in life," John Walsh, the father of Johnny Walsh, told the *News & Observer*. "We've all been hurt by the rush to judgment and the fact that nobody's looking at the injustice of this thing." Added Sally Fogarty, the mother of Gibbs Fogarty, "It's been tough. It's been scary. It was like a spin of the roulette wheel—that could have been any one of these kids."

Sports Illustrated, in a lengthy article titled "The Damage Done," examined the scandal from the perspectives of Mangum, Nifong, Pressler, Duke, and sev-eral of the accused but unindicted players. It was a powerful piece of journal-ism that showed, in the words of Donna Lisker, director of the Duke Women's

Center, "Everybody lost. No matter what happens." In the first section, the magazine's reporters spoke with Matt Zash, one of the three lacrosse cocaptains who lived at 610 North Buchanan. He revealed to the magazine he had suspected he would be indicted. "Nobody knew who it was going to be," he said. "But basically the three people living in the house thought, 'Hell, it's going to be us.'" He said that before Easter weekend, he had gone to see Pressler, his former coach. "I think there's a good chance I'm going to get indicted," Zash told him. "I've come to grips with it. I'm going to try to stay as strong as I can." Another player, Casey Carroll, who was not even at the party on the night of March 13—he was with his girlfriend—was still worried that he might be picked by Mangum in the photo lineup because his face was one of the ones put on the so-called "wanted" posters the Durham police put around town. "There I am, top right, every day when they show it," he said. "We all look the same, we're all generally tall, thin, white guys. I don't know how anybody would pick out someone [as a suspect]. I was nervous." He recalled how when he, along with the other white members of the team, was taken to Durham Police headquarters to give DNA samples, a policewoman examined his torso for marks. "There's some scarring right here," she said as she looked over his body. It turned out the marks were from when he had chicken pox, twelve years earlier. After the inside of his cheek was swabbed for a DNA sample, he heard a police officer say, as they were leaving, "Don't worry, guys. This will all blow over."

Of course, that did not happen. "I don't think any of us slept or ate much for a month," Zash explained. The magazine reported that Zash "spent the next week living out of his car and staying on friends' couches before checking into a hotel. His parents came down two weeks later to lend support, but in a lawyer's office, his mother, Nina, broke down sobbing, fighting for breath, unable to stand. 'You feel like you're drowning, and you just want it to stop,' she says. 'But it wasn't stopping. It was getting worse and worse.'" Over Easter weekend, Nina Zash repeated over and over the words, "Matthew's probably going to be arrested" and then her eyes would fill with tears.

Brian Loftus, a retired New York City fireman who spent thirty-six consecutive hours digging through the rubble at the World Trade Center after the September 11 attacks, had two sons, Dan (a goalie) and Chris (an attackman), on the Duke lacrosse team. The family lived in Syosset, Long Island, just east of New York City. "I thought that" September 11 "was the worst day of my life," he said. "You want to know something? This is the worst thing." The Loftuses repeatedly grilled their sons about what happened on the night of March 13. "How many times did I say to him on the phone? 'Danny, did anything happen?'" Loftus asked his wife, Barbara. "I asked him ten times. He goes, 'No, no, no, no.'" Added Barbara, "This is not a time to lie and cover up for your friends! Did anything happen?" They became convinced of their sons' innocence, but in the days before the first two indictments they were still afraid.

They spent Easter weekend at their Syosset home. "We sat here like zombies," he said. "I didn't want to talk to anybody."

Casey Carroll's father was also a fireman. Without his lacrosse scholarship, Carroll would not have been able to attend Duke. He was the first person in his family to attend college. "Without a scholarship I couldn't blink an eye at this place," he said. "There are a lot of kids on the team with a lot of money. I come from a completely different world. I'm just grateful: Now maybe I can help my family out." The Duke education and the lacrosse pedigree appeared to put the players in an elite, seemingly virtuous circle. "Every lacrosse coach came into my house, they all had the same line. The Hopkins guy, the Princeton guy: 'You're not coming to our school for four years, you're coming for the next forty,'" Brian Loftus told the magazine. "And they'll tell you they own Morgan Stanley or Dean Witter: 'We network.' Six months ago, going to Duke and playing lacrosse, you're going to get a job. Things are going to be good for you. Now? You're going to fight that the rest of your life." The three indictments of their friends and teammates had devastated them—and dashed their dreams. "They are ruined for life," said Nina Zash. Added her son, "It was a lottery drawing. We know it could be any one of us."

Crystal Mangum had not spoken to the media since giving an interview to the *News & Observer*, and she did not speak with *Sports Illustrated*. The magazine did what many other journalists had done: spoke with her parents, Travis and Mary. But since Mangum had not spoken with them for two months, their information was sketchy and mostly reflected—again—the odd ramblings of her father, who was fixing the cars that were scattered around the lawn of the Mangums' south Durham home, and those of her mother. "Duke did something to those DNA results so they would favor those boys," Mary Mangum told the magazine. She also said her daughter was angry with them for continuing to speak to the media. "We told her we were just trying to help her," she explained. "I asked my minister to pray with [her], but she won't come to church." She revealed that, in 2005, her own parents had thought Mangum was going to die of ovarian cancer. "But God healed her," she said.

With all the media attention focused on them, the Mangums seemed to be having trouble keeping straight what they had previously said, and to whom. According to the *New York Times*, Travis said Crystal was undergoing psychological testing and was in no condition to testify. "I don't know where they got that," he told *Sports Illustrated*. "A lot of times we hear stuff about [her] in the paper that we hadn't heard before." He thought she would testify. "That's just my feeling," he said. The magazine also revealed that Mary Mangum had met with Florida lawyer Willie Gary to see if he would represent the Mangums in a civil lawsuit against the players or the university (which owned the house where the party occurred) or both. There was a lot of confusion, Travis conceded. "Everybody has their opinions about this case: fifty people are going to have fifty different versions of the truth," he said. "People have to decide which version of the truth they want to believe." He said that making the case so much about race missed the nuances of life in the South. For instance, a white family had raised him from the time he was seven years old, after his family's home burned down in a fire. He also voted for Nifong, but had no illusions about his motivations. "Nifong doesn't care anything about my daughter," he said. "All he cares about is winning the case."

Nifong declined to comment. In his first interview since being fired, Mike Pressler told *Sports Illustrated* his troubles began on March 25, twelve days after the party but the day after he announced the forfeiture of two Duke lacrosse games. There were threats to his life. His wife, Susan, received scary e-mails. They moved their eight-year-old daughter out of town. When he woke up at 5 a.m., he would have to remove the signs that people had posted on the door of his house. "DO YOUR DUTY. TURN THEM IN," one read. Others were more horrific. Another time he was standing in his driveway when a car drove by and three eggs were thrown at him. "Boom, boom, boom," he said. The car sped away. He could barely sleep. "One eye open: you don't sleep at all," he said. "If something does happen, it's my home and my family, and I've got to be ready for that. And then there's the anxiety: What's next if the season's canceled? If changes are made? I've got to keep my cool for my family and the players. If the guys see I'm frazzled, it's going to filter down. But when I was alone, you can imagine what was going through my mind."

The catalyst for his career at Duke turned out to be the public release of McFadyen's e-mail. The magazine reported the McFadyen e-mail "symbolically" was "the Duke case's equivalent of the Superdome after Hurricane Katrina, confirming all the worst suspicions about the roles of class, race, sex, power, and privilege at the university." Thirty minutes after the McFadyen e-mail came out, Alleva asked to see Pressler. In the days leading up to the meeting, Pressler offered to resign if it would improve the overall situation. And at their meeting, Alleva gave Pressler the Hobson's choice of either quitting or waiting to be fired. Pressler didn't care to get into the details of their discussion. "I resigned," he told the magazine. Neither Brodhead nor Alleva tried to talk him out of the decision. His lawyer, Mark Anderson, elaborated. "Mike was the sacrificial lamb," he said.

Pressler reiterated that his late-afternoon meeting with the players was brutal. He hugged each of his players. He also cried. "All of us feel guilt," Zash said. "Whether we're choirboys or not, we were part of a team that got him thrown under the bus. To see him be the fall guy for something he wasn't involved in or had any clue about what was going on? It's horrible. We feel horrible for that."

The magazine noted that the Duke players gave Pressler a number of mixed messages. The players claimed to respect him but also regularly misbehaved—

fifty-six of them had been involved in thirty-six on-campus incidents since 2003, according to the Coleman report, and that did not include fifteen players cited by the Durham police for off-campus mischief. Pressler also was not given police reports about his players' bad behavior or the reports of on-campus problems unless there was a threat of a suspension. And then he handled the matter. The lacrosse players "were out of control," Coleman said. "As long as they thought [Pressler] wasn't finding out about it, they didn't have enough respect for him or enough self-discipline not to do it. But it wasn't as if they were doing this underground. It was the responsibility of the university to take effective disciplinary action, to make sure the athletic department knew about it and instructed them they wanted it to stop. If they had done that, my judgment is, Pressler would have responded." But another Duke administrator questioned Pressler's leadership of the team. "Do you think Mike Krzyzewski would've put up with this shit for five seconds?" he said. "The answer is no."

The magazine suggested that the reason the story had become such a national sensation was Duke's "long-standing and at times obnoxiously trumpeted sense of itself." In the previous twenty years Duke had "evolved into an educational force not far behind Harvard or Yale while expanding its reach as a sports power," *Sports Illustrated* reported. "Really, only two universities, Stanford and Duke, have been able to consistently utter the phrase 'We do it the right way' without hearing snickers; with three national titles in basketball since 1991 and a 96 percent athletic graduation rate, Duke seemed to have mastered the balance between high academic standards and big-time athletics." Then, as if on cue (and with more than a touch of irony), John Burness again stoked the flames. "If this was Mississippi or Penn State," he said, "it wouldn't be as big a story"—a point, although arrogantly made, that the magazine conceded was true. "Duke *is* special, yet for those inclined to schadenfreude, the school's need to remind everyone of that makes a Blue Devils scandal a bit more tasty," the magazine wrote. Added Donna Lisker, the director of the Duke Women's Center, "A lot of people hate, hate, hate Duke because it has this image of the golden child. They're happy to see the golden child fall."

To end the piece, *Sports Illustrated* accompanied Pressler on a return to the $2.4 million Koskinen Stadium on the day—June 5—that Broadhead announced he was reinstating the team and there was no hope for Pressler's return. Pressler recalled a "huge win" over Virginia in 2002 and a comeback victory over Penn State in 1997. He had, after all, turned the program around, bringing it to the final game in 2005 against Johns Hopkins, only to have the expected national championship, in 2006, snuffed out on the night of March 13. "All of that, gone now," the story ended. "He left the stadium on the verge of crying again. For a time he'd harbored the hope that he'd wake up and they'd give him his job back. Now Pressler began the walk home, forty-five minutes or so, and it hit him with the cold snap of finality: I'm done. This is good-bye.

For what? Why? 'I can't help it,' he says. 'I'd be a liar to say I'm over it.' Some people, he may never forgive. But the next coach? Pressler wants him to win the national title. He still flies a Duke flag on his house, still runs in Duke shorts, still wears his Duke lacrosse hat around town. He preached it and lived it, and he isn't about to change now. All in, all the way."

With each fresh piece of journalism, the tide of public opinion seemed to shift, palpably, away from the case Nifong had been making for months on Mangum's behalf. On June 19, Ruth Sheehan, the *News & Observer* columnist and one of the first people to condemn the lacrosse players publicly, wondered whether the time had come for Nifong to recuse himself and whether a special prosecutor should be appointed. "To think for a brief moment, I actually pitied Nifong for the attacks on his handling of the case," she wrote. "What a joke. . . . Whether he was shooting from the hip based on word-of-mouth inaccuracies or flat-out making stuff up, I don't know." What she did know was, "This case has affected the reputations of three young athletes, possibly unfairly. It has torn off the scabs on race and class—in Durham and beyond." Sheehan con-cluded with the thought that, "At this point, Nifong has damaged his own rep-utation and his own office to the point where he cannot possibly handle this case to its resolution. It's time for him to call in a special prosecutor and put himself—and the rest of us—out of our misery."

On June 19, *Newsweek*'s latest story about the lacrosse case hit the news-stands. There was little new in the story for anyone who had been paying atten-tion to the motions that defense attorneys had been filing. The lone exception was the opening scene the reporters described where attorney Bob Ekstrand offered the lacrosse players, many of whom were his clients, the legal strategy of not providing DNA evidence when Judge Stephens first ordered them to produce it—by having him appeal the order as too "overbroad" and "sweep-ing" in scope. Instead, they marched themselves down to the Durham police station to provide the DNA evidence. "Ekstrand was struck to see how little hesitation the players showed," *Newsweek* reported. "After all, if the DNA of any one of those men matched DNA found on the accuser's body, it could ruin his life: disgrace followed by many years in prison. But there was no talk of hiring individual lawyers or stalling for time; the players seemed to want to get on with it. 'I was watching to see if anyone hung back,' Ekstrand told *News-week*. No one did. It is possible, almost three months later, that the players are maintaining a conspiracy of silence. But it seems highly unlikely. Rather, court documents in the case increasingly suggest that Durham County Dis-trict Attorney Mike Nifong had very little evidence upon which to indict three players for rape."

The controversy over the lacrosse case brought out of the woodwork two new candidates—Lewis Cheek, a county commissioner and Democrat; and Steve Monks, the chairman of the Durham County Republican Party—both of whom sought to challenge Nifong in the November election for district attorney. Under normal circumstances, since there was no Republican running in the May primary, Nifong's victory in the Democratic primary over Freda Black and Keith Bishop would have ensured his November election but the entry of both Cheek and Monks into the fray showed how politically vulnerable many people thought Nifong had become in a month's time. "People feel Nifong totally sold out to the people of Durham," Monks said. "They don't feel comfortable with this case."

This became fodder for MSNBC. Dan Abrams, the Duke alumnus who had been outspoken in his criticism of Nifong, returned as a guest on his eponymous show. Someone had leaked to Abrams a set of the 1,300 pages of documentary evidence. "This case is even weaker than I originally thought," he said. But Abrams would not be pinned down about whether he thought Mangum was lying. "What I am willing to say is that there are so many contradictions in her story that this DA never should have brought this case," he said. "This is a case in serious, serious trouble."

That same day, *ESPN The Magazine* published a long article by Jon Pessah about what the infamous housemates Matt Zash and Dan Flannery were doing after graduating from Duke, not having been indicted. Zash had been a first-round draft pick of the Philadelphia Barrage of Major League Lacrosse, and Pessah caught up with him two days before a game against the Long Island Lizards in Uniondale, New York, not far from where Zash grew up in Massapequa.

They met on the small deck of the Zash family's three-bedroom split-level house. The lacrosse player was dressed in jeans and a T-shirt. "To me, rape is the most hated crime there is," Zash said, "and to be accused of that is completely horrifying. But nobody wanted to hear the truth. They wanted us to admit something that did not happen, and they wanted to see us pay for it." He recalled that how the media played the story on a given day had an outsized role in how the teammates were treated around campus. "If there were favorable media, maybe we wouldn't be harassed," he said. "It was tough to be a Duke lacrosse player on campus, and all of a sudden a mob of students crowd around and start yelling at you to step forward and tell what happened that night. Maybe I was young and naïve, but I thought that nothing bad was ever going to happen. The worst was when my name and home address was posted on a Web site, along with my picture and my parents' name, calling for vigilante justice. That really worried me. My parents live in that house and they were distraught. That's when it really hit me that anything could happen."

After graduating from Duke, Flannery, a five-foot-eleven-inch, 190-pound All-American attackman, was selected in the sixth round of the Major League Lacrosse draft by the Chicago Machine. He hadn't played yet because of a shoulder injury and so was at Zash's game in Uniondale. He had driven over from his parents' home in Garden City, Long Island. He had taken a year off to play professional lacrosse and take an accounting course before starting his job on Wall Street, at UBS. "I want to digest what happened this year," he told Pessah. He said his senior year at Duke was meant to be perfect: living in a primo location off-campus and being the cocaptain of a team that many assumed would be national champions. "It was perfect," he said of 610 North Buchanan. "That's where you wanted to be. Three bedrooms, backyard, a big living room. We had a big-screen TV that Dave's uncle was good enough to give us." They hosted parties, slept when they could, and played Xbox and Nintendo 64. "We had so much fun there," he said. He recalled that he returned to the house from a barbecue at a professor's when the police entered 610 North Buchanan. He rode in a squad car to join his two roommates at the police station. He gave his statement, his DNA, and offered to take a polygraph test, which was denied.

Eleven days later, he was listening as Pressler told the team he was leaving. "He walked in and told us that he had been forced out," Flannery recalled. "He was devastated. Coach is one of the best people I ever met, and he didn't do anything wrong. Everyone in the room just broke down and cried. It was the last time I was going to play for him, the last time I was going to play with guys like Matt Danowski. I just came home that weekend, I couldn't stay down there. We all felt abandoned." While watching Zash's team rally on the field, he said, wistfully, "This was going to be our year. We were going to do something really special."

The next day, at his annual summer press conference, Coach K broke his silence about the lacrosse case. No doubt many people hoped his thoughts would be revelatory, especially after nearly four months of keeping quiet. Instead, he served up a healthy helping of corporate pablum. Although many had argued Coach K was the most powerful person on the Duke campus— one noted: "He's not the power behind the throne; he sits on the only throne there is"—Krzyzewski said, "I think it is important for me to remember my place. I am the basketball coach. I am not the president, I am not the athletic director and I am not on the board of trustees. You have to be careful not to make statements outside of your realm." He said that behind the scenes, he had tried to be very supportive of Duke's "athletic department, the coaches, the players, our president, and the board of trustees. To me, the real story about this spring, without talking about the case because you have to let that run its course"—and here those hoping for something profound would be disappointed, especially since his comment made little sense—"is the community. I love our community because for the last few months, a number of people who have come into our community and raised a lot of questions, which they are entitled to do, that could have provoked things that were not a part of this situation. Our community is so darn good that they did not allow it. I don't look at this being a white community, an African-American community, a Hispanic community, I look at this being a great Durham community. The students at the two universities [North Carolina Central and Duke] should be applauded."

What planet had Krzyzewski been living on since March 13? How could he think that the Duke "community" had not allowed questions to be raised about the behavior of the athletes in the house at 610 North Buchanan? Wasn't that exactly what had been happening since the alleged incident become public?

But nobody asked him to explain his statement. Instead, he kept on spinning. "I do think for us as a university, we have to always be mindful of the fact of the major reason we are here is because of our students," he continued. "You have to be there to support them, to give them guidance, and to just to be there and say 'We are with you.' That is what I have tried to do behind the scenes. Giving support does not mean you are choosing sides; giving support is what a university should do, whether it be at North Carolina Central, Duke, Fordham, Illinois, or Army. We are in the kid business and that is what I have tried to do behind the scenes. I don't like the remarks that attack athletics, not just at Duke but anywhere, and I think that the people that do that are very narrow-minded in the total scope of what a university or college does." He continued on about the importance of athletics and learning to work together as a team—one of his favorite themes and the subject of several of his bestselling books.

Asked about the lacrosse team's new "code of conduct," Krzyzewski said he had his own rules for how his players should behave. "Our first rule with a team is, 'Don't do anything detrimental to yourself or to our program,'" he said. "That gives me a lot of latitude so that I can judge what is detrimental to them. You don't let a rule govern what you do; you let a principle govern what you do. Instead of a code of conduct, I would rather have a code of values."

Asked to expand what his behind-the-scenes role had been during the crisis, Krzyzewski again obfuscated. He said he would tell Alleva, "I'm with you" or ask Brodhead, "What can I do?" (As noted earlier, further behind the scenes, Krzysewski was critical of Alleva, claiming he had been a weak and ineffective athletic director, which caused at least one influential member of the Duke community to remind him that Duke chose Alleva specifically at Krzyzewski's request so that Krzyzewski would have free reign at the university.) He also said he continued to socialize with the Presslers, who had been his friends for years, and who were now exiled in Durham. "The Presslers are our dear friends," he said. "I don't know what Mike Pressler did wrong in this case; whether he's judged is a whole other thing that's another matter. He is a good man. My feeling is that he is here sixteen years; his players, former players, and families swear by him. As far as my friendship with him, he is going to be my friend."

At one point, Coach K was critical of William Bowen, the former president of Princeton and the outgoing president of the Mellon Foundation, and of the report Bowen wrote about athletics at Duke. "I think that's a report that's skewed," he said, according to the *New York Times* (the official transcript of Krzyzewski's press conference does not contain that minor criticism). "We have many great graduates of this university who participated in intercollegiate athletics who are running major corporations, who are operating on people, who are defending people, who are counseling people, and to say that intercollegiate athletics is not an integral part of any university is so ridiculously wrong. It is so narrow-minded and I'm glad that our administration and our board of trustees recognize this."

He also tried to explain his role as a special advisor to Brodhead, the position he had gained after agreeing to stay at Duke instead of going to the Los Angeles Lakers as head coach. He said it was not that formal a role. "Because of [the basketball program's] visibility, we obviously have an impact on our university," he said. "I am not saying we are the major thing or whatever, but obviously we have an impact. . . . I love Duke. Duke is a great school, and it will always be a great school. How it handles a situation like this will determine how much more it can grow and how it will grow. I wear my Duke stuff every day. I am proud of being the Duke coach. Being the Duke coach has given me more than I could ever give to Duke and I think most graduates would say the same thing."

In the end, Coach K conceded the scandal had put Duke through some very difficult moments. "This is the most trying time," he concluded. "That is the way it is. If you are going be here for the long run, you are going to have trying times. That is what happens, whether it is a business or a family, if you are in it for the long haul."

Also expunged from the official transcript of the press conference was any mention by Krzyzewski of the drunk-driving arrest—six days before—of former Duke basketball star J. J. Redick, who had graduated six weeks earlier. Police arrested Redick, who won the 2006 Wooden Award as the nation's top college basketball player and finished his career as the leading scorer in Atlantic Coast Conference history, around 1 a.m. on June 14 after he turned his car around as he was approaching a random license check by the Duke campus. The police followed him briefly, and he then pulled into a nearby apartment-building parking lot and stopped. His blood-alcohol level was 0.11, above the legal driving limit of 0.08. In his report, the arresting officer wrote that Redick had "very glassy eyes, strong odor of alcohol coming from breath." He posted bond of $1,000 at the Durham County Courthouse and was released. (In the end, Redick pleaded guilty to drunk driving, paid a fine of $410, had his license suspended for sixty days, and was ordered to perform twenty-four hours of community service. By then, the Orlando Magic had drafted him in the first round.)

While Coach K was trying to make sense of what clearly had become a very intractable and ambiguous situation, Mangum's cousin, Jakki—she would use only her first name—told the *Carolinian*, a small Durham newspaper focused on the black community, that "alums of Duke" had early on offered Mangum "a staggering $2 million" to drop the charges against the Duke players. "She told me they wanted to make the case go away," Jakki told the paper. But Mangum declined the offer because "It's not about the money to her," Jakki said. "It's about her [being] brutally raped, sodomized, called a 'nigger.' Can you imagine being choked and held down? The thought of it—it reminds me of slavery days when the women were brutally raped by the masters—makes me furious, because they want to make these [Duke players] out to be golden boys." Jakki said Mangum, who was in seclusion and could not be reached, told the family she wanted the trial to go forward so that justice could be done. Sam Hall, the communications director for Duke alumni affairs, denied the offer to Mangum had been made.

But the *Carolinian* insisted that "early in the case," unnamed "Black leaders" were "offered sums of money" for "themselves, NCCU" and Mangum "if they could influence her to retract her allegations." The paper reported that "those leaders flatly refused the offer." Jakki wanted to counter the perception that her cousin was trying to profit from her allegations. "She has not taken a dime from anybody," she said, "because she does not want it to be misconstrued that she is in it to get money." She said that since the allegations of her being raped became a national news story, Mangum had "lost a lot of weight," been "very fearful," had "cut her hair," and had "developed stomach ulcers." She also had trouble sleeping and was seeing a counselor. After Mangum had received "Die Nigger" death threats, she and her young children stayed at different locations around Durham and sometimes out of state. She even considered—briefly—dropping the charges. "She didn't realize how big a thing that this would become," Jakki said. "This has been traumatic for her. Not only was she raped that night, but she's being raped over and over every day, every night on some channel, in some newspaper."

Jakki also rejected the criticism of many—including those in the religious black community—that Mangum had brought the trouble onto herself by becoming an exotic dancer. "It's summertime, and these young girls who are walking around in these little shorts and [revealing attire], do they ask to be raped?" she asked. "No, they do not. I think it's ironic that America idolizes Marilyn Monroe and Pamela Anderson, and all of these women that pose for *Playboy*, but then if it's an African-American woman, it's a different situation. My cousin was doing a job, and unfortunately we as black people, for years, have had to do things [to support our families] we normally would not do. Did she deserve to be raped because of that? No, I don't think so. That's like saying because you're black, you deserve to be lynched, and that's ridiculous."

Jakki told the paper that for her and the Mangum family, there was "no doubt" Mangum "was raped and beaten" and that she was "slipped something in the drink she was given at the lacrosse party, severely disorienting her, resulting in an emotional and traumatic confusion" that led to the "contradictory versions" of events later described by police and the SANE nurse. "I'm privy to more information than people on the other side of [this are]," she said. "They haven't released the pictures of her . . . the bruises, the black eye. Where did she get that?" She said the daily leaks coming from the defense attorneys that were immediately seized upon by the media had left the impression that Mangum was a "false accuser" and that Nifong had lost control of the case. "They are crucifying my cousin," she said. Jakki said she was glad that Nifong had finally responded, on June 19, to the *Newsweek* article that had "mischaracterized" him. "I am so glad that he is still adamant about pursuing this case," she said. "We are pleased that he is not buckling to pressure, whether it's political or otherwise. [The families of the indicted Duke lacrosse suspects] are very wealthy people. They have a lot of influence, big people in big places. [Yet, Nifong is] sticking to his guns." She said she and the family understood the "high stakes" of the matter and were "very concerned." "These people have money [and] they want to make this go away," she continued. "They want to make my cousin look like a harlot, a Jezebel, and they want this to go away." Jakki said her cousin "needs a voice" and encouraged people to continue to pray for Mangum. "This could be their daughter, their sister," she said. "It could be their cousin. We all make mistakes, but she didn't ask to be brutally beaten and raped. They need to know that she's human." Asked by Durham police on June 30 if she had ever been offered money to drop the case, Mangum replied, according to police records, that she "never had any offers from anyone to drop the case," nor would she accept one.

Jakki's opinion seemed to be decidedly in the minority. MSNBC conducted an unscientific on-air poll asking viewers to vote on whether Nifong should drop the case against the three indicted lacrosse players. Of the 863 responses, 82 percent said he should. "Fair enough," the blog The Johnsville News opined on June 20. "Not everyone has had time to read the voluminous documentation and evaluate the alleged rape time line minute by minute. Millions watch *Law & Order* and believe the prosecutor is always the 'good guy.' That was [our] assumption when this Duke mess started. But, Mike Nifong has gone way off the 'good guy' reservation. He is in a different place now. He's an egotistical, pandering, lying bully who's been called out by most legal experts who have actually looked at the evidence. This case is a total hoax. It only continues as a dead man walking, ruining the lives of three innocent young men, for reasons known only to Mike Nifong.

"The false accuser," the blog continued, "Crystal Gail Mangum"—outing her in a more public way than had previously occurred—"is a sad person too.

But, she has sat through numerous police interviews and lineups (3?) and lied and lied and lied some more. Perhaps she became upset because the Duke players locked her out of the house and wouldn't let her get her shoe back. 'Mess with my shoe and you'll have hell to pay.' Accusing three young men of rape and trying to send them to jail because one of your white shoes is missing sounds like a pretty evil thing to do. But it is some stupid twisted logic like that which is guiding Ms. Mangum. She might also have other personal issues which are impacting her. So, thank you to Ms. Mangum, the perception of all future legitimate rape victims has been badly damaged." The blogger then wondered what the answer to the "real question" was. "Who is more evil: Mike Nifong or Crystal Gail Mangum?" Of the 170 votes submitted, Nifong garnered 84 percent of them.

At the court hearing on June 22, Nifong shared with defense attorneys another 536 pages of evidence—bringing the total to 1,814 pages—and immediately, after having somehow already parsed them, the lawyers declared yet again how the new documents exonerated their clients. Although the lawyers would not release the pages to the media, they said the pages contained a reference to Mangum claiming, at one point, that *five* players raped her—as she told Durham police officer Gwen Sutton early on—instead of three (or other numbers) and that she had been one of *four* dancers at the party, not two. "We've got none, we've got three, we've got five, we've got twenty," Joe Cheshire told reporters about the alleged number of rapists. "I mean, pick a number—any number you want to pick. She's told so many different stories I'm not sure how many there are."

Linwood Wilson, the investigator working with Nifong, barged onto the scene and asked Cheshire for a copy of the page where Mangum had made that claim.

"You're welcome to come get it," Cheshire told him.

"Yeah, I'd love to see it," Wilson replied, before he walked away and Cheshire continued his press conference.

Cheshire also addressed the report in the *Carolinian* that a group of Duke alumni had offered Mangum "$2 million" to recant her allegations. "These boys are innocent," he repeated. "No money has been or ever will be offered in this case. . . . There never will be a plea in this case, either. You don't plead innocent people."

The hearing and its attendant theatrics provided yet more evidence that the case had become a battleground between Nifong, on the one hand, and the defense attorneys, and an increasingly hostile press corps, on the other. For instance, before the June 22 hearing, Nifong walked up to Susan Filan, the MSNBC legal analyst, who was sitting in the courtroom gallery. Filan, who had once called Nifong a "rodeo cowboy" on the air, had asked Nifong for an interview. When she saw him coming over to her, she was thinking he was going to grant her the interview. "Two words: rodeo cowboy," Nifong said to her before turning away.

At the actual hearing, the judge agreed to lower the bail for Seligmann to $100,000 from $400,000 after his father, Philip, made another impassioned plea in an affidavit filed with the court that bail money was provided by a family friend who was losing the income on the money while it was tied up in court, not earning interest. "His loss of this income is substantial," Philip Seligmann wrote. "I feel an obligation to repay this gentleman for the loss of his imputed income. The obligation also creates a tremendous emotional toll on my son (who does feel a moral obligation to repay the debt) and my entire family." He added, "This case has taken an unbelievable and horrendous emotional toll on all my family, especially my wife. We are committed as a family, along with Reade, to do everything necessary to restore our good name." Seligmann's affidavit also allowed him to expound on the virtues of his son, who, he said, had turned down Harvard, Yale, and Princeton to attend Duke on a 90 percent scholarship and had "never been involved in the criminal justice system . . . before the filing of these charges." His son had been a camp counselor at the Lacrosse Camp at Delbarton, with the Tri-State Lacrosse Program and at the Princeton University Lacrosse Camp. In December of his junior year at Delbarton, Reade participated in the Appalachia Project to work with the "mountain children" of eastern Kentucky, the "poorest of the poor in the United States." There were pictures attached with Reade, dressed up as Santa Claus, with children from Appalachia.

He was a member of Bridges, another Delbarton program, where students "go into some of the poorest neighborhoods" in New York City "at night to bring food and clothing to the homeless during especially bad weather, such as severe cold and snowstorms."

His father also attached to the affidavit his son's Duke transcript, which showed that his grades had steadily dropped from As and a single B+ during his first semester (GPA 3.675 and Dean's List) to mostly Bs in the following two semesters. His cumulative GPA was a 3.33, but he had not received his grades for his four courses—elementary Spanish, entrepreneurship, African-American history, and anthropology of law—for the spring semester of 2006. "Reade is busily attempting to complete his course work . . . by working with his professors while remaining at his home in New Jersey." Philip Seligmann, who was born Jewish and raised by an African-American woman after a tree fell on his mother, seemed pleased to be able to boast about Reade's accomplishments. He also was not above seeking some sympathy. "I live near three country clubs," he once said. "I can't afford any of them, and two wouldn't have me as a member."

The day after the hearing, Cheshire couldn't resist tweaking Linwood Wilson by sending him a letter with a copy of Gwen Sutton's report with Mangum's comments about the number of men—five—that she claimed had raped her inside the house. "While being interviewed at Duke [Hospital], her story changed several times," Sutton wrote in her report, which Cheshire sent to Wilson. "Since you are [Nifong's] Investigator," Cheshire wrote, "the press could have assumed—falsely, as it turns out—that you had actually read your file"; he pointed Wilson to page 1,304 of the file and continued, "I can only assume your motivation in questioning my assertion was simple ignorance. A simple reading of your file might solve that problem in the future." But, Wilson told the Durham paper, Cheshire was "trying to twist what I asked him" and he, Wilson, was simply questioning Cheshire's reference to Mangum's comment about twenty rapists, not his comment about five rapists. "I was upset about the twenty," he said. "There ain't nothing about twenty in anything I've read. I wanted him to show it to me." (Actually, in a March 14 Duke police report, there was a reference to Mangum claiming that "she was raped by approximately twenty white males.")

The inconsistencies in Mangum's story were making defense attorneys angry. "These allegations are absolutely incredulous," attorney Bill Thomas said. "They have been unbelievable from the very beginning. As more information becomes available, they become more unbelievable. Any rational person reading this file could only conclude that a rape did not occur."

The end of June also saw David Evans convicted of a misdemeanor noise ordinance violation—arising from a January party at 610 North Buchnan—requiring him to pay a $110 fine. Even though a Durham judge found Evans guilty of creating a noise, around 1 a.m., that sounded to neighbors like someone banging away on trash cans, no record of the conviction would appear on his permanent record. As he had done previously for Seligmann, Judge Stephens also reduced the bail to $100,000 each for both Evans and Finnerty.

Then there was the release of a letter, dated June 7, from Duke to Ryan McFadyen reinstating him as a Duke student. Returning to Duke had been a goal of McFadyen's from the moment he was suspended two months earlier. To make it happen, he met one-on-one with Stephen Bryan, an associate dean of student affairs, and explained what had happened. "I walked him through the entire thing, four hours, just step by step by step to that point three months later, walking through every one of my e-mails, citing every reference of the movie, every reference of the inside jokes on the team," McFadyen recalled. A few days later, Bryan made the decision that McFadyen could return to school. Concluded Bryan: "After hearing from him, Ryan, one cannot help but see how his vilification is a gross misrepresentation of his true nature." The June 7 letter, written by Larry Moneta to Brodhead, now claimed that McFadyen wrote his infamous e-mail "in jest," after McFadyen cited to Bryan the parts of *American Psycho* he had been referencing in his e-mail. "He acknowledged the joke, especially given the context of the time, was not funny," Moneta wrote, adding that McFadyen accepted responsibility for an error in judgment. "I think he learned a valuable lesson in how words can be interpreted and mis-interpreted," Moneta told the Associated Press. McFadyen's return to Duke meant that he could also play again for the lacrosse team. (He also decided to play on the football team.)

McFadyen seemed contrite. "Ultimately, the shame I have brought upon myself and the indignity I have brought upon my family, friends, the Delbar-ton School, and Duke University overshadows the wrongs of those against me," he wrote. "I regret the consequences that have stemmed from my actions and accept full responsibility for what I did. Obviously I am grateful for the chance to once again play the sport I love with the men I am proud to call my team-mates. In the upcoming seasons my teammates and I will do all that is possi-ble to demonstrate the responsibility and professionalism that will eventually become synonymous with Duke lacrosse."

On June 30, Collin Finnerty's parents appeared on the *Today* show from their Long Island home, and were interviewed by Dan Abrams. Of the three defendants, Finnerty had been by far the least visible since his indictment. Unlike Evans, Finnerty had said nothing publicly after being indicted, and, unlike Seligmann, his attorneys had not produced any documentary evidence of an alibi for Finnerty's whereabouts during the time in question on the night of March 13. This was despite vague references to the fact that he supposedly was at Cosmic Cantina, a Durham restaurant several blocks away from 610 North Buchanan.

On the *Today* show, his parents, Kevin and Mary Ellen, were determined to change the public perception of their son. They declined to speak about the pending gay-bashing charge against him in Georgetown—set for trial on July 10—but seemed eager to defend Collin. They had previously turned down dozens of interview requests but told Abrams they had decided to come for-ward because, after they reviewed the nearly two thousand pages of "evidence" that Nifong had shared with defense attorneys, they had concluded that "there is no case," as Kevin Finnerty said.

Abrams asked Finnerty if his son had an alibi. "He does," he said. "And a very good one. From the outset, our legal team, our counsel, [has been] ada-mant that they will not reveal the evidence in the media. Collin has taken and passed with flying colors . . . no surprise . . . a polygraph test"—this was news—"[with] numerous eyewitnesses every step of the way . . . every minute of the night. Clearly, there were two DNA tests done and, obviously, no DNA. He has numerous phone calls around the time in question. Many incoming. Many outgoing. He has receipts. And he also swiped himself with his card into his dorm. For every minute of the night . . ." Abrams pressed them. So, like Seligmann, Collin had an alibi for the night, making it impossible for him to have committed the crime? "Yes," his mother said. "Impossible," his father said.

Although the Finnertys would not share the details of their son's alibi with Abrams, here it was: Between 12:10 a.m. and 12:20 a.m., after the dancing ended and when Roberts and Mangum were elsewhere in the house, Finnerty was in the living room "for a brief period" before "several" of his teammates said they saw him leave through the front door of the house. At 12:22 a.m., he made the first of a series of eight cell phone calls, including one to another team member asking if he wanted to get something to eat. Five minutes later, another teammate called him to discuss the topic du jour: getting something to eat. "By this point, Collin had gone to a house around the corner rented by two other senior lacrosse players" to pick up "his Playstation, which he had left at the other house." According to Finnerty's legal team, which had "all his calls triangulated," by 12:27 a.m., "Finnerty had unimpeachable electronic evidence that he was not at 610 N. Buchanan."

Three minutes later, he called Domino's Pizza to order a pizza. (At 12:31 a.m., there was that photograph of a smiling Mangum outside the back door of the house.) At 12:33 a.m., Finnerty called Domino's back to cancel his pizza order because he and his teammates (a freshman, a sophomore, and a senior) had decided to go to Cosmic Cantina instead. For the next twenty-three minutes, his lawyers claimed, Finnerty was chowing down at the restaurant and then paid the bill with a credit card. He then took a cab back to his dorm, which his key card confirmed he entered at 1:04 a.m. He bought some water from a vending machine. At 1:16 a.m. he made a cell phone call to his girlfriend in Boston. As for the lie-detector test, his attorneys said, Finnerty passed easily, and the tester told Wade Smith, "This boy is telling the truth and is innocent."

A few days later, Kevin and Mary Ellen Finnerty sat "stoically" in the packed Washington, DC, courtroom gallery, according to the *Washington Post*, as "dueling portraits of their son emerged" during Collin's two-day trial on assault charges stemming from a late-night "fracas" outside a Georgetown bar. To some, the *Post* reported, Finnerty was "an underage bar hopper who wouldn't walk away from a fight" while, to others, he was "a respectful, well-behaved young man who was an honor student at his Catholic high school and never received a demerit." As in the allegations in Durham, excessive underage drinking fueled Finnerty's behavior in Georgetown in the early morning hours of November 5. At the first day of the hearing, the federal prosecutors argued that Finnerty and his two friends from Chaminade High School "taunted, intimidated and threatened" Bloxsom and his friend, Scott Herndon, "hurling homophobic slurs and fake punches."

Finnerty's attorney, Steven McCool, said Finnerty was actually the victim and accused Herndon, whom he called a "hothead," of hitting Finnerty "in the back of the head." Prosecutors said Finnerty and his friends followed Bloxsom and Herndon for several blocks through Georgetown and "taunted" the men. Herndon went into a bar for help and when he came out he saw Finnerty "lunge" at Bloxsom. Herndon then grabbed Finnerty around the waist to get him to leave Bloxsom alone. Both Bloxsom and Herndon testified that Finnerty initiated the fight and "got in the face" of Bloxsom while shoving him and yelling: "Say you're a faggot. Say you're a faggot." Bloxsom said he "acquiesced" to avoid a fight, even though he was not gay and had just had dinner with his fiancée. Finnerty also supposedly urged Bloxsom to perform a sex act on him. When all was said and done, someone—not Finnerty—gave Bloxsom a bloody lip. "We don't think there's sufficient evidence to convict Collin Finnerty," McCool told the judge the next day. The witnesses' testimony showed "the character of the man," McCool said.

But the judge, John H. Bayly Jr., disagreed. "When he is sober," the judge said to McCool. "Do you think your character witnesses knew your client was using a fake ID to get into bars? People's character changes when they're drunk." He said he found Bloxsom's testimony the most convincing, and added that Bloxsom "rightfully feared for his safety" as a result of the repeated punches that Finnerty directed at Bloxsom that were intentionally designed to miss the mark. Bloxsom "was trying to get away," the judge said. "He didn't want to prolong this." Bayly sentenced Finnerty to thirty days in prison, with the jail time suspended in favor of a six-month youthful offender probation program. Judge Bayly also required Finnerty to "undergo alcohol testing and rehabilitation" and to "steer clear" of places where alcohol was served and stay out of Georgetown. Assuming Finnerty complied with his sentence requirements, the conviction would be expunged from his record. McCool said his client's sentence was "fair" and "lenient" but that he would appeal the verdict. "Judge Bayly found Collin Finnerty guilty of simple assault because he threw fake punches . . . and because he scared one of the complaining witnesses in the case," McCool said. "That's it." After Bayly's sentence, the Finnertys sought solace in a room off the courtroom, where Finnerty's girlfriend could be heard crying. His only comment during the trial was to say "Yes, your honor" when asked if he understood he had a right to appeal.

That there might be two Collin Finnertys—the choirboy and the obnoxious drunk—was the subject of Marc Fisher's subsequent *Washington Post* column, "Wolves in Blazers and Khakis." "They look like such upstanding young gentlemen in their blue blazers and pressed khakis," he wrote. "They say 'Yes, sir' and 'No, sir,' and they attend the finest schools. And they are such loyal friends. Oh, their stories matched up so prettily as they trooped up onto the witness stand to defend their boy, Collin Finnerty." He then described the scene in the courtroom. "Surrounded by family, friends, priests and a battalion of lawyers scratching away in the gallery on their yellow legal pads, Finnerty seems like the last guy in the world who would hurl vile insults and threats at two young men he'd never before seen," Fisher continued. "Michael Hannan, the father of Finnerty's girlfriend, tells the court that he watched Collin back home on Long Island at neighborhood parties and cotillion dances and concluded that this young man was 'a very warm and gentle individual,' 'extremely peaceful and extremely nonviolent.' Otherwise, of course, Hannan would never have permitted his daughter to go out with the kid. But on cross-examination, prosecutor George Varghese finds out that Hannan has never seen Finnerty under the influence of alcohol and therefore has no clue how the boy behaves when he's plastered. Now we're getting to the nub of the case. Because while no one in the courtroom makes much of an issue of it, this case is swimming in beer. The boys, all of them underage, testify that they were drinking back at the Georgetown University dorms, drinking in Georgetown bars—they were even heading back to campus to drink some more after they'd finished attacking two strangers."

Fisher then tried to draw a bow around the two Collins and what they might mean for the ongoing legal case in Durham, North Carolina. "How do you make sense of the disconnect between the proud, even arrogant claims of excellent character by Finnerty's friends and the disgusting descriptions of his behavior by the two men he humiliated that night in Georgetown?" he continued. "How is it that these polite youngsters spent half an hour shoving and taunting total strangers, making them announce to the world in the coarsest possible terms, right there on a public sidewalk, that they perform gay sex acts? What could gentlemen say that would cause Scott Herndon, one of the victims, to run into a restaurant seeking help because he thought he was going to be killed? Answer: When in the company of elders and teachers, these young men do behave admirably. When the stage lights go off and the guys head out to drink and drink and drink, anything goes. Hey, they're just kids! Or, as the priest who testified for Finnerty puts it, 'One incident doesn't make a gentleman's character.'"

In the end, Fisher saw wisdom in Judge Bayly's verdict, even if many wondered why valuable judicial resources were used to prosecute a simple case of drunken debauchery. "When you pick on a stranger, when you find fun in tormenting the innocent, when you believe it is in any way acceptable to attack another human being, then that incident does open a window onto a larger truth," he concluded. "Even if no rape occurred in the Duke case, even if that ugly incident was no more than a raucous party at which a bunch of drunken kids verbally abused a hired performer, it sounds like it was entirely within the character for these kids and the friend they tried to talk out of trouble in DC Superior Court. Sorry, Father, but one incident often does make a gentleman's character."

In the space of two weeks, both Evans and Finnerty had been convicted of misdemeanors related to drunken behavior—having nothing to do with their indictments for allegedly raping and kidnapping Crystal Mangum—and an intensely contrite Ryan McFadyen had been reinstated as an undergraduate at Duke. Meanwhile, that McFadyen's fellow Delbarton alumnus, Reade Seligmann, was even in trouble—of any kind—had *New York Times* columnist (and Duke graduate and parent) Peter Applebome stumped. Citing a letter from one of Seligmann's teachers at Delbarton—"If I had a son, I would hope he would be like Reade"—Applebome observed, making very much the same argument that the *Washington Post* had made about Finnerty, that it "can sum up the jarring disparity that characterizes Reade Seligmann's life now. On the one hand is the person his acquaintants know. On the other is his role as one of three white Duke lacrosse players accused of raping a black woman hired to dance at an off-campus party."

Like others, Applebome pointed specifically to Seligmann's alibi—the cell phone records, the ATM photos, the taxi driver's affidavit—to question whether he should have been indicted in the first place. "But to teachers, coaches and monks at Delbarton, to his neighbors in Essex Fells, N.J., and to his friends at Duke, the disparity between the indictment and these circumstances is not the biggest absurdity," he wrote. "Instead, it's that he is part of the story at all." People who knew Seligmann at Delbarton or at Duke were incredulous that Seligmann could have been part of what allegedly happened on the evening of March 13. "When I heard it was Reade, I knew 100 percent in my heart this was a completely false allegation," Katie Fisher, a recent Duke graduate, told Applebome. But, he continued, "you don't need ties to Duke to look at the details that have emerged about the case—the accuser's history of past accusations and differing accounts of the crime, a lack of DNA evidence, a police lineup of only Duke lacrosse players, a second dancer's original statement saying no rape could have occurred—and come away queasy. Maybe he and the others are the monstrous incarnation of white, male privilege, or maybe this has become a cautionary tale of a rush to judgment before facts were known, of a toxic brew of politics and race in the middle of an election for district attorney."

In the face of Nifong's ongoing silence and the onslaught of media stories far more sympathetic to the lacrosse players than had previously been the case, the *News & Observer* wondered if the worm had turned on the story and Nifong had lost control of the narrative. Irving Joyner, the NCCU law professor, said the defense attorneys had used the media expertly. "In the streets, we call it being played like a violin," he said. "Every time they pick up something that is seemingly exculpatory or casts some contradiction, they're putting it in the press." Michael Grinfield, an associate professor of journalism at the University of Missouri, described the defense attorneys' strategy as "press-release pleadings," while Jim Cooney, a Charlotte attorney, said Nifong's credibility was eroding. "You can't overcome what Mike Nifong did in one day or with a single press conference," he said. "What you've got to do is build it up over time, and it's got to be very fact-based." In the end, he said, nothing would be known for certain until a trial concluded. "The system has to play itself out," he allowed. "The media is not going to answer the question until the jury comes back."

Hal Crowther, a Williams College alumnus who had for years—as a columnist for the North Carolina *Independent*, a weekly based in Durham—served as the conscience of progressive thinkers in North Carolina, tried to put the still-unfolding drama into perspective. "We know for certain that one of these defendants, who lawyered his way around a gay-bashing incident in Washington, is an individual of questionable character and self-control," he wrote. "We know the team as a whole has a dismal history of disreputable undergraduate behavior, in which it was indulging when the alleged atrocity occurred." Regardless of the outcome, Crowther wrote, important lessons stood to be learned. "One is about transactions involving sex and money, and the stupidity of imagining that the one who sells surrenders more dignity or moral currency than the one who buys," he continued. "A race factor compounds the bitterness of this lesson, which many men never learn. But the great lesson they should have learned, if they're able to learn at all, is one that might make them better men and better citizens than the ones they would have become if no charges had ever been filed. It's a lesson learned too late by most children of privilege, blinkered well into adulthood by the myth of the affluent middle class—the myth that elite lives proceed smoothly from triumph to triumph with nothing but glory down the road. But the awful, class-blind truth—ask Duke lacrosse coach Mike Pressler, at the top of his world on Monday, unemployed and invisible on Thursday—is that we live our lives with one foot on the banana peel, the other on the well-oiled roller skate. How quickly fortunes change, how quickly it can all slip away. . . . Your world can upend itself in an instant, in the blink of an eye. If they've learned these things alone, the lacrosse team survivors are on a faster track to enlightenment than their university."

This last dig was a not-so-subtle reference to Crowther's view that elite schools, such as Duke, "will eventually learn to their great sorrow that coddling athletes and deifying coaches was a seductive wrong turn toward academic irrelevance and institutional ruin. The myth of the 'scholar athlete,' incorporating 'graduation rates,' 'clean programs' and the rest of that tired fraud, somehow survives daily bulletins on the multiple felonies and gross misdemeanors committed by current and recent college athletes." He couldn't help but mention Matt Wilson, the lacrosse player who was driving while impaired and in possession of marijuana at more or less the same moment that Brodhead was deciding whether to reinstate Duke's lacrosse program. "Sweet timing," he wrote, and figured that although Brodhead said he was "disappointed" by Wilson's behavior, what he really meant was that "Wilson may soon be found in a shallow grave with a big blue 'D' branded on his forehead." (If there had been a fourth player indicted, Chris Kennedy thought it would have been Wilson.

"If it had been my son who was the fourth one identified, I would have been scared to death," Chris Kennedy testified later.)

Then there was the matter of Duke's "most illustrious white athlete," J. J. Redick, and *his* drunk-driving charge. "Redick's gaffe brought Mike Krzyzewski up from the bunker to defend his boy and deliver, after more than three months of silence, his first public comments on the rape case," Crowther continued. "Offered in the form of a quarrel with the recent Bowen-Chambers report, which suggested that some de-emphasis of athletics might be in order, Silent Mike's remarks were agonizingly predictable." While Crowther wrote that it was very difficult to find in North Carolina "sympathy for the devil, if he's a Blue Devil," he conceded that it was hard not to "feel pity" for Brodhead, "an Ivy League scholar who took the helm at Duke just in time to test his survival skills on the perfect storm." While not overly impressed with Brodhead's handling of the case, he acknowledged that there was no happy ending likely. "If the party boys are found guilty, it's a permanent black eye, a setback no NCAA trophies can erase; if they go free—even without a shadow of doubt on their innocence—Duke's conspicuous presence as the rich white school in the poor black town is infinitely more precarious."

He lamented the "shock and awe media campaign" the defense attorneys, "on fat retainers," had employed against Mangum. He conceded they were "just doing their job, which isn't always a pretty one," but "If you feel a compulsion to believe them, you're the one who might catch a glimpse of your inner racist in the mirror." He also regretted the "Durham-after-dark scene" that journalists visiting town to cover the scandal seemed to be finding everywhere, particularly Janet Reitman at *Rolling Stone*. "If even half of this is true, why would any parent accept it and pay dearly to subsidize it?" he wondered. "A Duke education can cost close to a quarter of a million dollars, no bargain for a jock-dominated sex zoo where Junior can play Hugh Hefner to a hutchful of willing bunnies with high SATs."

Crowther's friend Peter Wood told Crowther that "A few years ago, a new kind of student began to show up at Duke. Cynical, arrogant, callous, dismissive—you could almost say openly hostile. They weren't all athletes, by any means. But some of the first ones I noticed were lacrosse players"— whereupon Crowther invoked Wood's June 2004 letter to Robert Thompson. "Wood's testimony supports grave misgivings about the demographic group that includes both the Durham dancer and the athletes she accuses," he continued. "It's a culture of expediency—a culture of shortcuts, which reminds me of a preacher I heard once, a Scottish Calvinist, who warned, 'There are no shortcuts; no shortcuts to heaven. Every shortcut leads to hell.' . . . It's a culture based on witless distraction, ruthless competition, and instant gratification, and if it's beginning to produce damaged specimens we can't easily recognize as our descendants, aren't we the ones to blame? If Huckleberry Finn and Holden Caulfield have been replaced by Sammy Glick [the fictitious and ruthless rags-to-riches character who stops at nothing to achieve his goals in Budd Schulberg's 1941 novel *What Makes Sammy Run*], isn't it time we confessed that American children have been criminally neglected and misled?"

In the end, Crowther allowed, "a court will decide whether this Neanderthal mindset is conducive to sexual assault. But . . . taunting racial minorities—a detail in the lacrosse case lawyers haven't bothered to deny—is behavior for which neither high spirits nor distilled spirits can account. It's fathoms below sub-baccalaureate; it's subhuman. Though cheating and plagiarism appear to be coeducational, and alcohol abuse is gender-blind, the sociopathic outer edge of undergraduate delinquency bears the sour reek of curdled testosterone. Where the gradual, cultural erosion of student character meets combustible machismo—a point never far from the athletic department—institutions designed for scholars are breeding and harboring common louts. . . . Whatever happens to this rape case, this is a devastating charge, one that Duke and other schools compromised by coach cults and athletic imperialism—its in-state rivals are in no position to gloat—will fail to address at a terrible price. What's at stake isn't reputation, recruiting, endowments or rankings in the *U.S. News & World Report*. What's at stake is their souls—their reason for existing. And they know it."

Despite the summer doldrums on campus, the legal case against the three players continued to progress. At a superior court hearing on July 17, Judge Kenneth Titus—one of the two judges, along with Judge Stephens, presiding over the case—warned both Nifong and the defense attorneys to keep their observations about the case out of the news media. At the hearing, Nifong turned over to defense attorneys more evidence, with a promise of more to come, and the two sides debated whether Nifong should be able to access the confidential records—such as home addresses and phone numbers—of the nonindicted Duke students in order to arrange to talk to them, since he said he considered everyone at the March 13 party a potential witness. "We're not trying to investigate them," Nifong said. "We want to be put in a position to call them, to tell the jury in Durham what they observed go on that night when this took place."

The animosity between Nifong and defense lawyers was hard to miss. While five defense lawyers for the nonindicted players were making their argument for why Nifong should not have access to their clients' private data, Nifong suggested in court that they were opposing his subpoenas in order to find a way into the case. "It looked sometimes over the course of the last few months that some of the attorneys were almost disappointed that their clients didn't get indicted so that they could be part of this spectacle here in Durham," he told the judge.

Not surprisingly—and despite Judge Titus's statement that comments outside the courtroom should be curtailed—the defense attorneys were offended. "Basic courtroom decorum, as well as our rules of court, require that all counsel conduct themselves with dignity and propriety and refrain from personal insults," attorney Bill Thomas said. He said Nifong's remark was "unprofessional and discourteous." On the contrary, Thomas said, "Every lawyer in this case has been greatly concerned, as we realized Mr. Nifong was going to indict young men who were factually innocent. Each and every lawyer felt great sadness to see these three young, innocent men having to endure a charge that should never have been brought." Added Butch Williams, "This lawyer, in particular, was overjoyed when his client wasn't indicted." By then, Nifong had left town, on vacation.

On July 21, Judge Titus ruled that Nifong could have access to the home addresses of the nonindicted Duke players but not their "key-card" data, in a partial win for the defense attorneys.

The same day, defense attorneys filed a seventeen-page motion urging the judge to let them speak publicly about the perceived wrongs done to their clients, despite the previous admonition to refrain from speaking publicly about the case. The lawyers argued that Nifong's repeated public statements solidified a narrative in people's minds. "Read and viewed together, Mr. Nifong's dozens of media interviews in March and April set a clear narrative of this case," they wrote, "that was embraced by most if not all of the media covering the case, as well as the public it served." His comments, the lawyers wrote, "are archived on dozens if not hundreds of Internet websites and have often been repeated, in hundreds if not thousands of stories written or broadcast in newspapers, on television, and on the Internet. In short, Mr. Nifong's narrative has thrived. But because the narrative is wrong, undersigned counsel are not only permitted, but ethically obligated to defend Dave Evans, Collin Finnerty, and Reade Seligmann against it. Moreover, under the First Amendment to the United States Constitution, their teammates on the 2006 Duke University men's lacrosse team have a right to respond freely to that government criticism."

Around the time that the defense lawyers were filing their provocative brief, Duke announced that fifty-two-year-old John Danowski, the father of star Duke lacrosse player Matt Danowksi and the longtime lacrosse coach at Hofstra, would be the new coach of the Duke lacrosse program. Danowski, whose father, Ed, played quarterback for the New York Giants, had compiled a 192–123 record in his twenty-one seasons at Hofstra. "This is going to be a lot of fun," he told the media at Cameron Indoor Stadium. He said he knew he and the team would face plenty of scrutiny. "I feel very confident that, with this particular group of young men, there will be very few if any issues," he said. "I just believe they'll have something to prove."

In a statement, Brodhead called him "a great choice" and added, "I had a long talk with him, and I too felt the force of his special qualities. Coach Danowski has compiled impressive winning records, but for him coaching is about far more than results on the field. [As] a former teacher, he sees his role as developing the human potential of his players in its fullest sense: in academics, in athletics and in the domain of character. . . . I look for him to continue everything that's best in the Duke lacrosse tradition and to build the new strengths we're committed to achieving." Alleva told the press "it never crossed my mind" to end the lacrosse program at Duke and that, after he checked on Danowski with the Hofstra campus police and student affairs officials, he concluded, "He's the real deal when it comes to the whole package." Matt Danowski, wearing a blue rubber bracelet with the word "Innocent" inscribed on it, said he thought his teammates would be "happy with my dad being the coach. I think they respect him. They know what he's done for Hofstra in the past, and, hopefully, he can carry that on at Duke." Kevin Cassese, the interim coach, was named an assistant to Danowski. Soon thereafter, on August 6, Mike Pressler was named lacrosse coach at Bryant University in Rhode Island. He had been vacationing on Block Island, Rhode Island, when he got a call from Bill Smith, a former Colgate lacrosse player who had just been named athletic director at Bryant. Smith read everything he could about the Duke lacrosse incident and then decided to interview Pressler for the Bryant job. "The interview was easy," Pressler recalled. "I just told the truth."

The reinstatement of the lacrosse team and the appointment of a new head coach did not prevent further criticism of Duke by Duke loyalists. In a July 18 jam-packed edition of the *Chronicle*, a group calling itself "Friends of Duke University," seemingly led by Jason Trumpbour, a 1991 graduate of Duke law school, ran a full-page advertisement in the form of an "open letter" to Brodhead and the board of trustees. Although friendly and well-reasoned, it was a devastating condemnation of the administration's handling of the scandal. "We address you as members of the Duke family, brokenhearted at the unfair treatment and portrayal" of the men's lacrosse team and by Duke's "acquiescence in this treatment," the Friends wrote in the ad. Furthermore, the Friends said, they believed Duke "cowered in the face of media pressure engineered by the unethical and probably illegal conduct" of Nifong and other law enforcement officials and virtually ignored the statements of the lacrosse team captains that the allegations against them were "totally and transparently false" and that, according to Dan Abrams, who had reviewed the full discovery file, "no sexual assault occurred." Yet, "Duke has remained hesitant in its support" and "has sacrificed its own students and values."

While conceding that Duke could "express no opinion about the ultimate outcome of pending legal matters," the Friends said, "we urge Duke to use all its influence and moral suasion to ensure that these three Duke students receive justice through a fair process" and "we also call upon Duke to formally demand that Mr. Nifong immediately correct, to the extent now possible, the grave errors that he has committed to date." The Friends argued that "at this point, no fair-minded person could any longer believe that a rape occurred. However, we are in no way apologists for the acknowledged conduct of the team. But necessary reforms must recognize that many of the team's problems exist within the larger Duke community. Therefore, any specific measures taken against the lacrosse team must be consistent with Kantian ethics, including a commitment to proportionate justice and treating the team as the end, not as the means."

On July 25, Brodhead responded to the Friends of Duke University. "In a situation as complex as the one we've been grappling with, where powerful passions have coexisted with rapidly changing 'facts' and where action has been required in the face of deep uncertainty, it was virtually inevitable that the University response would be open to question," he wrote. "It won't surprise you to learn that I have received critical comments from a great variety of points of view, including diametrically opposite ones. I accept that, and would only say that those of us in positions of responsibility have acted as best we could to make two points: that what the players were accused of was, if true, a heinous act; and that it would be equally unjust to prejudge their guilt in the absence of proof and certainty. This dual message has been at the heart of virtually every public statement I have made on the case."

Without tackling the ad point-by-point, Brodhead noted, "I am well aware that, after many weeks of media stories that made it seem almost self-evidently true that a rape had occurred, recent stories have offered extensive evidence exonerating the indicted students and questioning the legitimacy of the case. But the University does not have direct access to the full truth of the case now any more than we did earlier, and we can't speak with certainty of matters that only the criminal justice system can resolve." But, he continued, "We are eager for our students to be proved innocent. We share the wish for a speedy resolution of all the matters that are now in doubt."

On July 28, Nifong held his first formal news conference after months of silence. Nifong's ostensible reason for holding the session was to talk about his campaign for district attorney in light of the decision the night before by Lewis Cheeks, a Durham County commissioner, not to run against Nifong in November for the seat, despite obtaining enough signatures to be on the ballot. If the lacrosse case were taking its toll on Nifong, it was not apparent. He made sure to get a few digs in at the assembled media, who seemed obsessed by the lacrosse case, even though Nifong tried—naively—to make it off limits. Asked to explain his barrage of seemingly inflammatory public statements at the outset of the case, Nifong said that he hoped to convey two messages, early on: "The first message that I intended to portray was that the community was in good hands with respect to this case and did not have to worry about it," he said. "My second message during all this period of time was a message to the people who were present but not involved, in the hope that they would come forward and give us information that would help us." He conceded the strategy did not work. Would he do anything differently? "Actually, my reaction at this point would be just not to talk to you guys at all," he said. "But it was my hope [that] by speaking to you in the first place, we could actually help the community."

As for whether the November election was becoming a referendum on the lacrosse case, Nifong said, "Certainly there are those people who want to do that. I understand somebody is calling this the Anybody but Nifong campaign, and that I guess comes with the territory." He said he hoped voters would look at the entirety of his nearly twenty-eight-year record in the District Attorney's Office and not just the last few months on one case. But, "If, after looking at all that, a voter still thinks the election should be about a specific case, that probably is not a voter I will be able to reach." He added that, in the end, the lacrosse case "remains a Durham problem and it demands a Durham solution. The suggestion that it should be handed off to a neutral authority misunderstands the nature of the prosecutor's job. He is supposed to be the committed advocate for the truth, not a disinterested surrogate for public sentiment. At the end of the day, this case, like every criminal case, will be decided by a jury of twelve Durham citizens sworn to base their decision not on prejudice or emotion, but on the facts presented and the rule of law. I intend to be the prosecutor who presents those facts and argues that law."

Despite Nifong's assertions, he could not control the media's relentless curiosity. It was just a matter of time before the print media got hold of—and started digging through—the same document and evidence cache that defense attorneys had leaked on June 19 to Dan Abrams at MSNBC. The difference was that print journalists had more space to share the revelations about the evidence. On August 1, the *Durham Herald-Sun* reported on its front page that, according to "sources," the semen found on a towel from the bathroom at 610 North Buchanan matched David Evans's DNA. The towel, apparently, also contained non-semen DNA from someone else, although that "someone else" was neither Mangum nor the other lacrosse players who gave DNA samples to the police. "The implication is that Evans had sex with someone other than the accuser," the paper reported, "then used the towel to clean himself." DNA "consistent" with Evans's genetic makeup had also been found on one of Mangum's fake fingernails found in the bathroom, although that match was "not 100 percent conclusive," according to previous reports. The paper also reported that its sources said that "semen from an unindicted lacrosse player" was discovered on the bathroom floor where Mangum claimed to have been raped.

The experts, though, were not unified about the implications of the public revelation of Evans's semen on the towel. "If there is semen there that matches one or more of the players, I think it's crucial," attorney John Fitzpatrick told the paper. "It is evidence to show that some kind of orgasm occurred. It gives more credence to the prosecution's theory that something happened. It is a potential link to a crime. It is a big thing. The prosecution can say the semen was there because the alleged victim was right. Of course, the defense will probably try to explain it by saying the guys just masturbated." Irving Joyner, the NCCU law professor, also said the new evidence was important. "It would tend to support the prosecution's case," he said. "Of course, the prosecution will need to establish how the semen got there and its relevance to the young lady. There are still some hurdles, but this will help the prosecutor. The defense will have to go to some lengths to explain it." He added, though, that Evans's semen on the towel "would not be conclusive" because "there are plenty of ways the semen could have wound up there."

But other attorneys were less willing to think the new evidence would help Nifong's case. "It means nothing," said attorney Mark Edwards, who, like John Fitzpatrick, was not involved in the case. "These are college-age males full of testosterone. So what if there is semen found in the house? If the accuser's story was true, their semen should have been found in her, too." Bill Thomas, who represented an unindicted player—but not the one whose semen was found in the bathroom—agreed with Edwards. "Every person who uses a bathroom on a daily basis will have his DNA present in that bathroom in some form," he said. "But in this case, none of the accuser's DNA whatsoever was found. The only significant DNA is semen from a third party unconnected to the case. There still is no evidence whatsoever linking any of these [lacrosse players] to allegations made by the accuser." Kerry Sutton, who represented Matt Zash, said, "Finding a healthy young man's semen or DNA on a towel near his bedroom or in his own bathroom couldn't possibly be less shocking. It would be more surprising if you didn't find it."

The next day, Sutton told the News & Observer that it was Zash's semen that was found on the floor of the bathroom at 610 North Buchanan. "The fact that Mr. Zash's DNA in any form was found in his own bathroom is evidence of nothing related to his case," she said. Zash had long been elimated as a suspect because he was watching television in his room during the party. Brad Bannon, one of David Evans's attorneys, said the fact that his client's DNA was on a towel in his bathroom meant nothing. "It seems to me that the state of North Carolina has spent thousands of dollars to prove that a young college man's DNA is in his house," he said. And Mark Edwards, sharing his views again, said, "What this evidence tells you is that when you're walking aound these guys' house, make sure you have your shoes on."

On Sunday, August 6, the News & Observer delved deeply into the more than 1,800 pages of documents and evidence that Nifong turned over to the defense. After going through much of the tick-tock of events culled from the documents—surely a revelation for most readers—Joseph Neff, the reporter, found "that the accuser gave at least five different versions of the alleged assault to different police and medical interviewers and made shaky identifications of suspects. To get warrants, police made statements that weren't supported by information in their files. The district attorney commented publicly about the strength of the medical evidence before he had seen it. He promised DNA evidence that has not materialized. He suggested the police conduct lineups in a way that conflicted with department policy."

A few weeks later, on August 25, the *New York Times* published on the front page its own comprehensive, 5,600-word analysis of the same documents. "Whether the woman was in fact raped is the question at the center of a case that has become a national cause célèbre, yet another painful chapter in the tangled American opera of race, sex and privilege," reporters Duff Wilson and Jonathan Glater wrote. "Defense lawyers, amplified by Duke alumni and a group of bloggers who have closely followed the case, have portrayed it as a national scandal—[saying] that there is only the flimsiest physical evidence of rape, that the accuser is an unstable fabricator and that Mr. Nifong, in the middle of a tight primary campaign, was summoning racial ghosts for political gain. By disclosing pieces of evidence favorable to the defendants, the defense has created an image of a case heading for the rocks. But an examination of the entire 1,850 pages of evidence gathered by the prosecution in the four months after the accusation yields a more ambiguous picture. It shows that while there are big weaknesses in Mr. Nifong's case, there is also a body of evidence to support his decision to take the matter to a jury."

Within hours of the publication of the *Times's* story, the blogosphere went wild, viewing the story with disdain and considering it highly—and unfairly—biased toward Nifong and the prosecution of the three lacrosse players. "Imagine you are the world's most powerful newspaper and you have invested your credibility in yet another story line that is falling apart, crumbling as inexorably as Jayson Blair's fabrications and the flawed reporting on Saddam Hussein's supposed WMD," wrote former *Times* reporter Stuart Taylor in *Slate*, referring to two of the *Times's* most notorious journalistic miscues of recent years. "What to do? If you're the *New York Times* and the story is the alleged gang rape of a black woman by three white Duke lacrosse players—a claim shown by mounting evidence to be almost certainly fraudulent—you tone down your rhetoric while doing your utmost to prop up a case that's been almost wholly driven by prosecutorial and police misconduct. And by bad journalism. Worse, perhaps, than the other recent *Times* embarrassments. The *Times* still seems bent on advancing its race-sex-class ideological agenda, even at the cost of ruining the lives of three young men who it has reason to know are very probably innocent."

And Taylor was just getting warmed up. "The Wilson-Glater piece high-lights every superficially incriminating piece of evidence in the case, selectively omits important exculpatory evidence and reports hotly disputed statements by not-very-credible police officers and the mentally unstable accuser as if they were established facts," he continued. "With comical credulity, it features as its centerpiece a leaked, transparently contrived thirty-three-page police sergeant's memo that seeks to paper over some of the most obvious holes in the prosecution's evidence. This memo was concocted from memory, nearly four months after the underlying witness interviews, by Durham police Sergeant Mark Gottlieb, the lead investigator. Gottlieb says he took no contemporane-ous notes, an inexplicable and indefensible police practice. Gottlieb had drawn fire before the alleged Duke rape—perhaps unbeknownst to the *Times*—as a Dukie-basher who reveled in throwing kids into jail for petty drinking infractions, noise violations, and the like, sometimes with violent criminals as cellmates. Gottlieb's memo is contradicted on critical points by the contem-poraneous notes of other police officers, as well as by hospital records seem-ing to show that the accuser did not have the injuries Gottlieb claims to have observed. The *Times* blandly mentions these contradictions while avoiding the obvious inference that the Gottlieb memo is thus unworthy of belief . . ."

Given the increasing controversy, what should have been a cakewalk November election for Nifong as district attorney, following his May win in the Democratic primary, was turning into a far more competitive race than he had anticipated. By mid-August it was clear he would have competition for the job, however modest. On August 9, Steve Monks, the chairman of the Durham County Republican Party, confirmed that he would be part of the November election as an unaffiliated write-in candidate. He failed to obtain the 6,300 signatures he needed to have his name printed on the November ballot but his close-to-five-thousand unverified signatures meant that voters could write in his name. He also said he had not raised the $50,000 he would need to run against Nifong but was confident he would. "The die is cast," he said. "We're going forward." If elected, he said his first task would be to inter-view Mangum—with sensitivity, of course—to determine whether to prose-cute the case.

CHAPTER TWELVE

Election Day

With students starting to return to both Duke and NCCU after the summer break, the *News & Observer* reported that Mangum was one of the students scheduled for classes at NCCU. Her father told the paper that if she did return to school to finish her studies, he would have "some sense that she's all right." Mangum had been studying psychology at NCCU and had a 3.75 GPA. He said his daughter had "virtually vanished" over the summer and cut off contact with her family. Although the "mainstream media" had not printed her name, the *News & Observer* reported her father saying, "Everyone knows who she is by now." He said he had not talked with his daughter since June, when he happened to see her sitting in a friend's car on a Durham street. "She said she was doing fine," he said. "I asked where her kids were, and she said they were out of town. . . . Then the light changed." He said he used to see his daughter "every day until all this stuff [happened]."

On the Duke campus, administrators worried whether the national media would return to campus after taking the summer off. "We've heard from students and some parents about concerns that they don't want microphones and reporters in their faces throughout the week," John Burness said. "We don't know what we're going to see. The media seems to come out of nowhere sometimes." One thing Duke administrators could conclude, unequivocally, at the start of the new academic year was that the lacrosse scandal had not hurt donations to the school. In fact, they reached a record in 2006: Duke collected $341.9 million in donations during the 2006–7 academic year, some $66 million more than the previous year and more than the all-time record of $302.6 million in 2000.

Meanwhile, at the Durham courthouse, the lacrosse case was deemed "exceptional" by Sarah Parker, the State Supreme Court chief justice, making it the first time a criminal case in Durham was so designated. This meant that Judge Stephens and Judge Titus would be replaced by W. Osmond Smith III, the senior resident superior court judge in the district for Caswell and Person counties. Judge Smith would preside over the entire case no matter its length, instead of rotating off the case after six months, which was the requirement in "non-exceptional" cases. Smith's first ruling in the lacrosse case, on August

25, was to ban the use of media cameras or recording equipment in the court-room, at least during the preliminary phases of the case. During that same closed-door hearing with Judge Smith, Nifong shared with defense attorneys the results of the date-rape drug test, done with a sample of Mangum's hair by Quest Labs in Las Vegas. The test came back negative, meaning there was no evidence of Mangum being slipped a "controlled substance" during the party. "We knew that was going to happen," Kirk Osborn, Seligmann's lawyer, said. "It certainly eliminates whatever Mr. Nifong hinted to *Newsweek* magazine [in April], that they had slipped her a date-rape drug."

In early September, the *New Yorker*'s Peter Boyer jumped into the fray. Boyer's singular contribution to the media scrum was to share Brodhead's unscripted thoughts on the crisis as it continued to unfold. Boyer had met with Brodhead in July and wrote that the alleged incident and its aftermath, "cast into doubt the central tenet of the school's identity—the fragile balance between sports and scholarship." He asked Brodhead for his views on the rela-tionship between the two, and the scholar referenced Homer. "If you go back and read *The Odyssey*, who is Odysseus?" he asked. "'Sing in me, Muse, and through me tell the story of that man skilled in all ways of contending.' And his ways of contending are intellectual, and they're strategic, and they're polit-ical, and they're athletic. And so it seems to me that that would actually be at the foundation of it—it's the image of excellence. I'm not saying that I would embrace athletics on any terms. But that's its relevance. And then you have to couch it in the right terms, to have it be consonant with the other values of the university. There are other things as well. It's about working in teams, about learning to do things together that people can't do alone. The metaphorical value of sports is actually quite deep, when you stop and think about it. Our culture doesn't ask us often enough to think about it."

Brodhead told Boyer he had learned of the order requiring the forty-six white players on the lacrosse team to report to the Durham police headquarters to be photographed and provide DNA samples as he and Duke Board Chair-man Bob Steel were heading to Atlanta in a private jet to watch the Duke–LSU basketball game in the NCAA tournament. "It suggested that [the alleged inci-dent] was being treated with a degree of gravity and scope very different from what I had been told heretofore," Brodhead said. Boyer reported that Brod-head and his fellow administrators "felt besieged, and a bit bewildered" by the fast-moving events. "The nature of the information kept changing," Brodhead said, "and was extraordinarily confusing. You don't have a playbook in the drawer. And what made it hard was not only the scale of emergency—it was the combination of the extraordinarily inflammatory versions of the story with very high degrees of uncertainty." As one example of how the rapidly unfold-ing events forced him to react quickly—and possibly to overreact—Brodhead cited the McFadyen e-mail. He told Boyer he now saw it "in context." He still said he would describe it as "sickening" and "repulsive"—Boyer's words—but recognized it as a "morbid joke" ripped from the pages of *American Psycho*.

It turned out that the events since the night of March 13 had not only brought Homer to Brodhead's mind but also Shakespeare, and specifically *Othello*, in the scene at the beginning of the play where Desdemona's father discovers his daughter's relationship with the Moor and remarks, "Belief of it oppresses me already." Brodhead explained to Boyer the relevance. "'Belief of it oppresses me already,' you know?" he said. "And the thing is, we actually can't blame people for being subject to this, because it is so deeply human. And if, from day to day, we've seen people in the throes of this, we recognize that as a dimension of our humanity. At the same time, it really is our obligation to resist it, because, you know, truth and justice, they are cant phrases unless we try to take the trouble to make them have a reality to them. And what do truth and justice mean? Truth and justice mean something opposite from our preconceptions."

Along with Brodhead's erudite musings, Boyer also shared a couple of newsworthy observations from Steel. Boyer reported that after absorbing the details of the activity at 610 North Buchanan, many of the adults at Duke were surprised to learn that the hiring of strippers was a "familiar practice," and, Steel told Boyer, some of the strippers that came to campus were men. "So it's not just men getting women," he said. Steel also contextualized the decision in late March to cancel the Georgetown game shortly before it was supposed to start, infuriating not only the players but also their parents, who believed the move was a huge overreaction to the facts of the party, at least as their sons had relayed them. Steel had been worried, it turned out, that the "endless video loop" of the Duke lacrosse players practicing and carrying on as if nothing had happened on the night of March 13 was not only callous and insensitive but also might hurt the "Duke brand," which he was responsible for defending. "We had to stop those pictures," Steel told Boyer. "It doesn't mean that it's fair, but we had to stop it."

Boyer also probed the debate still raging on campus about the proper balance between academics and athletics—which he described as Sparta and Athens in one package—at Duke. And, naturally, he spoke with Peter Wood and Orin Starn. Duke was "this place that's sort of divided against itself," Starn said. "On the one hand, you have this university that wants to be this first-class liberal-arts university, with a cutting-edge university press, these great programs in literature and history and African-American studies, that's really done some amazing things over the last twenty years, building itself from a kind of regional school mostly for the Southern elite into a really global university with first-class scholarship. But then you have another university. That's a university of partying and getting drunk, hiring stippers, frats, big-time college athletics."

Boyer recounted Wood's 2004 letter to Thompson and the fact that Wood suspected the author of the statement "I wish all the Indians had died; then we wouldn't have to study them" from the teacher evaluations to be a lacrosse student. "My dad was an All-American football player, but he was also a straight-A student," Wood told Boyer. "I grew up in a world where these things were supposed to fit together nicely, and they no longer do." Boyer wrote that Wood discerned among Duke undergrads "a widening milieu of studied vulgarity." "It's an infection that spreads out," Wood said. At the top of the social strata, Wood noted, were the lacrosse players and the "Lacrosstitutes," who, it appeared, were the focus of much campus attention and envy. "Let's not kid ourselves, what frat doesn't hate these fuckers?" Boyer quoted the blogger DukeObsrvr. "The Lacrosstitute is a notch higher on the social scale than the 'frat slut.' And dammit, that's something worth fighting over." Boyer also spoke with Elizabeth Chin, a visiting professor in anthropology from Occidental College, who was teaching a course on Margaret Mead when the lacrosse scandal broke. In the class were members of the Core Four, the sorority elite written about in Janet Reitman's *Rolling Stone* article. "The sorority women in particular were trying to convince me that the sexually free and exploratory world that Mead describes is pretty much the same thing as the hook-up culture," Chin recalled. "The whole hook-up thing is, you get really drunk so that, at some level, you can't be responsible," she continued. "And then you hook up, and then there's no obligation. It's bad manners, in fact, to sort of get emotionally connected to the person. But I don't think any of them like it that much. . . . It's dehumanizing. And it's very alienating. It's sort of like they have to deaden themselves before they can do it."

On the same day that Boyer's Duke article hit the newsstands, the lacrosse team practiced together for the first time in five months, under the direction of its new coach, John Danowski. To impress upon the team that it was under a new regime, Danowski scheduled the two-hour practice at 7:15 a.m., in part to prevent any interference with classes and in part to make it that much more difficult, as early morning is a college student's least favorite time of day. More than a dozen different media outlets attended the practice and Danowski allowed several players, including his son Matt, to be interviewed. The team's inspiration for the year, "Succisa virescit," had been taken from the motto of the Delbarton School, where Seligmann and McFadyen attended high school. "It means when 'cut down, it grows back stronger,'" Matt Danowski explained.

A week later, Alleva invited Duke's 850 varsity athletes to a "combination pep rally and revival meeting" at Cameron Indoor Stadium. Afterward, Coach K, who spoke at the meeting, told a reporter, "What this situation this spring did was that people wanted to put a cloud over all of athletics, and specifically lacrosse. I don't think that's fair, quite frankly, because we have so many great kids. If somebody did something wrong, then hold them accountable, but don't indict everyone."

The rally itself—and the fact that it occurred on September 11—irritated Orin Starn. In an opinion piece for the *Durham Herald-Sun*, he wrote that he had taught many Duke athletes over the years and agreed with Coach K "that most are great kids." But the September 11 meeting suggested that Coach K, Alleva, "and their powerful supporters" had "stubbornly refused to learn the lessons of these last months," Starn wrote, adding: "An arrogant sense of victimization and entitlement seems to have replaced any semblance of clear thinking or self-reflection in Duke sports circles." He said that an exclusive rally for athletes sent "completely the wrong message. . . . This should be a time for openness, reflection and dialogue instead of circling the sports wagons with the veiled implication that any negative words about Duke sports are the fault of pointy-headed professors, scandal-mongering journalists and weak-kneed administrators who fail to understand the noble role of athletics at Duke."

His modest proposal, not surprisingly, was for Duke to abandon Division I athletics "with their horrifyingly large time, training and travel demands on student-athletes and their crass, television-driven over-commercialization." He suggested Duke move to a club-level sports program where students could still learn the "virtues of leadership, teamwork and competition" at a much lower cost and use the money saved for merit scholarships for students from backgrounds underrepresented in the Duke firmament. As for Coach K, Starn wrote, he "would have the option of remaining on [the] Duke payroll," at a lower salary and coaching one of the club teams. He conceded it would never happen, but believed it to be the "right thing to do."

The court hearing on September 22 was the first one presided over by Judge W. Osmond Smith III, but the session featured the same bickering and one-upsmanship between Nifong and the defense attorneys, as did the other hearings. Nifong told the judge that Mangum would "most certainly" testify and that defense attorneys could ask her questions at that time. The judge also ruled that the defense attorneys were entitled to the full scientific data that the two DNA labs had used to analyze the players' DNA.

Nifong also gave defense attorneys new information about the case, including a further 615 pages of evidence, a cassette tape, and a compact disc, as well as a stack of e-mails from Durham police officials. But the topic that seemed to cause the most debate inside the courtroom was the odd coincidence that a New York marketing firm hired by defense attorneys had conducted a telephone survey of some three hundred Durham County residents on September 11 to gauge their reaction to the lacrosse case. One of the residents called was Cy Gurney, Nifong's wife and the local administrator for a state advocacy program for abused and neglected children. In an affidavit, Gurney wrote that she spoke with the interviewer for an hour. "She seemed more interested in telling a story than in getting my answers, as some of the questions were very long and tailored to a specific point of view," she explained. "She also did not appear to be recording my answers." The first question, Gurney reported, was, "If the prosecutor in a community took on a sensational case right before a primary election, do you think such a case would be handled for political gain?" The questions continued in that vein, she wrote. At one point, the questioner asked Gurney if she knew anyone involved in the case and she said her husband was the prosecutor, but the questions continued. "Many of the questions asked, however, actually constituted a thinly-disguised attempt to influence the opinions of the respondents," Nifong wrote in a motion to the judge in order to get the survey stopped, in part because he suspected the defense attorneys' goal was a not-so veiled effort to taint the pool of potential jurists in the case. In court, Nifong asked the judge to decide whether the poll was appropriate and whether it violated any ethical rules. Not surprisingly, defense attorney Wade Smith defended the use of the survey. "We have tried to think of any case in North Carolina history that comes close to the kind of interest that has been generated in this case," he told the judge. "There isn't a person at this table who would squint down his eyes and say, 'I think I will try to influence improperly the 240,000 people in this county.'" In the end, Judge Smith ruled that the survey's questions were designed to elicit opinions, not to influence them.

By the beginning of October, the burning question on many people's minds throughout the Durham and Duke communities was why Nifong had not dropped the case against the three Duke lacrosse players. It was remarkable to witness how dramatically the tide of public opinion—at least as articulated by and reflected in the media—had turned against Nifong and Mangum to favor Seligmann, Finnerty, and Evans. There was one prominent exception, though: the *New York Times*. The 5,700-word, August 25 front-page analysis of Nifong's case files by Duff Wilson and Jonathan Glater—including a review of Gottlieb's newly drafted thirty-three-page chronology of the case—seemed to have missed the memo. An October 8 essay by Kurt Andersen, one of the founders of *Spy* magazine and the Jedi Master of the zeitgeist, in *New York* magazine, which he had formerly edited, captured well the rapidly changing mood and the *Times*'s seeming obliviousness to it.

After explaining how a former *New York Times* writer had e-mailed him that "You couldn't *invent* a story so precisely tuned to the outrage frequency of the modern, metropolitan, *bien pensant* journalist"—to wit, "successful white men at the Harvard of the South versus a poor single mother enrolled at a local black college, jerky superstar jock versus $400 out-call strippers, a boozy *Animal House* party, shouts of 'nigger,' and a three-orifice gangbang rape in a bathroom"—Andersen began to deconstruct the Hollywood tableau. "Real facts are stubborn things," Andersen wrote. "And today, the preponderance of facts indicate that there is an injustice—committed, as it turns out, against those perfect offenders." Andersen blamed Wilson and Glater for "declining to expose" the injustice of the wrongly accused lacrosse players. "The only thing we can look forward to now," Dan Okrent, the former *Times* ombudsman, told Andersen, "is what the *Times* will say to the accused once the charges are dropped, or once acquittals are delivered."

Andersen recounted how Nifong had promised that the DNA evidence would reveal what happened, and when it didn't confirm the narrative he had been articulating, he first pushed for the indictments of Seligmann and Finnerty and then, after the second round of DNA testing proved inconclusive, pushed for the indictment of Evans. Anderson recounted the flaws in the photographic lineup and the inconsistencies in the stories told by Roberts and Mangum about what had happened in the house. And he wrote that Nifong found himself telling Judge Smith that despite Mangum's claim the rape lasted thirty minutes, "If I had to speculate, I'd say this whole event took five minutes, maybe ten minutes at the outside." And how Nifong had never actually interviewed Mangum about the events of the night of March 13 and refused to consider Seligmann's alibi. "So why on earth does a heretofore well-regarded prosecutor push so . . . crazily to bring indictments?" Andersen wondered. "The Occam's-razor answer seems compelling: politics."

Andersen revealed, after talking to a source at the newspaper, that over the summer, Duff Wilson, an investigative reporter at the paper, "was getting a lot of pressure from somewhere up above to reenter the [Duke] story in a big way." But when Andersen spoke with Wilson, the latter seemed nonplussed by the idea that he and Glater had failed to get with the program. He said his article was "thorough" and that he did not "have a strong opinion" about the lacrosse case. He told Andersen he didn't buy the theory that Nifong's behavior was driven by his political ambitions. And although he conceded to Andersen that he never interviewed Nifong, he seemed to agree with the *News & Observer*'s conclusion that Nifong was "just stubborn." Andersen was incredulous that "in a single dismissive boilerplate sentence," Wilson had brushed off the weaknesses in Nifong's case "to defense lawyers, Duke alumni, and obsessive bloggers." Andersen retorted, "What about Brooks, Kristof, and just about every other major national and local journalist and legal expert who's looked closely at the case? Forget them. Thus the *Times*'s front-page newshole takeaway: it isn't a witch hunt; Nifong's not so bad; these aren't the Scottsboro Boys; the accuser may well have been raped; these Duke guys might have done it; the case deserves to go to trial."

This was not just idle musing on Andersen's part; this conclusion seemed to be consistent with the thinking of at least some of the *Times*'s editorial leaders. Craig Whitney, the paper's "standards editor," told Andersen, "The thrust of this August story is that there's more to the prosecution case than the defense would have you believe." Andersen found that point to be obviously true, in nearly every case. "I don't know whether the men who've been accused are guilty," Whitney told Andersen. "That's what trials are for." Still, it wasn't hard for Andersen to dig up other, unnamed reporters and editors at the *Times* who were appalled by Wilson's article and the paper's placement of it on the front page. "I've never [before] been a source for anyone on any story ever written about the *Times*," one reporter told him. Why this one? "I've never felt so ill over the *Times*'s coverage," this person replied. (Added Andersen, "That's *ill* at a paper that published Jayson Blair's fabrications and Judy Miller on WMD.") Explained another editor, "It's institutional. You see it over and over again, the way the *Times* lumbers into trouble."

Andersen seemed quite taken by the blogger K. C. Johnson, whose daily musings about the case—and its unfairness to the players—on his *Durham-in-Wonderland* blog had been an early and articulate voice that there might be serious problems with Nifong's prosecution. Anderson seemed fascinated that Johnson had no ties to Duke or Durham but rather was a thirty-eight-year-old tenured professor of US history at Brooklyn College with Harvard degrees who lived alone in an small apartment in Bay Ridge, Brooklyn, and was an ascetic, a vegetarian, and a runner. Andersen asked Johnson why he thought Nifong didn't abandon the case. As others had thought, "This is someone whose career is on the line," Johnson said. "He has no choice." Then came Andersen's final condemnation of Wilson's article and his editors' decision to put it on the front page. "For the past few years, I've tended to roll my eyes when people default to rants about the blindered oafishness or various baises of 'the mainstream media' in general and the *Times* in particular," Andersen wrote. "At the same time, I've nodded when people gush about the blogosphere as a valuable check on and supplement to the MSM—but I've never entirely bought it. Having waded deep into this Duke mess the last weeks, baffled by the *Times*'s pose of objectivity and indispensibly guided by Johnson's blog, I'm becoming a believer."

But Andersen's musings were merely an *amuse-bouche* for the forty-minute feast that would fill the national airwaves on Sunday, October 15: A *60 Minutes* segment on the lacrosse case, featuring—for the first time—exclusive interviews with Seligmann, Finnerty, and Evans. The show's producers, Michael Radutzky and Tanya Simon, along with longtime correspondent Ed Bradley—who would die of complications from leukemia some three weeks after the segment aired—had been working with the families for months to arrange interviews—exclusivity was a prerequisite—and to air them at what seemed like the penultimate moment, a few weeks before the November election, with the prosecution of the case continuing. After all, if Nifong were somehow to lose his race for district attorney, the chances of the prosecution proceeding would be greatly diminished. Some 16.8 million people tuned in.

60 Minutes explained to viewers that during the previous six months it had reviewed the "entire case file," around "two thousand documents, including police reports, witness statements, and medical records." Although neither Nifong nor Mangum would talk to the program—thus opening the show to charges of being pro-defense—*60 Minutes* concluded that the evidence revealed "disturbing facts about the conduct of the police and the district attorney, and raises serious concerns about whether or not a rape even occurred." In his first public comments since his indictment in May, Evans told Bradley, "This woman has destroyed everything I worked for in my life. She's put it on hold. She's destroyed two other families and she's brought shame on a great university. And, worst of all she's split apart a community and a nation on facts that just didn't happen and a lie that should have never been told." Bradley asked Evans if he was worried about going to prison. "Would you?" Evans shot back. After Bradley conceded that he would be, Evans said, "Thirty years. I could go to jail for something that never happens." He said he had moved out of 610 North Buchanan because he started fearing for his life. "There were threats of drive-by shootings, acts of violence, assaults, people driving by Duke students and pretending to point guns at them and it was just very scary," he said. "We moved out after the first day because there were mobs in front of the house burning candles, putting terrible things up, asking us to get a conscience, show character. It was terrible."

Next, Bradley spoke with Finnerty, who for the first time publicly said he was equally incredulous about being indicted. "I never expected anything even close to that happening," he said. "I never expected anyone to get indicted, let alone myself." He seemed amazed that he was one of the ones Mangum had picked out of the photo lineup. "It's unbelievable," he said. "Don't know how, why that happened. But, try to figure that out, I really have no idea how that happened." Seligmann told Bradley, "Your whole life you try to, you know, stay on the right path, and to do the right things. And someone can come along and take it all away. Just by going like that. Just by pointing their finger. That's all it takes."

Bradley spoke with Kim Roberts on camera. Bradley noted that Roberts had changed her story several times over the course of six months, from saying that it was "a crock" that Mangum had been raped to a revised view that "they were guilty." Roberts was no longer making predictions. "I'm not a detective, I'm not the DA," she said. "I'm just a girl who was there. So honestly, what needs to happen is you hear my version, you hear their version, put it together. Sift through the bull. And hopefully come out with as much truth as possible."

Roberts told Bradley that neither Seligmann, Finnerty, nor Evans used any racial epithets with the two women. Seligmann told Bradley he did not appreciate having this stigma attached to him, too. "If that comment was said, it's disgusting," he said. "And there's no way I can defend that. You know, that's a horrible thing for anyone to say." He also told Bradley he would not accept responsibility for a rape that did not occur and that he could prove he was not at the house during the time the rape allegedly occurred. "It's impossible," he said. "It's impossible for it to have happened." He told Bradley he left the party because, "I didn't like the tone of the party, it made me uncomfortable. It's as simple as that. I thought it was a boring party and I didn't like the tone." He said he had never spoken to the police about what happened that night and that Nifong rebuffed his lawyer when he tried to present Seligmann's alibi. Bradley never asked Seligmann to explain what about the "tone" of the party he had not liked enough that it caused him to leave. This would have been nice to know.

Evans told Bradley he had done "everything he could" to help the police when the investigation began, after they showed up at the house with a search warrant and found him sleeping. "It was scary," he said. "I woke up from a nap to ten police officers in my living room with a search warrant. As they read the search warrant, I went through every part of it—told 'em where they could find things and that we'd fully cooperate and answer any questions they had." Bradley asked Evans what he thought would happen next. "I'd done everything that I thought I could do," he said. "I put my faith in the legal system and told them what happened. I gave my statement. I offered to take a polygraph. I gave my DNA over. I don't know what else I could do."

Finnerty told Bradley the forty-six white players on the team were happy to go down to the police station and give DNA samples. "I mean, we were kinda, I mean, shocked by the fact that we—that we had to actually go to a police station to give DNA," he said. "But everyone—we were told it would help to clear everything up. So we were happy to go." Finnerty said that while he would wait until the trial to present his alibi, he, too, was not in the house when the rape allegedly occurred. "I left soon after I saw them do their act in the room with everybody else," he said. "I saw them leave the room. I never saw them again in my life." As for Mangum's supposition that Evans had a mustache when he assaulted her, Evans told Bradley, "Absolutely not," he said. "And, I tried to provide the district attorney with photographs showing that I didn't, and he refused to view them."

Bradley spoke with James Coleman, the Duke law professor and author of the report about the lacrosse program. He was highly critical of the photographic lineup the police constructed using only Duke lacrosse players. Not only did the lineup violate accepted local, state, and federal police procedures but it also was like shooting fish in a barrel for Mangum. "Can't make a mistake," Coleman said. Bradley asked Coleman why Nifong would ask for such a procedure. "Well that's a good question for the DA," he said. "But I assume that, you know, after his initial performance in this case, he needed to indict at least three players. And charge them with what he said was a rape that had occurred." Coleman was highly critical of Nifong. "I think that he pandered to the community," he said, "by saying, 'I'm gonna go out there and defend your interests in seeing that these hooligans who committed the crime are prosecuted. I'm not gonna let their fathers, with all of their money, buy, you know, big-time lawyers and get them off. I'm doing this for you.' You know, what are you to conclude about a prosecutor who says to you, 'I'll do whatever it takes to get this set of defendants?'" He said Nifong was guilty of prosecutorial misconduct.

The final words went to Evans, Finnerty, and Seligmann. Evans told Bradley he was "haunted" by his decision to have the March 13 party at his house. He explained that the March 13 party was his "greatest failure as a leader" of the lacrosse team and that he had learned in the past months "that even the smallest action has great consequences and even the things you take for granted every day that might be just a little bit wrong can lead to terrible, terrible things." Explained Finnerty, "It's changed my life forever, no matter what happens from here on out. It's probably gonna be something that defines me my whole life." Bradley asked Seligmann if he ever asked himself if he should not have gone to the party. "No," he replied. "Not go to the party? I did nothing wrong. I did nothing wrong."

But it was the highly articulate Seligmann who lashed out at the Duke administration for the way it had treated him and the other players. "I chose Duke to be my home for four years," he said, "and to see your professors go out and slander you and say horrible, untrue things about you and to have your administration just cut us loose based on nothing, based on nothing [was unacceptable]. They have to know this is not true. But Duke took the stance that 'we wouldn't stand for this behavior.' They didn't want to take a chance on standing for the truth. It wasn't convenient for them to stand up for the truth. I can't forgive them for that." He said he would not likely return to Duke, no matter the outcome of the case. "I can't say that I would," he said. "I don't know what the circumstances will be. I don't know where I'll be a year from now or whenever I get the opportunity, but I mean, based on the way I've been treated so far, I just can't imagine representing the school that didn't want me to represent them. I couldn't imagine." And he was angry. "To see my face on TV in those little mug shots and above it saying 'alleged rapists,' you don't know what this does to me."

Aside from the scoop of getting the three players for the first time all together to declare their innocence on national television, the only news *60 Minutes* seemed to break was the odd—but highly damning—suggestion that despite complaining of neck, back, and knee pain during the weeks after the alleged attack, Mangum had returned to dancing at the Hillsborough nightclub within two weeks of the attack. *60 Minutes* stated that it had obtained a video of Mangum supposedly performing at Platinum Pleasures on March 25 and 26; the program then showed parts of her performance and an interview with the ex-manager of the club, H. P. Thomas, who said she showed no signs of injury or impairment. "She didn't seem different to me," he said. "She was

the same way." Thomas also told *Inside Edition* that Mangum had danced at
Platinum Pleasures on March 17, four days after the attack.

"It's enormous," Joe Cheshire said of the video of Mangum dancing at the
club. "We'll have testimony and demonstrative evidence that days later she's
in the strip club performing." But after the *60 Minutes* segment aired, Jakki,
Mangum's cousin, told ABC News that she thought the defense was trying to
"break" Mangum. "I think a lot of this is intimidation," she said. "I think they
want her to break, to say 'Enough is enough.'"

Two days after the *60 Minutes* episode aired, Officer Himan and Mangum
watched the clip that *60 Minutes* showed. If what *60 Minutes* had implied—that
she was dancing suggestively within days of her alleged rape, despite repeatedly complaining of injuries suffered during the attack—then her integrity as
a witness would be further compromised, and Nifong's case would be severely
impaired. Himan had to find out if the alleged timing of the video was true.
"Crystal Mangum believes that was the last week of February," Himan wrote in
his notes, not the end of March. "The boots that are shown in the video were
white stillettos she bought at Pri[s]cilla's two days before she danced in that
video. She believes it was on a Tuesday that she bought them and she believes
the video of the *60 Minutes* dance was on a Thursday. She stated she danced
twice in those boots. She stated she never danced in the boots after the rape."
Mangum told Himan that she "did not strip" on March 25, and that that day she
had been wearing a "light green outfit with flowers on it and matching bra and
panties," although how she could recollect what she was wearing six months
earlier to the day was not asked—or at least noted—by Himan. (In her 2008
book, *The Last Dance for Grace*, Mangum reiterated that she never danced at
Platinum Pleasures after the alleged rape incident and that the video that *60
Minutes* obtained was from before March 13. In his April 6 affidavit to Durham
police, Mangum's driver, Jariel Johnson, said he drove Mangum to Platinum
on the night of March 11, where he said she danced from around 11 p.m. that
night until the club closed at 4:30 in the morning.)

The next day, Himan and Linwood Wilson, Nifong's investigator, met with
Dr. Victor Olatoye, the owner of Platinum Pleasures, who swore out an affidavit. In the affidavit, Olatoye wrote that the *60 Minutes* video misstated the date
of Mangum's dance at his club. "The video is at my club and was prior to the
rape," Olatoye wrote. "I am certain of this because Mangum has not stripped
at my club since the rape occurred." Had *60 Minutes* goofed?

A few days later, Patrick Thomas, also known as "Fats," called Linwood
Wilson, in the DA's office, to say he was stopping by to show Wilson the DVD
of Mangum dancing at the Platinum Club. He just wanted to show the DVD
to Wilson alone. At around 5 p.m. on the afternoon of October 24, Fats and
his friend, who went by the name of "Black," arrived. Twenty minutes later,
Himan walked into the meeting. "Both acted very nervous when I walked in,"

he later noted. Fats kept getting calls on his cell phone and then would leave the conference room to take the calls. Fats had brought his own DVD player with him and hooked it up to the television in the room. He started to narrate the video as it played "images of black males that appeared to be drinking," Himan wrote in his notes. At one point, he saw the date—March 25, 2006—appear on the screen, on a black background. "The video altogether seemed to be edited," Himan continued. Fats and Black then fast-forwarded the video to show when they went to the Platinum Club. Himan reported that he saw a picture of the club and Fats in a suit. Up on the screen popped the same segment of Mangum dancing that had appeared on the *60 Minutes* broadcast. After Mangum appeared to be dancing, Fats shut the DVD off. Wilson and Himan asked Fats if they could show the DVD to Mangum. "He stated, 'No,'" Himan wrote. "We were not allowed to look at it further or make any copies of it."

Ten members of the newly reconstituted Duke lacrosse team had gathered to watch the *60 Minutes* segment at the Trinity Park house of the two cocaptains, Matt Danowski and Ed Douglas, a Duke graduate student who had received his engineering degree from Duke the previous May. "The segment was well done," Danowski said. "I hope people watched it." Douglas said he hoped that it would have "some impact within Durham, specifically within the DA's case." Another group of Duke students watched the show at the Bryan Center, the student union building. "They produced a very compelling, but one-sided, account of the issues," senior Malik Burnett, the head of the Black Student Alliance, said. "It seemed very sensationalized." Sophomore Mike Muniz said that, given Bradley's "very liberal reputation," the fact that he seemed to be siding with the lacrosse players "was very telling." But William Dixon, a Durham resident who happened to be watching the show at the Bryan Center, said, "There's nobody who's innocent here. They should not have had a party like that. This is a school of standards."

Nifong didn't watch the show. "I have a tape of it," he said the next day. "I have a transcript of it. I didn't watch it." Did Nifong think the segment would hurt his election chances? "We're not going to know [until] after the election is over whether it made any difference or not," he said.

A few days later, James Coleman, along with six journalists who had been actively reporting on the lacrosse case, came together on a panel at Duke law school to discuss their coverage. More than a hundred people attended the panel discussion, which featured Duke alumni Susannah Meadows, the *Newsweek* reporter who had written the April cover story about the scandal, and Jay Bilas, the ESPN college basketball analyst, as well as Seyward Darby, the previous editor of the *Chronicle*, plus the managing editors of the *News & Observer* and the *Durham Herald-Sun*. There were no bloggers at the law school event but there was no denying, as Kurt Andersen had pointed out in *New York* magazine, that bloggers, such as K. C. Johnson at *Durham-in-Wonderland* and

John from John in Carolina, among others, and their relentless daily focus on the case were having an impact, especially since they tended to side with the lacrosse players and the defense against Duke and Nifong. "Given the nature of the blogosphere, I'm not surprised anymore at anything like this," Andersen said of the growing influence of the bloggers in the Duke case. "There are 300 million people in this country—a few of them are inevitably going to take an interest. It's a compelling story. . . . Bloggers have the luxury to do things the mainstream media don't . . . because of their passion and their focus. Bloggers don't have the fetters of institutional standards and editors and those good things the mainstream media has. . . . It can work both ways and requires readers to judge them accordingly."

Johnson said he had started his blog, which he stated received about one hundred thousand visitors, because he was outraged at the Duke faculty's response to the alleged incident, as embodied in the Group of 88 statement. He found that the more he investigated the case, the less Nifong's arguments held together. "Usually when you learn more about something, it's more nuanced," he said. "There are more shades of gray as more information comes to light. This is a case where it's been the opposite." He said he was not aware of any bloggers who were writing in support of Nifong. "If you're inclined to take a pro-Nifong view, there's nothing much you can say beyond 'Trust Nifong,'" Johnson said. "That is, in my opinion, very unusual. Usually you get blogs that are sort of on both sides."

An example of the challenges the bloggers posed to Duke and its administrators could be found in an October 24 thread that developed online after K. C. Johnson posted that he would be speaking on a panel at Duke, sponsored by the local chapter of the ACLU, on October 26. Innocuous enough. But then a few hours later, in the comment section of Johnson's blog, an anonymous person posted the "NEWS!!" that a "Duke Official" had said that the school had given "considerable support" to the lacrosse players since March and then included the "fact" that an anonymous Duke parent, not associated with the lacrosse team, had sent an e-mail to Brodhead asking him why he and the school had not been more supportive of the players. The reply came back to the parent from one of Brodhead's deputies: "Let me assure you that we're in regular contact with them and their families and offering considerable support," it read. "As you know, for the reasons articulated by the president on numerous occasions, Duke cannot pre-judge the outcome of the case regardless of media accounts. We all hopes this ends soon."

The response from Duke set off William L. Anderson, another blogger. "Believe me," he wrote, "that response comes out of the back end of a bull. The lacrosse parents with whom I speak tell me that Brodhead completely abandoned them to the tender mercies of the Group of 88 and others. With a little bit of backbone, Brodhead could have stood up to the Group of 88 and others, and he could have let Nifong and the Durham police know that they were expected to follow the law. Instead, he encouraged the faculty, Nifong and the police to use the lacrosse players and their families as piñatas."

Some additional speculative back and forth in the comments section convinced Jason Trumpbour, the spokesman for the Friends of Duke University blog, to post his first comment on K. C. Johnson's blog. "I have been monitoring this board since the very beginning," he wrote. "I have never posted simply because I cannot check it consistently enough to keep up with the fast pace of discussions. I am posting here for the first time because the assertion made by Brodhead's assistant that the Duke administration has been 'in regular contact with [the lacrosse players] and their families and offering considerable support' is so absolutely outrageous that I believe you should know the facts." Trumpbour then explained that except for three instances, "Brodhead and the rest of the administration have had no contact with any of the lacrosse players or their families whatsoever."

According to Trumpbour, Brodhead's three conversations were: one, with the family of Devon Sherwood, the team's only black player. Brodhead "apologized for what they were going through." The second interaction came when the family of one of the unindicted players ran into Brodhead at a reception at the Duke University Medical Center, after the dedication of a new building. "Brodhead was very cold and uncaring toward them," Trumpbour wrote. "One of the trustees joined them and was supportive of the lacrosse players. The trustee asked them how to get lacrosse wristbands, and he indicated he wanted to get enough for a lacrosse team at the university where he teaches. As Brodhead watched silently, the family members gave him one of their own wristbands, and he put it on immediately. At this point, apparently, Brodhead walked away."

The third conversation was with the parents of Collin Finnerty, who, according to Trumpbour, had contacted Brodhead to get permission for Collin to transfer to Duke the credits that he had received studying at other colleges in New York since his indictment in April. "Both Collin and Reade Seligmann are taking classes this semester at colleges near their homes," Trumpbour wrote. "However, Duke will not let them transfer more than two courses, so they are unable to keep up with their studies while suspended unless they get permission to transfer more. Collin was supposed to do study abroad this semester, but Duke canceled that. Brodhead refused to meet with them despite several requests. Finally, the person in charge of the annual giving program told Brodhead that, unless he agreed to see the Finnert[y]s, he would resign. Only then did Brodhead agree to meet them. In the meeting Brodhead remained intransigent, and he and Mrs. Finnerty got into a terrible argument. The Finnert[y]s walked out because Brodhead started insulting them. There has not been a single note, card, or other expression of kindness from anyone in the Duke administration to any of the three accused students."

Whether Finnerty and Seligmann would return to Duke to complete their studies and to play lacrosse was an issue first addressed in Ed Bradley's conversation with Seligmann, in which Seligmann said on national television that "I just can't imagine representing [a] school that didn't want me to represent them." In the days after the *60 Minutes* broadcast, their teammates and Duke administrators seemed to go out of their way to make sure the two rising juniors knew they would be welcomed back at Duke. The fact that they would be allowed to return to Duke only if the felony charges were dropped seemed to have been relegated to the fine print. "Collin and Reade would be welcomed back with open arms," Ed Douglas, the team cocaptain, told the *Chronicle*, "and that's something they're strongly considering. We look forward to having them with us. . . . It's obviously going to be a very personal decision for both of those individuals, and I'd imagine it won't be an easy decision. We understand that." The lacrosse coach, John Danowski, didn't forsee much difficulty with having the two players return to the team. "Why wouldn't they be?" he said. "If the school says they're academically eligible and they're athletically eligible, if and when the charges are dropped, we would welcome them back." Chris Kennedy, the senior associate athletic director, said he did not forsee any athletic elegibility issue for Seligmann and Finnerty. "The only question is how long it'll take," he said. "If it stretches into spring and next fall, you would have to request some kind of waiver. If this fall is the only term they miss, it won't be a problem." The first 2007 lacrosse game was scheduled for February 24 against Dartmouth.

If any of this—the constant haranguing of the bloggers, the national media onslaught now turned against him, the holes in Mangum's narrative, the growing assumption at Duke that the players were wrongly accused—was getting to Nifong, he was careful not to let anyone know. "It's the difference between character and reputation," he said on October 26. "Character is what you are. Reputation is what people say you are. As long as you know who you are, you don't have to worry over what people say about you."

During the October 27 court hearing, Nifong dropped the bombshell that he had not heard with his own ears Mangum's story of what happened on the night of March 13. The defense lawyers had asked him to turn over whatever "written report" he had put together after his conversations with Mangum about the details of the case. Instead, he told the court there was no such report. Defense lawyers were incredulous that Nifong would have them believe the only conversation he had had with Mangum—contained in the documents he turned over to the defense—was that he had asked her if she had taken the drug Ecstasy on the night of the alleged attack. That was "stretching the bounds of credulity," Brad Bannon, a lawyer for David Evans, told the court.

But Nifong said the question about Ecstasy was it. "She said, 'I've never taken Ecstasy,'" Nifong told the court. "That was the end of that conversation." He said he had met with Mangum on April 11 but that she was still too "traumatized by this offense" during that meeting to recount the story. "I could not see anything that could be served by even talking to her about the case," he said. The purpose of the conversation was not to hear her story, he said, but rather to figure out "what course we would be taking, what steps we would be taking" during the investigation. "No statements were made about the case by her," he continued. "No questions about the case were asked of her." He said she "possibly did not speak fifteen words during the whole conversation," was unable to make eye contact with him and the police detectives, and seemed on the verge of tears throughout. "She had a way of, when she sat in the chair, she kind of shrunk," Nifong recalled. "She looked smaller than she really was." He said she could barely look up at him "and she just did not seem to be ready to talk about the facts of the case . . . my impression was that something really bad had happened to her and she wasn't ready to deal with it yet." (Himan's brief recollection of the April 11 meeting with Mangum was that Nifong talked about how the case would unfold procedurally and "how it's going to be done and over with in a day.")

Nevertheless, based upon the conversations she had with Durham police, as well as her own April 6 statement and Levicy's examination of her in the early morning hours of March 14, Nifong took the case to the grand jury and won the indictments of Seligmann, Finnerty, and Evans. Nifong told the court he had spoken to Mangum on the phone a few times since April 11. "I've had conversations with Mangum about how she's doing," he said. "I've had conversations with Mangum about her seeing her kids. I have not had any conversations with her about the facts of that night because I don't need to do that right now. I am not preparing to try this case next week. . . . This is another false issue to make it look like I call her up and say, 'Tell me more about this case.' . . . We're not at that stage yet." He said that as the trial date approached, he would likely ask someone in his office to interview Mangum. He said defense attorneys "seem not to be satisfied with that answer, but it's the only answer I can give. No matter how many times they ask the question, the answer will be the same. . . . [Albert Einstein] is quoted as having said that insanity is doing the same thing over and over again and expecting a different result. I'm not going to give them a different result because I can't. Integrity requires that I tell them the truth on this occasion like I have on every other. . . . There is nothing to provide involving the April 11 conversation."

Nifong then launched into a short speech that revealed—again—just how he was thinking about the case, and his role as a prosecutor. He cited a previous conversation he had had with David Smith, the director of the Friends of Durham, a political organization trying to defeat Nifong in his election bid.

"We hear all of these things on the news," he said Smith had said to him, "about all the discovery that's been turned over and all these people are saying, 'You don't have a case.' What do you have to say to that?' And I said, 'In this case, like in any case, you don't try the case based on pieces of paper. You put witnesses in front of a jury so that the jury can hear what the witnesses have to say and how they have to say it.' I said, 'None of these people who are writing these articles have ever spoken with this victim. I am the only person involved with this case who has spoken to her.' And that was my entire conversation about that." (During the hearing, Nifong realized he appeared to be in the situation where he said he had spoken to Mangum about the case while at the same time saying his conversations had not yet been substantive. He seemed fine with the apparent contradiction.)

Furthermore, he said that had he interviewed Mangum or, alternatively, spoken to Seligmann and Finnerty about their supposed alibis, he risked becoming a witness in the case himself, which would have prevented him from prosecuting it. He said that's why he told them and their lawyers to tell their stories to police investigators. "I can't think of any prosecutor who would fall for that," he said. "Because I'm not stupid, I would not have done what they seem to keep accusing me of doing."

But Joe Cheshire was not content to let that be the last word. "Mr. Nifong intimated that we were attempting to try to conflict him out of the case by calculatedly getting him to interview our clients at the beginning of the case," he said. "That is simply untrue. I have the letter that I wrote to Mr. Nifong that I'll be glad to share with anybody. We asked Mr. Nifong to meet with us, the lawyers, to give him exculpatory evidence that showed that our clients are innocent. We also did offer to let him or anyone else interview our clients. Other than a very rude response to a telephone conversation through his assistant, he never responded to that letter. So the assertion that he made this morning is simply untrue."

Kirk Osborn then explained how before Reade Seligmann's first appearance in court, he, Osborn, had gone to see Nifong to share with him "exculpatory evidence" about his client. "And the response I got was not from Mr. Nifong but from somebody in his office saying that, 'I saw you on television proclaiming your client's innocence, so what is there to talk about?' That is the response that I got." Osborn's comment prompted Cheshire to speak up again. "And I might add, Your Honor, it is rather stunning to me that Mr. Nifong can stand up as piously as he did . . . and [say] that he never talked to the alleged victim in this case, refused to talk to any of the lawyers, refused to see any of the exculpatory evidence but has indicted, his office has indicted, three men and put their lives in the jeopardy that he's put them in."

Outside the courtroom, Cheshire told reporters, somewhat hyperbolically, "One of the most interesting things to me of course is Mr. Nifong did admit that he in fact has basically never talked to this woman and has absolutely no idea what her story is, and yet he has chosen to go forward with this case." He added, "It's a very emotional case. The feelings run very high. The lawyers on the side of the young men are very committed to their innocence. This is an immense travesty of justice."

With a week to go before the election, Ruth Sheehan, the *News & Observer* columnist who had previously been supportive of Nifong, told her readers that the best way to dispense with the deeply flawed prosecution of the lacrosse case was to not vote for him. "To most of us, the Duke lacrosse case is such a disaster that" Nifong, "up for reelection, should be preparing for a trouncing. But not, apparently, in Durham." To her disbelief, a poll of six hundred likely votes in Durham County revealed that 46 percent said they planned to vote for Nifong, with the rest split among other candidates. This had her perplexed. "In a strange way, Nifong has become a symbol of Durham to the nation," she wrote by way of a possible explanation. "And in Durham, as in most dysfunctional families, it may be okay to holler and throw lamps at one another within the family, but let an outsider criticize and, honey, watch out." She urged the Durham voters to make the upcoming election for district attorney a referendum on Nifong's handling of the lacrosse case. "If Nifong wins," she wrote, "how can he do anything but take this case to trial? That is what's so scary." Instead, she concluded, "Here's a chance for voters to say, 'Not here. Not in Durham.' Durham voters can set this case before new eyes. If only they would."

In his first article about the case since his lengthy August 25 front-page dive into big chunks of the evidence, *New York Times* reporter Duff Wilson wrote about how odd the Durham district attorney election had become. There was Nifong, the current prosecutor and a Democrat, who had brought the case against the three lacrosse players. As Sheehan pointed out, if elected, he obviously would bring the case to trial. There was Lewis Cheek, a local lawyer and county commissioner, who was on the ballot as an independent but had said he would not serve if elected, a tactic that would pave the way for Governor Mike Easley, a Democrat, to appoint the next district attorney, just as he had appointed Nifong a year earlier. Cheek had been trying to get Nifong to recuse himself and hand the case over to the state attorney general, Roy Cooper. The third candidate, Steve Monks, a Republican and a new resident of Durham, was not even on the ballot and had mounted a seemingly unwinnable write-in campaign. He said that, if elected, he would review the evidence thoroughly but that "this case might very well have to go to trial." "We have a saying here—OID," explained Nifong's new campaign manager. "Only in Durham."

But rather than provide much new insight into the coming election, Wilson's piece seemed more like an opportunity to nudge the *Times*'s reporting out of the Nifong camp into the growing conventional wisdom. "Mr. Nifong has been under attack for months by the defense and supporters of the lacrosse players for aggressively pursuing a case based almost entirely on the account of the accuser, which he acknowledges he has heard only from police reports and written statements, and not directly by speaking with her," Wilson wrote. "The flaws and gaps in the evidence have mounted. No DNA from the defendants was found on the dancer. At least one of the accused appears to have a strong alibi. A second woman hired to strip at the party has said she saw no evidence of an attack. And the array of photographs that led to the identification of the three defendants was not presented according to federal, state and local police guidelines for lineups."

On the morning of October 28—the day after the hearing—the *News & Observer* reported that it had reviewed the full video of Mangum supposedly dancing at Platinum Pleasures in Hillsborough on March 26, at the same time she was regularly showing up at area hospitals complaining of intense pain supposedly caused by the alleged attack. The newspaper assembled the time line of Mangum's activities after the alleged attack from documents Nifong had turned over to defense attorneys. "The video . . . shows a limber performer," the paper stated. (*60 Minutes* had only shown a three-second clip of the video on its program.) Linwood Wilson, Nifong's investigator, told the paper that he had watched the full video "but could not say with certainty that it was the accuser dancing."

According to the paper, when Mangum was taken to the emergency room at Duke Hospital in the early morning hours of March 14, she said she was "gang-raped but not hit or struck" and complained of "excruciating pain" of ten, on a one-to-ten scale. The nurses and doctors, though, "found no obvious discomfort and no associated symptoms of pain, such as grimacing, sweating, or changes in vital signs or posture." But ten days later, according to Thomas, Mangum was dancing at Platinum Pleasures. The *News & Observer* reported that the minute-long video clip "shows the woman, introduced as Precious, as she approached a floor-to-ceiling pole on a stage, dressed in a thong and skimpy top. She grasped the pole and lowered herself into a squatting position, so that her buttocks almost touched the floor. With her hands on the floor, she stretched out her right leg vertically, as though she were kicking to the ceiling while squatting, and waved her leg several times to either side of the pole." In the *60 Minutes* segment, Thomas said that on the night of March 26, Mangum "danced like she always danced, good old Precious." Whether Mangum had danced at Platinum Pleasures after March 13 seemed as much a mystery as ever.

Two days later, Mangum returned to UNC Hospitals, complaining of "knee pain, neck pain, and vaginal bleeding." Mangum told the doctors that she "continued to have muscle spasms" in her neck and back and continued to use Flexeril and oxycodone, "which helped." As for her knee pain, Mangum told the doctors that "when she was assaulted," she fell and felt "a sharp pain when she hit her knee," and that it was now "popping out" and "locking" when she climbed stairs. "She has not had this pain before," the doctors noted. They also wrote that Mangum had "vaginal bleeding on and off for the last two weeks." Although Mangum told the doctors she had not been bleeding vaginally for two days, when she did bleed it was "greater than a pad an hour." Again the doctors noted that Mangum had a "history of depression," but denied any "suicidal or homicidal ideation at this time." The doctors prescribed more Flexeril and tramadol for her neck and back pain and requested that she get an MRI for her knee pain. They would continue to monitor her vaginal bleeding.

On April 3—three days before her written statement to police—Mangum returned to the UNC Hospital, again complaining of severe neck pain. Dr. Natasha Walzer noted that Mangum had "acute . . . chronic neck pain" and ordered an X-ray. The film came back "negative for any fracture"; Dr. Walzer "reassured" Mangum and told her to continue her physical therapy and to take Flexeril for her symptoms. "The patient is a well-appearing African-American female in no apparent distress," Dr. Walzer concluded. The *News & Observer* noted that on April 11, Nifong said he met with Mangum but that she was still too traumatized to speak or to make eye contact with him and seemed to be constantly on the verge of tears.

Speaking with Chris Cuomo on ABC's *Good Morning America* on October 30, Kim Roberts dropped another bombshell on Nifong's head. Roberts told Cuomo that after the dancers had driven away from 610 North Buchanan, Mangum asked Roberts to scratch her body to make it look like she had been assaulted. "The trip in that car from the house . . . went from happy to crazy," she told Cuomo, after confirming her reluctance to tell him because it might make her an unattractive witness for Nifong. "I tried all different ways to get through to her. . . . I tried to be funny and nice. Then I tried to, you know, be stern with her. . . . We're kind of circling around, and as we're doing that, my last-ditch attempt to get her out of the car, I start to kind of, you know, push and prod her, you know." Frustrated, Roberts said she then told Mangum, "Get out of my car. Get out of my car. . . . I . . . push on her leg. I kind of push on her arm. And clear as a bell . . . 'Go ahead, put marks on me. That's what I want. Go ahead.'" Roberts said Mangum's words "chilled me to the bone, and I decided right then and there to go to the authorities."

Roberts teared up and wanted to stop the interview. Why had this revelation made her so emotional? Cuomo wanted to know. "Because I think it's gonna make people rush to judgment," she said. "It's gonna make them stop listening. . . . And I don't like this at all. It's gonna make people not listen, and I, I'm sure you're probably not even going to play this. It's gonna make people not listen to any other part of the story. It's gonna make people so judgmental. It's gonna solidify their opinions so much, that they're not gonna want to hear the other aspects of the case, which I think are just as important."

The combination of Nifong's failure to interview Mangum about the events of the evening and Roberts' new description of what had happened between the two women in her car after they left the party left Linda Fairstein, a former sex-crimes prosecutor in the Manhattan District Attorney's Office, incredulous. "It belies anything a prosecutor would do before making charges," she told ABC News. "There was no need to rush to the charging judgment in this case. . . . To have witnesses appear on a media program revealing information that the prosecutor doesn't know is stunningly inappropriate." In an interview with the *News & Observer*, Nifong declined to comment on the specifics of Roberts's revelation but did offer the general advice, "If [witnesses] want to talk to somebody, they have every right to do that. If you do choose to talk to somebody, make sure to tell the truth because you're going to hear it again."

Chris Cuomo and *Good Morning America* struck again on Halloween morning with an exclusive interview with Devon Sherwood, the only black player on the lacrosse team, whose parents were both Duke graduates. His father had been the first black person to play lacrosse at Duke. Sherwood was a "walk-on" to the team, meaning he wasn't recruited (and likely had no athletic scholarship). He said his teammates had been stereotyped, not unlike what happens to many minorities in America. "It's just been all the stereotypes," Sherwood said. "I've even been stereotyped for being rich, being on full scholarship, [being] not in touch with my own black community at Duke. . . . So it's just amazing that the things you see and that [were] going on in this case and how the reversal from black stereotype to now rich white, privileged stereotype." And, not surprisingly, Sherwood said he did not believe Seligmann, Finnerty, and Evans raped Mangum. He said it was "impossible" that the rape occurred. "I'm 100 percent confident," he continued. Even though he was not present in the bathroom when the alleged attack was said to have taken place, he said he knew nothing happened because he knows the three accused players. "I don't hesitate," he said. "I believe in the character of my teammates. I believe in the character of specifically [the three defendants]." He said the party itself was boring. "We were just sitting around," he said. "And there was nothing to it. It was very boring. I was itching to get out of there, because it was. I'd rather be going to sleep, personally, to tell you the truth."

He said he had been prepared to join his teammates at the Durham police station to give a DNA sample. But then Pressler pulled him aside. "I remember the day vividly," he said. "I remember they got me to walk out with everybody else. And then Coach Pressler, our former coach who I love dearly, he said, 'Come here real quick.' I came over. He was like, 'You know, you don't have to go.'" Sherwood said he felt like he was abandoning his fellow Marines in the heat of a battle. He also said he received threatening e-mails from people he did not know. "One e-mail," he said, "[the] person basically said that if my teammates [go down] then I should go down as well, that I should, quote-unquote, rot in hell." He was confused. "I really don't care," he said. "But at that time I was like, 'Whoa. This guy wants me to rot in hell.' Like, he doesn't even know. He doesn't even know who I am. . . . I would get random e-mails saying I was letting down my race, that I should turn in my teammates, referring to me as a 'young black soldier,' basically saying I was letting down my race, I was letting down my forefathers, which is completely insane."

On the matter of the racial epithets hurled by a few of his white teammates at Roberts and Mangum as they drove away from 610 North Buchanan, Sherwood was torn. "If it is in fact true, it's disgusting," he said. But he added he had never heard his teammates even jokingly use offensive racial language. "It's not the first time I've—I would ever hear anybody call . . . me by the 'N-word' or anything like that," he said. "And it won't be the last. If it's true, everybody's human. Everybody makes mistakes. No one's Jesus. Like, no one's going to be perfect all the time. So you just forgive. Don't necessarily forget, but you forgive and you work to correct the mistake." Indeed, he said, the tribulations brought on by the events of March 13 had bonded the team together more closely than ever. "I had one brother when I came to Duke," he said. "Now I have forty-seven brothers. Forty-six of them just happen to be white. We're almost inseparable. We have a bond for life that no one else has."

Ever since the *60 Minutes* broadcast of a three-second clip of Mangum supposedly dancing suggestively at Platinum Pleasures in the early morning hours of March 26, questions remained about how she could possibly have been so limber given her ongoing complaints of severe pain caused by the alleged attack eleven days earlier. Mangum had denied to Himan that the timing of March 26 for the dance was accurate and there was no question that Fats and Black were surprisingly mysterious about the video when they shared it—briefly—with Himan and Linwood Wilson. And there was the affidavit that Victor Olatoye, the club owner, provided to Nifong on October 18 that said Mangum had not danced at his club since February and that the video had to have been made before March 13. But on November 2, in an interview with Duff Wilson, at the *Times*, Olatoye said that after he had submitted his affidavit, he "found" records that showed Mangum *had* danced at the club on March 23, 24, and 25. He said he recognized her dancing in the video, even though her face was obscured. "I saw the clip and I believe that was her, yes," he told Wilson, who reported that Olatoye said he would amend his affidavit. He said Mangum had worked at Platinum for about a year, was reliable, and would leave the club early on weeknights to attend her classes at NCCU. "The lady has to work," Olatoye said. "We shouldn't judge her for her work." The *Durham Herald-Sun* reported the same day that another dancer saw Mangum dance at Platinum Pleasures in March. The *News & Observer* reported that another former manager at the club, Yolanda Haynes, said that on March 11—two days before the party at 610 North Buchanan—Mangum was dancing at the club but got so ill (from what she did not say) that she had thrown up in the bathroom and taken her clothes off. When Haynes got to the bathroom, Mangum was passed out and naked. It took four people to carry Mangum out to a car in the parking lot, and at one point they dropped her onto the the gravel in the parking lot—a possible explanation for the bruises and cuts that doctors would find on her body two nights later.

Then, the paper interviewed Fats Thomas, who said Mangum told him on March 17 that "I'm going to get paid by the white boys," he said. "I said, 'Whatever,' because no one takes her seriously." He said she had showed him a hospital bracelet from her visits to both the Duke and UNC hospitals and some paperwork. He said Mangum gave no indication to him that she had been raped on the night of March 13. "She was as regular as pie," he said. "She didn't do anything different." Thomas said that had Mangum been raped, the other women at the club would have known about it. "If another dancer had been beat up or raped by a bunch of white boys, there would have been a ruckus," he said. (He added he had little to gain by coming forward, because he faced a pending criminal charge of cocaine possession.)

As usual, the defense attorneys offered their view that Olatoye's and Thomas's new information was plenty damning. Joe Cheshire said it was "powerful evidence" that contradicted Mangum's own claims of being in extreme pain and Nifong's observation that on April 11 Mangum was still "too traumatized" to coherently describe what had happened to her on the night of March 13. Bill Thomas, representing the unindicted players, said the video showed Mangum in a "vigorous dance routine" and that "someone who continues to dance and perform in these clubs as she has would be inconsistent with someone who was in great pain." Thomas also said, "She's at the hospital telling them she needs narcotics because of extreme pain, yet she was dancing normally at night. . . . It's troubling. The dike is going to break at some point. The truth is going to come out, and the whole world will know these boys are innocent."

On November 2, Linwood Wilson and Himan went to see Bill Thomas to talk to him about the DVD that included the short scene of what looked like Mangum dancing at Platinum Pleasures. Wilson told Thomas that he "had made himself a witness" with his comments about Mangum at the club. Overhearing the discussion, Butch Williams, another defense attorney, came out of his nearby office and asked the officers to come into his office to discuss the DVD. Himan told Williams that he was not allowed by Fats and Black to analyze the video and that the two men were "extremely nervous" when Himan walked into the room. He said the video had no time stamps or date stamps on it and "appeared" to have been "edited" and that Fats fast-forwarded the video to the segment about Mangum dancing and then shut if off. "Fats made statements that we couldn't show it to anyone, and there was no way for us to show it to Crystal," Himan wrote in his notes.

The two attorneys then made a reference to "where the truth was" in the lacrosse case and how it looked like Himan and Wilson were trying to find it but actually were just trying to "plug holes" in the time line. The comment set Himan off. "Since the very beginning, I have been trying to get cooperation and the truth from anyone involved in the case," Himan told them. "I have not received that cooperation. Everyone is being represented by a lawyer and not many people have been willing to talk with me. I have not received any calls from the lacrosse players willing to discuss anything about this case or the details of that night." Williams told Himan it was his "job to find this information out." Himan replied, "If there is information that he knows about or has information of who I should speak to then I am willing and want to be notified. Many people do not want to be involved in this case and probably are more willing to talk to you than me. I can only present evidence that is reported to me and that I discover." He said only two lawyers—for two unindicted players—had contacted him to share their clients' alibis for the night of March 13, but that when he asked to speak to the players about "information from that night," he was told they did not have any information to share. "There has been a wall of silence," Himan told Williams, "and I would look at all information that someone has to offer."

Himan's plea for information seemed to soften up the two attorneys. They shared with Himan that "numerous people" at Platinum "would verify" that Mangum danced at the club on the night of March 25. They also "hinted" about a dance club in Fayetteville that Mangum was "supposed to have danced at." They also told Himan he should "probably" speak to a Mr. "Van Hook," who they "implied" paid Mangum for sex at the Millenium Hotel in Durham in the early morning hours of March 11, after she had danced at Platinum Pleasures. "That was the first time I had heard of that information," Himan told them.

Himan then went to see Olatoye at the Platinum Club. He showed Himan how he signed in dancers to the club. Himan went to the Millenium Hotel and was told that a Mr. Van Hook had stayed there on the night of March 11. He spoke with the hotel's general manager, who told Himan that he would need a subpoena to get more information.

Unsure what to think about the suggestion that Mangum had danced at Platinum Pleasures on March 25, Himan and Wilson talked to Jariel Johnson, one of Mangum's drivers. They played for Johnson the *60 Minutes* video of Mangum supposedly dancing at the club. He told the police officers he was not sure but did not think the video was from the evening of March 25. "The room was packed with people," he told Himan, "and in the video there are empty chairs." He said there was a party at the Platinum Club on March 25 for the rap artist Big Delph. Himan asked Johnson if Mangum had ever had any problems with other dancers at Platinum Pleasures. He said he recalled she once was "attacked" by one of the white dancers who "was swinging her shoes at Crystal." Johnson said he did not know Mangum "to take any drugs," and had only seen her intoxicated once (at a club, the Crazy Horse, in nearby Garner, North Carolina.) He said he had not heard the name "Van Hook" before but agreed it could have been the name of the man at the Millenium Hotel. As for whether Johnson recalled Mangum "being dragged out to the car by a couple of people" on the night of March 11, he said that was not true and that she "was fine that night" and "walked out on her own" and there were no "scratches or marks" on her.

Himan asked Johnson when he first became aware of the alleged incident at 610 North Buchanan. He said Mangum called and told him that "something happened" although she was "hesitant on the phone" and didn't really want to talk about it. He asked again and she said she "got robbed" too but did not want to talk anymore about it. On March 25, he said, Mangum told him that "Brett, Adam, and Matt raped her" after he heard about the alleged incident and left a voice mail message for her. She asked Johnson not to ask him further about the incident and told him she was "fine." But Johnson told Himan that he always knew Mangum to be "upbeat" and that since the night of March 13, she had "lost her world" and was not "the same Crystal." She was now "very down, not the same person."

In search of Mr. "Van Hook," Himan obtained a subpoena and served it on the general manager of the Millenium Hotel and obtained the home address for a Josephus Van Hook. The police went to his home and spoke with his father, who said Josephus was in Durham, driving a truck, and gave Himan his son's cell phone number. Van Hook agreed to meet Himan and Wilson in the parking lot of the Durham Wal-Mart, across from the Outback Steakhouse. Van Hook told Himan that he had stayed at the Millenium in March and had called an escort service to have a girl sent to his room. Naturally, Van Hook wondered how Himan and Wilson got his name, and Himan told him that lawyers had shared his name and that he would provide information about what happened that night. Himan said the attorney had implied that "there was more than a dance that happened at the hotel." Himan asked if Van Hook had had sex with Mangum. He said "no" and added, "I don't know what the intention was, but I did not have sex with her and nothing happened." Himan told Van Hook he was investigating the Duke lacrosse case, and Van Hook wanted to know if the woman who came to the Millenium Hotel was the same woman who claimed to have been raped. "We were given information that she had been to the hotel that night and performed a dance," Himan said. Van Hook started talking about getting his lawyer, Butch Williams (who had helped him out on some speeding tickets), involved and then Wilson told Van Hook that Williams was the lawyer who had given Van Hook's name to him and Himan. "He stated he really didn't want to be involved in this any further,"

Himan noted before giving him his card. "Call Mr. Williams," Wilson told Van Hook, "and ask him why he told us about [you]." A bit later, Himan asked Van Hook if he would "write a statement" about what had happened on the night of March 11. Van Hook told Himan that his new lawyer, Jimmy Sharp, would contact him about that.

Himan and Wilson then went to see Yolanda Haynes, the former Platinum Club manager, at her apartment to talk about Mangum. Haynes explained she shared the story about Mangum with the media after she saw what "Fats" was "saying" and "didn't want him doing her like that," which Himan translated as "lying and making her look bad." Haynes said Fats "never even" spoke to Mangum. She said he just hung out in the DJ booth and was always "sweating" the "pretty girls" but he never paid any attention to "Precious." She said Fats was "a habitual liar, a thief, and was always doing criminal things" and that the problem with him was that he "always believes his own lies." She added that Fats was "a wannabe pimp and a wannabe drug dealer." His girlfriend's name was "Sweet Cream" and he "pimps her out." Haynes said Fats tried to "pimp" Mangum out and they went together to a party but returned with her within minutes. "That bitch ain't trying to make any money," Fats told Haynes.

Haynes said she tried to get through to Nancy Grace on her show to talk about Fats but when she couldn't, she went to the local newspapers to set the "record straight" about "FATS." She told Himan she never said Mangum was "dragged" through the parking lot. "She stated that they had found Crystal passed out with her clothes off in the bathroom" and that then "they picked her up and was bringing her to her boyfriend's vehicle"—a burgundy Jeep—"while bringing her out, they dropped her" but "they never dragged her through the parking lot." She said she thought the date of this incident was March 8, not March 11. "She said she never saw any scratches [or] marks on her from that night or any day after that," Himan noted.

Asked whether she knew whether Mangum drank or used drugs, Haynes said that she did not. She knew because Haynes was the "main bartender" at the club and she never saw Mangum drink. She also said she never saw Mangum use drugs. She said she knew because Mangum "used to complain" about two other dancers—Passion and Tickles—who "used to sniff powder [cocaine] in the dressing room." She said the other girls picked on Mangum for "telling on them about drugs." She said Passion got into a fight with Precious—"and hit her head with a shoe"—because Precious had been dancing with Passion's boyfriend. Haynes told Himan she thought Mangum "might have mental problems" and the only "drug" she ever saw her take was Vivarin, an over-the-counter caffeine pill.

A few days later, Himan spoke with Angel Altmon, the off-duty security guard at Kroger's that Roberts had approached for help in the early morning hours of March 14. Altmon told Himan how she had just gotten off work when

Roberts drove up in her car, around 1:15 a.m., and came inside the store and asked Altmon to help her contact a police officer. "I have a young lady in my car," Roberts told her. "She won't get out, and I have already called the police." Altmon smelled "a strong odor of alcohol" on Roberts. Roberts then lied to Altmon and said that she had picked up the woman near Duke's East Campus. "She had white shoes on," Roberts said, "and she saw guys calling her a nigger." She said she wanted to pick up Mangum because she did not want her to get hurt. Altmon said she then went outside to the parking lot to investigate, even though her official responsibilities were for inside the store only. She looked in the passenger's side of Robert's car and saw Mangum with hair on her face. She checked to see if Mangum was breathing but did not smell any alcohol on her breath. She heard Mangum making noises (but not speaking) and thought she might be on drugs.

The police arrived about ten minutes later and began their efforts to get Mangum out of the car after she grabbed on to the parking brake and wouldn't let go. Altmon said she "found out" a couple of months later that Roberts had concocted her story and that the passenger was Mangum and both women were part of the Duke lacrosse case. Altmon told Himan she thought it was odd that Roberts smelled of alcohol but not Mangum. She said that when the police pulled Mangum from the car, Altmon noticed "blood that had gone down her leg"—she thought her right leg—and also saw a "maxipad that was between her legs." She said that as she thought about the incident she sensed something "was not right" and that it made no sense that Roberts had picked up Mangum but did not take her either to a hospital or police station. Roberts told Altmon that she didn't want to get Mangum "in trouble." She said her boss told her not to talk to the media. Altmon told Himan she thought "the whole situation was weird from the beginning: "She's drunk"—Roberts—"and she's not drunk"—Mangum—"something is wrong with this girl. She never heard [the] victim"—Mangum—"make any statements, just noises and saying a name over and over again. She thought it started with a 'T,' but she was not able to think of the name she was saying."

As the police investigators probed basic details of the night in question, the election drew nearer. Just a few days before, Stephen Miller, a Duke senior and a *Chronicle* columnist, convinced himself that the best way to prevent an unjust prosecution from proceeding was to get rid of Nifong, so he tried to convince his readers to help. (Indeed, Duke students registered in surprising numbers to vote in Durham—more than four hundred students were signed up and most likely voted for Cheek. Students also carried signs, posted flyers around campus, and even painted the famed bridge near East Campus in support of Cheek.) In a piece published just before the election, Miller exhorted his fellow students to vote out Nifong. "To successfully unleash this depravity of justice, it seems our DA has managed to go against criminal procedure, legal precedent, constitutional protections, hundreds of years of common law, and thousands of years of ethics tracing back to the Old Testament. Nifong must have confused America with a police state." Miller argued that, "If anyone should be on trial here, it's Mike Nifong." And yet, Nifong had a "massive" 6–1 margin over Lewis Cheek in Durham County's black community. "If voters won't put a stop to this, then who will?" Miller wondered.

On Election Day, Nifong was visiting a polling location at Temple Baptist Church, in Durham, when he ran into Bob Harris, the longtime play-by-play announcer for the Duke football team. As he was getting out of his car, Nifong approached Harris to shake his hand. But Harris refused.

"You've got to be nicer than that," Nifong said to Harris.

"Get out of here," Harris said. "Don't pull this crap."

"This isn't about Duke," Nifong replied. "This isn't about Duke at all."

"No," Harris said. "It's about honesty. You're not honest."

In the end, the election was closer by far than it would have been had Nifong decided not to prosecute the lacrosse case. But Nifong still won handily, with 26,116 votes, or 49.1 percent of those cast. He won every precinct where blacks comprised a majority of those voting. Cheek, who of course had said he would not serve if elected (allowing the governor to appoint someone), still won 20,875 votes, or about 39.3 percent. Monks won the balance of the votes, 6,193, or 11.6 percent. Although Monks denied as much, it seemed clear—mathematically, anyway—that had Monks withdrawn from the race—as many people urged him to do, because he couldn't win—and had the people who voted for him voted for Cheek exclusively—a big if—then Cheek would have won and Nifong would have lost. Instead, Nifong won, and the prosecution of the Duke lacrosse players continued. The race had taken its toll on him, though. "I'm glad it's over," he said on election night at the Old Durham Courthouse, where the votes were being counted. "I will go back to work tomorrow and start moving forward. . . . I'm going to continue doing what I believe to be the right thing."

CHAPTER THIRTEEN

New Revelations

Not surprisingly, the reaction to Nifong's victory was extremely polarized. Duke senior Tony McDevitt, a defenseman on the lacrosse team, told the *Chronicle* that the hoped-for defeat of Nifong "was a way to possibly slow down Nifong or end [the case] earlier, but by no means are we destroyed. . . . In no way, shape or form are we negative or walking around with our heads down." Commented Jill Garrison, a Duke sophomore, "I can't believe Nifong won such a high percentage of the vote after all the stuff that has come out about him. People are just rooting against Duke and don't want to admit that they're wrong." But Harris Johnson, a Durham resident for fifty-six years who worked in an election precinct near NCCU, could not have been happier with Nifong's election. "This goes to show that justice can't be bought by a bunch of rich white boys from New York," he said. "Duke has a habit of sweeping things under the carpet. I guess this goes to show that no matter how much money you have, Durham is owned by its citizens . . .If Nifong had lost, every woman in America would have been at risk." Beth Brewer, the spokeswoman for an anti-Nifong voting group, was nearly apoplectic. "I hope the North Carolina State Bar will do what the Durham citizens could not," she said.

At least two Durham attorneys who had a passing involvement with representing unindicted players in the lacrosse case, said they were pleased that Nifong won. Although their comments were perhaps good politics, they were still surprising. "I believe the right person won," attorney Kerry Sutton said. "While I disagree with Mike's handling of the lacrosse case, he had the right to take the stance he did, and he is doing his job. If I ever mess up a case myself, I hope people won't judge my entire career based on that case alone." She also said that too many outsiders had been trying to influence the course of events in Durham. "The fact that people from around the nation put their noses and money into the politics of Durham kind of skewed people's perspectives on what goes on on here and what should go on here," she said. Attorney Butch Williams also agreed that Nifong's election was "a good thing" and added, "The citizens of Durham have voted, and it's time to move on. . . . The DA's race is bigger than the lacrosse case. People who saw the election as a one-case issue underestimated the voters."

Sutton's comments irritated Joe Cheshire, Evans's attorney. In a column in the *Herald-Sun*, he chided her. "I understand the need for lawyers whose livelihood and clients' fates are often governed by the whim of the elected district attorney to remain as close as possible to that DA no matter what he does," Cheshire wrote. "But it must be noted that Nifong's only 'right' and 'job' as prosecutor in this or any other case is to satisfy his oath and to see that justice is done. He has no right to take over the role of lead investigator from the police and then refuse to view exculpatory evidence, or to order an illegal and improper photo lineup procedure, or to make baseless public statements that pander to race, gender and class during an election cycle. Justice is not done in any criminal prosecution when a DA who assumed the role of chief factual investigator does not bother to talk with the chief prosecuting witness about her allegations to assess her credibility, and instead lets forth a stream of pure speculation about the 'facts' of the case to conform to the evolving investigation: speculation that, in fact, contradicts materials in his own case file and sworn statements made by his own investigators and assistants in the investigation."

Cheshire's comments infuriated Shadee Malaklou, a Duke senior from Orange County, California, who was a double major in women's studies and cultural anthropology. She wrote in her own column in the *Chronicle* that Cheshire's insistence that the lacrosse players were innocent "ignored the gender and racial prejudice of the March 13 party." She wrote that "if nothing else, Nifong is holding the lacrosse players accountable for that; and as a woman at Duke who knows just how much these men get away with, I'm thankful. Perhaps that's Cheshire's problem—he's not a woman, and he doesn't know the fear of rape. A rape may not have occurred on March 13, but as a woman on Duke's campus, as a women's studies major and as an activist for survivors of sexual assault, I assure Mr. Cheshire that these men are not innocent."

Other editorial writers around town—with far less invested in the outcome of the case than Cheshire—were more willing to see some gray in Nifong's victory. At the *Durham Herald-Sun*, the editors concluded that Nifong's failure to win more than 50 percent of the votes meant that more than a majority of the people disapproved of his prosecution of the lacrosse case. Steve Ford, the editorial page editor at the *News & Observer*, applauded Nifong for his "instincts" to come to Mangum's defense, "setting aside stereotypes that might have led others to scoff at her claims." In conclusion, though, Ford joined the growing chorus of people calling for the state bar to step in to the case. "Given the persistent questions about Nifong's handling of the case, the NC State Bar—which oversees the conduct of this state's lawyers—ought to be gearing up to take a look. If the case turns out to be [a] house of cards, the man who built it should have some explaining to do."

Ford was not alone. Scores of people, some local, some from out of state, some with no connection to the players, and some in their employ, had started a letter-writing campaign to the state bar, with copies to Governor Mike Easely and State Attorney General Roy Cooper. In an August 9 letter to the state bar, Edwin Beusse, a New York developer who worked with Kevin Finnerty, Collin's father, wrote: "I would think of this as misconduct by a DA and that for some reason, maybe political, he has painted a fabricated picture. Isn't there a check or balance for situations like this that are so far out there, that they're obviously false?" Molly McGuire, of Darien, Connecticut, a friend of the Finnertys, wrote on June 13, "It is frightening to think of any American being victimized by our own legal system and devastating to know that three promising lives are held hostage to a not-so-hidden political investigation."

Michael Cornacchia, a former prosecutor in New York and a member of Finnerty's legal team—he was also married to Mary Ellen Finnerty's sister—asked for a federal civil rights investigation. He wrote his letter to the US attorney general, to the director of the FBI, and, among others, to the congressional delegations of North Carolina and Long Island. He wrote that Nifong's handling of the lacrosse case violated the three players' civil rights and warranted an immediate investigation. Regardless of whether such an investigation were to happen, its request was unusual. Mary Ann Tally, a defense lawyer familiar with state bar proceedings, wondered how the state bar could not investigate the claims about Nifong's alleged malfeasance. "I guess the question I have is why isn't the bar doing anything about it right now?" she said. "It seems to me there's a tremendous amount of pressure on the bar and a lot of public expectation on 'Can you do the right thing, and can you do it in a timely fashion?'"

Cornacchia sent an e-mail to a friend in Palm Beach lamenting the Finnertys' fate. "Kevin has been working twenty-eight hours a day—eight days a week—to clear his son," he wrote. "This, while trying to get his fledgling hedge fund company off the ground. This is my family's defining moment. Everything is designated either before or after the Collin thing. We are all different people than before this happened. I used to enjoy the Palm Beach social thing, the black-tie charity galas, chaired several of them myself. All that is over—seems empty now. We have circled the wagons. . . . We are strong Irish stock—overachievers—and extremely close. Talk about a slap across the face wake-up call as to what really matters—this was it. Now we talk about things like the Innocence Project, the judicial system, academia in America, the press, judges, injustices of all kinds. It's all different now. Nothing petty anymore, lots of grace and empathy and positive action when necessary. Time with Collin is so precious."

On December 5, Nifong agreed to meet with Jim Cooney, Seligmann's new lead attorney, at his sixth-floor office at the Durham courthouse. As a gesture of goodwill, a few days earlier, Cooney had withdrawn the motion filed by his predecessor, Kirk Osborn, seeking to remove Nifong from the case. (It was a moot point by then.) Seligmann was hopeful that Cooney would be able to persuade Nifong to drop the case against him, especially since Osborn had never been able to arrange a similar meeting with Nifong.

Cooney told Nifong, "Trial lawyer to trial lawyer, you don't want Reade Seligmann in the case," referring to Seligmann's supposedly "airtight" alibi that Osborn had made public soon after Seligmann's April indictment. "It doesn't help your cause." But Nifong was unimpressed. "There is no such thing as an airtight alibi," Cooney said Nifong told him. Cooney offered to have Selig- mann meet with Nifong. He offered to open the entire case file to Nifong. But Nifong was not interested. "There is nothing you can show me that will change my mind," he told Cooney. "Only her and her story. As long as she is willing, we're going forward." And, Nifong added, "She is not intimidated." Cooney remembered that Nifong was also feeling sorry for himself and worried that his legacy would be defined by the Duke lacrosse case and would overlook the nearly three decades of good he had done as a Durham prosecutor. The two lawyers shook hands, and Cooney left. There would be no meeting between Nifong and Seligmann. Nifong remembered telling Cooney that Mangum had identified Seligmann as one of her attackers and that "I had not seen any evi- dence that showed that he could not have participated in the attack at the time it took place." With regard to Seligmann's alibi, he said Cooney told him, "'Well, it wouldn't have given him much time.' And certainly that would have been true, that there would have been a relatively narrow window of time when this could have happened. But certainly to say that somebody wouldn't have had much time is not the same thing as saying he couldn't have done it."

On December 7, Walter B. Jones, a longtime North Carolina congressman (and a Christian conservative) from Farmville, seventy miles east of Raleigh, wrote to Alberto Gonzales, the US attorney general, asking him to investigate Nifong's prosecution of Seligmann, Finnerty, and Evans "to detemine if it con- stitutes prosecutorial misconduct" and whether Nifong "has denied these stu- dents their civil rights as US citizens under federal law." Enclosing for Gonzales the *60 Minutes* "exposé" of the case, Representative Jones wrote that the show revealed two cases of what "appear to be blatant examples of prosecutorial mis- conduct." The first violation he cited was the photographic lineup that Nifong directed the police to use. "By doing so, Mr. Nifong ensured that the accuser could not make a mistake no matter who she identified because she would inevitably identify Duke athletes," he wrote. Then there were Nifong's numer- ous prognostications to the media early on that he had not violated the North Carolina Rules of Professional Conduct. "What is perhaps most concerning is Mr. Nifong's public admission and representation in court that he's never had the accuser tell him what she alleges occurred that night; Mr. Nifong has stated it was unnecessary to hear her version." He urged Gonzales to investigate. "After all," he wrote, "if the American people cannot trust those who they've empowered to pursue justice fairly, then hope for this democracy is lost."

In the days leading up to the hearing on December 15, the defense attorneys filed a series of motions that would transform the case. The first motion, filed just before 1 p.m. on December 13, was to compel the State of North Carolina to obtain from DNA Security, the private lab in Burlington that had performed the second set of DNA tests, a complete report of its analysis, rather than just the partial report that Nifong had turned over to the defense. The lawyers reminded the court that on March 14, "physical evidence" was taken from Mangum's "mouth, vagina, anus, and pubic region" after her "accusation that she had been gang-raped and beaten only hours earlier by multiple men who did not wear condoms, at least one of whom had ejaculated." The lawyers noted that pursuant to Judge Smith's October 27 order, Nifong's office had provided the defense with "thousands of pages of materials underlying the analyses performed by DNA Security" and that after "examining" these pages, the defense "discovered" that "DNA Security identified DNA from multiple males in the accuser's anus, in her pubic region, and on her panties. Enough of that DNA existed for DNA Security to conclude that none of it matched the" three indicted Duke players or any other teammates "or anyone else who submitted a DNA sample in the investigation."

The defense wrote in its motion that "this is strong evidence of innocence in a case in which the accuser denied engaging in any sexual activity in the days before the alleged assault, told police that she last had consensual sexual intercourse a week before the assault and claimed that her attackers did not use condoms and ejaculated." The DNA Security documents, the attorneys wrote, "show that male DNA was discovered, on *multiple* rape kit items, which did *not* match *any* Defendant in this case or their lacrosse teammates." Worse, they wrote, "There is not a single mention of this obviously exculpatory evidence in the final DNA Security report" that Nifong gave defense attorneys on May 18. "Indeed, had Defendants not undertaken an exhaustive examination of the underlying materials, which DNA Security objected to providing, this evidence would have remained unidentified in the mass of documentation underlying DNA Secuirty's work in this case."

The motion, replete with technical terms, raised questions about whether Nifong and DNA Security withheld evidence favorable to the defense, and meticulously walked through the time line of events related to the DNA analysis. The lawyers demanded that Nifong turn over the full DNA Security analyses and that Brian Meehan, the lab's director, submit to "questioning under oath" by one of them.

In a second motion filed some twenty-five hours later, defense attorneys asked Judge Smith to "suppress" the photographic lineup procedure that Nifong and the Durham police had concocted in April and that Mangum used to identify her three alleged attackers because it "violated due process," was "inherently suggestive," "inherently misleading," and "resulted in out-of-court identifications by the accuser that have been tainted and are unreliable." They

also asked the judge not to allow Mangum to identify, at trial, the three players she claimed attacked her because the identifications would be "inherently
unreliable" because of the "tainted procedure" used by Nifong and police and
would also violate their rights under the Fifth, Eighth, and Fourteenth Amend-
ments to the US Constitution.

In forty-two pages, the defense identified any number of inconsistencies
in Mangum's description of what had happened in the early morning hours
of March 14. "Within the first thirty-six hours of the events in this case, the
accuser denied being raped, claimed she was raped by twenty men, then five
men, then two men, and then three men, claimed that she was carried against
her will from a car by Nikki and 'Brett,' claimed that she was dancing with
three other women, multiple other women, and then only one other woman,
denied ever being struck with fists, claimed that Matt was getting married, told
the forensic nurse that Matt raped her vaginally and orally, that Adam raped
her anally and did not mention Brett raped her, while telling other personnel that Brett raped her vaginally without mentioning either Matt or Adam."
They explained how Himan kept contemporaneous notes of his investigation
but that Gottlieb did not, and then reconstructed what he was told during the
investigation from memory months later. Not surprisingly, this led to descre-
pencies in basic information, for instance in how Mangum described her
alleged assailants.

In their motion, the defense team also pointed out the flaws in the photo
arrays, in the DNA testing, and in Mangum's April 6 handwritten description
of events—they pointed out that neither Himan nor Gottlieb had mentioned
that this existed in their running compilation of events, even though they were
the two police officers who were with Mangum when she made the report.
Having been through the discovery documents in detail, the defense argued
that such basic questions as "Who did what?" "How long did the attack last?"
"Was she drinking?" "Was she beaten?" and "What did 'Nikki' do?" could not
be answered clearly. They pointed out that "no semen, blood, bodily fluid,
skin, saliva, hair, fibers, or DNA" from Seligman, Finnerty, or Evans "has been
found in the accuser, on the accuser, or on the accuser's clothing" and none
of those things from Seligmann or Finnerty were found in the bathroom at
610 North Buchanan where the accuser claims that they assaulted her. (The
defense did concede that a towel found in the bathroom did contain sperm
and DNA from Evans, who of course lived in the house but there was no non-
sperm DNA from Mangum on the towel.) The defense also included in the
motion Seligmann's alibi, how Mangum claimed that Evans looked like one of
her attackers if only he had had a mustache, except that he never had a mustache; and how Mangum never identified anyone who looked like Finnerty
as one of her attackers until the April 4 PowerPoint. "Putting to one side the
substantial evidence that no sexual assault ever occurred at 610 N. Buchanan,

there is quite simply no evidence that any of the accuser's identifications or descriptions of her alleged attackers are in any way reliable," they concluded. "Rather, the State is left with an incoherent mass of contradiction and error, one which not only raises the issue of a 'substantial likelihood of misidentification,' but which establishes that the accuser has in fact misidentified the defendants."

Some thirty minutes before the December 15 hearing was to begin, the defense attorneys dropped a third motion—to change the eventual trial's venue to outside of Durham—into the mix. Along with providing a compendium of the often-shocking commentary and conclusions found in the media—"literally hundreds of thousands of news accounts have been published about these cases"—about the so-called facts of the lacrosse case, the defense concluded that "there exists within this County among a significant percentage of residents so great a prejudice against [the three players] that they cannot obtain a fair and impartial trial" and that no jury, selected from people living within the county, will be able "to deliberate on the evidence presented in the courtroom, free from outside influence."

Whether Judge Smith would throw out Mangum's identification of the three indicted players based on the biased April 4 photo lineups or move the trial out of Durham County were matters that would be decided February 5, 2007, the date of the next hearing. Instead, it turned out—in a development kept secret (from the media, anyway)—that the December 15 hearing was devoted to the unexpected testimony of Brian Meehan, the director of DNA Security, the Burlington lab that had performed the second set of DNA testing in the case. While defense attorneys had asked in their December 13 filing for Meehan to appear in court, under oath, to answer questions about information supposedly not turned over to defense attorneys, there was no reason to believe that two days later Nifong would agree to have Meehan appear in court. In fact, Nifong had not notified the defense attorneys, either.

Before the hearing, Judge Smith met with Nifong and the defense attorneys in a small room near the grand jury room. Nifong told those assembled that he did not know the results about the other men's DNA had been withheld. "I got the motion and I was like, 'Whoa,'" Nifong said. "So I immediately faxed a copy to Dr. Meehan and said, 'Read this, and I will call you in the morning and get your opinions about this.' And we discussed it, and I said, 'This is a major issue for the defense. They are entitled to hear about, and I think it needs to be addressed right away.'"

In open court, Nifong told the judge that "the first I heard of this particular situation was when I was served with this motion on Wednesday of this week." He then explained that after he received the motion he contacted Meehan and asked him to testify at the December 15 hearing, if possible. "The nature of the subject matter in this motion is obviously very important," Nifong said. "Because of the nature of the items that were raised, I did feel it was appropriate to address these right away." Nifong also pointed out to the court that Meehan's "final" report that Nifong shared with defense attorneys on May 12 was twelve pages, and then, after the October hearing, Nifong turned over on October 27 some 1,800 additional pages of underlying data. On the morning of the December 15 hearing, he turned over another fifty pages of documents from Meehan. "It's crucial that everybody have access to all of the evidence in this case," Nifong said.

Brad Bannon, an attorney for David Evans, questioned Meehan in a packed courtroom. For the first time, Seligmann, Finnerty, and Evans were present. Bannon had been poring through the DNA documents ever since Nifong turned over the 1,844 pages on October 27. Eighteen-hour days had become routine. Although Bannon was an English major, he bought a textbook, *Forensic DNA Typing: Biology, Technology, and Genetics of STR Markets*, to help guide him through the pages of DNA evidence. That was how Bannon discovered that Meehan had found DNA from at least four other men on Mangum and in her underwear. He made his discovery at around 7 p.m. one evening. He went to see Cheshire, who was still in the office. "That's interesting," Cheshire told Bannon, "but we need to make sure that's right before we do anything with it." Bannon then called Jim Cooney. "Jim, I think I have found foreign male DNA that hasn't been reported to us and doesn't match our clients on the pubic hair, on one section of the pubic hair comb," he said. Like Cheshire, Cooney told Bannon he'd better make sure he was right. "You have to understand," Bannon said, "we had all been in court all summer and fall, being told that there wasn't anything that was found or discussed in these meetings with Dr. Meehan that hadn't been reported to us. . . . And then over the next couple of days, it just kept getting worse. I would find another one of the items that had male DNA that excluded our clients and their teammates, and then another and then another and then another. At the conclusion of that process, I drafted probably about a forty-page memo about it that cross-referenced all these materials and circulated that to the defense lawyers." The defense team had a big meeting in Washington on December 8 with various DNA experts that had been hired. The experts concluded that Bannon was right. "We set up a meeting to talk about it and agreed that what we needed to do was convert this information to a motion to compel production of additional discovery materials," he said.

Meehan's testimony was highly technical—words like "allele" and "YSTR loci" were slung around like so much hash—but there were a few key admissions that stirred up a new hornet's nest for Nifong. In responding to Bannon's question about the brevity of the May 12 report, Meehan admitted that he "did not release the full profiles of all the players in this case" after "discussions with

Mike Nifong because of concerns about getting those profiles into the public arena."

Meehan testified that Nifong asked him to analyze the rape kit, as well as other items, such as Mangum's panties, plastic fingernails, and a towel found in the bathroom at 610 North Buchanan, to see whether any male DNA was present. Then, after Meehan did determine there was male DNA on the items, Nifong submitted to Meehan the "reference specimens" from the lacrosse players. Meehan's job was to figure out who could be exluded because the male DNA on the items examined did not match the reference DNA from the players. "Who can [we] exclude in this reference group?" Meehan said. "That's what we do. We exclude suspects. . . . That's what we were asked to do, to find out if we can exclude everybody or offer anybody's match."

Bannon asked, "Did every item that we just talked about exclude the defendants in this case as a contributor to the DNA characteristics?"

"Yes," Meehan replied. He added that he told Nifong, Gottlieb, and Himan at their April 10 meeting that the DNA connection to the Duke players was "pretty weak." He said he had discussed with Nifong and the police the results of all the tests but his report contained only some of his findings.

Bannon wanted to know if Nifong told him to write the report that way. Meehan said Nifong did not "specifically" tell him to "write it that way," but they were in agreement that it was a better alternative than listing every player by name publicly, even if it excluded them from the alleged crime. Meehan said he initiated the idea of limiting the scope of the report, which he conceded violated his lab's own protocols. "I had no idea who these people were, where they were coming from," he said of the lacrosse players' DNA specimens. "They could have been the bus driver, okay?" Meehan said he made this decision "so as not to drag anybody else through the mud." He also testified that just because a person's DNA was not found in the material he examined, that did not mean definitively that that person was not part of the crime being investigated. "We run across this fairly often," Meehan said. "It is possible for a person to be raped and no semen left there, okay? So it doesn't, by itself, it does not show that the person was not there. And it's a CSI effect. We call it a CSI effect, okay. Just because a person doesn't leave DNA at the scene, it doesn't mean that he was not there. He may not have been there and he would have to be there to leave the DNA, but if the DNA is not there, it doesn't mean they are not there. Simple analogy, and it may be an oversimplification: A person can rob a bank and never leave a fingerprint. It doesn't mean they didn't rob a bank."

Eventually, Jim Cooney, an attorney for Seligmann, got a turn to ask Meehan questions, and he dispensed with the technicalities.

"Did your report set forth the results of all of the tests and examinations that you conducted in this case?" he asked.

"No," Meehan answered. "It was limited to only some results."

Cooney replied, "And that was an intentional limitation arrived at between you and representatives of the state of North Carolina not to report on the results of all examinations and tests that you did in this case?"

"Yes," Meehan replied.

There were audible gasps in the crammed courtroom.

Meehan said that because of the minimalist way he wrote the report, for Seligmann, Finnerty, and Evans to have figured out that the test results excluded them, they would have had to go through "six inches of paper to find them." And then Cooney asked Meehan if there were any DNA evidence linking Seligmann, Finnerty, and Evans—"from even a single cell"—to Mangum. Meehan said there was no DNA evidence linking them to an alleged sexual assault crime involving Mangum and that the three could be excluded "with 100 percent certainty."

Incredulous, Cooney asked Meehan how, if he knew by May 12 that the DNA tests excluded both Seligmann and Finnerty—who of course had been indicted almost a month earlier—from the the alleged crime scene, he would choose not to disclose that information in his report because he was afraid of violating their privacy rights? "It was just [simply] me trying to do the right thing, saying, 'Well, let's not put that information out there and who knows what's going to happen with that information,'" Meehan replied. "It certainly was not an intention to withhold information. It was a failed attempt to provide the minimal amount of identification to the public in a case that's going to be just out there and they'll be undressing people. . . . We were trying to do the best we could and respect everybody that was involved in this case and only release information that really felt like it had to be released . . ."

Sensing he had been wounded by Meehan's testimony, Nifong tried to clarify a few points. "Did anyone ever tell you to conceal or hide any of your results from anybody?" Nifong asked.

"No," Meehan replied.

"Did anybody ever tell you who you were supposed to come up with a result [or] who we wanted you to pick?" Nifong asked.

"No," Meehan replied. "No."

Nifong then reiterated that in addition to the May 12 report, his office had turned over to the defense an additional 1,822 pages of documents and evidence. Meehan agreed his entire case file was now in the hands of the defense.

Despite the setback with Meehan's testimony, Nifong remained determined to bring the case to trial, sooner rather than later, as he told the court when the discussion about when to schedule the next hearing came up. Before the hearing adjourned, Joe Cheshire, the attorney for Evans, raised one final point. It seemed, Cheshire told the court, that Mangum was pregnant and about to give birth. "We would like to have a paternity test done on that child to prove that none of these defendants could possibly be the father," he said.

(Indeed, the local Raleigh television station had reported that Mangum had given birth.)

But Nifong rose to tell the court the rumors were not true. Mangum was pregnant but was not due to give birth until the first week of February. "That would tend to indicate that this pregnancy could not have resulted from any incident that took place during the night of March 13 to March 14," he said. A motion prepared by the defense claimed that a paternity test on Mangum's child "would definitively prove that none of the defendants has fathered the child" and "as such, the test results would be powerful substantive evidence of their innocence." But Nifong was not buying that logic. "I fail to see how the fact that they were not fathers of a child that was conceived at least two weeks and probably longer after this incident would prove anything about their guilt or innocence that night," he told the court. In the end, Judge Smith did order a paternity test be administered to Mangum's child after it was born, even though both Nifong and the defense attorneys agreed that the three players could not have been the father. (She gave birth on January 4, via a Caesarian section.)

In a nearly breathless story about the hearing the next day, the *News & Observer* reported that Meehan and Nifong had agreed not to report DNA results that were favorable to the three lacrosse players and that "could create difficulties inside and outside the courtroom for Nifong" and "will provide grist for those calling for Nifong to be disciplined or prosecuted." The paper then mentioned Representative Walter Jones's letter requesting the FBI investigate and that the NC State Bar had received numerous letters requesting that Nifong be disciplined. "I tell you, the more you hear about his missteps, the more you have to question whether it's purely a matter of incompetence or worse," James Coleman, the Duke law professor, told the paper. Outside the courtroom, Nifong amended his opening statement to say that the first time he had heard about discrepencies in the DNA results was when he received the defense attorney's motion on December 13. "We were trying to, just as Dr. Meehan said, trying to avoid dragging any names through the mud, but at the same time his report made it clear that all the information was available if they wanted it, and they have every word of it."

The idea that a month after Seligmann and Finnerty had been indicted—and days before Evans would be—Nifong knew that there was no DNA evidence and chose not only not to release that information but rather to deliberately downplay it, left many people furious. None of the three players spoke to the media after the hearing. But Kevin Finnerty might as well have been speaking for them and their families when he asked rhetorically, "Where is the justice?" He continued, "There was a rush to indict. There was a rush to judgment. There was a lack of thorough assessment of evidence. And I'm not happy about that." Mike Pressler, the former lacrosse coach, was also at the hearing. "It's all about support," he said. "It's all about being there for them." Asked whether a vindication for his three former players would mean vindication for him, he replied, "Like I said, I'm here for the guys and all those things will happen in time." Were the players innocent? "We believe in the truth," he said. "That's what we believe."

Late that night, *Saturday Night Live* spoofed the lacrosse case in a skit that feautured comedian Amy Poehler as a "sour-faced" Nancy Grace, the outspoken television host, delivering a Christmas message. It turned out Poehler's Grace was upset that many people had now concluded that Mangum was probably lying about being raped by Seligmann, Finnerty, and Evans. "You see, in recent years, our society has shown much greater sensitivity and compassion to victims of sexual assault, but what about those whose claims of sexual assault are almost certainly false?" Poehler's Grace wondered. "Who's sticking up for them? Nobody. And where are the therapeutic support programs like the ones that actual victims get? There are none, and that's a national disgrace, since making an allegation of rape is almost as bad as actually being raped, considering that these would-be victims have to invent hundreds of false details that can later come back to show that they were lying. That's why we should show more support to that exotic dancer, lest we come to a point in our society where fake victims of sexual assault are afraid to come forward." Poehler's Grace concluded by vowing to "spend the rest of my life hunting down the Duke team who turned out to be innocent all along."

Between Representative Jones's letter to US Attorney General Alberto Gonzales, the motions in court to suppress the photo-identification procedure and to change the trial's venue, Meehan's surprising testimony about the DNA results, and the protests filed with the North Carolina State Bar, the heat was ratcheting up on Nifong to either drop the case or to recuse himself from it. The prosecution of the case also seemed to taking a toll on Duke, too. Early admission applications for the Duke class of 2011 were down 20 percent to 1,198, from 1,496 applicants the year before the lacrosse scandal. Although Chris Guttentag, the dean of undergraduate admissions, seemed sanguine overall about Duke's applicants, he said, "It would have surprised us if all of the media coverage hadn't had some effect."

The reduction of early applications caught the attention of the five bloggers at Friends of Duke University. Their spokesman, Jason Trumpbour, blamed Brodhead. "The administration's silence about Mr. Nifong's continued assault on the civil liberties of Duke students appears to be having an unfortunate, if inevitable effect," he said. "Surely any prospective parent would have to think twice about sending a son or daughter to an institution whose leadership has stood aside as a local prosecutor targets students through procedurally improper actions." Brodhead, who had been quiet for months, replied to Trumpbour, "Under American law, the legal system is the place to establish the facts and bring a case to a just resolution. For that reason, it is of the essence that everyone involved in the legal system act fairly in pursuing the truth and protecting the rights of the individuals involved. As I told Ed Bradley during a *60 Minutes* interview last summer, given the concerns that have been raised, when it goes before a judge and jury, the DA's case will be on trial just as much as our students will be. In the meantime, as I have said before, our students must be presumed innocent until proven otherwise."

Recent events had caused the editors of the *Durham Herald-Sun* to rethink their position, which had been generally supportive of Nifong. "There is immense pressure building in the Duke lacrosse case," they wrote on December 19. "The pressure is to toss out the rape charges against three players, and it's coming from the players' families, their defense lawyers and their many supporters on campus and across the country. It is directed against anyone who thinks the case should be decided in a court of law, not the court of public opinion, and it has two basic targets—the accuser and District Attorney Mike Nifong."

In a statement on December 19, DNA Security sought to mitigate some of the damage to the firm from Meehan's testimony in court. "Neither DNA Security nor any other private accredited lab is an investigatory or a prosecutorial entity," it read. "Although currently popular television shows regularly show forensic scientists and DNA experts independently working to solve a crime, convict the defendant, or have charges dropped, most DNA testing labs like ours work for a client who hires us. We do not voluntarily show up at crime scenes or hospitals with teams of scientists, and solve the crime in one episode. Rather, we are usually provided with samples from the client. That client specifies the testing to be performed, typically to determine whether evidentiary DNA (from a crime scene or victim) matches DNA of a known individual or individuals (reference specimens). That is basically the service we performed in the Duke Lacrosse Team case for our client, the Durham County District Attorney's Office."

That same day, Representative Walter Jones released a second letter that he had written to Attorney General Gonzalez following an appearance Gonzalez had made the previous weekend on Fox News, where he mentioned that he had received Jones's first letter. "Mr. Attorney General, I was encouraged to see that on Fox News yesterday you confirmed that you 'received' my December 7 letter and that the Justice Department is evaluating the facts it presents," Jones wrote. "The new revelations of potential prosecutorial misconduct exposed in last week's court proceedings also require the Justice Department's attention. At the request of a growing number of my constituents, I again urge you and your staff to fully investigate these matters to ensure that Mr. Nifong's conduct has not illegally denied these students their constitutional rights to due process."

• • •

On December 20, the fate of the lacrosse case changed in a profound way. After months of a concerted campaign, Nifong received a letter from Katherine Jean, counsel to the Grievance Committee of the North Carolina State Bar, informing Nifong that "a grievance alleging misconduct on your part as an attorney" had been filed by the state bar. "The complaint was controversial," the *News & Observer* reported, "and the sixteen-member committee split evenly over whether it should be filed." Jim Fox, chairman of the Grievance Committee, cast the deciding vote. It turned out the state bar had opened an inquiry into Nifong's prosecution of the case on March 30—two weeks after the party—and found on October 19 that there was "reasonable cause" to turn the case over to the bar's Disciplinary Commission for a trial. Nifong had not been aware of the proceeding, and he said he thought the complaint was a result of the December 15 hearing. "That was, fairly obviously, a response to the hearing that had taken place the previous week," Nifong explained in an interview years later. "My understanding, from talking to a lot of people—not at the time but after the fact—is that because the bar had attempted to discipline some prosectors in the past, after the fact, and had run into a statute of limitations issue in dealing with the bar, that there was some pressure being put on the state bar by the attorneys for the Duke lacrosse players, specifically Joe Cheshire—and when I say specifically I don't know that he was necessarily doing it but people were doing it on his behalf—to go ahead and initiate an investigation from the state bar into this case before it was over. Traditionally, of course, investigations do not happen during the course of the case, because one of the things that you have to look at, to put everything in an appropriate context, is what happened, when it happened, and how everything was resolved. The attorneys for the lacrosse players were not interested in that kind of a context being provided. They wanted action immediately. Of course, part of the reason for that would be to force me out of the case, and that would be something that would be accomplished by that. So I think that there was more than one motivation."

Nifong said "the word on the street" was that the state bar was "looking for a prosecutor to make an example of." He never thought it would be him. "The state bar exists to protect that group of lawyers, that subset of lawyers among which the Duke lacrosse attorneys number themselves," he said. "Every once in a while they'll throw a virgin in a volcano to quiet down the population or something like that, but they don't really take action against attorneys who are well connected. They only take action against attorneys who are not, and that's just to say, 'Look, we're tough. We can police ourselves. We do this. See what we just did to this guy.' I'm a nobody. I was an elected official in Durham County. I actually had a really good reputation in Durham County, but to the people in Raleigh I was nobody."

Still, he had been told early on that the state bar seemed out to get him. Some pointed to Joe Cheshire's March 30 letter to Nifong—"Your reported comments have greatly prejudiced any court proceedings that may arise," he wrote—as evidence that Nifong was warned, early on, that his public comments could be viewed as prejudicial. According to the *New York Times*, that same day, the state bar opened an investigation into Nifong's public statements, even though it had never before brought a complaint against a prosecutor in the middle of a case for his public comments. Tom Lunsford, the executive director of the state bar, told the *Times* that the complaint started with a grievance filed by a private lawyer. He declined to tell the *Times* who filed the first letter. But it was Cheshire and Bannon. "He has basically announced the criminal guilt of dozens of people for committing a racial gang rape, effectively saying they are either guilty as principals or aiders-and-abettors," their letter stated. "He has untruthfully suggested no one has cooperated with law enforcement. . . . Thus, one can scarcely imagine anything more likely to materially prejudice an adjudicatory proceeding in the matter." Defense attorney Kerry Sutton had tried to give Nifong a heads-up in late April that the state bar was investigating him. And sometime in the early summer, Nifong received an impromptu visit from attorney Kirk Osborn. "He was very agitated and on edge, and looked unhealthily wound up, I guess is the way I'd say it, which is why I asked him if he was on some sort of medication or something, because he just didn't seem like himself," Nifong recalled. "But what he said, as close as I can recall, was, 'What you need to do is call a press conference, and you need to say that Crystal Mangum is not telling the truth, and that you're going to dismiss these cases because you have determined that she is not telling the truth, and that none of this happened. If you do that, all your problems will go away.' I said, 'Kirk, what are you talking about?' And he looked at me like, 'You've got to be kidding me!' I mean, it was like, 'Surely you jest.' I said, 'What are you talking about?' and he said, 'Well, if you don't know, I'm not going to tell you,' and he left. What he was talking about was the fact that the complaint had been filed with the state bar on the pretrial publicity and all that kind of stuff, and I guess he assumed that I was thinking, 'Oh, my God, I'm in this horrible trouble with the state bar,' but I hadn't even been notified of it." Nifong quickly concluded that the state bar was "really acting as an agent for the defense lawyers."

In fact, it appeared that Nifong had misjudged the state bar's willingness to make an example of him. On August 21, Jean sent Nifong a "letter of notice" advising him that two grievances—numbered 06G0372 and 06G0679—had been filed against him "alleging misconduct." She enclosed for Nifong the "Substance of the Grievance" and noted it was "not a pleading of any sort but is simply a summary of what appears to be the basis of the grievances." Eight days later, Nifong sent a response to Margeret Cloutier, a staff attorney at the state bar, in which he wrote that he had spoken with Cloutier by phone, requesting copies of the actual grievances filed against him, and that his request had been denied. He wrote that since the people who had filed the grievances against him were allowed to remain anonymous, he requested that his response to Cloutier not be shared with those people. On August 31, Cloutier responded to Nifong and let him know that his response would be passed on to the chairman of the Grievance Committee.

Jean's December 19 letter contained three charges against Nifong. The first was that he had "failed to provide discovery" to the lacrosse defendants, in violation of state law, case law, and Judge Smith's order for him to do so. Second, that he had conspired with Meehan that the report that Meehan would provide to defense attorneys about DSI's DNA testing "would not include exculpatory evidence showing that DNA samples taken from" Mangum "were from unidentified male donors who the DNA lab had determined were not members of the lacrosse team." Third, that Nifong had "falsely represented" to the court that prior to the December 13 motion to compel, he "did not know that the DNA lab had determined that DNA taken from" Mangum "came from unidentified male donors who the lab had determined were not members of the Duke lacrosse team." Jean included the citations of the code that Nifong allegedly had violated and told him he had fifteen days to respond.

Nifong was concerned. He said his "first reaction" to Jean's letter was that "I had to defend myself. The allegations in the first complaint, about pretrial publicity, whether or not you agreed with the tenor of the argument that they were making, there wasn't really any question that there had been interviews and that things had been said in the press," he said. "I thought that what they did either lacked or misstated context, but clearly, there were actual statements that were made that were the subject of that" complaint. A group of his fellow district attorneys met with Nifong, also on December 19, in Raleigh and urged him to recuse himself from the case. "Mr. Nifong felt stunned and subdued, friends say, yet still could not bring himself to exit," the *New York Times* reported.

In the early afternoon of December 21, Nifong dispatched Linwood Wilson, his chief investigator, to interview Mangum alone. "Up until this point," Nifong recalled, "we had been in the investigation phase of the case, and at this point we were switching into the point where now we were going to try to get the case ready to try it." At that point, he recalled, he thought the "strongest case" for the prosecution was against Dave Evans. "Although she had only a 90 percent identification of him, she did say that he was the person who had been behind her and who she was struggling with to be able to breathe as he had his arm around her, and that it was in the course of trying to pull the arm down so that she could breathe that she had broken off her fingernails, the false fingernails that she was wearing for her dancing routine," he said. "And it was his DNA that was found on those fingernails." He said the "second best case" was against Finnerty "because he did not look like anybody else on the lacrosse team"—since he was tall and lanky—"Of all the people that were identified, he would be the one you would [be] least likely to confuse with somebody else." (He noted by contrast that when the *Chronicle* found out that Seligmann and Finnerty were going to turn themselves in on April 17, the paper ran a picture of Matt Zash instead of one of Seligmann, because, he said, "there were a lot of similar-looking people on the team.")

Usually, interviews are conducted in teams of two, but Wilson spoke with Mangum alone for two hours. He did not bring a tape recorder. Wilson said he had two missions for his conversation with Mangum: to tell her that Nifong might be recusing himself from the case and that there were discrepencies between her version of events and Roberts's version. In particular, there was one disagreement between the two women that Wilson was focused on trying to clear up. "Kim kept saying that Crystal wanted to have sex with the guys for money," Wilson remembered, "and Crystal kept saying it was Kim who wanted to have sex with the guys for money. So we wanted to clear that up."

In his subsequent "investigative report," Wilson conveyed Mangum's latest version of what had happened on the night of March 13. She told Wilson she arrived at the house "around 11:10 p.m." and saw a "bunch of guys" in the backyard of the house, along with the other dancer, Kim Roberts. "All the guys and the female (Kim) had cups and were drinking alcoholic beverages," she told Wilson. She and Roberts introduced themselves. Mangum was "Precious" and Roberts was "Nikki." Wilson noted that, "They talked about their children briefly and then they go into the house, through the back door, along with the guys." Mangum and Roberts then went into the bathroom to get ready. One of the players then knocked on the bathroom door and handed Roberts two alcoholic drinks, one of which she handed to Mangum. "During this time Mangum could hear the guys yelling and talking loudly," Wilson wrote. "Another guy came to the bathroom door and tried to push his way in, and 'Nikki' (Kim) said 'you have to calm down, we are getting scared.'" Mangum told Wilson that, at that point, "the guys were yelling bad words like 'whore' and things like that."

When the two women went into the living room to dance, she said, the "guys circled around them" and one of them said, "We are going to stick a broomstick up your asses." Mangum told Wilson that she and Roberts "got scared" and "started picking their clothes up off the floor." She told Wilson she "started feeling dizzy at this point" and then she and Roberts "ran out" to Roberts's car "and were getting ready to drive off when three guys came to the car." Mangum told Wilson that Evans was one of three guys that came out to the car and that Roberts was "negotiating" with them. After the three players "apologized," Mangum and Roberts went back into the house. But, Wilson reported, "As soon as they got inside the house, the guys started acting crazy again. People were running around screaming."

Somehow, Mangum said, the two women got separated. "Dave Evans grabbed me by the arm," Mangum told Wilson, "[and the] tall one, Colin [*sic*] Finnerty grabbed me around my waist and the other one[,] Reade, was holding my legs." She said there were "about twenty guys" in the bedroom "and some of them started pushing me into the bathroom" while Evans, Finnerty, and Seligmann were holding her. "Dave Evans was holding my arms," Mangum told Wilson, "and said, 'Sweetheart, you can't leave.'" Mangum told Wilson she was wearing "a white top, red dressy undertop, white skirt and white thong." She continued, "Once inside the bathroom, Dave Evans was behind me, Reade Seligmann was in front of me and Finnerty was on the floor under Seligmann. She said she "felt a sharp pain in my vagina" and one of the three men said, "We're gonna rape or fuck"—she didn't recall which word he used—"this nigger bitch." She then described how alternatively Evans, Seligmann, and Finnerty took turns being behind her, got under her on the floor or were in front of her. "At this point," Wilson reported, "she started feeling sharp pains in her ass and vagina, while Finnerty was behind her. Both Finnerty and Evans were trying to get Seligmann to 'do it' but he kept saying NO. Then Seligmann got behind her, Finnerty got on the floor under her and Evans got in front of her. Dave Evans started jacking his penis and ejaculating on her face and she (Crystal) started spitting."

Then, "someone" opened the door to the bathroom and handed in some towels, which they used to start "wiping me off, Dave Evans off, and wiping up the floor," Mangum continued. "When they opened the door with the towels, I saw Nikki standing in the doorway. Nikki said, 'We have to go[.] They want us to leave." She said the "guys" were saying, "Get that trash out of here." She said she sat there for "a few minutes" and then "ran outside screaming, trying to get away." Mangum told Wilson she "fell on the ground" and the "guys" "picked me up, put me in her (Kim's) car and we drove away." She added, "They were yelling names at us and calling us 'Nigger.'" Mangum told Wilson she asked Roberts to take her to Raleigh, but she said no and that she would call the police. "She tried to push me out of her car at Kroger," Mangum said, "but I wouldn't get out of the car." She said when the police came to the Kroger parking lot, "it was hard to talk and I couldn't walk. They (police) said I was drunk and they were going to put me in a twenty-four hour lockup. They took me to a place where there were five or six other police cars. I talked with an officer Jones and told her what happened and she said she would get me help. They (police) took me from that place to Duke Hospital."

Wilson then asked Mangum a series of questions: How much did she drink at the house? (half of the drink the players gave her); How quickly did they start dancing after getting to the house? (within two to five minutes of getting inside); what happened after the broomstick comment? (they left the house by the back door); where were her belongings at that point? (in her purse in the bathroom, along with her makeup); when and how much did she get paid? ($400, soon after she arrived at the house, which she put in her makeup bag along with her cell phone); what time was it when they went back into the house the second time? (11:35 p.m.) and what happened then? (the two dancers "got separated" and Roberts told the players to "keep their hands off her" and then Roberts left the house "and left me inside during the rape"); when did the rape start? (about three to five minutes after she went back in, around 11:40 p.m. and lasted about "10–15 minutes" until around midnight).

Then Wilson asked Mangum if she was still sure that a penis had penetrated her. "I can't say 100 percent that it was a penis that was used because I couldn't see it," Wilson wrote that Mangum told her. "They had me bent over and my face pushed down to the floor so I couldn't see what they were using but I believe it was their penis. It felt like a penis, but it was a sharp pain. I couldn't say 100 percent that I saw them use their penis but it was certainly something." What did she do after the rape ended? "I sat in the bathroom for a few minutes and then ran out of the bathroom," she told Wilson. "They (guys) dragged me out of the house and dropped me on the steps. I started beating on the door[;] all I wanted to do was get away from the people hurting me. I didn't know whether to go back inside or run out to the street because they (guys outside) were yelling names at me. So, I ran out in the yard and fell on the ground. The guys picked me up and put me in 'Nikki's' (Kim's) car."

Wilson then showed Mangum the picture of her on the back porch of the house, time-stamped at 12:30 a.m. She told Wilson the picture was taken when she was entering the house because "it was showing her putting her money in her purse." On the other hand, it also showed her with only one white shoe on and there were other pictures of Mangum inside the house with both of her shoes on. Wilson asked Mangum to tell him which nicknames the three indicted players were using the night of the alleged attack since she now knew their names. She said Evans used the names Dan, Adam, and Brett; Seligmann used the names Adam and Matt. She said she did not recall if Finnerty used a different name. Wilson then asked Mangum to describe Evans's mustache. "It wasn't a real mustache like yours," she said, "it was like a stubble or a shadow." Wilson wondered, "Like a five o'clock shadow?" Mangum replied, "Yes, like that." Mangum said she recalled that "one of the guys" wiped "her vagina with a white towel and left it on the floor" and that the "same towel" was used to "wipe her face, Dave Evans's penis, and the floor." She also said that contrary to what the Kroger security guard had reported to Himan, she did not "remember wearing a maxipad or bleeding."

For the first time, Wilson showed Mangum the series of photographs of the evening that Dan Abrams had obtained from his friend and classmate, defense counsel Bob Ekstrand, and that Abrams had shown on MSNBC months earlier. According to Nifong, he wanted Wilson to show Mangum the photographs and get her reaction to them. "It was really kind of hard to explain what the photographs showed," Nifong said, "but I think that the point of the photographs being shown was that they tended to discredit her story about what had happened because the allegation, for instance, was that, well, this photograph was taken at such-and-such a time and it shows her smiling, so if she were smiling, then obviously these things couldn't have happened." Nifong wanted Wilson to find out the "context" for the photographs. "We had never talked with her about that," Nifong said of the photographs from the party. "We hadn't heard her explanation with respect to any of these photographs. We only heard the other side about what the photographs showed from their point of view." These were the only photographs that Nifong thought that Wilson would show Mangum.

But as Wilson was pulling the MSNBC photographs out of his briefcase, Mangum saw the PowerPoint presentation of the Duke lacrosse players. She pointed to a picture in the PowerPoint. "That's Dave Evans," Mangum said.

"How do you know that's Dave Evans?" Wilson asked. He was surprised because Mangum had told him that she hadn't been reading the newspapers or watching TV.

"I know who he is now," she said.

"She recognized him from that night," Wilson recalled. He did not ask her, though, how she knew his name. He felt those questions should be asked with a police officer present.

Wilson did ask her some questions about Evans. "Well, now he doesn't have a mustache, though," he said. "I thought you said something about a mustache?"

"It wasn't a real mustache, like yours," Mangum replied.

"You mean like a five o'clock shadow?" he asked.

"Yes," she answered.

Soon thereafter, Mangum was not feeling well. "She started hurting," Wilson remembered. "She was getting this sick headache. She wanted to quit talking."

After Wilson finished interviewing Mangum, he typed up a report of his conversation for Nifong. He also made some notes for himself that he wanted to be sure to share with Himan when they spoke after the New Year. "Heard things not previously known to me," he wrote. "1) heard things. 2) different time line or Time Line different (off twenty minutes or so). 3) Not able to say 100 percent of penile penetration but believe it was a penis. Guys laying under her? I told Himan she needs to be reinterviewed after baby is born and find out why the discrepancies. Needs to be interviewed by all and not just me. I am concerned about these discrepancies." (Wilson relayed these thoughts to Himan when they spoke on Janaury 3.) Interestingly, Gottlieb—who had been pretty much removed from the investigation after having suffered a mild

heart attack—had a different recollection of the accuracy of Mangum's statements about what happened on the night of March 13. "The information that
we would have shared with Mr. Nifong"—early on in the investigation—"was
that between the uniformed police officer's initial response up to the SANE
nurse, things were inconsistent," he said. "But from the time she spoke with the
SANE nurse all the way up through December, her story really didn't change."

Around the same time that Linwood Wilson was speaking with Mangum,
Nifong was giving a three-hour interview to *New York Times* reporters Duff
Wilson and David Barstow. In the interview, Nifong spoke about the importance of the next hearing on February 5 and how, as part of litigating the
defense's motion about whether to allow the use of the photo lineup, it would
be crucial to see whether "my victim"—Mangum—could identify her alleged
attackers, whom she would see in a courtroom for the first time. "If she came
in and said she could not identify her assailants, then we don't have a case,"
he said. "If she says, yes, it's them, or one or two of them, I have an obligation to put that to a jury." He said that although she had identified the three
players from the photographs, the in-person indentification would be telling.
"You can't always tell from a photograph," he said. "The only real time that
you're able to say if you have a misidentification is to put the person in the
courtroom with the other people." Nifong said he would ask Mangum, on the
witness stand, how sure she was of her identification of the three players. "It's
an opportunity to say, 'Yes, I'm 100 percent certain these are the people who
did it,'" he said. "It's also an opportunity to express doubt." Any doubts on
her part, he told the paper, could end the prosecution of one or more of the
lacrosse players.

Nifong also clarified that he knew the test results before he pushed for the
indictments of Seligmann, Finnerty, and Evans the previous April and May.
He admitted knowing the results were "relevant" and "potentially exculpatory"
and that he should have given the results to the defense before May 18, when
he signed a court filing confirming that "the state is not aware of any additional
material or information which may be exculpatory in nature." But, he said,
there was no truth to the defense team's implication that he deliberately tried
to mislead them. He simply had not realized the information had not been
turned over to the defense. "That wasn't something I was concentrating on,"
he said. He told the *Times* that the defense attorneys were using the revelation
of the DNA results as part of a campaign of "character assassination" against
Mangum. "What is the best way to keep the case from coming to trial?" he
asked. "Probably the best way is to attack the victim. If you can keep the victim from coming to court, if you make the victim say, 'Gee, this isn't worth it.'"
But Mangum seemed determined to proceed. "You can't make everybody back
away from a fight," he said. In the interview, Nifong also "expressed remorse,"
the *Times* said, about some of his earlier public comments about the case. He

said he was "wrong" to refer to the Duke players "as a bunch of hooligans." He said, "I regret having used that word."

Late that afternoon, Wilson briefed Nifong on his conversation with Mangum—particularly the fact that she was no longer certain she had been penetrated by a penis. "He just said, 'She's no longer sure that they stuck their penises in her,'" Nifong remembered, adding that his first thought was, "That just streamlined the case. It didn't make any difference to the case, really. . . . What we had was a group assault of a sexual nature, and I didn't really care if it was fingers or penises or hair brushes or whatever." Nifong was struck immediately by two aspects of what Wilson conveyed. First, of course, was the fact that Mangum said she was no longer sure about what had penetrated her on the night of March 13. The second was her referral to the indicted players by name. "I don't remember the exact wording but it was something to the effect that she was now referring to the perpetrators of this offense by name, and that, probably because of the media coverage of the case, there were now names that she associated with the faces," Nifong recalled. "So I thought, well, that's probably unavoidable. It's unfortunate, but we can't really control what she sees in terms of coverage. . . . It was not news I was happy to hear."

Nifong sent Wilson's report to the defense attorneys. He received a letter from Jim Cooney, Seligmann's attorney, asking to know exactly which photographs Wilson had shown to Mangum. "A perfectly reasonable request," Nifong said. Nifong then asked Wilson and, to his horror, Wilson told him that not only had he shown Mangum the pictures that were taken at the party that had appeared on MSNBC but that he also had shown Mangum photographs of the three defendants.

"How did that happen?" Nifong wanted to know. "Why would you do that?"

Wilson explained that he had not intended to show Mangum the photographs of the indicted players but that they happened to be in the same file as the other photographs. Mangum saw the photographs and asked Wilson if she could look at them and he said she could. Nifong said he thought that because Wilson showed the photographs of the players to Mangum, there was an "80 percent chance" the February 5 hearing would go against the prosecution because "that action had certainly tainted the identification." Nifong said he was "dumbfounded by the fact that an experienced investigator would have done that. I mean, in the first place, he shouldn't have even taken those photographs with him."

Nifong was livid, but he took some of the blame himself. "It was my fault, as I saw it, because I didn't say specifically, 'Do not take anything but these photographs,'" he said. "I didn't think I had to. This was an experienced investigator."

It was yet another turning point in the case. "I didn't have any choice," Nifong said of sharing Wilson's mistake with Cooney. "It was a fact. I didn't tell him specifically, 'Oh, this is going to destroy our case.' I just told him, 'Yes, these were the photographs she was shown,' but I knew when I did that what the effect was going to be. I mean, it was pretty clear, and Jim Cooney is not an idiot. . . . This was great news for the defense team." He said, in his opinion, the answer to Cooney's seemingly innocent question about what photographs Wilson had shown Mangum was the single most damaging piece of evidence in the case. "I didn't yell and scream at [Linwood], because it wouldn't have accomplished anything," he continued. "The deed was done. . . . I was really disappointed. I think he knew when I left his office that I was really disappointed, but there was nothing I could do."

At 11:30 a.m. on December 22, Nifong told Himan that Mangum could no longer "be 100 percent certain a penis was put into her vagina" and that "due to that information," he "was dropping the rape charge" against Seligmann, Finnerty, and Evans. When Himan read Wilson's report about his conversation with Mangum, he remembered being flabbergasted. "It didn't make any sense," he recalled. "She had changed her story completely. The sexual positions she had of the suspects weren't even close to what she told me."

Seven minutes after he hung up with Himan, Nifong filed a notice with the court that he had decided to drop the rape charge against Seligmann, Finnerty, and Evans, but was still going to prosecute the three men on both the kidnapping and sexual assault charges. "In an interview with DA Investigator Linwood Wilson on December 21, 2006, the victim in this case indicated that, while she initially believed that she had been vaginally penetrated by a male sex organ (penis), she cannot at this time testify with certainty that a penis was the body part that penetrated her vagina," Nifong wrote. "Since penetration of the vagina by a penis is one of the elements of this offense that the State must prove beyond a reasonable doubt, and since there is no scientific or other evidence independent of the victim's testimony that would corroborate specifically penetration by a penis, the State is unable to meet its burden of proof with respect to this offense."

It was a stunning development that didn't even include the additional fact that Nifong had serious doubts he would be able to introduce the photographic lineup evidence into the trial. Nifong continued to press forward and told the *New York Times* in an e-mail that his decision to drop the rape charges showed he was "willing to go in whatever direction the evidence takes me." He subsequently received a new wave of criticism for waiting nine months to have his investigator interview Mangum, only to find that she could no longer be certain a penis had penetrated her. But Nifong was unapologetic. His logic was that she had never given any indication to him or the Durham police that her story wasn't holding together, and also, with the February 5 hearing at which Mangum would testify approaching, the time was right to start getting down to business. "There was no reason for me to talk to her until I was getting ready to put her on the witness stand," he said. "This wasn't a situation where the officers that were involved, nobody said, 'You know, there's something about this story that doesn't add up.' This wasn't a situation where, when I spoke with her about other things, I got the impression that she was not functioning as a normal human being. So there was no red flags that said this probably never occurred, nothing along those lines. And there have been cases where that has precisely happened, where you have something that, on paper, sounds like a pretty straightforward rape claim or sexual assault claim, but the officer will come in and tell me, and say, 'You know, everything that is said here makes some sense. It's not inconsistent with the evidence, but there's something wrong here. I think you need to talk to this witness yourself.' I remember one time I did that. The victim was very believable on the surface. She was somebody who was going to school. She talked about an ex-boyfriend having come to her apartment and raping her. It seemed very legitimate, but the officer had a question, and I sat down with her and with a female member of our staff, and we just started talking. At some point, I said, 'You understand that there are a lot of people who don't believe your story,' and she broke down and she told me that it wasn't true. So the officer's hunch in that case was exactly correct, and of course that charge got dismissed. There was nothing like that in this case."

The law offices of both Wade Smith, the attorney for Collin Finnerty, and Joe Cheshire, the attorney for David Evans, were planning to have their Christmas parties around lunchtime on December 22. But neither party happened, because at that same moment the two lawyers got the word that Nifong had dropped the rape charges. At first, Cheshire had said to himself, "Thank you, Lord, we finally have justice" before realizing that Nifong had dropped only the rape charge and the two other charges of sexual assault and kidnapping would continue and carry with them substantially the same prison sentences as the rape charge.

During a hastily called news conference that afternoon in Raleigh, it was obvious that Cheshire and Smith—who did the speaking for the defense attorneys—were livid at Nifong. "Almost the only consistent thing that the accuser has said, throughout the many varied different statements that she has made, is that a penis was used in the assault that she describes and that it was used in her vagina," Cheshire said, with barely controlled rage. "Last week, it was clearly demonstrated that significant exculpatory evidence had been purposefully withheld from the defense in this particular case. It should not be lost on you all, who have covered this case, that that significant exculpatory evidence proved that there was no sexual contact between these young men and this woman. Apparently, for the first time, yesterday, representatives of the District Attorney's Office talked to the accuser. This certainly begs the question, ladies and gentlemen, which I hope you all will ask, why, after all of these months, and all of what these young men have been through, did the

District Attorney's Office first talk to this accuser, which leads to the dismissal of one of these charges? Why are they investigating the case now after they've brought it for months? And when they did, ladies and gentlemen, it should be noted clearly by you that her story has now, yet again, changed, and she now cannot remember the use of a penis in the vaginal rape that she described, and which was used to indict these young men. And let me say to you that the transparent coincidence between the proving of the failure of the State to give exculpatory evidence which shows that there was no sexual assault, and this conversation leading to this young woman saying that she cannot now remember a penis being used, is palpable, and certainly is something that should give you all great pause in covering this case, and asking questions of the prosecutor about the coincidence of last Friday to this Thursday, and the dismissal this Friday. Questions could be asked such as, is this some way to try to explain why there was no DNA on any of these three individuals?

"At the beginning of this case," Cheshire continued, in another virtuoso performance, "the prosecutor in this case referred to these young men, and other young men on the Duke lacrosse team, as rapists. He now dismisses the charge of rape. When the DNA results came back from the State DNA lab, which found no DNA of these young men in or on the accuser, the prosecutor in this case supposed that they must have been using condoms, although the accuser had said they were not using condoms. Then, when it was shown that Reade Seligmann had an absolute alibi for the time frame that the accuser said she was raped, the prosecutor supposed that if he had to guess, he would guess that the rape really took place for five or ten minutes instead of the thirty minutes that the accuser said it took place. Of course, remember, he had never talked to the accuser. Now, last Friday, when it was proved that there was no penile penetration, because no DNA was found on or about the accuser, although DNA of multiple other males was found, all of a sudden we have a dismissal and a statement that 'I can't remember if a penis was used.' That, again, is a troubling, transparent coincidence. But let me also point out to you that if it's now going to be the shifting sands again, the shifting factual theory to meet whatever we understand the truth is by the prosecution, that if this woman had been penetrated with a finger, a penis, a mouth, or any other body part, there would have been DNA left in and on her of these young men, and there was none left in and on her. . . . In his dismissal, the prosecutor says, 'Since there is no scientific or other evidence independent of the victim's testimony that would corroborate specifically penetration by a penis, the State is unable to meet its burden.' Well, ladies and gentlemen, there is no scientific or other evidence independent of the victim's testimony that would corroborate any physical assault of any kind, sexual or otherwise, occurring to this woman."

Wade Smith said he had kept relatively quiet throughout much of the case, but that the events of the past week compelled him to speak out against what he perceived as the ongoing injustice. "What I want to do today, on behalf of all the lawyers here and all these families, is call on Mr. Nifong to end this case, end this suffering," he said. "You know, you could say this is a step in the right direction. He has done something. Do the rest of it, Mr. Nifong, if you are listening. Do the rest of this. Do the honorable thing. End this case, because there isn't a case to bring."

In contrast to the defense attorneys, Nifong would not talk to the media, which had camped outside of his sixth-floor office at the courthouse. The door to his office was locked and his assistant placed white sheets of paper over the narrow pane of glass that looked into the office. "NO MEDIA . . . PLEASE!!!!!!!!!!!!," the sign read. "Reporters waited anyway," the *News & Observer* reported. "After a few hours, members of the district attorney's staff offered slices of strawberry cake left over from the office's holiday party." At 5 p.m., Nifong ordered reporters to leave the building. Duke law professor James Coleman said he could not believe Nifong would hide out in his office and not discuss his decision with the media. "This is no way for a prosecutor who has accused three students of rape to dismiss the charges, especially the way he handled this case early on," he said. "This is a really sad mess this guy has created, and I think the quicker he gets out of the case the better it will be for all involved. It looks like they're trying to salvage a case that's falling apart on them."

Meanwhile, Mangum's father told the Durham paper he "wasn't surprised at all" by Nifong's decision and that he had heard that his daughter "was the one that stopped" the rape charge. He said she still had not contacted him, though. "We stand behind her, whatever she decides," he said. "We still love her. I just wish she would call me."

The condemnation of Nifong and Mangum was nearly universal. Brodhead issued a statement calling for Nifong to give up his prosecution of the case. "Given the certainty with which the district attorney made his many public statements regarding the rape allegation, his decision today to drop that charge must call into question the validity of the remaining charges," he wrote in the statement. "The district attorney should now put this case in the hands of an independent party who can restore confidence in the fairness of the process. Further, Mr. Nifong has an obligation to explain to all of us his conduct in this matter."

Friends of Duke, which had been hypercritical of Brodhead, applauded his statement. "We are glad to see our faith in President Brodhead has not been misplaced," it said. "[Brodhead's] bold words must be matched by equally bold deeds in the coming weeks. He must also continue to speak out and do so forcefully." Kevin Finnerty said that while he was pleased the rape charges were dropped, the remaining charges were still serious, if false. "I view this as a big step in the right direction, but we are not celebrating," he said. "We have two serious charges outstanding. We're not taking it for granted. These kids are innocent, and there is no case, but we still have a lot of work to do." Of Nifong, Finnerty said, "He's so dug in, I don't know if he's ever acted rationally in this process. We're not celebrating."

Others were. "It's a textbook case of why a lawyer, and certainly a district attorney, should be sure all the evidence is gathered before you decide what you should do," said Lewis Cheek, who had lost the DA's race to Nifong. "These indictments were sought prematurely." At Charlie's Neighborhood Bar & Grille, near Duke, Mike Cole, the owner, said, "I think Nifong's running scared. Everybody here thinks he's a fish-eyed fool, and he should be hanged from Five Points." Jackie Brown, who had been Nifong's campaign manager during the spring primary before defecting to a recall-Nifong campaign, said, "He's dead. Put a fork in him. He's done." Brittany Adams, a sophomore at NCCU, was upset at Mangum, her fellow student. "I think if she did lie, it was a waste of time, and it's making us as a school look bad."

John Fitzpatrick, the head of the Durham Criminal Defense Lawyers Association, applauded Nifong for dismissing the rape charges. "I think that if the DA has new information that a penis was not involved, there's no way he can proceed on a rape charge," he said. "It's admirable that he dismissed the charge." He said he thought the remaining charges could be easier for him to prove. "He no longer has to explain away the lack of semen," he continued. "If a penis was not used, it would automatically explain the lack of semen. Mike doesn't need the semen part now." But Fitzpatrick said Mangum's changing stories was a negative for the prosecution. "She claimed previously that she was raped," he continued. "Now she's saying she doesn't know. It just adds up to a pile of inconsistent statements that have come from her, and that the defense will use to cross-examine her. It tends to bolster the defense claim that she isn't believable."

Even Irving Joyner, the NCCU law professor who had long been supportive of Nifong and the prosecution, began to express his doubts about the case for the first time. Like others, he suggested that Nifong consider recusing himself.

Joseph Kennedy, an associate law professor at UNC, on the morning of December 21 called for Nifong to recuse himself from the case in an op-ed in the *News & Observer*. "Nifong's own witness essentially accused him of breaking the law," Kennedy wrote. "An actual conflict of interest now exists between Nifong's need to defend himself against possible charges of misconduct and his obligation to prosecute the case fairly and effectively. As someone who used to spend my time defending people, I'm sensitive to the idea that he may not have yet had a chance to fully air his side. But that's part of the problem. He's in a position where he's essentially accused by his own witness of hiding potentially exculpatory material." He said Nifong could voluntarily turn the case over to a special prosecutor, the defense could ask a judge to remove him—as it already had without success—or Judge Smith could take him off the case. "This would be a strange one for a court to get its hands around," he wrote.

Nifong also seemed to be losing whatever meager support he once enjoyed from newspaper editors across the nation. Since the *New York Times* had the only in-depth recent interview with Nifong, reporters David Barstow and Duff Wilson plumbed its depths again for a lengthy Christmas Eve piece to assess the case and Nifong's behavior. Their conclusion was that the turning point had come from Meehan's explosive testimony about how he and and Nifong agreed not to share the exculpatory evidence that none of the DNA evidence found on Mangum had come from the three indicted lacrosse players or their teammates. "Looking back," the reporters found, "defense lawyers describe Mr. Meehan's testimony as a moment that opened a window on the tactics of a prosecutor they say is all too willing to trample state law and ethical duties to get a conviction. In the most unvarnished terms, they accuse Mr. Nifong of deliberately hiding test results—results they say further confirm their clients' innocence. What's more, they say that Mr. Nifong's decision to recast his prosecution on Friday is a cynical attempt to sidestep damage from Mr. Meehan's testimony."

The editors of the *Los Angeles Times* were running out of patience. "We may never know exactly what happened the night of March 13," they wrote. "What is clear is that Nifong, whose election campaign for a full term overlapped with the investigation, lost control of his tongue and participated in the transformation of this incident from a case into a cause—usually an ominous development for the administration of justice."

And *USA Today* was ready to throw in the towel. "Today, the case is looking less like a vicious crime perpetrated by privileged athletes and more like an example of prosecutorial misconduct by the local district attorney." The *Washington Post* nearly eviscerated Nifong. The editors accused Nifong of misusing his power and demanded that he dismiss the remaining charges against the Duke players. "It's been clear for months that Mr. Nifong's case—to the extent he has a case—is riddled with flaws that raise serious questions about his motives and ethics," they opined. "He should be subject to further ethics proceedings by state bar authorities, who filed charges Thursday against him for making inflammatory and misleading comments about the case in its early days."

On the front page of the *Wilmington Star*, Nifong's hometown paper, the editors called for him to resign. "Mike Nifong has demonstrated that he is not ethically or professionally fit to prosecute a littering case, much less the sexual assault case involving three Duke lacrosse players," they wrote, forcefully. "We know the players are guilty of hiring two strippers for a party. Whether they are guilty of anything worse is something we may never know. The woman who accused them turns out to be about as credible as the Durham district attorney who sought publicity—during his campaign for reelection—by rushing to prosecute and publicly denounce the kids she picked from of a lineup of player photos." The editors were incredulous that Nifong did not speak with the local press after he dropped the rape charges. "Hiding behind paper hung over the windows of his office, Nifong issues written statements and refuses to talk with North Carolina reporters," they continued. "Yet Thursday he gave a three-hour interview to the *New York Times*. Nifong doesn't owe an explanation to the readers of a national newspaper. He owes an explanation to the people who elected him. He owes it to the people of this state. But he owes them more: his resignation."

On December 28, the state bar's Grievance Committee publicly filed its sixteen-page first complaint against Nifong, in which his "long list" of public statements was filleted. The gist of its first complaint against Nifong was that he had made "improper commentary" on the case. The state bar also accused Nifong of engaging "in conduct involving dishonesty, fraud, deceit, or misrepresentation" and called for "disciplinary action" to be taken against him, at his expense, in accordance with state law.

The state bar's Disciplinary Hearing Commission had between ninety and one hundred fifty days to consider the state bar's complaint against Nifong. One of the possible outcomes of the commission's examination of the complaint was "what his critics have sought for months," the *News & Observer* wrote, "removal from the case" and the possible loss of his license to practice law.

Both Nifong and the usually vocal defense attorneys declined to comment to the press about the filing of the complaint, which seemed to be without precedent in North Carolina. "From the time I was Wake County's elected district attorney until I was chief justice [of the state Supreme Court], I can't recall the Bar filing a complaint against a district attorney for pretrial publicity," said Burley Mitchell, a Raleigh attorney. "[It's] truly extraordinary." But the consensus seemed to be that Nifong would have little choice but to recuse himself from the lacrosse case, as his foes had long wanted. Lisa Williams, a former Durham prosecutor, said the state bar's complaint created an unambiguous conflict for Nifong. "I feel like this is the first shoe," she said. "And the second shoe is coming." James Coleman, at Duke Law, said he thought the state bar would find that Nifong "violated the Code of Professional Responsibility and will sanction him. I have thought all along that Mike Nifong ought to step aside. He has a cloud over his head. Now, his primary interest is going to be protecting himself and his right to practice law. It seems to me the public is entitled to a prosecutor who does not have a personal interest in the outcome. . . . It's just a really unfortunate situation. Mike Nifong used to have an excellent reputation among lawyers. For some reason, it seems he lost it on this particular case. It's too bad it's come to this."

. . .

The next day, defense attorneys filed a motion in court stating that they intended to call, among others, Brian Meehan, the head of DNA security, as a defense witness following Meehan's December 15 assertion that he and Nifong had together sought to keep exculpatory evidence from the defense. At the same time, the State Conference of District Attorneys demanded that Nifong recuse himself from the case. In the midst of these swirling tactical moves and criticisms, a reporter for the Associated Press caught up with Nifong outside his office and asked him for a comment. "I'm not really into the irony of talking to reporters about allegations that I talked to reporters," he said.

The bad news for Nifong kept coming, even as the year was drawing to a close. *Time* reported that the state bar's Grievance Committee was getting ready to file another complaint against Nifong in mid-January as a result of Meehan's December 15 court testimony. L. Thomas Lunsford II, the executive director of the North Carolina State Bar, told the magazine that Nifong would get a copy of the new complaint during the first week of January and that his hearing on both complaints would be in May, where his punishment could range from a warning to disbarment. An unnamed Durham attorney said he would "bet large amounts of money" that Nifong "will lose his license over this." He recommended that Nifong quit and that "it's entirely possible he'll dismiss all of the remaining charges before then. We see where this speeding train is heading."

That direction was obvious in two New Year's Eve missives to Nifong. The first, from Alan Dershowitz, the Harvard Law School professor, was frank and succinct. "The prosecutor in the Duke case appears to have withheld exculpatory evidence, failed to interview the complaining witness in a timely fashion, and refused to consider obvious evidence of innocence," he wrote. "His entire course of conduct in this case should be scrupulously investigated."

The second, from Michael Skube, an Elon University journalism professor and former *News & Observer* columnist, noted that as the year was ending, the voices of the pot-bangers, the New Black Panther Party, and even Jesse Jackson had been silenced. He called around to see if any of them had any thoughts about the twists the case had taken. He spoke briefly with Jennifer Minnelli, a North Buchanan Boulevard neighbor who had attended a candlelight vigil in front of 610 and had criticized the lacrosse players for their "wall of silence." Before she hung up the phone on Skube, she said, "I have no comment. Good luck with your research." He spoke with Ned Kennington, a former Duke professor who, in March, had said, "I am outraged that forty Duke students know what happened and won't come forward." Kennington told Skube in December, "I trusted Mike Nifong was talking in a careful, judicious way when he called the lacrosse players hooligans. It wasn't long after that that I felt betrayed, and I regret what I said at the time." He added that Duke "is populated by a faculty that is very socially conscious. I think I am guilty of that. But this [case] was fueled by Nifong's assertions, which fit into our preconceptions."

Skube observed that a new "posse prowls the airwaves and the Internet," and was determined to seek its revenge on both Nifong and Brodhead. "It was the university, these critics argue, that failed to stand up for its students and let it be cast as the original *Animal House*," he observed. He wrote that Duke's problems were different from Nifong's, "and they won't evaporate soon, even if Nifong were to drop the remaining charges of kidnapping and sexual assault against the students." He noted that early admission applications to the school were down 20 percent and that, to try to stem the tide, senior administrators, alumni, and students had embarked on a twelve-city nationwide tour—"A Duke Conversation"—to convey the message that "what you read and hear about Duke—drunken parties, out-of-control athletes, pervasive arrogance, and privilege—is far from the truth." John Burness told the *News & Observer* that he had told the Duke trustees it would take "two to five years" for the university to recover from the negative publicity generated by the lacrosse case. "Even a good story is a bad story if it's about lacrosse," Burness said, "because it's a reminder." Observed Skube: "Surely no other top-tier university has found itself so recurrently the butt of criticism, even ridicule. . . . It wants to continue competing with the Ivies and with Stanford, schools with longer traditions, bigger endowments, and no black eyes. None like the lacrosse case, anyway."

And then there was a third commentary, published just after the calendar flipped, from Ruth Sheehan, the columnist at the *News & Observer*. She was more contrite than ever about her earlier support for Nifong during the opening weeks of the case. She was incredulous that Mangum had said she could no longer remember whether she had been assaulted by a penis. "As the victim of a date rape more than twenty years ago myself," she wrote, " I can attest that there are some details you can train your mind to glance over. Whether a penis was involved is a detail one is unlikely to forget." She wondered if Nifong had taken the citizens of Durham for fools. "In the spring, I wrote that we may never know exactly what happened in the lacrosse players' house," she continued. "That may be the only statement that I can salvage from my earliest columns on this case. But at this point, we know all we need to about Nifong's case. I am no legal expert. But it doesn't take one to see that this case should long ago been turned over to an independent prosecutor. In fact, it doesn't take a legal expert to see that the charges, at this point, should simply be dropped. Not just the rape charges. All the charges. Today is the first day of a new year. Let this excruciating exercise in injustice end."

CHAPTER FOURTEEN

The Hunter Becomes the Hunted

On January 2, 2007, at 8 a.m., Nifong was quietly sworn in at the Durham District Attorney's Office by his former UNC law school classmate Judge Orlando Hudson for his own four-year term. The press was not invited to the ceremony. By contrast, in April 2005, when he had been sworn in as interim district attorney after his predecessor Jim Hardin became a state judge, there was an overflowing courtroom. When Hardin presented Nifong with a T-shirt with a bull's eye on it, the crowd laughed uproariously together. This time, he said he was not trying to keep out the media but rather had scheduled the event for thirty minutes before the building opened so that his staff and other people working in the building would not be disrupted. When reporters were finally let into the building some ten minutes after the swearing-in ceremony— which Judge Hudson said violated nothing "but common sense"—Nifong was sitting in a courtroom with his wife and son.

He declined to discuss the lacrosse case, but answered other questions that made clear—in some of his critics' minds—that he was in denial about the magnitude of the firestorm swirling around him. "I don't feel that I'm part of the problem," he said. "I feel that I have assisted in revealing the problem. Durham has some healing to do. And I need to be part of that healing process, and I need to have something to do with how we move forward." He declined to say whether he would recuse himself.

In yet another example of how a consensus seemed to be forming rapidly that Nifong's remaining case against the three players was unwinnable, Duke decided to offer Seligmann and Finnerty reinstatement at the university. In a memo to Brodhead, Larry Moneta explained that in consultation with other Duke administrators, he recommended that Seligmann and Finnerty be allowed to return to Duke even though the legal case against them continued—a reversal of months of refusing to take a position one way or another for fear of getting out front of the legal process.

He noted that Duke had tried to do the right thing for the two players under the circumstances. "Our measures to date have attempted to fit a wise and prudent general policy to the facts of an extraordinary case," he wrote. "As circumstances have evolved, we have attempted to balance recognition of the gravity of legal charges with the presumption of innocence, and concern for the well-being of the community with the students' needs to continue their education. As we approach a new term, I believe that the circumstances warrant that we strike this balance at a different point." Yet Duke's gesture was a hollow one for the two players. For his part, Seligmann had already made quite clear during his *60 Minutes* interview that he had little intention of returning to a school where the administration had not supported him and his teammates for months. Wade Smith, Finnerty's attorney, said, "This announcement speaks to Duke's integrity as an institution, to its mission and to its belief in Collin Finnerty's innocence, and that makes us very glad. It's an announcement to the world that this important instititution has confidence in these boys." His father Kevin said the family was surprised by Duke's change of heart and invitation for Collin to return to the school. But he also relayed his son's view that he did not want to return to Duke until the litigation was resolved.

The Finnertys had also turned their attention to rehabilitating Collin's public image in the wake of the Duke indictment and the Georgetown conviction. Two days before the first *60 Minutes* episode about the lacrosse case aired, the family invited Sharon Swanson, a freelance journalist from Chapel Hill, into their home on Long Island. In light of the Duke lacrosse allegations and worried about her twelve-year-old daughter and the kind of people she would meet at a summer lacrosse camp, Swanson had written a column for the *News & Observer* in the spring that prompted Mary Ellen Finnerty to invite Swanson to meet Collin and to talk "mother to mother." Swanson decided to go see her, because she could sense the "fear and pain" in her voice when they spoke on the telephone. Swanson later conceded about her *News & Observer* column, "When this case first made national news, I was viewing the scenario through the prism of white liberal guilt. I felt somehow responsible that young black women were still being exploited by affluent young white men in the South. I stereotyped the entire Duke lacrosse team."

In her subsequent *Metro Magazine* article, which appeared the first week of January, Swanson more than atoned for the sin of stereotyping. "What gets me so angry," Mary Ellen told her, "is that I held this child in my arms; I protected him. He was a good kid in high school. He was never a curfew breaker—and I was the strictest mother in America. . . . The boys always worked hard, and their spending money they earned. It was never handed to them, despite all these articles that talk about spoiled rich kids." (Her grandparents were Irish immigrants to the Bronx; her grandfather was a New York City firefighter.) Although Kevin Finnerty had become a successful and powerful Wall Street executive, when they first met, "he was working seven days a week and has supported himself basically since he was fifteen. He paid off college loans for the first ten years of our married life."

Mary Ellen told Swanson she was "a very private person" (notwithstanding her participation in any number of media events about the case, including *60 Minutes*) and that because of the lacrosse case "a lot of joy has been taken out of our lives. We've been robbed. We were a very happy family, and a monster"—Mike Nifong—"stepped in. It's hard to experience joy right now. I just sort of get through the day." As for Collin's conviction in Georgetown for "menacing behavior" and his six months on probation, Mary Ellen said it was an example of how the Finnertys were made out "to appear different than what they are." And, besides, she said, Collin never threw a punch, the accuser was not gay and "none of the boys ever thought he was," and no one involved—not the arresting officer, the DA, or the judge—"believed that the actions of the young men constituted a hate crime." (On December 28, the judge in the Georgetown case ended Finnerty's probation and wiped the conviction off his record.) She said she did not condone underage drinking. "I hate alcohol," she said, "because I don't like to see what it does." And the lacrosse party on March 13? "Was I thrilled that they had a stripper?" she said. "I was disgusted that they would have a stripper. . . . I've heard since that there were as many as twenty-two incidents of strippers at other Duke parties; this wasn't the only time it's happened."

Swanson spoke, too, with Kevin Finnerty—"a tall, handsome man, who retains the physique of the college scholarship swimmer he once was" who was "on a mission to vindicate his son." Uniquely among the lacrosse parents, Kevin Finnerty had been particularly involved in nearly every aspect of his son's defense and had not missed a court hearing. "I'd like to believe that something good will come out of this," he said. He remained incensed that Nifong had no interest in meeting with the players' attorneys. "They didn't want any evidence from any of the defense lawyers," he continued. "They didn't want it, didn't ask for it and didn't want to take it when it was offered. . . . To this day, nobody has asked Collin where he was, who he was with, what kind of exonerating evidence he has."

As for Mangum, Kevin Finnerty tried to be charitable. "My best guess is that this woman has had a hard life," he said. And then he unleashed a tirade against Gottlieb, the Durham police investigator, Duke, and the media. "You have a bully cop, who is so corrupt, he will say anything," he said. "You have Duke, which mishandled the whole situation. You have the media, the white guilt, and years of injustices. It is the perfect storm of a lot of things. And yet, Collin is not guilty. Collin is innocent. He works full-time, he goes to school at Hofstra two nights a week taking courses; he works out every day in hopes that someday he will get back out on the field."

Collin made a brief cameo. "People think that I have the toughest time," he said, "but it's harder for my mom. It's tough to see her deal with this day after day for something that never happened. . . . When it's over, I'll be happy to see my whole family relieved, but especially for my mom." "Standing at his mother's sink," Swanson concluded, "I saw a vulnerable, almost fragile young man. I saw the son that his mother knows. After talking to Collin for five minutes, I wanted to leave the room—to go somewhere he couldn't see me—so that I could sob or scream or throw something breakable. If these charges turn out to be false, as he and the other defendants claim, it's not possible to undo the damage that has been done to this seemingly gentle man."

Then it was *Newsweek*'s turn to paint Seligmann with a sympathetic brush. Susannah Meadows, the Duke graduate who had written many stories about the case, including a spring cover story with the mug shots of Seligmann and Finnerty, wrote that Seligmann still got "emotional thinking about what his parents have gone through" since he was indicted. "Out on bail and suspended from Duke, Seligmann went home nine months ago to cope with the prospect of serving thirty years in prison," Meadows wrote in January 2007. "The case is headed for trial, possibly this spring, even though there appears to be no convincing evidence that a crime was committed." Seligmann described the morning when he was taken into custody and saw the "backseat of a police car" for the first time, which was "surreal." He repeated what he had told others about the feeling he had upon being processed at the prison and then in his jail cell, even if he was only there for a few hours before his $400,000 bail was posted.

After Seligmann's release on bail, the family contemplated returning home to Essex Fells, New Jersey, but quickly realized their house was nearly surrounded by television trucks. They decided to spend the next two weeks at a friend's house in Connecticut. But after two days, Seligmann had an epiphany. "What are we doing?" he said to his mother. "I didn't do anything wrong. There's no reason for us to hide." They left Connecticut, and when they got back home, the saw that neighbors had tied ribbons around the trees.

Seligmann told Meadows he was not sure whether he would return to Duke, despite the offer. He seemed to long for his simpler life there or the times when his name would appear in the local paper because of his Pee-Wee football exploits. "I miss more than anything staying up and worrying about a miserable midterm," he said. One day he received a package from his Duke lacrosse teammates. In it were his lacrosse jersey and the name tag from his locker. The two momentoes joined the others downstairs in the family's shrine to the Seligmann brothers' athletic prowess. "There, dozens of lacrosse cleats and helmets from all four Seligmann boys are arranged neatly on the shelves," Meadows wrote. "He hung the tag on the wall. READE SELIGMANN, it says, DUKE BLUE DEVILS, #45. It's a reminder of a team and a school that he still misses, but also of a past that is not yet behind him."

The idea that the Duke administration had offered to reinstate Seligmann and Finnerty before the court case had been resolved infuriated Karla Holloway, a

Duke professor of English, a force behind the Group of 88 advertisement, and a member of the Campus Culture Initiative task force. "I will share with you what I have not previously shared publicly," she wrote in a January 3 e-mail to a group of Duke professors. "It has colored this matter for me since last spring. It is legally hearsay, but nevertheless speaks volumes to what I think are the intricacies of the event that deserve a legal hearing." Holloway conveyed how she had been sitting in John Burness's office a few days after the alleged incident when she overheard Burness's conversation with the Duke police. "The vice president took a call from the Duke police, who had returned from a meeting with the Durham police," she continued. "He repeated aloud what the person on the phone was telling him," which was: "So you are telling me that when the boys opened the door and saw the dancers, they said, 'Oh no, we're not going to f[uc]k a 'n[igger].'" Holloway's e-mail continued, "I cannot help but think that if I was privy to this, this statement had to have been shared with our administration. . . . So what does it mean to readmit students with an indictment for violent acts, without an internal investigation of our own regarding the event? I think it is a choice the institution has made. And it has led to my own that I cannot work in shared good faith at a time when principled conduct matters less than polls and parents' pleas."

Burness replied to Holloway. "The comments you overheard in my office which were attributed to the Durham police were as you described them," he wrote in an e-mail. "We both found them to be profoundly painful/disgusting. They clearly, if true, spoke volumes about the climate of the event, but I knew that it was not clear who had made them and I knew that conducting our own investigation would instantly be seen as compromising that of the Durham police. That would play into the hands of those who assumed—as many people in Durham did as the case first surfaced—Duke would use its power to influence the case and the process. . . . I also knew that the Durham police didn't clarify who apparently had said it, and I made no assumption that the students who ultimately were indicted did."

Holloway decided to resign from the Campus Culture Initiative. "The decision by the University to readmit the students, especially just before a critical judicial decision on the case, is a clear use of corporate power, and a breach, I think, of ethical citizenship," she wrote in her letter of resignation. "I could no longer work in good faith with this breach of common trust." Holloway's decision to resign from the Campus Culture Initiative harked back at least to the previous summer when she had written an impassioned essay for The Scholar and Feminist Online denouncing the ongoing subjugation of black women by white men that the behavior inside 610 North Buchanan symbolized. "When things go wrong," she wrote, "when sports teams beget bawdy behavior and debasement of other human beings, the bodies left on the line often have little in common with those enclosed in the protective veneer of the world of college athletics. At Duke University this past spring, the bodies left to the trauma of a campus brought to its knees by members of the Duke University's lacrosse team were African-American and women. I use the kneeling meta- phor with deliberate intent. It was precisely this demeanor toward women and girls that mattered here." Holloway spared few (although she made no mention of Nifong) and even criticized Kevin Cassese, the interim lacrosse coach, for his expressed belief that Seligmann, Finnerty, and Evans were innocent, which she wrote "was critical in weighing the significance of this event." She contin- ued, "In nearly every social context that emerged following the team's crude conduct, innocence and guilt have been assessed through a metric of race and gender. White innocence, means black guilt. Men's innocence means women's guilt. These capacious categories, which were in absolute play the night of the team's drunken debacle, continue their hold on the campus and the Durham community."

Six months or so later, the fact that Brodhead offered to reinstate Selig- mann and Finnerty well before the legal charges against them had been resolved was too much accommodation for Holloway. Indeed, Duke's offer seemed to resurrect many of the long-simmering tensions between the Duke faculty and the student-athletes and the Duke faculty and the Duke admin- istration. (Around the same time, Kyle Dowd, a member of the lacrosse team who had graduated in May 2006, filed a lawsuit against Duke and Kim Cur- tis, his professor, accusing Curtis of giving him a failing grade because of the March 13 party. Dowd's mother had previously had a vicious e-mail exchange with Holloway in November 2006 about an article Holloway had written condemning the lacrosse players. "I wondered," Tricia Dowd wrote, "do you attack our sons because you feel guilt for your own failures as a mother? Do you attack our sons because you are so selfish that you cannot stand the thought of our sons leading successful lives, when your son"—who was con- victed of rape and attempted murder and then died trying to escape from prison—"did not and cannot? Do you attack our sons to justify your own shortcomings?")

Nothing symbolized those tensions more than the infamous Group of 88 ad that had appeared in April 2006. Nine months later, Duke professors were still debating the wisdom of its content. In a January 5 opinion column in the *News & Observer*, Cathy Davidson, a chaired professor of English at Duke, defended her decision to sign the ad and noted that its content had been repeatedly mis- construed. One thing the Group of 88 had no way of knowing in April, she said, was that Nifong "may well have acted unprofessionally, irresponsibly, and unethically, possibly from the most cynical political motives." She was proud to have signed the ad and seemed prepared to do it again, if need be. "Studying this social disaster must be on the lesson plan for our future," she concluded, "no matter what happens next in this miserable incident."

While Davidson was defending her decision to sign the Group of 88 ad, some eighteen members of the Duke economics department wrote a letter to the *Chronicle*, published January 9, that noted that the ad had been used as part of the defense attorney's change-of-venue motion and seemed to stand as the sole collective view of the Duke faculty to the March 13 incidents. "We regret that the Duke faculty is now seen as prejudiced against certain of its own students," they wrote. Like Brodhead, they demanded an investigation of the allegedly "irregular acts" committed by the Durham police and by Nifong that were "inimical to students at our university." They stated that they "welcome all members of the lacrosse team, and all student athletes, as we do all our students as fellow members of the Duke community, to the classes we teach and the activities we sponsor." Thomas Nechyba, chair of the economics department, said he received "e-mails thanking" him and his colleagues "for standing up and saying something and creating an atmosphere in which students feel faculty respect them. There seems to be a sense that's something that needed to happen." More than 450 Duke alumni and supporters signed an online petition in support of the economics professors.

A few days later, a group of eighty-seven Duke faculty members, many of them the same as the original group, doubled-down on the Group of 88 statement. "For us at Duke, the issues raised by the incident, and by our community's responses to it, are not [winding down]," they wrote in "an open letter" to the community. After reminding people about the purpose of the original ad, they wrote that it "has been read as a comment on the alleged rape, the team party, or the specific students accused. Worse, it has been read as rendering a judgment in the case. We understand the ad instead as a call to action on important, longstanding issues on and around our campus, an attempt to channel the attention generated by the incident to addressing these. We reject all attempts to try the case outside the courts, and stand firmly by the principle of the presumption of innocence. As a statement about campus culture, the ad deplores a 'Social Disaster,' as described in the student statements, which feature racism, segregation, isolation, and sexism as ongoing problems before the scandal broke, exacerbated by the heightened tensions in its immediate aftermath. The disaster is the atmosphere that allows sexism, racism, and sexual violence to be so prevalent on campus. The ad's statement that the problem 'won't end with what the police say or the court decides' is as clearly true now as it was then. Whatever its conclusions, the legal process will not resolve these problems." They were not backing down. "There have been public calls to the authors to retract the ad or apologize for it, as well as calls for action against them and attacks on their character," they concluded. "We reject all of these. We think the ad's authors were right to give voice to the students quoted, whose suffering is real. We also acknowledge the pain that has been generated by what we believe is a misperception that the authors of the ad prejudged the rape case.

We stand by the claim that issues of race and sexual violence on campus are real, and we join the ad's call to all of us at Duke to do something about this."

Meanwhile, not surprisingly, Nifong had given up reading the newspapers—except for the *New York Times*—or watching television. Instead, he was increasingly focused on the state bar's actions, particularly after Katherine Jean informed him by letter on December 19 that an amended complaint—derived from Meehan's testimony at the December 15 hearing—was heading his way. On January 5, she wrote him again, following up on his December 28 response. Nifong gave a detailed explanation of his actions in a series of letters to Jean, but the state bar Grievance Committee was unmoved by Nifong's written defense. On January 24, in addition to the original charges about pretrial publicity, the state bar's amended complaint accused him of withholding the exculpatory DNA evidence from the defense and of making "misprentations" to Judge Smith. The amended complaint also accused Nifong of making "misrepresentations" and "false statements" to the state bar in his response to the charges about failing to disclose the "exculpatory" DNA evidence. In other words, the state bar was accusing Nifong of lying to Jean in his two letters on December 28 and on January 16. In addition to the claims about making statements to the press he should not have made, the state bar criticized Nifong for "not making timely disclosure" to the defense "of information that tended to negate the guilt of the accused" and for "fail[ing] to make a reasonably diligent effort to comply with a legally proper discovery request." He then compounded these problems by supposedly conspiring with Meehan to keep exculpatory evidence out of the hands of the defense in ways that "constitute a systematic abuse of prosecutorial discretion in the underlying criminal cases" and were "prejudicial to the administration of justice." His responses to Jean seemed to fall on completely deaf ears.

It didn't take long for Nifong to realize that the state bar's allegations in the amended complaint put Nifong in a very difficult legal position, even though he claimed them to be total fiction. "The concealment of evidence, conspiracy, all that kind of stuff, that just wasn't true," he said in an interview. "It also was quite apparent that once the claim against me, as a prosecutor, was that I had done these things that were, at the very least, dishonest, and perhaps even violative of the statute, above and apart from any bar rules, that I would not be able to continue in the prosecution of the case. So, at some point, pretty quickly after that, I began to make plans to transfer the case to the Attorney General's Office."

The amended complaint questioned Nifong's ethics and integrity, potentially damaging his credibility with a jury. "For that reason, not only could I not prosecute the case, but, from the point of view of what was best for the case, you shouldn't want me to prosecute the case because my presence in the case, at that point, could be a distraction—a harmful presence to the state, because here I was asking the jury to follow my line of reasoning and return a particular verdict and there was evidence to show that the jury shouldn't believe me, or there were allegations to show that the jury shouldn't believe me," he explained. "It was very clear."

Nifong quickly decided that the first step in deciding to recuse himself was to speak with Mangum to find out whether—given all that she had been though already and what was likely to come—she was still determined to testify against the three lacrosse players. "I felt that I had an obligation to Crystal Mangum to talk with her about this whole issue, and why I needed to do this before I did it, because I didn't want her to think that I was just all of a sudden, without explanation, backing away from the case," he explained. The immediate problem for Nifong, though, was that Mangum was then enduring a very difficult pregnancy at the UNC Hospital. "It was literally a threat to her own life," he said, "and there was some concern about whether or not she would be able to survive all this." (Linwood Wilson said he thought that Mangum's "placenta had grown to her bladder and stomach and they were going to have to surgically remove that, and there would be a lot of blood loss." Papers were drawn up transferring the custody of her children in case Mangum died on the operating table.)

Nifong resolved to wait until after she gave birth and recovered before he would discuss his decision with her. "I needed to get from her a sense of whether or not she was willing to go forward," he said. "There was no point in sending the case to the Attorney General's Office if, after everything that had happened and after all the things that she was going through personally, if she no longer felt like pursuing the case or didn't feel like starting over again with a different prosecutor."

Around this time, Nifong agreed to meet with Bill Cotter, one of Finnerty's defense attorneys. Cotter and Nifong knew each other well—dating back more than twenty years—and were on good terms, all things considered. Cotter was aware that Nifong intended to meet with Mangum and he took with him a file containing Mangum's health and legal records. "I encouraged him to read her records," Cotter recalled. "I wanted him to know the person he was betting his career on, the person he staked his case on. I wanted him to ask her the hard questions, to cross-examine her."

Mangum gave birth to a baby girl, prematurely by Caesarean section, on January 4. After she recovered, Himan brought Mangum to see Nifong in his Durham office. She still had stitches from her surgery. "It was the longest conversation that I'd ever had with her," Nifong said. "I would say that it was a minimum of an hour and a half long, and it could've been longer than that." He explained to Mangum that he needed to recuse himself from the case because of the state bar accusations against him and would turn it over to a special prosecutor in the State Attorney General's Office. "During that conversation I attempted to explain to her, as a layperson, how all these things affected my ability to prosecute the case," he continued. "And why it would be necessary for me not to be the prosecutor, and how my remaining on the case actually could be detrimental to her point of view. I think that her initial reaction to that was resistance, but she understood that that was the case. And then I wanted to try to explain to her what she was likely to face as the case went forward, both in terms of meeting and speaking with and developing a relationship with new prosecutors, and also just in terms of preparing herself for what was likely to be occurring in the case itself, because we'd never really talked in any depth about that."

Nifong wanted Mangum to know precisely how grueling the upcoming trial would likely be. "I presented as negative a perspective of what was likely to happen with the case as I could," he said. "Not only didn't I want to sugar-coat any of this, but I wanted to present to her, in effect, a worst case scenario, from her point of view, about what she could expect. . . . I said, 'It's possible that the trial itself will be a worse experience for you than what you experienced on that night, and you need to understand that going in, that you will be the subject of vilification that you have not yet seen, and the whole point of the defense strategy in this case will be to completely discredit you, not only as a witness but as a person.'"

Nifong told Mangum what she would need to do to cooperate with the investigators from the Attorney General's Office who would determine whether the case could be prosecuted. "I also explained to her that if she did not want to proceed at this point that I was not going to refer the case to the Attorney General's Office," he said, "that I would go ahead and dismiss it myself, because there was no point in either putting her through another round of interviews or in getting them to devote their time and energy to the case if she wasn't going to proceed. I let her know that it was really up to her. . . . There was no hesitation at all. She didn't even have to think about the answer to the question. She just said, 'No. I want to go through with this. I will do whatever is necessary.'"

Meanwhile, while Nifong was meeting with Mangum, the defense attorneys filed a supplement to their December 14 motion to suppress Mangum's "identification" of Seligmann, Finnerty, and Evans, which was still to be heard on February 5. The defense attorneys claimed, essentially, that Mangum's comments to Linwood Wilson on December 21 called into question—again—the validity of the April 4 identification procedure, which they wanted the court to suppress on February 5.

The defense wrote that Mangum "now claims that the attack took place between 11:35 p.m. and midnight, which, in addition to other objective evidence, is contradicted by the accuser's own cell phone records and the cell

phone records for Reade Seligmann and his girlfriend." On that point, the
defense included a copy of Mangum's cell phone bill, which showed that starting at 11:25 p.m., she spoke with someone at her father's house for seven minutes, spoke to someone else for a minute at 11:33, and to someone else at
11:36 for three minutes. "Thus, according to the accuser's most recent telling,"
the defense wrote, "she apparently spoke with someone at her father's home
for seven minutes during the time she was planning her nude dance routine,
during the time she was dancing and then as she was fleeing to the car. In
addition, the accuser was apparently talking with someone on her cell phone
at the time she was walking back into the house and being 'kidnapped' into the
bathroom. She finished her last conversation at the time the rape was beginning. None of these facts has ever been mentioned in any statement that the
accuser has given to date in this case." The defense also pointed out that Seligmann was on his cell phone for nearly ninety seconds at 11:40 p.m., speaking
with his girlfriend. "Thus, at the height of the sexual attack now claimed by the
accuser, Reade Seligmann was having a telephone conversation," they wrote.

There were other inconsistencies revealed in the December 21 interview
as well. According to the defense, Mangum "recants" her April 6 statement
that Seligmann "was the accuser [sic] who stood in front of her and made her
commit a sex act," and instead claimed "for the first time" that Evans "was that
person," and that furthermore Seligmann "did not commit any sex act on her."
Mangum also revised her view, according to the defense, that Evans had a
mustache "and now says that the attacker who looked like Dave Evans did not
have a mustache." The defense also claimed that Mangum was totally confused
about the fake names her attackers used, making it seem like a dizzying blur of
names, people, and questionable behavior.

The attorneys also wrote that the "most troubling" fact of the December 21
interview was that "rather than attempt to identify her accusers as Matt, Brett,
and Adam," Mangum used the names of Seligmann, Finnerty, and Evans "in
her most recent telling of her story." That Mangum knew the names of the men
accused of attacking her "indicates that she has learned their names from the
extensive publicity that this case has received," the defense wrote, "publicity that
has necessarily included the Defendants' faces as well as their names. . . . This,
in turn, means that the accuser's present recollection of who allegedly attacked
her and how, has been irreparably tainted by this publicity and weighs strongly
against any in-court identification by her" of Seligmann, Finnerty, and Evans.

Of Mangum's new version of events, James Coleman, the Duke law professor, said it was a blatant attempt to fix the problems in Nifong's case. "Who
would believe that a witness, nine months later, suddenly recalls facts that
coincidentally negate evidence produced by the defense?" he asked. "These
people are almost criminal. It's making a mockery of the system. It's like
Nifong is mooning the system. It's contemptuous."

By January 11, Dorothy Rabinowitz, an editorial writer at the *Wall Street Journal*, seemed to have lost whatever patience, if any, she had had with Nifong. In a bitter and angry column, Rabinowitz noted how the words "the Duke University scandal" had been so completely transformed in the course of ten months. "[T]he term is now almost universally understood as a reference to the operations of Michael Nifong, the Durham County district attorney, whose abandonment of all semblance of concern about the merits of the rape and assault accusations against three Duke University students was obvious from the first," she wrote. "So was his abundant confidence while broadcasting comments on the guilt of the accused. He seemed a man immune to concerns for appearances as he raced about expounding on the case against the accused lacrosse players and calling them hooligans." She also was highly critical of Brodhead and his handling of the allegations. "Soon after news broke of the Duke athletes' alleged brutish sex crimes against a black woman, the administration undertook a well-publicized campaign targeting the entire lacrosse team for offensive behavior," Rabinowitz continued. "President Richard Brodhead was, it seems, barely able to recover from the shock of his discovery that a party thrown by male jocks could occasion heavy drinking. And related loutish behavior. Not to mention a stripper. Lacrosse was suspended for the season, and the team coach, Mike Pressler, was shortly after forced to resign. Mr. Brodhead in due course reinstated the team, but on probation, and with conditions, i.e., no underage drinking and disorderly conduct, and no harassment. The members of other Duke organizations, sports teams included, which had sponsored parties where alcohol flowed freely and which had featured strippers—an informal count reveals at least twenty known to have done so—no doubt understood that they faced no similar disciplinary action. The reason for the moral-cleansing program devised for the lacrosse team could scarcely have been missed."

Rabinowitz wrote that Nifong's behavior was politically motivated. "The jury to which Mr. Nifong played—the black population of Durham—duly helped reelect him," she coninued. "This could not prevent his case of rape and abuse against the three Duke students from coming undone, thanks in part to his own heedless behavior but mainly to the accusing dancer herself, whose shifting stories and checkered past could not be hidden. . . . The accused Duke students can be grateful that the case against them has collapsed, and that Mr. Nifong now confronts a serious ethics complaint filed by the North Carolina State Bar. . . . But Reade Seligmann, David Evans and Collin Finnerty have this year had a look into an abyss that has claimed many others, and that is never less than terrorizing. It is a piece of their Duke education they are unlikely to forget."

Things were also coming to a head at Duke. On the morning of January 11, after months of silence, Provost Peter Lange spoke to the faculty, with Brodhead at his side, about the importance of preserving freedom of speech even though the lacrosse case had caused a huge polarization on campus between (and among) professors, administrators, and students. The meeting came, in part, as a response to Karla Holloway's dramatic decision to resign from the Campus Culture Initiative. "When the events of the spring unfolded we witnessed an unimagined intensity of vituperative language and distasteful and deeply hurtful caricatures of Duke students, our campus and its culture, our Durham community, and our relationship to our neighbors in the city," Lange said. "The wave of attacks lasted for weeks in the media, on the e-mails, and in the blogs. It was deeply disturbing, in many ways for our students, faculty, and whole community. It inflamed and polarized rhetoric on our campus as well." He said that while the "attacks" had subsided during the course of 2006, the turn of events in the case—increasingly toward the three players' version of events and away from those advanced by Mangum and Nifong—had caused a flaring-up of resentment toward those professors who had been involved with creating and then endorsing the Group of 88 advertisement. "The connection to the advertisement often has become attenuated and the ad has become rhetorically transformed into and manipulated as a symbol of all that was thought to be extreme and bad about Duke faculty, and, in some cases, universities more generally," Lange continued. "At the same time, the e-mails and blogs attacking what people wrote or said have sometimes been replaced by personal attacks, some of them directed at the faculty members' scholarship or intellectual credentials, some viciously personal, still others openly threatening or racist."

He said the increasing ubiquity of bloggers and the widespread use of e-mails and text messages, dashed off with uncensored venom, had become so problematic that Lange could no longer keep silent. He continued, "Any reading of the rhetoric, and of the blogger and e-mail traffic, on all sides of the lacrosse case, however, makes clear that at many times such self-awareness, not to speak of self-restraint, has given way to a speech intended not to clarify but to embarrass, punish, demean, or humiliate, a result which is likely to diminish the quality of speech over time and to undermine the advantages to individuals and the community of a free, open, intense, engaged but also respectful debate." Lange was especially concerned about a recent wave of e-mails directed at Duke professors in previous months. "Worthy of special mention—because they are so distasteful and beyond any form of acceptable speech—are the e-mails that I have seen in recent months which are nothing more or less than the anonymous racist—personally vilifying—rants sent primarily but not only to African-American faculty members," he said. Among the e-mail messages that Holloway received were ones that contained the phrases "You stupid, bitter black bitch. What a fool you made [of yourself] jumping on the 'guilty' bandwagon only as a pathetic attempt to appease your own anger for growing up ugly," and "The fate of black people is sealed because whites possess superior logic. We need to show more rape cases on television between black men and black women to further educate black women."

Lange also explained his silence during the nine-month ordeal, as well as in the face of the attacks on some members of the Duke faculty. "I was concerned that public statements of defense of the rights of the faculty to speak in the face of the blogger and e-mail attacks would only generate more of the same vituperative rhetoric that my speaking out would be intended to help quell," he explained. "The merciless attention that the e-mailers and bloggers have been paying to every word uttered, syllabus crafted, and article authored suggested that an intervention by me might simply turn up the heat which seemed, at moments, to be cooling. Further, I feared that in the often tense and polarized atmosphere of our campus discourse, statements by the Provost, while intended to calm might simply further divide and be interpreted as 'taking sides.' This might well then run the danger of stifling other voices that needed to be heard." He said he had decided to speak out because the level of vitriol had ratcheted up again in recent weeks. "With the passing of time, the heat has not gone down," he continued. "In the last weeks, faculty members have shared with me e-mails and blog material that is as merciless, distorted, and vituperative as in the past. The cumulative damage of the months of attacks on some of our faculty and the distress of those who sympathize with them is exceeding the limits of prudence about provoking external reactions. It *is* the Provost's job to defend the fundamental value and values of the faculty and at some point refraining from that defense because it might produce more of the same becomes itself imprudent."

It wasn't until Nifong became the Durham district attorney in April 2005 that he began to interact—in a minor way—with Roy Cooper, the state attorney general. Cooper, then fifty-one, was from rural Nash County and used to pick tobacco in the summer as a teenager before heading to UNC as a prestigious Morehead Scholar. After graduating from UNC Law School, Cooper practiced law in his family's firm in Rocky Mount before beginning his political career in 1986. Cooper began serving as attorney general in January 2001. Nifong would occasionally see Cooper at the biannual meetings of the district attorneys from around North Carolina. Nifong remembered seeing Cooper at one such meeting in the spring of 2006, a month or so after he had taken control of the lacrosse case. "He was very solicitous," Nifong recalled. "He said, 'If there's anything I can do, don't hesitate to call me.' That kind of stuff." Nifong saw Cooper again at the next gathering six months later and he was still friendly. "But obviously, at some point, things changed, as far as he was concerned," Nifong recalled. Nifong said he would speak regularly with Jim Coman, a special deputy attorney general, about cases and it was clear to him that the last case Cooper and Coman wanted any part of was the Duke lacrosse case. Nifong remembered calling up Coman during the summer of 2006. "I just wanted to let you know that I'm going to have to send you that lacrosse case," Nifong told Coman. "And it was total silence on the other end of the line. And I said, 'Jim, I'm just kidding.' He said, 'Oh, man, I didn't think that sounded like you. I didn't think you were the type of guy who would just duck on a case like that.'"

On January 11, 2007, after he had met with Mangum and heard her tell him she still wanted the case against the three lacrosse players to be prosecuted— "What they did to me was wrong," Nifong recalled as her parting words—he picked up the phone and called Coman, who was Cooper's head of special prosecutions. Coman was the son of a New Jersey police chief and a former head of the North Carolina State Bureau of Investigation, or SBI. In 1980, Coman prosecuted members of the Ku Klux Klan accused of murdering five Communist Workers Party members at a march in Greensboro in 1979. (One of the murdered, Cesar Cauce, was a Duke graduate and another, Michael Nathan, was a doctor at Duke Hospital.) The jurors ended up acquitting the Klansmen of the murders. "At this point, I can't imagine that my call to Jim Coman was unexpected," Nifong recalled. "He was very professional." He told Coman—no joking this time—"If you've been reading the papers, Jim, you probably know why I'm calling, but at this point I feel like I do have an unresolvable conflict, and I'm going to have to recuse myself from prosecuting the Duke lacrosse case, and I'm going to ask the attorney general to accept it for prosecution. I just wanted you give you a heads-up on that."

Nifong believed he had no choice. "By that point, I was probably beyond pissed off or angry, in this case," he recalled years later. "I was more, probably, resigned than anything. See, you also have to understand that it's not like I really wanted this case. It was something that I had a responsibility to do. If I couldn't do that, if I couldn't accept the responsibility, I shouldn't have been in the job at all. So there is a sense that you're letting somebody down."

Even as Nifong was letting the case go, he was convinced a crime had been committed in the bathroom at 610 North Buchanan on the night of March 13. "I still feel that today," he said seven years later in the small dining room of his Durham home. "Something happened in that bathroom, because as a result of that, [Mangum] experienced a post-traumatic stress reaction that governed her behavior over the next twenty-four hours or so. I don't know exactly what it was that caused that—I'm not an expert—but something did trigger that. I haven't seen anything that's changed my mind about that."

In retrospect, Nifong compared the behavior of the Duke lacrosse players to that of the members of a now-defunct "club" for elite Japanese university students, known as Super Free. (Someone had sent him a copy of a *Harper's Magazine* article about the group.) Between 1995 and 2003, Super Free members were believed to have raped "hundreds of women." The club's leader, Shinichiro Wada, once argued that "gang rape creates solidarity among members." The Super Free handbook outlined four "steps" that club members were to take to accomplish a rape on a given night—"steps" that, to Nifong, bore eerie similarities to what had happened in the house on North Buchanan Boulevard in March 2006. First, "create a fun and wholesome main show" and "promise women they can talk to top organization officials to lure them to the after-show party." Second, at the "after-show," usually at a bar, "decide which women are to be raped: Aim for new students from the countryside who have recently arrived in Tokyo and aren't used to partying. . . . Look for women who seem ill at ease and timid, and are unlikely to attend future events."

Step three was to "ply the woman with alcohol." The handbook then urged its members to "go in for the kill by giving plastered women drinks spiked with Spirytus"—a 96-proof Polish vodka—and "even if they say they can't drink any more, force them. Soft drinks are not to be served." Finally, "with the excuse of looking after the drunk woman, move her away from her friends. Only one person should leave with the woman at first, but afterward three to ten people may join them and take part . . ." Here, presumably, is the part that Nifong deemed most similar: "Set up a lookout and use cell phones to communicate. Take away the woman's shoes, purse, and cell phone so that she cannot get away before we have finished. . . . After finishing, make sure everybody has a tight cover story and be sure all information related to you is deleted from the woman's phone. Take pictures or a video of the rape and threaten to expose the woman publicly if she opens her mouth about what happened." Explained Nifong, "It is a fascinating parallel, where they say that what you do is you separate her from her friends, you separate her from her shoes, you separate her from her money, you separate her from her phone, and you take pictures."

Nifong also believed that, at the moment he turned the case over to Coman and Cooper, Mangum would be able to convince a jury that she had been the victim of a crime. "She seemed to really have everything together," he recalled. "I was surprised. I thought that she might say, 'This is a good point to get out of this,' not because there wasn't anything to it, but just because, just, kind of like, 'Man, what else could possibly happen?' I gave her every chance to do that. I probably made it easier for her to do that than to go ahead, and she went ahead and she did it in a very calm and reasonable manner. It was like, 'No, this is really something I need to do.'"

He said the reason he had not interviewed Mangum about the facts of the case was because he had no reason to doubt her story. "Every witness"— he mentioned by name Levicy and officers Himan, Gottlieb, Clayton, and Soucie—"that I had spoken to about the case believed that she was telling the truth, that she had in fact been assaulted, in which case the issue for the court or for the jury would only have been if she could identify the people who had committed the assault," he said. "None of [them] had expressed any question at all about what she said in terms of whether this assault had occurred. And never at any point in the four interviews that I had with her did I see any indication of any equivocation, any hiding of anything. There was nothing she ever gave—and we didn't talk about the case itself but we talked about other things—and she always answered everything appropriately. Her responses seemed to be the responses I would have expected. I never saw anything in the course of my conversations with her that made me think that she either was not capable of telling the truth or knowing what the truth was or that she was not being honest when she said that an assault took place."

Between Mangum's testimony (and despite the inconsistencies in her story, which he said was "not unusual in a sexual assault case"), Levicy's examination and testimony, and the evidence concerning David Evans's DNA on Mangum's fake fingernail, Nifong said he believed he was turning a winnable case over to Cooper. "To convince a jury that she had been sexually assaulted, I didn't think that would be difficult at all," he said. "I think the only question for the jury would have been whether she had correctly identified the people who assaulted her. I never viewed this as a case of whether or not she was assaulted. I viewed this as a case of eyewitness identification with very little corroborating evidence." He took additional comfort, he said, from the new revelation—from Wilson's interview—that Mangum (now) believed that it was David Evans who ejaculated in her face and then wiped her and himself clean with a towel that was then tossed in the hall outside the bathroom. "You look back to Dave Evans's DNA on a towel that was found at that residence from semen—that certainly is corroborative of what she told Linwood Wilson," he said. "I certainly never mentioned the existence of that towel to her. As far as I know, she does not today know that there was such a towel or that what was found on that towel."

On January 12, Mangum called Nifong and reconfirmed that she wanted to continue to pursue the case. Later that day, Nifong wrote to Coman, "there have been calls for me to remove myself, or for me to be removed, from the prosecution of these cases" from nearly the beginning. "I have resisted those calls because I did not believe that the circumstances of these cases fit your published criteria for accepting requests for assistance. Recent developments, however, have caused me to reevaluate that position." He cited the state bar's December 28 complaint against him. "I believe that, in addition to fueling any existing public perception that I have a conflict of interest in this matter, this filing has also created an actual conflict, as I am now personally the subject of an investigation and charges in this case." He noted that the North Carolina Conference on District Attorneys agreed and had called "for my recusal and the assignment of these cases to another prosecuting attorney." Nifong also explained to Coman that because of the "precariousness" of Mangum's "personal health," he had not been able to speak to her until the day before his letter to Coman. "After which she agreed that the case should be referred to you for prosecution," he continued. "She also assured me that she would give you her full cooperation in this matter." He concluded, fatefully, "For all of the foregoing reasons, I am hereby requesting that the Special Prosecutions Section of the North Carolina Department of Justice immediately assume full responsibility for the prosecution of the above-captioned cases."

Nifong's critics were thrilled. "He is a rogue prosecutor," Kevin Finnerty told the News & Observer. "He indicted these boys after he had exculpatory evidence clearing them, and we are thrilled that the attorney general will take over the case." Finnerty told the Chronicle, "The Attorney General's Office is going to bring very professional and objective oversight of the evidence in this case, which is something that had been missing from the outset." He said he was thinking about filing a civil suit against Nifong, and others, but that would wait until the criminal charges were resolved.

Other, more objective observers praised Nifong for making the tough decision to give up the case. "Excellent," said Tom Keith, the Forsyth County district attorney. "Good for him. Certainly, I think this is good news for Mike to have someone else take a look at the case, talk to the victim, give a fresh perspective. . . . That person might come up with the same conclusion he had. It's good for the court system, so that people have confidence in the justice system in Durham and in North Carolina. It's good all the way around." Garry Frank, the district attorney in Davidson County (and president of the Conference of District Attorneys), said, "The case was becoming about Mr. Nifong instead of the merits of the case. It's in the interest of justice that the case be evaluated and go forward or not go forward based on its merits, not on public opinion about the prosecutor."

Bill Bell, Durham's mayor, said not everyone in Durham would be happy with the decision. "That's a decision Mike had to make on his own," he said. "And to say why didn't he do it earlier, that's something Mike has to answer as well. I think people will be satisfied that the judicial process will move forward." Durham Police Chief Ron Hodge said Nifong's decision wouldn't affect the evidence that the Durham police had collected and would share with the attorney general. "I don't think it changes anything that we've done," he said. "It just means that we'll have to deal with a different attorney." At the James Joyce Irish Pub, a bar in Durham popular with Duke students, the reaction to Nifong's decision was mostly predictable. "It's about time," said Sarah Harden, from Cary, North Carolina. "Nifong's a joke. He ruined three lives just to get reelected." But, like Nifong, Scott Kushner, a graduate student at Duke, said he still believed something had happened in the bathroom at 610 North

Buchanan. "The thing that worries me," he said, "is that there's a whole lot of room between a rape and an innocent barbecue." Still, Kushner was no fan of Nifong's. "If Mike Nifong is taking donations for his legal defense fund, he should not call me," he said.

The next day, Coman called Nifong at home to tell him the attorney general had agreed to take over the case. What's more, Nifong said Coman assured him that he would be investigating the case along with Mary Winstead, another deputy attorney general; together they had fifty-six years of combined prose-cutorial experience, and would be taking it seriously.

At 2:30 that afternoon, Cooper held a press conference in Raleigh announc-ing his decision to take over the prosecution of the lacrosse case. He said the first step would be to get the complete case file from Nifong's office, read it and then begin the process of reviewing the evidence and speaking with the indicted players, as well as their attorneys, Mangum, Roberts, and the Durham and Duke police. "I wish I could tell you that this case will be resolved quickly, but it's my understanding there are numerous documents and other informa-tion in the district attorney's files and in the court record," he said. "Since we have not been involved in the investigation or the prosecution of these cases, all of the information will be new to our office. Any case with such serious criminal charges requires a careful and deliberate review. Our goal is to seek justice and truth while respecting the rights of everyone involved. We accept these cases with our eyes wide open to the evidence but with blinders on to all other distractions. In the final analysis, the path that these cases travel will be lighted by the law and the evidence alone."

Joe Cheshire and Wade Smith praised Cooper's decision to take control of the case. Smith especially, as one of the deans of the Raleigh bar, had close ties to Cooper and to his two special prosecutors. "I think people admire public officials who just rare back and do their job, just rare back and do what's right," Smith said, wasting little time in appealing to the new authority in the case. Cheshire told the *New York Times*, "For the first time, someone who is honest and objective and doesn't have an agenda will look at this case. We feel confi-dent that when they do, these young men will be exonerated."

On January 14, *60 Minutes* broadcast another segment about the Duke lacrosse case, this one featuring correspondent Lesley Stahl—she had taken the task of covering the case in the wake of Ed Bradley's death—interviewing Brian Meehan, the DSI lab director, as well as the parents of the three indicted players. Stahl pushed Meehan about whether it was an error not to include in his May 12 report the finding that DNA from men other than the lacrosse sus-pects was found in Mangum's underwear and rectum. "I said it was an error," Meehan replied. "It was an error in judgment on my part."

Stahl pressed Meehan to explain whether it was his decision alone to leave that information out of his report. "It was my decision based on my understanding of what was asked in this case from when the case began," he said. He added that Nifong never asked him to exclude the information from the final report, nor did he ask him to specifically include it. Meehan said he figured Nifong would eventually ask for that information to be included in a second report but that did not happen, until Judge Smith ordered that the complete file be turned over to the defense. Was Nifong lying? Stahl asked. "Well, I know that I told him," Meehan said. "I sat down in our conference room and went over all of the information in this case with him."

Stahl then pointed out how, without any DNA evidence, the case rested solely on Mangum's word. (She made no mention of the possibility that Evans's DNA was on Mangum's fake fingernails.) She explained that *60 Minutes* had uncovered the fact that Mangum had a "long psychological history" and had taken antipsychotic medications such as Depakote and Seroquel. Rae Evans, David Evans's mother and a former government relations executive at CBS, Inc., told Stahl she believed Nifong had abused Mangum, too, just like many of the men in her life. "When I'm trying to get over the rage I am thinking about, so deeply, this young woman who has been abused by men all her life," she said. "And nobody has abused her more than Mike Nifong." Evans was also angry with Duke and the Duke administration.

What about the all-day underage drinking and the hiring of strippers? Stahl wanted to know. Did the parents ever speak to their sons about those decisions? "It was a mistake, that was poor judgment," explained David Evans, Sr. "But then what you need to do is separate that from felony charges, talking about moral questions. These are felony charges. And if they did make a mistake, even though they did what many other students have done, they have paid for it dearly."

What did the parents have to say to those people—like Nifong, Mangum, and others—who alleged that "something must've happened" in the bathroom at 610 North Buchanan?

"Something happened—an incredible hoax was concocted that night," Kathy Seligmann responded.

"But don't you think there were people who aren't going to think it's a hoax, no matter what?" Stahl wondered.

"You know what?" Seligmann replied. "I believe you'll never change those people's minds. And what's so sad to me is, I almost get the feeling they're disappointed that something didn't happen. You don't have to feel sorry for our families. You don't have to pity these boys. We'll be okay. What we're asking [is], for justice's sake, look at the facts."

The Finnertys worried that the stigma of the accusations would never go away, even if Collin were found not guilty. "I think that in this day of Googling people," said Kevin Finnerty. "If you Google any of these three boys, you'll get . . . reams and reams and pages about this case." Added Mary Ellen Finnerty, "It will never go away for us or the boys. I mean, it might end. But it will have a lasting effect on all of us."

And what would they say to Nifong, if he walked into the room at that moment? "I guess I'd say, with a smile on my face, 'Mister Nifong, you've picked on the wrong families. You've picked on the wrong families that you've indicted. You've picked on the wrong family of the Duke lacrosse team. You've picked on the wrong family of Duke University, and you will pay every day for the rest of your life,'" Rae Evans said. More than 25 million people were watching.

On January 16, Coman sent Nifong a letter, in reponse to Nifong's January 12 letter, putting in writing what was already obvious: that Cooper had agreed to take over the lacrosse case. Late that afternoon, six boxes and two folders of files were scooped up by the SBI and brought to Cooper's office in Raleigh. "Our attorneys will immediately begin examining this material," Cooper explained. "These files contain a substantial amount of information, and we will work carefully to ensure a full and fair review." Nifong remembered that moment. "They just came over," he said, "and I showed them all the stuff, and they gave me a receipt for how many ever pages it was, and took stuff with them. And that, really, ends my official involvement with the case."

For Ruth Sheehan, the *News & Observer* columnist, Nifong did the right thing, for the wrong reason. "By turning over the miserable Duke lacrosse case to the Attorney General's Office for handling by a special prosecutor, he did the right thing," she wrote. "But he did so more than seven months later than he should have. And here's the stunner: he did it to save his own hide." Sheehan wrote that Nifong did not relinquish the case to acknowledge "any mistakes or misdeeds." Rather, Nifong was "feeling heat from the state bar, and a chorus of fellow DAs, regarding ethical violations. (Finally, we might see the wussy Bar take some action against a prosecutor. Stay tuned.) So forgive us, Mike, if we don't stand up and applaud." But it was not only Nifong for whom she had contempt. She was critical of the Durham investigators as well as, to a lesser degree, the lacrosse players "who I believe are innocent of the crimes with which they are charged but whose peer group's behavior on the night in question was appalling. . . . Strippers and racial slurs? If I found one of my sons was involved in such a scene, I'd jerk a knot in his neck." Then there was the performance of the parents on *60 Minutes*. "One came off as mighty arrogant as well," she wrote. "Nifong messed with the 'wrong families' indeed." As for Mangum, "she can't seem to get her story straight. She will never be punished sufficiently if her allegations are as bogus as they appear." She figured Brodhead had not acquitted himself well, nor had the Group of 88 professors. The only good guys? "There's Elmo, the cab driver whose testimony cleared Reade Seligmann in the accuser's first version of events," she concluded. "Oh, and the accuser's newborn baby, who, it's safe to say, will never play Duke lacrosse."

With little question that the legal and political momentum had shifted definitvely in favor of Seligmann, Finnerty, and Evans, Brodhead decided to sit for his first, extensive one-on-one interview with a print journalist, Rob Copeland of the *Chronicle*. To be sure, there were still demands in the blogosphere for Brodhead to resign. But he was feeling confident enough, for the first time in months, to answer pointed questions about his handling of the case.

Copeland questioned Brodhead's decision to fire Pressler and cancel the remainder of the 2006 lacrosse season. Brodhead said if he were to do it all over again, he would make the same decisions. "When the coach's resignation was announced on April 5, I tried to take great care to indicate that I was not fingering him as responsible for this," he said. "What I said was that given the history that we were in the middle of living through, if and when we started the replaying of lacrosse, it couldn't be on the same terms as in the past. We needed to close one chapter and start a new chapter. Changing the coach was just one of the necessities that came along with that. There was no pleasure to be taken in any of these decisions, but I think they were inevitable and it's all very well ten months later to look back and say, 'You should have done things differently.'" Copeland wondered why Brodhead had not fired Joe Alleva, the athletics director, or Larry Moneta and other Duke administrators who were aware of the bad behavior of the lacrosse players but had done nothing to curtail it. Brodhead ducked the question. "The party was a team event," he said. "It wasn't just a group of people; it was something convened by the captain of the team. The Pressler resignation was not my attempt to say that he was responsible for the situation. It was simply a resignation of the inevitability that, given where we were, we would need to make some differences to go forward with lacrosse." Why just pick on the lacrosse team and its coach, when underage drinking and "documented" examples of strippers dancing at frat parties were not all that unusual at Duke? "You said there are documented cases," Brodhead said. "I would say that to my knowledge, there are rumored cases. The difference between this and other cases is that this one came to our attention. . . . It's not my idea of how to run an undergraduate school to have dragnets and police officers to investigate people and trap them in bad behavior."

Copeland asked whether Brodhead thought some members of the Duke faculty had been too critical of the students and their behavior and had been too quick to condemn them? Critcizing professors is, of course, the third rail of university politics, as no less a figure than Larry Summers, the president of Harvard, discovered much to his dismay in 2006 when the Harvard faculty gave him a vote of no confidence. Summers resigned in June 2006, and there was little question that his dramatic departure from the nation's top university weighed on Brodhead. He answered Copeland diplomatically. "The president of a university has to exercise great care when commenting on the individual utterances of faculty members," Brodhead said. "Faculty members do not, and should not, speak for my pleasure or my approval. I was careful not to make statements that could make it seem like I was on one person's side rather than another, or to say, 'Watch out when you engage in free speech, because the president is watching.' . . . If faculty members talked about those underlying issues, that is their right. Quite a number of people have assured me that the [Group of 88] ad said the students were guilty, but if you go back and look, that's not what the ad says. I look forward to the day when we can all look back and draw a box around that whole situation and everything that arose from it and [say], let's come together as a community, show respect for each other, find ways to engage and listen to people who don't already agree with us."

The reaction around Duke to Brodhead's public comments was mixed. Those, like John Burness, who were paid to burnish the university's reputation were laudatory of Brodhead. Chemistry professor Steven Baldwin, who had argued in October that firing Pressler was a mistake, said he doubted the sincerity of Brodhead's recent decisions, for instance to reinstate Seligmann and Finnerty. "Cynically, you wonder how sincere they are," he said. "I've heard people suggest that they're positioning themselves for possible litigation. I don't want to be viewed as an attack dog, but . . . I just wonder what Nifong would have done if he thought that the things he was doing were, in fact, not supported by the university."

On January 22, during an hour-long speech to students at New York University about public service, North Carolina Governor Mike Easley, a former state attorney general and the person who had appointed Nifong district attorney in April 2005, was highly critical of Nifong, not only for his handling of the lacrosse case but also for his decision to run for district attorney in 2006. Easley said he had selected Nifong to fill the district attorney's seat in Durham—after Jim Hardin became a state judge—on the recommendations of Hardin and Ron Stephens, another predecessor (and the first judge in the lacrosse case) and because Nifong had told him he would not run for the office outright in 2006. "I almost un-appointed him when he decided to run," Easley said. "I rate that as probably the poorest appointment I've [made]."

After the speech, an audience member asked Easley to evaluate Nifong's performance in handling the rape case. He said Nifong had done a poor job. "You don't need me to tell you that," he said. Easley criticized Nifong for his initial statements about the case. "That's how all this mess got started," he said. "He challenged the defense lawyers by talking about the case, calling the kids 'hooligans.'" The defense lawyers were cornered, and had to fight back. "You can't comment on that except in the courtroom," Easley continued, "and when you do, then the defense lawyers have to stand up for their client. Then it's on. All the rules are out the window, then you have chaos, and that's why the rules are so important and that's what you got in this case. It's chaotic. It looks bad for North Carolina. It looks bad for the DA's office. It looks bad for the criminal justice system in general."

Easley's talk, which was recorded by NYU and then released, caught Nifong off-guard. Neither he nor his attorney, David Freedman, would comment about Easley's observations. And the governor would not, either. Years later, Nifong expressed no love for Easley, who in 2010 became the first governor, or former governor, of North Carolina, to plead guilty to a felony, when he agreed he failed to report on a required campaign disclosure form that he had accepted a $1,600 helicopter ride with a supporter in October 2006. Easley paid a $1,000 fine and $153 in court costs. "He pled guilty to a felony and never got disbarred," Nifong said. "He got his license suspended for a few years." (Ironically, Joe Cheshire was Easley's attorney during the proceedings and Judge Smith, then a Wake County judge, accepted Easley's plea agreement.)

On the morning of January 24, reporters swarmed around Nifong and his two attorneys as they entered the headquarters of the state bar in downtown Raleigh for Nifong's first procedural hearing in the civil case against him. On the way in, Rodney Tillery, a Raleigh resident, shouted to Nifong, "It's going to be all right, Mr. Nifong." He thanked Tillery. Once inside, Nifong sat at the defense table, hands folded in front of him, throughout the thirty-minute hearing. He stared straight ahead, never once looking at Katherine Jean or Douglas Brocker, the two lawyers prosecuting him.

The chairman of the three-member Disciplinary Hearing Commission, Lane Williamson—a classmate of Nifong's at UNC law school—noted that "the defendant, Mr. Nifong, is present." Williamson and the other two commissioners, Sharon Alexander, a lawyer, and R. Mitchell Tyler, a nonlawyer, acted as both judge and jury for Nifong's hearing. At the end of the hearing, when the new, amended complaint was shared with Nifong—he had already been aware of it—Williamson said he would not impose a gag order on Nifong or the lawyers. "I simply ask that you use your good judgment and discretion," he said. Outside, Nifong had nothing to say to reporters. But David Freedman said, "Any time any charges are filed with the state bar, they're all serious, and we want to make sure we handle them properly." To the *New York Times*, Freedman denied that Nifong had engaged in "any sort of intentional unethical conduct," stating that he had had "a flawless record" for ethics in his twenty-eight years as a prosecutor and that he had "great confidence the panel will render a just and fair verdict."

Nonetheless, as the *News & Observer* noted presciently, "The hunter is now the hunted."

CHAPTER FIFTEEN

"She Believed Many of the Stories She Was Telling"

As others had, David Rademeyer, a Duke junior and *Chronicle* columnist, hoped the increasing passions on all sides would somehow cool. "Caricatures are remarkable things," he wrote at the end of January. "It now seems obvious that the bright, well-spoken young men from good families were set up by that lying black stripper, as it once did that a poor single mother reduced to escort work to pay her college bills was kidnapped, sexually assaulted and raped by the drunk, rich, white hooligans. Many on both sides of the issue have attempted to deconstruct, unpackage or debunk (verbs vary with ideology) these stereotypes, often raising the hackles of the other side in the process." He invoked Karla Holloway's "famous" conclusion from the previous summer that "white innocence means black guilt" and "men's innocence means women's guilt" and wondered why. "Why is it that, at every stage, the presumption of innocence is so difficult?" he asked. He wrote that it was "only natural" to sympathize with the victim and loathe those seen as her attackers and explained why "there was such a frenzy of condemnation for the lacrosse team" and why "there is such loathing" now for Nifong and Mangum. "We will never know exactly what happened that fateful night," he concluded.

Yet there seemed to be no waning of the passion. In early February, six members of the Duke faculty—five of whom had signed the Group of 88 ad—convened a panel discussion titled "Shut Up and Teach?" where they refused to be intimidated into silence by their critics, who argued that they had not been sufficiently supportive of the lacrosse players during their legal ordeal. "We're talking about decades of rhetorical tarring and feathering of faculty who step outside the confines of their research or their classroom," said Wahneema Lubiano, an associate professor of African and African-American studies and one of the organizers of the Group of 88. The professors on the panel spoke about the "thousands" of pieces of hate mail that the Duke faculty had received after some of them expressed their views about the behavior that had occurred at 610 North Buchanan. "There are all different forms of fear-making," said Diane Nelson, an associate professor of cultural anthropology. "But eventually you become the change you were looking for." Added Pedro Lasch, an assistant professor of the practice of visual arts, "Crisis historically has often been critical to the production of new knowledge. When we are engaging in knowledge, we have to be listening." The panelists insisted they would not be quiet. "It seems to me that the only way for professors to be professors is to enter the public discourse," said Maurice Wallace, an associate professor of English and African and African-American Studies.

A week later, the *Chronicle of Higher Education* published a story about the continuing intellectual debate at Duke caused by the lacrosse scandal. On one side were the professors who had signed the Group of 88 ad and the eighty-seven faculty members who had signed the January follow-up ad refusing to rescind the April ad, while on the other side were the seventeen economics professors who had signed the letter to the *Chronicle* expressing their regret about the perception that some professors were prejudiced against some students. There was the sense that the Group of 88 had engaged in an unwarranted rush to judgment of the lacrosse players while the economics professors were jumping on the anti-Nifong bandwagon now that it was convenient. It was all a fine mess. "Faculty members aren't known for their thick skin, but at Duke sensitivities are running especially high," the newspaper observed. "Nearly a year after a rape allegation against three men's lacrosse players became a news-media maelstrom, the controversy shows little sign of abating. The case against the players appears to be falling apart, the original prosecutor has stepped down and the accuser has changed her story several times. The protesters who banged pots and hung 'Wanted' posters picturing the players have gone silent. But as the case has dragged on, the spotlight has shifted from rowdy jocks to outspoken professors. Countless columnists, talk-show hosts, and bloggers have used the incident as an opportunity to lambaste professors at the elite university, in some instances mocking their scholarship or hurling racial epithets."

Wahneema Lubiano told the *Chronicle of Higher Education* that she thought the contents of the Group of 88 ad were taken out of context and exploited by overzealous bloggers eager to come to the defense of the three indicted players. "In the moment when the ad came out, I did not hear from one colleague that there was something wrong with the ad," she said. "To some extent, what we're talking about it is how it has been read in the moment of organized agitation." Karla Holloway, who had originally come up with the idea for the ad, while Lubiano was the scribe, shared with the paper one of the more vile e-mails she was sent as a result of her outspoken stand: "gives me a check honky, i's got a lowe iq and me's a full profssah." Both Holloway and Lubiano insisted they would not change one word in the ad, had they the opportunity to do it over again. There was no "rush to judgment," Holloway maintained. The phrase "what happened to this young woman?" in the ad does not refer, necessarily, to her being raped, she said. "Something did happen on Buchanan," she said.

"A party happened. Drunkenness happened. If you want to read 'happening' in one particular way, that's the bias you bring to your reading."

The *Chronicle of Higher Education* reporters spoke with some professors who had signed the original ad, and would again, some who didn't sign the original ad but who signed the second ad in its defense, some who regretted signing the first ad and some, like chemistry professor Steven Baldwin, who remained irritated with his fellow professors for signing any ad. In an opinion column in October, Baldwin spared no punches. "My biggest concern has always been with Duke's treatment of the student athletes at the center of the storm," he wrote. "These kids were abandoned by their university. At least one of the indicted students, perhaps all three, was [forced off] Duke property. They were denied the presumption of innocence, despite the mounting evidence that the case against them is made of smoke and mirrors and is fatally flawed procedurally. They have been pilloried by their faculty and scorned by the administration. They are pariahs. . . . The faculty who publicly savaged the character and reputations of specific men's lacrosse players last spring should be ashamed of themselves. They should be tarred and feathered, ridden out of town on a rail and removed from the academy. Their comments were despicable." Even though Baldwin was later criticized for his choice of words, he was not backing down, either. "My personal view is that their social agenda was at the forefront of their thinking," he said of the Group of 88 professors. "I think there was a collision between political correctness and due process, and I think political correctness won."

Paul Haagen, the law professor and head of the Academic Council, had made a proposal the previous year—which many of his colleagues did not even know of—whereby Duke professors would spend time with athletic coaches in order to try to gain a better understanding of what they were hoping to accomplish at Duke. A professor would get paired with a sports team, meet the coaches and players, attend practices, and travel with the team to away games. He said it was important—if the two hemispheres of the Duke brain were to work together—that professors understand the athletes' mindset. About eighty professors signed up for the program, and Haagen said he thought it had helped diffuse tensions. But to show that no good deed goes unpunished in such a highly charged atmosphere, two professors—Frederick Nijhout, a biology professor, and Richard Hain, a math professor—thought Haagen had his calculus exactly wrong. It was the coaches who should be exposed to the professors and sit in on their classes and labs, not vice versa. They wrote and distributed a parody of Haagen's idea. "They called us immature," Nijhout said about his colleagues, and he was surprised to learn that Haagen's idea had actually been implemented.

Then there was Michael Gustafson, an assistant professor of electrical and computer engineering and an outspoken opponent of the Group of 88.

When he came across an eyebrow-raising cultural anthropology course—"The Hook-Up Culture at Duke," the description of which read in part: "What does the lacrosse scandal tell us about power, difference, and raced, classed, gendered, and sexed normativity in the US?"—he e-mailed Provost Lange, in disgust. Lange suggested Gustafson speak with the professor, Anne Allison, the chairman of the cultural anthropology department and a signatory of the Group of 88 ad. At first, Allison was offended by Gustafson's e-mail. "The very query seemed hostile," she said. "I mean, I'm not asking him about his class." But after the two professors sat down and discussed the course at length, each of them expressed optimism that the conversation had helped. "If this discussion had happened the way discussions have been happening, I would have written a letter to the newspaper, and she would have written a letter, and there would have been an escalation," Gustafson said. "It was better to actually communicate with each other." Allison remained a bit unsure. "He heard me," she said, "but did he really hear me? I don't know." In any event, she didn't change the class. "It was a small victory for civility, but the war over the lacrosse scandal is far from over," the *Chronicle* reporters concluded.

There seemed to be no letup in the backlash against those who sided early and often against the lacrosse players. On Sunday, February 4, starting at 11 a.m., a group of about a hundred people supporting the three indicted lacrosse players participated in a community walk from the Durham County Courthouse—Nifong's office—to Koskinen Stadium, the home of the Duke lacrosse team, which was practicing in anticipation of its opening game against Dartmouth on February 24. The marchers carried Nifong's campaign signs, with his name crossed out, and wore buttons with messages such as "Innocent Until Proven Innocent" and "Fantastic Lies." The walk organizers also handed out wristbands with "Duke Lacrosse 2006" on one side and "Innocent! #6, #13, #45" on the other. Madge Dooley, a nurse at Duke University Medical Center, said she was walking to protest Nifong's handling of the case. "I just think it was a travesty of justice from the very beginning," she said, "that what they are doing to these boys—doing to their families—is just terrible. Regardless of how it turns out, they've ruined their lives. They've ruined their reputations." Courtney Kremers, a Duke senior and the girlfriend of a former Duke lacrosse player, agreed with Dooley. "We want to send a message that injustice has occurred," she said. Marge Enberg and her husband participated in the more-than-three-mile walk because they believed, like the others, that Nifong had mishandled the case. Their son, Jon Enberg, had played lacrosse at Duke a few years before and was now serving in Iraq, in the Navy. "I'm more disappointed than angry," she said. "You believe so much in the justice system, and so far it hasn't worked out the way it was supposed to." When the group arrived at Koskinen Stadium and saw the lacrosse team practicing, they faced the team and applauded. They chanted "Let's Go, Duke!" for a while before dispersing.

In the absence of genuine developments in the lacrosse case, the media began to fill the void with curiosities. There was news that the nonprofit legal defense fund for the players—the Association for Truth and Fairness—had figured it would need to raise $5 million to pay for legal fees if the case went to trial. Approximately $3 million had already been spent. "Unfortunately, that is accurate," Kevin Finnerty told the *News & Observer*. The nonprofit raised $750,000 of the money needed and was looking for more. The players' former teammates sent around a letter asking for donations. "As you can imagine, these three families have been taxed to their emotional and financial limits," they wrote, "Your support will convey to these families that you stand by them in their fight for truth and justice." In one creative donation, George Jennison, the father of lacrosse player Jay Jennison, put up for auction four tickets to the Duke–UNC basketball game at Cameron Indoor Stadium on February 7. As the bidding was nearing $7,000 for the tickets, Jennison decided he wanted to keep them, bid $7,600 and then donated $10,000 to the legal defense fund. He gave the tickets to his sons. "Whatever the rest of us have spent on this just pales to what the three accused have spent," Jennison said. "To me, that's just one of the tragedies of this whole thing—the financial burden placed on these families." (Duke lost the game, 79–73.)

Then two of the grand jurors who had agreed to indict Seligmann, Finnerty, and Evans in 2006 appeared anonymously on ABC's *Good Morning America*. "Knowing what I know now and all that's been broadcast on the news and in the media, I think I would have definitely . . . made a different decision," the first grand juror said. "I don't think I could have made a decision to go forward with the charges that were put before us. I don't think those charges would have been the proper charges, based on what I know now." The second grand juror said he did not regret his decision to indict the players but was not sure what had happened that March night. "I don't know for sure whether she was raped, you know, because of everything that . . . came out," he said. "I'm not sure, to tell you the truth." They were both bothered by Mangum's December 21 conversation with Linwood Wilson where she said she could no longer recall if she had been raped. "What do you mean you're not sure whether you got raped or not?" the second grand juror said. "That . . . didn't add up."

Given that grand jurors pledge not to speak publicly about what happens inside the grand jury room, at least one North Carolina judge—Orlando Hudson, senior resident Superior Court judge in Durham—was furious and considered finding the two jurors in contempt and sentencing them to thirty days in jail. "What the grand jurors did was clearly against the laws of the state of North Carolina," he said. "The grand jury is to discuss nothing about what went on in the grand jury proceedings, nor anything about the grand jury proceedings." In the end, Hudson decided not to punish the grand jurors for fear of discouraging people from serving in that role.

Then there were the requisite stories about how, on February 24, under the direction of new coach John Danowski, the revived Duke lacrosse team—all thirty-five players of which had opted to return to Duke rather than transfer— would open its 2007 season against Dartmouth. In an unscripted comment to *USA Today*, Danowski said the behavior of the lacrosse players on the previous year's team might have been unduly influenced by the behavior they witnessed on Wall Street during their summer jobs. "They're around forty- and fifty-year-old men all summer," he said. "During that time they see that for those men, hiring strippers and dancers is acceptable behavior. But the rules of private behavior on Wall Street are different than the rules at college. I'm teaching values every day. I'm holding them accountable to their team- mates. These guys have great futures ahead of them. They're the next masters of the universe." The new coach insisted that his players attend every class and demanded to know immediately about any infraction, no matter how slight. "I get the first phone call," he said. "I don't care if it's 3 a.m. There will be hell to pay if I don't get the first call. I'll go to bat for them as long as I know the truth." He said there had been "five or six very minor incidents, some of them ludicrous," such as beer cans found in a hallway. "They're under a micro- scope," Danowski said, "and they know that." He said the team's early morning workouts—some as early as 6:30 a.m., four days a week—were not a "punish- ment" but rather "a way to find out who was committed. . . . You get that when you're out working as the sun is rising. . . . On the field, you see the schoolboy giddiness coming out. They've got a stick and a helmet and they're running around. My fear is that they are trying to be too perfect. They're feeling guilty about what happened, and they'd like to go back in time before Coach Pressler lost his job."

For the Dartmouth game, the lacrosse players intended to wear warm-up shirts with the numbers 6, 13, and 45 on them, as well as sweatbands and stick- ers with those numbers. Many of the players also wrote "MP" on their helmets for their former coach and wore a sticker to remember Jimmy Regan, a 2002 Duke graduate and lacrosse player who had been killed in northern Iraq on February 9 after his vehicle was struck by an explosive device. And just days before the opening game, came reports—confirmed by Danowski—that it was unlikely that either Seligmann or Finnerty would return to Duke. The *Brown Daily Herald* reported that Seligmann was looking to enroll at Brown, while Danowski said he had been working with Kevin Finnerty to find a new place for his son to play lacrosse and finish his college education.

Meanwhile, it hardly seemed like Mike Nifong's political and legal situation could get any more precarious—until on February 9, it did. That day, Beth Brewer—a longtime Durham County resident with no connection to Duke who had been determined to drive Nifong from the District Attorney's Office (she was chair of the Recall Nifong—Vote Cheek political action committee)—filed a civil affidavit with the clerk of the Durham County Superior Court, charging Nifong with "willful misconduct" and "conduct prejudicial to the administration of justice" that brought the District Attorney's Office "into disrepute." In calling for a Superior Court judge to remove Nifong from office, Brewer cited a North Carolina statute regarding the removal of district attorneys. "Recent revelations show further, much more serious misconduct including statements made by Mr. Nifong in court in knowing contradiction of the truth," Brewer, a billing manager at Verizon, said in her press release accompanying her filing. "There can be no faith in our justice system with a district attorney who, in a very public case, conspires to withhold exculpatory evidence from the defense and repeatedly makes misrepresentations and false statements to the court and opposing counsel about the matter."

Brewer's affidavit replicated many of the state bar's criticisms of Nifong, from the charge of withholding "exculpatory evidence" to making a plethora of public statements that prejudiced the case. As the defense attorneys had, she also criticized Nifong for the photographic lineup used by Mangum to identify her alleged attackers, and for failing to interview Mangum, and for refusing to meet with defense attorneys about the alibis of their clients.

As much as Nifong might have wished to ignore Brewer's seemingly gratuitous affidavit, he could not. By state law, Judge Orlando Hudson—the man who had just sworn Nifong into office a month earlier—had thirty days to review the complaint. Because many of its allegations parallelled those of the state bar, he intended to postpone any decision on the complaint until after Nifong's state bar trial, in June, and would issue a stay to that effect. Brewer was not happy. "I don't think Orlando Hudson can put it off," she said. "I think the law says he has to [adhere to the time limits]." Even so, she figured Nifong would soon be gone. "I have confidence that the Bar will remove him from office," she said, "but 7A-66"—the state statute—"will remove him quicker."

Irving Joyner, the NCCU law professor, said that by design it would not be easy for Nifong to be removed from office. "What they will have to present is evidence of malfeasance," he said, "more that just a personal disagreement, a disagreement with legal strategy, which is within the province of the district attorney. I've not seen anything that would warrant a judge doing that, although clearly a lot of things involved with this case are controversial. At this stage, Mike Nifong is an easy person to beat up on. . . . Everybody's going to do it."

Nifong issued a statement that his critics could not help but find terribly ironic. "I'm looking forward to having the case heard and having the opportunity to have my side told publicly," he said. "I would really hope that everybody would be willing to withhold judgment until that procedure that is already in place has been given an opportunity to work."

• • •

Despite the Duke community's heightened sensitivity to issues of sexual misconduct, the alleged rape case had not prevented rape from again occurring on the campus. On Saturday night, February 10, Katharine Rouse, an eighteen-year-old Duke freshman from Long Island, went to an off-campus party in Durham at 405 Gattis Street, a house rented by a number of Duke students affiliated with the Phi Beta Sigma fraternity, one of the predominantly black student fraternities at Duke. Rouse, who was white, had a 3.5 grade-point-average during her first semester at Duke, despite working two part-time jobs to help pay the cost of her tuition. She was also involved with Dance Black, a student organization that used dance to celebrate African-American culture. An invitation to the Phi Beta Sigma party, sent to about three hundred people on Facebook, listed the hosts as "Phi Beta Sigma and Gattis St. Residents." About a hundred people showed up for the party—not all of them Duke students—and enjoyed an alcohol-based punch spiked with Everclear, a pure grain alcohol illegal in many states.

As the alcohol flowed and it got later, Rouse started dancing and making out with Michael Jermaine Burch, a twenty-one-year-old black man from Durham, who told people at the party his name was "Chris" and that he was not affiliated with Duke. He was wearing black jeans, a long white T-shirt, and a Do-Rag. At 2:45 a.m., Rouse went to the bathroom, and then Burch followed her in and locked the door. They kissed some more, but Rouse told Burch she did not want to have sex with him. Burch did not heed Rouse's request and forcibly raped her. "Once inside the bathroom, [Burch] forced [Rouse] to the ground causing her to hit her head on the sink," according to a search warrant issed on February 19. "He then sexually assaulted her." A witness at the party—a friend of Burch's—told Durham police, "During the course of the party everyone was dancing and having a good time. At one point during the party, Michael Burch began dancing with and getting close to a white female wearing a striped polo shirt (victim)." The witness said he "turned around for a minute" and "when he looked back he saw Michael Burch enter the bathroom and close the door. Burch was in the bathroom for a long time and he could hear a thumping noise coming from the room. Since Burch was taking so long, he decided [to] leave the party and go home."

Two friends of Rouse's who were at the party told police that they were "unable to find" Rouse for "approximately one hour" during the party, when they saw Burch leave the bathroom. A few minutes later, they saw Rouse leave the bathroom "and started crying." Rouse then told her friends "what had happened." Rouse sat in the car while her friend, Nicole Feeling, went back into the house and tried to find out who Burch was and how to contact him. She learned he was a student at Durham Technical Community College, allowing police to track him down.

Rouse returned to her dormitory. She was understandably upset. At 4:51

a.m., other residents of the dorm called the Duke police and reported what had happened to Rouse. The Duke police arrived and took Rouse to the Duke Medical Center emergency room, where she met with a SANE nurse and a rape kit was administered. The Duke police informed Duke's Student Affairs Office that Rouse had been raped, and shortly thereafter both Sue Wasiolek and Larry Moneta became aware of the situation. The Duke police called the Durham police, who quickly took over the investigation, identified Burch and a week later, armed with a search warrant, went to his home in Durham, which he shared with his mother. They collected a black bag with clothes in it, including several white shirts, fifteen unopened condoms, one condom wrapper, and one dietary supplement pill. Burch soon pled guilty to raping Rouse, as well as to other charges, and was sentenced to about six years in prison.

Although the prosecution was straightforward, the incident took a strange twist. On February 13, Moneta suspended a Duke student who lived at 405 Gattis Street after he was caught throwing "drugs" out the window of the party house when the police were searching it in the aftermath of the party. That night, Moneta received an e-mail from Aubrey McClendon, an alumnus of the class of 1981 and the billionaire chairman and CEO of Chesapeake Energy Corporation. McClendon, who was one of Duke's largest benefactors, told Moneta in the e-mail, "Larry, this house is my house. I own this house. Here are the names of the renters. . . . Let me know what else I can do to help." Moneta immediately forwarded McClendon's e-mail to the Duke vice president for fundraising and development, along with the message "Shit." He then sent McClendon's e-mail to Brodhead with the message "Unbelievable."

According to allegations in a suit Rouse brought against Duke, the university curtailed its investigation into what role the fraternity had in sponsoring a party where spiked punch was served to underage students and where one of them had been raped. "After receiving the e-mail from Mr. McClendon, Duke did not conduct any subsequent investigation of the 405 Gattis Street party," the judge wrote in her order dismissing Rouse's lawsuit against Duke. "At some point, Assistant Dean of Students Todd Adams spoke with the president of the fraternity, who said that the fraternity did not host the party and that the majority of the members of the fraternity were not involved in the event. Adams concluded that Phi Beta Sigma had not hosted the party, and he apparently terminated his investigation. There does not appear to have been a formal Greek Judicial Board investigation of Phi Beta Sigma, and the Board did not sanction any fraternities or students."

During one of the court hearings related to Rouse's unsuccessful lawsuit against Duke, her attorney, Bob Ekstrand—the Durham lawyer was still representing many of the nonindicted lacrosse players in their suit against Duke—claimed that when the Duke administration discovered that McClendon owned the house where the rape occurred, it ended the investigation into what happened. Ekstrand claimed, among other things, that a "hostile environment" had been created at Duke. "In response to a horrific rape in a bathroom at a fraternity party where Katie was first served alcohol spiked with Everclear," Ekstrand said, "the university decided, apparently, that it would be better to just not do anything and not learn anything about this and not make waves with their biggest donor . . . worth $2.1 billion. He has three buildings named after him, all of them constructed around the time of this event."

Compounding the tension caused by Rouse's rape—which would have been bad enough even if it hadn't happened in the middle of the lacrosse saga—were the comments Moneta was reported to have made to a local television station in the days after the party. "It's part of the reality of collegiate life and of experimentation," he said, "and some of the consequences of students not necessarily always being in the right place at the right time. This happens around the country. Duke is no different in that respect. Part of the problem is who is defining social norms. . . . TV shows and popular music celebrate drugs, drinking, and casual sex. Students seem to want an accelerated approach to relationships so that it becomes utilitarian." It was not difficult to see why Rouse might want to transfer from Duke after her rape, the university's lame effort at an investigation, and Moneta's public comment.

Meanwhile, the lacrosse case continued. On February 21, at around 11:30 a.m., Mangum met with Coman and Winstead, the investigators for the attorney general. Mangum had been in favor of the case moving away from Nifong. "It was not because I did not like Mike Nifong," she explained in a subsequent interview. "I believed that things were so out of hand that the only way to come to any conclusion was to have a special prosecutor." She told the investigators about her three children: Richard, age seven, Ariana, six, and the newborn, Kayla Murchison. Mangum said she was enrolled at NCCU, was taking thirteen credits that semester and thought she was twenty-one credits short of her degree. She said she wanted to be a nurse. She told the investigators that her doctor at UNC, Dr. Roberts, had prescribed Depakote and Seriquil for her after she had entered the psychiatric hospital Holly Hill, in July 2005, because she was depressed after losing her job because of a disagreement with her boss. She said she took Flexiril for back pain. She told them she started dancing at Platinum Pleasures on February 25, 2006, and worked for the "escort agency" after she met a woman at a Burger King who told her about it. She said she only had a "problem" with "Passion" at Platinum Pleasures because she had "danced with one of her boyfriends." She said she had last danced at Platinum Pleasures on either March 20 or March 25 of the previous year—in any event, soon after the alleged March 13 assault—for an "album release party."

For her part, Mangum thought this first meeting with Coman and Winstead went well. Although she was a bit nervous, she thought they were both professional and were "representing me" and she did not expect them to be "hostile" toward her. She said Winstead introduced herself, said she knew Nifong and had "confidence in his ability as a district attorney." Mangum thought Winstead "was going to do everything she could to help." Coman, Mangum thought, was "more matter-of-fact" and focused on what needed to be done "to move forward." He told her, "The most important thing to me is to say you don't know rather than to guess when I ask you a question." Mangum said she had always taken that approach when talking about the events of March 13 and that she would continue with Winstead and Coman. "I was feeling good about how things went," she said.

There was huge anticipation on campus, and in the media, for Duke lacrosse's February 24 opening game against Dartmouth. The game, which was to be nationally televised on ESPNU, gave the fans who packed Koskinen Stadium the chance to express their unmitigated support for the players and the team. "Saturday at Duke will be the most scrutinized regular season college lacrosse game ever," Quint Kessenich wrote at *Inside Lacrosse*. "The entire sports nation will be on notice. This game transcends the sport. It's the rebirth of Duke lacrosse, and it promises to be an event of unusual magnitude."

But Moneta wanted to make sure the enthusiasm for the team's return to the playing field did not get out of hand. "We expect the game to attract considerable attention from reporters, both local and national," Moneta wrote in an e-mail to students on February 20. "Given this reality, it's important that we demonstrate outstanding sportsmanship and appropriate fan behavior." Moneta said the Duke athletics department "has requested that no signs be brought into Koskinen Stadium. Paint your faces but leave your posters and other signage at home." He added thoughts such as "I trust I can count on all of you to show up in your Duke blue" and "We have much to gain as a community with our best effort and even more to lose with our worst."

Moneta's e-mail raised some hackles. Two Duke graduate students, Leigh Campoamor and Kinohi Nishikawa, questioned whether Moneta's assumption was accurate that the campus was ready to move on from the March 13 party. "We reject Moneta's false claim to consensus," they wrote in a letter to the *Chronicle*. "Superficial measures such as putting on our 'Duke blue' cannot heal the deep fissures in our community. We believe that these fissures should be addressed through sincere and respectful dialogue and with the acknowledgment that no one involved in this situation is exempt from criticism."

And despite most everyone's best efforts to assume the case had been resolved, it had not been. *Sports Illustrated* visited Duke days before the opening game to watch the team practice, giving writer S. L. Price the chance to recount where the case stood against Seligmann, Finnerty, and Evans—none of whom were even playing, of course. Even with Danowski, the new coach, Price wrote that "the program remains shaded by anger, doubt, even survivors' guilt. 'Everybody feels almost helpless,' Danowski says . . . [and] any hope of turning the experience into motivational fodder 'is jaded by the fact that three of our close friends are undergoing a horrible experience,' says senior cocaptain Ed Douglas. 'For me to try to find a good thing in this whole process seems almost smug.'" Price also pointed out what few were willing to admit, at least publicly: that the team's behavior on the night of March 13 (and before) had cost Pressler his job. "That's why they are keeping a lower social profile on campus this year, why the seniors have pledged themselves to what Douglas calls 'a sober preseason.' That's why, just minutes before they walked out to practice last Thursday, Sue Pressler, Mike's wife, addressed the team in the locker room, something she never did in all the years years her husband was coach. . . . She told the players that the Pressler family has never blamed them for what happened, told them she loved them, told them it was time to stop running and be proud again."

In the end, everyone behaved, and Duke beat Dartmouth 17–11 before a packed stadium of 6,845 fans. The Duke police issued no citations. Alex Senior, a sophomore in the Delta Sigma Phi fraternity, told the *Chronicle* that the fraternity had decided to have a party near its house, rather than tailgate by Koskinen Stadium as fraternities had done in years past. "We got an e-mail from Larry Moneta saying they'll arrest us if we're caught drinking, and nobody wants to be caught in public throwing down booze," he said. Brodhead himself was happy. "It was a great crowd, a beautiful afternoon, and it was great to have the team playing again," he gushed. Moneta, too, was pleased not to see any protestors. "I just saw a crowd of students thrilled to be there to support the team." He was glad that the fans heeded his request to behave responsibly. "They exhibited a terrific fan loyalty," he said.

George Vescey, the *New York Times* sports columnist, also attended the game. He noted that despite the victory, he saw bumper stickers in the parking lot that read, "Free the Duke 3" and realized that "no matter what comes out of the continuing legal case, the players have learned that some people right around them were quick to judge them not only as possible witnesses to an alleged crime but also as arrogant." Vescey watched as John Danowski told the lacrosse players that "party boys do not win national titles" and put them "through body-fat tests that horrified them into cutting way back on liquid calories." The players were also committed to doing five hundred hours of community service. "Critics will see the volunteerism as cosmetic, something to obscure whatever happened last March," Vescey observed. "The players may never totally undo what they set in motion. Even for achievers at an elite university, that's not a bad lesson to take out of college."

On February 28, Nifong responded to the state bar's amended complaint. In forty-nine pages, Nifong's attorneys David Freedman and Dudley Witt reiterated, in legalese, the answers that Nifong himself had given to the state bar on December 28 and January 16. He admitted to making many of the public statements early on about the case cited by the state bar, but his lawyers said he did so only because he wanted to encourage witnesses to come forward and because he wanted to reassure the public that he was personally taking charge of the case. He denied he was trying to sway public opinion about the case and had spoken about the players generally, as opposed to any specific individual. Nifong "did not fully understand the extent of the national media interest" in the story when he made his first group of comments, his lawyers argued. After April 3, they wrote, Nifong limited his comments to "arguments he made in open court, press releases issued from his office, and responses to questions directed at him at public forums he attended in Durham County." Nifong's lawyers asked the state bar to dismiss the charge that he withheld "exculpatory evidence" from the defense because, they argued, he had turned over the evidence in toto well before a trial date had been scheduled, and in any event he was not required by the state law to summarize the findings of the DNA testing if instead he turned over the entire dossier of the DNA evidence to the defense, as he eventually did once the court ordered him to do so.

While asking for the state bar's complaint against him to be thrown out, Nifong pointed out that if, instead, the grievance panel found that he had violated any "Rule of Professional Conduct," it was "not intentional, nor the result of a dishonest or selfish motive, but rather that any discipline entered [should] be based upon a finding that" such violation "was the result of a mistaken belief that any of the actions taken by defendant were not prohibited by said rules."

In interviews with the media, Witt said, "There have been a lot of people rushing to judgment on this case and the underlying case. It's important to allow a full hearing on this." He told the *New York Times*, "I think it will do everybody good to sit back and allow the process to work." But Thomas Metzloff, a Duke law professor, said he thought Nifong's response to the state bar complaint missed the point. "This is a very different type of case," he said. "This is now the state bar saying, 'You did not provide the information you should have provided the way you should have provided it.'" He said Nifong's argument about his public comments was also a weak one. "All members of that team suffered potential media scrutiny and suffered the kind of injury that the rule is meant to prevent," Metzloff said.

As if the lacrosse scandal had not ruffled enough feathers at Duke already, the long-awaited recommendations of Brodhead's Campus Culture Initiative threw the university into further turmoil at the end of February, especially since some of the proposed changes to campus life—moving frats and other "selective" living groups off West Campus and a concerted effort to curtail underage drinking—would likely never have surfaced without the events of

March 13. There were other proposed changes as well: raising the admission standards for athletes and decreasing their practice and travel schedules; reorienting "campus life" to reduce the role that alcohol played in the social scene and establishing "attractive venues" around campus "for controlled distribution of alcohol" to students older than twenty-one; requiring that undergraduates take a course on "racial, ethnic, class, religious, and/or sexual/gender difference in the United States"; hiring more women and racially diverse professors and encouraging all professors to spend more time teaching and socializing with undergraduates; and expanding residential, dining, and social facilities on both the West and East campuses to allow for greater interaction and a way to socialize outside the fraternities and changing the "philosophy" of dining services on campus "so it isn't run as a business" but rather as a way to encourage social interaction across groups of students. The committee behind the recommendations, while appreciating Duke's position of "prominence in the top echelon of the nation's research universities," nevertheless found that it had come "to better understand how Duke is experienced differentially by different members of its community, that there are often pressures for conformity which work against our institutional vision as an inclusive academic community, and that engaging the notion of 'difference' more deeply and directly will enable the University to accelerate its rise to the top."

For his part, Brodhead said that none of the report's recomendations was a "done deal" and he hoped the report would "launch a conversation" at the school. "The questions for this conversation are deeply important: how can we create a Duke where every student will get the richest development of his or her personal powers while contributing to and benefiting from the larger community?" he wrote. He observed that a number of the topics raised by the report—"the role of alcohol in social life" and the "experience of race and other forms of difference"—were not unique to Duke and represented "challenges" for every institution.

The Duke administration braced for a powerful backlash. "To some . . . the report was a politically correct treatise by leftists intent on social engineering and a top-to-bottom remake of a great university," the *News & Observer* found. Not so, said Brodhead. "It's the very nature of these subjects that they require thought and participation by the community," he explained. Added Larry Moneta, one of the two co-chairs of the committee, "The culmination of the report is the initiation of the conversation. I hope our students won't either immediately adopt or immediately dismiss anything at hand." Brodhead sensed the greatest reaction would be to the suggestion that effectively would loosen the fraternities' viselike—and long-standing—grip on the best real estate on West Campus. There was no question that, at Duke, the fraternities' ability to control the social life on campus depended largely on their control of the choicest places to live. There was also no longer much doubt that the fraternities added a highly corrosive element to Duke social life, which Brodhead was correct to understand and want to change. But, in terms of campus taboos, there was none more dangerous to explore. "The students at this place are creative, civic-minded people," Brodhead said. "Let's ask them to bring their creativity to the questions."

But some wondered whether Duke needed fixing. Jason Trumpbour, the outspoken Duke alumnus, told the *News & Observer* the CCI report started from a "faulty premise" because, when Brodhead created it, the near-universal supposition was that the three lacrosse players had sexually assaulted Crystal Mangum. Now that many people had serious doubts about that premise, the report could just be trashed. K. C. Johnson, the Brooklyn College history professor and popular blogger about the Duke case, referred to the idea of requiring students to take a class on cultural diversity as the "Group of 88 Enrollment Initiative."

While controversy still raged on campus, Durham police investigators kept making inquiries into what had happened on the night of March 13, 2006. On March 11, Himan attended an interview between Kim Roberts and Coman and Winstead. Coman told Roberts that the purpose of the interview was for her, if she could, to explain the discrepencies in Mangum's stories about last year's events. "Kim [Roberts] became visibly upset," Himan noted, "and started questioning why she was even there." She said she had already given a statement about what happened that night. Coman said he just wanted to clarify some of the information he had been given. Roberts said they would have to "subpoena her" if they wanted her testimony. She asked if she had to be there and Himan told her the interview was voluntary. At that point, Roberts got up and left.

The one-year anniversary of the March 13 party at 610 North Buchanan occasioned any number of assessments of what it all meant and what could be learned. Coach K appeared on an HBO special, *Costas Now*, with sports broadcaster Bob Costas. For only the second time in a year, Krzyzewski had something to say publicly about the lacrosse case. He told Costas that Duke should have been more supportive of the lacrosse team. "The one thing that I wish we would have done is just, out publicly, say, 'Look, those are our kids. And we're gonna support 'em, because they're still our kids,'" he said. "That's what I wish we would have done. And I'm not sure that we did—I don't think we did a good job of that." And, like many others on the one-year anniversary, Coach K was critical of the eighty-eight professors who signed the "Social Disaster" ad. "We had almost one hundred professors come out publicly against certain things in athletics," he continued, "and I was a little bit shocked at that. But it shows there's a latent hostility, or whatever you want to say, toward sports on campus. I thought it was inappropriate, to be quite frank with you." (After hearing Krzyzewski's statement, Professor Paula McClain commented, "I don't think there's a latent hostility. The questions about athletics are not just related to Duke. I'm sorry Coach K really feels like it's hostility toward athletics and such, because most faculty really appreciate Duke athletics.")

In the year or so since the Group of 88 ad had appeared, its signatories had received hundreds of racist and demeaning e-mails. Three professors received death threats. Many were accused of fomenting a "lynch-mob mentality" on campus. In January, on a Saturday morning, Fox News cameramen—from the *O'Reilly Factor*—appeared at the homes of two of the professors who had signed the ad, demanding to know if "they felt bad . . . for convicting the players." Lee Baker, an associate professor of the culture of anthropology, was just waking up. "I was really caught off guard," he said. "I had not had my coffee, and the sun was in my eyes. Once I sort of woke up and figured out what was really going on, I said repeatedly that we did not rush to judgment and presumed that they were innocent. . . . They only aired me mumbling something unintelligible." O'Reilly called the professors who signed the ad "irresponsible."

Once again, some of the professors were put on the defensive by the renewed attacks. "Black students were being told, 'There isn't any racism or sexism, and if you talk about that, you're attacking the lacrosse players,'" recalled Wahneema Lubiano. "Every time we raised it, people told us to shut up." She said the professors' comments were well within the bounds of free speech and "talking about" an issue. "Think of O. J.," she said. "Did anyone say, 'You can't talk about criminal justice inequality?' You can't not talk about things because of this huge spectacular event going on. Otherwise, O. J. would sue millions." Mark Anthony Neal, a colleague of Lubiano's in the African-American Studies department wrote in his blog, "Regardless of whether or not anyone is indicted and convicted in the case, the reality is that women will continue to be raped, and those sexual assaults will continue to be met with silence and a degree of dismissiveness that holds the victims accountable for attacks on their bodies."

William Chafe, the history professor and a former dean of the faculty of arts and sciences, observed, "There's a whole industry out there seizing on the opportunity to pillory a group of faculty members as leftist, racist, elitist, avant-garde Marxist people. They are creating a wonderful straw person to attack." Chafe's comment enraged Jason Trumpbour. "This isn't about ideology," he said. "What we're criticizing them [for] doing is prejudging the guilt of the lacrosse players and using the players' troubles to call attention to their own social issues." Chafe also found himself having to defend his March 2006 opinion column in the *Chronicle* about the long history in the South of white men taking advantage of black women. As a historian, he said, it was his responsibility to put events into context. "It didn't have any reference toward the guilt or innocence of anyone," he said. "This generation has very little historical sense of the depth of the issues in Southern history, and I was trying to talk about the pervasiveness of those linkages, all the way back to Thomas

Jefferson and Sally Hemings. We're talking about something integral to the history of the country and the South."

K. C. Johnson said the Group of 88 injected questions of racism into the debate, while ignoring what he called "black racism"—where blacks voice prejudice against whites—on Duke's campus. "The eighty-eight claim that sexism and racism are prevalent on campus," he said. "That's an extraordinary allegation. It's also reckless and untrue, and they have not been able to produce much evidence to substantiate it." But James Coleman, the law professor, said the near-civil war on Duke's campus had drained energy from what should be the main focus of people's animosity: Mike Nifong. His actions, Coleman said, were "symptomatic of the way prosecutors railroad [an] innocent victim for personal gain." He added, "Everyone is acting like these students are the only people treated unfairly by the justice system. It happens every day, and nobody cares because they are usually poor minorities and everyone assumes they're criminals."

On March 15, Roy Cooper and his two investigators, Jim Coman and Mary Winstead, spent twenty-three minutes inside the house at 610 North Buchanan. Durham police officers Ben Himan and A. H. Ashby walked through the house with the attorney general and his investigators and answered their questions. Winstead asked Ashby "to take measurements of Bathroom B and of an area at the back steps on the southeast side," Ashby noted. Ashby took the measurements and also took six photographs of "Bathroom B." Later that day, a spokeswoman for Cooper said, "We expect the investigation to wrap up in the next few weeks."

By then, Cooper's investigators had met once with Mangum, as well as with defense attorneys. They had met with the Durham police officers, as well as with Brent Saeli, a Duke student at the March 13 party who was not on the lacrosse team. They had watched a video of Mangum at the party—made by lacrosse player Kevin Coleman—that showed Mangum appearing to be "impaired" and, incredibly, claiming to be "a cop." (Coleman had also taken photographs of the party but Durham police never subpoenaed his camera or his time-stamped photographs, even after they appeared on MSNBC.) According to Himan, the video showed Mangum "walking around and stumbling with one shoe on." At one point during their investigation, they asked Nifong to come to Raleigh and answer questions about what some of the defense attorneys had told Coman and Winstead were reasons not to prosecute the players—for instance, Seligmann's alibi or Mangum's inconsistent statements. "My responses apparently were pretty much what they were already thinking were the correct responses," he recalled. But, beyond that single invitation, Nifong was in the dark.

As for Nifong's case before the state bar, his lawyers had asked for a dismissal of the charge that Nifong intentionally withheld exculpatory DNA evidence from the defense. But the lawyers representing the state bar argued against a dismissal and claimed that Nifong's statements in his defense were "semantic hairsplitting." If convicted of the charges, Nifong stood to lose his license to practice law. In another interesting twist, then Illinois Senator Barack Obama called for a federal investigation of Nifong, endorsing the previous call for such an investigation by Representative Walter Jones of North Carolina. Obama's endorsement of a federal investigation came a day after North Carolina Senate leaders introduced legislation that would permit a governor to remove a district attorney from office if a state bar investigation into his behavior was sufficiently serious.

On March 23, Paul Caufield, a writer for *Inside Lacrosse* magazine, appeared on Fox News and said his sources had told him the remaining charges against the three former Duke lacrosse players would soon be dropped. "There is no case here and they will be hearing a dismissal in the coming days," he said, adding that after the case was dropped, the three players planned to bring civil charges against Nifong and others. "This is something that will wait in the wings," Caufield, a former prosecutor, said. "Once the criminal case is dropped, we are going to see this and I believe we'll see it quite quickly. . . . We're going to see the tables turned on Mike Nifong in the media and in the courtroom because he still continues to defend his name."

Philip Seligmann confirmed to the *Chronicle* that a dismissal was imminent. "We don't know exactly what day it is," he said. "All I can say as far as [the families] are concerned is it can't be soon enough." But Noelle Talley, a spokeswoman for Cooper, said no decision had been made and the investigation was continuing. Meanwhile, Mangum's family told Fox News that she had been summoned to the Attorney General's Office and "just wants this to be over." Her father told the *Durham Herald-Sun* that his daughter was tired and isolated and "hates that she ever reported it." (Just as the case seemed to be unwinding, Kirk Osborn, who had been the Seligmann attorney who crafted Seligmann's alibi documents soon after he was indicted, suffered a heart attack in the early morning of March 25 and died. "Kirk stood up for Reade at great personal cost," the Seligmann family said in a statement. "He passionately believed the truth would emerge.")

Other lacrosse parents also believed the case would soon be dropped. "That's what we've been hearing," Sally Fogarty told the *Baltimore Sun*. She and other parents had gathered in "a damp parking lot" in Georgetown, prior to the Duke–Georgetown lacrosse game. While they ate sandwiches and drank Bloody Marys, they allowed themselves to indulge in the thought that the nightmare would soon be over. "Let's have those three boys get exonerated," said Tricia Dowd. "That's the only win that really matters." The parents said the year had been "horrible" and "surreal." John Walsh remembered going to cocktail parties where people would say to him, "Well, something must have happened." He would look at them, incredulously, and reply, "C'mon, you know my son." David Evans showed up at the tailgate party before the game and received "hugs and well wishes," according to the *Baltimore Sun*. Evans's parents were at the game as well. Despite the optimism, a number of the Duke parents were still furious about the indictments.

Like others, Selena Roberts, the *New York Times*'s sports columnist who had previously been highly critical of the Duke lacrosse team's behavior and culture, sensed the end of the case might be near. She wondered what the implications would be of dropping the charges against the three players. "There is a tendency to conflate the alleged crime at the Duke lacrosse team kegger on March 13, 2006, with the irrefutable culture of misogyny, racial animus and athlete entitlement that went unrestrained that night," she wrote. "Porn-style photos of two exotic dancers—one of whom was the accuser—emerged from cell phone camera downloads. Heated exchanges between players and dancers occurred. Racial slurs were heard. And in an *American Psycho* reference, a repulsive e-mail message depicting the skinning of strippers was sent by a player, Ryan McFadyen, who, to his credit, has since apologized. To many, the alleged crime and culture are intertwined. No trial, all vindication. This microview has some passionate, respectful followers, but also a few loquacious bullies. Some of them have expressed their anger with threatening e-mail messages to Duke staff members who had voiced opinions on the scandal. And, certainly, several hostile lacrosse advocates have burned a hole in my in-box as well over the past year."

While she noted that other college sports programs had worse infractions—and again mentioned the "sex-for-recruits rape saga" at the University of Colorado—she seemed taken aback by the ferocity of the response by the Duke family. "To shine a light on its integrity has been treated by the irrational mighty as a threat to white privilege," she wrote. "Feel free to excoriate the African-American basketball stars and football behemoths for the misdeeds of all athletes, but lay off the lacrosse pipeline to Wall Street, excuse the khakipants crowd of SAT wonder kids." She rightly acknowledged that there was no justice in prosecuting young men who did not commit a crime, but credited Mangum's rape charges for exposing a culture of "misogyny" among the lacrosse players.

On the morning of March 29, Himan picked up Mangum and took her to the State Bureau of Investigation lab, where she met with Coman, Winstead, and Greg Tart, an SBI agent. Although Himan did not keep notes of the meeting—he wrote that an SBI agent took "handwritten notes"—the attorney general later reported that Mangum "made several new statements" to the investigators and officers that she "had never made before." For the first time, Cooper wrote, Mangum "was not with 'Nikki' [meaning Roberts] when the 911 call regarding the racial comments outside 610 N. Buchanan Blvd. was made; that she and Nikki left the house in Nikki's car at 11:50 p.m. and then "rode around for an hour after leaving the house." She said Evans and Seligmann "threw her onto the back porch after the alleged assault" and that all three of the indicted players "kicked her in the neck while she was on the back porch after the alleged assault" and "ten" of the partiers "assaulted her in the back-yard by pushing her around." She also said that Evans and Finnerty put her in Roberts's car. Unfortunately, Cooper reported, "Verified and credible pho-tographic, documentary, and testimonial evidence contradicts each of these seven statements."

There was more, too. Whereas in her December 21 interview with Linwood Wilson she had said Seligmann was not one of her attackers after all, on March 29, she said he was one of her "active" attackers. "She stated to the special prosecutors that the players took off her underwear and lifted her into the air," Cooper reported. "Finnerty crouched below her in a squatting position and held her up. Evans got behind her. She felt a sharp pain in her vagina. She felt a sharp pain in her anus. Finnerty got up and went behind her. Seligmann got under her and held her up in the air. Evans was then in front of her. Evans told Seligmann, who was crouched holding her up, to relax and do her. Evans ejac-ulated in her mouth, and she spit it on the floor. She indicated to the special prosecutors that all three individuals were active participants in the assault." She also told the special prosecutors that she "feigned unconsciousness during the early morning hours of March 14" and claimed she "arrived at the party at 11:10 p.m. and dancing started shortly thereafter."

But, Cooper noted of the March 29 meeting, "When shown credible pho-tographic evidence to the contrary, she claimed that the pictures had been altered." Mangum claimed they danced in a bedroom, not the living room. "When confronted with credible photographic evidence to the contrary," Coo-per continued, "she claimed Duke paid someone to alter the photos. She rou-tinely denied she made various earlier statements that were attributed to her by law enforcement officials. She denied that she had made statements attributed to her in medical reports both the night of the alleged attack and in the ensu-ing days." Mangum also "claimed that the photograph of her on the back porch at 610 N. Buchanan Blvd., time-stamped at 12:30 a.m. and in which she is smiling broadly, is a picture of her arriving at the party." But when the special prosecutors pointed out that she was wearing only one shoe, "she persisted in her position that the picture was taken when she arrived at the house."

In the same interview, "the credibility of the accusing witness's ability to identify the alleged attackers was further called into doubt," Cooper claimed. "When asked how she could recall with such certainty who allegedly attacked her, she claimed she was good at remembering faces. When the special pros-ecutors brought Officer Gwen Sutton of the Durham Police Department into the interview room, the accusing witness claimed she did not know Officer Sutton and had not seen her before that day. Officer Sutton had spent more than five hours with the accusing witness during the early morning hours of March 14, 2006. Similarly, when the special prosecutors asked her about behavior during the party that had suggested impairment, the accusing witness stated that she was dizzy and fuzzy when the two women began dancing that night. She said she was dizzy after the alleged assault, and that was why she was stumbling in the backyard. When asked how she could be certain of her identifications of her attackers, she said she was dizzy when the dancing started, but she 'woke up' in the bathroom and then was dizzy afterward."

Mangum conceded the second meeting with the special prosecutors did not go nearly as well as the first one, during which she had felt confident that they were on her side. She was not nearly as comfortable in the conference room, in part because there were six additional people in the room—four white men (three of whom were SBI agents), a white woman, and a black woman. She had come alone, without an attorney. "The demeanor of those watching did not make me feel they were on my side," she remembered. She was given a long pointer and asked to go to an easel that had been set up and go over in detail the events of March 13. While this was not unexpected, Mangum was ill at ease. "I struggled with my words," she said, "and felt confused at times because I could not stand the looks I was getting. I was told I needed to describe again in detail what had happened. It was excruciating and humiliating, trying to tell my story to people who were visibly hostile." She had expected a "strategy session about the case" and instead felt like she was being cross-examined on the witness stand. "After about two hours, I was reduced to tears and was forced to stop," she explained. "During our break for lunch, I completely lost my composure. I cried uncontrollably."

She eventually calmed down with the help of the black woman who was also at the meeting. But then Coman started asking Mangum precise questions, in rapid succession: "Where were you raped? Which door did you enter and exit? Were they the same doors? Did Mr. Nifong tell you the names of your attackers?" Mangum felt like she had answered the same questions many times before, and she found Coman's staccato approach intimidating. "Maybe he was getting me ready for being on the stand," she confessed, "but it was still painful. I started to cry again. I could not take it anymore and left the room in tears." She went back to the bathroom to try to calm down. This time, Winstead came into the bathroom and told her to try to relax, because the tough questioning was just meant to prepare her for testifying. She felt disrespected, a feeling she had never felt from either Nifong or the police.

When she went back into the conference room, Coman "lit" into her "from all directions," she recalled. The other people in the room sat silently. She later reflected that had someone at least said to her "We don't believe you," then "I would have been clear on where they were coming from" and that this was a "way to tell the world that I was crazy and delusional." Unable to take Coman's persistent questions any longer, she "blurted" out: "They are going to get away with it because Duke has paid everyone to be silent." She quickly recognized "it was not the smartest thing for me to do," but she "did not know what else to say at that point. It was my word against everything the defense attorneys had been able to amass." Despite her impolitic outburst, she left the meeting thinking the case would still go to trial.

On the morning of April 4, police officers Himan and Clayton went to the thousand-square-foot home where Mangum was living on Dauphine Place. They had planned to meet her and then to take her to Raleigh to meet again with Coman, Winstead, and Tart, the SBI agent. But when Himan went to the door, the woman who answered—"Mrs. Pettiford"—said Mangum was not home and she did not know where she was. Himan called Winstead and told her Mangum was not around and they would be late for the 10 a.m. meeting. They agreed Himan should wait for Mangum. He tried her on her cell phone but she did not pick up. At 9:30, an unidentified man drove Mangum to the house. Himan asked her if she was ready to go to Raleigh. She said she was but just wanted to go into her house for a few minutes. When Mangum returned, "I noticed that she was not walking as she normally walked," Himan observed. As she approached the car door to get in, Himan asked Mangum if she was okay. She said she was "fine," but Himan noticed that "her eyes were wandering" and "her demeanor was different than any time I have been around her." Himan asked Mangum a few questions. He concluded she was "intoxicated." He asked if she had taken any medication, and she said she had taken an "Ambien" at around six o'clock the previous night. He did not smell alcohol on her, but he felt "there was some kind of impairment" with her. "She wasn't walking right," Himan recalled. "When I spoke with her, she was very lackadaisical. She wasn't making sense, some of the comments she was making."

Himan called Tart "to advise him of the situation." Tart said he would call Coman and Winstead and report back. All three agreed to come to Durham and meet Mangum at a Durham police station, rather than meet in Raleigh. On the way to the police station, Himan and Mangum made small talk. He asked her about her son. As they were passing by NCCU, he asked her if she was thinking about returning to school. She replied she "thinks about it every day" but was thinking of moving "out of the country" to Amsterdam. Did she have family there, Himan wondered? Mangum started laughing. She was just kidding, she told Himan. She was actually just thinking of moving to Miami.

At the police station, Mangum was led to a conference room and then asked to use the bathroom. She was gone so long—about fifteen minutes—that Himan asked a female assistant to go see if she was okay. Just then, Mangum returned.

While waiting for the state investigators to arrive, Mangum watched the Food Channel on television and drank two Mountain Dews. At 10:30, Mangum noted that Coman, Winstead, and Tart were "late" but Himan explained that the meeting was originally scheduled for Raleigh but was changed to Durham because Mangum was late coming home.

Eventually, the three investigators arrived and began to question Mangum. "They noticed she was impaired and asked to do some tests," Himan noted. "Crystal stated she didn't think she was impaired and she felt like she usually does." Agent Tart took notes of the session with Mangum and it was also videotaped. Mangum eventually agreed to have a blood sample taken so that she could be tested for drugs. Just before noon, the interview ended and Himan took Mangum back to Dauphine Place.

On the car ride back home, Mangum told Himan "she had messed up again." Himan wanted to know what she meant. "She stated that she messed it up and that she was kicked out of the meeting," Himan wrote in his notes. He told her it was "probably a good idea to get some sleep" and that Ambien should not be mixed with alcohol. "She agreed and stated that she did need sleep," Himan noted.

At her home, Himan and Clayton helped Mangum out of the car and were helping her up the stairs into the house when "her body went limp and she fell back into me," Himan recorded. Himan and Clayton then put Mangum into Himan's vehicle and called 911. Paramedics arrived, and Himan told them how Mangum had been acting and that she had eaten "a small breakfast" and that he had "witnessed her drink three Mountain Dews." The medics "took possession" of the medication in Mangum's purse and told Himan they were going to take Mangum to Durham Regional Hospital. Her aunt, Mrs. Pettiford, rode in the ambulance with Mangum. Throughout the course of the day, Himan wrote that he checked in with Mangum at the hospital. He also stated he spoke with her cousin and with her boyfriend, Matthew Murchison. Mangum told Himan the doctors thought she was "dehydrated" but also that "she had overdosed on the pills." She said she told the doctors she had just taken the pills "too early" in the day.

In his subsequent report, Cooper wrote that at the April 4 interview, Mangum "demonstrated unsteady gait, slurred speech, and other mannerisms that were consistent with behaviors observed by numerous witnesses who were at the party" on March 13 and that were "confirmed" through Kevin Coleman's video of that night. Cooper wrote that the "special prosecutors confirmed" that Mangum had taken "Ambien, methadone, Paxil, and amitriptyline"—for which she had prescriptions—"prior to meeting with special prosecutors that day." It was a year to the day after Mangum had identified her alleged attackers in a PowerPoint presentation of their faces.

• • •

Even as Mangum's confused behavior continued to weaken her credibility, Duke began a sophisticated maneuver to try to protect itself legally. On April 9, John Burness and another, unidentified Duke administrator gave interviews to Steven Marcus, a columnist at *Newsday* on Long Island. That the paper was metaphorically in Finnerty's backyard was probably no coincidence. Burness, on Duke's behalf, seemed concerned about potential civil lawsuits from the players now that it looked like they would be cleared and he conveyed no remorse about how the Duke administration had handled the matter. "We're expecting that there's probably going to be civil suits from folks trying to get money out of us, that comes with the turf," he told Marcus. He noted that there were people who wanted Duke to apologize to the players, assuming Cooper exonerated them. "I said," Burness replied, "for what?" The other Duke administrators interjected that Seligmann, Finnerty, and Evans were "no choirboys." Burness also took on Pressler and his coaching style. "One of the things we certainly have to come to understand in this case is that coaches in general in each of our sports is responsible for the behavior of their teams." He said the difference between Pressler and Danowski, the new coach, was "night and day" and added about Danowski, "As our president said, 'This guy's a mensch. This guy gets it.'" Concluded Burness: "Duke as an institution has a reputation to repair and that is paramount over clearing the names of the players involved in last spring's party."

Burness—and Duke Board Chairman Robert Steel—later apologized for Burness's lack of diplomacy. "I apologize for the content and tone of my comments," Burness confessed. "They are not consistent with the viewpoint or sentiment of the leadership of Duke University." Stuart Rojstaczer, a former Duke professor, explained that Burness was likely just trying to warn the players and their families that Duke would fight their civil suits. "One public thing you do is have your PR guy call in a chit to an old buddy who happens to be a reporter for a newspaper in the neck of the woods where the lacrosse players' families live," he said. "You tell him your side of the story. The kids are bad apples. The coach was rotten. Duke did nothing wrong. It's your way of signaling to those families that this is a 'teachable moment.' They are about to be taught a lesson that, when attacked, Duke fights back."

The next day, as rumors intensified that Cooper would soon exonerate Seligmann, Finnerty, and Evans, the three former Duke lacrosse players and their families returned to North Carolina. Television trucks lined up outside the Attorney General's Office in Raleigh. Duke issued guidelines for the journalists expected to again descend on the campus. Even Katie Couric, the anchor of CBS News, traveled to North Carolina in anticipation of Cooper's announcement. ABC News reported the charges would be dropped. "We have gotten at least fifty-seven media calls," said Noelle Talley, Cooper's spokeswoman. "We've gotten calls from both people far and near, from people flying in to town and people who are here." Kevin Finnerty told the Associated Press that he and his family had come to Raleigh for the announcement but did not know when it would come.

At around 8 a.m. the morning of April 11, Winstead called Himan and told him that Attorney General Cooper was going to "make an announcement" during the day regarding "the dropping of the charges." Thirty minutes later, Himan spoke with Mangum and told her that the Attorney General's Office wanted to meet with her and that "it was very important that they meet with her today." Himan told Mangum that he would bring her to the Attorney General's Office. When Himan arrived at 19 Dauphine, Mangum was not there, and her aunt, Mrs. Pettiford, said she had not been staying there. He tried calling Mangum and left several messages for her. Himan then went to 2518 Barrack Drive, where Mangum sometimes left her children to be watched, but she was not there, either, and the woman whom Himan spoke to was of no help. "At that point it was apparent that they were not going to tell me where she was," Himan noted. He reported to the Attorney General's Office that he could not find Mangum. He learned from them that they could not find Mangum, either. Himan spent another few hours unsuccessfully trying to find Mangum.

Around the same time, Nifong received a call from Coman and Winstead. He was at his attorneys' office in Winston-Salem preparing for his upcoming state bar hearing on April 13. "They told us that Cooper had decided not to prosecute the case, that he was going to dismiss the charges because he didn't have sufficient prosecutable evidence to use, that he thought that there had been a rush to judgment, but that he was not going to come down on me," Nifong recalled. "He was just going to say something general about the importance of not rushing to judgment and stuff like that, and that it was pretty much what we could expect in a news conference. . . . I got the impression from them that the only thing that was really going to happen in the press conference was that they were going to say that there is not any basis to prosecute and therefore the charge is going to be dismissed, and maybe say a few things, a few little Roy aphorisms that he thinks are going to help him in his next election or something like that." (Cooper's morning press conference ended up being delayed until the early afternoon, after the attorney general reported not feeling well and was taken to the hospital for an examination.)

Just before 2 p.m., Mangum called Himan. "What is going on?" she asked. Himan said he had been looking for her for more than three hours. "Oh, I dozed off," Mangum told Himan. He told Mangum that the Attorney General's Office wanted to meet with her; he arranged to pick her up at Dauphine Place in fifteen minutes. At 2:15, Himan showed up at Dauphine Place, but Mangum was not there.

While Himan was waiting for Mangum to return, he turned the radio in his police cruiser to Roy Cooper's 2:36 p.m. press conference. After apologizing for the rainy North Carolina weather, Cooper announced to the local and national media that had assembled, "The result of our review and investigation shows clearly that there is insufficient evidence to proceed on any of the charges. Today we are filing notices of dismissal for all charges against Reade Seligmann, Collin Finnerty, and David Evans. The result is that these cases are over, and no more criminal proceedings will occur." What's more, he said, "We believe that these cases were the result of a tragic rush to accuse and a failure to verify serious allegations. Based on the significant inconsistencies between the evidence and the various accounts given by the accusing witness"—and here he dropped a bombshell—"we believe these three individuals are innocent of these charges."

Cooper said that while he recognized that rape and sexual assault victims often have trouble remembering the specifics of such a traumatic event, in this case "the inconsistencies were so significant and so contrary to the evidence that we have no credible evidence that an attack occurred in that house on that night." He said that Mangum did want to move forward with the case and had "offered information" to Coman and Winstead and had answered their questions. But again, Cooper said, "the contradictions in her many versions of what occurred and the conflicts between what she said occurred and other evidence like photographs and phone records, could not be rectified. Our investigation shows that the eyewitness identification procedures were faulty and unreliable. No DNA confirms the accuser's story. No other witness confirms her story. Other evidence contradicts her story. She contradicts herself." He said a future report would contain his investigation's "important factual findings" and "some of the specific contradictions that have led us to the conclusion that no attack occurred." Asked afterward whether he thought Mangum was "mentally unstable," Cooper said his investigators came to believe that "she believed many of the stories she was telling" and "that they worked real hard with her" but that "it just doesn't make sense. You can't piece it together."

Having dispensed with Mangum, Cooper then attacked Nifong, although not by name. He said the district attorney "pushed forward unchecked" and added "there were many points in this case where caution would have served justice better than bravado, and in the rush to condemn a community and a state, lost the ability to see clearly." He said, "Regardless of the reasons that this case was pushed forward," the "result was wrong" and people needed to learn from the mistakes made so that they did not happen again. He observed that while there were many "good" district attorneys in North Carolina who were both "tough and fair" and that while prosecuting criminal behavior remained a central component of the justice system—to say nothing of protecting the public—"this case shows the enormous consequences of overreaching by a prosecutor. What has been learned here is that the internal checks on a criminal charge—sworn statements, reasonable grounds, proper suspect photo line-ups, accurate and fair discovery—all are critically important." Accordingly, he said, he was going to propose a new law whereby the North Carolina Supreme Court—as opposed to the governor, as the state Senate had suggested—could remove a district attorney under certain limited circumstances. "This would give the courts a new tool to deal with a prosecutor who needs to step away from a case where justice demands," he said.

In answer to a question about what he would say now to Seligmann, Finnerty, and Evans, Cooper responded, "We have looked at the charges. We have looked at the law. And we have cleared them of all of these charges. And it is important to note that the Durham County district attorney is now facing ethics charges with the North Carolina Bar Association." As for what he surmised Nifong could have been thinking while pursuing the charges against the three men, Cooper said, "I'm concerned that statements were made publicly about things that turned out not to be true. That's a concern. And right now I think it's appropriate that the North Carolina Bar Association is looking at these ethics charges." Asked how the case would reflect on the public perception of justice in North Carolina, Cooper observed, "Any state in the country, including the federal government, can have a rogue prosecutor who goes on out on his own. . . . Here in North Carolina we have solved the problem, we've corrected the problem. But I propose today a way that I think it can be done more quickly, and I think that that's important."

Asked whether he thought Nifong had ever interviewed Mangum or whether she had ever told the "same story twice," Cooper replied that Mangum had "told many stories" and that "some things are consistent within those stories." He said the subsequent report would make clear the discrepencies in her stories. As for Nifong speaking with Mangum, Cooper said he did not know for sure whether he had spoken with her before the indictments were brought but that he thought Nifong had spoken with Mangum "at some point" during the case. He also said he considered—but ultimately decided against—bringing criminal charges against Mangum. "Our investigators who talked with her and the attorneys who talked with her over a period of time think that she may actually believe the many different stories that she has been telling," he said. "And in reviewing the whole history, there are records under seal that I'm not going to talk about, but we believe it's in the best interest of justice not to bring charges, and we have made that decision as well."

For the players, their families, and the defense attorneys, a state of near-euphoria quickly ensued. "Amid laughter, applause, and tears," at a press conference at the Sheraton Hotel, in downtown Raleigh, attorney Joe Cheshire cautioned against excessive emotion. "This, ladies and gentlemen is not a great day of celebration," he said. "This is a great day for justice. . . . It is a great day of relief. . . . When Roy Cooper said a word today, the word is i-n-n-o-c-e-n-t, and I want to make sure that everyone heard that and knows how to spell it. These young men were, are and always have been innocent." Cheshire also criticized Nifong as "a man who had not a care in the world about justice—only about himself and his agenda." He said the filing of civil suits was likely. Wade Smith praised Coman and Winstead. "They didn't leave a stone unturned," he said. And Jim Cooney, Seligmann's attorney, blasted the media and the Duke professors. "One wonders, if the newspapers had stood up for proper processes and the teachers had stood up for proper processes, whether this would have slowed down the last coward." He blamed the *Durham Herald-Sun* in particular for not questioning many of Nifong's decisions. Cheshire, though, decided that the media deserved some praise, especially since he would see the same reporters and editors soon enough in the next case. "I do not believe we would have avoided the trial if you all in the media had not been courageous enough to . . . reexamine your positions and realize that you were wrong and start[ed] telling the truth about this case," he said. "I know it's hard to say you're wrong . . . but you helped justice. You saved lives."

In recalling that moment, Reade Seligmann could barely keep from crying. "In a single word, the man gave us our life back," he said of Roy Cooper. "In a single word. Everything that had happened, all the bad stuff that we had to go through, all the tough times, were erased when he said it. I think the funniest part was when we were sitting in the room—there was a bunch of us—all in a hotel room, and we were watching it. I've probably never been that nervous in my entire lifetime. We're all watching it and it felt like an eternity. He talks really slow. . . . [When] he said, 'We believe these boys are innocent,' the room just erupted. Just erupted. If there was a changing point in my life, that would be the point, that moment. My whole life turned around on that one word."

In his prepared remarks at the press conference in Raleigh, Seligmann was slightly more composed. He started by saying how "deeply saddened" he was that his onetime defense attorney Kirk Osborn was not around to witness "this very emotional day." He said Osborn "stood by my side from the very beginning of this travesty and did all that he could to proclaim my innocence. Not only has North Carolina lost one of its finest attorneys, it has lost a man who embodied the words honor and integrity. We will never forget his sacrifices and our thoughts and prayers are with his family." He then launched into his speech. "Today marks the end of a yearlong nightmare that has been a destructive force in so many people's lives," he said. "The dark cloud of injustice that hung above our heads has finally cleared."

Seligmann concluded with the announcement that he intended to finish his academic and athletic careers—he would enroll at Brown University in the fall—and to put to good use what he had learned in the year after March 13. "This case has shown me what the important things in life really are as my entire perspective on the world has changed," he said. "I view this situation as a unique opportunity to make a difference and I know that there are many people who can benefit from the lessons I have learned. . . . My ultimate aspiration, moving forward, is to live a life that will make all of those who stood by my side throughout this injustice proud to know that they defended the truth."

Finnerty was more low-key than Seligmann, and his comments at the players' joint press conference were in keeping with his personality. Like Seligmann, Finnerty thanked Cooper, his investigators, his attorneys, his teammates, his friends and girlfriend, his high school, the people from around the country who supported him—and K. C. Johnson, "for his diligent work exposing the truth every day." He thanked his parents and family especially, as well as the Seligmanns and the Evanses. "We have become one big family through all this," he said. "We have a bond that will last forever. It's been a very long and emotional year for me and for all of us." He said he would not miss the constant barrage of the news media and looked forward to returning to college—he would end up at Loyola University in Maryland—and to the lacrosse field. He also said he could not understand why grand juries in North Carolina do not keep records of what they do, making it impossible to understand the evidence on which the three players had been indicted. And he urged "checks and balances" on the power of district attorneys. "This experience will be with me forever and I will never forget all those who stood right next to me throughout it all," he concluded. "The truth finally did prevail, as so many told me it would."

For his part, David Evans started his speech with the fact that he and his family had gotten stuck, briefly, in the hotel elevator and almost missed the press conference. "It has been 395 days since this nightmare began, and finally today it has come to a closure," he said. "From the very beginning, many of the men sitting at this table, including myself, Reade, and Collin, said that we are innocent. And we are just as innocent today as we were back then. Nothing is changed. Facts don't change and we've never wavered on our story." Toward the end of his talk, he said, "These allegations are false. These charges were false and should never have been brought against us. We fully cooperated. From the beginning there was never a 'Blue Wall of Silence'! Look at the facts of the case and you will see that. It's painful to remember what we went through in those first days. It's a testament to our character that we never lashed out; we stood there strong. If you want to know what character is, walk around a campus and see a photo of yourself with 'castrate' signs on it and people in the media relating you to Hitler and other terrible people in history—when you have done nothing wrong. That is character, to sit there and take that, as the young men in the Duke University lacrosse team did."

Evans added that the sport of lacrosse had been unfairly maligned since March 13. "The stereotypes are just not true," he continued. "They sell magazines, they sell newspapers, but they are not anything that represent us as a sport, as a school, as a university, or as a team. And, they are wrong." He also acknowledged Mike Pressler, "who has sacrificed everything" and spent sixteen years building the Duke lacrosse program. "He fell on the sword so that we could continue as a team at the university that he loved," Evans said. "We owe him everything." Evans said he wanted to get on with the rest of his life. "It has been a long year, longer than you could ever imagine," he said. "I hope these allegations don't come to define me"—he would soon be offered a job as an analyst at Morgan Stanley—"I hope that the way I could be remembered is sticking up for my name, my family and my team against impossible odds. . . . My family and I can sleep at night knowing that I did everything that I was told to do. I never lied. I fully cooperated, starting the day after the party. I can walk with my head high and sleep at night knowing that I could not have done anything else to prove my innocence. This day has been coming for a long time."

At one point, a reporter asked the three players if they regretted attending the party at 610 North Buchanan and hiring the strippers. They were silent. Jim Cooney rushed to answer. "No one's proud of that party, and they've expressed regret for it," he said. "I don't want to be judged by the worst things I did when I was twenty. These young men shouldn't, either. They almost lost their productive lives because of it." Added Wade Smith, "These boys and these families have suffered terribly, and they didn't deserve it. North Carolina didn't deserve it, either. . . . We expect amazing things from these boys. They have been tested in heavy fire. Roll on, boys. Roll on like the rivers of North Carolina to better days. Roll on."

The Duke men's and women's lacrosse team members were on a bus to Raleigh during Cooper's press conference and heard him proclaim their former teammates' innocence on the radio. "When everyone was listening, it was kind of just like shoulders back and a deep breath like, 'Finally, finally, it happened," Matt Danowski said. "We thought it should have been over Day One, but there's so many curveballs and so much going on that you never knew if it was actually going to happen. . . . Finally, there's some completion to it." After the bus arrived in Raleigh, members of the two teams—seventy-two players in all—lined up at the back of the press conference to show their support. "The guys on the team and even outside the team—they've meant a lot to us," Danowski continued. "I know they were kind of far and few between in the first couple of months, but I think ultimately we found out who our true friends are." He said the implications of what had happened between March 13 and April 11 would be pondered for years. "It's a feeling of guilt that we have, being that we've brought this upon ourselves, and the aftermath is going to linger on," Danowski continued. "It's just not going to go away. People are not going to stop talking about it." After the press conference, the players hung around the Sheraton, reveling in the moment. Danowski said he told Seligmann, Finnerty, and Evans that "they've been an inspiration to us the entire

year in how strong they've been and how they've really shown the true character of why they are throughout this whole thing. We actually joked with Collin
and Reade and told them that we have practice at 8 p.m. tonight, so get their
cleats on and get ready to go."

Then there was the fate of Mike Pressler—one of the many elephants in the
room that day. His wife, Sue, had been on the team bus to Raleigh and, the
day before, Pressler had addressed the team after attending a memorial service at Duke Chapel. "Today is the celebration of the two words we've attached
our lives to for almost thirteen months—the truth," Pressler said at his own
press conference at Bryant University. "You can talk about loyalty, honesty, and
trust. They all apply to the 2006 Duke men's lacrosse team, but in the end, it all
comes down to the truth." (Ironically, the title of Pressler's book about the incident was *It's Not About the Truth*.) Added John Danowski, Pressler's successor,
"It was very painful for a lot of us today. That, though this is a vindication, a
good man is not here, and ironically I am here in his place . . . I struggle with
that often—to know that I'm here because of this unique set of circumstances."

There was one odd, personal question that a reporter asked Cooper at the
Raleigh press conference. Had he gone to see a doctor the day before? Cooper looked pale at the press conference and seemed to slur a few words. Had
making the decision to drop the charges against the three players taken a toll
on him? "Well, what happened yesterday is, I was out running and got a little
bit dehydrated," Cooper said. "I run four, five days a week. Got a little dehydrated. I wanted to make sure that I got it checked out. That's all. I'm fine. I
wanted to run to this press conference, but my staff wouldn't let me. So I'm
doing just fine."

But Nifong, for one, did not believe Cooper. He said in an interview that
there was much more to Cooper's visit to the doctor than a simple case of dehy-
dration while he was out running the day before. Nifong said that between the
time that Coman and Winstead called him and told him what would tran-
spire at the press conference, a period of several hours, Cooper "suffered some
kind of a health issue"—Nifong said he thought it might have been "shortness of breath"; others thought he might have suffered a heart attack—"that
required medical attention, which is what I characterize as 'selling your soul
to the devil,' which involves a painful extraction. When he showed up at the
press conference, he had a little bit different agenda than the one that was
announced beforehand." Nifong said he remembered "being just stunned by
the tenor of the remarks, and I have to believe, based on my knowledge of Jim
Coman and Mary Winstead, that they were every bit as sandbagged by what
happened as I was, that they were told to tell me what they told me and that the
remarks that were made were not the remarks that they were expecting either.
And I remember thinking, as I was sitting in the office, with the context of

the remarks that were made, thinking about the fact that the attorney general had to postpone his press conference to go to the hospital with shortness of breath, that what he'd experienced was what you felt when you sold your soul to the devil, because if you watched that press conference, it was pretty clear who was calling the shots." He said he felt "like you've been punched in the gut, and you go on."

Nifong said while he was being "figurative" about Cooper making a pact with the devil, nonetheless, "Roy Cooper had some real doubts about what the defense board wanted him to do—that is to declare the boys to be actually innocent—which, of course, is something that's well beyond the purview of the criminal justice system, and, in essence, is relief that's available to no one. I think he had misgivings about that." Nifong said Cooper had to know that by declaring the players "innocent," he stepped outside the legal boundaries. "He's a lawyer," Nifong said. "How could he not know? I think every first-year law student understands that. I mean, the man is not an idiot. He may be some other things. I don't know. It's been reported to me that his coffers were enriched by tens of thousands of dollars by law firms in the Northeast. I don't know. Seventy thousand was the number that somebody gave me. It doesn't sound like a lot, but you don't know why lawyers in New York are supporting a North Carolina attorney general at this particular moment of his career." (According to followthemoney.org, in his 2008 election Cooper received $228,124, or 19 percent of his contributions, from outside North Carolina.) He added, for good measure, "Roy Cooper would've lied if he thought it would help him. Roy Cooper is the state's chief prosecutor and he's never prosecuted a case in his life. He's never been a district attorney or an assistant district attorney. He was in private family practice and then he ran for state office."

He had other impressions of Cooper's decision, too. "The most interesting part of what Roy Cooper did was that—obviously, the other side really wanted Crystal Mangum hammered—they wanted the case dismissed, but they also wanted her discredited, because there were going to be some people who were always going to say, 'Well, the case got dismissed but I still believe that something happened.' Heck, I said that. . . . But what we're dealing with in this situation is that if she is really discredited, where the attorney general says that he's going to indict her for making a false report, then that kind of enhances the idea that they could really be innocent. But what he did here, when he was asked specifically, 'Are you planning on indicting Ms. Mangum?' he said, 'No. Our investigation indicates that she really believes what she said.' That's a very unusual comment to make about somebody. We can't prosecute this because we don't have any believable evidence. However, we're not going to prosecute the person who made these charges because the evidence is believable to her. Don't you think that's odd?"

He was also miffed by Cooper's allusion to his being a "rogue prosecutor."

"If you listen very carefully to his words," Nifong said, "he never says specifically 'Mike Nifong is a rogue prosecutor,' but he talks about Mike Nifong and then in the next sentence it's 'rogue prosecutors do this,' and certainly the implication is that I'm included in the rogue prosecutors categorization." He said that what Cooper had decided to do that morning was "to throw the case under the bus, and then threw me along with it."

As for whether Cooper truly believed Seligmann, Finnerty, and Evans were innocent, Nifong said, "I don't know what he believed. I have no way of knowing that. I know that there is a difference in believing something and in stating it as a consequential fact of your public position. In other words, Roy Cooper may very well, presumably does, believe in God, but it would be inappropriate for him to make proclamations, as the attorney general, based on what he thought God had in mind for North Carolina. Those two things are normally kept separate. You have your issues of your personal faith, for which you are personally responsible and to which you are personally committed. You have your public duties and responsibilities as a result of your position, and you're not supposed to mix those two up. That's First Amendment stuff. Well, to truthfully answer that question, you have to know what is justice, in this particular case. Am I in a position to know what justice in this case is? I don't think so. That really is a God decision, isn't it? Is justice done? It's not a human decision.

"But what I would say, in general terms," he continued, "is that I don't think that justice is ever served by somebody making a statement that goes beyond his legal authority to make, and that is to declare somebody actually innocent, because the justice system, of which he is an officer, does not have that as an option. A person can be declared guilty or not guilty, and both guilty and not guilty are matters of legal conclusion that have nothing to do with states of grace. They may be proved beyond a reasonable doubt or not proved beyond a reasonable doubt. Of course, as we've seen, on multiple occasions, in many states, the whole question of proof beyond a reasonable doubt is, in and of itself, a less-than-precise term, because guilt must be proven beyond a reasonable doubt, but that doesn't always mean that the people that are convicted are guilty. If you convict only upon an absolute certainty, then nobody would ever get convicted. So, everything that the justice system does is a balancing test." He then added, a bit snarkily, "Now, up until that point, I had not realized that Roy Cooper had been there that night, because we certainly would've wanted to talk to him, if we'd known he was present and could've told us what really happened. But after that, I realized that we'd missed another opportunity to interview a witness that we just didn't know was present. Of course, he's the only person who could." He then said, turning serious, "The criminal justice system could never say that, because they don't find people actually innocent. They find people to either be proven to be guilty or to be not proven to be guilty. . . . The fact is that innocence is a state of grace that no human system is able to parse out, and we do the best we can with what we have, and when we make a mistake, we try to correct it."

Needless to say, by April 2007, Nifong may have been nearly alone in questioning Cooper's decision. He did not speak with reporters after Cooper's press conference. His attorney, David Freedman, told the *New York Times* he was "devastated" by Cooper's criticism of Nifong's handling of the lacrosse case. He said that Nifong had "no problem" with Cooper's decision to "exonerate the players," but that he was deeply wounded by Cooper's attack on his judgment and performance. "He's a person who has dedicated himself to public service for twenty-nine years," Freedman said. "All he cares about is public service."

After Cooper's press conference concluded, Himan was still at Dauphine Place waiting for Mangum to meet him, as she had said she would. Himan waited more than ninety minutes for Mangum to come home; at one point she called and said she would be there soon. But, by then, she had obviously heard about Cooper's decision. One last time, Himan called Mangum's cell phone. Was she still coming? Himan wondered. "I don't think I am going to show up today," she told him. Himan told her "Okay," and she asked him, if it was over, if she could get her phone and her purse, two of the items of evidence she had left behind at 610 North Buchanan on the night of March 13. Himan told Mangum there was "a process" by which evidence was released and he had to sign a form. She then hung up the phone. Himan returned to Police Station 2 and informed Coman, Winstead, and Tart of his conversation with Mangum. While he was at the station house, Mangum called back again. Could she come by to pick up her property? Mangum wanted to know. Again, Himan told Mangum there was a process he needed to initiate to return the evidence to her. "She then hung the phone up," Himan noted, the last entry in his case diary.

Himan had worked closely with Cooper's special prosecutors between January and April 2007. He concurred with Cooper's decision to drop the case against the three lacrosse players. "There is significant evidence that proved her story wrong," he said. Himan said he came to the conclusion that Crystal Mangum "was not telling the truth about anything. That she was improvising everything that she said. That everything she was contradicted with, she would make up an improvisation of what actually happened, of why this happened, why this didn't happen. And she just thought it was a big coverup, and she accused me of being paid by Duke. That was like one of the first times she accused me. I had a pretty good rapport with her, and she accused me of basically being paid off by Duke and that she didn't trust me anymore."

In her October 2008 book, *Last Dance for Grace*, cowritten by Vincent Clark, Mangum devoted only about a page to the events of the night of March 13,

2006. "I know people want me to name names and point fingers but that would just be opening up a whole can of worms," she wrote. "The criminal case is closed! But that does not mean I do not believe I was violated. It just means that there is no way for me to do any more about it." She wrote that once she and "Kim/Nikki" got separated, she "was forced into the bathroom with three of the partygoers, grabbed by the throat, and quickly subdued. There were two people in front of me and one in the back." She tried to get away, without success. "The one holding my arm said, 'Sweetheart, you can't leave.' He then stood behind me while another man stood in front. I could hear yelling in the other room. I screamed, too,"—this was the first time she had mentioned screaming—"hoping someone would hear me but the noise coming from the other room was very loud."

She wrote that the more she tried to break away, the tighter they held her. "I was in a great deal of pain," she continued. "Then I felt as though I was being penetrated, first in my vagina and then in my anus. I tried to focus on other things while being attacked. 'Next!' my first attacker said. The second attacker was now standing in front of me as the first held me from behind. 'What are you going to do?' he said. 'Are you going to be still or am I going to have to kill you?' He penetrated my vagina. I pulled at his shirt, trying to make him stop. Quickly, he was done. From all of the struggling my tightly glued fingernails began to pop loose, causing my fingertips to have a burning sensation." She wrote that she remembered the "three attackers" had a conversation. She couldn't recall all of it because there was a lot of noise coming from the living room. But she did hear the "third attacker" tell the other two, "I don't want to. I love my fiancé and we are going to get married." But, she continued, they convinced him to take his turn. "When he finally did," she wrote, "each thrust hurt, and it felt like my insides were being ripped out. I also believe I may have been penetrated with a foreign object. I genuinely believed I was going to die in there, but I did not want to." Then, she explained, the "second attacker" decided "to penetrate me again. This time anally and painfully. He removed himself just before he had an orgasm and ejaculated on the floor."

Soon thereafter, she wrote that she heard Roberts's voice and then "the guys wiped me off quickly and attempted to straighten my clothes." Then Roberts came into the bathroom "and helped them finish fixing my clothes," another new detail. Mangum wanted out of there—as did the players, she wrote—and she eventually made it to the back door. She couldn't stand and remembered being dragged toward the car. "I was afraid and did not know what to do," she allowed. "They put me in the front passenger seat. I sat in the car with my eyes closed and pretended to be asleep. Nikki got out of the car, and when no one was looking I started to cry. I could tell she was yelling at the guys but I could not make out what she was saying."

Mangum wrote that she remained convinced the doctors and nurses at

Duke Hospital, who examined her in the early morning of March 14, "did their jobs," and although she never spoke to them again, "I assure you they were not manufacturing the injuries they reported finding on me." Indeed, she wrote, "the damage to my body was much more extensive than was ever reported in the media." She had X-rays and MRI exams that revealed "bruising to my neck and knee that were not present before the attack. I had to have pain medication for my neck and had to wear a knee support. The pain lasted for weeks afterward."

She recounted with considerable pathos what it was like to be hounded by the media at all hours of the day and night and how, to get her away, the police moved her from one safe house to another. After she became pregnant with her third child, she was utterly fatigued. She wanted to clear up several reporting errors. First, despite what *60 Minutes* reported, she never danced at Platinum Pleasures again after the events of March 13 (in contrast to what she told Cooper's investigators). She did return to the Club in March to attend a party to celebrate the release of a band's CD. "The alleged videotape of me dancing at the club was several months *before* the incident at 610 North Buchanan," she wrote. "There was evidence that the tape was analyzed and verified—something other than what some people wanted to believe." She also wrote that the bouncer at the club was lying when he said Mangum wanted to "make money" from the "Duke boys." She noted that he "was facing drug charges" and was being represented by one of the attorneys for the lacrosse players.

As for the DNA testing, she did not feel qualified to opine on it, but wrote that "others have exaggerated their unscientific assessments of the DNA reports." She wrote that since she lived with her boyfriend, Matthew Murchison, "it stands to reason that his DNA would be on me and my clothing." She wrote that she believed "there are DNA tests in the case file that may tell a different story" than the one that "none of the people charged left DNA on me," and that, in fact, there was evidence consistent with David Evans's DNA on her fake fingernails. She called for Roy Cooper to "release all records to the public"—something Cooper has refused to do—because "perhaps once and for all it would clear up any misconceptions about what DNA really exists." She continued, "Calling for the entire case file to be made public is not something I take lightly. I know there are pictures and video that will not flatter me. Unfortunately, I do not believe there will be any clarity in the case unless everything is finally exposed. I am willing to take that risk. Can everyone at that party on March 13, 2006, say the same thing? Little, if any, real information about what was said and done at the party has ever been made public. *Instead the discussions have always been about what did not happen.* So I have to be skeptical when I hear people from the Attorney General's Office say the records are being suppressed in the interest of the public." She wrote that the Durham police found "one other DNA sample" that the media rarely mentioned. It was "near the sink in the bathroom" at 610 North Buchanan and was "semen from one of the individuals who had been at the party. Again we will never know unless the case file is made public."

(Noelle Talley, the spokeswoman for the NC Attorney General, at first wrote in an e-mail message to me, "There is a federal court order in place sealing the file." Weeks later, she wrote that she was mistaken. The files existed and have been preserved, she wrote, but since they were "criminal files," North Carolina State law keeps them out of public view, and she would not make them available despite their importance to the determination of the outcome of the case. Despite numerous requests, Talley also said Cooper would not be interviewed.)

Mangum remained convinced she was attacked that night. "I know these events will follow me the rest of my life if I do not deal with them now," she wrote. "The only thing I stand to gain now is some dignity. Long after everyone has forgotten about the Duke lacrosse case, I will always wake up knowing that something happened to me and it went unpunished. I also realize that a lot of people believe they have suffered, too. Nevertheless, I have felt stifled and unable to talk on account of all the vitriol directed at me. It still does not matter that I never did want or ever would want anyone to suffer injustice on my behalf. I will forever be labeled 'the accuser.' I cry sometimes and cannot sleep because I think about how others have profited from my pain and suffering."

Wearing a "conservative gray suit and sporting a stylish bob," Mangum held a press conference at the Know Bookstore & Restaurant near the NCCU campus to promote her book shortly after its 2008 publication. "This is very difficult for me, but this is something that I have to do," she said quietly, in her brief remarks before leaving the store. "God has given me the grace and the courage to stand up. No one deserves to be sexually assaulted, regardless of their profession. . . . Many people have tried to use my name and my past to intimidate me, to make me believe that I was a nobody. I'm a real person. I'm not just an exotic dancer. I'm not just someone who tried to frame someone who was innocent of sexual assault. My only intentions were for justice, and I wanted justice for myself." She declined to answer most questions, but in answer to one, said, "No one has ever offered to take a statement by me that came from me. I had to write the book for closure. In order to go on with my life, I need to use my experience and what I've learned to help other people. I don't mind being sort of sacrificed in order to help others, as long as I can share my experiences in a positive way." She graduated from NCCU in May 2008 and said she hoped to enroll in a PhD program at the University of Georgia and then open a home for troubled young women.

Joe Cheshire had no sympathy for her. "Her press conference and her continued assertion that an assault happened is really pathetic," he said at the time. "She says she's writing this book to help other people, and what she's continuing to do by lying is continuing to hurt people, including women who really are victims of sexual assault. She's clearly doing this to make money. By continuing to lie, she makes everything in the book, everything she says, a lie." And Philip Seligmann threatened to sue her. "We are presently evaluating all legal options," he said in a statement. "If Ms. Mangum and those associated with her continue to slander Reade, we will have no choice and will not hesitate to utilize these options."

I visited with Crystal Mangum in November 2012, more than four years after the publication of *Last Dance for Grace* and nearly seven years after the alleged incident at 610 North Buchanan. She was in Durham County Jail awaiting a November 2013 trial for the alleged murder of her then boyfriend, Reginald Daye, whom Mangum stabbed on April 3, 2011, in what she claimed was "self-defense" after an argument at their Durham apartment. In the warrant for her arrest, Durham police wrote that there was "probable cause" to believe that Mangum "unlawfully, willfully, and feloniously did assault" Daye with a "KITCHEN KNIFE, a deadly weapon, with the intent to kill and [inflict] serious injury." In a 911 call from Daye's nephew to police, after Daye had been stabbed, the nephew said to the dispatcher, "It's Crystal Mangum. THE Crystal Mangum! I told him she was trouble from the damn beginning." Daye died eleven days later at Duke Hospital. "His death was a result of medical malpractice at Duke Hospital," Mangum told me from jail. "Everything was fine. He was getting ready to be discharged. All of a sudden they put that endotracheal tube—instead of putting it in his trachea, they put it in his esophagus. So it went into his stomach, so they filled the stomach up with air while his lungs were deflating. By the time they realized what had happened, he was in cardiac arrest, and he passed shortly after that. Before that, he was fine."

Mangum was indicted on April 19 for Daye's murder. According to the autopsy report, "This forty-six-year-old black male was the victim of a single stab wound to his left side with subsequent hemorrhage within the chest and abdominal cavities secondary to perforation of the left lower lung lobe, diaphragm, stomach, colon, left kidney, and clinically the spleen. . . . After review of the historic and autopsy findings contained herein, it is my opinion that the deceased, Reginald Daye, died as the result of complications of a stab wound to his chest."

At the Durham jail, Mangum was dressed in a standard-issue orange jumpsuit and had orange Crocs on her feet. She was on the inside of a closed visiting room on a high floor inside the jail; I sat on a stool on the outside of the room. We were separated by thick Plexiglas. She seemed nervous but more petite and attractive than I expected after seeing one mugshot after another of her. She seemed sad but also, on occasion, smiled warmly. We had had one previous communication, by letter, dated June 17, 2012, after I had asked to interview her. "I, as you probably have guessed, have been here for quite some time (fourteen months) and I am anxious to reunite with my angels (children) ages five, twelve, and thirteen," she wrote. "If we could come to some sort of arrangement concerning my release, that would be a plus. If not, I don't feel that I would be interested. My bond is currently placed where I may be released with eight thousand cash, or property/land. I'm being very upfront [*sic*] because I do not want to waste your time or resources."

She agreed to speak with me at the jail, even though I made it clear I would not help her post bail. (For what it's worth, an unidentified person posted Mangum's $200,000 bail on February 20, 2013, far more than the $8,000 she suggested would spring her.) Mangum said her "emotional issues" had begun at an early age. "There's been a lot of abuse in my life," she said. "And it all began when I was young—when I was quite young. And it started off with family members touching me and me not saying anything about it, which led to me being attracted to older men 'cause I always felt like I was safe with an older man. And then more like a father figure, I guess. So I got into the exotic dancing profession. And, again, a lot of it had a lot to do with emotional issues. I was seeking validation from the wrong sources. Also, I found out that exotic dancing carried a substantial income as well"—about $1,500 a week, she said, for dancing and escorting. And she enjoyed the work. "Well, I'm a people pleaser anyway," she said. "And I love guys. So it fit. It fit with everything else. And I love music. I love to dance. There was some degrading things about it that I didn't like, but the good outweighed the bad up until that point."

She said that the lacrosse players had paid her and Roberts $400 each, and then another $400 each—for a total of $800 each—when they decided to go back into 610 North Buchanan the second time. (If true, this was new, as previous reports had the dancers' pay at $400 each.) "I'm just trying to get it over with," she said about going back into the house. "I'm just like, 'Okay, we're gonna do our routine and then we're gonna go.'" Mangum said the players started to get "riled up again," so Roberts left for good. "She was smart enough to leave," Mangum said. "I was obviously intoxicated." She said she believes the lacrosse players slipped her a Mickey Finn. "I honestly believe there was something in my drink because to this day I never felt that way before," she continued. "It felt like my heart rate had dropped really quickly. I was dizzy. I couldn't maintain my balance. My thoughts were kind of mixing together. And it seemed like I was seeing Kim, but she really wasn't there. It was weird. It was a weird experience. . . . I feel dizzy. I feel different, but it's kinda a good feeling but a weird feeling. So I felt really good, but I felt really weird at the same time. So I went back in, and Kim was behind me. I could hear her. And then I hear her arguing again. She was like arguing the whole night. And then one of the guys, when we go inside, they were like, 'You're gonna finish your job. You're not leaving until you finish.'"

Then she and Roberts got separated. "I ended up in the bathroom," Mangum continued. "And I could hear Kim outside. And I noticed, like when I left, Kim was still sitting in the car. So I guess she wasn't even in the house that long. In the bathroom there's like a door before you get to the bathroom. The guy named Dan, or that calls himself Dan, closed the door. And he looked at me. He's like, 'Sweetheart, you're not leaving.' And I got this chill, like this weird feeling, like, 'Oh no, this is not good' kind of feeling. And they took me in the bathroom. And I kept hearing all these people yelling like 'Yeah, yeah. Give it, black bitch.' And they were just yelling like different things. And I could hear people banging on stuff. It was like really loud." She said the door to the bathroom remained half open. But as soon as she was in there, the three guys "just started taking my clothes off. And next thing I know, I feel this excruciating pain in my anal area, and I started crying and telling them to stop. But they wouldn't stop. They just kept doing it. And when I got to the hospital and they took the samples, it was like my skin was coming out like from the inside in my vaginal area and my anal area. And they found, like, wooden pieces. Like, I guess they used a broomstick."

None of the records of the medical exams mentioned the discovery of wooden shards in Mangum's vagina or anus. They used a broomstick? I asked. "The broom did it," she said. She was sure. "I felt like I was gonna die," Mangum continued, "like my stomach was cramping really bad. Like I felt like I was having a baby. My stomach was hurting really bad. And the guy that was in front of me, he kept telling the other guys to stop, like he didn't want them to—he was like, 'Man, you're gonna' kill her. Stop.' He was like telling him to stop. And the other guy was like, 'We're not gonna' kill her. We just wanna' make her feel good.' And they were laughing at me and stuff. And they were like, 'Are you in pain? Are you hurting?' And it was like, 'I thought black girls liked it like this.' And I was crying and telling them to stop, but they just kept doing it." She said she thought to herself that while she had "flirted" with the players when she first arrived at the house, she could not understand why they were attacking her. "I kept asking them, why are you doing this to me?" she continued. "Why? And they just kept saying that, 'I thought black girls liked it rough. Thought they liked it like this.' And I kept asking them, like, why? Like I didn't do anything to do deserve this. So all I thought about was, why? It didn't have to be that way."

She said the man standing in front of her was David Evans. The other guys were behind her shoving the broomstick up her anus. She said Evans forced her to give him oral sex by trying to put his penis in her mouth, and then he ejaculated. "I know for a fact that it happened," she said. "I've been carrying a lot of guilt because I was drinking and I was flirting. And I went back in the house. And my memory is kinda fuzzy. So it's a possibility that I may have picked the wrong people." She said the attack went on for "fifteen to thirty minutes" but she was not sure how or why it stopped. "All I know is that a door opened, and I was so happy 'cause I thought I was gonna die," she said. "All I know is, that door opened. I thought they were gonna kill me. Yeah, because like seconds earlier or minutes earlier, they were nice. I mean, they were sweet. It seemed like they turned into a different person, and I just couldn't under-stand how they changed so fast. So I'm figuring, if they changed in that man-ner, then maybe they'll try to kill me next. All I know is they picked me up and put my clothes back. They picked me up and take me outside and just dumped me on the porch. They just threw me outside on the porch and closed the door. And then, like, one of the guys picked me up and puts my arm around his neck. And I kinda' felt like he kinda felt bad about what had happened. And he placed me in the back of Kim's car."

She said she thought Reade Seligmann was the one who felt guilty and car-ried her to the car. What about his alibi? She said she never saw the evidence of his alibi. "My problem with that is none of the evidence was actually veri-fied in court," she said. "I don't really know what to believe. It never made it to court. Anybody can stand on television and say 'I have an alibi.'" She said she had asked the Attorney General's Office for access to the evidence. "I was told all the evidence was destroyed for my case," she said. "I can't even get access to my own hospital records." (She said she was going to the UNC Hospital after the attack to get "therapy" to help her "have a bowel movement"; she said they also gave her muscle relaxers and painkillers.)

She said her life did not turn out as she had planned. She never expected to be in jail for supposedly killing her boyfriend. She never thought she would be reviled for accusing the three lacrosse players of attacking her. "It's very frustrating when you know something is true but you can't prove it," she said. "And then you have people that hate you, and you don't even know why. I have like millions of people around the country that hate me, and they've never met me. I guess they feel like I'm a vindictive person. And so that's their reaction or retaliation. I guess because my case never made it to trial [and] that the actual truth never came out. And the way the media makes it sound is that I just went to the police station and said, 'These guys raped me, get 'em.' That's the way they make it sound. But that's not the way it happened. I never even pressed charges. I went to the hospital for help. I mean, if it really had been up to me, I probably woulda just said leave it alone and went on with my life. I probably woulda kept it to myself. And a lot of times I wished I had. I used to think that the judicial system was so straightforward. If it's true, it'll come out and every-thing will be fine. Now I have a completely different view. It's not even a mat-ter of innocence or guilt. It's a matter of who's more powerful or who has the most resources or who can persuade public opinion. And it's very frustrating. I think that our system needs to be built on something stronger than public opinion. And basically that's what my case came out to, popular opinion." As I got up to leave, Mangum stood up and put her hand against the Plexiglas. "Get me outta here," she said.

CHAPTER SIXTEEN

Insufficient Credible Evidence

At Duke, after the public exoneration of Seligmann, Finnerty, and Evans, the powers-that-be were nearly tripping over themselves to jump on the players' bandwagon. "This announcement comes at the end of an extraordinarily painful year for the young men and their families," Brodhead said. "They have carried themselves with dignity through an ordeal of deep unfairness. Let's be clear about what was said today. The attorney general did not dismiss the allegations on narrow, equivocal, or legalistic ground. He determined our students to be innocent of the charges and said they were 'the tragic result of a rush to accuse.' In short, he used the strongest language of vindication. From the outset, I have been careful to note that these students were entitled to the presumption of innocence and I looked to the legal system to determine the merit of the charges. Now, finally, that process has given us a decision based on a thorough and objective review of the evidence."

Bob Steel, the chairman of the Duke Board of Trustees who had been nearly invisible to the public during the ordeal, wrote a letter to the Duke community. The case against the three lacrosse players should never have been brought, he concluded. "This announcement explicitly and unequivocally establishes the innocence of David, Collin, and Reade, who with their families have suffered an unimaginable year of accusation and public scrutiny," he wrote. "They deserve our respect for the honorable way they have conducted themselves during this long legal ordeal that ends with their exoneration." Steel emphasized that Cooper had blamed Nifong for the "miscarriage of justice" and reiterated that while "these three young men and their teammates" could have "been spared the agony of the past year," it was essential for Duke "to defer to the criminal justice system" because, as "imperfect and flawed as it may be, it is that process that brings us today to this resolution." While neither Brodhead nor Steel apologized for the university's initial reactions to the allegations—and indeed defended the decision to let the justice system work—there was little doubt that civil lawsuits awaited them and the university, as defense attorneys had made clear. "This isn't a day when I'm thinking about lawsuits," Brodhead told the *Chronicle.* "This is a day when I'm thinking about relief at the end of this long ordeal."

Meanwhile, there was tremendous fury directed at Nifong—some of it thinly veiled, most of it palpable. "High-profile criminal cases dramatically increase the press coverage and curiosity," the North Carolina Conference of District Attorneys said in a statement. "This creates an environment in which there is an incredible amount of pressure for the public, press, and decision-makers to rush to judgment. The responsibility and duty of a prosecutor is to deliberately assess the case presented, evaluate the evidence and witnesses and then make a determination as to how to proceed in the case so as to attempt to obtain justice for the public, alleged victims, and the defendant. The prosecutors of this state grapple with thousands of decisions involving these issues on a daily basis. We are confident that Deputy Attorney General Coman and Mary Winstead have diligently conducted their analysis of the Duke lacrosse cases and acted accordingly." Freda Black, a longtime nemesis of Nifong who still wanted his job, seemed to relish the outcome. "It was clear to me and a lot of other people that [Nifong] used this case to win the election," she said. "The sad thing about it is that it worked. I found that to be very discouraging about the political process. . . . He had no name recognition before this case. I don't think anybody outside the courthouse knew who he was."

And there were the columnists and editorial writers who called for Nifong's head. "Cooper's comments come amid an ongoing ethical investigation evaluating Nifong's behavior into this case," wrote the *Chronicle*'s editors. "And now, all eyes are turned to Nifong. It is now quite apparent that he abused his position as the prosecutor in this case and blatantly failed to obey rules governing the ethical conduct of attorneys. . . . Mike Nifong can no longer be Durham's district attorney and should be disbarred."

Howard Kurtz, the media critic for the *Washington Post*, was particularly critical of the media's role in fomenting the rush to judgment. "It was an awful performance," he said. "No question about it. News organizations took one woman's shaky allegations and turned them into a national soap opera, pillorying the reputations of the players. . . . Remember all the 'trend' stories about 'pampered' and 'privileged' student athletes being 'out of control'? Remember how the lacrosse players' homes were shown on TV? How the coach lost his job? How this case was depicted as being about the contrast between a white elite institution and a poor black community? All of that was built on what turned out to be lies." Like Kurtz, the editors of the *Washington Post* were also critical of the news media that, "eager to pursue a 'Jocks Gone Wild' story line, aided and abetted by [Nifong's] rush to judgment, all but pronouncing the students guilty before the facts were in. A notable early skeptic was Stuart Taylor Jr. of the *National Journal*, whose precise analysis of the evidence stands as a rebuke to less careful colleagues. Similarly, the Pavlovian politically correct response among some at Duke University, who bemoaned 'white privilege' and were quick to dispense with any presumptions of innocence, is embarrassing in hindsight."

On the night of April 11, Katie Couric led the CBS evening news with the story of Cooper's dismissal of the case. After an interview with Reade Seligmann's parents, a *CBS News* reporter tracked down Nifong in the driveway at his home in Durham. "Don't come in my yard," Nifong said to him. "Don't come in my home."

"What would you say to the boys' families, Mr. Nifong?" the reporter called after Nifong, who did not respond.

The next day, he did. In a public statement, Nifong said that, while "I certainly take issue with some of Mr. Cooper's comments," he had confidence in his investigation and had high regard for both Coman and Winstead, whom he had known for more than twenty years. He noted that they had had access to all the evidence he had, plus additional evidence they "developed" during their twelve-week investigation. Sounding a bit like a dry run for his state bar defense, Nifong reminded people that he had requested Cooper to take over the investigation and had turned over to him "every document, every photograph, every piece of evidence of any kind that had been turned up in the Durham Police Department's investigation of these cases" as well as his office's investigations. "If I did not want to subject either that investigation or my own performance to such scrutiny—if, in other words, I had anything to hide—I could have simply dismissed the cases myself," he continued. "The fact that I, instead, chose to seek that review should in and of itself call into question the characterizations of this prosecution as rogue and unchecked."

He then mustered what seemed like an apology, or as close to one as Nifong could stomach. "Finally, it is, and always has been the goal of our criminal justice system to see that the guilty are punished and that the innocent are set free," he said. "We all want that system to work perfectly. At the same time, we all know that no system based on human judgment can ever work perfectly. Those of us who work within that system can only make the best judgments we can, based on the facts available to us, with the understanding that those judgments may have to be modified as more facts become known. That is the process I used in these cases, and that is the process the attorney general used in these cases. To the extent that I make judgments that ultimately prove to be incorrect, I apologize to the three students that were wrongly accused. I also understand that whenever someone has been wrongly accused, the harm caused by the accusations might not be immediately undone, merely by dismissing them. It is my sincere desire that the actions of the attorney general will serve to remedy any remaining injury that has resulted from these cases."

Nifong's speech did not go over well. "It's a very weak, tepid, Kool-Aid type of apology," Wade Smith said, "coming a year after these people started to endure the things they endured. . . . It doesn't seem real. It seems conditional."

Smith recalled how he and the other attorneys had once met with Nifong, before the players were indicted and before the primary, and urged him to "slow down, because the rush to prosecute" as the election approached was "unsavory." Recalled Smith, "He was cordial. He was pleasant to us, courteous in every way. But he didn't listen. And he didn't stop." Evans's attorney, Joe Cheshire, was appalled. "This is not an apology," he said. "This is another attempt by Mr. Nifong at revisionist history."

Nifong suffered a further setback at the first hearing of the state bar's case against him. At issue was whether the three-member state bar panel hearing the case would accede to his lawyers' request to throw out the most serious charge against him—that of withholding the exculpatory DNA evidence from the defense—on the basis that, essentially, Nifong did turn over all the DNA evidence well before any trial date had been set. But, after consulting with his fellow panel members, F. Lane Williamson, the chairman of the panel, ruled that the charge against Nifong would stay.

In arguing to throw the charge out, Nifong's attorney Dudley Witt told Williamson, "We have an allegation that Mr. Nifong should have memorialized his discussions with Dr. Meehan. There is no allegation that a court ordered him to do it." But Williamson countered that the relevant North Carolina statute read, in part, "Make timely disclosure to the defense of all evidence or information known to the prosecutor that tends to negate the guilt of the accused or mitigates the offense."

Witt focused on what the meaning of the word "timely" was. "If he gets a report in on August 28, does he need to mail it off September 1?" he wondered. "If he needs time to study something, can he have time to study it?" Williamson agreed that the question of timeliness was a good one and that there weren't many legal precedents that addressed the issue. He said, though, that a Colorado case from 2002 made the "pretty good" point that, "If the exculpatory evidence is material, then the prosecutor must disclose that evidence in advance of the next critical stage of the proceeding, whether the evidence would particularly affect that hearing or not." Witt countered that, applying that standard to the lacrosse case, "there were not, I would submit to you, any critical proceedings that had occurred in the criminal case." Williamson wondered, though, "Should a prosecutor . . . who intentionally tries to withhold that information get a free pass just because somehow it has come to light prior to trial?"

He offered to play devil's advocate. "Say this was a civil case and you had an interrogatory to the effect of, 'Tell me what the results of the DNA are here,'" he said. "And you have 1,844 pages of stuff you've got to go through to try to figure it out; you wouldn't be happy with that, if that's the response you got. . . . An uncharitable person would say, if you were trying to hide the information— that not only did the DNA testing not match any of these lacrosse players under

THE PRICE OF SILENCE

suspicion, but also there were positive results from other people—you would do exactly that. You would dump the information, rather than simply say, 'Yeah, there were four other guys' DNA found.' You know, the one statement you would want to know. And so intent is important here. And we're going to have to figure out at the hearing, as best as we can from the evidence, what Mr. Nifong's intent was here. And again, an uncharitable person would say, 'Well, that's the way you do it if you're trying to hide it, is to do this the way he did.'"

Witt tried to argue that the DNA testing was complex and that Williamson was putting the onus on the prosecutor to figure it out and convey that judgment to the defense. But Williamson disagreed. "As a layman, I understand when the person who does the testing tells me, 'I didn't find anything on these lacrosse players.' I also understand as a layperson if he tells me, 'But we found DNA from other men.' I also understand as a lawyer . . . the old thing, 'absence of evidence isn't evidence of absence.' But here, knowing that there's testing that has found DNA from other people, that is 'evidence of absence.' I don't need to understand anything about the science. That's all I need to understand."

Williamson argued that, in the end, the issues he and the panel were going to evaluate were really pretty simple: "Did he talk too much in the pre-trial statements? Is there a legitimate law enforcement purpose for those statements? If so, what is it? Let's hear it. And on the DNA evidence, did he reveal what he should have revealed by the time he should have revealed it? And then, suffusing all of that is, what was his intent?" He said Nifong, Meehan, and members of the Durham Police Department would testify to "shed light on those issues."

For her part, Katherine Jean, the state bar counsel, said the timeliness of when Nifong had shared the DNA evidence was irrelevant. She cited a statute regarding the collection of pre-indictment DNA evidence that stated that such evidence must be turned over to the defense "as soon as the reports are available." Said Jean: "The state bar has alleged that Dr. Meehan gave an oral report to Mr. Nifong before he sought and obtained the indictments" of Seligmann and Finnerty, but Nifong did not share the results of it with the two men. "This isn't about how you interpret the word 'timely,'" Jean continued. "This says it must be provided as soon as it is available." She said Nifong had other meetings with Meehan where additional information about the results of the DNA testing was conveyed and still—not until forced to by a judge did Nifong share the results with the defense (although that was not entirely true, as Nifong had turned over both the SBI lab results and the summary document of DSI's findings to the defense). "But what is bothersome here," Jean said, "is that in 95 percent of the criminal cases in North Carolina, there's a plea bargain. There's not a trial. . . . It's scary, when you think about a case like this case, because this is DNA evidence that the district attorney has in his possession that certainly could be argued by a defendant to be exculpatory—'Some other man deposited the DNA on this woman. It's not me'—and yet if this hadn't come to light through the extraordinary diligence of the defense counsel in these criminal cases, who knows. These men might have pled guilty, never knowing that the DNA evidence was exculpatory of them."

When she thought about it for a minute, though, she said Seligmann, Finnerty, and Evans would have continued to fight the charges because their families had deep pockets. But what Nifong and his attorneys were arguing, she said, was that "for the defendants who don't have the means to fight, and haven't been shown that there's DNA evidence that's exculpatory and end up pleading guilty, no harm, no foul. It's a scary concept."

After the panel ruled against Nifong, a crush of TV cameramen and reporters flanked him as he made his way to his car. "You'll look good in an orange jumpsuit," a heckler said. Nifong would not comment on the ruling. "I'll do my talking inside the courtroom," he said. "My statement [Thursday] is in really plain language. I think it speaks for itself." His attorney, David Freedman, said there had been no discussion of the possibility that Nifong might resign. "Here's a man who's devoted his whole life to public service," he said. "He still wants to serve people."

The weekend following Cooper's announcement that the state of North Carolina would drop its charges was alumni weekend at Duke. In a speech to an auditorium full of alumni—that was off-limits to television reporters and photographers—Brodhead said he and his fellow administrators had attempted to handle the lacrosse case with equanimity. "But I also do think it is time for us to look each other in the eye and say we have suffered this story for a year, and now let us figure out how to move on to a constructive future," he said.

That weekend there was also a Duke–Virginia lacrosse game, which Duke won in sudden-death overtime. Dom Starsia, the Virginia coach, told the *Chronicle*, "Last spring there was a sense of terror among college lacrosse coaches that they were coming to get the rest of us. In a very close community like college lacrosse, it affected us all in a very real way, and quite dramatically." Before the three Duke lacrosse players were indicted, Starsia said he had many opportunities to speak to the media about lacrosse culture, but he declined them. "It was never about the sport of lacrosse," he said. "It was more a college athlete issue, and it happened to be a men's lacrosse team. . . . They could have found similar things on any college campus." (Starsia would have his own crisis when one of his star players, George Huguely V, was charged in May 2010 with murdering his girlfriend, Yardley Love, also a lacrosse player, during a drunken rage at the University of Virginia campus. In February 2012, Huguely was convicted of second-degree murder and grand larceny—

of Love's computer—and sentenced to twenty-three years in prison.) Scott Anderson, Harvard's men's lacrosse coach, said "there were a million lessons to be learned" from the Duke case, "one of which is that athletes are very much in the public eye and subject to the sensationalism that was applied to this case by all different forms of media. You can't ignore that. It's part of the additional responsibility that comes with the privilege of being an athlete and representing your school."

The final installment of the *60 Minutes* trilogy about the case came on the evening of April 15. Correspondent Lesley Stahl spoke with the three players and Roy Cooper. Cooper told Stahl that Nifong had gone off the reservation. "When we have a prosecutor who takes advantage of his enormous power and overreaches like this, then yes, it's offensive, and yes, it's my duty as the chief law enforcement officer of this state to call him out on it," he said. While Nifong's motives for his decisions promised to be a major topic of examination during his state bar hearing in June, as Williamson had made clear, Cooper said that, regardless of Nifong's motives, "the result was wrong. What happened was wrong." Cooper said he and his investigators could not figure out if, or when, Nifong or Linwood Wilson, Nifong's investigator, ever asked Mangum the "tough questions" about the many inconsistencies in her version of events. "When our investigators and attorneys started interviewing her again, new stories came out that had never been told before that did not fit with the evidence," he said. "So we went in and tried to get all of it rectified, and the way it turned out, it was much worse than we thought."

Was Mangum lying? Stahl wondered. "The people who talked with her, and these are trained investigators who have been around for a long time, a number of them said to me, 'I've never seen anything like this.'" Cooper recalled for Stahl Mangum's second interview with Coman and Winstead and how she had described yet another version of the events of the night of March 13. "She was suspended in midair and was being assaulted by all three of them in the bathroom," Cooper said Mangum told them. "And I've been in that bathroom. And it was very difficult for me to see how that could have occurred. And then we got *another* new story."

Why, because the bathroom was so small? Stahl asked.

"It was a small bathroom," Cooper said. "Yes. And you would've had to have four people in there in different positions that she was describing to us being attacked. Including being suspended in mid-air. It was just difficult for any of us to see how that could have occurred."

Cooper said Mangum's "new" story was about what had happened outside the house. "She says that Reade Seligmann and David Evans pushed her out onto the back porch," he told Stahl. "And then all three of them went out and started kicking her and beating her on the back porch. And then there were ten other lacrosse players in the backyard who were assaulting her and pushing her around. And there was absolutely no evidence that any of that had occurred." Indeed, there was the picture of Mangum lying on the back stoop of the house, with a half smile on her face. Mangum had said that that was before the rape occurred, but the "verified" time-stamp indicated it was taken afterward. "She was smiling on the back porch," Cooper said. "It was a picture that our prosecuting attorneys and investigators said they would've had a real hard time explaining to a jury."

It all seemed so sad, Stahl said. "All of this was a tragedy, because it should have been stopped somewhere along the line," Cooper said. "Good prosecutors, we demand them to look hard at the facts, look hard at the law. We also demand them to change their minds if the facts so dictate. Here, these contradictions were clearly pointing to the fact that this attack did not occur. And it's disappointing and really outrageous that it was not stopped sooner."

The segment then turned to Mangum's emotional state, which Stahl reported Cooper had determined was "clearly mentally unbalanced." Stahl cited Nifong's records of her "long psychological history" and her use of the anti-psychotics Depakote and Seroquel. "It was amazing how she could continue to tell different stories," Cooper said. "And she actually believed the many stories that she told." By then, Stahl had heard about Mangum's early April 2007 meeting at the Durham police station house, where she was incapacitated. "Our investigative team believed that she was under the influence of something," Cooper confirmed to Stahl. He said Mangum was disappointed to hear that Cooper was dropping the case. "She wanted to move forward with the case," he said. He also told Stahl, in answer to her question, that part of his consideration for not filing charges against Mangum was to help Durham recover from the whole episode.

Stahl asked the three players to share their opinions of Mangum. "I think she's a very troubled woman," Evans said of Mangum. "We're not vindictive people. We don't want to take her away from her children. We hope that she gets help. And hopefully . . . we won't have to hear her name ever again." Cooper's decision to leave her alone was troubling, however, to Finnerty. "You know, we went through a lot," he said. "If no one has to pay for it, it's tough to imagine that that was all, you know, fine; nothing should happen. But I feel like something should happen."

As for Nifong, the players were less charitable. "It's hard to put into words what you would say to a person that was trying to put you in jail for thirty years," Seligmann said. "And he caused our family so much pain and heartache for so long. . . . He tried to take away my name. He tried to take away my life." He said Nifong should "absolutely" be punished. Added Evans, "I can only imagine it's very difficult for him to go home and have go look his son in the eyes and have to answer the questions that he probably has for him." Should he resign? Stahl asked. "I want to give him the respect that he didn't give us,"

Evans said. "And he's got a legal situation to deal with. . . . The legal system determines guilt or innocence, and [to] go out here and say that he is guilty, I don't think that's right. And I've learned my lesson." About Nifong's apology, Finnerty elaborated, "This has been a year of decision after decision after decision to keep doing the wrong thing. He's had so much time to say he's sorry over the last year. And now he comes the day after we're exonerated. I don't think anyone's going to feel better after that apology." What would you say to Nifong? Stahl asked Finnerty. "Why?" he said. "Why? I just wish I could just get it answered—why us?"

Seligmann said he was happy, but also in an unforgiving mood. "I'm angry at so many people, and there are so many people that I think need to be held accountable," he said. "But for the time being, I'm just so happy to get back on with my life. I want to move forward. I want to be back at school. I'm out for getting my name back. I want to smile again. I don't want to have to be vengeful." Evans said he thought the healing process would be a long one—for all involved. "I don't think it really will ever be over," he said. "No matter what, you can try to move on, but rape will always be associated with my name. Innocent might be a part of that, but when I die, they'll say, 'One of the three Duke lacrosse rape suspects died today. He led a life and did this, but he was one of the three Duke lacrosse rape suspects.'"

On April 17, Michael Cornacchia, a New York City–based attorney for Collin Finnerty, made clear what the Finnertys thought should happen to Nifong. In a letter to Governor Easley and Attorney General Cooper, Cornacchia outlined four requests. First, he wanted the two men to "call on" Nifong to "resign immediately." He noted that when Easley was in New York, he had told the audience at New York University that Nifong was the "worst appointment" of his career and that Nifong had "lied" to him when he said he would not run for election in 2006. Cornacchia also, of course, cited Cooper's description of Nifong as a "rogue" and "unchecked" prosecutor and said Nifong continued to make "life-altering decisions about who should be subject to prosecution" and how cases were to be prosecuted. He did not mention, but could have, that Nifong was still prosecuting a quadruple homicide case and was fighting the release of a man imprisoned for twenty-eight years for stealing $173. "Mr. Nifong has not done the honorable thing and tendered his resignation," he wrote. "He may do so if you both publicly and unequivocally call for that resignation."

Cornacchia was not satisfied that the state bar's procedure against Nifong was "sufficient"; he noted it "will not, and cannot, address the conduct of the members of Mr. Nifong's office, the officers of the Durham Police Department and others such as Mr. Meehan" in what he wrote "can only be characterized as a 'frame-up' of three young men whose parents had sent them to your state for an education." Cornacchia's final request was that an investigation be started into Meehan's ability to continue to operate his DNA lab in the state.

While Nifong was being spit-roasted, others were willing to give Duke, the institution, the benefit of the doubt for how it had handled the case. "I'm not sure what more the university could have said that would have been supportive of the students and would not have appeared to be Duke trying to interfere in the judicial process," said law professor James Coleman. He said the school had to balance the "gravity of the charges" against the players with the "potential consequences" of using its power and prestige to influence the legal process. "Nifong had already basically attacked students as being wealthy, white, privileged students whose fathers could go out and buy them the best lawyers," Coleman said. "I don't think the university could have asserted that the students were innocent under those circumstances." The players, too, could have lost their absolute victory had Duke been more forceful on their behalf. "It would have been difficult for the Bar to intervene in the middle of the case because of the appearance that the Bar was acting under the influence of the university," he continued. "And the same is true for Cooper. If it looked like Duke was pressing for exoneration, it would be difficult for him to say they are innocent."

Brodhead seemed to concur with Coleman's logic. In an e-mail to the *Chronicle* he wrote, "The University urged everyone to defer to the legal process for two reasons. First, that's the way our society has agreed to resolve disputes of fact and judgment, and we undermine that system only at great public risk. If Duke had used its institutional power to attack the case, [Nifong] might well have said, 'How am I to stand up to pressure like this?' and folded his hand—leaving an ambiguous, unsatisfactory result."

As for Bob Steel (going against the wishes of Duke, which had asked him not to talk to me about the lacrosse case), the chairman of the board of trustees reflected back on what the lacrosse scandal had been like for him. "When I first heard about it, I didn't know all the details, but you had the idea there was an incident, and you wondered if it was kind of garden-variety misbehaving," he explained. "And then it became clear it wasn't garden-variety misbehaving. It had other aspects to it." Once the board realized how serious the allegations were, it kicked into a higher gear. "We're stewards of the university," Steel said. "Here you have an institution that's one hundred years old. Universities in America are extremely durable institutions. How do you manage through this in the best way that's consistent with the values that you think should be undergirding the institution, and what are the values? It's complicated, because here you have an incident that developed a scale and an interest and a complexity that was outside the normal things we do. The press office at Duke issues press releases, copies of reports, presidential speeches, and discusses, in Duke's case, national championships. All of a sudden, you have multiple TV cameras outside, reporters all over the campus, national news covering events, and we weren't prepared to deal with that. We just weren't."

Steel said the university did its best to deal with the situation in real time but sometimes events overtook it. "Everyone wanted instant resolution or instant perspective when, in fact, facts came out over time," he said. "And certain things came out as facts that later turned out not to be facts. So I think that it's complex, is the real issue." One of the crucial principals that the Duke board stuck to—which was often parroted by Brodhead—was that there was a legal process that had started and there was little the university could do until that legal process resolved itself. "You have a legal system, you have a university judicial system, and you have a sense of fairness in how you're trying to manage people's understanding of the situation," Steel said. "Universities are exciting because of all the different cohorts and perspectives that exist there, and all these cohorts, I think, have a focus and the ability to pull together, whether it's students, faculty, blue-collar workers, the community, alumni, or the administration, and the board. These were all groups trying to deal with this. So the strategy, I think, from the board was to provide guidance and be available to the management of the university, which is the executive office, and so that's what we tried to do. We're lucky because we had, on the board, people that understood legal issues. We had a State Supreme Court justice. We had a dozen attorneys, several from North Carolina, some of whom were African-American, some of whom were white. We had people that understood the politics of North Carolina, [one] who had been president of the North Carolina State Legislature. So we had a group of people, and we had previous trustees that did our very best to give advice to the president."

But often, chaos reigned. "It was pretty clear this situation had accelerant," he said. "It's a bit like the McNamarian 'Fog of War,' that when you're in war, it's not going to be clear what's going on around you." Adhering to established principles was essential. "I believe boards have four functions," he said. "Number one is they choose the strategy; two, they choose the leader; three, they monitor the leader's actions relative to strategy; and four, they're available for consultation. That's what boards should do, in my opinion. It's pretty straightforward."

He said that while the board made a few mistakes, overall the situation was handled well. "Our principles were right, that, one, the legal process has to be the predominant thing," he said. "I think there are some things we could have done better. I think our support of the students was deficient, and if I could wave a magic wand, I think we could've done a better job. It was complicated by the decisions that the coach should be relieved, because the coach would be the normal person that you would use as your valve to the students. . . . The key person in these boys' lives was the coach, and when the decision was made to relieve the coach, who takes the place in these boys' Duke lives as their key contact, confidante, looks them in the eye and basically says, 'If you have any problem, call me'? Who takes that job? I don't think we did it very well." Steel also said he wished he could have a "do-over" on Brodhead's April 20 statement to the Durham Chamber of Commerce, "If they didn't do it, whatever they did is bad enough." Steel said, "I think Dick's vocabulary, on occasion, strayed. . . . Dick is a talker. Sometimes you have to have a message and you don't say anything more. You get in, you get out. Dick tends to go on. We were practicing for depositions and [Duke's lawyer said], 'Dick, you're the worst person I ever tried to teach about depositions. You talk too much. You're a professor. You explain everything.' The answer is, 'That's not something I can recall.' Then you're through. 'That's not something about which I have a recollection.' I've done this, unfortunately, a lot of times, but Dick wants to pontificate. He's an English professor."

Steel, then sixty-one years old and the deputy mayor of New York City, seemed to be understanding of the "bad boy" behavior that had occurred in the house at 610 North Buchanan. "I think that part of growing up is doing things that aren't right," he said. "That's how you learn what's right. As I tell my kids all the time, if we have a contest of who's made the most mistakes, I win. Making mistakes is part of life. Whether I think having bars that have exotic dancers is right or wrong, that's completely legal and they exist in our community and in our society, so you and I can have an opinion. So I made a decision: when I became a partner of Goldman Sachs, I would never go to a strip club again, because I said I can't go and have some kid from Goldman Sachs see me and tell everyone at Goldman Sachs he saw Bob last night in a strip club, and then me look at a woman employee in the eye, and have her think that I'm going to view her in a balanced way. I can't, so I have never been since then. My brother's bachelor party, at his wedding, was the last time. I used to joke with my wife: someday, when all this is over and I don't have a job, I'm going to go to Las Vegas for a week and go to strip clubs so I can make up for it, but I haven't done that yet. So I made that decision . . . that it's not really what we should do, for a variety of reasons, and my life hasn't been adversely impacted. I haven't missed that much. But I think the idea that kids do dopey things is kind of what kids do. Do I think that it was a pretty heavy dose of dopey things at this event? Yeah, and I can tell it in a way that sounds insidious. I might personally think the cumulative impact of having strippers, swearing, making ethnic comments, using a broomstick as an alleged sex toy, rifling their purses, and things like that—assuming those things are all true—I personally might feel that that's pretty unattractive. So I do, but kids do dumb things. Did you ever drive after drinking too much? I did. And could something terrible have happened? Could I have injured someone? Yes, and I did that. You know, boy, am I lucky."

As for what he believed happened in the bathroom that night, Steel said, "I felt there was zero chance that there was a group activity, that thirty guys saw something that was incredibly unattractive or whatever. These guys are like your and my kids. They're babies. Someone would've told their parents that

'I saw this' or whatever. I don't believe there's any group thing that happened, something that they all saw. I just don't buy it, because I just think some kid would've broken to his mom, or some dad [would have] said, 'Tell me the truth or I'm taking away your car.' We have no idea what happened in a bathroom with one person or two persons. I have no clue, no idea. And again, you and I have dealt with things where you don't know, so you have to hope for the best and plan for it not being the best, but I have no idea. Today, what do I think? I just don't know. And then you get the issue of, there are like seven clicks on this dial of what it could be. I don't need to be graphic. You can imagine seven clicks, some of which you can go, 'That's not so great,' or other clicks you can imagine, 'That's pretty unattractive.'" Was justice served? "We have a legal system that has a process by which the wheels of justice turn," he said. "I believe that that process, after it wound its way to the right conclusion, I believe that it was an extremely unusual and messy, non-normal process this time, but in the end, yes, the exoneration seems like the right outcome."

Steel said he felt good about most of his decisions along the way and suggested that he had yet to receive the credit he deserved for navigating Duke through rough waters. "My biggest fear, some nights when I went to bed," he said, "was that I used to remember the exact distance, 3.8 miles from Duke was North Carolina Central, and that this could've turned into a very messy black-white confrontation with people driving by, shooting guns and things like that. It could've happened in a second. They had Black Panthers on campus, and things like that. No one's ever written about the management of that dynamic, point one. And there were reports of guns being shot. There were Black Panthers on campus who had guns. And the fear of an incident spiraling out of control. No one's ever said, 'You guys did a good job.' No one's ever said there wasn't anything violent; it never turned into a black-white situation. No one's ever given anybody any credit for managing that. We discussed that a lot. No one's ever written it. It's fine with me. I don't care."

Then, he said, "Number two, I busted my ass to keep the board on the same page. We've got a lot of strong personalities on the board. You never heard the board break apart once. They were managed to be on the same page, and I must have spoken to every board member a bunch of times, basically saying, 'Listen, what do you think?' because my view was having the board break apart—and there were some people that were more student-sensitive on the board—John Mack [the former chairman and CEO of Morgan Stanley]—he's a handful. So keeping the board together was, I thought, my job, and I give myself a good grade on that." He said the decision to suspend the season was particularly unpopular. "There are people that will go to their grave being angry at me because we robbed their boys of the ability to play," he said. (Duke successfully appealed to the NCAA to allow the lacrosse players to have a fifth year of eligibility to make up for the lost season.) "So," he continued, "suspending the season, relieving Pressler, very controversial at the time. We had very little support for that from anyone. That was a lonely decision. . . . And then the decision to hire Danowski. We had three or four choices and I think we chose the right guy. I don't need a thank-you note from anybody. I'm just telling you I feel pretty good about it."

Not that Seligmann, Finnerty, and Evans needed more evidence of having been wronged, but they got it anyway on April 27, when Cooper released his twenty-one-page report on how he had decided to drop the case against the three players and to declare them innocent. "The State's cases rested primarily on a witness whose recollection of the facts of the allegations was imprecise and contradictory," Cooper wrote. "This alone would have made it difficult for a prosecutor to prove the allegations. However with additional evidence uncovered in the new investigation, it was clear that there was no credible evidence that these crimes occurred at 610 N. Buchanan Blvd. in Durham that night." The combination of the lack of evidence and additional "affirmative proof" that "these crimes" did not occur "during this time" caused Cooper, Coman, and Winstead to declare the three players "innocent of these charges."

Here was what Cooper wrote happened on the night of March 13: During the afternoon, Dan Flannery called the escort service to arrange for two white dancers to come to the house at 610 North Buchanan at 11 p.m. He did not use his real name. At 11 p.m., "Nikki"—Roberts—arrived at the house. She waited at the house for some thirty minutes for Mangum to arrive. At 11:10, Flannery made three calls to the escort service, wondering where Mangum was. Between 11:11 p.m. and 11:39 p.m., Mangum received four calls and made one call. At about 11:40 p.m., Mangum was dropped off at the house, forty minutes late. At the start, Mangum was described as "unsteady on her feet." Each of the dancers was paid $400 in cash. Flannery took them to the bathroom to get ready for the performance. Mangum was already in her dance outfit, but Roberts needed to change. In the meantime, Flannery confirmed with the forty or so party attendees that they were interested in seeing two nonwhite women dance. They were. He also confirmed with Mangum and "Nikki" that they were cool with dancing before forty guys, not at a bachelor party as promised. They agreed to perform.

Just before midnight, the two women left the bathroom and went to the living room to dance. Mangum appeared to be "unsteady on her feet" and "fell to the ground." During the performance, there was "sexual banter" between "Nikki" and "some of the party attendees" involving the use of "sex toys," which "culminated" in one of the "attendees" holding up a broomstick "and suggesting its use as a sexual object for the dancers." This upset Roberts, and the "performance abruptly ended." At 12:04 a.m., "Nikki" and Mangum retreated to the back of the house. Flannery and Evans ("and possibly others") went to speak with the two women and "assuage" their hurt feelings about the broom-stick comment. They reminded the women that they had been paid $800 but the show had lasted all of about four minutes. They dancers then returned to the bathroom "where they had left their belongings."

Shortly after the dancing ended, at 12:05 a.m., Seligmann started making phone calls—to his girlfriend and others—and then, at 12:14 a.m., he called the cab company. He left the party at around 12:19 a.m. with another player and walked around the corner to get into the cab. Then he was off to the ATM, the Cook-Out, and then back to his dorm room at 12:46 a.m. Finnerty, meanwhile, decided to leave the house after the dancing ended, too. He and some friends left 610 North Buchanan and headed around the corner to 1105 Urban Street, where other lacrosse players lived. At 12:22 a.m., he used his cell phone to call another lacrosse player. They spoke for two minutes. Five minutes later, another player called him and wondered where he was; he said he was at 1105 Urban. At 12:30 a.m., and again three minutes later, Finnerty called Domino's Pizza. Sometime thereafter, Finnerty and three other players walked to Cosmic Cantina, picked up some food and paid for it at 12:56 a.m.

Meanwhile, back at the party house, some of the players who stuck around were miffed that the performance had been so short. They wanted a refund or a continuation of the dancing. According to Cooper, "eventually" Mangum and "Nikki" left the bathroom and went outside to the backyard. Flannery spoke to them. He again apologized for the broomstick comment and urged them to return to the house to continue dancing. They went to Roberts's car. Then Evans came to the car, with other players, to talk to the women. In the meantime, several of the players used the bathroom and noticed that the danc-ers' cosmetic bags were there, with the money inside. Feeling cheated, they removed some of the money. But both Flannery and Evans told them to put the money back, which they did.

Eventually, the two dancers returned to the house through the back door, although by then more of the players had left. Those that remained at the house also apologized for the broomstick comment. For some reason, the player who had made the comment—Peter Lamade—"approached the danc-ers," which made "Nikki" angry again and caused the two dancers to go back to the bathroom "alone together" and "refuse to come out." Flannery went to the bathroom and tried "to coax" the dancers to leave the house. Then Evans and Matt Zash, the other cocaptain living at the house, urged everyone to leave the house because they were concerned the police might show up and arrest people for noise and underage drinking violations, as had increasingly been the pattern in the neighborhood.

Sometime "before 12:30 a.m.," the dancers opened the bathroom door and left the house through the back door "for the second time." Flannery and "Nikki" walked back to her car using the sidewalk in the front of the house.

Mangum lingered in the back of the house. With the two dancers outside the house, as well as most of the players who had stuck around, Zash locked the door at the back of the house to prevent anyone from getting inside. Mangum began banging on the door to get back in but Zash refused to let her in. At 12:26 a.m., Mangum called the escort service. Four minutes later, she was photographed on the back porch "smiling and rummaging through Evans's shaving kit." Under her arm was her cosmetics bag, in which was "an object that appears to be her cell phone." A video made at 12:31 a.m. shows Mangum "talking incoherently" and telling the players she was "a cop." She also appeared to be unsteady on her feet as she walked down the back porch steps. At 12:37 a.m., Mangum was photographed in a "prone position" on the back porch. Flannery, who had been with Roberts in the front of the house, was told of the "problem" with Mangum in the back of the house and he found her lying on the back porch. He then helped carry her to "Nikki's car." By 12:42 a.m., both dancers were in the car. The flinging of racial epithets on both sides soon followed, and then Roberts and Mangum drove away.

And that was that. There was not even the remotest indication in Cooper's report that anything like a sexual assault or rape occurred in the house at 610 North Buchanan in the early morning hours of March 14.

Cooper focused on Mangum's credibility as a witness at trial. "With no evidence other than the accusing witness's word, a jury would have to conclude that her word was sufficient to prove guilt beyond a reasonable doubt," he wrote. He concluded unequivocally that she had no credibility left—"insurmountable credibility issues," is how Cooper put it. After citing Mangum's erratic behavior at the March 13 party—the stumbling around, the drinking, passing out— he noted that the special prosecutors saw "similar behavior firsthand" when Mangum met with them on April 4, 2007.

Her recollection of events was faulty. "She denied to the special prosecutors that she had made statements attributed to her in medical reports both the night of the alleged attack and in the following days," the report claimed. "She denied making statements attributed to her in police reports. Significantly, on several occasions, when confronted with evidence that contradicted her assertions, she changed her story." The report continued, "In meetings with the special prosecutors," Mangum, "when recounting the events of that night, changed her story on so many important issues as to give the impression that she was improvising as the interviews progressed, even when she was faced with irrefutable evidence that what she was saying was not credible. [Mangum] attempted to avoid the contradictions by changing her story, contradicting previous stories, or alleging the evidence had been fabricated." Asked to explain her behavior during the party, which suggested she was impaired, Mangum told Cooper's special prosecutors "she was dizzy and fuzzy" when the two women began dancing and that she was "dizzy after the alleged assault," and "that was

why she was stumbling in the backyard." As for her certainty about the identification of Seligmann, Finnerty, and Evans, she explained she was "dizzy when
the dancing started, she 'woke up' in the bathroom, and then was dizzy afterward." Mangum "gave numerous differing statements to law enforcement and
medical personnel" about what happened on the night of March 13, Cooper
wrote: "While witnesses often have inconsistencies in details when recounting
events over time, the volume of inconsistent statements and the fact that many
of these were substantial and were in regard to significant events rendered the
truthfulness of the accusing witness in serious doubt."

The attorney general then traced a litany of Mangum's inconsistent statements, with the most incredible coming during an interview with the special
prosecutors on March 29 when she explained how the three indicted players
raped her in the bathroom after lifting her up in the air. This particular description of events caused Cooper, in the April 11 press conference, to remark that
after visiting the bathroom at 610 North Buchanan, he could not imagine how
three big guys and Mangum could have possibly contorted themselves into
the positions she described in such a small space. Cooper was simply incredulous. He also expressed his doubts about her differing descriptions of whether
the attack occurred over ten minutes, twenty minutes, or thirty minutes. "It
was evident to the special prosecutors that there was no opportunity for an
attack to occur for even ten minutes, much less the twenty or thirty minutes
as alleged," Cooper wrote.

In sum, Cooper wrote, Mangum's assertions of what had happened on the
night of March 13 seemed to be the stuff of pure fantasy. Along with Mangum's
inconsistencies, there was no evidence to support her version of events: "No
DNA evidence confirmed her stories," he wrote. "No medical evidence confirmed her stories. . . . No other witnesses confirmed her stories." Even in the
face of the mounting discrepancies in her version of events and the lack of evidence to support them, Cooper wrote, Mangum "was unwilling" in her meetings with the special prosecutors to admit that "she might be mistaken about
the identification of the defendants." Cooper wrote that, "While prosecutors
acknowledge that rape and sexual assault victims often have some inconsistencies in their accounts of a traumatic event, in this case, the inconsistencies
were so significant and so contrary to the evidence that the State had no credible evidence that an attack occurred in that house that night."

Cooper also addressed the possibility that David Evans's DNA was on one
of Mangum's fake fingernails, noting that, "while analysts could not confirm
the DNA matched Evans, he could not be excluded." He found, however, that
this "failed to confirm that a sexual assault occurred, for several reasons,"
including that "statistically, the chance of randomly selecting an individual
from the populations that would be included in this sample would be approximately one in one thousand"; "a visual examination at the SBI lab" of the

fingernails indicated that there was no skin or body tissue attached, despite Mangum's claim that they had been ripped off during the attack; and "the SBI experts confirmed that the DNA could easily have been transferred to the fingernails from other materials in the trash can."

And after reviewing seven thousand documents, six hundred photographs, interviewing forty-seven people, including seventeen members of the lacrosse team, as well as Nifong, Mangum, and Linwood Wilson, Cooper had closed the book on the incident.

The unraveling of the lacrosse case was also having serious repercussions at Duke. Some of these reverberations were showing up in online commentary. "The fact is that, with the current state of the university, an inept and feckless leader and at least one-fifth of the faculty extreme left wing airheads, a few of us do not give a rat's patoot whether you survive or not," one angry alumnus wrote about Duke. "I will not contribute to this idiocy, my wife [also a Duke graduate] will not give, my daughter [also a Duke graduate] will not give and eight of twelve fraternity brothers I have contacted will suspend contributions." Another Duke alumnus wrote on an online message board that he had changed a family bequest from Duke to Claremont McKenna College because "Duke and Durham have just been rewarded for their [bad] behavior. We will see more of it." He wrote that, "If one of my grandchildren really, really wants to go to Duke, the trust will not pay for it. They will have to figure out the money on their own."

The university appointed a committee to conduct a review of the performance of Joe Alleva, the athletic director. One of the committee members was Jim Coleman, who had produced the report about the lacrosse program a year earlier and revealed that Alleva and his team had failed "to adequately convey to [Mike] Pressler any sense of alarm" with regard to the team's off-the-field activities. "These reviews are done very conscientiously at Duke," Brodhead told the *Chronicle*, "and I will value the committee's findings." On July 24, Brodhead reappointed Alleva to another term as director of athletics, citing the "emphasis on integrity that [Alleva] has infused in[to] our programs and [the] central place he gives to the idea of scholar-athletes." He added, "The situation of college athletics is changing rapidly and in challenging ways. We want to be foresightful in being prepared for these changes."

To the outside world, the impression was given that Alleva had received a new five-year contract. But in fact, although Alleva had asked for a new five-year contract, Brodhead had really given him a one-year extension. Four months before his one-year contract was up, Alleva told Duke, "LSU is after me. . . . I don't really want this job. I want to stay at Duke." But Steel told Alleva, "You owe it to yourself to consider alternatives." Alleva then told Duke that LSU was going to offer him the job. "Can you tell me that my contract will be extended for a five-year normal period when the one-year probation comes up?" he asked. But Duke told him, definitively, "We're not in a position to be able to consider that now." Alleva left Duke in April 2008 to become the athletic director at Louisiana State University. "I am grateful to Joe Alleva," Brodhead said after Alleva announced he was leaving Duke. "Duke athletics sets an example of success and integrity of the highest order and Joe has played a key role in achieving these results." Observed one highly placed Duke official, "He's lucky to get what he got."

During two days in mid-May, Nifong gave his deposition to the state bar attorneys, Katherine Jean, from the state bar, and Douglas Brocker, a Raleigh attorney hired by the state bar. If there was any remaining doubt about the weight of the charges against him, his comments revealed that he understood the gravity of the situation and how his previous public comments could be used against him. It turned out he had never been deposed before. Much of the two days was spent having Nifong recall events as they had unfolded during the nine months he was prosecuting the case. But occasionally he reflected on his decisions and whether he would still have made the same ones again.

He did not think he had violated the state bar's Rules of Professional Conduct by making the statements he did about his belief that a crime had occurred and asking why the players did not come forward voluntarily to tell police what had happened at the party. "If they found a body on the front steps of the courthouse with three bullet wounds in the back and I said that I believed a homicide occurred, that would be stating a fact that I think most people would come to the conclusion of," he said. "I had medical evidence, the evidence from the SANE nurse, and the statement of a victim that she had been sexually assaulted, and I had no reason to question that statement. What I was saying was not directed toward any specific defendant because no defendant had been identified [at that time], no class of defendants had been identified other than she said three white males. We did not know who those people were or who they might be. So I certainly didn't see that classifying something as a crime was bringing any type of public disrepute toward any individual or any class of individuals. I believe I was making a statement that was accurate based on the information that I had and that was informative to the people of Durham that we believed that this crime had taken place."

Then, perhaps sensing for the first time what was at stake during his deposition—that he was at serious risk of being disbarred—Nifong showed some contrition. "I believe that it's permitted for the DA to indicate publicly that a crime has occurred," he said, "but obviously if I'm wrong about that, the Bar will certainly tell me. Certainly I did not intend at that point—and we had nobody who was even a suspect at that time—and so I certainly wasn't commenting on any individual person as having been involved in the crime, just that a crime had taken place and we were trying to identify the people who were involved." He also seemed remorseful about his numerous pre-trial public statements between March 27 and April 3. "If I had to do it all over again, I've indicated I probably wouldn't have made any of these statements. . . . In retrospect, not only were the statements probably inadvisable [as] a practical matter but they were inadvisable [as] an ethical matter as well."

Asked whether once a suspect is identified, it was proper, under the Rules of Professional Conduct, to express an opinion about whether he thought a crime had occurred, Nifong said that once suspects in the lacrosse case had been identified—which seemed to have happened, however inadvertently, at the April 4 photo identification session—he stopped making those kinds of statements. He noted, though, that journalists continued to ask him if he had changed his mind through the course of 2006 about whether a crime had occurred. "My statement, generally speaking, was, 'I have not changed my mind about what has occurred,'" he said. "But it was not specifically a statement. During this period of time, obviously, the defense attorneys were putting out lots of information that was being reported in the newspaper about why these people could not have been guilty of crimes and so on. That was unchallenged because I didn't think it was appropriate—whether or not it was appropriate for them to say anything, I didn't think it was appropriate for me to say anything specifically to that—although we were getting to a point, I think, where there were statements made in response to some, I think, false information that was given to the press. But I would say that I was attempting to get across by making the statement that I had not changed my mind [and] that the evidence that was being reported by the defense team was not something I believed." He continued, in a direct answer to a question, "It seems to me that if I take a subject to the grand jury, prepare a bill of indictment and submit it to the grand jury, and if thereafter take a case before a jury and start to pick, those are acts, in and of themselves, [that] say I believe a crime occurred. I believe it would be unethical for me to prosecute a person if I did not believe he committed a crime."

As to whether or not some of his public comments "inflamed" the racial tensions in Durham, Nifong replied that, "If I had this all to do over again, I probably would not have spoken with the press at all because one thing that I have seen in all of this is, my intentions notwithstanding, things that are said are going to be twisted in various ways by different people and are going to be used in certain ways that are clearly not of benefit to the case. And certainly had I understood at the time that any of these statements were made, that they would have an adverse impact on the case, I would not have made them."

As for the inconsistencies in Mangum's statements about what had happened to her on the night of March 13, Nifong said that he believed he could explain "such inconsistencies" to a jury. "The case really would be based on how a jury evaluated her," he said. "And there was not a lot of corroborating evidence. And we haven't had this issue since I was prosecuting rape cases, but certainly we have what we call 'the CSI effect' now where people watch TV and they expect a lot more out of evidence than can sometimes be there. And, generally speaking, if jurors are disappointed with the quality of the evidence, they hold that against the state." He said that when he decided to go to the grand jury seeking the indictments of Seligmann and Finnerty, he was not thinking about whether the case would be a difficult one to prove. "I don't normally evaluate cases based on how difficult I think they would be to win if I believed the victim was, in fact, a victim of the crime and the victim wanted to go forward," he continued. He said Mangum's testimony on the stand, in court, would have been the ultimate determinant of whether there was a case to be made for the alleged crimes. "It is certainly possible that if none of this had happened in this case, none of the Bar complaints or any issues, and we had gone forward and had actually had the hearing with respect to the photographic array . . . and she had gotten on the witness stand and had exhibited any of the behavior that was referred to in the attorney general's report that we never saw or had [she] been unable to say convincingly that she knew what happened or who had been her assailant, we wouldn't have gone forward with the case at that point. But I never would have attempted to evaluate the case without having heard that testimony."

While Nifong did interview Mangum four times, he said he never saw her display anything remotely like the kind of behavior she exhibited with both Cooper and his investigators, and with Himan on the day Cooper issued his decision. "And I never got reports of that [behavior] from anybody else who spoke with her other than some reports of that night, the night that it happened," he said. "Obviously there were some reports that she was out of it or apparently impaired or something prior to her arriving at the hospital."

Crucially, Nifong also said he blew it with regard to Brian Meehan's May 12 report, on a variety of different levels. "I will concede that I made a real mistake in not going over the report more carefully," he said. "I should have done that. . . . I did not give the report the attention that I probably should have at the time I received it. . . . My primary concern was to get the report back to Durham, make copies, and get it out to the lawyers, because it was late in the afternoon on a Friday." He said that when he read the December 13 defense motion that revealed positive DNA results from non-lacrosse players, "my first reaction upon reading this was, 'Oh, crap,' . . . or a sinking feeling like getting punched in the stomach, that how did I miss this? . . . because that really was the first time that I had even thought about that since the time we discussed it back in April. It just had not really crossed my mind. My second thought was, 'Thank God they found this stuff in the stuff that we gave them on October 27,' because what I was thinking about [was] what if they hadn't found it? I mean, clearly this was something that they were entitled to have. Clearly I had not provided it. And I had just dropped the ball on that and did not think about it between the April meeting with Dr. Meehan and receiving that December 13 motion. But I thought the only thing I could do to correct—I mean the motion seemed to be that we hid it intentionally, which was not the case—and so the only thing I could think to do was call Dr. Meehan, let him testify and just say what really happened."

Nifong then admitted he had not shared information that was "at least arguably exculpatory in nature" and "Frankly, whether it was exculpatory or not, they were entitled to have it as far as I'm concerned. It has always been my policy that the defense attorney should have everything that the state has and that was my policy twenty years before the law required that. I just really dropped the ball on this one. And I have no explanation for why it happened. . . . There's no question, however, that the information could be viewed by the finder of fact as exculpatory in nature, and there's no question that they were entitled to it. It just did not register in my mind at the time."

As for the explosive moment during the December 15 hearing when Cooney asked Meehan whether his May 12 final DNA report "set forth" the results of all the tests and examinations that he performed in the lacrosse case and Meehan said "No. It was limited to only some results" and that it was "an intentional limitation" between him and "the State," Nifong said that this particular testimony was "contradicted" by Meehan's earlier testimony "to the opposite effect." He said he chose not to cross-examine Meehan that day because of the conflicting testimony. But, he said, "I think it's pretty clear from Dr. Meehan's testimony that his understanding was not the same as the understanding that I thought he would have from our discussion."

One reason Nifong gave for not focusing on the DNA results on Mangum from the non-lacrosse players was he did not think it was "specifically exculpatory." "To my mind when I was talking to Dr. Meehan about it, it neither showed that the lacrosse players had committed the assault or had not committed the assault," he said, "or for that matter that any person had or had not committed the assault. Because read in the context with what I already knew from the SBI, I believe[d] this to be a nonejaculatory event, so that I would not have expected them to find anything that would have resulted from an ejaculation. Obviously had we found ejaculate from three men who were not members of the lacrosse team, then that would be a perfect result that exonerated all the members of the lacrosse team. If we had found ejaculate from any members of the lacrosse team, then that would have been a circumstance that implicated them. But the fact that there was no ejaculate, as far as I was concerned, meant that the results neither proved that the lacrosse players did it or proved that they did not do it. And so in that sense I did not view it as specifically exculpatory. That might be one of the reasons that I didn't pay more attention to it at the time. Part of the problem with DAs determining what's exculpatory evidence and what's not, and one of the reasons that I've always believed that open file discovery should be the case, is that you don't know what somebody can make of evidence. And clearly evidence like that is potentially exculpatory, and it could perhaps be used in some fashion in the trial of the case. And so I'm not denying that they should have had it."

The inevitable question was asked: Did Nifong believe—on May 18, 2007, anyway—that Mangum was sexually assaulted on the night of March 13, 2006, at 610 North Buchanan? After several long pauses—"I'm considering how to phrase my answer," he explained—he said, "Based on the information in the attorney general's report about the investigation that they did after the case was sent to them and the information on which that report was based, I would say that I agreed with their conclusion that there was not sufficient credible evidence to take the case to trial."

As for Cooper's finding of innocence, Nifong paused again before answering and repeated what he had said after Cooper's press conference a month earlier: "My personal understanding of actual innocence would be something that would be based on conclusive proof that either an event never happened or that a person other than the person who was accused, therefore who we're considering the innocence of, had commited that. . . . Short of something like that, I am not sure that I would ever feel comfortable in any case saying that anybody is actually innocent. I was not there that night. I do not know what happened that night, so I cannot say. I certainly cannot say under oath that I could make the judgment about whether or not anybody is innocent. I can certainly make the judgment based on their findings that there was insufficient credible evidence to go forward with a trial."

Nifong was increasingly contrite as the deposition proceeded. "It would be inappropriate to seek an indictment on less than probable cause," he said, "and I think it would be inappropriate to take a case to trial if you believe that you did not have sufficient credible evidence to convince a jury beyond a reasonable doubt. In retrospect, I believe that there may be things that I could have done either in a different fashion or at an earlier time. I believe, however, based on what I know about the case that had these allegations of ethical violations not been lodged against me so that I did not have to withdraw from the case, I believe it is likely the case would also not have gone to trial; based on what I now know about the case, I believe following a hearing in which Ms. Mangum were placed on the stand that—based on what the Attorney General's Office says—we would probably have come to the conclusion that we did not have sufficient credible evidence to proceed to a jury trial."

CHAPTER SEVENTEEN

"The Only Person Incarcerated"

Despite the ongoing fallout from Cooper's investigation—the pending state bar hearing on Nifong, a coming investigation of the Durham police, the verdict on Alleva's tenure as athletic director, and the expected litigation from the lacrosse players (both from the three who were indicted and the others) what was almost overlooked was that in his first year as head coach of the Duke lacrosse team—a year of redemption!—Danowski had brought the Blue Devils to the NCAA championship game, against longtime rival and perennial lacrosse powerhouse Johns Hopkins. A Hollywood ending was in the making. But it was not to be. On Memorial Day 2007, Hopkins prevailed 12–11, the second time in three years that Duke had lost to Hopkins in the championship game. After the game, Danowski invited Pressler back into the locker room to congratulate his team. "It was unbridled emotion," Pressler recalled. "It was wonderful. It closed things out."

The slightly less than storybook ending occasioned much editorial hand-wringing, with the most pointed once again coming from John Feinstein, the outspoken Duke alumnus and best-selling author. Writing in the *Washington Post*, Feinstein pulled no punches in his criticism of Duke's handling of the lacrosse incident. "So the Duke lacrosse team's saga will not be a Disney movie after all," he wrote. "You know the story: unfairly accused group of athletes finds redemption by coming back from a season canceled to win a national championship." Despite the loss to Hopkins, Feinstein noted, the combination of getting so far in the NCAA tournament and Cooper's declaration of innocence for the three players meant that "a lot of Duke people" believed that "all is well and good with Duke athletics."

Feinstein was not one of them. "It is almost pointless to argue with the Duke loyalists who have bought into the notion that the lacrosse players were guilty of nothing more than 'boys being boys,'" he wrote. He mentioned an e-mail sent to him by a friend—another Duke alumnus—who, in recounting the events of the night of March 13, tossed out the parenthetical that "Some racial epithets were directed at the strippers" as if it were no big deal. "Oh is that all?" Feinstein wrote, incredulously. "Just a few racial epithets? He also pointed out that the players had requested a white stripper and a Hispanic stripper but were sent two African-Americans. Don't you just hate when that happens? Poor kids. No wonder the party got out of control."

He wrote that there had been "enough apologizing and enough martyrdom" because "it was a known fact on the Duke campus for years that the lacrosse team overdid it when it came to partying." He cited the 2004 Duke report about the lacrosse team's behavior and the facts that both Alleva and Tallman Trask, his boss and Duke's executive vice-president, did nothing about it. The fact that Alleva made Pressler the fall guy in the early stages of the crisis appalled him. "Here's what's wrong with all this: No one at Duke is ever wrong," he continued. He criticized the previous Duke president, Nan Keohane, for hiring Alleva in the first place. "Everyone at Duke knew that Alleva was a pleasant man whose next original idea would be his first, someone whose main asset when applying for the job was the fact that his racquetball partner was Mike Krzyzewski. Five years later, Alleva had lived down to everything expected of him . . ."

After listing Alleva's major failings—making a bad football program worse, firing a "crony" baseball coach who had assembled a lousy team and then encouraged the players to use steroids, and hiding behind press releases because he "looked foolish" when he opened his mouth in public—Feinstein wrote that he did what others had done at Duke: "Rode the coattails of Krzyzewski's successful basketball team." He then faulted Keohane for giving Alleva a new contract based on a lousy record of performance. "Why?" he asked, rhetorically. "Because she was a typical academician: completely unable to admit a mistake. Keohane finally left in 2004, going off to write tedious, self-righteous academic tomes." Then came Brodhead who was "saddled with the lacrosse scandal. And handled it horribly." He thought Brodhead should have reinstated the lacrosse season after the DNA tests came back negative and he criticized Brodhead's "closest advisors"—Trask, Alleva, and Burness (all appointed by Keohane, he pointed out)—for not giving him proper advice. "It is an indictment of Brodhead's leadership that, in spite of the fact that Trask, Alleva, and Burness have consistently proven themselves incompetent, he hasn't brought in his own people to replace them." After railing about the missed opportunities regarding the Duke football program—there was the chance to hire Bobby Ross (not taken), who managed a national championship at Georgia Tech—Feinstein concluded that "no one really cares" about Duke football, anyway. "That's because Krzyzewski built a national power in basketball, winning three national titles and reaching ten Final Fours," he wrote. "Therefore, money continues to flow into the athletic department, and people just make jokes about the football team." As for the vaunted encomium about the graduation rates of the Duke athletes, Feinstein wrote, "Trust me when I tell you graduating from Duke isn't all that hard. What's hard is graduating AND representing the school well. The lacrosse team represented the school poorly off the field, and the football team is an embarrassment on the field."

He hoped that the lacrosse players had learned from the "disaster" of 2006. "What's sad is that the adults appear to have learned nothing," he continued. "Brodhead continues his Mr. Chips act, sending out lengthy e-mails to alums about how everything is going just fine now. Trask is still employed. Burness is still employed and so is Alleva. No one from Duke has apologized to the lacrosse kids for throwing them under the bus—the kids are hardly victims here but the school chose to protect its image rather than its athletes—and the entire athletic department is in disarray. People like me get angry mail from Duke people saying that, really, everything is just fine—that it's the media (people like me) who are causing all these problems." Not even close, he wrote. "There is a lesson in all this: it isn't about overzealous prosecutors or media running amok," he concluded. "It's a lesson about a society in which no one ever wants to admit they're wrong (see G. W. Bush and R. Cheney as exhibits 1 and 1A), especially allegedly smart people. Smart people make mistakes too. Mistakes are forgivable—but only after you admit them. No one at Duke has admitted to a single mistake yet. Until they do, they don't deserve forgiveness."

Days after his former teammates lost to Johns Hopkins, Reade Seligmann made official what had been rumored for months: He was not returning to Duke. Instead, he would be transferring to Brown, where he would also play lacrosse. On Duke's behalf, Burness tried to put the best spin on the inevitable decision. "We are pleased that Reade Seligmann is resuming his education and wish him only the best at Brown," he allowed. Then Burness announced that Duke and Pressler had reached a financial settlement in late March related to his firing a year earlier. He would not disclose the amount of the settlement but said, in delicious corporate-speak, "We regret the negative consequences this decision had on Coach Pressler. He and Duke reached an amicable, fair financial settlement in which Duke recognized his contributions to the lacrosse program and the circumstances of his departure."

The settlement with Pressler came on the eve of the publication of *It's Not About the Truth*, his book, written with Don Yaeger of *Sports Illustrated*, about the scandal. In Raleigh to promote the book, Pressler told WRAL-TV, "We're all here for the students in the education business, and part of the education process is when you're wrong, you admit you're wrong and you tell those people that you've wronged that you're sorry. An apology to the players, especially the three indicted boys and all the parents and certainly the former coach and his family would go a long way in healing this episode in our lives and allowing both parties to move on and move forward." (The settlement also stipulated that "Duke and Pressler agree that neither they nor their agents, principals, or representatives will make disparaging or defamatory comments regarding the other party . . . ," a provision that Pressler would later claim had been violated by Burness's comments about him to *Newsday* and the Associated Press. Pressler later sued Duke for slander and libel because of Burness's comments.)

The flurry of activity in the wake of Cooper's announcement gave the impression that the severely frayed strands of the Durham cultural, political, and economic fabric—occasioned by events of the previous year—were being stitched back together. But it was an illusion. Still to be resolved was a hefty financial settlement between Duke and Seligmann, Finnerty, and Evans. Still unfiled were any number of expected civil lawsuits against any number of potential defendants. Then there was Beth Brewer's request, before Judge Orlando Hudson, to have Nifong removed from office. And on June 4—almost a week before Nifong's anticipated auto-da-fé before the state bar was set to begin—Superior Court Judge Osmond Smith, who had presided over the bulk of the lacrosse case before Cooper took it over in January, filed a memorandum—in case anyone had forgotten about him—declaring that there was still unfinished business in his courtroom regarding the Duke lacrosse case. "Significant concerns regarding discovery issues arose from the December 15, 2006, hearing," he wrote. "Since the hearing was recessed without completion . . . these concerns were not addressed by the court at that time, and due to subsequent developments have not yet been addressed by the court." Those concerns included whether to expunge the court records, seal them or dispose of them, and, more important, also included "matters related to disciplinary actions involving attorneys before the court." It was in Smith's power to discipline Nifong: he could admonish him; he could disbar him; or he could find him in contempt and send him to jail.

James Coleman, the Duke professor, argued that Smith should not abdicate his responsibility to discipline Nifong. "Judges should not tolerate this crap," he said. "They see it all the time. If they don't do anything about it, that's how it keeps going on. [Nifong's] behavior was a total affront to the court. . . . Prosecutors can ruin lives very easily, they do it and clap their hands and say never mind and move on. Courts have basically ignored it. I've seen misconduct by prosecutors in a capital case where everyone recognizes the misconduct, but the judge declares it a harmless error. Then the prosecutors show up at the execution."

Nifong's five-day state bar trial had all the trappings of a sacrificial slaughter. Whereas once the news media would camp outside his Durham office, hanging on Nifong's every word, with the tables turned—and Nifong in the hot seat—it seemed almost as if he had a communicable disease. "Heads turned and throats cleared," when Nifong walked into the hearing room at the NC Court of Appeals Building, the *News & Observer* reported, "but little more than a heavy silence greeted Durham County's top prosecutor as he took his seat at the defense table." While Court TV was airing the trial live, as was local television, "absent is the frenzied, almost insatiable attention that surrounded the case in the initial stages in the spring of 2006." At the Fayetteville Street Tavern, around the corner from the courthouse, the menu featured a Wednesday special of Toasted Nifong with a Side of National News. But that was about the extent of the excitement in downtown Raleigh that Nifong's trial occasioned.

Indeed, it seemed clear from the opening statements of the opposing attorneys that Nifong stood little chance of coming out of the hearing alive, at least metaphorically. Where Katherine Jean, on behalf of the state bar, seemed well prepared and confident (if not a bit dowdy), David Freedman, representing Nifong, seemed disorganized, at times inarticulate, and appeared to ramble. Jean's version of events presented a devastating portrait of an out-of-control prosecutor, making intentional mistakes at every turn. "The state bar's evidence will demonstrate that Mr. Nifong intentionally sought out the world's attention, went on television, talked about this case; when the world was focused squarely on North Carolina and its justice system, Mr. Nifong repeatedly and intentionally misled the media, and therefore the public, about a very serious case, caused racial unrest in Durham, intentionally concealed evidence to which he now admits the defendants were entitled, but which was extremely harmful to his theory of the criminal case, and made false representations to two judges in an effort to keep the defendants from discovering it," she said. "The harm done to these three young men and their families, and to the justice system in North Carolina, is devastating. The public perception is that justice can't be had in North Carolina unless you know how to play the shell game. If you can figure out how to play the shell game, you might get justice. The public perception is that the justice system in North Carolina has no integrity. This didn't have to happen, and the horrible consequences were entirely foreseeable."

While Jean made the state bar's case against Nifong seem obvious, Freedman tried to tell the story from Nifong's perspective. He said the state bar was not there to judge the merits of the sexual assault case against the three former Duke lacrosse players—two of whom, Seligmann and Finnerty, were in the audience—since Cooper had already made that judgment, nor were they assembled because Nifong wanted to bring the case against the three men to trial in Durham. "It is not unethical to pursue what someone may believe to be an unwinnable case," he said. Rather, Freedman said, Nifong was on trial to assess whether he intentionally withheld evidence and, through his public statements, villfied the players.

The media's focus on the Duke lacrosse case was not Nifong's fault, Freedman claimed. "In hindsight, I would contend you look at the man, you look at his career, you look at what he had on his plate when he was handling this case," he continued. "The talk about political gain—I contend to you there is nothing political about Mike Nifong. This is his first run for office. He did not seek this office. Mr. Nifong, I contend the evidence will show, is someone who sees things, something he believes to be right, and that's what he pursues. I contend that this case has been complicated a great deal, both initially and obviously even up to this point, by the intense media interest. Mr. Nifong didn't create the media interest in the Duke case. Mr. Nifong didn't ask for the media to come down here and start asking about the Duke case, and Mr. Nifong quit talking about the case in April, early April, which obviously has not dissuaded the media interest in this case, I think as evidenced by this courtroom today proves. . . . So I contend to you, when you hear all the evidence, you'll realize Mr. Nifong at no time committed any intentional violations of the state bar."

Nifong sat generally motionless during the opening statements, according to the *Times*, "often holding his chin and cheek by thumb and forefinger," while his wife, son, brother, and sister sat behind him. But he was not happy.

Police investigator Ben Himan was the first to testify. He seemed uncomfortable and did Nifong no favors. He described the details of the March 27 meeting between Nifong, Himan, and Gottlieb, during which Himan recalled that Nifong said, "We're fucked." There was little elaboration, so the profane sound bite—bleeped out on television—hung in the air like exhaled cigar smoke. It was devastating. Himan followed with the story about how he had questioned Nifong's decision—through his superiors—to indict Seligmann. "I think I made the response, 'With what?'" Himan testified. "We didn't have any DNA. We didn't have [Seligmann] at the party. It was a big concern to go forward with the indictments when we didn't have him there. . . . I didn't want to indict someone who shouldn't have been indicted." (There was some minor excitement on the first day of the state bar hearing when Victoria Peterson, a staunch supporter of Nifong, approached Mary Ellen Finnerty, Collin's mother, and told her that the "people of Durham still thought a rape occurred at a lacrosse team party." Peterson was ejected from the hearing and barred from attending future hearings.)

On the second day of the hearing, Dudley Witt, Nifong's other attorney, cross-examined Himan. Asked whether he had told Nifong early in the case that Mangum was believeable, Himan said, "Yes."

The media coverage of Himan's testimony ignored two shocking revelations about what had gone on in the house at 610 North Buchanan on the night of March 13. Himan explained that Dan Flannery had reported to him that on that night, he had heard one of his teammates say to Roberts, as the party was breaking up, "Go feed your kids. We ordered white girls, not niggers." Then Himan testified about the e-mail that Matt Zash, one of the residents of the house, had sent to some friends from his Blackberry, to wit that, "He doesn't split dark wood," a reference, apparently, to his preference for not having sex with black women.

The surprise testimony of the hearing, though, came from Brian Meehan, who despite being a witness for the state bar, seemed to want to atone for his damaging testimony—to Nifong—from December 15. He said it was his decision alone not to include the DNA results from the non-Duke lacrosse players in his May 12 report. "Mr. Nifong never directed what should be in or out of the report," Meehan testified, causing the hearing's chairman, Lane Williamson to ask him to put himself in the role of a potential juror. That bit of role-playing made Meehan uncomfortable. "I know I have to answer the question," he said, a bit miffed. "I don't feel that I should be trying these children, these kids, or these young men." Williamson persisted and soon labeled Meehan "Mr. Obfuscation." "Does the fact that you find no DNA that matches the people who are on trial, but you do find DNA of other unidentified people . . . does that fact have any bearing on your deciding in your own mind as to whether these three men did it?" he asked. After a pause, Meehan answered. "If I were a juror and the only information I had was that one-line sentence that said there was DNA there, I would want to know that," he said. "I would want to know what the hell are you talking about. . . . I would want to know what this DNA is, because this could be crucial to this case." He later added, "Yes, a juror should have this information." Meehan said his May 12 report had just been "an interim report" and that he had planned to write a final report that contained all the DNA findings, but Nifong never asked for a final report.

Freedman, Nifong's lawyer, said he was pleased with Meehan's testimony because "I thought it was fairly clear from the evidence there was no agreement, no attempt at all to hide the evidence in this case." But, of course, Cheshire wasn't buying that logic. "There would never have been a 'final' report," he said. "That's the whole problem here. They together conspired to withhold exculpatory evidence from the people who were charged." He told the *News & Observer*, "It is now clear, it's no longer in doubt, that Mr. Nifong lied to the court."

The day's final witness was Brad Bannon, the defense lawyer who had studied the piles of DNA data before figuring out that Meehan had discovered DNA on Mangum that came from four men who were not Duke lacrosse players. Bannon said Nifong's comment, early on, that the Duke lacrosse players had constructed "a stone wall of silence" was untruthful. "David Evans, who ended up being my client, and Matt Zash and Dan Flannery, who lived with him at 610 North Buchanan, had cooperated fully, essentially in every way that they had been asked to," he said. "When any figure of authority, whether it was a figure of authority from Duke University or the Durham Police Department or the Durham District Attorney's Office or anybody who acted on their behalf had asked Dave Evans to do anything or say anything, he had done it. Most especially that was illustrated on March 16th, which has been discussed here as the night that the search warrants were executed at his house." But, Bannon said, he learned quickly that for Nifong, "cooperation" was "somebody saying that a sexual assault had occurred."

More pummeling for Nifong came the next day when Marsha Goodenow, the chief homicide prosecutor and an assistant district attorney in Mecklenburg County, North Carolina, testified that Nifong did nearly everything wrong during the prosecution of the lacrosse case. She criticized Nifong's decision to wait nine months before interviewing Mangum. She criticized him for making his series of inflammatory public statements about the lacrosse players. She criticized Nifong for questioning the players' decision to hire legal counsel and then taking their legal advice. She criticized the April 4 photo identification procedure and said that it was relied upon, in large part, to indict Seligmann, Finnerty, and Evans. She criticized his decision to withhold from the defense the potentially exculpatory DNA evidence Nifong heard from Meehan during the April 10 meeting. That information, she testified, "is about the most important thing you possess. . . . You have an obligation to turn it over right away." She criticized Nifong for not meeting with defense attorneys on the numerous occasions when they made offers to visit with him. "If you're playing poker with someone and they offer to show you some of their cards, I'd look," she said. She said she worried the way Nifong handled the case had set back the cause of justice in North Carolina. "There is a perception that justice might depend on who your lawyer is, it might depend on how much money you have, it may depend on whether you're white or black," Goodenow said.

The next morning, Nifong was scheduled to testify in his own defense. But before he did, the state bar called Seligmann to the stand. His testimony was some of the most emotional of the proceeding. After explaining how he got to Duke from Delbarton and that he had the chance to play in the NCAA championship game in 2005 after breaking his hand and foot earlier in the season, he told the tribunal that his teammates called him "Mr. Flustered" because he was "always the nervous Nellie of the group." Yes, he was at the party on the night of March 13, but he had left after calling a taxi at 12:14 a.m. He spoke about reading about the rape allegations in the *Chronicle* and how he was eager to comply with the nontestimonial order. "I was always a nervous character," he said. "I watched *CSI* and shows like that, and you think you know about DNA, but it was one of those things where some of the lawyers were saying, 'Oh, they can't make you give DNA. Let's fight this.' I mean, I had tape on my ankles, still, from what we thought we were going to practice that day, and I said, 'This is great. This will be the easiest way to resolve the situation, to go right away and give DNA.'"

He testified that Nifong's relentless barrage of public statements about what supposedly happened on the night of March 13 changed the whole dynamic of the situation. "It really turned our world upside down," he said. "We'd always been really respected on campus, and we had a lot of friends on campus, and we all got along with our teachers really well. Everyone looked at you differently. . . . Previously, everyone had given you a pat on the back and said . . . 'Who are you guys playing this week?' and 'Hope you guys are number one. Hope you win the national championship,' to nobody really wanted to talk to you. . . . Teachers certainly looked at you differently, and just the feeling on campus was, I mean, it was as lonely a feeling as you can ever imagine." He recounted the protests on campus against the team. He recalled how his classmates in his American history class started looking at him differently as a result of the accusations. "There were wanted posters. . . . We'd go to the gym. I remember specifically going to the gym once. I step onto a treadmill next to a girl who was wearing a shirt that said, 'Speak Up. You Know What You Did,' written on her T-shirt. Everywhere you looked, everywhere you went, and that's what we had to deal with."

At first he and his teammates thought nothing would come of Mangum's allegations. "To be honest," he said, "we all knew it was so transparently false that no charges would ever be brought, but as time went on, we always thought that nothing would ever come of this, particularly after going to Sergeant Gottlieb [when] the DNA tests came back and they said there was no match, as we expected. As time grew on, Mr. Nifong said that they were going to do things the old-fashioned way, and to us, I've never had to deal with the court system before and I didn't know what the old-fashioned way was, but as he pressed forward, everyone started to get—'this is really going to happen to us; something is going to happen.'"

But Seligmann never thought he would be indicted. "I never thought, in a million years, that I would ever be a suspect, and I was being told, there's no way," he said. "I wasn't even listed as having been at the party. In my mind, it could never be. It could never be me. 'I left the party. The people probably don't even want to talk to me. I have nothing to say.' As time went on, we realized that indictments really were going to come down." Seligmann told the state bar how he thought for sure Nifong would see his documented alibi and that would be the end of it or that the finding of DNA on Mangum from men not associated with the lacrosse team would be a stop to the prosecution. He was wrong. Then came the dropping of the rape charges. "That was the hardest point," he said, "because this entire thing—this is called the Duke Lacrosse Rape Case, and the rape charges were thrown out, and we continued to live this life of the cloud hanging over our head, sexual assault and kidnapping. And it always felt that way, but at that point it felt almost like a sick joke, like we were being toyed with, like he was doing it maliciously, on purpose, to us." Then came the news of Nifong's recusal. "To be honest with you, I couldn't believe he did it," he said.

Seligmann recounted the euphoria he had felt listening to Cooper's press conference and then recalled how, a few weeks later, Delbarton, his high school, honored him. "I received what's called the Delbarton Medal, and it's the highest honor that the school gives out, and it's for any number of reasons," he said. "They said the way I conducted myself through this difficult situation was admirable, and they were so proud to have me be part of their community, and I couldn't be prouder to be a part of their community. It was, by far and away, the most incredible award I ever received. It was incredible." That summer, Seligmann worked as an analyst in the fixed-income group at Bear Stearns, the Wall Street investment bank, and told the audience he hoped to be an attorney one day.

In an interview, Nifong said he was told the original plan was to have David Evans testify at the state bar hearing, not Seligmann. "They did some mock trial stuff, where they put these people through their paces," he said. "They thought that Dave Evans, as the oldest and most experienced—and presumably wisest—would be the best person to do this. He apparently tested very badly in their test panels, and they were very surprised to find that Reade Seligmann came across very well, even though some of what he said might not have been true. And actually, he did come across very well. . . . Not everything he said was true, but he did come across well." Nifong was reluctant to specify what exactly Seligmann had said in his testimony that wasn't true. "Some of the things that he said about the party, we had other things to show otherwise," he continued. "There's no point in getting into any of that. I've already talked to you about how his actions after the party indicated that in leaving he showed that he knew that there was something about that that he had to distance himself from. There were some other things that I pointed out that he said, about [how] he was going to get married, which, of course, is exactly what Crystal Mangum said about the person she identified as Seligmann, as having said as the reason that he did not want to have intercourse with her, why he was begging off from them doing that, because he was going to get married. Anyway, he came across well, but I don't think he was very sincere."

Nifong said his wife had "a more chilling encounter" with Seligmann at the state bar hearing. "She actually tried to say something nice to him and she said that she was kind of frightened by the way he looked at her," he continued. "He's not an angel, but he did come across well. There's no question of that. Even I, as a trial lawyer, appreciate a good performance as a good performance. It has nothing to do with who the person actually is or what the truth of the matter is, but it was a good performance."

As Nifong's direct testimony was winding down, he began to make some major concessions. Asked what he thought of Seligmann's testimony, Nifong said he "was a very impressive young man." Witt asked him if it would have made any difference to his thinking if he had met Seligmann before seeking his indictment. "I believe that if I had done so, and that Mr. Seligmann had presented himself the way he did today, at the very least I would have sat down with Ms. Mangum and talked with her about the situation and reevaluated the case under those circumstances. Yes, I think I probably would have done that."

Then Witt asked Nifong if he had anything else he wanted to say. He knew the question was coming but had not told Witt how he would answer. "Throughout the years that I have served as a prosecutor in North Carolina, I have always tried to do the right thing," he said. "In this case, I was trying to do the right thing. Much of the criticism that has been directed against me in this case is justified. The allegations, however, that I'm a liar are not justified. I felt that it was important to come before this commission to defend myself against allegations that I intentionally misrepresented anything to the court at any time because I have never done that, and I would never do that. . . . I take responsibility for the things that I have done in this case that in any way contributed to the injustice being done. But I do not take responsibility for lying, and any misrepresentations that I made about anything in this case were unintentional. And it is important for me to say that.

"As you may know," he continued emotionally, tears welling up in his eyes, "I've been here this week with my wife"—she was starting to cry as well—"and son and other family members and friends. When I saw Mr. Seligmann on the stand today, I thought that his parents must be very proud of him. I'm very proud of my son. I want him to be proud of me. And I felt that it was important for him to see this, because I've always told him that in this case, although I have made mistakes, I was trying to do the right thing and that I was going to come in here and I was going to defend my good name, and that's why I'm here. But it has become increasingly apparent during the course of this week, in some ways that it might not have been before, that my presence as the district attorney in Durham is not furthering the cause of justice. It is not fair for the people in my community to be represented by someone who is not held in high esteem by either members of the community or members of the profession. It does not contribute to the cause of justice in Durham for me to serve as the sitting district attorney. Every time I walk into the courtroom, people are going to be pointing their finger at me and saying, 'There's the guy from the Duke lacrosse case.' . . . I think that I can't do justice, I can't do the right thing if I am district attorney. So it is my intention, whatever the decision is for me, to resign as district attorney in Durham. I came here as district attorney to defend my name, but it would not be fair to my community to put them through a recall kind of motion. . . . My community has suffered enough. . . . Although honorably intended, [my actions did not have] the consequences that I desired [them] to have. So to the extent that my actions have caused pain to the Finnertys, the Seligmanns, and the Evanses, I apologize. To the extent that my actions have brought disrespect or disrepute to the Bar, and to my community, I apologize. I cannot admit that I told a lie that I didn't tell. And I still intend to defend myself against those allegations."

After Nifong's announcement, he had to endure three more hours of cross-examination. There was an element of pathos in his ongoing testimony, in the wake of his hari-kari; but it didn't take long for him to exercise his new freedom to explain—probably for the first time—what he really thought about his prosecutorial judgments and what he thought happened in the house on the night of March 13. His career as a district attorney over (and his disbarment a near certainty), Nifong began to let loose.

But first, Douglas Brocker, representing the state bar, had to sling a few last arrows in Nifong's direction. For instance, Brocker tried to get Nifong to admit that he had taken over the investigation of the lacrosse case and hit the airwaves in an effort to boost his election chances. Brocker trotted out a March 27, 2006, poll (the same day Nifong started talking to the press, at 12:45 p.m.), conducted on behalf of his primary rival Freda Black, that showed that she had 37 percent of the vote and Nifong had 20 percent, with a 40 percent plurality needed to win the primary. While Nifong had to admit to Brocker that if the poll were accurate, Black needed only three percentage points more to win the primary—had the vote been held March 27—he wasn't buying Brocker's argument. "But I'd also say that the poll is not a very realistic picture of the situation in Durham in terms of elections," primarily because it also showed Keith Bishop—the lone black in the race—to have only 3 percent of the vote.

Brocker kept at it. He noted that Nifong had fired Black soon after he became the district attorney in 2005 and that had she won, chances were good she would have returned the favor. "I knew that if Ms. Black prevailed in that election, I wouldn't have wanted a job in the District Attorney's Office," Nifong said.

"So, if you lost the primary, you essentially would have been out of the only job in which you had had an office as an attorney, correct?" Brocker asked.

"Yes, sir," Nifong replied. "That's what's going to be happening after this hearing anyway. But yes, sir."

Although the defense attorneys and the state bar made much of the fact that on April 10 Meehan had told Nifong there was DNA found on Mangum that belonged to four men who were not lacrosse players and Nifong had not shared that information with the defense until after receiving the December 13 motion, one of the more burning unanswered questions was, why did it matter? Except for the fact that Nifong should have turned that information over to the defense sooner, why was it important that the so-called exculpatory evidence was not turned over? The truth was, it didn't matter, and even if Nifong had turned the information over sooner, he was still basing his entire case against Seligmann, Finnerty, and Evans—rightly or wrongly—on Mangum's testimony. The charge was a red herring. A PR disaster for sure, but a red herring nonetheless. Under Brocker's cross-examination on June 15, Nifong finally explained his thinking.

"When you were sitting with Dr. Meehan and he was going through this unidentified male DNA that did not match any of the lacrosse players, did you realize at the time that it was exculpatory, or at least potentially exculpatory?" Brocker asked.

"Well, certainly any evidence is potentially exculpatory, because the only way you can determine the exculpatory value of evidence is to view it in light of the other evidence in the case," he said. "The problem is, as I indicated, that there was specifically exculpatory information in the tests; that is, none of the DNA on these rape kit items matched any of the Duke players. That is specifically exculpatory. With respect to the fingernails, there was DNA on one of the fingernails that matched David Evans and that is specifically inculpatory. Now the presence of other DNA is not specifically exculpatory because since, as I indicated Dr. Meehan said, and I believe as he has testified, if you can't determine when it was deposited, how long it's been there, where it came from, then its relationship to this particular case is [not relevant]. So it is potentially exculpatory only because there may be some way it can be used in conjunction with other evidence, but it doesn't prove, either, that an assault did not take place or that specific people involved in the complaint did not commit the assault. The absence of DNA evidence does not prove, either, than an assault took place or that a person didn't commit it. The presence of DNA from someone other than the people who are charged with a crime doesn't mean that they committed the crime or that the crime was committed."

This was truly the heart of the matter, although Nifong's cogent explanation would likely come too late to save him from his fate.

"So you're saying that the fact that there's male DNA on an alleged rape victim that does not match the suspects is not exculpatory?" Brocker said.

"Yes," Nifong answered.

"That's your answer?" Brocker retorted, incredulous, causing Williamson to admonish Brocker for being argumentative.

"A piece of DNA, or a segment of DNA that fell into that very category was the vaginal swab, the sperm fraction, that was recovered that did not match any of the players," Nifong continued. "It did, however, match the the victim's boyfriend. The victim's boyfriend was not involved either in a sexual assault on her that night or for that matter sexual activity with her on that date. So that's an example of something that does not match the players. The DNA found does not match the players. It is not exculpatory, because the fact that she had sex with her boyfriend three days earlier doesn't prove anything of what happened that night." Nifong continued his long-overdue explanation. "The difference between exculpatory and *potentially* exculpatory is that something that is clearly exculpatory would be something like—there's no DNA from Duke lacrosse players there. That is exculpatory. It doesn't prove they didn't commit a crime, but it's exculpatory because it shows that there is no evidence that they did," he said. He said he did not think that what Meehan told him about the DNA from other males "proved anything at all in this case, in light of the profession of the victim and also in light of the fact that no determination, no conclusions could be drawn about where the evidence came from, how long it had been there or anything like that."

Williamson wondered why a "lightbulb" didn't "go off in your head" after Meehan told him about that finding, as in "Whoa, what is that?"

Nifong said he recognized that the defense was entitled to have that information but not that it was all that important to the case. "I didn't think it proved anything at all about the facts and circumstances of what occurred on March 13 and 14, that evening." That did not mean Nifong and the police did not try to investigate the origin of the DNA. "I'm just saying that it wasn't something that was so prevalent in my mind . . . ," he said. "With respect to the lacrosse players, their DNA, if there was no assault, they should have no DNA on any of the clothing or items from the rape kit of the victim in this case. And, in fact, they did not. But the reason it was being tested was to determine whether there was any evidence, because that would be probative or at least suggestive of potential guilt. There was no such evidence. The fact that she had male DNA on her, on the other hand, was not suggestive that somebody else committed this crime or suggestive that the crime hadn't taken place. It was simply a fact that was there, and a fact that should have been reported."

In answer to another question from Williamson, Nifong elaborated further. "The perfect result in this case would have been to find fresh sperm or fresh semen, whether or not that was identified with any lacrosse player or even not identified," he said. "Because that would show sexual contact. If there were no lacrosse players or person that we could identify associated with that, then that would have meant there would have been no charges. That would have been specifically exculpatory, even, that would have prevented any charges having been brought, because it would have shown that there was some kind of sexual contact but that none of these people that we were looking at were involved. Had there been such evidence, that would have been good news because it would have resolved the case. The problem is that the evidence that you're asking about was not evidence in my mind that resolved the case. It was nothing that got us to that. It wasn't about its being exculpatory or inculpatory."

Once again, as he had in his deposition, Nifong reiterated his view that at the time he turned the case over to Cooper, he had believed a sexual assault had occurred. Then came the inevitable question about whether Nifong still believed—"as you sit here today," Brocker said—a sexual assault occurred. "At this point, I think what I would have to say, honestly, is, I think something happened in that bathroom," he said, "but I'm not sure I can actually say that I now at this point believe it was a sexual assault. A nonsexual assault, an intimidation, something. Something happened to make everybody leave that scene very quickly."

The reaction to Nifong's offer to resign as district attorney appeared to be uniform: it was inevitable. Joe Cheshire called Nifong's "tepid" apology "a cynical ploy designed solely to save his law license" and "far too little, far too late." Brodhead said, "When Mr. Nifong accepted his appointment as Durham's leading law enforcement officer, he committed to ensure the fairness and integrity of the legal system that we rely on to resolve conflicts in our society. His handling of the Duke lacrosse case was deeply unfair to the young men involved and damaged the criminal justice system itself. Mr. Nifong brought great harm to these Duke students and their families, to the Durham community and to Duke University and all who care about it. Even though his decision to resign comes under threat of sanctions by the North Carolina State Bar, I welcome it. It sets the stage for a healing process to which we all are committed."

Thomas Stith, a Durham city councilman, said, "If you look at the totality of it, it's clear that this was a situation where there was a miscarriage of justice. When you have that type of failed leadership, it merits you removing yourself." But Jim Cooney, the defense lawyer, was more focused on Nifong's statements that he still believed something had happened in the bathroom. "For him to apologize," Cooney told the *New York Times*, "and then to continue to slander forty-six innocent people about a crime that did not happen, is outrageous." Not surprisingly, Freda Black could barely contain herself. "Today marks a new start for Durham," she said. "Mr. Nifong's resignation will allow the community to lift itself up out of this dark scandal. I sincerely hope that Mr. Evans, Mr. Finnerty, and Mr. Seligmann understand that they got caught up in the perfect storm, where a district attorney was more interested in politics rather than protecting the rights of the innocent." She said she would be interested in being appointed by the governor to fill out the remainer of Nifong's four-year term.

On Saturday afternoon, Lane Williamson announced the commission's findings. As Jean-Paul Sartre might have written about Nifong: *Les Jeux Sont Faits*—the gig was up. "At least part of Lane Williamson's sentencing memo was done the night before I testified," Nifong said. "At least part of that had been written. . . . I could've said anything. I could've called Jesus Christ as a witness, and He could have testified and ascended into heaven, and they would've said, 'Well, obviously you can't make anything of that testimony. That doesn't mean anything. You're obviously guilty.'" First, Williamson read aloud the tribunal's decision that twenty-seven of the thirty-two legal charges against Nifong—that formed the amended complaint against him—had been proved against Nifong with "clear, cogent, and convincing evidence." When Williamson finished, the hearing entered "Phase II," in which each side offered testimony, ostensibly to help the three commissioners decide how to punish

Nifong. David Evans Sr., the father of David Evans, and Mary Ellen Finnerty, Collin's mother, testified on behalf of the state bar. The defense turned over a stack of letters to the commission testifying to Nifong's good character.

David Evans Sr., a patrician attorney at Reed Smith in Washington, described his son as "a great kid, fun, focused, hard-working, athletic" who went out of his way to make others feel welcomed. He said his son chose Duke and played on the lacrosse team during his first two years without a scholarship and eventually earned a scholarship during the spring semesters of both his junior and senior years. While acknowledging that his son was one of the hosts of the fateful party on the night of March 13, Evans Sr. noted that it was not unusual. "The captains hosted a party that had been a tradition during spring break for over fifteen years," he said. He first heard about the party, and its aftermath, from his son on March 17. "Dave called me on Friday, the day after the police had begun their investigation and showed up at the house with a search warrant," he recalled. "I remember sitting in my office and getting a call a little after one in the afternoon, and seeing on the caller ID 'Coach Pressler,' and picked it up and it was Dave. He explained to me the situation, what happened the night before. The first thing he said was, 'I made a mistake, and we know that, but I want to describe the situation to you.' Over the course of the next ten days to two weeks, Dave, with other captains, met with senior officials at Duke. They stepped up to the plate. They apologized for hosting the party and hiring dancers. They then, after meeting with the president of Duke University, prepared a written statement, and in that written statement they accepted responsibility and apologized for the shame that they had brought upon their families and the university."

Evans said his son did not try to call him during the seven or so hours he was in police custody. "He was there uncounseled," he said. "He had not called either of us, his parents. Two days before, Dean Sue Wasiolek of Duke had actually contacted Coach Pressler, indicating that there had been some report, and I could get into the details of that, but I think the most important thing is to say that while Dave did not speak with her, Matt and Danny did; that she advised them to cooperate fully and tell the truth if the police came to see them, and they did precisely that without counsel and without consulting with parents." He said he could not believe it when Nifong started to make comments suggesting the lacrosse players were not cooperating with police. "We were floored," he said. "Our son had cooperated fully. The police had told a local paper that the residents at 610 North Buchanan were cooperating fully. We just couldn't figure out why Mr. Nifong was making these statements when, in fact, it was obvious that the three residents of the house had cooperated to the best of their ability." He said the players had a constitutional right to legal representation and was dumbfounded that Nifong had questioned that right. "As an attorney, I remember being taught that everyone had a constitutional right to a lawyer, and I notice Mr. Nifong has lawyers, which he has the right to do," he testified. "To me, it called into question: here are forty-seven members of the team. The three who were residents had fully cooperated. The others wanted to talk with their parents. The parents wanted them to consult with lawyers before going down and talking with the district attorney, who had begun to malign the entire team. It seemed to me that it was beyond what any prosecutor should ever say, to make the players of the team look bad for seeking counsel when, under the circumstances, it was the appropriate thing to do and it was their right to do it."

He said the family knew by the end of April that Nifong had targeted his son for indictment. "We continued to hope that through cooperation and reason, and looking at the evidence that was coming out, that that wouldn't happen," he said. "We actually went to [the] baccalaureate at Duke Chapel [on May 13]." They came out of the service and called Brad Bannon for an update. Bannon obfuscated a bit. He did not want to ruin the family moment on graduation weekend. But his son said he needed to know and called Bannon back. "Brad said, 'You're going to be indicted on Monday.' So we, over that weekend, had that information. We knew what was going to happen. We knew that if Mr. Nifong or witnesses from the police department sought an indictment, it would absolutely occur. We had a dinner Saturday night with all the senior players and their families, but couldn't really talk about it. On Sunday, Mother's Day, it was graduation day, so Dave graduated one day before he was indicted."

When news of his indictment reached his new employer, JPMorgan Chase, in New York, the Wall Street bank rescinded his offer. "JPMorgan indicated that they had to withdraw the offer because of felony charges," he said. "Joe Cheshire talked with them and their human resources department, in an effort to see if Dave could be given a job that didn't involve securities, and they indicated that no, that would not be possible. And then we tried to determine whether once the charges were dropped—because we knew this was all a lie; we knew this was going to go away—whether or not he would be able to have the job waiting for him, and they said no, in fact, that he would need to reapply. I am very happy, though, to report that, I think it was April 12, one day after Attorney General Roy Cooper pronounced Collin, Reade, and Dave innocent, that the head of investment banking for JPMorgan called Dave to renew the offer, but Dave had already accepted another offer" from Morgan Stanley after interviewing with both John Mack, the CEO, and Gary Lynch, the general counsel—both of whom were Duke graduates.

Evans Sr. said that the stigma of Mangum's accusations against his son had not gone away, despite Cooper's declaration of innocence for the three men. "I'm sure that the Finnertys, the Seligmanns, and the Evanses will tell you that it's not like turning off a switch," he continued. "The emotion is still there. After listening to yesterday's testimony, I lost sleep again last night, hearing what I heard yesterday. I heard a number, from the witness before, about a week and a half ago, I searched Yahoo!, 'Dave Evans Duke lacrosse,' and had 5,130,000 hits. I think it's going to be a while before that goes away"—it's now down to about 56,200 hits. The fourteen-month ordeal had taken a toll on the elder Evans's health, too. "I thought I was pretty strong and unflappable," he continued. "I began to lose weight, and also had a very difficult time sleeping. I mean, I can remember, if you have those digital clocks, looking at 2:00, 3:00 in the morning, and 4:30, worried every hour, thinking there's got to be something I can do to help my son. He's innocent. All we have to do is get that out. But, of course, we learned we had to prove his innocence, and Collin and Reade's innocence. I did find that I lost a lot of weight. I went and had it checked out and learned that I had Type 1 diabetes. We don't know exactly what caused that. I'm told that it probably was stress-induced. Type 1 diabetes is something you normally get when it's called juvenile diabetes, but if you're over forty-five—and I'll be sixty-two this year—and hit fifty, it's uncommon. So it's either caused by stress or some viral infection. I don't know about the viral infection, but I know I had a lot of stress, and it was for over a year."

Asked for his reaction to Nifong's apology from the day before, Evans said, "Mr. Nifong said it with great emotion," he said. "I can tell you that I did feel, and it resonated with me, when Mr. Nifong said that he wanted his son to be proud of him. It particularly hit me, since tomorrow is Father's Day." But that was the extent of Evans's empathy for Nifong. "I would be less than candid if I didn't tell you how disappointed I was, and the Finnertys and the Seligmanns [too], when, asked by the chair whether he felt that a sexual assault had occurred, [Nifong] had a difficult time answering that and then said that he thought something happened that night in that bathroom," Evans continued. "I have a real hard time with that. I don't accept it. The attorney general of North Carolina [and] Jim Coman and Mary Winstead for ninety days investigated this case, and what did they find? They found that the accuser was a liar with a mental health history. They found that the accuser, whom I don't know—yesterday, during Mr. Nifong's testimony, he referred to her as the victim. They"—pointing to Seligmann, Finnerty, and his son, in the audience—"are the victims, not Crystal Mangum. And he placed his career and reputation on a woman he didn't interview and persisted with this case, and then gave up the case because of a conflict of interest, and then the word of the attorney general of North Carolina says they didn't do it, it didn't happen, she wasn't touched, she's a liar, she has a mental health record, and he says he still thinks something happened that night."

Not surprisingly, Evans's father made no mention of the evidence regarding the possibility that his son's DNA was on Mangum's fake fingernail when he took the stand. In an interview, Nifong explained why he thought neither the defense nor the media made more of the fingernail evidence. "The first thing you have to understand is that when these tests are done, it would be an ethical violation for me to, for instance, provide to the press a copy of this," he explained. "The same would be true of the defense, although they certainly had a reason for not doing it. So none of that was ever made public. The press never got a hold of any of that. . . . You have to remember that one of the things that the lawyers for the other side said was, 'These results exonerate everybody.' He reiterated that it would have been unethical for him to provide that information to the press. "I was trying to try this case, and if I did something like that, then the case might go away for prosecutory misconduct," he continued. The irony was not lost on Nifong. "Yes, isn't it?" he said.

"The irony was intended, but that's part of the problem that I faced; I was kind of screwed if I didn't respond, and I was kind of screwed if I did." Nifong remained convinced that Roy Cooper had downplayed the evidence concerning the DNA on Mangum's fingernail in his report and his public statements. He had a very different view from that in Cooper's report of what the DNA evidence showed. "Roy Cooper was trying to justify his decision," Nifong said. "He had decided that he was going to not prosecute this case, and if he had emphasized that the one DNA result that we had showed that there was a 98 percent probability that one of the three accused people had been the person who was on her fingernails, and also her statements indicated that he was the one who was behind her, struggling with her at the time that her fingernail broke off, then you'd have an uproar from all the people who wanted it prosecuted. So he had a real incentive not to let that get out."

After Evans finished his testimony, the commissioners began their deliberation. Soon enough, Nifong concluded he should be disbarred and *voluntarily* offered to turn in his law license. Williamson declined Nifong's offer. He decided that the commissioners needed to deliberate and make their ruling. "I've been at executions," Joe Cheshire said later. "It's kind of like the day before you're executed, if you cut up your sheet and hang youself so you're in control of your own destiny."

At around 5:15 p.m. Saturday, Williamson announced that the three commission members were "in unanimous agreement" that for Nifong "there's no discipline short of disbarment that would be appropriate in this case given the magnitude of the offenses we have found and the effect upon the profession and the public." He then explained why he, Mitchell Tyler, and Sharon Alexander had reached the conclusion that Nifong would be disbarred. Williamson was relentless. "This matter has been a fiasco," he said. "There is no doubt about it. It has been a fiasco for a number of people, starting with the defendants and moving out from there to the justice system in general. We've heard evidence over the last several days of how that came about. Though we are lawyers and a school administrator—we're not psychologists—you have to ask yourself, 'Why? Why did we get to the place that we got?' It seems that at the root of it is self-deception arising out of self-interest. Mark Twain said that, 'When a person cannot deceive himself, the chances are against his being able to deceive other people.' Well, what we have here, it seems, is that we had a prosecutor who was faced with a very unusual situation in which the confluence of his self-interest collided with a very volatile mix of race, sex, and class, a situation that if it were a plot of a John Grisham novel, it would be considered to be perhaps too contrived."

He said that while Nifong may have been "politically naïve," his public statements starting in the lunch hour on March 27 were designed to "forward his political ambitions" and then he was caught in a trap of his own making: Nifong had to keep pushing his version of events forward even in the face of "developing evidence" that contradicted his statements. "And even today one must say that in the face of a declaration of innocence by the attorney general of North Carolina, it appears the defendant still believes the facts to be one way and the world now knows that is not the case," Williamson said.

By its rules, the commission had to consider various "aggravating" and "mitigating" factors in the case against Nifong. On the "aggravating" side of the ledger, the three commissioners found that Nifong had a "dishonest or selfish motive," a "pattern of misconduct," a "refusal to acknowledge wrongful nature of conduct" in the "handling of the DNA evidence" and his treatment of the "three young men who were wrongfully charged." On the "mitigating" side, the commission found that Nifong had a clean "prior disciplinary record" and a "reputation for character"—whatever that means—but, in any event, the "aggravating factors outweigh the mitigating factors."

He said the fourteen-month incident seemed to be outside the norm. "It appears to be an aberration in the life and career of Michael Nifong," Williamson continued. "It appears also to be an aberration in the way justice is handled in North Carolina. It's an illustration of the fact that character—good character—is not a constant. Character is dependent upon the situation. Probably any one of us could be faced with a situation at some point that would test our good character and we would prove wanting. And that has happened to Mike Nifong. But the fact that it has happened and the fact that we have found dishonesty and deceitful conduct requires us in the interest of protection of the public to enter the most severe sanction that we can enter, which is disbarment." He then turned his focus to the "victims" of the situation. "The victims are the three young men to start with, their families, the entire lacrosse team and their coach, Duke University, the justice system in North Carolina and elsewhere," he said. "And indeed prosecutors—honest, ethical, hard-working prosecutors throughout the nation—as we've heard through anecdotal evidence, are victims of this conduct. And in particular the justice system is a victim of the way this was taken out of"—quoting Wade Smith's testimony—"the courtroom and put in the hands of the public and not only the public in general but into a media frenzy unprecedented in anyone's experience."

He said the justice system in North Carolina "righted itself somehow" through the state bar's complaint against a sitting district attorney in the middle of a high-profile case—that he acknowledged was controversial and probably engendered "serious debate" at the bar—forcing Nifong to recuse himself and turn the case over to Cooper. "And that led to something really very extraordinary, a declaration of actual innocence of the three defendants—something that could never have been accomplished even if the criminal case had proceeded before Judge Smith," he continued. "And while we don't know, it seems reasonably clear that one would predict that at the suppression hearing in February, the case would have been dismissed. But it would have been dismissed with no declaration of innocence and indeed this entire controversy regarding the wrongful prosecution [would be] still hanging over the heads of the defendants and the justice system of North Carolina. So perhaps that was the good thing that happened, if one can find much of anything good out of this situation."

But he suggested that these "extraordinary" measures that turned the case around were a fluke and therefore a serious reminder of how powerful a district attorney can be. "The person who is the most powerful in the criminal justice system is not the judge and, except at the end of the process, it's not the jury, it's the prosecutor who makes the charging decision to start with," Williamson said. "The prosecutor, as any defense lawyer will tell you, is imbued with an aura that if he says it's so, it must be so. And even with all the constitutional rights that are afforded criminal defendants, the prosecutor merely by asserting a charge against defendants already has a leg up. And when that power is abused, as it was here, it puts constitutional rights in jeopardy. We have a justice system, but the justice system only works if the people who participate in it are people of good faith and respect those rights. And Mr. Nifong, it must be said, for whatever reason it does appear to us to be out of self-interest and self-deception, not necessarily out of an evil motive, but that his judgment was so clouded by his own self-interest that he lost sight of it and wandered off the path of justice and had to be put back on course again by very extraordinary means."

Williamson tried to find some good in the outcome. One was that Nifong had been disciplined with the Bar's "most severe sanction." He then focused on Nifong's initial statement after he received the state bar complaint: The "word on the street" was that the Bar was looking for a scalp. Not so, Williamson said. "Every case is different but the case we have here is a clear case of intentional prosecutorial misconduct," he said. "So in addition to this being a deterrent to any prosecutorial misconduct, I would say that this should be a reminder to everyone that it's the facts that matter. It's not the allegations." He also said the hearing had put many of the actors in the drama on the record for the first time in fourteen months. "We've had an opportunity over the last several days to hear additional evidence—and while it is really not within the purview of the panel to make such a pronouncement—I want to say again that we acknowledge the actual innocence of the defendants," he said. "And there is nothing here that has done anything but support that assertion."

Out of good things to say, Williamson concluded, "It's been truly—a 'fiasco' is not too strong a word. But it could have resulted from a lapse of character of practically anyone, not just in particular Mike Nifong. We've heard anecdotal evidence of the harm that it has caused. The actual harm is very difficult to get one's arms around. But I certainly hope that this process will help assuage the harm and stop the ripples that seemed to start when the stone was thrown in the pond. They just got bigger and bigger. But hopefully they will ebb from this point forward." He said a formal, written order would come from the commission in due time. On July 24, on behalf of the commission, Williamson filed the formal order disbarring Nifong, giving him thirty days to turn in his law license to the state bar; he was also required to pay all costs of the hearing, within ninety days.

After the hearing, Seligmann, Finnerty, and Evans and their families "exchanged hugs and good-byes," according to the *News & Observer*. "The mood in the courtroom was one of relief after more than a year of stress and uncertainty." Said Dave Evans Sr.: "We take no joy in this proceeding. It brings closure to a very sad period in our lives and we're gratified to the North Carolina justice system for seeing to it that justice has been done."

Nifong did not speak at the hearing on Saturday. He sat with his arm around his wife, Cy Gurney. They were both in tears. David Freedman, one of Nifong's two lawyers, told the *New York Times*, "He wants this over. He wanted the process to play out and to receive a fair hearing, and he believes he has received a fair hearing and accepts the findings of the commission." He said Nifong had been "devastated" by the testimony. Speaking on her husband's behalf, Gurney said, "It's a day of resolution—for us and, hopefully, for the court system." Steven Michael, the president of the state bar, took a victory lap. "The bar's strong response to this situation made clear that the ethical rules restricting pre-trial public comment and requiring prosecutors to turn over exculpatory evidence will be strictly enforced," he wrote in a statement. "Those rules are important, because they ensure the fundamental right to a fair trial that every citizen is guaranteed in our Constitution." It was left to Joe Cheshire to put the moment into some perspective. "Until a prosecutor who was willing to cheat got disbarred or went to prison, [prosecutorial misconduct] would not end," he said. "[The decision] was, as the English say, spot-on, and probably hard for him to hear. It's a shame he didn't listen to people who were trying to tell him that months ago. . . . I would be surprised if the saga of Mike Nifong is over."

The defense lawyers said they intended to file a motion with Judge Smith to "sanction" Nifong for his behavior in court and to hold him financially responsible for the nearly one hundred hours of legal work required for Bannon "to ferret out the hidden test results" in the 1,844 pages of DNA documents. The legal bills for the three families were estimated to be more than $3 million, and after Nifong's statement Friday that he still believed something happened in the bathroom, Cheshire said the families weren't in a particularly charitable mood toward him. "His continued efforts to smear the members of the Duke lacrosse team, which were recognized by the panel, did not endear him to the players' families or anyone else hurt in this," he said.

Years later, Nifong reflected on what it was like for him to endure the state bar hearing. "For somebody who has gone through what it takes to become a lawyer, and has then worked from the bottom of his profession to the top of at least that particular place, this is not the way you want your career to end," he said. "Just the idea of having to go into this situation, especially when everybody is out to get you, apparently, so you don't really feel like you have any friends in the courtroom, it is excruciating. The whole situation was kind of like the cancer treatment, in the sense that you had the feeling that no matter how this came out, it was never really going to be okay again, that there wasn't really any winning for you. There were only different ways of losing. I think that's such a hopeless feeling. Whatever you think about me as a person, if you talk to people who actually knew me, I was somebody who tried to do everything right, and who took pride in doing things right. It was about as low as you can feel, professionally." Did he think the fix was in? "It was pretty clear, during the examination, that, yes, it was over," he said, "they'd made up their minds, and that my career as a lawyer was over, but that also was what frees you from the pain."

On Monday, June 18, Brodhead and Steel, the chairman of the Duke board of trustees, announced that Duke had reached a financial settlement with Seligmann, Finnerty, and Evans. They did not announce the amount that Duke forked over to the three men in an effort to put the incident behind them, and none of the parties to the settlement will talk about it to this day. Instead, there was the usual corporate pablum about putting the matter behind everyone and moving on. "This has been an extraordinary year for Duke students David Evans, Collin Finnerty, and Reade Seligmann, who were accused of serious crimes they did not commit," the trustees' statement reads. "In April, after a thorough review, the North Carolina attorney general declared that they were innocent of all charges and that the charges never should have been brought. We welcomed their exoneration and deeply regret the difficult year they and their families have had to endure. They conducted themselves with great dignity during their long ordeal. These young men and their families have been the subject of intense scrutiny that has taken a heavy toll. The board of trustees and the president have also determined that it is in the best interests of the Duke community to eliminate the possibility of future litigation and move forward. For these reasons, and after considerable deliberation, the trustees have agreed to a settlement with each student. Beyond this statement, the resolution is a private matter among the students, their families, and Duke. This past year has been hard for many people who care about Duke—for students, faculty, staff, alumni, families, and friends—and for the three students and their families most of all. We resolve to bring the Duke family together again, and to work to protect others from similar injustices in the criminal justice system in the future."

Part of what Duke bought that day from Seligmann, Finnerty, and Evans was their silence, and neither they nor Duke has ever spoken publicly about the terms of the settlement. The secrecy was immediately controversial. "The question is now: For all its timeliness, does this settlement sweep important questions under the rug?" wondered Kristin Butler, a Duke senior, in the *Chronicle*. "It would be a real disappointment to see some administrators (Brodhead included) get a free pass in the spirit of 'closure,' as there remains much to answer for. . . . Moreover, it's hard to see how this administrative secrecy is compatible with Duke's mission as an educational community; such policies make it impossible for students, faculty and alumni to comment intelligently on University affairs. If other world-class institutions routinely make this information public without injury [on the same day the Duke settlements were announced, the *Chronicle of Higher Education* reported that the University of Wisconsin at Madison had paid $135,000 to settle a claim with a former administrator], Duke can surely do the same. Administrators have yet to provide a compelling reason why they choose not to, or how their choices benefit anyone outside of the Allen Building."

The consensus around Duke and Durham was that the university paid the three former lacrosse players a total of $60 million—$20 million each—to put the matter to rest. Duke noted that the money came from a "legal fund" and not from the Duke endowment. When, in February 2011, the IRS slapped a nearly $6.5 million tax lien on Seligmann for the tax year 2007—the year he received his settlement payment—a little reverse mathematical calculation lands at the $20 million figure. (His lawyer, Richard Emery, not only said the tax lien was filed in error but that the tax the IRS claimed he owed was not calculated based on his settlement.) Nifong said he, too, had heard the settlement number for the three players was $60 million. "Part of the message [of the settlements] is that Duke's got a shitload of money," Nifong said. "It apparently was worth it to them to spend whatever was necessary to make this go away."

As part the settlement, the three former lacrosse players agreed to release every member of Duke's faculty from future litigation. The agreement ended whatever potential liability existed—however slim—for the faculty members who had been outspoken against the players during the ordeal or who had affixed their name to the infamous Group of 88 ad. "This was an unprecedented situation, the likes of which we believe will not recur, and it was dealt with accordingly," John Burness said. "The settlement covers all matters related to the situation to date involving Duke and its employees, including members of the Duke faculty." The settlement with the three players was Duke's third settlement since the crisis began, following agreeements reached with Mike Pressler, over his firing and his being slandered and libeled, and with lacrosse player Kyle Dowd, who sued Duke over his belief that a professor had given him a poor grade in the spring 2006 semester because he was a lacrosse player. "I don't know if any faculty really felt any liability," said Professor Paula McClain, the incoming head of the Academic Council. "But in a very litigious society, anyone can sue for anything." (Indeed, in November 2008—of all times—Duke sued its insurance company, an affiliate of AIG, for refusing to pay any portion of the $60 million settlement with the three players.)

It fell to the three players to pay their attorneys' fees, which had accumulated to somewhere in the range of $3 million to $4 million total. But at least one attorney hired by the Seligmanns—Kirk Osborn—apparently did not get paid. Sometime in the fall of 2006, the Seligmanns replaced Osborn (and another attorney, Ernest L. "Buddy" Conner, from Greenville) with Jim Cooney, from Charlotte. Whereas Osborn was reticent to use the press to try the defense's case, Cooney had had no such concerns. Osborn seemed content to support Seligmann's case in his seemingly airtight alibi. In any event, Osborn died on March 25, 2007, after suffering a massive heart attack. At that time, the Seligmanns said in a statement, which read in part, "We are heartbroken over the death of Kirk Osborn." Two weeks later, on April 11, when Cooper declared Seligmann innocent, the first words out of Seligmann's mouth were his regret that Osborn had not been able to share the moment with him and his family. Nevertheless, according to Ann Petersen, one of Nifong's attorneys, "Kirk never got paid. Buddy never got paid. . . . Buddy and Kirk worked hard on that case. I mean, at a minimum, [Cooney] could've called the Seligmanns and said, 'Hey, guys, you need to pay up.' Seligmann got millions. There was no reason why he couldn't afford to pay his bill." Nifong, too, says Osborn's law firm was not paid for representing Seligmann. "I know that's what his wife told Ann Petersen," he said. "She was the one that reported that to Ann, because she tried to collect the money, and she called Seligmann's father about that and couldn't get paid." (Neither Conner nor Tonia Osborn, Kirk's widow, responded to repeated requests for comment.)

A lingering question remained as to why Duke—which found itself caught in the middle of a very difficult situation—would agree to pay the three indicted players $60 million, especially if Duke did nothing wrong? This is not a popular topic around the university. But one person familiar with the settlement discussions explained the settlement decision this way: After Cooper decided he was going to drop the case, the Duke board of trustees hired an independent counsel to investigate whether Duke had acted properly. The counsel told the board, in conclusion, "I don't think it could have been handled a lot differently." But there were "a couple of things that were done wrong, in hindsight, during the first twenty-four or forty-eight hours." The person explained that the incorrect advice given to the players early on had to do with the somewhat logical idea that they should just cooperate with the Durham police and tell them everything they know. That advice, in part, resulted in Zash, Flannery, and Evans spending hours with the Durham police—without having counsel present and without informing their parents—and providing a written statement as well as DNA and blood samples, and agreeing to have their house searched. "With hindsight, we shouldn't have said that," this person explained. "Not our job. Again, most times you would say, 'If this thing blew up amongst your students, yeah, get them to cooperate with the police and then it'll go away if it didn't happen. The best way they can get out of this is to go cooperate.'"

"But," the person continued, "when it turns out you're dealing with lying cops and a rogue prosecutor, you just gave them bad advice. In hindsight, you learn. The advice is, call your lawyer or call your parents. But people in the university aren't thinking that way. They're thinking, 'How do we smooth this over?'" The issue for the Duke board of trustees was that the players had been given poor legal advice: "'Why would you tell them to cooperate with the police? Why didn't you tell them to go get a lawyer before they went to the police? And, oh, by the way, did they pay a price for that?' They went in and gave them blood samples. Would any lawyer let them do that without first saying 'blah-blah-blah'? Well, the answer is maybe, but the answer would be of course not, because once you know you're dealing with a rogue prosecutor . . . It was thirty-six hours later they went and got lawyers, and the parents didn't hear about it the first night. . . . You got exposure. It's probably unfair, and when you've got exposure to somebody, you're sympathetic to them, and you'd rather not have to go fight over that." Another member of the Duke board of trustees summed up the situation simply: "Duke is good at teaching; it's not good at learning."

On the same day as Duke's settlement, Nifong submitted his resignation letter to both Judge Orlando Hudson and Governor Mike Easley. A few days later, he was locked out of the courthouse and not allowed to return to his elected office. "I never went back into my office again," he said, wistfully. Judge Hudson ordered Durham Sheriff Worth Hill to go to Nifong's house—after a courtesy call to let him know he was coming—to confiscate Nifong's office keys and access card for the courthouse. Arrangements were made for Nifong to separately obtain his personal items from his office. And just like that, the door to Nifong's twenty-nine-year prosecutorial career was slammed shut. Within a day, Governor Easley had appointed Nifong's predecessor, Jim Hardin, to replace him temporarily until Easley selected a full-time district attorney. One of Hardin's first moves was to fire Linwood Wilson, Nifong's investigator. He then asked the State Bureau of Investigation to determine whether any law enforcement officials, including Nifong, should be prosecuted because of their handling of the case.

"Frankly, this board hopes the door bumps Nifong on the way out," the *Chronicle* editors wrote the next day.

But even with his unceremonious resignation as district attorney and his disbarment, Nifong's legal troubles were not over. The same day as the hearing in Judge Hudson's courtroom, Judge Smith, in Superior Court, issued an order that informed Nifong there was sufficient evidence to charge him with "willfully and intentionally" making "false statements of material fact to the court," most of which had occurred during the September 22 hearing. Judge Smith assigned yet another attorney—Charles Davis—to act as his prosecutor and scheduled a hearing for July 26. To Nifong, it was all just gratuitous piling on. "Everybody is looking for more stuff to hang on me, this whole time, so that Mike Easley won't look bad," he said. "It's all covering their ass, because they're getting the blow-back from this, and I guess it just never occurred to them that somebody might actually want to do his job. They're not used to that, so they have to look for other people who have their interests at heart, and in a political patronage system, you can always find somebody like that."

Sporting a neatly trimmed Van Dyke beard and mustache, Nifong appeared at the July 26 preliminary hearing with two new lawyers, Jim Glover and Ann Petersen, of Chapel Hill. His first order of business was to apologize again. "The last sixteen months have proven to be a difficult and painful journey for my family and myself," he said. "This has also been a difficult and painful journey for Reade Seligmann, Collin Finnerty, and David Evans; for their families; for Durham and the state of North Carolina. We all need to heal. I believe, however, that this healing process cannot truly begin until all proceedings involving this matter are concluded and everyone is able to go forward." He said he had resigned. He said he had read Cooper's report, "including his recitation of evidence that I did not have, obtained from his own investigation," and he agreed with Cooper's finding "that there is no credible evidence that Mr. Seligmann, Mr. Finnerty, and Mr. Evans commited any of the crimes for which they were indicted or any other crimes during the party that occurred on March 13 and 14 of 2006 at 610 N. Buchanan Blvd." He continued, "Mr. Seligmann, Mr. Finnerty, and Mr. Evans were entitled to the presumption of innocence when they were under indictment. Surely they are entitled to more than that now as they go forward with the rest of their lives. And that is what the attorney general tried to give them in his declaration that they are innocent. I have admitted on more than one occasion that I have made mistakes in the prosecution of these cases. For that, I sincerely apologize to Mr. Selig-mann, Mr. Finnerty, Mr. Evans, and to their families. It is my hope that all of us can learn from the mistakes of this case, and that all of us can begin to move forward. It is my hope that we can start this process today."

After his apology, the defense attorneys—the same cast as before—took some pity on Nifong. They no longer demanded that he pay the cost of Brad Bannon's hundred or so hours of work ferreting out the DNA evidence from the 1,844 pages of raw data. But Judge Smith was not accommodating to Nifong's lawyers, who asked that a grand jury be convened to indict Nifong before con-tinuing with the contempt case against him—denied—and also asked that any trial against Nifong be held before a jury—also denied. The next hearing was scheduled for the end of August. If Judge Smith found Nifong guilty, he could fine him and sentence him to as many as thirty days in jail.

But despite his apology and his contrition, Nifong remained very much ambivalent about the denouement of the case. He was careful in his July 26 apology to note the new information Cooper had come across in his inves-tigation as the reason for why he believed there was no longer any "credi-ble evidence" with which to prosecute the three former lacrosse players. But he never said he agreed with Cooper's finding of innocence, and he still believed—believes—that "something happened" in the bathroom at 610 North Buchanan on the night of March 13. Then there was his belief that the North Carolina legal system had risen up against him. It was not unlike how, Voltaire explained in *Candide*, the British executed one of their own admirals who lost an important battle "*pour encourager les autres*" (to encourage the others). Nifong's ongoing feistiness could be seen in the August 7 letter he sent to the state bar turning in his law license. "You will note that it contains a misspelling of my middle name (which unfortunately I did not notice until after my swear-ing in), and damage subsequently by a puppy in her chewing stage," he wrote. "Consequently, it has never been framed or displayed." He wrote that he could not comply with the order to "surrender" his state bar membership card, "as I have never been sent one," and "since I never encountered a situation in which I needed the card, I have never requested one."

Nifong's two-day contempt trial on August 30 and 31 featured many of the same characters and much of the same testimony as had the state bar hearing two months earlier. After Nifong pleaded not guilty to the charges that he had lied to Judge Smith during the September 2006 hearing, Brad Bannon took another star turn, testifying against Nifong, as did Ben Himan and Katherine Jean, the state bar prosecutor. Brian Meehan and David Saacks testified for Nifong, as did Nifong himself. (Days later, Governor Easley would appoint Saacks to fill the remainder of Nifong's term as district attorney.) "I now under-stand that some things that I thought were in [Meehan's] report were in fact not in the report," Nifong testified. "So the statements were not factually true to the extent that I said all the information had been provided." But, he continued (as he had many times previously), "It was never my intention to mislead this or any other court. I certainly apologize to the court at this time for anything I might have said that was not correct. . . . At the time I made the statements, I believed them to be true."

Within minutes of the completion of the hearing, Judge Smith delivered the inevitable. Nifong was found guilty of intentionally lying to him during the September 2006 hearing. Judge Smith sentenced Nifong to spend twenty-four hours in jail, starting at 9 a.m. on September 7. Judge Smith said he did not believe Nifong's testimony that he did not know there was DNA evidence from non-lacrosse players at the time of the September 2006 hearing. "He was aware he had not provided such information to the then-defendants," he said, and declared that Nifong's statements to the court about the DNA evidence were "willfully contemptuous." Sentencing a district attorney to jail time was nearly without precedent. "This just doesn't happen," Duke law professor Thomas Metzloff told *Newsday*. "This was a very important moment, because it showed that the court system really cared about what happened in this case."

As usual, the defense attorneys crowed about Judge Smith's findings. Whatever empathy they had for Nifong was gone, again. "I believe this is one of the most historic days in American criminal justice," said Joe Cheshire. "It sends an enormous message to prosecutors all over this country." He told *Time* magazine, "I think what [Nifong] did was willful and intentional and damaged seriously this state and the lives of these boys and their families. I don't feel sorry for Mike Nifong. Sorry if that sounds cruel, but I don't." Added Jim Cooney, "I guess I have an overwhelming sense of watching the end of a tragedy. None of us take any joy in what happened today or in what's going to happen to Mr. Nifong."

While understandably not happy with Judge Smith's legal ruling or his one-day jail sentence, Nifong conceded it could have been worse. He said the prosecutor in the case—Charles Davis—was incompetent. "I thought that the prosecution in the contempt hearing was among the most inept that I have ever seen, and that I would not have expected anybody to ever be convicted on the evidence that was presented against me, but that didn't keep that from happening," he said. Indeed, he expected to get the full thirty-day sentence. In an interview, he said his attorneys had told him that about a month before the hearing, Judge Smith was at a wedding and was overheard saying, "after he convicted me of contempt, he intended to sentence me to thirty days in jail. Now, after he convicted me of contempt, he sentenced me to one day in jail, and I think that's because even a corrupt judge couldn't sentence me to thirty days in jail on the case that was presented against me. It was really bad—but that's all beside the point, anyway."

Nifong said he decided not to appeal Judge Smith's ruling because he wanted to be done. "I wanted it over," he said. "I just wanted it over. It didn't matter. He convicted me of being in contempt of court. As I told somebody, I wasn't in contempt of court as time was going on, but by the time I had been adjudged to be in contempt of court, I pretty much was. I pretty much had nothing but contempt for that court at that point, so I said fine, I'll pay that price." Ann Petersen, one of Nifong's attorneys said, "We did everything we thought we could, and when that judge stood up there with his already-written, eight-page document, it was clear that no matter what we did, that was going to be the result."

Generally speaking, Petersen said—as have many others—that the wealth of the indicted players' families played a big role in the case, both in its build-up and in its unraveling. "I have never had a question about the fact that the rich get different justice than the poor, and that's not based on the quality of lawyers, necessarily," she said. "They just have more resources. They had more resources, in this case, to hire experts. They had more resources to use the media. . . . There was absolutely no question that wealth played a role in this case."

Petersen paused, and then conceded that as a graduate of the University of North Carolina, it was part of her—ahem—DNA to have a bias against Duke. "The classic portrayal of the Duke students, it's the Harvard of the South, or Yale of the South," she continued. "They're rich kids that come from the North, and that's particularly true of the lacrosse players, because the Northeast is lacrosse country. And because it was a sport that was played at the prep schools, it's also primarily rich kids that play that sport, and to some extent that's changing. So all of my biases, that I felt that lawyers and judges would protect against, didn't happen in this case. I felt like the kids that were charged were treated differently than normal kids charged with this kind of offense would have been. There was a sense that, 'Oh my goodness, you're ruining the Duke lacrosse team by doing this.' I mean, how many times can you think of where a kid gets charged with rape and the kids sue the university because they didn't get to play lacrosse? And win. And the coach gets fired. I mean, it's one thing if they had gone to trial and been acquitted by a jury, and testimony had come out that would have implicated either the lacrosse coach or Duke University or given some basis for a lawsuit, but that didn't happen in this case.

"How many times has an innocent person been charged with an offense and recovered millions of dollars because they were charged?" she continued. "So what makes this case, and these kids, so exceptional and different from all of the other people who have been mistakenly charged with a criminal offense? Money. And I understand that money works with lay jurors—they sort of don't know the system—but judges should. People at the state bar should. Lawyers involved in this case should. I think part of what happened in this case, too, is that Mike—like I said, it was a perfect storm; I've said this a thousand times—there were two or three [earlier] cases that came to the state bar that were clear cases of prosecutors who had gone way over their responsibilities and ethical standards, and nothing could be done, for various reasons, or nothing was done. And there was an uproar because everybody felt like, if that's the case, the prosecutors have carte blanche to do whatever they want, whether it's right, wrong, or indifferent. The state bar had done nothing, and so I felt like [the Nifong case] was going to be [made the example]. Mike was going to be it, for no other reason than it was the next case up, and it had all the money behind it, it had all the press behind it, it had all the notoriety behind it. . . . That shouldn't happen. Those factors should not be factors. Yes, Mike made statements. Even if he had violated—which he didn't—but even if he had violated some discovery rule, you don't disbar somebody for that. I don't know of a lawyer that's been disbarred for something like that, ever. This case took on proportions that were beyond my comprehension, in all respects."

She was not completely disillusioned by what had happened to Mike Nifong. "I wouldn't say that I don't believe in the judicial system," she said. "What I now believe is that there are factors that are outside our judicial system that have a greater impact, and shouldn't have an impact, but do have an impact. And I was naïve. I was naïve to think that those factors don't count, and I was naïve for thirty years. I have no regrets about what we did. That's correct. I feel bad. I feel bad for our system. I feel bad for Mike. I feel bad that those kinds of factors can have an impact on our judicial system when they shouldn't, but I don't have any regrets about the way we approached it and what we did." Still, she said she was "terribly angry" with Judge Smith for finding Nifong in contempt. "I was angry at Judge Smith for doing what he did," she said. "One day is not a big deal in prison, but finding him guilty was." She said she believes Nifong still has not recovered from the case. "It all got turned," she continued. "Everything. Everything he had believed in, everything he had fought for, for twenty-eight years as a prosecutor, turned on him. Lawyers turned on him. Judges turned on him. The community turned on him, and it wasn't just the Duke community. It was other parts of the community. Durham was his community, and it all turned on him. I think it just devastated him."

At 8:40 a.m. on Friday morning, September 7, a group of about twenty supporters joined Nifong as he walked south on South Roxboro Street in Durham, over the railroad tracks and across Pettigrew Street to the jail. Suzanne Eisman, a family friend from Raleigh, and Victoria Petersen, the political activist, carried red signs that read: "We believe in your integrity and goodness." Dressed in a cream-colored golf shirt, tan pants, and brown loafers, Nifong held hands with his wife and his attorney, Ann Petersen. Asked if he had anything to say, Nifong responded, "Nice day." Petersen filled in the silence. "No comment, keep moving," she told the assembled reporters. "The sign says it all." One man, standing near the entrance to the jail, said of Nifong, "He's guilty. He's a dirtbag." Duke lacrosse player Thomas Clute intentionally missed lacrosse practice to watch Nifong turn himself in at the jail. "I wanted to watch vindication, the culmination of everything ending," he said.

At the jail, police issued Nifong a standard orange jumpsuit and soft sandals. He was put in a jail cell away from the general inmate population. His dinner consisted of spaghetti with meat sauce, green beans, a salad, a fruit drink, and cake. "In a way it was almost embarrassing," he said. "I mean, I had a whole cellblock to myself, I had two jailers who had to be there, and I'm sure they were embarrassed by the situation. I had an orange jumpsuit. I was in a cell where the light stays on twenty-four hours a day, which doesn't make for the most restful sleep, but that's what you do. You have to do that for everybody, because you don't want somebody hanging themselves, if you can figure out a way to do it, because they can't see in the cell. It was an interesting experience. It was not a bad experience in any way. Of course, almost by definition, it's not really a good experience. It's just something that you've never done before that you've now done. I would imagine that any time that you're incarcerated, not knowing when you're going to get out—although, as many people pointed out, I was the only person incarcerated for any length of time in the Duke lacrosse case. Nobody else was incarcerated at all."

Looking back, Nifong said if the white players on the Duke lacrosse team had only voluntarily agreed to provide DNA evidence to the police, there would have been "no Duke lacrosse case." He said that if the players had followed Pressler's original instinct—cooperate with the police and provide DNA voluntarily—things would have been very different. "There was only a Duke lacrosse case because they made the police put all this stuff in this affidavit that was part of the public record," he said. "If they give the sample voluntarily, there is never any doubt raised. Nothing ever happens. There's never a Duke lacrosse case. Even if somebody gets charged, it's not the Duke lacrosse case. It's members of a Duke sports team that have been charged, but it's never the Duke lacrosse case. That was a decision made when people decided that, oh no, we don't want to voluntarily give these samples, even though we didn't do anything because that document is a public record, and if they do it voluntarily, there is never any paper trail like that at all. All the allegations contained in that don't exist. Of course, that was all done before I ever even knew about this case." He said Bob Ekstrand's stridency exacerbated the situation. "What happened was Bob Ekstrand came in—and I could talk for days about Bob Ekstrand—but Bob Ekstrand came in and said, 'Everything's going through me now,' and put up this stone wall, and the only way you could do anything was with a subpoena or a search warrant. There was no possibility of talking reasonably to somebody at that point."

Nifong also said that he got e-mails from people suggesting he wanted to prosecute the Duke lacrosse players because he was a UNC fan. "I bet you wouldn't be prosecuting this case if it were members of the Carolina lacrosse team doing this," was how the typical e-mail in this vein read. "I was thinking," Nifong said, "well, if they came over to Durham to do it, I sure as hell would be." He said he had never been to a lacrosse game and had little knowledge or appreciation of the game. "When I grew up I never heard of lacrosse," he said. "When I was in college I saw people carrying these funny sticks, from the Northeast, and they had brought them with them. . . . I don't have anything against lacrosse. I don't really know anything about it. I know more about it now than I knew before this story, but I certainly didn't have any bias against it. . . . The fact is that jocks of any sort, if they get into a group of people that are egging them on, they probably follow along. I've seen that with all kinds of teams. But there are people who seem to think lacrosse is different. They say, 'We're not like other helmet sports.' Well, I don't know."

He started to talk about Mike Krzyzewski. "When he came to Duke, I hated the son of a bitch," he said. "He was arrogant, he was nasty, and he didn't like Dean Smith, whom I loved. Poor Dean. But I actually met Mike because I had two cases involving his children. I had one case involving—get this—a barroom assault on a Duke lacrosse player, where his eyeball got cut. I prosecuted the guy, a local, who I had a little history with, since I sent his mother to prison for murder when he was about twelve. I prosecuted that case, and Mike's oldest daughter"—Debbie—"was a witness. She was in the bar the night that this happened. She was actually a very good witness. So I met Mickie"—Krzyzewski's wife—"early on, and then Mike came to the testimony and sat in the courtroom, and I met him briefly. Later, Lindy, who I think is their middle daughter, she was assaulted and robbed at Northgate Mall, and I prosecuted that case. Mike and Mickie were in the courtroom for the whole thing. They were perfectly nice people—and here's the thing. When Mike Krzyzewski no longer was in anybody's shadow, when he made his own reputation, when he was no longer the new guy at Duke, when he was now someplace that, 'Wow, this guy can coach,' he stopped being an asshole. Now he's the best coach in college basketball. He might be the best coach in basketball, period. I don't like basketball very much, but I still recognize that he is a great coach, and he is a class guy. I know people who went to Carolina who can't stand Mike Krzyzewski because he coaches Duke. I know people probably hated Dean Smith because he coached Carolina. I'm an old Roy Williams fan. He's not nearly the basketball coach that Mike Krzyzewski is. He's a good recruiter. Frankly, I wouldn't have thought that he would've won even one championship at Carolina. I didn't think he was that kind of a coach. But still, Krzyzewski is the gold standard for college basketball coaches. I don't know how he feels about me at this point. Before, when I'd see him in places, he'd be friendly."

Nifong reiterated his view that the defense strategy—which he never thought would work—was to remove him from the case. "Their whole strategy—and this amazes me—was that this case never come to trial," he said, reflecting back. "And I really didn't think they could do that. I didn't think they had the power to have that happen, but I was wrong."

He again said that he believed—and believes—that Crystal Mangum was attacked in the bathroom. "Here's what I believe," he said. "I believed something occurred to Crystal Mangum that night that triggered a post-traumatic stress reaction. That's what I believe. Now, just what the nature of that was—whether it was a physical assault or whether something that occurred here—and we don't know everything that occurred and we'll never know that. It's not something that's knowable at this time. But, I believe that she reacted the way she did that night because she was under the influence of a post-traumatic stress reaction. I think that explains her behavior in the car when Shelton came to the scene. I think it explains her behavior in the emergency room when she's taken there. And the problem is that at this point, we'll never be able to get to the bottom of that. From my point of view, the case probably became un-tryable at the point that Crystal began to show some signs of instability, when she was working with the Attorney General's Office at a point after the case had left. There had been none of that before. She was always real lucid, always focused. . . . I never had any reason to question that there was an assault until at a time that I no longer had the case."

Nifong expressed disappointment with the way things turned out. "I won't say that I was happy about how any of this stuff went down," he said. "I was very disappointed in certain things. . . . The attorneys who were involved on the other side of this case, what they did was not really appropriate and it was not really permissible, but I don't begrudge them any of that because that's what defense lawyers do. They live in that 'What we're doing is not really appropriate but we get away with it because we have to' kind-of-world, and I've dealt with that all my life. . . . I guess what really disappointed me was the state bar, who, in essence—and I don't know to what extent they were egged on by the specific attorneys that were involved, although that was part of it—they decided that I needed to be removed, and the only way they could do that would be to find a crime that justified disbarment, and I didn't commit a crime. I mean, if I committed anything at all, it was talking to the press too much, and as my lawyer said, 'Nobody in the United States has ever been disbarred for talking to the press.' So they tried to make it look like I'd lied about some stuff, which I clearly didn't lie about. When they filed this motion based on stuff that they'd discovered in the discovery I just gave them—and it's not like I'd hidden it, or that I denied them the evidence—they got all the evidence that I had all along. They got it as soon as I got it. I'm disappointed that the state bar did what it did, but you have to understand that although they would want you to feel otherwise about it, the state bar does not exist to protect the public from lawyers. It exists to protect the lawyers from the public. There's a lot of money involved for a lot of people, and this case was probably one of the biggest money cases that criminal law has ever seen in North Carolina. I can't imagine that any case had more money spent on it in the criminal courts than this one; it was a situation where they really sold out to the monied interests of the state bar. It's the same model with the NCAA and with the Mafia and so on. You have this group of people that decide who can be a member, they decide what the rules are, they decide who's broken the rules, and they decide what the punishment is, and there's basically no oversight over any of those steps of the procedure. And they would do anything to keep that power from being taken from them. The last thing that the state bar wants is any kind of citizen oversight, any kind of group outside of the bar itself, to review their actions. I mean, they vote on what's improper or not."

When he picked up that nontestimonial order from the copy machine on the afternoon of March 24, Nifong said he did not give a thought to what the outcome of the case might be. "No, not like it came out, but I wasn't outcome-oriented," he said. "I was process-oriented. I was, 'This is what we need to do. This is what my mandate is, as district attorney in Durham. This is what I'm supposed to do. It doesn't have to be fun. It doesn't have to be self-aggrandizing. It may not be the way I want to spend my time, but it's why I'm in this job, and if I can't do this job, then I don't need to be here.' Which is why the loss of the law license was such an insignificance, because my law license, by the time they took it away, meant nothing. Absolutely nothing. They showed me that it never meant anything in the first place. All that crap that I thought I was fighting for, it was just crap. The state bar should be a real embarrassment to North Carolina. I mean, it exists for the purpose of protecting the rich lawyers from the people. It has nothing to do with protecting the people from the lawyers. Every once in a while, as I said, they'll sacrifice some low-hanging fruit, some dumbass who should never have been a lawyer in the first place, who does something unforgivable. They're the easy targets. But the people who are corrupting the system are essentially immune from being dealt with by them, and that's their decision that they make by having the lawyers police the lawyers. There's no public oversight."

He said the outcome of the Duke lacrosse scandal triggered in him his own post-traumatic stress reaction. "After a while it kind of gets to you, and you do the best you can, and you try to go on about your life, and you try to put things behind you, and you try to move on and I have moved on, but, as I said, as thinking about sitting down with you today over the course of the last few days I have felt a lot of this—not exactly anxiety. It's more like this sense of inevitability I guess: That I'm going to have to face this sort of thing again and that probably I'm going to have to keep facing this. It's not like it's ever really going to go anywhere, is it? So, it's something that I'm never through dealing with and I may never be through dealing with, and cancer is like that, because you do everything that you can do to try to get rid of the cancer, but you can never be sure that you've gotten rid of the cancer."

On his way out of jail on Saturday morning, Nifong thanked his jailers for "the professionalism" with which he was treated "and the respect which I was shown." He told the assembled press, "Other than that, I just want to go home and spend time with my family." He said of the twenty or so people who came out to support him, "It means a whole lot to me, it really does." As he made his way to a car, the supporters surrounded Nifong and kept reporters at bay. "We love you here in Durham," Victoria Petersen told him. "The people love you. We support you and we feel that you are innocent." Gloria Parker, a Durham resident, watched Nifong leave the jail. "He didn't deserve to go to jail, not one day," she said, "because he only did what he thought was right. I think they took his dignity from him. That was wrong." Others, of course, thought the day-long sentence was too short.

"I don't have anything else to say," Nifong told the crowd.

CHAPTER EIGHTEEN

Bad Karma

As Nifong had been gearing up for his contempt trial and day in jail, a special committee of the Durham City Council that had been investigating the behavior of the Durham police after the alleged rape at 610 North Buchanan abruptly stopped its probe on the advice of the city's insurance company—a subsidiary of AIG, the giant insurer. The insurance company worried that a report that detailed the mistakes the police had made during the investigation would provide "ammunition," according to an article in the local press, for any number of civil lawsuits against Durham. The anxiety was warranted. After Cooper found Seligmann, Finnerty, and Evans innocent in April, the three men had hired high-priced attorneys to represent them in civil suits against various defendants, one of which was to be Durham and its police force. Seligmann hired the high-profile New York City attorney Barry Sheck, who not only once had been a member of the team of lawyers that won an acquittal of murder charges for O. J. Simpson but also was the founder of the Innocence Project, which uses DNA and other evidence to try to free the wrongly imprisoned. Finnerty and Evans hired Brendan Sullivan, the superstar Williams & Connolly partner who had once represented Oliver North in the Iran-Contra hearings.

Durham officials announced that on the advice of the city's insurer, its investigation was in a "holding pattern" pending a settlement meeting between the players' lawyers and Durham's. "I think, after a while, the city may end up feeling like General Custer at Little Bighorn," remarked Councilman Eugene Brown. "He looks around and, to paraphrase, says, 'Where . . . are all those lawyers coming from?'" For his part, Willis Whichard, a former justice of the North Carolina Supreme Court who was leading Durham's investigation, said he had wondered "if this would be a problem" from the beginning, as Durham had a $5 million liability policy with a $500,000 deductible, meaning that any settlement above $5 million with Seligmann, Finnerty, and Evans would be borne by Durham taxpayers.

On September 5, Sheck and Sullivan met secretly for two hours with Durham officials—including Mayor Bill Bell and City Manager Patrick Baker—to discuss a potential settlement between the players and the city. In a rare legal misstep for the former lacrosse players, their lawyers offered to settle the civil suit against Durham for $30 million—$10 million each—or $142 for each of the city's 210,000 residents. Along with the financial settlement, the city council would be required to pass resolutions to urge the North Carolina State Legislature to enact reforms to the criminal justice system—for instance, requiring the recording of grand jury proceedings and creating a state ombudsman to hear, and act upon, complaints against local prosecutors.

On September 6, the city council met to consider the settlement proposal. Legal experts believed Durham was vulnerable on a few points: the April 4 photo-identification lineup violated established police procedures because Mangum was shown only the photographs of the forty-six white Duke lacrosse players; there were discrepencies between Himan's description of who Mangum said had attacked her and Gottlieb's description, especially since Gottlieb did not prepare his notes until July 2006, some four months after his conversation with Mangum; and a Crimestoppers poster used by police had claimed a woman was "sodomized, raped, assaulted, and robbed" and that a "horrific crime . . . sent shock waves throughout the community." (In general, municipalities are immune from civil lawsuits except when a government violates a citizen's constitutional rights, when a federal civil rights lawsuit can be filed; in that case, plaintiffs must prove "a pattern and practice" of civil rights violations. The city, rather than the state—Nifong's employer—was the focus of the players' potential lawsuit because North Carolina law limited the state's liability in civil rights cases to $500,000.) Sheck and Sullivan gave the city thirty days to consider the settlement or face the filing of a federal civil rights lawsuit.

The blowback was immediate against the players' $30 million settlement demand, which had been leaked to the press. Barry Saunders, the *News & Observer* columnist, was livid. "Only a heartless misanthrope would argue against giving something to the dear, sweet former Duke lacrosse players who have been through such an ordeal," he wrote on September 10, with considerable sarcasm. "Why, I think one of them even spent an hour in custody—not in jail, but waiting for a magistrate to finish his lunch so daddykins could post bail." He said the $30 million "seems a bit high for the inconvenience they suffered, but they deserve some recompense. After all, the strippers they hired didn't even finish their hootchy-kootchy dance." (Another $10 million each from Durham must have seemed logical to Sheck and Sullivan after the players got $20 million each out of Duke, given the relative wealth and theoretical culpability of Duke and Durham.) As a compromise, "instead of $30 million," Saunders suggested, "how about a fish sandwich, a Yoo-hoo, and one-way Greyhound bus ticket." He wrote that the Duke lacrosse case was "like a bad rash" that had "become the gift that keeps on giving." While he acknowledged that settling the matter was the "only medicine that would make it go away," his less Swiftian proposal was for the city to agree to pay the players' legal fees and also to institute reforms to its "dysfunctional cop shop to ensure that no one else suffers what they did." After noting that Seligmann, Finnerty, and Evans never went to jail, Saunders said that if Durham paid them "an exorbitant amount without a fight," he himself would be spending time in jail after he went to city hall and assaulted the councilmen. For Saunders the problem was simple: "Much of the media were too quick to demonize the little darlings when charges surfaced that they had raped an exotic dancer. As if to make up for that, most media have gone the other way, deifying the Blue Demon 3 and making them out to be victims of an evil woman and an even more evil judicial system. Judging by the amount they're seeking, it appears they themselves have come to believe the hype that they are somehow heroic and deserving."

He then penned a ditty to the three players, based upon Dion's 1968 classic song, "Abraham, Martin, and John":

Has anybody here seen my old friends Dave, Reade & Collin?
Can you tell me where they've gone?
They hired themselves a stripper
But they're the ones who got paid
I just looked around, and they were gone
Probably to an island they purchased with the $30 million they extorted
*   from the City of Durham.*

He conceded the players deserved "something" for their troubles but wondered if they honestly believed they "deserve" more than Dwayne Dail, an innocent Goldsboro, North Carolina, man who had been imprisoned for eighteen years for a rape he didn't commit. Dail got $20,000 for each of his years in prison. "The Dukies have gone beyond seeking justice," Saunders concluded. "They're being greedy and retributive. If they get $30 million, they will have done to the city what Mike Nifong said they did to that dancer." Even the *Chronicle*'s editors believed the $30 million settlement was excessive. "Although the families need to be repaid, $30 million is pretty steep," they agreed. "After all, the 'bad guys' in this case are not the Durham citizens who will be paying the lion's share of that settlement, but rather Nifong and certain members of the Durham Police Department."

Others quickly joined the protest. Mayor Bill Bell had heard from many of his constituents. "They think it's ridiculous," he said. "People have heard there was a settlement with Duke. [The players] didn't spend any time in jail, didn't go to trial and now they're giving demands that could affect people's pocketbooks as taxpayers." Even Jackie Brown, Nifong's former campaign-manager-turned-enemy, believed the $30 million may have been an overreach. "I've had people call me and say, 'I've supported these guys all the way, but $30 million is way over the top,'" she said. "Then I've had people call and say [the players] deserved the money for what they went through and what they have to carry with them through the rest of their lives." Sandy Ogburn, a former city council member, e-mailed Bell, "I am unwilling to give those boys a single penny. The very last thing that these parents want is for the evidence to be heard. While a court case would be costly, it would be worth every penny to me as a taxpayer. At least then we will be able to hear the entire case—and have the evidence in the public view. All we know right now is what the defense attorneys have parsed out—oh, as well as their million-dollar PR campaign."

Not surprisingly—as happened throughout the case—those in support of the demands of Seligmann, Finnerty, and Evans were equally virulent. "Thirty million dollars is the least of Durham's worries," Kenneth Larrey, a Duke senior and the founder of Duke Students for an Ethical Duke, wrote in the *Chronicle*. "Residents should be asking how a corrupt District Attorney's Office could remain silent throughout this affair, how an entire police department could do the same, how a man like Sergeant Mark Gottlieb can still carry a badge, how consecutive judges could allow this charade to continue and actively enable it, how a population could nominate and elect an overwhelmingly corrupt prosecutor, and how the *Herald-Sun* continues to sell papers after maneuvering the county into precisely this sort of legal quagmire." He acknowledged that while not every citizen of Durham had voted for Nifong and very few Duke students and alumni were involved in the incident, both Duke and Durham would suffer for years. Kristin Butler, another *Chronicle* columnist, agreed. "I hope the families get every penny," she wrote. "If attorneys can establish that the players' civil rights were violated—and clearly I believe Sheck and Sullivan can—then they have a right to damages. There is, of course, no magic to the $30 million figure, but after taxes, attorneys' fees and other expenses, $10 million per family does not seem unreasonable in light of the financial and emotional toll this case has taken."

In the end, the city of Durham rejected the $30 million settlement demand, and, on October 5, Seligmann, Finnerty, and Evans filed a federal civil lawsuit against a rash of defendants, including Nifong, Durham, its police department, and Dr. Brian Meehan, arguing that they had conspired against the players to violate their constitutional rights under the Fourth and Fourteenth amendments. The lawsuit sought unspecified financial damages as well as broad reforms of the way the Durham police department operates. The lawsuit described the lacrosse case as "one of the most chilling episodes of premeditated police, prosecutorial, and scientific misconduct in modern American history, which resulted in charges brought and maintained against three innocent Duke University students and lacrosse players over a period of more than one year." The suit dredged up, in impassioned detail, the whole sorry episode.

Meanwhile, as Durham was grappling with how to handle the demands of

Sheck and Sullivan, Duke was eagerly trying to put the matter further into the rearview mirror. On September 19, the university announced it would spend $1.25 million in the coming five years to expand the law school's Wrongful Conviction Clinic and its Innocence Project, and that none other than James Coleman would lead the development of the new program. "Three of our students suffered a grave injustice at the hands of the legal system," Brodhead—now fully converted—said in a statement announcing the new initiative, "and we were relieved when their innocence was finally established. Their ordeal reminded all of us that our legal system is imperfect and innocent people can be accused unfairly. I am determined that we will make some good come out of the grave injustice that took place."

Ten days later, Brodhead was at it again, at another Duke Law School event—examining the role the media played in the case—where he made his first, full-throated, scripted apology. He had originally declined to be involved in the conference but later asked for fifteen minutes to address the audience. After some general observations about the case, he said:

We are now in the aftermath of this extraordinary case, and the aftermath, we have to hope, is a time for learning. Having spent my life in the cause of teaching and learning, I am not at all unwilling to learn lessons of my own. I am happy for this chance to share some of those lessons.

First and foremost, I regret our failure to reach out to the lacrosse players and their families in this time of extraordinary peril. Given the complexities of the case, getting this communication right would never have been easy. But the fact is that we did not get it right, causing the families to feel abandoned when they most needed support. This was a mistake. I take responsibility for it, and I apologize.

Second, some of those who were quick to speak as if the charges were true were on this campus, and some faculty made statements that were ill-judged and divisive. They had the right to express their views. But the public as well as the accused students and their families could have thought that those were expressions of the university as a whole. They were not, and we could have done more to underscore that.

Third, I understand that by deferring to the criminal justice system to the extent we did and not repeating the need for the presumption of innocence equally vigorously at all the key moments, we may have helped create the impression that we did not care about our students. This was not the case, and I regret it as well.

Fourth, this episode has taught me a hard lesson about the criminal justice system and what it means to rely on it. Given the media circus and the public reactions it fed, I thought it essential to insist that the matter be resolved within the legal system, not in the court of public opinion. As far as it went, this was right. But what this case reminds us is that our justice system—the best in the world—is only as good as the men and women who administer it. In this case, it was an officer of this system itself who presented false allegations as true, suppressed contrary evidence and subverted the process he was sworn to uphold.

Relying on the criminal justice system in this case proved to have serious limits. But for the university to strive to set the system to rights—for instance, by attacking the district attorney—presented problems as well. For one thing, none of us can lightly speak as if the system itself is tainted because some of our own have been accused of a crime. I was also concerned that if Duke spoke out in an overly aggressive fashion, it would be perceived that a well-connected institution was improperly attempting to influence the judicial process, which could have caused the case to miscarry in a variety of ways. Finally, there was no legal recourse against the district attorney, for me or anyone else. Under North Carolina laws, no one had authority to take an active case from a DA absent the DA's own request, as finally happened in January.

Even with all that, Duke needed to be clear that it demanded fair treatment for its students. I took that for granted. If any doubted it, then I should have been more explicit, especially as evidence mounted that the prosecutor was not acting in accordance with the standards of his profession.

The larger problem for society is how to create and maintain the optimal balance between the independence of the legal system and protection of individuals from false prosecutions. If this state should ever again have a rogue prosecutor on the loose with no more remedies than were available last time around, the failure to have learned the lesson of the Duke lacrosse case would be intolerable. I do not want to create some instant legislative solution that opens the door for new injustices tomorrow. I recognize that it is not easy to get the checks and balances right when two such important interests are at stake. But it's essential for all relevant parties to work to create these mechanisms, and I trust the current conference will contribute to this cause.

Closer to home, this case highlights challenges universities face when students are tied to serious criminal charges. This challenge has many aspects: how the university advises a student in these circumstances, how the university regulates the presence on campus of students charged with serious crimes, how the university interacts with parents and many more. My colleagues in the Duke administration are going over all our procedures to see what we can learn from our experience. But these are complex questions, and they aren't ones Duke can or should hope to solve on its own. To work through these difficulties and see that their lessons are learned not only here but around the country, we will be hosting a national conference of educators, lawyers, and student affairs leaders to discuss best practices in this important field.

I'll end with the deepest lesson this case taught me. When I think back through the whole complex history of this episode, the scariest thing, to me, is that actual human lives were at the mercy of so much instant moral certainty, before the facts had been established. If there's one lesson the world should take from the Duke lacrosse case, it's the danger of prejudgment and our need to defend against it at every turn. Given the power of this impulse and the forces that play to it in our culture, achieving this goal will not be easy. But it's a fight where we all need do our part.

Much of me hopes the Duke lacrosse case will be forgotten someday. But if it is remembered, let's hope it is remembered the right way: as a call to caution in a world where certainty and judgment come far too quickly.

The speech earned Brodhead a standing ovation from the audience. And he left the symposium soon thereafter, without answering any questions. He remained under fire, though, for his handling of the crisis. One of his most prominent critics was Jay Bilas, the ESPN college basketball analyst and a gradute of both Duke and Duke Law School. In a letter he wrote—that was not published but quickly appeared online—to the Duke alumni magazine, Bilas said, "A true leader has the vision and courage to recognize what is right, especially in the face of adversity, and fears not the consequences of unreasonable response. A true leader needs not the benefit of hindsight to make clear the right path. From March 2006 to date, President Brodhead's mishandling of the challenges presented has proven him incapable of effectively leading Duke into the future."

He conceded that Brodhead could "point to a few ineffectually communicated words here and there for a feeble claim that he 'emphasized' the protection of the rights of Duke's students," but added that such a claim "fails the laugh test," since the "vast majority of his words and actions, and in many cases his silence, emphasized an aura of guilt of the students and of the university." Bilas wrote, "From the beginning," Brodhead "abdicated his responsibility as Duke's leader to stand up for fairness and truth." Instead Brodhead "chose the path of political expediency" and "failed to effectively counter factually inaccurate and inappropriate statements about Duke and its students, failed to forcefully speak out against procedural irregularities, and failed to take appropriate action in response to repeated attacks upon the due process rights of Duke's students. That is unacceptable."

He wanted Brodhead to go. "If such failures in leadership are not enough, for the same reasons that President Brodhead forced the resignation of lacrosse

coach Mike Pressler—because confidence in his ability to lead had been compromised, and a need [arose] to move forward in a new direction—President
Brodhead should resign or be dismissed." And he thought that Steel and any
other board members who likewise had supported Brodhead's actions and
statements throughout the ordeal should also resign. Contacted after Brodhead's September 29 apology, Bilas said it was "appropriate" but "woefully late."
He told the *News & Observer* about Brodhead, "The confidence in his ability to lead has been eroded. While Dick Brodhead is a terrific person and
would make a wonderful head of the English Department, he has demonstrated his ineffectiveness and his inability to lead, especially in a crisis." He
told the *Chronicle* the apology was "woefully insufficient." "What President
Brodhead apologized for was his weakness and failures as a leader," Bilas continued, "but what we're left with is a weak leader. I respect him very much as a
scholar but I think he's proven himself incapable to lead Duke into the future."
He wondered why his alma mater was "more concerned with liability than
responsibility."

But John Burness said Brodhead's speech was unrelated to the fact that a
large number of the non-indicted lacrosse players had hired an attorney and
were thinking about whether to bring a lawsuit against Duke and others.
And he said that it was unrelated to the fact that a number of trustees were
on campus and that a trustee and faculty committee had begun the process
of reviewing Brodhead's tenure as president. James Coleman agreed that he
didn't think Brodhead's speech was motivated by any effort to mitigate a new
lawsuit against the university. "I think he did the right thing," Coleman said,
"and the fact that he did the right thing in the face of a threatened lawsuit is
[commendable]. . . . I think there was almost a sense of relief, that a kind of
final piece has been put into place. He recognized the university had not [done
enough] and, as president, he took responsibility for that. He made no excuses,
and I think that was appropriate." Others were less sure of Brodhead's motives.
Ken Larrey, a Duke senior, said he believed Brodhead gave the speech because
the board of trustees ordered him to do it. "I'm not even sure he believed what
he was saying," he said.

In a letter to the *Chronicle*, Ole Holsti, a professor emeritus of political science, spoke what many thought but rarely communicated out loud. "President Richard Brodhead was very gracious, as always, in his apology for Duke's
handling of the lacrosse case," he wrote. "Indeed, he went far beyond what
was necessary. When will we get an apology from members of the lacrosse
team for their irresponsible behavior, including hiring a stripper, that initiated
this sad affair? When will we get an apology from the parents of the lacrosse
players for not raising their sons to understand that hiring strippers constitutes wholly unacceptable behavior?" Of course, Holsti's letter brought its own
retort, from Jon Jackson, the associate director of athletics for communication,

who reminded Holsti of the three cocaptains' "apology" after meeting with Brodhead on March 28. "The statement proved to be entirely prophetic," Jackson wrote. "Perhaps Holsti, along with many others deceived by the 'wall of silence' propaganda being put forth by the former district attorney, missed the many sincere apologies by the players at the time. It is a shame that there are still those who believe the young men and their families have not been through enough." And another response came from Mike Munger, the chair of the polical science department, who agreed with Jackson that the players had apologized. "Whether the events at the party required an apology is moot," he wrote. "Those responsible have apologized, and the entire team had its season canceled. Surely that is enough—more than enough—apology and punishment."

Actually, it wasn't. The litigation related to the Duke lacrosse case was only just starting. At the end of October 2007, Jim Cooney, Seligmann's lawyer, asked the federal government to join with Roy Cooper to conduct a criminal investigation into Nifong's prosecution of the case. In early December 2007, federal prosecutors declined to launch the criminal probe Cooney requested. "This matter involves the conduct of a state prosecutor applying state law in a state criminal trial," Craig Morford, acting federal deputy attorney general, wrote. "We believe the state of North Carolina has the primary interests in this matter: protecting the integrity of its judicial proceedings, holding Mr. Nifong accountable for his actions as an officer of its courts, and vindicating the principles of justice under state law."

Then, on December 18, three of the other, nonindicted lacrosse players—Ryan McFadyen, Breck Archer, and Matt Wilson—decided, in a four-hundred-page complaint, that no less than a "consortium" of people had "railroad[ed]" them and the other lacrosse players "based upon the transparently false claim of rape, sexual offense, and kidnapping made by a clinically unreliable accuser." The list of defendants ranged from Duke, Brodhead, and Steel to Nifong and Meehan and nearly everyone in between. Duke called the new lawsuit "misdirected" and "another unfortunate result" of Nifong's failed prosecution. "No, it isn't," wrote *News & Observer* columnist Barry Saunders. "It is the unfortunate result of these three chumps' lack of values. Instead of trying to make money off shameful misbehavior, they should be trying to make up for the bad karma the team unleashed onto the world before the March 2006 rape allegations. So all-encompassing is their four-hundred-page complaint that I'm surprised Alexander Graham Bell wasn't listed as a defendant: if he had never invented that darned telephone contraption, the players would never have been able to dial up the booty-shaking duo of Crystal Mangum and Kim Roberts."

Not to be outdone, another group of thirty-eight nonindicted Duke lacrosse players filed their own lawsuit against twenty-nine different defendants. The only three Duke lacrosse players on the 2006 team who were not part of any lawsuit were Matt Danowski, the son of the Duke lacrosse coach; Kevin Mayer, who had been "passed out" at the party, according to Evans, McFadyen, and others; and Matt Zash, one of the three cocaptains who had lived at 610 North Buchanan, told his friends that he "doesn't split dark wood" and was the one who told police that he had placed Mangum's broken fingernails in the trash after the party. (Nifong observed that Zash's lack of involvement with the lawsuits "is interesting if it shows nothing other than restraint on his part.")

Incredibly, their attorneys and publicist—Bob Bork Jr., the son of Robert Bork, the unsuccessful Supreme Court nominee—commandeered the National Press Club in Washington, one block from the White House, to announce the lawsuit. At the same time, they also launched a website to accompany the filing of the lawsuit. "This is kind of a media center," Bork said, "and Durham isn't. Sorry." The players' attorney, Chuck Cooper, described the people who came out against the lacrosse team in the days after March 13 as an "angry mob" and said the players were "reviled almost daily in the local and national press." From this, he said, the players suffered "grievous, lasting injuries." Cooper said the players had decided to sue "reluctantly" but "to hold Duke accountable." No players appeared at the National Press Club, Bork said, because they did not want to attract attention. Steven Henkelman, an architect from Philadelphia and the father of player Erik Henkelman, appeared at the press conference and spoke about the anguish his son faced after the allegations against the team became public. He had to move out of his Durham home, out of a fear of retribution, and was "devastated" when Brodhead canceled the season. Duke was "willing to sacrifice a few—our sons—for the good of the administration," he said. As Duke had with the first lawsuit filed by the nonindicted players, it claimed that the new suit was "misdirected and without merit" and that if the players had a legal beef, "it [was] with Mr. Nifong," who some compared to a cross between Wyatt Earp and Elliot Ness. Of the lawsuit from the nonindicted players, Nifong said simply, "That just shows you why you don't negotiate with terrorists."

At least one Duke parent felt the same way. "I am delighted to see that Duke is defending itself vigorously against the specious claims of the LAX players," he wrote. "I have always found it incredible that these clowns, whose actions did more damage to Duke than anything else in the entire history of the university, would have the gall to assume the victim pose and claim that the university damaged them. What a joke. One of the problems with this case is that from the very beginning, people like K. C. Johnson have tried to spin the case in a way that portrays the LAX players as 100 percent pure and innocent and Duke and its administrators as 100 percent evil and malicious. Because this analysis relieves the players of any personal responsibility for their actions, they and their parents were quick to buy into the analysis and even went so far as to file lawsuits against Duke, which are predicated on this analysis. I have news for you. While this analysis may play well with the players and their families and the small group of fanatics who inhabit this website and are still flogging this case more than five years after the fact, it will not play in a court of law. The judge in this case sees through the nonsense. He has already dismissed most of the claims against Duke and its administrators and has criticized the players and their lawyers for wasting his time with so many frivolous claims. Now, a Duke law professor who is an expert in the area of civil litigation and has no connection to the case states that the causation issues raised by the university in its response to the complaint are very real and pose a significant problem for the players. The handwriting is on the wall. These cases are going nowhere."

Somewhat ironically, though, Nifong was not a defendant in the new lawsuit because five weeks earlier, on January 15, 2008, he had filed for personal bankruptcy in federal court, listing assets of $243,898 and liabilities of the astounding sum of $180.3 million, including $30 million for each of the six Duke lacrosse players—Seligmann, Finnerty, Evans, McFadyen, Archer, and Wilson—who had sued him. He listed his monthly income from his pension of $4,957.48 and that of his wife of $4,252.48. Unless his actions were found to be "willful and malicious"—a charge he disputed—his bankruptcy filing would remove him from the lawsuits. His house, owned jointly with his wife, would also be protected from creditors' claims. He did not list another house his wife owned in Ashe County, North Carolina. In his initial filing, he forgot to list his three vintage guitars—a Fender Deluxe Nashville Telecaster, a Martin D-41, and a PRS Custom 24—as his separately owned assets. The three guitars were sold at auction in October 2008 in less than thirty minutes for $5,100. "He's basically throwing in the towel [on the lawsuits]," Jeb Jeutter, a Raleigh attorney, told the *News & Observer*. "He has said either I don't want to or I don't have the resources to defend this lawsuit, so I will file for bankruptcy and I can walk away with the exempt assets I have."

Since he had been a state employee at the time his offenses supposedly occurred, Nifong had previously asked the state to pay for his legal counsel to help defray the costs of the mounting lawsuits against him. But the state declined to pick up the tab for Nifong's legal defense. "I felt like, okay, this is hardly a surprise, but of course I was extremely disappointed," he said. "When you consider that Jim Coman and Mary Winstead, who were the two people who investigated this case for Roy Cooper, when they told him that they thought that the state should pay for my defense and he said no, then that's very disappointing. . . . It meant that I had to be sacrificed, and he was willing to do whatever was necessary to do that."

Cooper's decision not to pay for Nifong's legal defense made the latter's subsequent bankruptcy filing nearly inevitable and added yet another extraordinary twist in one of the most improbable legal sagas in American history. "I sacrificed some guitars," Nifong explained of the bankruptcy filing. "I never defaulted on anything. Mortgages, whatever, I went to the bank and signed a note after the bankruptcy saying that I still intended to be liable on all that. The only thing that was ever implicated were the official results of the lawsuit, and the costs of the state bar hearing. I threw that in [to his list of liabilities] because I figured that if they were going to spend all that money to do a hearing that runs three or four times as long as their average hearing, and subpoena all these witnesses, and weren't even going to give me a fair hearing—if they're going to do all of that as a dog-and-pony show, when the results had already come in, then I really shouldn't have to pay for it. So I also included the costs of the hearing, which were about $11,000. I didn't have to pay anything. The [net] assets were around $3,000 from the sale of the guitars, and that was the bankruptcy estate and all the claimants had to deal with that." The state bar was the only claimant against Nifong in bankruptcy court and ended up receiving around twenty cents on the dollar for its claim for the costs of the hearing.

Ironically, after McFadyen got suspended from Duke for writing his infamous e-mail, his lawyer, Glenn Bachman, asked Nifong to write a letter on McFadyen's behalf in order to help him get reinstated at Duke. Nifong wrote the letter. "Duke didn't tell me to write the letter," he said. "His lawyer came and told me he needed it. If there were ever anybody that I could probably justify not doing anything for, without feeling like a total asshole, it would be somebody like him, because what he did was just so—there's no justification for it. It was senseless, insensitive, thoughtless. Everything about it was wrong. Of course, what was in it was bullshit, although they couldn't know that at the time. But I wrote him the letter, because he's a kid. He did something incredibly stupid, that should not cost him the rest of his life. Everybody makes mistakes." McFadyen never thanked him. "Are you kidding?' Nifong said. "His lawyer thanked me. No, he probably still resents me for it. I never did anything to Ryan McFadyen. He probably still thinks I'm a piece of shit. So, no, I'm not expecting anything from Ryan."

For his part, McFadyen only saw Nifong once—from a short distance—when he attended the December 15, 2006, hearing. McFadyen was sitting in the front row of the audience section and remembered being stunned when Meehan testified that he and Nifong had agreed not to include the exculpatory DNA evidence in Meehan's report. "There's a rape case being accused here and the DNA of five"—four, actually—"other people was found inside this woman, and not ours, and you just didn't think that was important," he said. "The signs of vaginal trauma maybe could have been brought on by these other gentlemen. But, no, we'll just leave that out. It's not a big deal. You've been harping on, 'The DNA will show,' for three weeks and all of a sudden somehow it's not that big of a deal?" He sat back, stunned. "I was just like, 'What the hell is this guy doing?' I remember just being—I didn't hate him; maybe I was just angry at him. I didn't know what the guy was thinking. . . . Maybe there was something I was missing. You question yourself for a second. 'Did something actually happen?' Nothing happened. Well then, what the hell is this all about? How is this happening? It was so surreal."

He also wondered what he would say to Nifong if he ever happened to run into him in Durham. One day, during the time McFadyen was a graduate student at Duke, he and a couple of his friends were at a shopping mall in Durham. He went to Bojangles restaurant to get some food, and his buddies went to the K-Mart. Nifong was in front of them in line. They didn't say anything to him. McFadyen was incredulous that his friends didn't speak to Nifong. "I swore if I ever saw him I would say something," he said. "I never thought about it, but I would just go up to him and shake his hand and say, 'Hey, Mike, I'm Ryan McFadyen, one of the Duke lacrosse players.' I don't know the guy. I don't know what his motivations were. It's fucked up. It's a fucked-up life. I can walk. I can talk. I have a job. But he changed my life for sure. He changed the way I look at things, probably affected me in some way that I won't realize until forty years from now or something."

National Championship

On Memorial Day, 2010, in John Danowski's fourth year as head coach, the Duke men's lacrosse team defeated Notre Dame five seconds into overtime to win the school's first national lacrosse championship, 6–5. It had been a tense and thrilling game until sophomore C. J. Costabile won the opening face-off in overtime and seemed to float on air through the Notre Dame defense to launch a rocket past goalie Scott Rodgers. "It is a storybook ending for the Duke seniors with their first national championship in school history!" the ESPN announcer roared.

Some six weeks later, on July 12, at nine in the morning, a big backhoe "with a jawlike grapple" began taking apart big chunks of the simple white, hundred-year-old, 1,407-square-foot house at 610 North Buchanan Boulevard. The house had sat idle for more than four years, until—without warning or explanation—the house's owner, Duke University, ordered it demolished. "It was an eyesore in the neighborhood," a Duke spokesman told the local television station. "While the decision to tear it down was not made for any symbolic reasons, certainly there will be people who will be relieved to see it gone." Adam Sobsey, a reporter for the *North Carolina Independent*, had received a heads-up that Duke planned to demolish the house and was on hand to witness it. "From start to finish," he subsequently wrote, "the entire demolition had taken about as long as a lacrosse match." Sobsey noted that Duke's explanation that 610 North Buchanan had become an "eyesore" was "disingenuous" if for no other reason than "Duke had, of course, made the house an eyesore over the last few years, as if waiting for the right level of communal forgetfulness before razing four years of squalid remorse."

He wondered what might rise in its place. "One suggestion was offered, perhaps inadvertently, by another onlooker, who strolled by with his young daughter during Monday's demolition," Sobsey wrote. "He wondered aloud if the building materials would be recycled or reused, then turned to his daughter and added, 'They could build you a playground.'" As of December 2013, the small lot remained empty.

Around the same time that Duke was winning its first national lacrosse championship, Karen Owen, a Duke senior, thought it would be a good idea to put together a PowerPoint presentation entitled "An Education Beyond the Classroom: Excelling in the Realm of Horizontal Academics." Owen sent the presentation to three friends and hoped that it would not go beyond them. But she miscalculated, and the subsequently so-called Duke Fuck List soon went viral. In often-graphic terms, Owen included the names and photographs of thirteen Duke male athletes she had had sex with during her four years at Duke. She also decided it would be interesting and informative to rank the athletes by prowess and performance and to include in her presentation a narrative description of her experience with each man. As the PowerPoint went viral, the national media's interest ratcheted up, despite the explicit nature of the presentation's content. Owen was horrified. "I regret it with all my heart," she told the media. "I would never intentionally hurt the people who are mentioned."

Maybe so, but Owen's "thesis" did nothing to dispel Duke's "work hard, play hard" image or the idea of the school as a "hook-up" culture gone wild as documented in Janet Reitman's 2006 *Rolling Stone* article. Of course, Owen's favorite "subjects" were lacrosse players. Numero uno, with a score of 10.25 on a scale of 1 to 10 was a junior attackman on the 2010 championship team. "I and several friends had been discussing which men at Duke merited entry into the exclusive 'township' we referred to as Woodcock Pocket," Owen wrote. "Entry was based exclusively on the size of their male appendages. Although none of us had experienced the wonders of this particular Subject, my friend Ali submitted him as a candidate based on an incident when he randomly whipped his dick out in the middle of working on a class project. We had laughed about it, but I hadn't given it much thought until we were introduced (and then it was all I could think about)."

Owen summed up the "memorable moments" of her time with him as "His ridiculous, ridiculously sized dick and accompanying incredible talent. His insistence that I come before him, each time. At one point he looked at me for a while, and when I asked him what was up he replied: 'I just think you have a really beautiful body.' He was the first guy I have hooked up with that kept an intense level of eye contact throughout the hook-up, which honestly brought the entire experience to a level of hotness that I had never before experienced. His talented hands. His goodnight line: 'Maybe, if I get really lucky, you'll wake me up with a kiss in the morning.' The next morning, although hung-over, when I told him I could leave with my friend then or stay a while, he looked at me and said 'Stay . . . I'm exhausted, but I want to fuck you again.' His incredible stamina; after a five-minute break in between morning sessions, he would look over at me and ask 'Do you want to do it again?' His refusing to allow me to leave before noon (although I did not exactly try all that hard to escape). Around 11:30, I mentioned that I was getting hungry and he peeked at me, only his eyes visible above the blanket and said 'Oh. Well . . . are you horny? Any chance you want to fuck again?' Of course I did.

I have never had the opportunity to conduct that much research in one session with a Subject."

Not surprisingly, Owen's major opus revived memories of the lacrosse scandal at Duke. *Today* show reporter Jeff Rossen said the Fuck List was "a new sex scandal" and reminded him of the lacrosse case. "In 2007, the charges were dropped, but the damage was done," he said on the show. Larry Moneta, Duke's vice president for student affairs, said of the document, "On a personal basis, I'm saddened by the behavior. Many of the circumstances that are referenced in it continue to make me really concerned about some of the judgments and some of the norms that persist." But freshman Grace Benson told the *Chronicle* she didn't think it was that big a deal. "A lot of college campuses are really promiscuous," she said. "I don't think [Duke] should be singled out."

A January 2011 *Atlantic* magazine article by Caitlin Flanagan took Owen to task for demeaning women generally and for perpetuating the stereotypes of women at Duke. "Clearly, the very last thing Karen Owen would want is for the reader of her thesis to perceive her as a vulnerable creature whose desire for sex with campus bigshots was at least partly motivated by a powerful and unmet desire for affection," Flanagan wrote. "But in the sheer amount of anecdotal detail, and in particular in her relentless descriptions of the anatomical shortcomings of various partners, she reveals that the thesis is motivated by the same force that has prompted women through the ages to describe with savage precision their liaisons with men who discarded them: revenge."

Flanagan argued that Owen's PowerPoint presentation revealed a campus stuck in time. "In some respects, Duke has never moved on from the values of the 1980s," she continued, "when droves of ambitious college students felt no moral ambivalence about preparing themselves for a life centered largely on the getting and spending of money. With a social scene dominated by fraternities and sororities (a way of life consisting of ardent partying and hooking up, offset by spurts of busywork composing angry letters to campus newspapers and taking online alcohol-education classes), with its large share of rich students displaying their money in the form of expensive cars and clothing, and with an attitude toward campus athletics that is at once deeply Southern (this is a part of the world where even high school athletes can be treated with awestruck deference by adults) and profoundly anti-intellectual, it's a university whose thoughtful students are overshadowed by its voraciously self-centered ones. It was both from within this world and outside it that Karen Owen emanated."

In March 2011, while the lacrosse players' lawsuits raged on against Duke and a rash of other defendants, J. Donald Cowan, an attorney for Duke at Ellis & Winters, in Greensboro, wrote a memorandum to a number of Duke professors and administrators reminding them of their obligation to preserve any records they had in their possession related to "the claims that a woman was raped by members of the Duke University lacrosse team" five years before. That meant no deleting or "otherwise destroying" anything related to the case or to the members of the lacrosse team, whose names and nicknames were listed in the back of the memo. Then came the chilling part, at least if one has any respect and admiration for the First Amendment. "I would also like to bring to your attention that comments about the lacrosse case, even if made in a small circle of people, inevitably reach the authors of the various blogs about the lacrosse case and are publicized," Cowan wrote. "Such comments, even if seemingly innocent, may have an effect on the position of Duke University in the ongoing litigation. In addition, such comments have also been the bases for lawsuits against the speakers of such statements."

In February 2013, Duke settled a lawsuit—*Carrington v. Duke University*—brought against the university by thirty-eight members of the lacrosse team, supposedly, according to one insider, for something like $50,000 per player, or around a total of $2 million. Some eight months earlier, in July 2012, as part of trying to defend itself against the *Carrington* lawsuit, Duke had taken the extraordinary step of subpoenaing the private communications, e-mails, documents, and other journalistic recordings and records of K. C. Johnson, the Brooklyn College professor who had been blogging about the lacrosse case since its start on his *Durham-in-Wonderland* blog and who, along with legal journalist Stuart Taylor wrote the 2007 book *Until Proven Innocent* about the case. (For some unexplained reason, Duke did not go after Taylor's notes and records.) After Johnson understandably objected to Duke's attempts to subvert the First Amendment by forcing him to turn over his confidential notes, Duke eventually sued Johnson in a Maine court—where Johnson lives—to obtain his records. After—incredibly—Magistrate Judge John Rich awarded Duke a partial victory in the initial legal round, Johnson appealed Rich's decision to a Maine federal district court, where his legal team argued—correctly—that Duke's demand violated Johnson's constitutional rights under the First Amendment.

When Duke settled the *Carrington* litigation, it also dropped the request to get Johnson's private communications with his sources. On his blog, Johnson wrote that two aspects of Duke's gambit were especially offensive to him. First, was that Duke seemed to be singling him out for special treatment by demanding his source material. He surmised this happened because, as Duke wrote in a legal brief, Johnson "continue[d] to this day to blog about the events underlying this litigation." Then, of course, he struggled to comprehend how an institution devoted to academic freedom could not appreciate the irony of trying to obtain a journalist's private source notes and records. While conceding that too many "institutions of higher learning don't respect the First Amendment" in some of their policies, Johnson wrote. "Nonetheless, major research universities rarely launch a frontal attack on First Amendment and academic freedom privileges as Duke did in this instance, lest they create a precedent that could be used against their own faculty members in the future. A major research university that deems itself 'happy' with forcing researchers to turn over internal correspondence in a civil suit to which the professor isn't a party—as Duke's attorneys described the university's attitude to Maine District Court Judge Brock Hornby—will have trouble attracting quality scholars, at least those whose research in any way touches on controversial, contemporary matters. In short, self-interest almost always leads universities to *defend*, rather than *undermine*, First Amendment academic privileges." Of all the truly chilling aspects of the Duke lacrosse case—and there are many—Duke's willingness, five years after the fact, to subpoena Johnson's private records may be the most jaw-droppingly astounding.

Also, in early February 2013, the national television spotlight once again returned to Duke's campus after the Kappa Sigma fraternity at Duke—which had recently been allowed back on campus after being kicked off eleven years earlier—sent out invitations to a party it called Asia Prime: "Herro Nice Duke Peopre!! We are proud to announce the return of Kappa Sigma Asia Prime this Friday! We look forward to having Mi, Yu, You, and Yo Friends over for some Sake. Chank You." There was also a picture of the late North Korean leader, Kim Jong Il, from the satirical movie *Team America: World Police* and the phrase "You Had Me at Herro." After the invitation got around and a number of students complained to the Duke administration that the themed party was offensive and racist, the leaders of Kappa Sigma sent around a revised invitation. "The Brothers of Kappa Sigma regret to inform you that our forebrothers' secrets of the Far East have not survived the move back onto campus. Without them, Asia Prime cannot go on and must be canceled. Instead, Kappa Sigma presents: International Relations. A celebration of all cultures and the diversity of Duke."

But the new invitation was a ruse and the Asia-themed party went on as scheduled on February 1, replete with people dressed up in sumo wrestler costumes and as geisha girls. After the party, offended students called for campuswide protests and put up posters with pictures taken at the party and a Twitter hashtag, RacistRager. "If you're not outraged, you're not paying attention," the protestors wrote. "None of the Dukies in this photo are Asian (Not that it would make it any better.)" Observed one Asian student, "Their costumes made a mockery of our culture, reducing our way of life into a crude joke for one drunken night of so-called fun." Of course, the party did not offend all Asian students at Duke. "I'm Asian and I think that the theme is hilarious," one tweeted.

Kappa Sigma president Luke Keohane—no relation to the former Duke president Nan Keohane—wrote a letter of apology to the *Chronicle*. "On the evening of Tuesday, January 29, we, the Eta Prime chapter of Kappa Sigma, distributed an e-mail to a significant portion of the student body for a party then-titled 'Asia Prime' which contained offensive and racially insensitive language," he wrote. "We wish to deeply apologize to any individual whom we offended and to the greater Duke community for our contributions to the marginalization [sic]. Our actions bring us great regret and have led us to examine our beliefs, both as individuals and as a brotherhood. Upon learning of the deeply damaging effects of our e-mail to our fellow students, we should have completely canceled the aforementioned party. Instead we chose to hold a different party at the same place and time, and the event encouraged party attire representative of any culture or ethnicity, which included demeaning cultural misrepresentations specific to Asian and Asian American individuals, and individuals of Asian descent." Despite Keohane's apology, the national chapter of Kappa Sigma suspended the Duke chapter of the fraternity pending an investigation of the incident.

On campus to cover the story, reporters for the *Today* show interviewed Larry Moneta, who is still the vice president of student affairs. He told *Today* he took the incident seriously, but said he had no plans for any formal disciplinary action. "At the moment, we're not aware of any overt violation," he said. "Acting boorish and foolish is not in and of itself a violation."

On Memorial Day, 2013, Duke won its second national lacrosse championship under Danowski's leadership of the program, defeating Syracuse 16–10. Bob Steel—who had been replaced as chairman of the board of trustees at Duke first by Rick Waggoner, the former CEO of General Motors, and then by David Rubenstein, the billionaire cofounder of the Carlyle Group, the powerful publicly traded Washington private-equity and asset-management firm—was very tempted to e-mail Brodhead. "When Duke lacrosse won the national championship this year, and you looked at Danowski and you looked at the quality of kids, and you say the decision to basically replace the coach, take a pause, have Dick talk to the boys and look them in the eye and explain to them what being an athlete at Duke meant to be, had them think about whether they wanted to come back in this way, and the hiring of Danowski—you know, I sleep pretty well," he said. "But no one is ever going to write me a thank-you note from the 150,000 alumni at Duke and say, 'Good work, guys.'"

THE DENOUEMENT

The Duke lacrosse rape scandal affected those involved in ways both expected and not. Perhaps most remarkable was how disparate were the fates of the individual participants, with some seeming to recover quickly while others continue to suffer consequences. And although the case received unprecedented publicity and analysis, whatever lessons that might have been learned from it appear to have had little to no effect on the nation's college and university campuses—at least judging from the plethora of comparable cases that followed it.

David Evans

After graduating with an MBA from the Wharton School of Business at the University of Pennsylvania in May 2012, David Evans rejoined Apax Partners, a private equity and venture capital firm in New York City, as a senior associate. He declined repeated requests to be interviewed for this book. At one point, his attorney at Williams & Connolly in Washington objected to my efforts to try to contact Evans at Wharton because, he said, incredibly, the Wharton School administrators had not been aware of Evans's involvement in the Duke lacrosse case, and my contacting them might bring him unwanted attention from his classmates and the school administrators. He told me Evans "reserved the right" to talk to me about what happened if he chose to, but he never did. One person who interviewed Evans while he was looking for a job on Wall Street told me that at one point he asked Evans if he were angry at Duke about what happened to him. Evans replied that while of course he was, he also conceded that by hiring two strippers for the March 13 party, the Duke lacrosse players had not done themselves any favors and had opened themselves to criticism. This was a view shared by other players of the team, too. Asked in a March 2012 deposition in the *Carrington* lawsuit whether he regretted attending the party six years earlier, Thomas Clute, now an analyst at Paladin Capital Group, a venture capital firm, replied: "I regret having all this happen. . . . I regret attending the party because of what happened. . . . I regret ever meeting or coming near Crystal Mangum and Kim Roberts, yes."

Evans's father retired from Reed Smith in January 2012 to become president of the Evans Capitol Group, a Maryland-based lobbying firm started by Rae Evans, David's mother.

What remains unresolved is, if in fact it was David Evans's DNA on Mangum's red plastic fingernails, how did it get there?

Collin Finnerty

In May 2010, Finnerty graduated from Loyola University in Maryland after studying communications. He was cocaptain of the Loyola lacrosse team. At his graduation, Finnerty wore a silver medallion of St. Raymond—the patron saint of the falsely accused—under his gown, a gift from David Evans. He has done some work for the Innocence Project, a national organization dedicated to helping the wrongly convicted, as well as for the Boomer Esiason Foundation, which is dedicated to fighting cystic fibrosis, and for the Fortress Investment Group, a New York City hedge fund. In the summer of 2008, he interned at NBC Sports in Baltimore, and between November 2010 and April 2012 worked as an account services representative at ESPN in New York City. Since July 2012, he has worked as a stockbroker at Deutsche Bank Securities on Wall Street. His father, Kevin, a former member of the board of directors at Bear Stearns & Company, Inc., where he also was a senior managing director and head of the mortgage-backed securities department, was a founding partner of the Fortress Investment Group. He was also the founding partner of Galton Capital Group, a residential mortgage-credit fund manager, which is now part of the hedge fund Mariner Investment Group, started by Finnerty's former Bear Stearns partner, William Michaelcheck.

Collin Finnerty did not respond to numerous requests to be interviewed for this book.

Reade Seligmann

After graduating from the Emory University School of Law, in May 2013, Seligmann moved to Philadelphia and serves as a law clerk at the US District Court in Camden, New Jersey. He has said repeatedly that his experience during the lacrosse case motivated him to go to law school and pursue a legal career. He has spoken publicly about what happened to him on behalf of the Innocence Project, which one of his attorneys, Barry Sheck, founded. (Sheck invited Evans, Finnerty, and Seligmann to an Innocence Project benefit dinner weeks after the three men were exonerated.) During a speech in March 2012 in Atlanta—sponsored by the Georgia Innocence Project—Clarence Harrison, who had been freed from prison thanks to the efforts of the Project, introduced Seligmann. "It was clear that he and Reade were not strangers," according to someone who was at Seligmann's talk. "Reade clearly differentiated between the lacrosse players' situation and that of the men who had been incarcerated. He then gave a personal account of the events that took place. It was incredibly interesting." The Georgia Innocence Project declined to make a video copy of Seligmann's speech available to me, despite numerous requests for it, and Sheck declined to make it available, either, explaining that it was not relevant to the Duke case anyway, because Seligmann does not speak publicly about the case, even though he clearly did during his Atlanta speech.

Seligmann declined my numerous requests to be interviewed. At one point, in September 2013, another of Seligmann's attorneys, Richard Emery, contacted me and told me Seligmann would like to speak with me. A protracted negotiation among Emery, Sheck, and me ensued about what the rules of engagement with Seligmann would be, with Sheck taking an especially hard line that the conversation be completely off the record, could not be referred to in the book, and could not be recorded. Seligmann's lawyers would record the conversation, but would not provide me a transcript of it. I would be permitted to take notes while Seligmann spoke at the meeting, which was to occur at Emery's office in Rockefeller Center in New York City.

At one point, on September 15, 2013, Seligmann took over the negotiations himself, marking the first time we had ever communicated. "Rather than coordinating through Richard," he wrote, "I figured it would be easier to contact you directly. I would like to start by apologizing for failing to respond to your initial inquiry this past spring. I had received your message from Emory's communication department, but chose not to pursue your request at the time because I was trying to focus on finishing my final year of law school.

"That being said, I am certainly open to meeting with you in person, completely off the record and not for attribution, on Thursday, September 19," he continued. "Additionally, I would ask that my attorney, Richard Emery, be permitted to record our conversation, to ensure that my words are not taken out of context and that there is a record of what was said. While I entirely appreciate your interest in relying on, or rejecting, if you choose, what I tell you to give context to your work, and while I understand it's your job as a journalist to obtain as much information as possible, my decision to meet with you stems not from a desire to be a named source in your the book (as you can tell from the terms of this arrangement), but rather a hope that I can give you a better perspective on what it was like to live through the Duke case.

"As you might imagine, sharing my personal story about the most trying period of my life is incredibly difficult for me, but I am willing to open up about my experience for the sole purpose of allowing others to learn from our case and to prevent future injustices from occurring. To date, I have yet to contribute to any book relating to our case, and try to limit my interactions with the media to interviews pertaining to criminal justice reform and advocacy work. My goal in meeting with you is not to proclaim our innocence, nor is it to condemn the actions of others. The incontrovertible facts of the case speak for themselves, and I doubt my words could ever persuade those who ignore the irrefutable evidence of our innocence. However, despite my concerns about meeting with you, given the title and description of your book, I am willing to trust that you will be fair and honest in your reporting. For those reasons, I would welcome an opportunity to sit down with you, face-to-face, completely off the record, without notes or use of my quotations, to provide you with insight into a case that changed my life forever."

In the end, Seligmann, his attorneys, and I could not work out an agreement, despite one more go at it. No meeting occurred.

Ryan McFadyen

Although he was not indicted, perhaps no Duke lacrosse player has suffered more from the consequences of the events of March 13, 2006, than Ryan McFadyen. Not only did his ill-considered e-mail get him temporarily suspended from Duke, it also led to a series of events that resulted in the firing of Mike Pressler and the cancellation of the 2006 lacrosse season. Eventually, with Nifong's help, McFadyen was allowed to return to Duke. He graduated with a degree in history in 2008, and then received a master's degree in liberal studies, economics in 2010. He wrote his thesis on Russia's economic system.

But his fateful e-mail haunts him to this day. As Ryan McFadyen, he had much difficulty finding a job, because a Google search of his name would reveal, immediately, the e-mail he had written in jest and poor taste. "I had a 3.7 coming out of Duke," he told me. "I had two degrees after I finished my graduate school. I would send in résumés under Ryan John McFadyen and not get anything back." He got far down the road with a San Francisco–based venture capital firm, but then his e-mail popped up and that was that. He worked as a junior analyst at W. R. Huff Asset Management in Morristown, New Jersey. He also worked as an intern at Guerilla Fitness CrossFit in Morristown. Eventually, to try to get on a higher career trajectory consistent with his Duke degrees, he changed his name to John McFadyen. "I figured if I could get in front of people, they would look at a résumé and say, 'He's good enough. Bring him in,' and I can speak to them and they'll see that I'm not what the Internet makes me out to be," he said. "I'm not the kind of monster that a lot of people preconceive me to be." Since April 2012, he has been an associate developer at Post Road Residential in Fairfield, Connecticut, a developer of multifamily residential homes started by the father of one of his Duke lacrosse teammates.

Like Finnerty and Evans, McFadyen would like to work on Wall Street. "[Collin's] dad was a big finance guy," McFadyen said. "So he had an in. I didn't come from that background. I wanted to work in finance. It's an attractive industry. When I was young I was really interested in the market, so I wanted to trade commodities. . . . I never had that opportunity."

He is still grappling with the fallout from that night. "I've been through a lot," he explained. "I put most of it behind me, but I don't think anybody can really comprehend, because to really understand what happened to me, how it affected me, I'm still not fully realizing what I've been through six years down the road. There's still things that are coming out that I'm realizing: 'Wow, this is how I live my life now because of what happened in 2006 and the two or three years after that.' . . . I look at things a lot differently than a lot of other people who go about life in similar circumstances, whether it's just personal relationships, professionally, the way I behave in an office, or meeting other people. It's different. So I can't even fully comprehend what the effect those years had on me."

As of December 2014, his lawsuit against Duke, in which he is joined by two of his teammates, remains unresolved. It is the last remaining piece of outstanding litigation against Duke stemming from the events of March 13, 2006. Not surprisingly, the lead attorneys for the lacrosse players regularly appear across the country trumpeting their triumph—for a fee—as "Anatomy of a Hoax: Prosecutorial Misconduct and the Duke Lacrosse cases." In January 2014, Jim Cooney offered to share with me "Anatomy of a Hoax." A few months later, he sent me an expurgated version of the presentation.

Richard Brodhead

In May 2012, the Duke Board of Trustees appointed Brodhead to a new five-year term as the university's president that is set to end at around the same time as the university's new $3.25 billion fund-raising campaign for the Duke endowment. (There are those who believe the main reason Brodhead's contract was renewed was because of the capital campaign; after all, it was explained to me, a company would not change its CEO as it was embarking on its IPO, or initial public offering.) In 2011, Brodhead was paid nearly $1.2 million, according to university records. (His wife, Cindy, a "senior advisor" at Duke, was paid $136,500.)

He declined repeated requests to be interviewed for this book. When I spoke with him briefly in February 2013 to tell him I was writing it and to request an interview, he was not happy. "Why do you have to write this book?" he asked me. "We are just getting over the events of March 2006." He told me there was "much about what happened" that "people don't know," but he declined to elaborate and never made himself available to be interviewed. A few weeks after the publication of this book in April 2014, Brodhead and I did speak briefly outside his Allen Building office. We shook hands, but it was a pained encounter.

Coach K

Mike Kzyzewski, of course, remains Duke's men's basketball coach, a position he has held since 1980. With a record, as of January 1, 2014, of 968 wins and 299 losses, he remains the winningest coach in Division I college basketball history, surpassing the 903 wins of his mentor and onetime coach, Bobby Knight. Kzyzewski's record at Duke, as of early January 2014, was 895 wins and 240 losses, the second-most victories at one school in Division I history. At Duke, Coach K has won four national championships and appeared in eleven Final Fours. Under Kzyzewski, Duke has won the Atlantic Coast Conference Championship twelve times and the ACC Tournament Championship thirteen times. In 2012, according to Duke records, Kzyzewski was paid nearly $9.7 million.

In October 2013, Duke became the first university to allow "player-tracking cameras"—all the rage in the NBA—to be installed at Duke's Cameron Indoor Stadium to enable a near-constant tracking of individual player movements on the court during both games and practice, allowing the Duke basketball coaches a more-complete understanding of a player's strengths and weaknesses. On November 15, 2013, both the number 1 and number 5 most highly touted high school basketball players—Jahlil Okafor and Tyus Jones, respectively—committed to play at Duke. That night, number 4–ranked Duke trounced Florida Atlantic University, 97–64.

E-mails and depositions that came to light as a result of the lacrosse players' civil lawsuits against Duke and others revealed that senior Duke administrators were desperate to have Coach K come to Duke's defense during the lacrosse scandal by commenting publicly on the case. But, the e-mails show, John Mack, the Duke board member and then-CEO of Morgan Stanley, among others, advised Coach K not to get involved in the scandal and to remember that he was the basketball coach, not the lacrosse coach. Kzyzewski heeded Mack's advice.

Mike Pressler

Since 2007, Pressler has been the head coach of the men's lacrosse team at Bryant University in Smithfield, Rhode Island. In 2013, Pressler coached Bryant to the school's first-ever bid to play in the NCAA lacrosse tournament. (It lost to Syracuse in the opening round.) In May 2014, Pressler coached Bryant to its first-ever NCAA tournament victory, a 10–9 upset defeat of Syracuse. That win resulted in a *New York Times* feature story about how far Pressler had come since Duke fired him in April 2006. Bryant lost its next game in the 2014 NCAA tournament to Maryland, 16–8. On March 31, 2010, Duke and Pressler reached a confidential settlement on a breach-of-contract suit that Pressler had brought against Duke after John Burness made disparaging comments to *Newsday* about him. Pressler had successfully argued that Burness's comments about him had violated the terms of his settlement agreement with Duke after Duke fired him.

Through his agent, Lee Southren, Pressler declined to be interviewed.

Duke University

In the ways that seem to matter most to people, Duke University has emerged from the lacrosse scandal in extraordinarily fine shape. Its $6 billion endowment increased 13.5 percent in the year ended June 2013, a better annual return than that achieved by the Harvard endowment (up 11.3 percent) and the Dartmouth endowment (up 12.1 percent). As of July 2013, Duke had raised half of the $3.25 billion it is seeking to add to its overall endowment. If successful—and there is little doubt of success—Duke's pro-forma endowment of $9.25 billion will put it about $1 billion below that of the Massachusetts Institute of Technology, and behind only the endowments of Harvard, Yale, Princeton, and Stanford. In the annual 2013 *U.S. News & World Report* rankings of top universities, Duke was tied for seventh place with both MIT and the University of Pennsylvania.

Meanwhile, it is harder than ever to gain admission to the university. Of the 31,785 applications Duke received for admission to the Class of 2017, the university admitted 2,929 students, or 9.2 percent, the lowest percentage in its history. (For the same class, Harvard admitted a tiny 5.8 percent of its 35,022 applicants.) Since 2007, annual applications to Duke have risen to 31,785 from 19,206, a 65 percent increase. Of those admitted to the Class of 2017, some 45.6 percent matriculated, the school's highest yield since 1987. Early admission applications for the Class of 2018 increased to 3,180, up 25 percent from the year before, and 797 (nearly 23 percent) of those who applied early were admitted. Duke's athletic prowess continues to increase, especially after Coach K brought Duke its fourth NCAA basketball championship in 2010 and Danowski won NCAA championships in lacrosse in both 2010 and 2013. Also in 2013, the Duke football team, with a season record of ten wins and three losses, had its best record in school history and played Texas A&M on New Year's Eve in the Chick-fil-A Bowl. (Duke lost.)

One might almost think Duke had reached academic nirvana but for, among other things: the inexplicable $60 million settlement with Evans, Finnerty, and Seligmann; the $2 million settlement with most of the other players; the legal efforts to try to pry out of K. C. Johnson his confidential source material; Karen Owen's Fuck List; and the mind-boggling, insensitive "Asian-themed" fraternity party. Indeed, between the ruinous financial settlements and the cost of legal and public-relations advice, the cost to Duke—in monetary terms—of the March 13 party is said to be near $100 million.

To show that the more things change, the more they stay the same, in September 2013, a Durham bar—Shooters II Saloon—decided to double its cover fee for students under twenty-one years old to $10 due to "rowdy freshmen" and the "extensive property destruction" they caused, according to the *Chronicle*. Property damage at the club included "destroyed cabinets" and torn-off bathroom doors "four times in past two weeks." One Duke freshman, Alex Brunson, told the *Chronicle* he did not think the higher entry fee would deter the students or get them to change their behavior. "I think the opportunity to be drunk out of your mind and to go somewhere where that is acceptable is far too enticing," he said. "Especially for freshmen taking advantage of their newfound autonomy." But Kim Cates, the club's owner, said she hoped the bad behavior would change. "Something about these kids is totally different this year," she said. "I don't know what's happened to them."

Of course, "bad-boy" behavior and drunken debauchery is hardly unique to undergraduates at Duke. Indeed, there appears to be nothing less than an epidemic of alcohol-driven crimes and scandals at America's elite colleges and universities. The media are packed with these stories. Below is a brief survey of the most appalling:

- On February 25, 2011, George Desdunes, a nineteen-year-old sophomore at Cornell University, from Brooklyn, died after a night of heavy drinking during an initiation ceremony at the Sigma Alpha Epsilon fraternity. According to a $25 million wrongful death suit filed against the fraternity and four of its members by Desdunes's mother, her son was "kidnapped" in the early morning of February 25, and fraternity pledges, who bound his wrists and ankles with "zip ties" and "duct tape," then forced him to drink until he passed out. He was found unconscious the next morning on a couch in the fraternity with hands and feet still bound. "One SAE pledge tried to interfere with the crime scene by having the zip ties removed before police arrived," the suit alleged.

  Desdunes had a blood-alcohol level of 0.409 percent, five times the legal limit for New York State. A judge acquitted three of the fraternity brothers of the charges against them—the fourth was underage and his case was handled separately. At one point during the trial, a prosecution witness testified that she had had sex with Desdunes prior to the "kidnapping game" and that he "was not intoxicated then." But the defense presented testimony that "far from being forced to drink," he was "free to stop the kidnapping game at any time." Desdunes's mother was "in shock" about the verdict, according to what her lawyer told the *New York Times*, "and terribly saddened that her son could be killed by these individuals and there be no criminal responsibility." In an August 2013 opinion piece in *USA Today*, David Skorton, the president of Cornell, cowrote his view that "Alcohol is a common element in hazing" and that "drinking games can lead to alcohol poisoning—especially when inexperienced, underage drinkers are served hard liquor (a few vodka bottles are easier to hide than a keg)." He wanted hazing to stop at Cornell, but decided not to go so far as to ban fraternities from campus.

- Following his February 2012 conviction for murdering his girlfriend, lacrosse player Yardley Love, in a drunken rage, the former University of Virginia and Landon School lacrosse player George Huguely V—now known as prisoner #1458946—remains in a high-security state prison in southwest Virginia, where he continues to serve his twenty-three-year sentence for Love's murder. The prison warden has decided to put Huguely in "protective custody" to keep him away from other inmates. There was reportedly a concern that Huguely did not yet have the "street smarts" to interact with other prisoners. In a court appearance prior to his sentencing, Huguely told Love's mother and sister, "I'm so sorry for your loss. . . . I hope and pray you find peace."

  Huguely is appealing his conviction, claiming he did not get a fair and impartial trial.

- In June 2013, four Vanderbilt University football players were arrested and accused of raping an unconscious twenty-one-year-old female student in an on-campus dormitory. The four players—Cory Batey, nineteen; Brandon Banks, nineteen; Jaborian McKenzie, nineteen; and Brandon Vandenburg, twenty—were each charged with five counts of aggravated rape and two counts of aggravated sexual battery. They all pleaded not guilty. After being arrested in August, the four men were released on bail, ranging from $50,000 to $350,000. By serendipity, the campus police had spotted "unusual activity" on a surveillance video while looking into another matter.

  The victim, said to be "good friends" with one of the accused players, is cooperating with police in the ongoing investigation. Five members of the Vanderbilt football team are on the witness list. "Whenever you claim the moral high ground, as Vanderbilt has, and it should, every time you get in trouble, people will be there to remind you," E. Gordon Gee, a former chancellor at Vanderbilt, told the *New York Times* in September 2013. "The fall from the high ground is much greater."

  The four football players, who had not played a single down for the Vanderbilt team, were dismissed from the team and suspended from the university, pending the outcome of the legal process, which, as of December 2013, was ongoing. Some in Nashville wondered whether, in an effort to be more competitive in football, Vanderbilt had lowered its academic standards to attract better athletes. During the 2012 season, Vanderbilt won nine games and finished among the top twenty-five football teams in the country for the first time since 1948. The team's home opener in 2013 was sold out; it finished the 2013 season 8–4.

- After a "yoga and toga" party in 2012 near the US Naval Academy in Annapolis, Maryland, three Navy football players were accused of sexually assaulting a twenty-year-old female midshipman and then lying about what happened. At first, the victim would not cooperate with the investigation, but later, with her help, two of the three players—Eric Graham and Joshua Tate—were ordered to face a court-martial proceeding. The third player was cleared of the charges against him. The victim arrived drunk to the party and had no recollection of the events of the evening and discovered she had been assaulted via social media. (In January 2014, the case against Graham was dismissed as a result of "insufficient evidence.")

- On May 25, 2011, Angie Epifano, a former member of the Amherst College Class of 2014, was raped by an "acquaintance" in a dormitory on the campus. In October 2012, she wrote a "wrenching account," according to the *New York Times*, of what had happened to her in the campus newspaper, which subsequently was viewed by hundreds of thousands of people. "When you're being raped, time does not stop," she wrote. "Time does not speed up and jump ahead like it does when you are with friends. Instead, time becomes your nemesis; it slows to such an excruciating pace that every second becomes an hour, every minute a year, and the rape becomes a lifetime. . . . Everything I had believed myself to be was gone in thirty minutes."

  At first, Epifano tried to forget the incident had occurred and decided not to report it. But, over time, as she frequently found herself running into her assailant on Amherst's small campus, she became increasingly desperate and despondent. She reached out to the campus counseling center, only to be told, "No, you can't change dorms, there are too many students right now. Pressing charges would be useless; he's about to graduate, there's not much we can do. Are you SURE it was rape? It might have just been a bad hook-up. . . . You should forgive and forget. How are you supposed to forget the worst night of your life?" She has since withdrawn from Amherst.

- On October 13, 2010, a group of Delta Kappa Epsilon pledges at Yale University marched passed the Yale Women's Center chanting, "No means yes, yes means anal" and "My name is Jack, I am a necrophiliac, I fuck dead women." Although there was some dispute about who said what, the entire episode was captured on videotape and put on YouTube, where it quickly went viral. When the Yale administration asked that the fraternity be suspended from campus for five years, the DKE national organization decided that only the pledging activities should be curtailed for one month. According to the *Yale Daily News*, "The DKE incident sparked a yearlong debate on campus about Yale's sexual climate and the University's response to instances of sexual misconduct. Deeming the fraternity's antics as the 'last straw' in a long chain of public incidents, a group of sixteen students and alumni filed a complaint with the Department of Education's Office for Civil Rights, claiming that Yale had violated Title IX regulations—a federal law that prohibits gender discrimination in schools that receive federal funding—by allowing a hostile sexual environment to persist on campus."

- In May 2006, Northwestern University suspended the upcoming season of its women's soccer team after a blogger posted photographs of the female team members—which he found on a file-sharing server while looking for photos of the Duke lacrosse players—on his website. The photos had been shared by one of the soccer players. According to the *New York Times*, "The photographs showed women's soccer players wearing only T-shirts and shorts or just underwear. Many of the players were covered in marker, and some appeared to be drinking beer. Other photographs showed players giving lap dances for what the captions said were Northwestern men's soccer players. The captions said the dances were a punishment. In some photographs, the players are in lines, blindfolded, their hands bound behind their backs." The *Times* did not mention that the women had pictures of penises drawn on their bodies with magic markers and had been drinking tequila and were simulating sex acts with the male soccer players.

- At Wesleyan University, at a Halloween party in 2010, a female student—known only as "Jane Doe"—claimed she had been raped by John O'Neill, a visiting friend of one of the fraternity brothers at the Beta House on campus. In 2012, O'Neill pleaded guilty to lesser charges and was sentenced to fifteen months in prison. Also in 2012, the woman filed a $10 million civil rights suit against Wesleyan and the Beta House fraternity for failing to protect her from the fraternity, which was known around campus as a "rape factory." In September 2013, the case was settled confidentially.

- In 2008, Princeton University surveyed nearly 1,600 of its undergraduate women to try to gauge the incidence of sexual assaults on campus. The response the university received was shocking. Some 15.9 percent of the women who responded to the online survey said they had been "vaginally penetrated without their consent"; another 14.3 percent said they had experienced attempted oral sex without their consent; and 12.3 percent said they had given or received oral sex without their consent. The number of incidents was larger than expected, especially since between 2008 and 2011 only fifty-eight incidents of sexual assault were reported on the campus.

Faced with these surprising results, Princeton chose not to release the survey, claiming it was for "internal planning and programming." In March 2013, the *Daily Princetonian* got hold of the unpublished survey results, causing uproar on campus. Amada Sandoval, the director of the campus women's center, told the paper that she believed the results weren't publicized at the time because no other universities make such statistics available. "Anything about Princeton goes international, practically, and no other universities do that, so does Princeton want to be the one to say that this many of our students are sexually assaulted?" she said. "I don't think so."

Meanwhile, at Harvard University, the number of confidentially reported rape cases on campus increased to twenty-three in 2012, from twelve in 2011. In August 2012, two women reported being raped on the Harvard campus in the span of two weeks.

• In October 2013, the *New York Times* reported that Philip Hanlon, the new president of Dartmouth College, found himself grappling with such less than scholarly concerns such as "binge drinking, sexual harassment and fraternity hazing." The paper also reported that the Department of Education was investigating a "civil rights complaint" against the college "alleging that Dartmouth has not met its duty to prevent and respond to sexual harassment." Continued the *Times*, "The turmoil is particularly unwelcome at a place whose enviable academic reputation and bucolic New England setting have long coexisted with issues revolving around drinking and fraternity life."

In April 2013, the paper reported, at the annual event for newly admitted high school seniors, a group of Dartmouth students "pushed their way" in and started "shouting about sexism, homophobia, racism and harassment" on the campus. This did not go over well. In June 2013, the Alpha Delta fraternity pleaded guilty to a criminal charge of serving alcohol to "underage people" and agreed to pay a fine and adhere to court-imposed restrictions on parties and who may attend them. Weeks later, at a "Bloods and Crips" party sponsored by a Dartmouth fraternity and sorority, there were "complaints of callousness." Then, in September 2013, a fire broke out in a fraternity house and was investigated for possible arson.

According to the *Times*, Dartmouth student Andrew Lohse raised "questions about alcohol abuse, hazing and the treatment of women" in an essay he wrote for *The Dartmouth* in January 2012. "I was a member of a fraternity that asked pledges, in order to become a brother, to: swim in a kiddie pool of vomit, urine, fecal matter, semen, and rotten food products; eat omelets made of vomit; chug cups of vinegar, which in one case caused a pledge to vomit blood; drink beer poured down fellow pledges' ass cracks . . . among other abuses," he wrote. Dartmouth's seventeen fraternities, eleven sororities, and three coed houses—to which about half the students on campus belong—perpetuated a culture of "pervasive hazing, substance abuse and sexual assault," as well as an "intoxicating nihilism" that dominates campus social life.

In March 2012, Janet Reitman wrote about Lohse and his essay in *Rolling Stone*. He told her, "One of the things I've learned at Dartmouth—one thing that sets a psychological precedent for many Dartmouth men—is that good people can do awful things to one another for absolutely no reason. Fraternity life is at the core of the college's human and cultural dysfunctions." Lohse, who came from a family of Dartmouth men, described to Reitman the importance of being "a true bro." When she asked him what constituted "true bro-ness," he told her a "true bro" was "good-looking, preppy, charismatic, excellent at cocktail parties, masculine, intelligent, wealthy (or soon to become so), a little bit rough around the edges," and not a "douchey, superpolished Yalie."

By May 2014, the issue of sexual assaults on college campuses had become a nationwide crisis, following President Barack Obama's creation of a task force of cabinet members to focus on the problem and the release by the US Department of Education of the names of fifty-five colleges and universities under investigation for the mishandling of sexual assault cases on their campuses. The list included Harvard, Princeton, Dartmouth, and Amherst, but not Duke. On May 15, 2014, *Time* magazine made the topic of sexual assault on campus its cover story.

Kim Roberts

Roberts, who graduated from high school with a perfect 4.0 GPA and studied psychology at UNC-Chapel Hill, once envisioned herself "one day wearing a power suit and carrying a briefcase," according to the *News & Observer*. Instead, she got pregnant during her junior year at UNC, dropped out of college, and married the child's father. When her marriage quickly fell apart, she was left a single mother. In 2001, she embezzled $25,000 from her employer and eventually took up exotic dancing to pay her bills. The Duke lacrosse scandal made her infamous. Her current whereabouts are unknown.

Crystal Gail Mangum

On November 22, 2013, Mangum, then thirty-five years old, was found guilty of second-degree murder in the death of her boyfriend of one month, Reginald Daye, forty-six years old, whom Mangum had stabbed with a kitchen knife at his Durham apartment following an argument. She told me she stabbed Daye in self-defense and that he survived the stabbing, only to die ten days later, in April 2011, at Duke Hospital. She claimed that the doctors and nurses at Duke Hospital were responsible for Daye's death. The jury disagreed. She was sentenced to as many as eighteen years in prison.

She told me, when I visited her in jail, that she admired Nifong for rising to her defense. "I admire him because he was doing his job," she said. "And quite honestly every DA, every prosecutor, bends the rules. I guess that's what I'm trying to get at. If you got a strong hunch about something, you push it over a little more. . . . Yeah, I admire him for sticking up for what he believes in spite of what other people think. It's unfair. If they should disbar him, they should disbar all the DAs, because every last one of them every day does something that they're not supposed to do. They put the standard for him so high that he could've sneezed wrong and they woulda disbarred him." She said she remained hopeful she would get justice in the lacrosse case. "I still have faith this thing is gonna come out right," she said. "Regardless of what it looks like right now, I honestly feel like it's gonna turn out. It's gonna come in the right direction." And if she had it do all over again, "I would never have even considered exotic dancing," she said.

She said that ever since her father died, her mother developed Alzheimer's disease, and her children were taken away from her, "I'm really all I have right now." She told me that if she were to be acquitted of the murder charge against her, she would leave Durham. (She had once suggested to Himan that she would move to Miami but had changed her mind.) "Durham is all right," she laughed. "But I think it's time for me to go. I'll probably move back out to the West Coast. Maybe California, Santa Rosa or somewhere like that."

Mark Gottlieb and Benjamin Himan

On March 2, 2008, Gottlieb resigned from the Durham police force for "personal reasons" after a brief stint as a uniformed officer. Himan had resigned a few weeks before Gottlieb for similar reasons. On July 5, 2014, Gottlieb committed suicide in Dekalb County, Georgia, where he moved after leaving the Durham police force and where he worked as a paramedic.

On May 16, 2014, the three indicted—and then exonerated—lacrosse players settled their lawsuit against the City of Durham, and by extension its police department, for a onetime donation by the city of $50,000 to the North Carolina Innocence Inquiry Commission, well below the $30 million the three players had sought initially. In the end, they received no cash compensation from Durham.

Mike Nifong

Since his disbarment, his removal from office, his day in jail, and his personal bankruptcy filing, Nifong has spent the past six years living quietly in his modest but tidy Durham home, along with his wife, Cy Gurney. He does not work and lives off the pension he earned during his years in the Durham District Attorney's Office. He gardens and has been known to sing—quite beautifully, actually—when asked, which he did recently at a neighbor's funeral.

His son, Bryan, was a sophomore in high school in 2007 and attended nearly every day of his father's state bar hearing. He had been thinking about becoming a lawyer, like his father, but after what happened, he decided to pursue a career in business. He graduated from the University of North Carolina at Wilmington, with a degree in business administration with an emphasis on economics. He lives in Wilmington and has started a job in finance. "He is a very fine young man, and I'd like for him to meet you someday," Nifong said of his son during our last visit in June 2013. "He's done very well with all this. I've never talked to him exactly about how he felt about some of these things. Other than little bits and pieces, we never sat down and had a conversation about that. I would imagine that if I were to do so, or if somebody else that he trusted were to do so, it would result in some angry words. But I think that he's really handled it all extremely well, and I think he's going to be fine. I think probably the person who was most adversely affected by all this was my wife, and there's nothing you can do about that; that's just part of who she is."

Earlier in 2013, Nifong suffered a heart attack, from which he has recovered. His cancer has not recurred. Like the City of Durham, in May 2014 Nifong also reached a final settlement with Evans, Finnerty, and Seligmann: he agreed to pay $1,000 to the North Carolina Innocence Inquiry Commission. The players' attorneys had sought from Nifong a payment to the Innocence Inquiry Commission of $25,000 and an agreement that he would no longer speak publicly about the lacrosse case. He refused both of those demands. Does he wish he had never found the nontestimonial order on the copy machine outside his office? "It's like any other wish," he told me in April 2013. "It doesn't do any good. It's not an option. Now, do I wish I'd never had cancer? Do I wish I'd never had a heart attack? Do I wish I'd had a better fastball? There are a lot of things you can wish, but you're wasting your time. It is what it is. I'm where I am because of what I did, and that's okay with me. I don't have a problem with that."

AFTERWORD

If anything, nationwide concern about sexual assaults on college campuses has only ratcheted up since the night of the party at 610 North Buchanan Boulevard. And finally, in January 2014, the problem landed in the Oval Office. On January 22, President Obama convened a summit meeting of his cabinet to create the White House Task Force to Protect Students from Sexual Assault. "An estimated one in five women is sexually assaulted at college—and that's totally unacceptable," Obama said. "We're going to help schools do a better job of preventing and responding to sexual assault on their campuses. Because college should be a place where our young people feel secure and confident, so they can go as far as their talents will take them."

Four months later, the task force issued a report that urged colleges and universities to take a number of steps to make it easier for victims to get justice, since only a fraction—12 percent—of those sexually assaulted on campuses actually report the crime. These steps included ensuring the confidentiality of those reporting sexual assaults; taking regular, anonymous surveys of students about sexual assaults; and starting a website, NotAlone.gov, to provide information and to track enforcement about incidents of rape on campus. On May 1, the Obama administration took the further unprecedented step of releasing the names of fifty-five colleges and universities under investigation for their mishandling of sexual assaults on their campuses. By naming names, the government put pressure on the schools to be more proactive about confronting the scourge. The stick was the implicit threat that if they didn't get their act together, the government would withhold essential federal funding from those schools. "Colleges and universities need to face the facts about sexual assault," Vice President Joseph R. Biden Jr. said. "No more turning a blind eye or pretending it doesn't exist. We need to give victims the support they need, like a confidential place to go, and we need to bring the perpetrators to justice."

Among the fifty-five schools were Harvard, Dartmouth, Princeton, Swarthmore, the University of Chicago, the University of Southern California, and Florida State University. Duke was not on the list. At the same time, FSU was the subject of controversy over the handling of an alleged sexual assault on its campus involving Jameis Winston, the school's Heisman Trophy–winning quarterback, who supposedly raped a woman—he claimed the sex was consensual—after which the local police bungled the investigation because, according to the *New York Times*, Winston was, well, Winston, and a star. On May 15, *Time* made sexual assault on campus its cover story.

There has also been no slowdown in the concern about rampant underage drinking on college campuses, which—no surprise—is highly correlated to the increase in sexual assaults. After a yearlong investigation that resulted in a February 2014 cover story in the *Atlantic* about "bad-boy" behavior at college fraternities, writer Caitlin Flanagan explored incident after incident of binge drinking on campus resulting in asinine behavior, sexual assaults—even death. "One warm spring night in 2011, a young man named Travis Hughes stood on the back deck of the Alpha Tau Omega fraternity house at Marshall University, in West Virginia, and was struck by what seemed to him—under the influence of powerful inebriants, not least among them the clear ether of youth itself—to be an excellent idea: he would shove a bottle rocket up his ass and blast it into the sweet night air," Flanagan began. "And perhaps it *was* an excellent idea. What was not an excellent idea, however, was to misjudge the relative tightness of a 20-year-old sphincter and the propulsive reliability of a 20-cent bottle rocket. What followed ignition was not the bright report of a successful blastoff, but the muffled thud of fire in the hole."

Whether fraternities' days are numbered remains to be seen. In May 2014, partially in reaction to the campus conflagration that accompanied the alleged rape of former student Angie Epifano, prestigious Amherst College, in Amherst, Massachusetts, announced that it was banning its students from joining fraternities and sororities, either on- or off-campus, effective July 1. (Previously, participation in fraternities and sororities at Amherst had been tacitly allowed, with students being permitted to join them as long as their activities were kept off-campus and underground.)

Then, as if on cue to further prove Flanagan's point about the misogynist thinking of some fraternity brothers, a cache of highly embarrassing e-mails written by Evan Thomas Spiegel, the founder and CEO of Snapchat—the social networking service that allows online communication to disappear—ironically surfaced on the Internet. In one example of the Spiegel oeuvre, written in October 2009 when he was a student at Stanford University—shouldn't he have known better by then?—Spiegel lamented that nobody seemed to be paying attention to his e-mails, so "who gives a fuck if I send another one[?]" He continued, "[O]ur pledge class"—at Kappa Sigma, which had been temporarily kicked off campus for violating the university's controlled substances and alcohol policy—"is currently dominating the fuck out of everything and if I hear one more freshman tell me how much they love kappa sigma I'll probably get so excited I'll punch them in the face. [T]his has happened because we have all been having a fucking blast together. [S]o give yourself a pat on

AFTERWORD

the back or have some girl put your large kappa sigma dick down her throat because you fucking HANDLED this weekend. Can't wait to see everyone on the blackout express soon." The e-mails went downhill from there.

Of course, Spiegel, who in 2013 turned down a $3 billion offer for Snapchat from Facebook, apologized. He explained how deeply embarrassed he was for his immature behavior. In response, Stanford's provost, John Etchemendy, sent an e-mail to Stanford's undergraduates that read, in part, "I have no reason to doubt [Spiegel's] statement or the sincerity of his regret. But that does not change the fact that the e-mails were sent. And in my mind, that raises a troubling question for the rest of us. Because the e-mails were also received, and no doubt received by others who found them crude, offensive, and demeaning to women—others who had already matured enough to see them as, in fact, worse than 'idiotic.'"

As troubling as the twin epidemics of underage drinking and sexual assaults on college campuses continue to be, equally disturbing has been the mean-spirited reaction to the publication of *The Price of Silence*, which raises the existential question: Whose story is it, anyway?

Does a traumatic narrative—one that deeply affects, even shatters, the lives of those involved, as well as scores of others dragged into it, willingly or not—belong to the people caught up in it at the moment, or does it belong to those who come later, after all the dust has supposedly settled, and who decide that the incident needs a new, fresh look? Is the only way to study dramatic, life-altering events to visit them in some exquisite diorama at the Museum of Natural History or after lava has toppled them midstride? Or can such sagas be deconstructed and examined from different angles, or through the prism of time and distance? Do the winners always get the last word?

These questions are especially relevant for writers who tackle controversy while it remains fresh in the minds of the people who experienced it firsthand. Who controls the narrative of the Duke lacrosse scandal? The understandably aggrieved players, their families, and their high-priced lawyers, among them Barry Sheck and Brendan Sullivan, no doubt armed for battle at a moment's notice? Their high-pitched surrogates, with easy access to the media, who performed their duty despite their heavy axes to grind? Are other voices to be heard above this din? Should Mike Nifong be allowed to reflect on the events that destroyed his career, his reputation, and his livelihood? Is Crystal Mangum to be forever marginalized as a bit player in the drama because she regularly changed her story, was diagnosed as being bipolar, and suffered from drug addiction, or because, years later, her abusive boyfriend ended up dying from the stab wounds she inflicted in self-defense, or so she claimed? Is Duke allowed to silence the voice of Bob Steel because his reflections on the events of 2006 and 2007 might prove inconvenient to the institution whose board of trustees he once headed?

It soon enough became clear that there was an effort under way to discredit *The Price of Silence*, even though the book did nothing more than take a new, dispassionate look at the lacrosse scandal eight years on and included, for the first time, a complete analysis of the documentary record as well as the reflections of those people who had been central to the scandal but whose voices were somehow deemed to be irrelevant and unworthy of being heard.

The campaign began even before *The Price of Silence* was published. Television host Charlie Rose, a prominent Duke graduate, asked me on several occasions when we happened upon each other in New York City why I was bothering to write the book, since he was certain there was nothing new to be said. Dick Brodhead wondered the same thing. As did Peter Applebome, another prominent Duke graduate and a *New York Times* columnist who had written about the lacrosse scandal while it was happening and could not fathom what could be left to write about. On the late afternoon of March 28, 2014, I spoke with Joseph Neff, a reporter for the *News & Observer* in Raleigh, who proudly told me that the paper's coverage of the Duke lacrosse scandal was all wrong until he took it over a few weeks after the March 13, 2006, party. Neff had received an advance copy of the book, was writing a story about it, and wanted to ask me a few questions. It turned out that he was utterly indifferent to what I had to say and was merely checking the box for having spoken to me. A few hours later, Neff's story appeared online. His lede was "Former Durham District Attorney Mike Nifong has held his tongue since his career imploded in the Duke lacrosse case. But his thoughts are about to land in bookstores, at length and virtually unchallenged."

The idea that a fellow journalist would criticize an author—in a news article, no less—for having the audacity to interview Nifong, one of the main players in the drama, about what he did and what the consequences of his actions were and then claim that the author had allowed Nifong to go on "at length" and "virtually unchallenged" was patently absurd, on many levels. Forgetting for a moment that all but a few of the 615 pages in the book are devoted to one criticism after another of Nifong's behavior throughout the fifteen-month ordeal, isn't the job of a responsible journalist to interview, if he or she possibly can, the people who were central figures in the story? And to let them have their say, especially if, for whatever reasons, they have not spoken about the crucible for years? Of course it is. And had Nifong granted Neff an interview, wouldn't Neff have gladly given the former district attorney all the column inches he needed to explain why he did what he did?

The mission was clear. Regardless of the actual content of *The Price of Silence*, its critics could not allow, for even a moment, anyone to consider it anything but a tired and inaccurate rehash of the story, the narrative of which was already firmly established: the three players were innocent; Nifong was a politically ambitious and ruthless rogue prosecutor; and Mangum was an utterly discredited bipolar nut job. K. C. Johnson re-started his daily posts on his still-extant blog, *Durham-in-Wonderland*, dissecting with relish the perceived affronts to the established narrative he found in the book. Stuart Taylor called in to my hour-long April 14, 2014, appearance on the *Diane Rehm Show* on NPR to denounce both the book and me. Rehm told me before the show began that she and her producers had never before received so many calls trying to get an author tossed off her program. Taylor wrote a diatribe in *The New Republic*. Johnson followed up with his vitriol in *Commentary*. Nearly six weeks after the book's publication, and seemingly out of nowhere, Dorothy Rabinowitz weighed in with a lengthy harangue in the editorial pages of the *Wall Street Journal* under the headline "A Dishonest Rewrite of the Duke Lacrosse Case." None of them, of course, bothered to seek me out and ask for my thoughts before they penned their screeds. Their effort was to attack—and to demean—the substance and relevance of this book, which they claimed had the audacity to tamper with the narrative they had carved in stone seven years earlier.

The attacks stopped at nothing. A Twitter campaign bombarded me with an endless stream of criticism. Within hours of the book's publication, there was a push on Amazon to get mostly anonymous reviewers, many of whom clearly had not even bothered to read the book (some by their own admission), to slap one-star reviews on *The Price of Silence* long before any genuine, objective reviewers had had the time to receive the book or to read it. (Incredibly, Amazon allows such disinformation campaigns, claiming they add to the overall public debate.) As of this writing, of the 108 customer reviews on Amazon, 81 are of the one-star variety, and of those, Amazon was able to verify that only a small handful had actually bought the book (and presumably read it).

Preserving the existing and accepted narrative in amber remains the most important priority. This was just one more battle in a war that began in the early morning hours of March 14, 2006, when Crystal Mangum told Mariecia Smith, at the Durham Access Center, that she had been raped by a bunch of Duke lacrosse players at an off-campus party. For these people, the debate about what did or did not happen at 610 North Buchanan Boulevard is long over. And woe to anyone who dares to question the story they like to tell.

Of course, not everything could be controlled. In appearances on *The Daily Show*, NPR, MSNBC, CNN, and C-SPAN, among others, I was given plenty of airtime to recount the story of the Duke lacrosse scandal, including some of its persistently troubling aspects. A diverse group of reviewers from *The New York Times*, *The Wall Street Journal*, *The Economist*, *The Financial Times*, *Salon*, *Entertainment Weekly*, and *Sports Illustrated* praised the book for its even-handedness, thoroughness, and fresh take on a complex and disturbing tale. Wrote Caitlin Flanagan in her *New York Times* review of the book, "[W]hat Cohan has done, to superb effect, is to bring a forensic level of reporting to the event, so that we are forced to throw out its long-accepted narrative and look at it with new eyes." That had to aggravate my critics to no end.

But if the story of the Duke lacrosse scandal has such a beautiful bow on it, why did Duke pay $100 million to shut everyone up? Why has Roy Cooper never explained why and how he reached the conclusion that the three players were "innocent," a word that does not even exist in the jurisprudence lexicon? Why has Cooper kept access to his investigation files under lock and key, away from prying journalistic eyes? Why did Brodhead refuse my repeated requests to be interviewed and nix the participation of the other Duke administrators involved? Why did Duke's lawyers send ominous-sounding letters to current and former Duke professors warning them not to talk to the media about the case? Why did Sheck and Sullivan (unsuccessfully) try to prevent Nifong from talking to the media about the case as part of the May 2014 settlement between the three indicted players and the City of Durham? Why did Reade Seligmann want the taxi to pick him up around the corner from the house where the party was, and why was no one home when police stopped by the house after 1:00 a.m. on March 14 to see what was going on? If in fact it was David Evans's DNA on Crystal Mangum's fake red fingernails, how did it get there? Why is there now just a pile of rubble where the house at 610 North Buchanan Boulevard used to be?

Who owns a narrative, indeed.

ACKNOWLEDGMENTS

I have been blessed in the writing of *The Price of Silence* by having, in Colin Harrison, my superb editor at Scribner, someone who shared from the outset my vision of what this book could be and its relevance to the increasingly important national debate about the role played by our elite, private universities in developing future generations of Americans while also contributing to the growing divide among the nation's rich and poor. His ability to see the narrative arc contained in my manuscript and to pare from it the extraneous has been nothing short of brilliant, and I am immensely thankful that we found each other.

At Scribner, I would also like to thank Susan Moldow, the president of the Scribner Group, and Nan Graham, the publisher, for their faith in me and in this book. As Colin did, both Susan and Nan understood intuitively what the book needed to be, and they kept me on path to get there. I would also like to thank at Scribner, in alphabetical order: Katrina Diaz, Colin Harrison's assistant; Tal Goresky, the art director; Benjamin Holmes, the production editor; Liese Mayer, another Scribner editor who gave the manuscript an essential read and edit; and Katherine Monaghan, the associate publicity director.

In a class by herself, and worthy of special thanks, is Pat Devine, a former North Carolina district court judge who took it upon herself to create a lengthy oral history of the Duke lacrosse case from Mike Nifong's perspective and made her meticulous recordings available to me. Without Pat and her inspiration, this book would likely not have been possible. (Transcripts of both of my interviews with Nifong—as well as Devine's—will be available in 2014 as part of the Southern Oral History Program at the University of North Carolina in Chapel Hill.) Special thanks also go to Elizabeth Palumbo, who selflessly helped me to collect a large chunk of the research material that I used in writing the book. In October 2012, Hurricane Sandy turned Elizabeth's world upside down, and my best wishes go out to her. Tiffany A. Ross, at the courthouse in Durham, helped me immeasurably to obtain hard-to-find records of the court proceedings against the three lacrosse players. For whatever reason, it seems, some people would have been more than happy to have some of those records disappear; Tiffany made sure that did not happen.

I also want to single out for taking the time to meet with me—and for their generosity of spirit—Mike Nifong, the former Durham district attorney; Bob Steel, the former chairman of the Duke board of trustees, even though Duke urged him not to meet with me; Ryan McFadyen—now known as John McFadyen; and Crystal Mangum, who met with me while she was in a Durham jail awaiting her November 2013 trial on the charge of murdering her one-time boyfriend. Fortunately, Crystal did not insist on me bailing her out as a pre-condition to our conversation, as she first suggested. There were many others who were extremely generous with their time, too, including Anne Petersen, one of Nifong's attorneys; Dudley Witt, another of his attorneys; John McPhee, one of the world's great writers and an authority on college lacrosse; Robert Scott, the Hall of Fame lacrosse coach at Johns Hopkins University; and John Feinstein, the Duke alumnus and world-famous sports journalist and author. There were, not surprisingly, others in and around Duke, Durham, and North Carolina who were immensely helpful to me along the way but—given Duke's highly litigious nature—preferred that our conversations remain unacknowledged publicly. You know who you are, and I thank you.

    I also want to thank my extraordinary friends and colleagues at *Vanity Fair*, the *New York Times*, the *Atlantic, BloombergView, BloombergBusinessWeek*, the *Financial Times, ARTnews*, BloombergTV, CBS This Morning, CNN, MSNBC, the BBC, NPR, and WOR radio, who gave me plenty of highly enjoyable opportunities throughout the past two years to divert my attention from the writing of this book. I am extremely grateful to you all for allowing me to share my thoughts, opinions, and journalism. Among them are: Max Abelson, Suzanna Andrews, Martin Bashir, Deirdre Bolton, Brian Burrough, Dominic Chu, Graydon Carter, Robin Cembalest, Sewall Chan, Laura Chapman, Sue Craig, Mark Crumpton, Paula Dwyer, Sara Eisen, Milton Esterow, Ted Fine, Pimm Foxx, Scarlet Fu, John Gambling, Trish Hall, Christine Harper, Toby Harshaw, Sylvia Hochfield, John Hockenberry, Al Hunt, Julie Hyman, Bob Ivry, Emma Jacobs, Jonathan Kelly, Tom Keane, Gayle King, Andy Lack, Betsy Lack, Jaime Lalinde, Tim Lavin, Susan Lehman, Brian Lehrer, Hugo Lindgren, Betty Liu, Leonard Lopate, Jane Mayer and Bill Hamilton, Ian Masters, Sue Matthias, Bethany McLean, Matt Miller (both of them), Tim O'Brien, Norah O'Donnell, Don Peck, Richard Plepler, Ken Prewitt, Ben Protess, Trish Regan, David Rhodes, Stephanie Ruhle, Charlie Rose, Andrew Rosenthal, Erik Schatzker, Maryam Shahabi, David Shipley, Eliot Spitzer, Doug Stumpf, Josh Tyrangiel, and Chitra Wadhwani. I apologize in advance to anyone I might have omitted; it was not intentional.

Once again my usual cast of faithful and charming characters sustained me on the lonely two-year trek up the mountainside, which actually included a three-week excursion to the Mt. Everest Base Camp, in Nepal (that's another story). They always knew when to administer the proper dose of criticism and encouragement. Among them are: Peter Davidson and Drew McGhee (once again they insisted on being first and I oblige them happily), Kurt Andersen and Anne Kreamer, Jane Barnet and Paul Gottsegen, Charlie and Sue Bell, Seth and Toni Bernstein, Clara Bingham and Joe Finnerty, Joan Bingham, Bryce Birdsall and Malcolm Kirk, Michael Brod, John Brodie, Mary and Brad Burnham, Jerome and M. D. Buttrick, John Buttrick and Alex Ching, Mike and Elisabeth Cannell, Alan and Pat Cantor, Jay Costley, Marc Daniel and Suzanne Herz, Robert Douglass, Tom Dyja and Suzanne Gluck, Don and Anne Edwards, Stuart and Randi Epstein, the Feldmans (all of them), John and Tracy Flannery, Charles and Patricia Fuller, Al Garner, John Gillespie and Susan Orlean, Alan and Amanda Goodstadt, Jessica and Drew Guff, Stu and Barb Jones, Michael and Fran Kates, Jamie and Cynthia Kempner, Jeff Kuhr, Peter Lattman and Isabel Gillies, Jeffrey Leeds and Elizabeth Marshall, Sandy and Barbara Lewis, Tom and Amanda Lister, Patty Marx and Paul Roosin, Dan McManus, Steve and Leora Mechanic, Hamilton Mehlman, Chris and Amy Meininger, David Michaelis and Nancy Steiner, Mary Murfitt and Bonnie Hundt, Esther Newberg, Joan Osofsky, Eric Osserman, Jay and Massa Pelofsky, Nat and Melissa Philbrick, Ron Pillar, Michael Powell, Adam Reed, David Resnick and Cathy Klema, Scott Rostan, Andy and Courtney Savin, Charlie Schueler, Pam Scott and Phil Balshi (photographer *extraordinaire*), Gil Sewall, Robert and Francine Shanfield, Jim and Sue Simpson, Andrew Ross Sorkin, Lesley Stahl and Aaron Latham, Jeff and Kerry Strong, David Supino and Linda Pohs Supino, Rick Van Zijl, Silda Wall, David Webb, Andy and Lauren Weisenfeld, Kit White and Andrea Barnet, Jay and Louisa Winthrop, Dan Yergin and Angela Stent, Tim and Nina Zagat, and, of course, Gemma Nyack (last but not least).

I also want to thank my in-laws and relatives, the Futters and Shutkins, in toto, as well as various other Cohans and Hiekens, also in toto. My parents, Suzanne and Paul, as well as my brothers, Peter and Jamie, and their wives and families, continue to be hugely supportive of me, and I thank my lucky stars to have them again and again and again (as in every day) in my life.

To Joy Harris, my dear friend and literary agent, who has taken this journey with me four times now (with many more to come), I literally cannot thank you enough. And yet, I still try.

Then there is my amazing, loving, supportive, and nurturing family, Deb Futter, Teddy Cohan, and Quentin Cohan. I could not have done it without you; I love you all very, very much.

Needless to say, any errors in fact, of omission or commission, are my responsibility alone.

A NOTE ON SOURCES

In an era when digital access to documents of all stripes is becoming increasingly ubiquitous, the idea of providing page after page of notes on the sources of my research—as I did in my previous three books—seems somewhat superfluous, especially when writing about events that started to unfold primarily in 2006.

That said, thanks to invaluable research assistance from Elizabeth Palombo, I was able to access many hundreds of newspaper and magazine articles and blog posts—in both printed and digital forms—about the Duke lacrosse case. Throughout the narrative, my reliance on these articles and blogs is indicated clearly, and the vast majority of them are easily accessible to anyone online, often at little or no cost. It should be clear to the reader—since I cited them when used in the text—that the through-line of the story came from sources such as the *News & Observer*, in Raleigh; the *Durham Herald-Sun*; the *Chronicle*, Duke's daily student newspaper; the *New York Times*; the *Washington Post*; *Newsday*; the *North Carolina Independent*; the *Carolinian*; the *Los Angeles Times*; the *Wilmington Star*; and the *Wall Street Journal*, as well as, among others, *Newsweek*; *Vanity Fair*; the *New Yorker*; *Rolling Stone*; *Inside Lacrosse*; and *Time*. There is also a treasure-trove of contemporaneous video recordings—from WRAL-TV in Raleigh—of events and press conferences as they unfolded. These are available online. WRAL-TV's website also provides a fairly complete document archive. I owe a tremendous debt of gratitude to the daily journalists and bloggers who covered the story meticulously from its inception, with special appreciation reserved for the ever-changing cast of reporters and columnists at the *Chronicle*; for Joseph Neff and Benjamin Niolet at the *News & Observer*; for Susannah Meadows and Evan Thomas, formerly at *Newsweek*; for K. C. Johnson, who, despite his obvious bias, proved—and still proves—on his *Durham-in-Wonderland* blog to be a tireless chronicler of the often hard-to-believe events as they unfolded; and, yes, even for Duff Wilson at the *New York Times*.

I was also able to get access to the public record—including thousands of pages of documents, depositions, and original source material—of Mike Nifong's 2007 state bar hearing. There were also transcripts of the hearings.

Contained in this record were many—but not all—essential source documents, including the daily logs of Ben Himan, the Durham police investigator,
as well as the diary entries made retroactively by Mark Gottlieb, Himan's boss.
There were also numerous on-the-record statements made by a number of the
lacrosse players, as well as by the two dancers. Statements by Crystal Mangum's
various boyfriends and drivers were also in this record, as were statements by
important but secondary players in the drama such as Tara Levicy, the SANE
nurse who examined Mangum on March 14, 2006, and various Durham and
Duke police officers who were involved in the events of March 13 and 14. All
of this is easily accessible online for anyone wishing more information. The
North Carolina State Bar should, after some prodding, make available its files.

Then there is the voluminous public file of the various lawsuits that the
lacrosse case occasioned, from the charges Nifong brought against Evans, Finnerty, and Seligmann—some of which is still available at the courthouse in
Durham, some of which has been sealed—plus the lawsuits brought by the
players against Duke, Durham, Nifong, et al. Many of these records are also
available at courthouses or online at PACER. Of course, none of this is made
easy for a researcher, in part because the nature of litigation is that some key
documents—such as e-mails, depositions, and transcripts of hearings—are
kept sealed, which is highly frustrating, and in part because—much to my surprise, there was a reluctance on some people's parts to be cooperative in sharing information that should be public, or on the public record. A case in point
is the ongoing refusal of North Carolina Attorney General Roy Cooper—who
is said to be running for governor in 2016—to not only be interviewed about
the case but also to share any of the documentary or other information he
received in the course of his four-month investigation—between January 2007
and April 2007—that resulted in his unprecedented announcement that the
three players were "innocent" of the charges brought against them.

Noticeably absent as well in making themselves available were David Evans,
Collin Finnerty, Reade Seligmann, Richard Brodhead, and Mike Pressler. The
good news is that these individuals were not shy about speaking publicly along
the way, so their voices—and their points of view—are included throughout
the book. The other good news is that many others in and around Duke and the
case spoke to me off the record—for fear of legal repercussions—about what
happened from their perspectives. The reader gets the benefit of their thinking,
if not their names.

There is no question Duke and its lawyers tried to put the kibosh on nearly
everyone in its control—from administrators to coaches to professors and to
the former players—mainly through the time-honored method of paying settlements and extracting pledges to remain silent, through so-called confidentiality or non-disparagement agreements.

Finally, there are four books that are must-reads for anyone interested in learning more about this topic:

Don Yeager and Mike Pressler, *It's Not About The Truth: The Untold Story of the Duke Lacrosse Case and the Lives it Shattered* (New York: Threshold Editions, 2007).

Crystal Mangum with Vincent Clark, *Last Dance for Grace: The Crystal Mangum Story* (Raleigh: fire! Books, 2008).

Daniel Golden, *The Price of Admission: How America's Ruling Class Buys Its Way into Elite Colleges—and Who Gets Left Outside the Gates* (New York: Crown Publishing Group, 2006).

Stuart Taylor Jr. and K. C. Johnson, *Until Proven Innocent: Political Correctness and the Shameful Injustices of the Duke Lacrosse Rape Case* (New York: Thomas Dunne Books, 2007).

INDEX

in Mangum's allegations, 444–45; case notes of, 37, 122, 172–73, 174, 202, 394, 430, 582; critics of, 394, 458; crusade against Duke students, 56, 57, 58–59, 117; DNA results and, 195, 240, 276, 277–78; Evans's arraignment and, 334; indictments and, 249–50, 260, 278; investigation into Mangum's rape allegations, 60–63, 64, 65–66, 72–81, 226, 232–33, 276; key-card report from Duke police and, 182; learns of Mangum's rape allegations and involves himself in the case, 37–38, 59; March 27 briefing with Nifong, 111–13; March 29 "command staff" meeting, 172–73; March 29 new photo lineup created, 174; McFadyen's *American Psycho* e-mail and, 110–11, 113, 115; media statements about rape allegations, 70; neighborhood "canvass" by, 199; Nifong and, 81; NTO order and, 75–77, 78, 79, 80; postings on digital bulletin board, 38, 67, 70, 233; PowerPoint presentation of Duke lacrosse players shown to Mangum, 189–93; questioning at Edens dormitory by (April 14), 254–56; questioning of Zash, Evans, and Flannery by, 65; removed from beat, 59; search of 610 North Buchanan Blvd. and, 64, 66; search of Finnerty and Seligmann's dorm rooms, 269–71; search of McFadyen's dorm room and, 115–20; time line prepared by, 199

Grace, Nancy, 244–45, 422; *SNL* spoof of, 436–37

Graduate and Professional Student Council, 197–98

Graduate Employees and Students Organization (GESO), 156–57

Graham, Eric, 609

Grape, Matthew, 44

Graves, Aaron, 255–56

Green, Jacinta, 120

Greene, Betty, 105

Greer, Zack (lacrosse player), 255

Grinfield, Michael, 386

Group of 88, 408, 460–63, 494; critics of, 222–23, 462, 476, 482–83; grade dispute involving Kyle Dowd and, 223–24; Holloway and, 222; Krzyzewski criticizes, 495; liability of avoided, 569;

members of, 220, 222, 461–62, 483, 495–96; reiteration of stance, 462–63, 482; "Social Disaster" ad, 220, 221–22, 224, 460, 461, 468, 478, 480, 481, 482, 495; Tricia Dowd's response and Baker's reply, 223; vitriolic attacks on, 468–69, 495

Guardian newspaper, 320

Gunter, Dale, 50, 52, 58

Gurganus, Allan, 233–36

Gurney, Cy, 95, 134, 401, 555, 567, 613

Gustafson, Michael, 482–83

Guttentag, Chris, 437

Haagen, Paul, 103, 214, 292, 482

Hain, Richard, 482

Hall, Sam, 376

Hanlon, Philip, 611

Hannan, Michael, 384

Hanson, Brian, 126

Harden, Sarah, 473

Hardin, Jim, 81, 89, 91, 96, 280, 456, 478, 571

Harding, Lindsey, 186

Harrington, Mike, 288

Harris, Bob, 424

Harris, Charles A., 260

Harris, Eddie, 258

Harrison, Clarence, 602

Harvard University: athletics at, 139–40; endowment, 606; lacrosse at, 140, 528; reported rape cases, 611; Summers's resignation, 166, 477; William Barry Wood and, 139; William Barry Wood, Jr. and, 139–40

Hauver, Jeni, 28

Haynes, Yolanda, 422

Height, Dorothy, 345

Heinsohn, Eric, 349

Henderson, Gerald, 344

Hendricks, Kate, 103, 193

Henkelman, Erik (lacrosse player), 37, 190, 590

Hill, Thomas, 5

Himan, Benjamin, xi, 471; AG's dropping of all charges against players and, 513–14; alleged crimes listed on search warrant for 610 North Buchanan Blvd., 63; case notes of, 122, 430; code of silence/wall of silence allegations by, 420; conclusions about rape allegations, 514;

Limbaugh, Rush, 281, 345
Lisker, Donna, 367, 371
Lithwick. Dahlia, 291
Little, Danielle, 246
Livingston, Shaun, 1, 2, 5
Loflin, Tom, 114, 126
Lofton, Ashley, 244
Loftus, Barbara, 368
Loftus, Brian, 367–68
Loftus, Chris (lacrosse player), 190, 191, 255, 368
Loftus, Dan (lacrosse player), 21, 191, 368
Lohse, Andrew, 612
Lopresti, Mike, 273–74
Los Angeles Clippers, 1
Los Angeles Lakers, 1–10
Los Angeles Times, 3, 178, 244, 259, 452
Louisiana State University, 540
Love, Yardley, 528, 608
Loyola University, 508, 602
Lubiano, Wahneema, xii, 166, 222, 480, 495–96
Lunsford, L. Thomas, II, 439, 454
Lyman, Rick, 177–78
Lynch, Gary, 561

Mack, John, 535, 561, 606
Mack, Julian, 261–62, 263, 270, 271, 364
Mack, Tiana, 109
Macur, Juliet, 198, 199
Maier, Charles, 141
Major League Lacrosse, 350; drafting of Duke players, 346, 349, 372, 373
Malaklou, Shadee, 426
Malveaux, Julianne, 345
Mangum, Crystal Gail, xi: account of March 13 events, 15–22, 61–62; account of March 13 events, compiled by AG Cooper, 535–37; account of March 13 events, interview with author (November 2012), 518–20; account of March 13 events, Wilson interview and report (December 21) 440–45, 465; account of March 13 events, written statement of (April 6), 227–29; account of March 13 events in her book, 514–17; accuses husband of attempted murder, 101; AG Cooper's investigation of rape allegations, 473, 474, 489–90, 494–97; AG's dropping of all charges against players and, 503–4, 513; alleges raped

by twenty men, 29, 34, 35, 319, 380, 430; alleges she scratched her attackers, 78; artificial fingernails lost, 36, 76, 121, 231; author's interview with, 517–21; avoidance of the press, 368; background on, 100–102; belongings recovered from 610 North Buchanan Blvd., 64; boyfriend of (Murchison), 227; children of, 26, 101, 249, 489; condemnation of, 450; cousin of, media and, 278 (*see also* "Jakki"); credibility questioned, 27, 28, 29, 34, 35, 36, 37, 99, 173, 232, 241, 292–93, 294, 306, 307, 319, 330, 342–43, 363, 378, 379, 393, 407, 502; 537–39; criminal record of, 101–2, 259, 284, 363; CSI investigator photographs of, 62; dancing at clubs, after March 13 events, 312, 489, 515; demonstrations supporting, 198, 268, 310–12; description of alleged assailants, 62; desire to pursue rape case, 428, 465, 472; DNA evidence and, 120, 171, 240, 278, 325, 393, 429, 432, 515; at Duke Hospital and rape examination/investigation, 26–34, 171, 173; first rape allegation made by, 26; Gottlieb and Himan interview, 60–63; Himan visits about DNA evidence, 121–22; identifying attackers (April 4, third attempt), 189–93, 248–49, 254, 283, 306, 405, 406, 428, 440; impaired state (April 4, 2007), 500–502; impaired state (March 13–14, 2006), 17, 18, 20–21, 23, 24–26, 29, 61, 66, 73, 276–77, 280, 342, 361, 422–23, 499, 502, 538; inconsistencies in identification of players, 191–92, 431, 499; inconsistencies in versions of alleged assault, 393, 430, 444, 447, 465–66, 484, 498–500, 505, 506, 528–29; indictment and conviction on murder charge, 517–18, 613; institutionalization of, 301; interview at Durham police station, 73; interview with AG investigators, (March 29, 2007), 498–500; life after lacrosse case, 613; media statements about rape allegations, 99–100; medication taken by, 475, 489, 502, 529; meeting with AG investigators (February 21, 2007), 489–90; meeting with Nifong, 249; motivation for rape allegation, 173, 416, 419; name revealed

ABOUT THE AUTHOR

William D. Cohan, the author of the *New York Times* bestsellers *Money and Power*, *House of Cards*, and *The Last Tycoons*, worked on Wall Street for seventeen years. He spent six years at Lazard Frères in New York and two more at Merrill Lynch and Co., Inc., and later became a managing director at JPMorgan Chase.

Cohan is also a contributing editor at *Vanity Fair*, a columnist at *BloombergView*, and writes frequently for the *Financial Times*, the *New York Times*, the *Atlantic*, *ArtNews*, and the *Washington Post*. He is a graduate of Duke University, Columbia University School of Journalism, and Columbia University Graduate School of Business. He lives in New York City.